American Cancer Society

Atlas of
Clinical Oncology

Published

Blumgart, Fong, Jarnagin	*Hepatobiliary Cancer (2001)*
Cameron	*Pancreatic Cancer (2001)*
Carroll, Grossfeld	*Prostate Cancer (2002)*
Char	*Tumors of the Eye and Ocular Adnexa (2001)*
Clark, Duh, Jahan, Perrier	*Endocrine Tumors (2003)*
Droller	*Urothelial Tumors (2004)*
Eifel, Levenback	*Cancer of the Female Lower Genital Tract (2001)*
Fuller, Seiden, Young	*Uterine Cancer (2004)*
Ginsberg	*Lung Cancer (2002)*
Grossbard	*Malignant Lymphomas (2002)*
Ozols	*Ovarian Cancer (2003)*
Pollock	*Soft Tissue Sarcomas (2002)*
Posner, Vokes, Weichselbaum	*Cancer of the Upper Gastrointestinal Tract (2002)*
Prados	*Brain Cancer (2002)*
Raghavan	*Germ Cell Tumors (2003)*
Shah	*Cancer of the Head and Neck (2001)*
Silverman	*Oral Cancer 5th Edition (2003)*
Sober, Haluska	*Skin Cancer (2001)*
Wiernik	*Adult Leukemias (2001)*
Willett	*Cancer of Lower Gastrointestinal Tract (2001)*
Winchester, Winchester	*Breast Cancer (2000)*

Forthcoming

Richie, Steele	*Kidney Tumors (2005)*
Volberding, Palefsky	*Viral and Immunological Malignancies (2005)*
Yasko	*Bone Tumors (2005)*

American Cancer Society
Atlas of
Clinical Oncology

Editors

GLENN D. STEELE JR, MD
Geisinger Health System

THEODORE L. PHILLIPS, MD
University of California

BRUCE A. CHABNER, MD
Harvard Medical School

Managing Editor

TED S. GANSLER, MD, MBA
Director of Health Content, American Cancer Society

American Cancer Society
Atlas of
Clinical Oncology

Urothelial Tumors

Michael J. Droller, MD
Katherine and Clifford Goldsmith Professor of Urology
Mount Sinai School of Medicine
Professor of Oncology
Derald Ruttenberg Cancer Center
Program Director
Mount Sinai Medical Center
New York, NY

2004
BC Decker Inc
Hamilton • London

BC Decker Inc
P.O. Box 620, LCD 1
Hamilton, Ontario L8N 3K7
Tel: 905-522-7017; 1-800-568-7281
Fax: 905-522-7839; 1-888-311-4987
E-mail: info@bcdecker.com
www.bcdecker.com

ISBN 1–55009–173–5
Printed in Spain

Sales and Distribution

United States
BC Decker Inc
P.O. Box 785
Lewiston, NY 14092-0785
Tel: 905-522-7017; 800-568-7281
Fax: 905-522-7839; 888-311-4987
E-mail: info@bcdecker.com
www.bcdecker.com

Canada
BC Decker Inc
20 Hughson Street South
P.O. Box 620, LCD 1
Hamilton, Ontario L8N 3K7
Tel: 905-522-7017; 800-568-7281
Fax: 905-522-7839; 888-311-4987
E-mail: info@bcdecker.com
www.bcdecker.com

Foreign Rights
John Scott & Company
International Publishers' Agency
P.O. Box 878
Kimberton, PA 19442
Tel: 610-827-1640; Fax: 610-827-1671
E-mail: jsco@voicenet.com

Japan
Igaku-Shoin Ltd.
Foreign Publications Department
3-24-17 Hongo
Bunkyo-ku, Tokyo, Japan 113-8719
Tel: 3 3817 5680; Fax: 3 3815 6776
E-mail: fd@igaku-shoin.co.jp

UK, Europe, Scandinavia, Middle East
Elsevier Science
Customer Service Department
Foots Cray High Street
Sidcup, Kent
DA14 5HP, UK
Tel: 44 (0) 208 308 5760
Fax: 44 (0) 181 308 5702
E-mail: cservice@harcourt.com

Singapore, Malaysia, Thailand,
Philippines, Indonesia, Vietnam,
Pacific Rim, Korea
Elsevier Science Asia
583 Orchard Road
#09/01, Forum
Singapore 238884
Tel: 65-737-3593; Fax: 65-753-2145

Australia, New Zealand
Elsevier Science Australia
Customer Service Department
STM Division
Locked Bag 16
St. Peters, New South Wales, 2044
Australia
Tel: 61 02 9517-8999
Fax: 61 02 9517-2249
E-mail: stmp@harcourt.com.au
www.harcourt.com.au

Mexico and Central America
ETM SA de CV
Calle de Tula 59
Colonia Condesa
06140 Mexico DF, Mexico
Tel: 52-5-5553-6657
Fax: 52-5-5211-8468
E-mail: editoresdetextosmex@prodigy.net.mx

Brazil
Tecmedd
Av. Maurílio Biagi, 2850
City Ribeirão Preto – SP – CEP: 14021-000
Tel: 0800 992236
Fax: (16) 3993-9000
E-mail: tecmedd@tecmedd.com.br

India, Bangladesh, Pakistan, Sri Lanka
Elsevier Health Sciences Division
Customer Service Department
17A/1, Main Ring Road
Lajpat Nagar IV
New Delhi – 110024, India
Tel: 91 11 2644 7160-64
Fax: 91 11 2644 7156
E-mail: esindia@vsnl.net

Contents

Preface.. vii

Contributors ix

1   **Demographics and Epidemiology of Urothelial Cancer of the Urinary Bladder** 1
Neil Fleshner, MD, MPH, FRCSC, Filippos Kondylis, MD, FACS

2   **Cell-Cycle Aberrations in Human Bladder Cancer**.................................... 17
Jay E. Reeder, PhD, Edward M. Messing, MD

3   **Molecular Carcinogenesis and Pathogenesis of Proliferative and Progressive (Invasive) Urothelial Cancer** 28
Dan Theodorescu, MD, PhD

4   **Molecular Pathogenesis of Proliferative and Progressive (Invasive) Urothelial Cancer Development**.. 44
Paul Sweeney, MD, Colin P.N. Dinney, MD

5   **Clinical Pathogenesis and Staging of Urothelial Bladder Cancer** 59
Peter Lagenstroer, MD, MS, William See, MD

6   **Diagnosis and Diagnostic Pitfalls in Urothelial Bladder Cancer** 73
Markus D. Sachs, MD, Theresa Chan, MD, Stephen B. Solomon, MD,
Frank König, MD, Mark P. Schoenberg, MD

7   **Pathology of Urothelial Tumors of the Bladder** 92
David G. Bostwick, MD, MBA, Rodolfo Montironi, MD, PhD, FRCPath,
Antonio Lopez-Beltran, MD, Liang Cheng, MD

8   **Urinary Cytology, Cytometry, and New Approaches in the Assessment and Monitoring of Urothelial Cancer** 112
Hans Wijkström, MD, PhD, Barbara Du Reitz, MD, Anna Tolf, MD

9   **Quantitative Cell Biomarkers in Transitional Cell Carcinoma of the Bladder** 143
Peter W. Hamilton, PhD, Kate E. Williamson, PhD, Rodolfo Montironi, MD, PhD FRCPath

10   **Bladder Tumor Markers: Current Concepts and Status** 160
Vinata B. Lokeshwar, PhD, Francisco Civantos, MD

11   Intravesical Chemotherapy in Approaches to Treatment and Prophylaxis 206
Gregory L. Alberts, MD, Sam S. Chang, MD, Joseph A. Smith Jr, MD

**12   Intravesical Bacille Calmette-Guérin in the Treatment and Prophylaxis of
Urothelial Bladder Cancer** 219
Michael A. O'Donnell, MD, Jennifer A. Burns, MD

**13   Outcomes and Quality of Life Issues Following Radical Cystectomy and
Urinary Diversion** 248
Erin E. Katz, MD, R. Corey O'Connor, MD, Gary D. Steinberg, MD

**14   Neoadjuvant and Adjunctive Systemic Chemotherapy in the Treatment
of Invasive Urothelial Cancer of the Bladder** 261
Amnon Vazina, MD, Derek Raghavan, MD, PhD, Seth P. Lerner, MD

15   Cystectomy in the Elderly 272
Peter E. Clark, MD, John P. Stein, MD

16   Bladder-Sparing Approaches in Treatment of Muscle-Invasive Bladder Cancer 290
Arthur I. Sagalowsky, MD, Kenneth S. Koenemann, MD

17   Laparoscopic Aproaches in Cystectomy for Urethelial Cancer 311
Jihad H. Kaouk, MD, Inderbir Singh Gill, MD, MCh

18   Demographics and Epidemiology of Urothelial Cancer of the Renal Pelvis and Ureter 318
Neil Fleshner, MD, MPH, FRCSC

19   Diagnosis and Staging of Upper Tract Urothelial Cancer 324
Murali K. Ankem, MD, Kenneth B. Cummings, MD, FACS

**20   Endoscopic and Radiologic Imaging of Urothelial Cancer of the Upper Urinary Tract
and Bladder** 333
David I. Lee, MD, Jaime Landman, MD

21   Percutaneous Upper Tract–Preserving Approaches in Urothelial Cancer 340
Robert Marcovich, MD, Avrum Jacobson, MD, Arthur D. Smith, MD

22   Ureteroscopic Upper Tract–Preserving Approaches in Urothelial Cancer 353
Demetrius H. Bagley, MD

**23   Laparoscopic versus Open Nephroureterectomy for the Treatment of Upper Tract
Transitional Cell Carcinoma** 369
Michael C. Ost, MD, Stephen J. Savage, MD

24   Systemic Chemotherapy for Metastatic Urothelial Cancer 388
Gurkamal S. Chatta, MD, Donald L. Trump, MD, FACP

Index 402

Preface

Bladder cancer is the second leading cause of cancer of the genitourinary tract, the fourth leading cause of cancer death in men, and the seventh leading cause of cancer death in women. In addition to its recognition as an important health problem because of its significant incidence and prevalence, bladder cancer has also drawn increasing attention because of the accessibility it provides to study generic aspects of the overall cancer process, its characterization, and a variety of approaches to its treatment.

The focus of this new text on urothelial tumors (encompassing both the urinary bladder and upper tracts) is an exposition of the dramatic advances that have characterized this area over the past few years. These include an understanding of epidemiology and the events in carcinogenesis of urothelial cancer, delineation of distinct aspects of pathogenesis of the different forms of urothelial cancer, explication of new means of diagnosing and characterizing the prognosis of various types of urothelial cancer, and a definition of standard and new approaches in treating the different types of urothelial cancer.

The authors of this text have provided a critical evaluation of their particular area, creating the context for their presentation of directions for further advances and future prospects. The text is designed to give the reader, be they clinician or laboratory investigator, an overall understanding of the cancer process in the context of urothelial cancer. At the same time, the various chapters are intended to provide a compendium of information on each of the various areas addressed.

In constructing a project such as this, one depends on one's colleagues who are in large part responsible for many of the advances that have been made, and who have contributed to the general knowledge in this area. Each of the contributors has been extraordinarily generous with their time in making substantive contributions in the development of this monograph. In keeping with our intent to provide the most current scientific and clinical information, they have also offered their critical assessment of what the future might hold. This text thus assumes the additional purpose of stimulating new thinking to create opportunities for new advances to be made.

As editor of this monograph, I have been privileged to work with each of the contributors, first in examining their contribution, and then in interacting closely with them to enhance each presentation. Each of the contributors has selflessly collaborated in making their contribution adhere to the highest standards in offering objective information and thoughtful insights. For their efforts, collaboration, and support I am profoundly grateful. My hope is that each contributor will feel that his or her presentation has amplified our understanding of each area and contributed to an expansion of knowledge and thoughtful appreciation by all who take the time to explore this text.

Michael J. Droller, MD
New York, New York
May 2004

Contributors

GREGORY L. ALBERTS, MD
Department of Urologic Surgery
Vanderbilt University Medical Center
Nashville, Tennessee
*Intravesical Chemotherapy in Approaches to
    Treatment and Prophylaxis*

MURALI K. ANKEM, MD
Department of Surgery
Robert Wood Johnson Medical School
University of Medicine and Dentistry of New Jersey
New Brunswick, New Jersey
*Diagnosis and Staging of Upper Tract
    Urothelial Cancer*

DEMETRIUS H. BAGLEY, MD
Department of Urology
Thomas Jefferson University
Philadelphia, Pennsylvania
*Ureteroscopic Upper Tract-Preserving Approaches
    in Urothelial Cancer*

DAVID G. BOSTWICK, MD, MBA
Bostwick Laboratories
Philadelphia, Pennsylvania
Pathology of Urothelial Tumors of the Bladder

JENNIFER A. BURNS, MD
Department of Urology
University of Iowa
Iowa City, Iowa
*Intravesical Bacille Calmette-Guérin in the
    Treatment and Prophylaxis of Urothelial
    Bladder Cancer*

THERESA CHAN, MD
Department of Pathology
Johns Hopkins Medical Institute
Baltimore, Maryland
*Diagnosis and Diagnostic Pitfalls in Urothelial
    Bladder Cancer*

SAM S. CHANG, MD
Department of Urologic Surgery
Vanderbilt University Medical Center
Nashville, Tennessee
*Intravesical Chemotherapy in Approaches to
    Treatment and Prophylaxis*

GURKAMAL S. CHATTA, MD
University of Pittsburgh Cancer Institute
Pittsburgh, Pennsylvania
*Systemic Chemotherapy for Metastatic Urothelial
    Cancer*

LIANG CHENG, MD
Indiana University
Indianapolis, Indiana
Pathology of Urothelial Tumors of the Bladder

FRANCISCO CIVANTOS, MD
Department of Urology
University of Miami School of Medicine
Department of Pathology
Columbia Cedars Medical Center
Miami, Florida
*Bladder Tumor Markers: Current Concepts
    and Status*

PETER E. CLARK, MD
University of Southern California Norris
    Comprehensive Cancer Center
Los Angeles, California
Cystectomy in the Elderly

KENNETH B. CUMMINGS, MD, FACS
Department of Surgery
Robert Wood Johnson Medical School
University of Medicine and Dentistry of New Jersey
New Brunswick, New Jersey
Diagnosis and Staging of Upper Tract
   Urothelial Cancer

COLIN P.N. DINNEY, MD
Department of Urology
The University of Texas, MD Anderson
   Cancer Center
Houston, Texas
Molecular Pathogenesis of Proliferative and
   Progressive (Invasive) Urothelial Cancer
   Development

BARBARA DU REITZ, MD
Department of Clinical Pathology and Cytology
Huddinge University Hospital
Stockholm, Sweden
Urinary Cytology, Cytometry, and New
   Approaches in the Assessment and Monitoring
   of Urothelial Cancer

NEIL FLESHNER, MD, MPH, FRCSC
Department of Surgery
University of Toronto
Toronto, Ontario
Demographics and Epidemiology of Urothelial
   Cancer of the Urinary Bladder and
   Demographics and Epidemiology of Urothelial
   Cancer of the Renal Pelvis and Ureter

INDERBIR SINGH GILL, MD, MCH
Department of Urology
Urological Institute
Cleveland, Ohio
Laparoscopic Approaches in Cystectomy for
   Urethelial Cancer

PETER W. HAMILTON, PhD
Department of Pathology
Queen's University Belfast
Belfast, United Kingdom
Quantitative Cell Biomarkers in Transitional Cell
   Carcinoma of the Bladder

AVRUM JACOBSON, MD
Department of Urology
Long Island Jewish Medical Center
New Hyde Park, New York
Percutaneous Upper Tract-Preserving Approaches
   in Urothelial Cancer

JIHAD H. KAOUK, MD
Department of Urology
Cleveland Clinic Foundation
Cleveland, Ohio
Laparoscopic Approaches in Cystectomy for
   Urethelial Cancer

ERIN E. KATZ, MD
Department of Surgery
University of Chicago
Chicago, Illinois
Outcomes and Quality of Life Issues Following
   Radical Cystectomy and Urinary Diversion

KENNETH S. KOENEMANN, MD
Department of Urology
University of Texas, Southwestern Medical Center
Dallas, Texas
Bladder-Sparing Approaches in Treatment of
   Muscle-Invasive Bladder Cancer

FILIPPOS KONDYLIS, MD, FACS
Division of Urology
University Health Network
University of Toronto
Toronto, Ontario
Demographics and Epidemiology of Urothelial
   Cancer of the Urinary Bladder

FRANK KÖNIG, MD
Department of Urology
Charite Medical School
Berlin, Germany
Diagnosis and Diagnostic Pitfalls in Urothelial
   Bladder Cancer

JAIME LANDMAN, MD
Washington University School of Medicine
St. Louis, Missouri
Endoscopic and Radiologic Imaging of Urothelial
   Cancer of the Upper Urinary Tract and Bladder

PETER LAGENSTROER, MD, MS
Department of Urology
Medical College of Wisconsin
Milwaukee, Misconsin
Clinical Pathogenesis and Staging of Urothelial
Bladder Cancer

DAVID I. LEE, MD
Department of Urology
University of California, Irvine
Irvine, California
Endoscopic and Radiologic Imaging of Urothelial
Cancer of the Upper Urinary Tract and Bladder

SETH P. LERNER, MD
Department of Urology
Baylor College of Medicine
Houston, Texas
Neoadjuvant and Adjunctive Systemic
Chemotherapy in the Treatment of Invasive
Urothelial Cancer of the Bladder

VINATA B. LOKESHWAR, PHD
Department of Urology
University of Miami Medical Center
Department of Pathology
Columbia Cedars Medical Center
Miami, Florida
Bladder Tumor Markers: Current Concepts and
Status

ANTONIO LOPEZ-BELTRAN, MD
Department of Urology
Mount Sinai School of Medicine
New York, New York
Pathology of Urothelial Tumors of the Bladder

ROBERT MARCOVICH, MD
Department of Urology
Long Island Jewish Medical Center
New Hyde Park, New York
Percutaneous Upper Tract-Preserving Approaches
in Urothelial Cancer

EDWARD M. MESSING, MD
Department of Urology
University of Rochester
Rochester, New York
Cell-Cycle Aberrations in Human Bladder Cancer

RODOLFO MONTIRONI, MD, PHD, FRCPATH
Department of Pathological Anatomy and
    Histopathology
University of Ancona
Ancona, Italy
Pathology of Urothelial Tumors of the Bladder and
Quantitative Cell Biomarkers in Transitional
Cell Carcinoma of the Bladder

R. COREY O'CONNER, MD
Department of Surgery
University of Chicago
Chicago, Illinois
Outcomes and Quality of Life Issues Following
Radical Cycstectomy and Urinary Diversion

MICHAEL A. O'DONNELL, MD
Department of Urology
University of Iowa
Iowa City, Iowa
Intravesical Bacille Calmette-Guérin in the
Treatment and Prophylaxis of Urothelial
Bladder Cancer

MICHAEL C. OST, MD
University of Cordoba
Cordoba, Spain
Laparoscopic versus Open Nephroureterectomy
for the Treatment of Upper Tract Transitional
Cell Carcinoma

DEREK RAGHAVAN, MD, PHD
Department of Medicine
USC Keck School of Medicine
Los Angeles, California
Neoadjuvant and Adjunctive Systemic
Chemotherapy in the Treatment of Invasive
Urothelial Cancer of the Bladder

JAY E. REEDER, PhD
Department of Pathology and Laboratory Medicine
University of Rochester
Rochester, New York
Cell-Cycle Aberrations in Human Bladder Cancer

MARKUS D. SACHS, MD
Department of Urology
Johns Hopkins Hospital
Baltimore, Maryland
*Diagnosis and Diagnostic Pitfalls in Urothelial
    Bladder Cancer*

ARTHUR I. SAGALOWSKY, MD
Department of Urology
University of Texas
Dallas, Texas
*Bladder-Sparing Approaches in Treatment of
    Muscle-Invasive Bladder Cancer*

STEPHEN J. SAVAGE, MD
Department of Urology
Memorial Sloan Kettering Cancer Center
New York, New York
*Laparoscopic versus Open Nephroureterectomy
    for the Treatment of Upper Tract Transitional
    Cell Carcinoma*

MARK P. SCHOENBERG, MD
Johns Hopkins Medical Institute
Baltimore, Maryland
*Diagnosis and Diagnostic Pitfalls in Urothelial
    Bladder Cancer*

WILLIAM SEE, MD
Department of Urology
Medical College of Wisconsin
Milwaukee, Wisconsin
*Clinical Pathogenesis and Staging of Urothelial
    Bladder Cancer*

ARTHUR D. SMITH, MD
Department of Urology
Long Island Jewish Medical Center
New Hyde Park, New York
*Percutaneous Upper Tract-Preserving Approaches
    in Urothelial Cancer*

JOSEPH A. SMITH JR, MD
Department of Urology
Vanderbilt University Medical Center
Nashville, Tennessee
*Intravesical Chemotherapy in Approaches to
    Treatment and Prophylaxis*

STEPHEN B. SOLOMON, MD
Johns Hopkins School of Medicine
Baltimore, Maryland
*Diagnosis and Diagnostic Pitfalls in Urothelial
    Bladder Cancer*

JOHN P. STEIN, MD
Department of Urology
University of Southern California
Los Angeles, California
Cystectomy in the Elderly

GARY D. STEINBERG, MD
Department of Surgery
University of Chicago
Chicago, Illinois
*Outcomes and Quality of Life Issues Following
    Radical Cystectomy and Urinary Diversion*

PAUL SWEENEY, MD
Department of Urology
Mercy University Hospital
Cork University Hospital
Cork, Ireland
*Molecular Pathogenesis of Proliferative and
    Progressive (Invasive) Urothelial Cancer
    Development*

DAN THEODORESCU, MD, PhD
Department of Urology and Molecular Physiology
University of Virginia
Charlottesville, Virginia
*Molecular Carcinogenesis and Pathogenesis of
    Proliferative and Progressive (Invasive)
    Urothelial Cancer*

ANNA TOLF, MD
Department of Clinical Pathology and Cytology
Huddinge University Hospital
Stockholm, Sweden
*Urinary Cytology, Cytometry, and New
Approaches in the Assessment and Monitoring
of Urothelial Cancer*

DONALD L. TRUMP, MD, FACP
Roswell Park Cancer Institute
University of Buffalo
Buffalo, New York
*Systemic Chemotherapy for Metastatic Urothelial
Cancer*

AMNON VAZINA, MD
Department of Urology
Baylor College of Medicine
Houston, Texas
*Neoadjuvant and Adjunctive Systemic
Chemotherapy in the Treatment of Invasive
Urothelial Cancer of the Bladder*

HANS WIJKSTRÖM, MD, PHD
Department of Urology
Huddinge University Hospital
Stockholm, Sweden
*Urinary Cytology, Cytometry, and New
Approaches in the Assessment and Monitoring
of Urothelial Cancer*

KATE E. WILLIAMSON, PHD
Department of Pathology
Queen's University Belfast
Belfast, United Kingdom
*Quantitative Cell Biomarkers in Transitional Cell
Carcinoma of the Bladder*

Demographics and Epidemiology of Urothelial Cancer of the Urinary Bladder

NEIL FLESHNER, MD, MPH, FRCSC
FILIPPOS KONDYLIS, MD, FACS

DEMOGRAPHICS OF UROTHELIAL CANCER OF THE BLADDER

Urothelial cancers of the bladder are a heterogeneous group of tumors. Incidence refers to the number of newly diagnosed cases of a certain disease over a specified time period.[1] It is usually expressed as an incidence rate—the number of cases per 100,000 persons per year. Bladder cancer is a common malignancy, ranking fourth among cancers in terms of disease incidence for men and eighth for women.[1] In 2004, 60,240 US residents are expected to be diagnosed with bladder cancer. This compares with 217,440 and 230,110 residents diagnosed with breast and prostate cancer respectively in that year.[2] The majority of bladder cancers are not life-threatening. This is reflected in the number of deaths attributable to bladder cancer, which is predicted to be 12,710 in 2004.[1] The case-fatality ratio is thus approximately 4.7. The consequences of this are important in terms of disease prevalence. Prevalence reflects the total number of afflicted individuals with a given disease within a specified time point. In this context, bladder cancer is the second most prevalent cancer among men (prostate cancer is the first).

Bladder cancer is not a disease that is limited to the developed world. Increased industrialization and tobacco use in the third world have increased the global incidence of this disease, although significant variation (~10-fold) exists.[3] Rates are particularly high in North America and Western Europe and are relatively low in Asia and Latin America. Certain areas of the Balkans such as Yugoslavia and Bulgaria have a high incidence in association with nephropathy.[3] In Northern Africa, exposure to schistosomiasis has created an endemic pattern of bladder cancer in Egypt and Northern Sudan.[4]

Current trends suggest that, even when adjusted for the aging population, the incidence of bladder cancer is increasing.[5] There has been approximately 39% increase in the incidence of bladder cancer in the United States over the past 15 years. The cause for increased rates of bladder cancer remains largely unknown. It is unlikely that diagnostic bias or screening efforts can account for this as incidental autopsy-detected tumors are not common.[6] The incidence of bladder cancer increases exponentially with age, with rare cases among persons less than 30 years and most occurring in patients over age 50 years.[7] The trend in most neoplasms among patients less than 20 years is toward low-grade superficial tumors, which, in contrast to those in older patients, rarely recur.[8] Tumors in patients between 20 and 40 years behave in a similar fashion to those in older patients.[9]

Gender differences in the incidence of bladder cancer remain an important area of ongoing research. Bladder cancer is roughly 4 times more common in men than in women.[5] Historically, this difference was felt to be related to differential opportunity for exposure to known bladder carcinogens such as industrial carcinogens and tobacco. However, recent data suggest that this does not explain all of the differences. Over the past 30 to 40 years, tobacco exposure among women has dramatically increased, as has the entry of women into the workforce. These changes, particularly with respect to smoking, have been well reflected in the increased incidence of lung cancers in women.[10] Surprisingly, however, although rates among women have increased, they have not increased to the degree predicted by changes in carcinogen exposure. The reason for the relative "protection" from transitional cell carcinoma (TCC) among women remains unknown but may reflect anatomic, hormonal, or reproductive factors.[11–13]

Racial differences in incidence and survival have also been noted in urothelial cancer.[5] White men and women are 2.8 and 1.6 times more likely to get bladder cancer than black American men and women, respectively. It is estimated that a white male has a 3.9% lifetime chance of developing bladder cancer compared with 0.8% for a black American female.[14] Hispanic Americans have approximately half the risk of bladder cancer as do white Americans.[15] Despite racial differences in risk, clinical, epidemiologic, and genetic evidence suggests that tumors among blacks are more aggressive.[16,17]

CAUSATION IN EPIDEMIOLOGY

Background and Introduction

The variations in the risk of disease in different geographic locations suggest that the environment plays a vital role in disease causation. The purpose of this chapter is to review some of the hypothesized and well-known risk factors for urothelial cancer. In addition, because new risk factors for urothelial cancer are being researched, it is important that the reader be able to recognize and interpret various types of epidemiologic studies and to realize their limitations.

The primary goal of epidemiologic investigation is to determine risk factors for disease causation. It is important to note that these risk factors can either cause or prevent the disease in question. Once these risk factors are determined (eg, tobacco and increased risk of TCC), primary prevention programs can be initiated to limit disease incidence. Other epidemiologically discovered risk factors cannot be modified (eg, family history); however, their importance in disease causation is still relevant as they can lead to early detection and treatment of dis-

ease (so-called "secondary prevention") for individuals at high risk. Nonpreventable risk factors can also provide clues for basic science endeavors that aim to discover disease mechanisms.

Although, on a superficial level, it may seem trivial to determine these risk factors, in practice it is often very difficult. Unlike laboratory science, epidemiology aims to study free-living persons with diverse genetic, geographic, and cultural traits. Owing to this lack of experimental control, minor errors in study design or analysis can have a profound impact on study outcome, often leading to spurious associations or inconsistencies in the published literature. In addition, the labeling of a specific risk factor (also known as exposures or agents) as a definite causal factor for a specific disease rarely results from one study. It is invariably a slow accumulation of knowledge that arises from many studies (of various epidemiologic designs) carried out in different study populations. For example, the causal association between smoking and urothelial cancer took decades to prove.[18]

Ecologic Studies

Ecologic studies (also referred to as correlational) are epidemiologic studies in which groups of people, rather than individuals, form the basis of the study. Three types of correlational studies exist: international, regional, and time trend. International studies correlate disease incidence (or mortality) rates and level of exposure in various countries. Regional studies compare intranational disease incidence (or mortality) and correlate them with exposure level.[1] Time trend studies examine changing levels of exposure within the same population over time and attempt to correlate this with changing disease incidence.

On the surface, ecologic studies appear compelling and are also easy to perform, usually with readily available data. However, they are generally regarded as the weakest of all epidemiologic methodologies in terms of causal inference. Reasons include the following: (a) there is no information about exposure at the level of the individual; (b) proxy measures (such as food production), rather than true measures (ie, food consumption), are often used for exposure classification; and (c) these studies cannot assess if other exposures rather than those of interest are responsible for the association. This is referred to as confounding.

Despite their limitations, these studies can signal the presence of a disease exposure association worthy of study. However, they should be viewed only as hypothesis generating, not hypothesis testing.

Case-Control Studies

Case-control studies are investigations that compare exposures in persons with a particular disease (case) with exposures in a similar group of persons who are not diseased (controls).

The conceptuality of case-control studies makes them the most efficient of all epidemiologic studies. In addition, they can be completed in a relatively short time. Associations from case-control studies are usually expressed as an odds ratio (OR; Table 1–1), which compares the odds of exposure in diseased individuals with the odds of exposure in the controls.

The major limitation of case-control studies is the possibility of bias, in particular recall bias, which refers to the inaccurate reporting of exposure in cases compared with controls. This can create an artificial association. It is very easy to imagine how, for example, a cancer patient overestimates his exposures to environmental carcinogens (diet, smoking, etc) as he/she may be introspective and self-blaming compared with a healthy control.

In general, however, case-control studies are efficient and, if done correctly, can provide powerful insight into risk factors for disease causation. The well-accepted association between transplacental diethylstilbestrol exposure and clear cell vaginal cancer was derived from case-control studies.[19]

Cohort Studies

Cohort studies are the most robust of observational epidemiologic studies and most closely simulate a controlled trial. In cohort studies, disease-free individuals are questioned about environmental exposures. They may also have tissue (eg, blood, toenails, hair) procured for laboratory analysis. The individuals are followed forward in time. As time elapses and persons begin to develop disease, one compares the rates of disease in the exposed with the unexposed

Table 1–1. CASE-CONTROL AND COHORT STUDIES

Exposure	Disease Present	Disease Absent	Total
Present	a	b	e
Absent	c	d	f

Case-control study: odds ratio = (a*d)/(b*c).
Cohort study: relative risk = (a/c)/(c/f).
As incidence decreases, odds ratio approximates relative risk

persons. The measure of association is referred to as a relative risk (RR; see Table 1–1).

The obvious advantage of cohort studies is that exposure is determined prior to the development of the disease; thus, it is free of recall bias. The major limitations of these studies are their cost and length of time to complete. Loss of participants over time is another limitation of these studies. The Health Professional Follow-Up Study and Framingham study are well known examples of cohort studies.[20,21]

Causal Criteria

It is important to realize that elevated risks of disease in persons with a particular exposure are merely an association. In epidemiology, we are not interested in general associations but in causal associations. Hill developed a set of criteria (Table 1–2) that can be used for causal inference in observational epidemiologic studies.[22]

Strength

Strength refers to the degree of association between an exposure and a disease. Strong associations (RR or OR > 3) are more likely to be indicative of causation because weak associations may be alternatively explained by bias. Nonetheless, the fact that an association is weak does not eliminate the potential for that exposure to be causal.

Table 1–2. HILL CRITERIA

Strength
Consistency
Specificity
Time order
Dose response
Biologic plausibility
Coherence
Analogy
Experimental evidence

Consistency

Consistency refers to the degree with which different studies done by various methodologies, investigators, and populations conclude that an exposure and a disease are associated. It is important to realize that not every observational epidemiologic study may reveal a hypothesized association. Limitations owing to methodology in study design, bias, and chance may prevent 100% consistency.

Specificity

This criterion stipulates that a single exposure can produce only one disease. This criterion is not consistent with a modern view of disease. For example, cigarette exposure is causally related to many diseases. Many investigators now find this criterion unnecessary and misleading.[1]

Time Order

This criterion is intuitive. It refers to the necessity that the exposure to the causal agent precedes the development of the disease. This is the only criterion that must be satisfied to infer causality.

Dose Response

This criterion suggests that those individuals exposed to more of a causal agent are more likely to be afflicted with the disease. Not all causal associations, however, follow a traditional dose-response relationship. Other models of dose response, such as threshold, critical period (eg, particular week of gestation), or parabolic responses, have been hypothesized.[23]

Biologic Plausibility

This criterion mandates that an hypothesized association be scientifically plausible. The limitation of this criterion is that a discovered association may precede scientific knowledge.

Coherence

This refers to the fact that the hypothesized association should not conflict with the well-accepted facts about the natural history of the disease under study. Absence of coherence, however, should not be regarded as evidence against causality.

Analogy

Analogy suggests that if similar mechanisms of causation exist in other diseases (eg, diet and cancer), it can enhance the credibility of a newly discovered potential causal agent. The limitation of this criterion is that it constrains inventive and alternate ways of thinking about risk factors for disease.

Experimental Evidence

This criterion suggests that a controlled study should exist to confirm the relationship. In practice, this is rarely available. This criterion is usually applicable when the exposure is a preventive agent (eg, vitamins and cancer) as it is not ethical to carry out studies of risk factors for disease (eg, smoking and cancer).

Using the Hill Criteria

It is important to understand that the aforementioned criteria are not meant to hinder the discovery of disease risk factors but to provide general guidelines for investigators and public health policy makers. The only criterion that must be satisfied is the time-order association. For most risk factors, many of these criteria will never be satisfied.

In this review, many associations are listed and described. Associations are categorized as follows:

- *Sufficient evidence.* This suggests that there is ample evidence of a causal association.
- *Limited evidence.* This suggests that although evidence exists for causality, alternative explanations are credible.
- *Inadequate evidence.* This indicates that either the data are consistently negative or the studies are seriously biased, confounded, or underpowered.

ETIOLOGY OF UROTHELIAL CANCER OF THE BLADDER

Environmental Factors

General Concepts

Cancer is a disease characterized by accumulated genetic mutation. The origins of these mutations are either hereditary or environmental. There is little

UTI.[122] However, the risk seemed only to exist proximate to the date of diagnosis (ie, and not remote). Although one could hypothesize that this represents a late-stage progression effect, it could also represent a manifestation of the disease as many patients have UTI or similar symptoms that ultimately may lead to the diagnosis of bladder cancer. Similar studies from Denmark and Spain demonstrated no association.[123,124]

Cystitis glandularis is a metaplastic inflammatory lesion of the bladder often seen in association with inflammation or pelvic lipomatosis.[125] This condition is widely considered to be a premalignant lesion of bladder adenocarcinoma. Despite this reputation, there are few cases documenting the transition of cystitis glandularis to bladder cancers.[126,127] Close surveillance, not cystectomy, is recommended for patients with this inflammatory condition. There is insufficient evidence supporting an association between recurrent UTI and urothelial cancer.

Human Papillomavirus

Human papillomavirus (HPV) is a common sexually transmitted disease and is causally linked to cancers of the cervix and penis.[128] Given the anatomic proximity of the bladder to the genital tract, it has long been postulated that HPV could play a role in urothelial cancer. Most investigations that have assessed this association use molecular techniques to identify HPV-associated molecules in bladder cancer specimens.[129–131] Depending on the technique and methods used, 0 to 50% of bladder cancers contain molecular evidence of HPV.[132] Unfortunately, none of these studies used age-matched controls to determine if this prevalence was greater than in persons without bladder cancer. It is thus impossible to know if this is merely an epiphenomenon. Given this major limitation, there is insufficient evidence to support this association.

Iatrogenic Causes of Bladder Cancer

Phenacetin

Phenacetin is an analgesic that was commonly used in the 1950s through 1970s. In Australia, use was quite prevalent, with regular use reported by 12% and 7% of female and male residents in New South Wales, respectively.[133,134] Owing to its nephrotoxic and carcinogenic effects, phenacetin was banned in most countries by 1980. There is sufficient evidence for a causal association between phenacetin exposure and urothelial cancer.

Acetominophen/Paracetamol

Phenacetin was largely replaced by acetominophen and paracetamol as the over-the-counter (OTC) analgesics of choice in the Western world. Both of these agents are metabolites of phenacetin and, in theory, may also be carcinogenic. At least five case-control studies have assessed the association between OTC analgesics and bladder cancer, and all have been consistently negative.[31,135–136] Although, at this point, there is insufficient evidence to support an association between urothelial cancer and OTC analgesics, latency issues demand that this association be revisited in 10 to 15 years.

Cyclophosphamide/Ifosphamide

The cytotoxic agents cyclophosphamide and ifosphamide, through the action of the metabolite acrolein, are known uroepithelial toxins.[137,138] Recent molecular analyses of *P53* mutations in cyclophosphamide-induced bladder cancers suggest that phosphoramide mustard, another metabolite, may play a more important role than acrolein.[139] Both acrolein and phosphoramide mustard are known mutagens and have been shown to induce bladder cancer in animal models.[140,141] Chemotherapy-induced bladder cancers are not rare; some studies suggest that the 12-year risk of developing bladder carcinoma following high-dose cyclophosphamide therapy is 11%.[142] The disease phenotype in these bladder cancers tends toward an aggressive biology and poor outcome.[143] The overall data supporting this association are strong. Patients with good-prognosis neoplasms are at highest risk.[142] The latency period for these tumors is in the range of 6 to 20 years.[144,145]

Prevention of bladder cancer induced by these agents is plausible. Although not proven in randomized trials, pragmatic use of adequate hydration and, when necessary, sodium 2-mercaptoethane sulfonate (MESNA) may minimize this risk.

Pelvic Radiotherapy

Radiation is a well-accepted mutagen and carcinogen.[146] Recent data suggest that persons who reside in the Chernobyl nuclear plant area have an increased incidence of urothelial dysplasia, tumors, and urothelial *P53* mutations.[147] The use of therapeutic radiotherapy has yielded tremendous benefit in treating many pelvic malignancies, including those of the cervix and prostate. Women treated with radiotherapy for cervical cancer have a reported two- to fourfold increased risk of TCC of the bladder.[148–151] Furthermore, men treated with radiotherapy for prostate cancer have a 1.5 times risk of bladder cancer than men treated surgically.[152] This association is less strong than chemotherapy-induced TCC. It remains difficult to disentangle shared risk factors for these cancers from treatment effects. For example, smoking and sexually transmitted diseases (especially HPV) are well-accepted risk factors for cervical carcinoma.[153] Men who receive radiotherapy for prostate cancer often possess more comorbidities than men who are not treated with radiotherapy. Because many comorbid conditions are smoking related, it is possible that smoking history is more prevalent among men treated with radiotherapy than not. Because all studies have been unable to control for these confounders, there is insignificant evidence to support this association. In addition, there is no evidence for an association between bladder cancer and carcinoma of the anal canal, another common neoplasm treated by radiotherapy (in field).

Laxatives

Experimental tumor systems have demonstrated that certain laxatives possessed carcinogenic properties. Toyoda and colleagues demonstrated that bisacodyl could induce bladder tumors in F344/Du Crj rats.[154] In a clinical context, one case-control study has demonstrated that habitual laxative use, a common practice in Germany, doubled the risk of urothelial cancer.[155]

Host Factors

Carcinogen metabolism plays an important role in bladder cancer, although this risk factor could be attributed to the carcinogen per se, polymorphisms of a host of enzymatic systems are increasingly being recognized as risk factors for urothelial cancer.

Glutathione-S-Transferase M1

Smoking is a well-accepted risk factor for urothelial cancer. The product of the glutathione-S-transferase M1 (GSTM1) is involved in detoxification of polycyclic aromatic hydrocarbons (PAHs).[156] A homozygous deletion of this gene, present in approximately 50% of Asians and whites, results in diminished activity, which allows for higher concentrations of PAHs and potentially a higher risk of urothelial cancer.

A host of studies have addressed the issue of GSTM1 and risk of bladder cancer. The most complete was the pooled analysis by Engel and colleagues, which reviewed almost 2,000 cases and 1,500 controls among 10 countries, including the United States, Europe, and Asia.[157] All considered, it was concluded that a modest 30 to 50% increase in risk was noted among those deficient in GSTM1. There is sufficient causal evidence for GSTM1 dysfunction as a risk factor for urothelial cancer.

Acetylation

Aromatic amines are well-accepted bladder carcinogens.[158] Aromatic amines, particularly monoamines, can be detoxified by acetylation. Humans possess two major *N*-acetyl-transferase genes (*NAT1* and *NAT2*). A wide body of epidemiologic data has examined the role of *NAT1* in bladder cancer; these studies have been consistently negative.[158,159]

In the context of bladder neoplasia, it would appear that *NAT2* is more important.

NAT2 is a polymorphic gene in which homozygotes are known as "slow acetylators." Subsequent studies have demonstrated a significantly increased risk (two- to fourfold) of bladder cancer among these patients.[159] Most Asians are fast acetylators, which may explain their relative protection from bladder cancer.[158] There is sufficient evidence for the role of *NAT2* in bladder carcinogenesis.

Cytochrome P-450

The CYP1A2 isozyme of the P-450 family is particularly important in the metabolism of aromatic amines such as 4-aminobiphenyl.[158] CYP1A2 causes metabolic activation of 4-aminobiphenyl by *N*-hydroxylation. Persons with this polymorphism seem to form more 4-aminobiphenyl adducts than those without it; however, there does not appear to be a higher risk of urothelial cancer among carriers of the CYP1A2 isozyme.[160]

Occupational Risk Factors

Industrialization of the Western world over the past century resulted in exposure of a large number of workers (mostly men) to chemicals previously unknown to cause harm. The causal link of these occupations or chemical exposures to bladder cancer was first described in 1895 by Rehn, who noted bladder cancers among workers in the aniline dye industry.[141] In 1954, Case and colleagues described an increased incidence of bladder cancer among men employed in the rubber and dye manufacturing industry.[161,162]

Over the past 50 years, numerous occupations have been linked to urothelial cancer. Distilling the literature is not easy as, in many cases, controlling for confounders such as smoking was not performed. In addition, it is often difficult to disentangle a certain occupation from a particular chemical exposure. Accepted bladder carcinogens include 2-naphthylamine, 4-aminobiphenyl, benzidine, benzidine-related azo dyes, 4,4-methylenebis, 4-cholor-*o*-toluidine, *o*-toluidine, and methylenedianiline.[141,161–165] In the following section risk is classified by work type with the hypothetical agent(s) mention within.

Chemical Dye/Aromatic Amine/Rubber/Plastic Manufacturing

As alluded to earlier in this chapter, there is strong evidence linking occupation in the chemical dye industry to urothelial cancer.[161–169] Many of the aforementioned carcinogens are found in this environment. Measures of increased risk associated with exposure to these agents are over 100-fold and are dependent on duration of employment (dose response).[170] As few as 6 months of exposure confer an increased risk.[171] Patients with significant exposures should be screened for bladder cancer. Rubber manufacturing involves many of these solvents.[172]

Textile/Dry Cleaning Industry

Employees in the textile and dry cleaning industry possess a two- to fourfold increased risk for bladder cancer, although the data are not consistent.[173] Perchloroethylene, an organic solvent used in dry cleaning, is felt to be the culprit, although exposure to smoke is also plausible.[173–176] The textile industry uses many known carcinogens, including chemical dyes and aromatic amines.[176]

Hair Dyes

Seven cohort and 11 case-control studies have assessed risk in hairdressers, barbers, and beauticians.[176–178] The overall risk estimate is 1.4 in the cohort studies and modestly above unity in the case-control studies. Although these data suggest a modest increase in risk, lack of controlling for confounders (especially smoking) renders this issue open to debate. Five case-control studies have looked at personal use of hair dyes, and all were negative.[178] There is limited epidemiologic evidence for a causal association between hair dyes and bladder cancer.

Automobile/Oil Industry

Inconsistent data suggest that workers in the petroleum industry are at higher risk of urothelial cancer.[179–181] The precise carcinogen is unknown.

Coal Gasification/Tar Distillation/Carbon Black

Persons in the aforementioned industry are exposed to high levels of PAH at their workplace. Considerable evidence demonstrates that workers in this industry are at higher risk for urothelial cancer.[182]

SUMMARY

Bladder cancer is one of the most common cancers in humans. Bladder cancer is also highly preventable with approximately 60% of global cases attributed to tobacco exposure or schistomiasis infection. In this chapter we explored the incidence and international variation of the disease. We also reviewed the accepted epidemiological criteria of Bradford Hill and used these criteria to derive scientifically credible risk factors of developing bladder cancer.

Of the well-accepted risk factors, schistosomiasis, tobacco exposure, and exposure to industrial carcinogens, are all strong risk factors. Similarly, some less common and less well known, but likely equally strong risk factors exist, such as pelvic radiotherapy, cyclophosphamide exposure, arsenic poisoning, and ingestion of certain Chinese herbs. All of these risk factors, in addition to other well studied, but non-existent risk factor associations, have been discussed.

The genetics of bladder cancer, as well as the field cancerization theory of bladder and upper tract urothelial cancers, have also been reviewed in this chapter. Heritable genetic risk factors of carcinogen metabolism, such as N-acetyl-transferase 2 and glutathione-S-transferase M1, were also extensively reviewed. Clearly more research is required to better define unidentified risk factors for bladder cancer. Research is also needed to better obtain control of tobacco use and addiction worldwide.

REFERENCES

1. Rothman KJ. Modern epidemiology. 1st ed. Boston: Little, Brown and Company; 1986
2. Jemal A, Tiwari RC, Murray T, et al. Cancer Statistics, 2004. CA Cancer J Clin 2004;54:8–29.
3. Cohen SM, Shirai T, Steineck G. Epidemiology and etiology of premalignant and malignant urothelial changes. Scand J Urol Nephrol Suppl 2000;205:105–15.
4. el-Mawla NG, el-Bolkainy MN, Khaled HM. Bladder cancer in Africa: update. Semin Oncol 2001;28:174–8.
5. Ries LAG, Eisner MP, Kosary CL, et al. (eds). SEER Cancer Statistics Review, 1975–2000, National Cancer Institute. Bethesda, MD, http://seer.cancer.gov/csr/1975_2000, 2003.
6. Kryger JV, Messing E. Bladder cancer screening. Semin Oncol 1996;23:585–97.
7. Cohen SM. Urinary bladder carcinogenesis. Toxicol Pathol 1998;26:121–7.
8. Iori F, DeDomincis C, Liberti M, et al. Superficial bladder tumors in patients under 40 years of age: clinical, prognostic, and cytogenetic aspects. Urol Int 2001;67:224–7.
9. Yossepowitch O, Dalbagni G. Transitional cell carcinoma of the bladder in young adults: presentation, natural history and outcome. J Urol 2002;168:61–6.
10. Brennan P, Bray I. Recent trends and future directions for lung cancer mortality in Europe. Br J Cancer 2002;87:43–8.
11. Meisel P. Cancer, genes and gender. Carcinogenesis 2002;23:1087–9.
12. Rizk DE, Raaschou T, Mason N, Berg B. Evidence for progesterone receptors in the mucosa of the urinary bladder. Scand J Urol Nephrol 2001;35:305–9.
13. Au WW. Lifestyle factors and acquired susceptibility to environmental disease. Int J Hyg Environ Health 2001;204:17–22.
14. Messing EM. Urothelial tumors of the urinary tract. In: Walsh PC, Retik AB, Vaughan ED, Wein AJ eds. Campbells Urology, 8th ed. Philadelphia: WB Saunders; 2002. p. 2732–84.
15. Davis FG, Persky VW, Ferre CD, et al. Cancer incidence of Hispanic and non-Hispanic whites in Cook County, Illinois. Cancer 1995;75:2939–45.
16. Prout GR, Wesley MN, Greenberg RS, et al. Bladder cancer: race differences in extent of disease at diagnosis. Cancer 2000;15:1349–58.
17. Fleshner NE, Herr HW, Stewart AK, et al. The National Cancer Data Case report on bladder carcinoma. The American College of Surgeons Commission on Cancer and the American Cancer Society. Cancer 1996;78:1505–13.
18. Berrino F. The combined effects and smoking and other agents. IARC Sci Publ 1986;74:167–71.
19. Herbst AL, Ulfelder H, Poskanzer DC. Adenocarcinoma of the vagina. Association of maternal stilbestrol therapy with tumor appearance in young women. N Engl J Med 1971;284:878–81.
20. Michaud DS, Clinton SK, Rimm EB, et al. Risk of bladder cancer by geographic region in a US cohort of male health professionals. Epidemiology 2001;12:719–26.
21. Kannel WB, Abbot RD. Incidence and prognosis of unrecognized myocardial infarction. An update on the Framingham study. N Engl J Med 1984;311:1144–7.
22. Hill AB. The environment and disease: association or causation? Proc R Soc Med 1965;58:295–300.
23. Willet W. Nutritional epidemiology. New York: Oxford University Press; 1990.
24. Kiemeney LA, Moret NC, Witjes JA, et al. Familial transitional cell carcinoma among the population of Iceland. J Urol 1997;157:1649–51.
25. Patton SE, Hall MC, Ozen H. Bladder cancer. Curr Opin Oncol 2002;14:265–72.
26. Silverman DT, Hartge P, Morrison AS, Devesa SS. Epidemiology of bladder cancer. Hematol Oncol Clin North Am 1992;6:1–30.
27. Donato F, Boffetta P, Fazioli R, et al. Bladder cancer, tobacco smoking, coffee and alcohol drinking in Brescia, northern Italy. Eur J Epidemiol 1997;13:795–800.
28. Chyou PH, Nomura AM, Stemmermann GN. A prospective study of diet, smoking and lower urinary tract cancer. Ann Epidemiol 1993;3:211–6.
29. Wynder EL, Goldsmith R. The epidemiology of bladder cancer: a second look. Cancer 1977;40:1246–53.
30. Hartge P, Silverman D, Hoover R, et al. Changing cigarette

habits and bladder cancer risk: a case-control study. J Natl Cancer Inst 1987;78:1119–25.

31. Burch JD, Rohan TE, Howe GR, et al. Risk of bladder cancer by source and type of tobacco exposure: a case-control study. Int J Cancer 1989;44:622–8.

32. Fortuny J, Kogevinas M, Chang-Claude J, et al. Tobacco, occupation and non-transitional cell carcinoma of the bladder: an international case-control study. Int J Cancer 1999;80:44–6.

33. Bartsch H, Malaveille C, Friesen M, et al. Black and blond tobacco risk: molecular dosimetry studies implicate aromatic amines in bladder carcingenesis. Eur J Cancer 1993;29:1199–207.

34. Vizcaino AP, Parkin DM, Bofetta P, Skinner ME. Bladder cancer: epidemiology and risk factors in Bulawayo, Zimbabwe. Cancer Causes Control 1994;5:517–22.

35. Thun MJ, Apicella LF, Henley SJ. Smoking vs other risk factors as the cause of smoking-attributable deaths. JAMA 2000;284:706–12.

36. Pitard A, Brennan P, Clavel J, et al. Cigar, pipe and cigarette smoking and bladder cancer risk in European men. Cancer Causes Control 2001;12:551–6.

37. Chao A, Thun MJ, Henley SJ, et al. Cigarette smoking, use of other tobacco products and stomach cancer mortality in US adults: the Cancer Prevention Study II. Int J Cancer 2002;101:380–9.

38. Carpenter AA. Clinical experience with transitional cell carcinoma of the bladder with special reference to smoking. J Urol 1989;141:527–8.

39. Thompson IM, Peek M, Rodriguez FR. The impact of cigarette smoking on stage, grade and number of recurrences of transitional cell carcinoma of the bladder. J Urol 1987;137:401–3.

40. Michalek AM, Cummings KM, Pontes JE. Cigarette smoking, tumor recurrence and survival from bladder cancer. Prev Med 1985;14:92–8.

41. Koch M, Hill G, McPhee M. Factors affecting recurrence rates in superficial bladder cancer. J Natl Cancer Inst 1986;76:1025–32.

42. Zeegers MP, Goldbohm RA, van den Brandt PA. A prospective study on active and environmental tobacco smoking and bladder cancer risk. Cancer Causes Control 2002;13:83–90.

43. Fleshner N, Garland J, Moadel A, et al. Influence of smoking status on the disease-related outcomes of patients with tobacco-associated superficial transitional cell carcinoma of the bladder. Cancer 1999;86:1337–45.

44. Sarkis A, Dalbagni G, Cordon-Cardo C, et al. Association of p53 nuclear overexpression and tumor progression in carcinoma in situ of the bladder. J Urol 1994;152:388–92.

45. Esrig D, Elmajian D, Groshen S, et al. Accumulation of nuclear p53 and tumor progression in bladder cancer. N Engl J Med 1994;331:1259–64.

46. Zhang ZF, Sarkis AS, Cordon-Cardo C, et al. Tobacco smoking, occupation and p53 nuclear overexpression in early stage bladder cancer. Cancer Epidemiol Biomarkers Prev 1994;3:19–24.

47. Bernardini S, Adessi GL, Chezy E, et al. Influence of cigarette smoking on p53 gene mutations in bladder carcinomas. Anticancer Res 2001;21:3001–4.

48. Spruck CH, Rideout WM, Olumi AF, et al. Distinct pattern of p53 mutations in bladder cancer: relationship to tobacco use. Cancer Res 1993;53:1162–6.

49. LaVecchia C, Airoldi L. Human bladder cancer: epidemiological, pathological and mechanistic aspects. IARC Sci Publ 1999;147:139–57.

50. Badawi AF, Habib Sl, Mohammed MA, et al. Influence of cigarette smoking on prostaglandin synthesis and cyclooxygenase-2 gene expression in human urinary bladder cancer. Cancer Invest 2002;20:651–6.

51. Yu MC, Ross RK, Chan KK, et al. Glutathione S-transferase M1 genotype affects aminobiphenyl-hemoglobin adduct levels in white, black and Asian smokers and non-smokers. Cancer Epidemiol Biomarkers Prev 1995;4:861–4.

52. Burger MS, Torino JL, Swaminathan S. DNA damage in human transitional cell carcinoma cells after exposure to the proximate metabolite of the bladder carcinogen 4-aminobiphenyl. Environ Mol Mutagen 2001;38:1–11.

53. Vineis P, Marinelli D, Autrup H, et al. Current smoking, occupation, N-acetyltransferase-2 and bladder cancer: a pooled analysis of genotype-based studies. Cancer Epidemiol Biomarkers Prev 2001;10:1249–52.

54. Donato F, Boffetta P, Fazioli R, et al. Bladder cancer, tobacco smoking, coffee and alcohol drinking in Brescia, northern Italy. Eur J Epidemiol 1997;13:795–800.

55. Brownson RC, Chang JC, Davis JR. Occupation, smoking, and alcohol in the epidemiology of bladder cancer. Am J Public Health 1987;77:1298–300.

56. Kabat GC, Dieck GS, Wynder EL. Bladder cancer in non-smokers. Cancer 1986;57:362–7.

57. Mills PK, Beeson L, Phillips RL, et al. Bladder cancer in a low risk population: results from the Adventist health study. Am J Epidemiol 1991;133:230–9.

58. Thomas DB, Uhl CN, Hartge P. Bladder cancer and alcoholic beverage consumption. Am J Epidemiol 1983;118:720–7.

59. Pohlabeln H, Jockel KH, Bolm-Audorff U. Non-occupational risk factors of cancer of the lower urinary tract in Germany. Eur J Epidemiol 1999;15:411–9.

60. Woolcott CG, King WD, Marrett LD. Coffee and tea consumption and cancers of the bladder, colon and rectum. Eur J Cancer 2002;11:137–45.

61. Zeegers MP, Volovics A, Dorant E, et al. Alcohol consumption and bladder cancer risk: results from The Netherlands Cohort study. Am J Epidemiol 2001;153:38–44.

62. Pera M, Pera M. Recent changes in the epidemiology of esophageal cancer. Semin Oncol 2001;10:81–90.

63. Papadimitralopoulou VA. Chemoprevention of head and neck cancer: an update. Curr Opin Oncol 2002;14:318–22.

64. Murata M, Takayama K, Choi BC, Pak AW. A nested case-control study on alcohol drinking, tobacco smoking and bladder cancer. Cancer Detect Prev 1996;20:557–65.

65. Pelucchi C, Tavani A, Negri E, et al. Alcohol drinking and bladder cancer. J Clin Epidemiol Community Health 2002;56:78–9.

66. Morgan RW, Jain MG. Bladder cancer: smoking, beverages and artificial sweeteners. Can Med Assoc J 1974;111:1067–70.

67. Risch HA, Burch JD, Miller AB, et al. Occupational factors and the incidence of cancer of the bladder in Canada. Br J Ind Med 1988;45:361–7.

68. Hartge P, Hoover R, West DW, et al. Coffee drinking and risk of bladder cancer. J Natl Cancer Inst 1983;70:1021–6.

69. Gonzalez CA, Lopez-Abente G, Errezola M, et al. Occupation, tobacco use, coffee and bladder cancer in the county of Mataro (Spain). Cancer 1985;55:2031–4.

70. Pannelli F, La Rosa F, Saltalamacchia G, et al. Tobacco smoking, coffee, cocoa and tea consumption in relation to mortality from urinary bladder cancer in Italy. Eur J Epidemiol 1989;5:392–7.

71. Akdas A, Kirkali Z, Bilir N. Epidemiological case-control study on the etiology of bladder cancer in Turkey. Eur Urol 1990;17:23–6.

72. Hopkins J. Coffee drinking and bladder cancer. Food Chem Toxicol 1984;22:481–3.

73. Stensvold I, Jacobsen BK. Coffee and cancer: a prospective study of 43000 Norwegian men and women. Cancer Causes Control 1994;5:401–8.

74. Slattery ML, West DW, Robison LM. Fluid intake and bladder cancer in Utah. Int J Cancer 1988;42:17–22.

75. Jensen OM, Wahrendorf J, Knudsen JB, et al. The Copenhagen case-control study of bladder cancer. II. Effect of coffee and other beverages. Int J Cancer 1986;37:651–7.

76. Rebelakos A, Trichopoulos D, Tzonou A, et al. Tobacco smoking, coffee drinking, and occupation as risk factors for bladder cancer in Greece. J Natl Cancer Inst 1985;75:455–61.

77. Sala M, Cordier S, Chang-Claude J, et al. Coffee consumption and bladder cancer in non-smokers: a pooled analysis of case-control studies in European countries. Cancer Causes Control 2000;11:925–31.

78. Lina BA, Rutten AA, Whitersen RA. Effect of coffee drinking on cell proliferation in rat urinary bladder epithelium. Food Chem Toxicol 1993;31:947–51.

79. Ellwein LB, Cohen SM. The health risks of saccharin. Crit Rev Toxicol 1990;20:311–26.

80. Auerbach O, Garfinkel L. Histologic changes in the urinary bladder in relation to cigarette smoking and the use of artificial sweeteners. Cancer 1989;64:983–7.

81. Armstrong BK. Saccharin/cyclamates: epidemiological evidence. IARC Sci Publ 1985;65:129–43.

82. Sacchrain. Review of safety issues. Council on Scientific Affairs. JAMA 1985;254:2622–4.

83. Cohen SM, Anderson TA, de Oliveira LM, Arnold LL. Tumorigenicity of sodium ascorbate in male rats. Cancer Res 1998;58:2557–61.

84. Howe GR, Birch JD, Miller AB, et al. Artifical sweeteners and human bladder cancer. Lancet 1977;ii:578–81.

85. Najem GR, Louria DB, Seebode JJ, et al. Life time occupation, smoking, saccharine, hair dyes and bladder carcinogenesis. Int J Epidemiol 1982;11:212–7.

86. Yu Y, Hu J, Wang PP, et al. Risk factors for bladder cancer: a case control study in northeast China. Eur J Cancer Prev 1997;6:363–9.

87. Moller-Jensen O, Knudsen JB, Sorensen BL, Clemmesen J. Artifical sweeteners and absence of bladder cancer risk in Denmark. Int J Cancer 1983;32:577–82.

88. Cohen SM. Role of urinary physiology and chemistry in bladder carcinogenesis. Food Chem Toxicol 1995;22:715–30.

89. Michaud DS, Spiegelman D, Clinton SK, et al. Fluid intake and the risk of bladder cancer in men. N Engl J Med 1999;340:1390–7.

90. Bruemmer B, White E, Vaughan TL, Cheney CL. Fluid intake and the incidence of bladder cancer among middle-aged men and women in a three-county area of western Washington. Nutr Cancer 1997;29:163–8.

91. Vena JE, Graham S, Freudenheim J, et al. Drinking water, fluid intake and bladder cancer in western New York. Arch Environ Health 1993;48:191–8.

92. Lu CM, Lan SJ, Lee YH, et al. Tea consumption, fluid intake and bladder cancer risk in southern Taiwan. Urology 1999;54:823–8.

93. Geoffrey-Perez B, Cordier S. Fluid consumption and the risk of bladder cancer: results of a multicenter case-control study. Int J Cancer 2001;93:880–7.

94. Claude J, Kunze E, Frentzel-Beyme, et al. Life-style and occupational risk factors in cancer of the lower urinary tract. Am J Epidemiol 1986;124:578–89.

95. Wannamethee SG, Shaper AG, Walker M. Physical activity and risk of cancer in middle-aged men. Br J Cancer 2001;85:1311–6.

96. Balbi JC, Larrinaga MT, DeStefani E, et al. Foods and risk of bladder cancer: a case-control study in Uruguay. Eur J Cancer Prev 2001;10:453–8.

97. Wakai K, Takashi M, Okamura K, et al. Foods and nutrients in relation to bladder cancer risk: a case-control study in Aichi Prefecture, Central Japan. Nutr Cancer 2000;28:13–22.

98. Michaud DS, Spiegelman D, Clinton SK, et al. Fruit and vegetable intake and incidence of bladder cancer in a male prospective cohort. J Natl Cancer Inst 1999;91:605–13.

99. Michaud DS, Spiegelman D, Clinton SK, et al. Prospective study of dietary supplements, macronutrients, micronutrients and risk of bladder cancer in US men. Am J Epidemiol 2000;152:1145–53.

100. Airoldi L, Orsi F, Magagnotti C, et al. Determinants of 4-amino-biphenyl-DNA adducts in bladder cancer biopsies. Carcinogenesis 2002;23:861–6.

101. Vinh PQ, Sugie S, Tanaka T, et al. Chemopreventive effects of a flavonoid antioxidant silymarin on N-butyl-N-(4-hydroxybutyl)nitrosamine-induced urinary bladder carcinogenesis in male ICR mice. Jpn J Cancer Res 2002;93:42–9.

102. Hursting SD, Perkins SN, Phang JM, Barrett JC. Diet and prevention studies in p53-deficient mice. J Nutr 2001; 121:3092–4.

103. Brown KG, Chen CJ. Significance of exposure assessment to analysis of cancer risk from inorganic arsenic in drinking water in Taiwan. Risk Anal 1995;15:475–84.

104. Chiang HS, Guo HR, Hong CL, et al. The incidence of bladder cancer in the black foot disease endemic area of Taiwan. Br J Urol 1993;71:274–8.

105. Shibata A, Ohneseit PF, Tsai YC, et al. Mutational spectrum in the p53 gene in bladder tumors from the endemic area of black foot disease in Taiwan. Carcinogenesis 1994;15: 1085–7.

106. Chiou HY, Hsueh YM, Liaw KF, et al. Incidence of internal cancer and ingested inorganic arsenic: a seven year follow-up study in Taiwan. Cancer Res 1995;55:1296–300.

107. Brown KG, Beck BD. Arsenic and bladder cancer mortality. Epidemiology 1996;7:557–8.

108. Chiou HY, Chiou St, Hsu YH, et al. Incidence of transitional cell carcinoma and arsenic in drinking water: a follow-up study of 8,102 residents in an arseniasis-endemic area in northeastern Taiwan. Am J Epidemiol 2001;153:411–8.

109. Arnold LL, Cano M, St John M, et al. Effects of dietary

dimethylarsinic acid on the urine and urothelium of rats. Carcinogenesis 1999;20:2171–9.

110. Pu YS, Hour TC, Chen J, et al. Cytotoxicity of arsenic trioxide to transitional cells. Urology 2002;60:346–50.

111. Feifer AH, Fleshner NE, Klotz L. Analytical accuracy and reliability of commonly used nutritional supplements for prostate disease. J Urol 2002;168:150–4.

112. Nortier JL, Martinez MC, Schmeiser HH, et al. Urothelial carcinoma associated with the use of a Chinese herb (*Aristolochia fangchi*). N Engl J Med 2000;342:1686–92.

113. Cukuranovic R, Ignjatovic M, Stefanovic V. Urinary tract tumors and Balkan nephropathy in the South Morava River basin. Kidney Int Suppl 1991;34:S80–4.

114. Pfohl-Leszkowicz A, Petkova-Bocharova T, Chernozemsky IN, Castegnaro M. Balkan endemic nephropathy and associated urinary tract tumors: a review on aetiological causes and the potential role of mycotoxins. Food Addit Contam 2002;18:282–302.

115. Cohen SM, Johansson SL. Epidemiology and etiology of bladder cancer. Urol Clin North Am 1992;19:421–8.

116. Pycha A, Mian C, Posch B, et al. Numerical aberrations of chromosomes 7, 9 and 17 squamous cell and transitional cell cancer of the bladder: a comparative study performed by fluorescence in situ hybridization. J Urol 1998; 160(3 Pt 1):737–40.

117. el-Mawla NG, el-Bolkainy MN, Khaled HM. Bladder cancer in Africa: update. Semin Oncol 2001;28:174–8.

118. King CH, Muchiri EM, Mungai P, et al. Randomized comparison of low-dose versus standard-dose praziquantel therapy in treatment of urinary tract morbidity due to *Schistosoma haematobium* infection. Am J Trop Med Hyg 2002;66:725–30.

119. El-Sheikh SS, Madaan S, Alhasso A, et al. Cyclooxygenase-2: a possible target in schistosoma-associated bladder cancer. Br J Urol Int 2001;88:921–7.

120. Bedwani R, el-Khwsky F, Renganathan E, et al. Epidemiology of bladder cancer in Alexandria, Egypt: tobacco smoking. Int J Cancer 1997;73(1):64–7.

121. Kantor AF, Hartge P, Hoover RN, et al. Urinary tract infection and risk of bladder cancer. Am J Epidemiol 1984;119:510–5.

122. La Vecchia C, Negri E, D'Avanzo B, et al. Genital and urinary tract diseases and bladder cancer. Cancer Res 1991;51(2):629–31.

123. Kjaer SK, Knudsen JB, Sorensen BL, Moller Jensen O. The Copenhagen case-control study of bladder cancer. V. Review of the role of urinary-tract infection. Acta Oncol 1989;28:631–6.

124. Gonzalez CA, Errezola M, Izarzugaza I, et al. Urinary infection, renal lithiasis and bladder cancer in Spain. Eur J Cancer 1991;27:498–500.

125. Heyns CF, De Kock ML, Kirsten PH, van Velden DJ. Pelvic lipomatosis associated with cystitis glandularis and adenocarcinoma of the bladder. J Urol 1991;145:364–6.

126. Farina LA. Pelvic lipomatosis associated with cystitis glandularis and adenocarcinoma of the bladder. J Urol 1992; 147:1380.

127. Gordon NS, Sinclair RA, Snow RM. Pelvic lipomatosis with cystitis cystica, cystitis glandularis and adenocarcinoma

of the bladder: first reported case. Aust N Z J Surg 1990; 60:229–32.

128. Sanclemente G, Gill DK. Human papillomavirus molecular biology and pathogenesis. J Eur Acad Dermatol Venereol 2001;16:231–40.

129. Soulitzis N, Sourvinos G, Dokianakis DN, Spandidos DA. p53 codon 72 polymorphism and its association with bladder cancer. Cancer Lett 2002;179:175–83.

130. Sur M, Cooper K, Allard U. Investigation of human papillomavirus in transitional cell carcinomas of the urinary bladder in South Africa. Pathology 2001;33:17–20.

131. Simoneau M, LaRue H, Fradet Y. Low frequency of human papillomavirus infection in initial papillary bladder tumors. Urol Res 1999;27:180–4.

132. Agliano AM, Gradilone A, Gazzaniga P, et al. High frequency of human papillomavirus detection in urinary bladder cancer. Urol Int 1994;53:125–9.

133. McCredie M, Stewart J, Smith D, et al. Observations on the effect of abolishing analgesic abuse and reducing smoking on cancers of the kidney and bladder in New South Wales, Australia, 1972–1995. Cancer Causes Control 1999;10:303–11.

134. Johansson S, Wahlquist L. Tumors of the urinary bladder and ureter associated with abuse of phenacetin-containing analgesics. Acta Pathol Microbiol Scand 1977;85:768–74.

135. Piper JM, Tonascia J, Matanowski GM. Heavy phenacetin use and bladder cancer in women aged 20 to 49 years. N Engl J Med 1985;313:292–5.

136. McCredie M, Stewart JH. Does paracetamol cause urothelial cancer or renal papillary necrosis? Nephron 1988;49: 196–300.

137. Agarwala S, Hemal AK, Seth A, et al. Transitional cell carcinoma of the urinary bladder following exposure to cyclophosphamide in childhood. Eur J Pediatr Surg 2001; 11:207–10.

138. Vlaovic P, Jewett MA. Cyclophosphamide-induced bladder cancer. Can J Urol 1999;6:745–8.

139. Khan MA, Travis LB, Lynch CF, et al. p53 mutations in cyclophosphamide-associated bladder cancer. Cancer Epidemiol Biomarkers Prev 1998;7:397–403.

140. Cai Y, Wu MH, Ludeman SM, et al. Role of O6-alkylguanine-DNA alkyltransferase in protecting against cyclophosphamide-induced toxicity and mutagenicity. Cancer Res 1999;59:3059–63.

141. Cohen SM, Johansson SL. Epidemiology and etiology of bladder cancer. Urol Clin North Am 1992;19:421–8.

142. Pederson-Bjergaard J, Ersboll J, Hansen V, et al. Carcinoma of the urinary bladder after treatment with cyclophosphamide for non-Hodgkin's lymphoma. N Engl J Med 1988;318:1028–32.

143. Fernandes ET, Manivel JC, Reddy PK, Ercole CJ. Cyclophosphamide associated bladder cancer—a highly aggressive disease: analysis of 12 cases. J Urol 1996;156:1931–3.

144. Messing EM, Catalona W. Urothelial tumors of the urinary tract. In: Walsh PC, Retick AB, Vaughan ED, Wein AJ eds. Campbells Urology: urothelial tumors of the urinary tract, 7th ed. Vol 3. Philadelphia: WB Saunders; 1998. p. 2327–410.

145. Volm T, Pfaff P, Gnann R, Kreienberg R. Bladder carcinoma associated with cyclophosphamide therapy for ovarian can-

cer occurring with a latency of 20 years. Gynecol Oncol 2001;82:197–9.

146. Phillips TL. 50 years of radiation research: medicine. Radiat Res 2002;158:389–417.

147. Romanenko A, Morimura K, Wei M, et al. DNA damage repair in bladder urothelium after the Chernobyl accident in Ukraine. J Urol 2002;168:973–7.

148. Duncan RE, Bennett DW, Evans AT, et al. Radiation induced bladder tumors. J Urol 1977;118:43–5.

149. Sella A, Dexeus FH, Chong C, et al. Radiation therapy associated invasive bladder tumors. Urology 1989;33:185–7.

150. Quilty PM, Kerr GR. Bladder cancer following low or high dose pelvic radiation. Clin Radiol 1987;38:583–6.

151. Hemminki K, Dong C, Vaittinen P. Second primary cancer after in situ and invasive cervical cancer. Epidemiology 2000;11:457–61.

152. Neugut AI, Ahsan H, Robinson E, Ennis RD. Bladder carcinoma and other second malignancies after radiotherapy for prostate carcinoma. Cancer 1997;79:1600–4.

153. Wyatt SW, Lancaster M, Bottorff D, Ross F. History of tobacco use among Kentucky women diagnosed with invasive cervical cancer: 1997–1998. J Ky Med Assoc 2001;99:537–9.

154. Toyoda K, Imaida K, Shirai T, et al. Relationship between bisacodyl-induced urolithiasis and rat urinary bladder tumorigenesis. J Toxicol Environ Health 1993;39:59–78.

155. Pommer W, Bronder E, Klimpel A, et al. Urothelial cancer at different tumour sites: role of smoking and habitual intake of analgesics and laxatives. Results of the Berlin Urothelial Cancer Study. Nephrol Dial Transplant 1999;14:2892–7.

156. Lee SJ, Cho SH, Park SK, et al. Combined effect of glutathione S-transferase M1 and T1 genotypes on bladder cancer risk. Cancer Lett 2002;177:173–9.

157. Engel LS, Taioli E, Pfeiffer R, et al. Pooled analysis and meta-analysis of glutathione S-transferase M1 and bladder cancer: a HuGE review. Am J Epidemiol 2002;156:95–109.

158. Cohen SM, Shirai T, Steineck G. Epidemiology and etiology of premalignant and malignant urothelial changes. Scand J Urol Nephrol Suppl 2000;205:105–15.

159. Inatomi H, Katoh T, Kawamoto T, Matsumoto T. NAT2 gene polymorphism as a possible marker for susceptibility to bladder cancer in Japanese. Int J Urol 1999;6:446–54.

160. Vaziri SA, Hughes NC, Sampson H, et al. Variation in enzymes of arylamine procarcinogen biotransformation among bladder cancer patients and control subjects. Pharmacogenetics 2001;11:7–20.

161. Case RAM, Hosker ME. Tumour of the urinary bladder as an occupational disease in the rubber industry in England and Wales. Br J Prev Soc Med 1954;8:39–50.

162. Case RAM, Hosker ME, McDonald DB, et al. Tumours of the urinary bladder in workmen engaged in the manufacture and use of certain dyestuff intermediates in the British chemical industry. Br J Ind Med 1954;11:75–104.

163. Silverman DT, Levin LI, Hoover RN, et al. Occupational risks of bladder cancer in the United States: I. White men. J Natl Cancer Inst 1989;81:1472–80.

164. Carli A, Peto J, Piolatto G, et al. Bladder cancer mortality of workers exposed to aromatic amines: analysis of models of carcinogenesis. Br J Cancer 1985;51:707–12.

165. Rubino GF, Scansetti G, Piolatto G, et al. The carcinogenic effect of aromatic amines: an epidemiological study on the role of o-toluidine and 4,4'-methylene bis (2-methyl-aniline) in inducing bladder cancer in man. Environ Res 1982;27:241–54.

166. Puntoni R, Bolognesi C, Bonassi S, et al. Cancer risk evaluation in an area with a high density of chemical plants. An interdisciplinary approach. Ann N Y Acad Sci 1988;534: 808–16.

167. Vineis P, Magnani C. Occupation and bladder cancer in males: a case-control study. Int J Cancer 1985;35:599–606.

168. Boyko RW, Cartwright RA, Glashan RW. Bladder cancer in dye manufacturing workers. J Occup Med 1985;27: 799–803.

169. Morrison AS, Ahlbom A, Verhoek WG, et al. Occupation and bladder cancer in Boston, USA, Manchester, UK, and Nagoya, Japan. J Epidemiol Community Health 1985; 39:294–300.

170. Bulbulyan MA, Figgs LW, Zahm SH, et al. Cancer incidence and mortality among beta-naphthylamine and benzidine dye workers in Moscow. Int J Epidemiol 1995;24:266–75.

171. Risch HA, Burch JD, Miller AB, et al. Occupational factors and the incidence of cancer of the bladder in Canada. Br J Ind Med 1988;45:361–7.

172. Sorahan T, Hamilton L, Jackson JR. A further cohort study of workers employed at a factory manufacturing chemicals for the rubber industry, with special reference to the chemicals 2-mercaptobenzothiazole (MBT), aniline, phenyl-beta-naphthylamine and o-toluidine. Occup Environ Med 2000;57:106–15.

173. Serra C, Bonfill X, Sunyer J, et al; Working Group on the Study of Bladder Cancer in the County of Valles Occidental. Bladder cancer in the textile industry. Scand J Work Environ Health 2000;26:476–81.

174. Weiss NS. Cancer in relation to occupational exposure to perchloroethylene. Cancer Causes Control 1995;6:257–66.

175. Schumacher MC, Slattery ML, West DW. Occupation and bladder cancer in Utah. Am J Ind Med 1989;16:89–102.

176. Gago-Dominguez M, Castelao JE, Yuan JM, et al. Use of permanent hair dyes and bladder-cancer risk. Int J Cancer 2001;91:575–9.

177. Steineck G, Plato N, Norell SE, Hogstedt C. Urothelial cancer and some industry-related chemicals: an evaluation of the epidemiologic literature. Am J Ind Med 1990;17:371–91.

178. La Vecchia C, Tavani A. Hair dyes and bladder cancer: an update. Eur J Cancer Prev 2001;10:205–8.

179. Wong O, Raabe GK. A critical review of cancer epidemiology in the petroleum industry, with a meta-analysis of a combined database of more than 350,000 workers. Regul Toxicol Pharmacol 2000;32:78–98.

180. Iscovich J, Castelletto R, Esteve J, et al. Tobacco smoking, occupational exposure and bladder cancer in Argentina. Int J Cancer 1987;40:734–40.

181. Zaridze DG, Nekrasova LI, Basieva TK. Increased risk factors for the occurrence of bladder cancer. Vopr Onkol 1992;38:1066–73.

182. Boffetta P, Jourenkova N, Gustavsson P. Cancer risk from occupational and environmental exposure to polycyclic aromatic hydrocarbons. Cancer Causes Control 1997;8:444–72.

2

Cell-Cycle Aberrations in Human Bladder Cancer

JAY E. REEDER, PhD
EDWARD M. MESSING, MD

Disregulated cellular proliferation is a fundamental characteristic of cancer. This loss of regulation is the direct result of genetic aberrations that occur in somatic cells leading to quantitative or qualitative changes in protein expression. Most known carcinogenic agents are also genotoxic, and through damage to specific genes, they alter cellular proliferation by altering primary protein structure or expression levels. Promotion of cellular proliferation can in itself be carcinogenic through disruption of the normal regulation of tissue homeostasis at the cellular level, leading to an increased risk of acquired somatic mutations.[1]

In cancers, the most frequently detected acquired somatic mutations are in genes that directly or indirectly affect cellular proliferation. In the transition from normal to neoplastic, cells acquire specific phenotypic characteristics. Hanahan and Weinberg have described six categories of acquired capabilities of cancer cells: self-sufficiency in growth signals, insensitivity to antigrowth factors, evasion of apoptosis, sustained angiogenesis, limitless replication potential, and tissue invasion and metastasis.[2]

Each of these characteristics has been associated with aberrations in one or more genes whose products influence cellular proliferation. Self-sufficiency in growth signals is the capacity to proliferate independently of external signals, and insensitivity to antigrowth signals confers the capacity to proliferate in spite of the presence of external negative signals. Evasion of apoptosis leads to proliferation of cells with genomic aberrations (which normally would be destroyed by homeostatic defense mechanisms), resulting in inheritance of these aberrations in clonal descendent cells. Angiogenesis requires proliferation, albeit of nontumor cells. The limited replication potential of normal cells is correlated to telomere length, and this limit is abrogated in tumor cells through increased telomerase activity. Finally, cells with the capacity for tissue invasion and metastasis must proliferate in the process.

CELL CYCLE

Evolutionary Transition from Unicellular Organisms to Metazoons

The evolutionary transition in eukaryotes from unicellular organism to metazoon required a fundamental change in regulation of cell proliferation and specialization, but the basic mechanisms of cell-cycle control were conserved to the extent that much of what is known about cell proliferation in metazoons has been learned through the study of cell proliferation in yeast. Many of the crucial yeast genes have homologs in higher eukaryotes, but control of proliferation from an evolutionary standpoint in yeast is essential to the success of the individual cell and its progeny, whereas in metazoons, the individual cell can be sacrificed for the benefit of the organism. Cancer can be seen as a microevolutionary process in which the individual cell abandons this "greater good" collaboration and reverts to the "simple survival of the fittest" paradigm to the detriment of the host organism. The cell cycle is a paradigm for cellular proliferation that fits the life cycle of unicellular organisms and cancer cells in that their mitoses are generally symmetric and limited only by the hospitality of the local environment.

The cell cycle can be divided into four phases based on a sequential series of cellular events that occur at various levels. These phases are G_1, S, G_2, and M (Figure 2–1). Normal human cells have 46 chromosomes in two sets, or a 2N number of chromosomes. They also have a 2C deoxyribonucleic acid (DNA) content in the G_1 phase of the cell cycle, where C is the amount of DNA in the haploid 1C genome. The G of the G_1 phase refers to "growth" or "gap." G_1 is a period in which the cell may grow in size or may have no observable morphologic changes and appear to be in a gap between more dramatic morphologies. There is a series of events known as checkpoints that drive a cell to commit to the S or DNA synthesis phase of the cell cycle. During the S phase, the DNA content doubles as the genome is replicated. It is important to note that whereas the DNA content increases to the 4C value, the actual

number of chromosomes remains fixed at 2C as the replicated strands remain paired in each chromosome composed of two chromatids. At the conclusion of the S phase, the nucleus has a 4C DNA content, with each and every segment of the genome having been replicated once. The M phase (mitosis) is morphologically the most distinctive phase of the cell cycle as the chromosomes condense on the metaphase plate and the chromatids are separated into two daughter cells with 2C DNA content.

Each step in this process is precisely controlled. The commitment to exit G_1 is dependent on both intrinsic and extrinsic regulation. The process must alternate DNA replication with cytokinesis. It must have input from systems that sense both the need for replication and the availability of resources to complete the process. Cell survival is dependent on successful completion of these steps, and elaborate control mechanisms have evolved to ensure its success. Cancer can be viewed as a failure of the control mechanisms to subjugate the evolutionary success of an individual cell to the survival of the host.

Homeostasis of Epithelial Tissues and Maintenance of the Urothelial Barrier

In transformation to the malignant phenotype, a cell population acquires a set of genetic aberrations that abrogate the normal control of cellular proliferation and tissue homeostasis. This homeostasis, resulting in a relatively constant cell number, is maintained by regulating cell division to match cell loss. A rudimentary understanding of how this is accomplished is slowly emerging for some tissues. A general paradigm for epithelial tissues proposes a stem cell compartment composed of cells with no practical limit in proliferation, a compartment of transit amplifying (TA) cells[3] with limited proliferative potential, and terminally differentiated cells with no proliferative potential. In this model, somatic mutations acquired in terminally differentiated cells have a very low or no potential to yield transformation to a malignant phenotype. Somatic mutations in stem cells or the TA cells may disrupt normal cell-cycle control and lead to inappropriate expansion of the pool and malignant transformation. Presumably, normal control of stem cell proliferation and TA proliferation

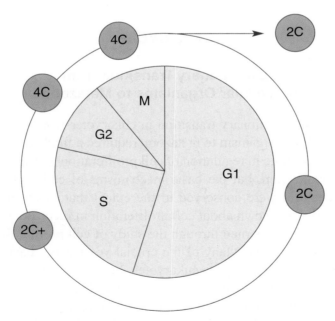

Figure 2–1. The eukaryotic cell cycle is a tightly regulated process divided into four phases. G_1 is a growth phase in which diploid (2C) cells increase in size. Mitogenic signaling can trigger a transition to S phase, a period during which the genome is replicated and total DNA content increases to a 4C value. S phase is followed by another G_2, another growth or "gap," which proceeds mitotic segregation of the replicated chromosomes into two diploid daughter cells during the M phase.

share many common features but may differ sufficiently to account for differences in the biologic and clinical behavior of tumors with similarly acquired somatic mutations. Alternatively, stem cells and TA cells may have different sensitivities and capacities to repair DNA damage. It has been proposed that stem cells lack DNA repair mechanisms and therefore trigger cell death programs as a strategy to avoid clonal expansion of cells with acquired somatic mutations and unlimited replicative potential.[4]

Cancers of the bladder arise primarily in the urothelium. Traditionally, the urothelium has been called a transitional epithelium to reflect its intermediary morphology between stratified and pseudo-stratified epithelium. The term urothelium, however, recognizes that this very specialized tissue is unique to the urinary tract. A thorough review of the bladder urothelium has recently been written by Lewis.[5] Lewis lists four properties of the urothelium essential to performance of its role in storage of urine. These are minimization of surface area (which is accomplished by the spherical shape of the bladder) to limit movement of substances between blood and urine, passive permeability, active sodium resorption, and inertness to the substances found in urine. The bladder urothelium acts as a barrier for urine storage but is not metabolically inactive. Procarcinogens may be activated by the bladder urothelium, and the urothelium actively secretes proteins into the urine.[6]

Relatively little is known about normal cellular proliferation in the urothelium. Martin divided the guinea pig urothelium into three distinct cell layers: basal, pyriform, and surface cells.[7] This same author investigated proliferation in the urothelium using tritiated thymidine following hydrodistention.[8] Nuclear labeling was seen only in occasional basal cells in control animals. Hydrodistention triggered a rapid increase in basal cell labeling, followed by migration of the labeled cells upward into the pyriform and surface layers. Over time, as the labeled cells differentiated into pyriform and surface cells, unlabeled and labeled nuclei were observed within the same cell, indicative of frequent cell fusion events. In addition to cellular fusion, nuclear fusion within these cells was implied by nucleophilic staining of hourglass-shaped objects, with half of these objects labeled and the other unlabeled. The basal

layer of normal urothelium has proliferative potential and is equivalent to the TA compartment described by Lavker and Sun and almost certainly also contains the urothelial stem cells.[3] No specific morphologic compartment for urothelial stem cells has been identified, unlike in the epidermis.[3]

Although a urothelial stem cell compartment has not been identified, a painstaking study by Tsai and colleagues sheds some light on cell population dynamics.[9] Random inactivation of one of the two X chromosomes occurs in early embryogenesis of females. This inactivation event can be used to demonstrate cell lineages by determining which of two polymorphic alleles on the X chromosome is expressed. Because inactivation is a random event, sampling of large populations of normal cells will show expression of both alleles. Inactivation of the X chromosome is dependent on methylation of cytosine residues in gene promoter regions; thus, genomic DNA can be analyzed for methylation to determine which allele is methylated and inactivated. Clonal populations will show clonal methylation. By sampling small populations of cells from the urothelial layer, Tsai and colleagues were able to show clonality of X inactivation in normal urothelium. They estimated the largest area of monoclonality to be approximately one square centimeter in size and that the normal bladder is populated by approximately 200 such patches. Presumably, each patch is a clone derived from a single stem cell or clonal stem cell population.

Tissue Specificity of Oncogenes and Tumor Suppressor Genes

Oncogenes have protein products that exert a positive, dominant effect on cellular proliferation. Oncogenes are activated in somatic cells through several mechanisms, including chromosomal translocations, gene amplification, and coding sequence mutations that alter the activity of the expressed protein

Tumor suppressor genes exert a negative effect on cellular proliferation. Mutations of these genes in tumors lead to inactive protein products. As such, the recessive, inactive phenotype requires that both alleles of a tumor suppressor gene be inactivated to produce the null phenotype. The one exception to this generalization is the rare production of a dominant negative mutant in which both a normal and a mutant protein are expressed, and the mutated protein inactivates the normal protein, such as through the formation of nonfunctional hybrid oligomeric complexes.

Examination of human tumors has revealed that the frequency of acquired somatic aberrations in both oncogenes and tumor suppressor genes is specific to the tissue of origin. This fact is particularly evident in familial cancer syndromes. Presumably, because activated oncogenes are dominant and would disrupt normal differentiation and development, there are no examples of familial cancer syndromes linked to germline inheritance abnormal oncogenes. The majority of these syndromes have now been linked to specific mutations in tumor suppressor genes. The inheritance pattern at the organism level is dominant, but the inherited tumor suppressor gene mutation is recessive at the cellular level until a second mutation is acquired in the normal allele. Remarkable tissue specificity is observed in these syndromes, indicating tissue-specific mechanisms for regulating cellular proliferation. So loss of retinoblastoma (Rb) protein function is nearly obligatory in both sporadic and familial retinoblastomas, but mutations in the *CDKN2A* gene have been linked to familial risk of melanoma. The *RB* and *CDKN2A* genes are components of the same cellular proliferation control pathway that is modulated in different tissues to achieve appropriate cell population homeostasis.

Redundancy in proliferation control pathways is a mechanism to fine-tune proliferation control to the requirements of specific tissue types. This review considers three pathways of cell-cycle control in bladder cancer, and the discussion is restricted to the genes with demonstrated impact on urothelial tumorigenesis. These may be altered in other tissues as well, just as there are cell-cycle control genes that are rarely, if ever, found to be mutated in bladder cancer.

CELL-CYCLE PATHWAYS ALTERED IN BLADDER CANCER

Growth Signals

Mitogenic signaling between cells is essential for maintenance of epithelial tissues. Figure 2–2 has the basic elements of a mitogenic signaling pathway with demonstrated aberrations in bladder cancer. Epidermal growth factor (EGF) was first isolated from urine as urogastrone. The origin of urinary EGF is still controversial, as is its role in maintenance of the normal urothelium. EGF binds to the epidermal growth factor receptor (EGFR) and triggers homo- and heterodimers to form and autophosphorylate. Through several adaptor proteins, the RAS guanosine triphosphatase (GTPase) is activated, which, in turn, initiates the mitogen-activated protein kinase cascade. Through this cascade, various transcription factors are activated, such as Myc, Fos, and Jun, which increase transcription of genes directly involved in progression through the cell cycle. Genetic aberrations and abnormal protein expression levels of EGFR, erbB2, RAS, and Myc have been reported in bladder tumors. Details of these observations are discussed below.

The EGFR family of receptor tyrosine kinases contains four highly similar proteins that are apical signaling proteins in a phosphorylation cascade that stimulates cellular proliferation. Largely owing to methods of discovery, a variety of names appear in the literature for these proteins. The family is unified under the erbB1, erbB2, erbB3, erbB4 naming scheme. The viral *ERBB* oncogene from the avian erythroblastic leukemia virus is a truncated version

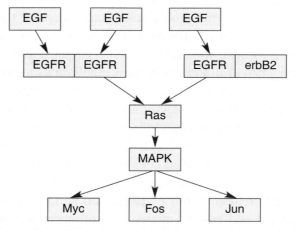

Figure 2–2. Cell-cycle control pathways with known genetic aberrations in bladder cancer. The epidermal growth factor (EGF) receptor (EGFR) family of receptor tyrosine kinases is apical signaling molecules in a phosphorylation leading to increased activity of transcription factors that up-regulate genes essential to cellular proliferation. EGFR and erbB2 have both been shown to be aberrantly expressed and/or mutated in bladder tumors, as have RAS and Myc.

of the cellular gene for EGFR (*ERBB1*). Messing, Neal, and Mellon and their respective colleagues have independently shown that abnormal expression of the receptor for EGF occurs in bladder cancer cells and increased expression is associated with more aggressive biologic behavior.[10–13] Because a major ligand for this receptor, EGF, is excreted in urine in very high quantities in a biologically active form, abnormally high expression of the EGFR may be an example of a cell exploiting its unique environment to provide it with a growth advantage.[14,15] Additionally, EGFR signaling not only induces growth, but also cancer cell motility and matrix metalloproteinase 9 expression, both steps necessary for invasion and metastasis.[16,17] Mechanisms of EGFR overexpression are uncertain because even when the protein is overexpressed, amplification of the *EGFR* gene has not commonly been seen in bladder cancer.[18]

Another member of this gene family with known alterations in bladder cancer is the *ERBB2* oncogene.[19–22] Sauter and colleagues found overexpression of the erbB2 product in 61 of 141 bladder cancers; however, gene amplification was found in only 10 cases.[20] Ding-Wei and colleagues found that 33% of 56 bladder tumors had increased expression of the erbB2 protein by immunohistochemical detection, which correlated with higher grade, higher stage, and tumor recurrence.[21] However, not all authors have found a significant correlation between erbB2 protein expression and aggressive bladder cancer behavior.[19,23,24]

Abnormal expression or function of growth factor receptors can enhance proliferative capacity of malignant cells, a major component of the invasive process. Under normal circumstances, receptors for EGF are confined to the basal layer of urothelial cells. However, in both transitional and squamous cell carcinomas, the EGFR protein is expressed not only on basal cells but throughout the urothelium, including cells at the luminal surface.[11] This abnormal distribution of EGFR is also seen in dysplastic and normal-appearing urothelium adjacent to and remote from transitional cell cancers.[11,25] Even tumor cells that invade deeply into the bladder wall express the EGFR.[11] Both Messing and Neal and colleagues have independently demonstrated that the degree of EGFR expression directly correlates with the inva-

sive phenotype.[11,12] Neal and colleagues, with extensive follow-up, have demonstrated that abnormally high expression of EGFR in bladder cancers is an independent predictor of poor survival.[12,13]

Additionally, other ligands that work through EGFR, such as transforming growth factor α and heparin-binding EGF-like growth factor, may also play a role in bladder tumor progression and proliferation.[16,26–28] EGFR ligands not only induce mitogenesis but also cellular motility. Stimulation of EGFR on malignant urothelial and normal endothelial cells may encourage angiogenesis and malignant cell motility—all processes important for invasion to occur.

Oncogenes that have been associated with bladder cancer include those of the *RAS* gene family, which, at least in some studies, has been found to correlate with a higher histologic grade.[29–31] This is a GTPase that transduces signals from the cell membrane (and receptor tyrosine kinases at the cell surface, such as the EGFR) to the nucleus, affecting proliferation and differentiation.[32] Whereas some reports have claimed that nearly 50% of transitional cell cancers have *RAS* mutations, others have reported far lower levels.[30,33]

In a transgenic mouse model of bladder carcinogenesis in which an activated *HA-RAS* gene was spliced to the urothelium-specific uroplakin II promoter, mice developed superficial papillary bladder tumors in contrast to the invasive and metastatic bladder cancers that developed in mice with urothelium-specific expression of the SV40 T antigen protein. The SV40 T antigen protein produces functional inactivation of both p53 and pRb.

Retinoblastoma Pathway

The retinoblastoma protein is a key player in regulating the G_1- to S-phase transition of the cell cycle (Figure 2–3). In its hypophosphorylated form, pRb interacts with the E2F transcription factors, most notably E2F1. E2F1 is an essential transcription factor for several genes involved in synthesis of new DNA and thus S-phase processes. The pRb–E2F interaction suppresses this transcriptional activity. It is thought that the pRb-E2F1 complexes actually form on promoter regions of target genes. The interaction is disrupted on phosphorylation of Rb

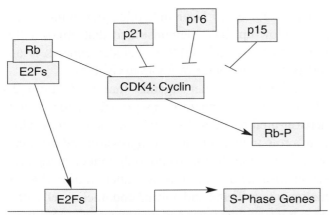

Figure 2–3. Cell-cycle control pathways with known genetic aberrations in bladder cancer. Phosphorylation of Rb is a critical step in the transition from the G_1 to the S phase of the cell cycle. Rb may be lost or mutated in bladder tumors, but more often, proteins that block Rb phosphorylation are the targets of somatic mutation. Loss of p16 is the most frequently documented genomic aberration in bladder cancer of all grades and stage. In some tumors, there is increased expression of CDK4 and/or cyclin D_1.

through the activity of cyclin-dependent kinases 4 and 6 (CDK4, CDK6). CDK4 is active when associated with cyclin D protein. CDK activity is reduced through interaction with several small inhibitor proteins known colloquially as p15, p16, and p21. With the exception of E2F, all of these genes have been implicated as oncogenes or tumor suppressor genes in human bladder cancer.

Inhibitors of the CDKs (which phosphorylate Rb, disassociating it from E2F), serve as regulators of the cell cycle. Such regulators include p15 and p16, proteins coded for on neighboring regions of chromosome 9p, which normally complex with CDK4 and CDK6, inhibiting the phosphorylation of Rb. Similarly, two other nuclear proteins, p21, whose expression is induced directly by p53, and p27, whose level of expression is determined by proteosome-mediated degradation, also inhibit CDKs' phosphorylation of Rb.[34–36] Inactivation of any of these proteins thus would permit Rb to become phosphorylated, resulting in uncomplexed E2F driving the G_1 to S transition and cellular proliferation. Hence, reduced or abnormal expression/function of the products of genes coding for p15, p16, p21, or p27 would be expected to result in uninhibited proliferation and perhaps malignant transformation and tumor progression. Again, all of these genes have been reported to be bladder cancer tumor suppressor genes.

Abnormal expression of Rb (deletion or "overexpression") detected immunohistochemically also appears to occur primarily in aggressive transitional cell cancers.[37,38] Loss of heterozygosity (LOH) of the *RB* gene locus is associated with a higher-grade and -stage tumor, with an overall incidence around 20% of all bladder cancers.[39] Loss of Rb immunoreactivity is seen at a similar frequency.[40,41] *P21* deletions also correlate with more aggressive bladder cancers, and abnormal expression of either p21 or pRb, along with p53, may have additive adverse prognostic implications.[42] The genes encoding the CDK inhibitor proteins p16 and p15, *CDKN2A* and *CDKN2B*, respectively, are located in the p21 band of chromosome 9. Although the LOH of both genes is frequent, *P16* appears to be the predominant target gene as there are examples of p16 loss with retention of the *P15* gene. Some studies point to a more aggressive phenotype in tumors with p16 loss, whereas others are far less clear, revealing losses equally in nonaggressive and aggressive urothelial cancers.[43–45]

Urothelial cell lines with loss of Rb show an increase in p16 expression.[46] These data imply a dependence of p16 expression on Rb. Further work by this group using E6 and E7 HPV (Human papilloma virus) proteins for immortalization of human urothelial cells[43] also supports Rb regulation of p16 expression. Loss of Rb may up-regulate p16 (in an attempt by the cell to inactivate E2F's stimulation of the cell cycle), but it also may make p16 interaction with CDKs irrelevant. The possibility that Rb and p16 could be surrogate markers for each other is intriguing.

Tumor suppressor proteins p53 and Rb are rarely mutated in cells transformed by viral proteins such as E6 and E7. The viral inactivation of these cell-cycle control proteins makes mutations irrelevant. A study of cell lines with cyclin D_1 aberrations found that a high proportion also had *CDKN2A* alterations, suggesting that alteration of one does not make the other irrelevant.[47] In contrast, Rb-deficient cell lines do not contain aberrations in the genes encoding these upstream regulatory proteins (eg, cyclins, CDKs, or their inhibitors), indicating that mutations in these genes and proteins must enhance tumor gene growth primarily through a functioning Rb protein.

Initial reports of *CDKN2A* DNA sequence analysis in bladder tumors found a very low frequency of mutations in the retained allele of tumors with chromosome 9p21 LOH.[44,48] Subsequent analysis and further understanding of the structure of the *CDKN2A* and *CDKN2B* genes allowed these initial negative results to be placed in context.

A comprehensive analysis of 16 bladder cell lines and 140 bladder tumors revealed homozygous deletion of the *CDKN2A* gene in half of the cell lines.[49] Overall, LOH and/or deletion or mutation were found in 55 tumors (39%). The tumors included in this study had a lower frequency of chromosome 9 loss than has been found in other studies. In a nonselective sampling of bladder tumors, approximately 50% have LOH at all informative markers on chromosome 9p. Molecular allelotyping and LOH studies, most notably by Cairns, Habuchi, and Knowles and their colleagues, narrowed the common region of deletion in bladder cancer to chromosome 9p21.[50–53] Subsequent mapping of the p16 complementary DNA to this locus strongly suggested that the *CDKN2A* gene was a target gene in bladder cancer.

There are three possible routes to *CDKN2A* inactivation: homozygous deletion, hemizygous deletion and mutations of the remaining allele (rare), and hemizygous deletion with hypermethylation at a 5' CpG island in the promoter. Methylation of cytosine nucleotides in CpG palindromes occurs in regions of DNA rich in CpG. In promoter regions, this methylation process can silence transcription of genes.[54] Hypermethylation of *CDKN2A* and transcriptional silencing have been observed in bladder tumors and cell lines.[55]

P53 Pathway

A simplified scheme of the role of the p53 protein in cell-cycle control is presented in Figure 2–4. As it is perhaps the most extensively studied tumor suppressor gene, any attempt to summarize the vast p53 literature requires such simplification. When DNA is damaged, such as strand breaks from ionizing radiation, the half-life of the p53 protein is greatly increased, and, acting as a transcription factor, p53 up-regulates the expression of several genes. One of these is the p21 CDK inhibitor. Through this mechansim, p53 alters phosphorylation of the Rb protein (see Figure 2–3).

Considering the critical role that p53 has in controlling normal cell growth and the neoplastic process, it is not surprising that its own stability is under tight regulation. MDM2, a protein whose expression itself is induced by p53, binds to p53's amino terminal, targeting it for ubiquitization and proteosomic degradation.[56] Failure of this process stabilizes p53. Indeed, wild-type p53 normally lasts only very briefly in the cell nucleus, whereas mutated forms will often accumulate for longer times and hence be more easily detected by immunohistochemistry.[57] The abundance of p53 protein is tightly regulated through transcription and protein degradation via ubiquitination, which is promoted by the MDM2 protein. MDM2 is, in turn, down-regulated by the p14/ARF protein, an alternate splice variant sharing the same genetic locus with p16.

The *P53* gene is frequently reduced to homozygosity and mutated in bladder tumors. LOH is also frequently observed at the p16/p14/ARF locus, and the promoter is silenced by methylation. The *P53* gene and p53 protein have been surveyed in solid bladder tumor tissues, exfoliated cell specimens, and DNA extracted from urine. The primary conclusion from these studies is that p53 aberrations are a marker for higher-grade urothelial cancers.

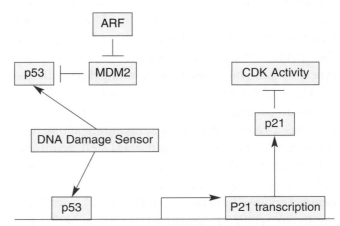

Figure 2–4. Cell-cycle control pathways with known genetic aberrations in bladder cancer. *P53* aberrations are generally associated with high-grade and -stage bladder tumors. Loss of p53 activity decreases p21 expression, resulting in increased cyclin-dependent kinase (CDK) activity, and contributes to replication of damaged DNA, yielding increased genomic instability. Loss of the ARF protein, which can occur in concert with loss of the p16 and p15 proteins (the other products of the 9p21 tumor suppressor gene locus), is another mechanism whereby p53 activity is decreased though MDM2-mediated p53 degradation.

Immunohistochemical detection of nuclear p53 antigen is strongly correlated with detectable p53 mutations.[58] The sensitivity of p53 nuclear reactivity for p53 mutations is 90%.[59] These results lay a foundation for p53 immunohistochemistry as a marker for p53 mutation and essentially equate immunoreactivity with accumulation of mutant protein. Several groups have closely correlated p53 accumulation in cell nuclei (immunohistochemically detectable) with genetic mutations in the *P53* gene and have employed immunohistology as a fairly simple means of screening cancers to assess whether p53 is mutated. Unfortunately, some important mutations in the *P53* gene will result in expression of a sufficiently truncated form of the protein (or no protein) that no nuclear "overexpression" is seen, a circumstance that is indistinguishable immunohistochemically from one in which wild-type p53 is expressed.[34] Similarly, deletion of both alleles of the gene (homozygous deletion) will also not be detectable immunohistochemically. This may explain some of the discordance between immunohistochemical and LOH or other molecular data in some reports.[42] Additionally, because the wild-type p53 protein functions as a tetramer, the altered product of a mutant allele stabilizes (permitting nuclear accumulation) but inactivates the tetrameric protein (resulting in tumorigenesis) even when the nonmutated allele is expressed normally. This dominant negative effect offers a theoretical hurdle to genetic therapeutic strategies that attempt to insert a wild-type *P53* gene into tumors with mutated p53 alleles.

The *P53* gene is the most frequently altered gene in human cancers.[60,61] The normal protein, wild-type p53, has a variety of functions, including acting as a transcription factor that suppresses cell proliferation, directing DNA damaged cells toward apoptosis before DNA replication (S phase of the cell cycle) occurs (reviewed in Harris and Hollstein), contributing to the repair of damaged DNA by inducing the production of deoxyribonucleotide triphosphates in the nucleus (reviewed by Lozano and Elledge), and other mechanisms.[42,60–63] Because p53 directs cells with genetic abnormalities toward apoptosis, p53 mutations have been associated with genomic instability, leading to progressive development of further mutations.[61] Thus, it is not surprising that bladder cancers with p53 abnormalities appear to have more aggressive behaviors.[34,64]

Tetu and colleagues examined initial superficial bladder tumors and found a low frequency of p53 overexpression (14.7%).[41] Although p53 expression correlated to a shorter interval to first recurrence, it was not an independent predictor in multivariate analysis. In contrast, patients whose tumors overexpress p53 and undergo cystectomy have significantly shorter 5-year survival than those whose tumors lack such expression.[64] Similarly, patients with muscle-invasive tumors that have low p53 expression have better 5-year survival than those with elevated p53 expression or who are treated with methotrexate, vinblastine, doxorubicin, and cisplatin combination chemotherapy.[65] Sarkis and colleagues also found an association between p53 immunoreactivity of stage Ta and carcinoma in situ lesions and progression to higher stages.[66] Finally, p53 immunoreactivity is correlated with metastases of bladder tumors.[67]

Studies of p53 in exfoliated cells have been few. This may be attributable to the difficulty in establishing criteria for positivity. Cytoplasmic staining is frequently observed in bladder tumor tissues; thus, flow cytometric assays may be complicated by this phenomenon. One report of p53 and DNA cytometry of bladder irrigation specimens found correlations of p53 staining with the presence of tumor and tumor grade and stage. The presence of aneuploid populations correlated to p53 immunoreactivity.[68]

For tumors to exceed 1 or 2 mm in diameter, new blood vessels must feed them. Wild-type p53 induces the expression of a potent inhibitor of angiogenesis, thrombospondin 1 (TSP-1), a normal constituent of the extracellular matrix, whereas mutant (or absent) p53 does not. A correlation of abnormal p53 immunostaining with down-regulation of TSP-1 and neoangiogenesis has been reported in bladder cancer.[69] Additionally, whereas wild-type p53 may repair DNA damage caused by chemotherapeutic agents such as cisplatin, impaired p53 function, although contributing to a more aggressive phenotype, may paradoxically enhance sensitivity to some chemotherapeutic agents.[42,70]

Through study of the normal functions of the products of deleted genes, particularly their roles in regulating cellular proliferation, investigators have tried to correlate identified deletions with the known differences in behavior of the two major types of transitional cell carcinoma: low-grade, papillary, superficial tumors and high-grade cancers that rapidly become invasive and metastasize. Through such correlations, several groups have now identified chromosome 9 and particularly 9q losses as an early event in the development of low-grade superficial tumors. [44,53,71–74] Alternatively, high-grade cancers are much more commonly associated with p53 abnormalities and chromosome 17p deletions. [44,75] This observation is not surprising because accumulated genetic errors expected in a cell with a nonfunctioning p53 protein encourage continued genetic instability and selection for aberrant (ie, aggressive) behavior and anaplastic morphology. Such abnormalities are beginning to be used to predict future tumor behavior (see below).

CLINICAL IMPLICATIONS

Current treatment strategies for both superficial and invasive bladder cancer do not exploit aberrant cell-cycle control genes. This information has the potential to improve patient care by allowing treatment to be fitted to a particular tumor's specific complement of genetic aberrations. For instance, antibodies to cell-surface receptors and small molecule inhibitors of the EGFR family of receptor tyrosine kinases might abrogate the mitogenic drive of some tumors, but a tumor with an *H-RAS* mutation might not be responsive to these drugs as this lesion is downstream in the signaling pathway of the apical EGFR signaling.

Inhibition of the dominant activity of oncogenes is perhaps more easily accomplished by pharmacologic agents than restoration of recessive tumor suppressor gene activity. Drugs that inhibit CDK activity might decrease Rb phosphorylation in tumors with intact, wild-type Rb expression, but CDK inhibitors will fail to control tumors that lack Rb expression, and restoration of Rb expression through gene therapy requires restoration in all cells of malignant potential.

The problem, however, has become finite because we are close to knowing the finite combinations of genetic events that can contribute to loss of proliferation control. These genetic aberrations occur in genes that are components of pathways that are highly conserved across species but also exhibit tissue specificity. The tissue specificity increases the possibility that therapeutic strategies can be devised that are tumor specific. The unique accessibility of the bladder lumen to topical agents should overcome some of the potential difficulties, in terms of reliable delivery and toxicity, that systemic administrations face.

REFERENCES

1. Cohen SM, Ellwein LB. Genetic errors, cell proliferation, and carcinogenesis. Cancer Res 1991;51:6493.
2. Hanahan D, Weinberg RA. The hallmarks of cancer. Cell 2000;100:57–70.
3. Lavker RM, Sun TT. Epidermal stem cells: properties, markers, and location. Proceeding of the National Academy of Sciences. 2000;97:13473–5.
4. Cairns J. Somatic stem cells and the kinetics of mutagenesis and carcinogenesis. Proceeding of the National Academy of Sciences. 2002;99:10567–70.
5. Lewis SA. Everything you wanted to know about the bladder epithelium but were afraid to ask. Am J Renal Physiol 2000;278:F867–74.
6. Deng FM, Ding M, Lavker RM, Sun TT. Urothelial function reconsidered: a role in urinary protein secretin. Proceeding of the National Academy of Sciences. 2001;98:154–9.
7. Martin BF. The effect of distention of the urinary bladder on the lining epithelium and on its histochemical reaction for alkaline phosphatase. Ann Histochim 1962;7:51–62.
8. Martin BF. Cell replacement and differentiation in transitional epithelium: a histological and autoradiographic study of the guinea-pig bladder and ureter. J Anat 1972; 112:433–55.
9. Tsai YC, Simoneau AR, Spruck CH III, et al. Mosaicism in human epithelium: macroscopic monoclonal patches cover the urothelium. J Urol 1995;153:1697–700.
10. Messing EM, Hanson P, Ulrich P, Erturk E. Epidermal growth factor—interactions with normal and malignant urothelium: in vivo and in situ studies. J Urol 1987;138:1329–35.
11. Messing EM. Clinical implications of the expression of epidermal growth factor receptors in human transitional cell carcinoma. Cancer Res 1990;50:2530–37.
12. Neal DE, Sharples L, Smith K, et al. The epidermal growth factor receptor and the prognosis of bladder cancer. Cancer 1990;65:1619–25.
13. Mellon K, Wright C, Kelly P, et al. Long-term outcome related to epidermal growth factor receptor status in bladder cancer. J Urol 1995;153:919–25.
14. Fuse H, Mizuno I, Sakamoto M, Karayama T. Epidermal growth factor in the urine from the patients with urothelial tumors. Urol Int 1992;48:261.
15. Messing EM, Murphy-Brooks N. Recovery of epidermal growth factor in voided urine of patients with bladder cancer. Urology 1994;44:502–6.

16. Theodorescu D, Laderoute KR, Guilding KM. Epidermal growth factor receptor-regulated human bladder cancer motility is in part a phosphatidylonositol 3-kinase mediated process. Cell Growth Differ 1998;9:919–28.

17. O-Charoenrat P, Modjitakedi H, Rhys-Evans P, et al. Epidermal growth factor-like ligands differentially up-regulate matrix metalloproteinase 9 in head and neck squamous carcinoma cells. Cancer Res 2000;60:1121–28.

18. Neal DE, Smith K, Fennelly JA, et al. Epidermal growth factor receptor in human bladder cancer: a comparison of immunohistochemistry and ligand binding. J Urol 1989; 41:517–21.

19. Wright C, Mellon K, Johnston P, et al. Expression of mutant p53, c-erbB-2 and the epidermal growth factor receptor in transitional cell carcinoma of the human urinary bladder. Br J Cancer. 1991;63:967–70.

20. Sauter G, Moch D, Carroll P, et al. Heterogeneity of erbB-2 gene amplification in bladder cancer. Cancer Res 1993; 53:2199–2203.

21. Ding-Wei Y, Jia-Fu Z, Yong-Jiang M. Correlation between the expression of oncogenes ras and c-erb B-2 and the biological behavior of bladder tumors. Urol Res 1993;21:39–43.

22. Swanson PE, Frierson HF, Wick MR. C-erbB-2 (HER-2/neu) oncopeptide immunoreactivity in localized, high grade transitional cell carcinoma of the bladder. Mod Pathol 1992;5:531–6.

23. Mellon JK, Lunec J, Wright C, et al. C-erbB-2 in bladder cancer: molecular biology, correlation with epidermal growth factor receptors and prognostic value. J Urol 1996;155: 321–6.

24. Orlando C, Sestine R, Vona G, et al. Detection of C-Erb-B-2 amplification in transitional cell bladder cancer using competitive PCR technique. J Urol 1996;156:2089–93.

25. Rao JY, Hemstreet GP III, Hurst RE, et al. Alterations in phenotypic biochemical markers in bladder epithelium during tumorigenesis. Proc Natl Acad Sci U S A 1993;90: 8287–91.

26. Cooper CS, See WA, Crist SA. Urine from iatrogenically traumatized bladders promotes transitional carcinoma cell growth in a manner consistent with a growth factor dependent mechanism [abstract]. J Urol 1992;147:262A.

27. Brown LF, Berse B, Jackman RW, et al. Increased expression of vascular permeability factor (vascular endothelial growth factor) and its receptors in kidney and bladder carcinomas. Am J Pathol 1993;143:1255–62.

28. Freeman MR, Yoo JJ, Raab G, et al. Heparin-binding EGF-like growth factor is an autocrine growth factor for human urothelial cells and is synthesized by epithelial and smooth muscle cells in the human bladder. J Clin Invest 1997;99:1028–36.

29. Burchill SA, Neal DE, Lunec J. Frequency of H-ras mutations in human bladder cancer detected by direct sequencing. Br J Urol 1994;73:516–21.

30. Czerniak B, Cohen GL, Etkind P, et al. Concurrent mutations of coding and regulatory sequences of the Ha-ras gene in urinary bladder carcinomas. Hum Pathol 1992;23:1199–204.

31. Viola MV, Fromowitz F, Oravez S, et al. Ras oncogene p21 expression is increased in premalignant lesions of high grade bladder carcinomas. J Exp Med 1985;161:1213–18.

32. Barbacid M. Ras oncogenes: their role in neoplasia. Eur J Clin Invest 1990;20:225–35.

33. Knowles MA, Williamson M. Mutation of H-ras is infrequent in bladder cancer: confirmation by single-strand conformation polymorphism analysis, designed restriction fragment length polymorphisms, and direct sequencing. Cancer Res 1993;53:133–9.

34. Cordon-Cardo C. Mutation of cell cycle regulators—biological and clinical implications for human neoplasia. Am J Pathol 1995;147:545–60.

35. Loda M, Cukor B, Tam SW, et al. Increased proteasome-dependent degradation of the cyclin-dependent kinase inhibitor p27 in aggressive colorectal carcinomas. Nat Med 1997;3:231–4.

36. Xiong Y, Hannon GJ, Zhang H, et al. P21 is a universal inhibitor of cyclinkinases. Nature 1993;366:701–4.

37. Cote RJ, Dunn MD, Chatterjee SJ, et al. Elevated and absent pRb expression is associated with bladder cancer progression and has cooperative effects with p53. Cancer Res 1998;58:1090–4.

38. Cairns P, Proctor AJ, Knowles MA. Loss of heterzygosity at the RB locus is frequent and correlates with muscle invasion in bladder cancer. Oncogene 1991;6:2305–9.

39. Miyamoto H, Shuin T, Ikeda I, et al. Loss of heterozygosity at the p53, RB, DCC and APC tumor suppressor gene loci in human bladder cancer. J Urol 1996;155:1444–7.

40. Johnson S, Karlsson MG. Predictive values of p53 and pRb immunostaining in locally advanced bladder cancer treated with cystectomy. J Urol 1998;160:1291–6.

41. Tetu B, Fradet Y, Allard P, et al. Prevalence and clinical significance of HER/2neu, p53 and Rb expression in primary superficial bladder cancer. J Urol 1996;155:1784–8.

42. Cote RJ, Chatterjee SJ. Molecular determinants of outcome in bladder cancer. Cancer J Sci Am 1999;5:2–15.

43. Reznikoff CA, Belair CD, Yeager TR, et al. A molecular genetic model of human bladder cancer pathogenesis. Semin Oncol 1996;23:571–84.

44. Spruck CH III, Ohneseit PF, Gonzalez-Zulueta M, et al. Two molecular pathways to transitional cell carcinoma of the bladder. Cancer Res 1994;54:784–8.

45. Friedrich MG, Blind C, Milde-Langosch K, et al. Frequent p16/MTS1 inactivation in early stages of urothelial carcinoma of the bladder is not associated with tumor recurrence. Eur Urol 2001;40:518–24.

46. Yeager T, Stadler W, Belair C, et al. Increased p16 levels correlate with pRb alterations in human urothelial cells. Cancer Res 1995;55:493–7.

47. Lukas J, Aagaard L, Strauss M, Bartek J. Oncogenic aberrations of p16INK4/CDKN2 and cyclin D1 cooperate to deregulate G1 control. Cancer Res 1995;55:4818–23.

48. Cairns P, Tokino K, Eby Y, Sidransky D. Homozygous deletions of 9p21 in primary human bladder tumors detected by comparative multiplex polymerase chain reaction. Cancer Res 1994;54:1422–4.

49. Williamson MP, Elder PA, Shaw ME, et al. P16 (CDKN2) is a major deletion target at 9p21 in bladder cancer. Hum Mol Genet 1995;4:1569–77.

50. Cairns P, Shaw ME, Knowles MA. Initiation of bladder cancer may involve deletion of a tumour-suppressor gene on chromosome 9. Oncogene 1993;8:1083–5.

51. Cairns P, Shaw ME, Knowles MA. Preliminary mapping of the deleted region of chromosome 9 in bladder cancer. Cancer Res 1993;53:1230–2.

52. Habuchi T, Ogawa O, Kakehi Y, et al. Accumulated allelic losses in the development of invasive urothelial cancer. Int J Cancer 1993;53:579–84.

53. Knowles MA, Elder PA, Williamson M, et al. Allelotype of human bladder cancer. Cancer Res 1994;54:531–8.

54. Jones PA, Baylin SB. The fundamental role of epigenetic events in cancer. Nat Rev Genet 2002;3:415–28.

55. Gonzalez-Zulueta M, Bender CM, Yang AS, et al. Methylation of the 5' CpG island of the p16/CDKN2 tumor suppressor gene in normal and transformed human tissues correlates with gene silencing. Cancer Res 1995;55:4531–5.

56. Carr AM. Piecing together the p53 puzzle. Science 2000; 287:1765–6.

57. Finlay CA, Hinds PW, Tan TH, et al. Activating mutations for transformation by p53 producer gene products that forms an HSC-70-p53 complex with an altered half-life. Mol Cell Biol 1988;8:531–9.

58. Esrig D, Spruck CH III, Nichols PW, et al. P53 nuclear protein accumulation correlates with mutations in the p53 gene, tumor grade, and stage in bladder cancer. Am J Pathol 1993;143:1389–97.

59. Cordon-Cardo C, Dalbagni G, Saez GT, et al. P53 mutations in human bladder cancer: genotypic versus phenotypic patterns. Int J Cancer 1994;56:347–53.

60. Vogelstein B. A deadly inheritance. Nature (Lond) 1990; 348:681–2.

61. Harris CC, Hollstein M. Clinical implications of the p53 tumor-suppressor gene. N Engl J Med 1993;329:1318–27.

62. Lozano G, Elledge SJ. P53 sends nucleotides to repair DNA. Nature 2000;404:24–5.

63. Smith ML, Chen IT, Zhan Q, et al. Interaction of the p53 regulated protein Gadd45 with proliferating cell nuclear antigen. Science 1994;266:1376–80.

64. Esrig D, Elmajian D, Groshen S, et al. Accumulation of nuclear p53 and tumor progression in bladder cancer. N Engl J Med 1994;331:1259–64.

65. Sarkis AS, Bajarin DF, Reuter VE, et al. Prognostic value of p53 nuclear overexpression in patients with invasive bladder cancer treated with neoadjuvant MVAC. J Clin Oncol 1995;13:1384–90.

66. Sarkis AS, Dalbagni G, Cordon-Cardo C, et al. Association of p53 nuclear overexpression and tumor progression in carcinoma in situ of the bladder. J Urol 1994;152:388–92.

67. Moch H, Sauter G, Moore D, et al. P53 and erbB-2 protein overexpression are associated with early invasion and metastasis in bladder cancer. Virchows Arch 1993;423:329–34.

68. Griffiths TR, Mellon JK, Pyle GA, et al. P53 and ploidy assessed by flow cytometry in bladder washings. Br J Urol 1995;76:575–9.

69. Grossfeld GD, Ginsberg DA, Stein JP, et al. Thrombospondin-1 expression in bladder cancer: association with p53 alterations, tumor angiogenesis, and tumor progression. J Natl Cancer Inst 1997;89:219–27.

70. Hawkins DS, Demers W, Galloway DA. Inactivation of p53 enhances sensitivity to multiple chemotherapeutic agents. Cancer Res 1996;56:892–8.

71. Tsai YC, Nichols PW, Hiti AL, et al. Allelic losses of chromosomes 9, 11, and 17 in human bladder cancer. Cancer Res 1990;50:44–7.

72. Habuchi T, Luscombe M, Elder PA, Knowles MA. Structure and methylation-based silencing of a gene (DBCCR1) within a candidate bladder cancer tumor suppressor region at 9q32-q33. Genomics 1998;48:277–88.

73. Simoneau M, Aboulkassim TO, LaRue H, et al. Four tumor suppressor loci on chromosome 9q in bladder cancer: evidence for 2 novel candidate regions at 9q22.3 and 9q31. Oncogene 1999;18:157–63.

74. Czerniak B, Chaturvedi V, Li L, et al. Superimposed histologic and genetic mapping of chromosome 9 in progression of human bladder neoplasia. Implications for a genetic model of multi-step urothelial carcinogenesis and early detection of urinary bladder cancer. Oncogene 1999;18:1185–96.

75. Gruis NA, Weaver-Feldhaus J, Liu Q, et al. Genetic evidence in melanoma and bladder cancers that p16 and p53 function in separate pathways of tumor suppression. Am J Pathol 1995;146:1199–1206.

3

Molecular Carcinogenesis and Pathogenesis of Proliferative and Progressive (Invasive) Urothelial Cancer

DAN THEODORESCU, MD, PhD

Carcinoma of the urinary bladder is the second most common urologic malignancy (Chapter 1). In addition, these tumors are one of the best understood genitourinary neoplasms with a well defined etiology, natural history, tumor biology, treatment options, and outcome. This level of understanding arises as a consequence of multiple factors and represents a convergence of knowledge from diverse scientific disciplines. Insight provided by these disciplines, coupled with unique features of this neoplasm which make it assessable for detection, monitoring and treatment, combine to make this disease a model system for modern oncology. The intent of this chapter is to provide the reader an overview of our current understanding of this tumor from the standpoint of its molecular biology as related to tumor development and progression.

MOLECULAR BASIS OF TUMOR DEVELOPMENT

The first insight into the etiology of transitional cell carcinomas (TCC) of the urinary bladder began with the observation of an increased incidence associated with industrial development. Workers in the aniline dye industry in Germany were noted to be at increased risk for the development of this tumor.[1] This association made bladder neoplasms the first of what would subsequently be recognized as many chemically induced tumors. Subsequent understanding has come to identify the process of uroepithelial transformation as one of contact carcino-

genesis. Carcinogens ingested by one of multiple routes, either inhaled, consumed, or absorbed through the skin, are concentrated in the urine and subsequently come in contact with the lining of the urinary tract. This diffuse exposure predisposes to what has come to be known as "field change." Thus the entire uroepithelium to which urine has been exposed may have multiple areas of frank or preneoplastic transformation.

Early clinical observations regarding the biology of the "at risk" field suggested that sites of preneoplastic changes could follow several distinct clinical courses. It is possible that areas of dysplasia remain simply dysplastic. Alternatively, the urinary epithelium can progress either to superficial bladder neoplasms, characterized by recurrence but rarely life threatening progression, or along the path towards invasion with its well recognized risk of mortality. Evidence in support of these disparate pathways comes from the low progression rate of the majority of superficial bladder tumors, coupled with the fact that many invasive neoplasms present as such initially. An example of a clinical evidence–based pathway detailing these distinctions in tumor biology is illustrated in Figure 3–1.[2] Insight afforded by these clinical observations has played a central role in generating hypotheses, developing models, and directing basic research in bladder cancer. Not only have these clinical observations served as the basis for research undertakings, but these subsequent research activities have in turn provided strong evidence to support the validity of these clinical models.

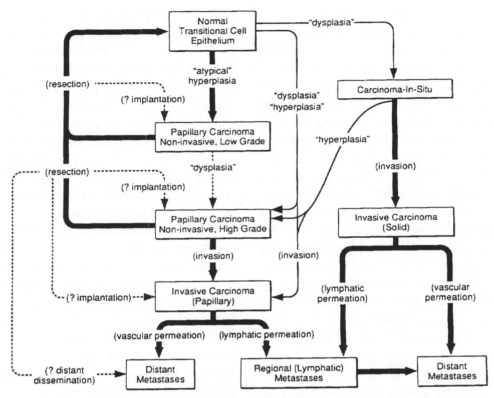

Figure 3–1. Proposed pathway for bladder tumor development derived from clinical observation. Note that the superficial and invasive pathways are distinct, with divergence early in the process of tumorigenesis. (From Jones PA, Droller MJ. Pathways of development and progression in bladder cancer: new correlations between clinical observations and molecular mechanisms. Semin Urol 1993;11:177–92.)

Carcinogenesis

Models of molecular carcinogenesis must explain the relevant clinical natural history and aspects of tumor behavior such as uncontrolled cellular proliferation, neovascularization, and altered apoptosis. In addition, models of neoplastic transformation should account for other clinically relevant features of the neoplasm in question. For superficial and invasive transitional cell carcinomas of the urinary bladder, these would include tumor recurrence and tumor metastasis, respectively.

The historic view of two-stage carcinogenesis in which tumor initiation (mutation) is followed by tumor promotion (epigenetic changes) has been conceptually important but is currently thought to be too simplistic. It is now believed that there may be six or more independent mutational events[3,4] necessary for carcinogenesis. Furthermore, chemical carcinogens may be geno-

toxic, nongenotoxic[5] or induce epigenetic effects[6] with dose-response relations being linear or nonlinear.[7,8] Endogenous mutagenic mechanisms such as DNA oxy-radical damage, de-purination, and polymerase infidelity also contribute to carcinogenesis[3,9–11] leading to a debate regarding the relative importance of endogenous versus exogenous mutagenic events and the value of animal bioassays or short term mutagenic assays for assessment of human cancer risks.[4,10,12,13] In this chapter, two of the best characterized molecular paradigms leading to transitional cell carcinoma will be discussed. Together, these will highlight how the effect of a chemical carcinogen may be altered by the characteristics of the host and serve as both a model system and framework for further research in this area.

Many different exposures and risk factors have been identified in bladder cancer. In the late 19th century, the German physician Rehn observed an association between the occurrence of bladder cancer and exposure of workers to aromatic amines (arylamines) and polycyclic aromatic hydrocarbons (PAH), compounds found in the dyestuff industry. In addition to these environmental exposures, tobacco smoking has also been associated with an elevated risk for multiple types of human cancers.[14] Several of the chemicals identified in tobacco smoke have been shown to cause cancer in laboratory animals.[15] The property that is common to all of the diverse types of genotoxic chemical carcinogens is that they can form directly or are metabolized to highly reactive electrophilic forms.[16] These electron deficient species can attack the many electron rich or nucleophilic sites in molecules such as proteins and nucleic acids to form covalent adducts or induce mutagenesis.[17] There is considerable evidence to suggest that DNA is the molecular target of these agents. Damage to DNA induced by these adducts is hypothesized to lead to mutations in proto-oncogenes and/or tumor suppressor genes. Two components of tobacco smoke, benzopyrene, a PAH, and 4-aminobiphenyl, an arylamine, form adducts with DNA, suggesting that these components may be direct mutagens contributing to the development of bladder cancer.

Interestingly, neither PAHs nor arylamines are direct carcinogens and therefore it would seem that additional steps are necessary for their activation and metabolism (Figure 3–2A). The normal role of the host enzymes that act on chemical carcinogens is to convert these foreign lipophilic compounds into more hydrophilic forms that can be readily excreted. How-

ever, in attempting to create a hydrophilic product, these enzymes inadvertently form a reactive product. Most of these reactions are catalyzed by cytochrome P450–dependent monooxygenases located predominantly in the liver. In the case of carcinogenic arylamines, the first step in this process is N-oxidation catalyzed by hepatic cytochrome P450 1A2 isoenzyme (CYP1A2).[18] This enzyme has been shown to be inducible by several environmental factors including cigarette smoke, which has resulted in significant individual and population variability when the activity of this enzyme is measured.[19] Due to its critical role, it is not surprising to find indirect evidence that a phenotype associated with enhanced CYP1A2 activity, may be a risk factor for bladder cancer.[20] These electrophilic metabolically active forms of arylamines or hydroxylamines can form adducts with hemoglobin or circulate freely as glucuronide conjugates and be excreted in the urine.[21] Hydroxylamines are then hydrolyzed in the acidic urinary environment allowing formation of adducts with nucleophilic sites in the transitional bladder mucosa.

Fortunately, alternative processing of arylamines can occur in detoxifying pathways (see Figure 3–2A), with the most studied of these pathways being N-acetylation. Two isoenzymes of N-acetyltransferase (NAT1 and NAT2) have been identified in humans.[17] The NAT2 enzyme is encoded by a single polymorphic gene, with individuals having any two of several possible mutant alleles displaying a slow acetylator phenotype and hence exhibit impaired detoxification of carcinogenic arylamine (Figure 3–2B).[22] Several

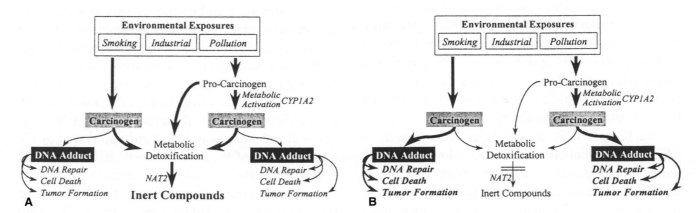

Figure 3–2. Hypothetical model of carcinogen activation and detoxification and resulting cellular consequences in patients with normal detoxification (*A*), and in individuals with abnormal detoxification mechanisms (B). CYP1A2 = hepatic cytochrome P450 1A2; NAT2 = N-acetyltransferase 2; GST-M1 = glutathione S transferase M1.

recent case-control studies have investigated the relationship of NAT2 phenotype or genotype and bladder cancer risk[23-25] and have demonstrated that "slow aceltylators," namely, individuals who detoxify arylamines slowly due to decreased activity of these pathways, have a substantially higher risk of bladder cancer. On the other hand, NAT2 does not appear to play a role in bladder carcinogenesis induced by PAHs.[26] In addition to NAT2, glutathione-S-transferase M1 (GST-M1), a family member of a class of enzymes which detoxify reactive chemicals by promoting their conjugation to glutathione has also been studied in relation to bladder cancer risk.[27] Metabolites of several PAHs that are present in cigarette smoke as well as arylamines are known or potential substrates of GST-M1.[27,28] Thus, NAT2 and GST-M1 likely play key roles in the risk for bladder cancer development in individuals exposed to similar doses/durations of carcinogens. In addition, the status of these enzymes may explain, in part, the wide variation in bladder cancer risk in different ethnic and racial groups.[29,30] Both NAT2 and GST-MI have shown racial/ethnic variations, which may explain in part why similar smoking habits result in different risks of bladder cancer.[23,28,31]

A number of specific genes are known to be mutated by chemical carcinogens. Two of the genes, *H-RAS* and *P53*, have also been implicated in bladder tumorigenesis and progression. The *H-RAS* gene codes for p21Ras, a small guanosine triphosphatase (GTPase) involved in signal transduction,[32] that was the first proto-oncogene found to be mutated in the T24 bladder cancer cell line.[33] Evidence from clinical studies using immunohistochemical techniques has demonstrated a correlation between the levels of the Ras protein and the degree of tumor invasiveness and that the expression of *H-RAS* is an independent prognostic variable for tumor invasion.[34] In addition, an in vivo study[35] has implicated this molecule in several of the steps involved in tumor invasion, supporting the notion that *H-RAS* overexpression is causally related to tumor progression and not merely an epiphenomenon. Detailed staining for *H-RAS* in normal bladder tissue has revealed that the basal (progenitor) cells of the multilayered transitional epithelium stain with the highest intensity while more superficial (differentiated) compartments stain to a much lesser degree. Thus the level of normal *H-RAS* protein diminishes

considerably with differentiation. However, *H-RAS* overexpression per se is not restricted to the malignant state in bladder tissue. It is thus conceivable that a deregulation of *H-RAS* gene expression[34] or expression of a mutant protein[33] can occur and result in the induction of bladder cancer. Support for this idea comes from results demonstrating that transfection of an *H-RAS* gene will convert SV40 immortalized human urothelial cells into invasive transitional cell carcinomas.[36,37] Recent reports[38,39] utilizing polymerase chain reaction (PCR)-based methods, revealed that approximately 40% of bladder tumors harbor *H-RAS* codon 12 mutations.

For genotoxic carcinogens, the interaction with DNA is likely not to be random, and each class of agents reacts selectively with purine and pyrimidine targets.[40,41] In addition, targeting of carcinogens to particular sites in DNA is determined by the nucleic acid sequence,[42] by specific DNA repair processes and host cell type, making some genetic sequences more at risk than others. As expected from this chemistry, genotoxic carcinogens are potent mutagens, able to cause base mispairing or small deletions, leading to missense or nonsense mutations,[40] but the spectra of mutations seems to be dependent on the agent. For example, the mutations found in activated *RAS* proto-oncogenes associated with tumors of animals exposed to N-nitroso compounds are predominantly G:C $\rightarrow$ A:T base substitutions.[43] Although there are several guanine residues in *RAS* codons that would generate a transforming protein if substituted by adenine, these experiments have revealed that the mutations detected in tumors occur overwhelmingly at only one of the possible mutation sites. PAHs, on the other hand, produce a different mutation spectrum,[44] and other chemical classes, such as tobacco-specific nitrosamines, have yet other spectra.[45] In vitro studies using either prokaryotic or human cells, indicate that human exposure to mutagens may result in a narrow nonrandom spectrum of mutations.[46] Finally, adding another layer of complexity in humans, the spectra of *K-RAS* gene mutations in adenocarcinomas vary according to tissue sites, indicating that mutational spectra may be dependent on the causal agent, the target gene, and the tissue involved.

Another important genetic target for chemical carcinogenesis is the *P53* tumor suppressor gene.

This gene is of particular relevance in bladder cancer because of its putative roles in both transformation[47] and progression.[48] Mutations in the *P53* tumor suppressor gene are a frequent event in both transitional cell and squamous cell carcinomas of the bladder,[49] with up to 40% of bladder cancers harboring such lesions. Especially valuable have been studies of the timing of occurrence of these mutations during different stages of bladder cancer pathogenesis. Mutations are rare in low-grade papillary tumors but are common in carcinoma in situ (CIS) and more invasive high-grade bladder cancers, suggesting that *P53* may play a role in both transformation[47] and progression.[48] Recent immunohistochemical studies of patients with bladder TCC have revealed a significant correlation between the number of cigarettes smoked and the incidence of positive *P53* immunohistochemistry. Studies comparing cases of bladder cancer from smoking and nonsmoking patients showed an increased frequency of G:C → C:G transversions in both groups. While smokers did not have a different mutational spectrum than nonsmokers, they did exhibit a higher frequency of double mutation events.[50,51] Mutations in *P53* are particularly detrimental due to this gene's multiple cellular regulatory and supervisory roles.[52]

Genetics of Tumor Development

The molecular basis of urothelial transformation and progression can be deduced from numerous studies carried out over the last several years. Using cytogenetic, molecular genetic, and immunohistochemical methods, a general pattern seems to be emerging as to which genes and/or chromosomal locations are important for tumor development and progression. In this section we will highlight the genetic abnormalities associated with neoplastic transformation and focus on those associated with progression later on. Multistage carcinogenesis is regarded as a consequence of the accumulation of somatic genetic alterations, which include activation of cellular proto-oncogenes, and the inactivation of tumor suppressor genes. As outlined above for *RAS* and *P53*, environmental carcinogens can induce alterations of both gene types. In addition, to these studies, a large number of reports have surveyed the cytogenetic

changes found in TCC.[53] Studies of TCC revealed consistently high incidence of chromosomal abnormalities in chromosome 9[54] and 17p.[55]

Currently, it would appear that chromosome 9 [56] and *P53* [57] changes can occur relatively early in the genesis of TCC while other changes such as epidermal growth factor receptor (EGFR) and E-cadherin are associated with progression. Chromosome 9 deletions are often found early in bladder tumor development, a finding also observed in other cancers such as lung,[58] ovary,[59] and kidney.[60] A candidate tumor suppressor gene *CDKN2A*:p16 was recently identified in the 9p21 region,[61] an area commonly altered in bladder cancer.[53] *CDKN2A* encodes a protein that is part of a new group of cell cycle inhibitory molecules known as cyclin dependent protein kinases (CDK).[62] Among these are also p15 (*INK4B/MTS2*) which together with p16 can inhibit the phosphorylation of the retinoblastoma protein (RB), thereby inhibiting the cell cycle. Loss of either of these genes may have profound implications on the cell cycle and result in uncontrolled growth and tumor formation. The loss of p16, often accompanied by p15 loss, is a very frequent occurrence in bladder cancer, occurring in up to 40% of cases.[63] The importance of *P53* in bladder tumorigenesis was suggested by the high frequency of loss of heterozygosity (LOH) of chromosome 17p where this gene is located (17p13.1). *P53* codes for a 53kDa phosphoprotein with DNA binding properties which is involved in multiple cell functions including gene transcription, monitoring the fidelity of DNA synthesis, and apoptosis.[64] *P53* mutations may be induced by carcinogens as outlined above, resulting in a selective growth advantage of cells harboring these defects. The role of *P53* as a target for chemical carcinogenesis was discussed earlier. Whereas there is significant evidence to support the role of *P53* in bladder tumor progression, the role of *P53* has only recently been clarified in tumorigenesis of TCC. Recent genetic evidence has suggested that different clinical forms of TCC may result from different genetic lesions.[47] A model has been recently proposed which hypothesizes two different pathways leading to the development of superficial bladder tumors including CIS (Figure 3–3). This model postulates that chromosome 9 alterations in normal cells lead to papillary superficial TCC whereas *P53* muta-

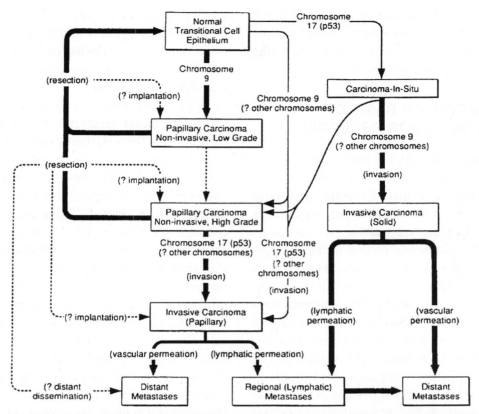

Figure 3–3. Proposed pathway for bladder tumor development derived from molecular epidemiologic data. The divergent, distinct pathways for superficial and invasive tumors parallels the model developed from observations of clinical biology (Figure 3–1). (From Jones PA, Droller MJ. Pathways of development and progression in bladder cancer: new correlations between clinical observations and molecular mechanisms. Semin Urol 1993;11:177–92.)

tions lead to CIS (CIS/Tis). Both *P53* and chromosome 9 losses can play a complimentary role further downstream in tumor progression in concert with other genetic changes.

In addition to these changes, microsatellite instability at loci on chromosome 9, was found in TCC.[65] Microsatellites are sequences of polymorphic nucleotide repeats found throughout the human genome,[66,67] which are routinely used in the analysis of LOH in human cancers. In addition, abnormalities or instabilities consisting of alterations of the number of repeats of a specific microsatellite in tumor DNA when compared to normal tissue DNA, indicate that replication errors have occurred.[68] The persistence of these errors is an indication of the reduced ability of cancers to repair mutations. The greater the instability, the less the capacity of repair, the greater the potential for the generation of heterogenous populations, some of which exhibit novel

and more malignant attributes such as enhanced growth, growth factor independence, and drug resistance among many others. In colon cancer, microsatellite instability has been linked to alterations in the *MSH2* gene, located on 2p16,[69] which codes for an enzyme involved in DNA repair. Since microsatellite abnormalities found in TCC appear to be early changes,[54,65,70] they may be reflecting severe deregulation of cellular DNA which if left unchecked may lead to unrepaired mutations in key regulatory genes such as *P53*. In addition, genes such as *MSH2* may themselves be targets of carcinogenic insults. Finally, a case study by Schoenberg and colleagues[71] describes a patient who developed TCC of the bladder and renal pelvis at an early age. The patient was found to have the germline translocation t(5;20)(p15;q11), which may have been an initiating factor in the disease. A recent literature review by Kiemeney and Schoenberg[72] examined case reports and epidemiological studies on TCC and concludes that there is evidence for a familial bladder cancer gene, which is a distinct entity from the known cancer predisposition syndromes.

MOLECULAR BASIS OF SUPERFICIAL TUMOR RECURRENCE

A central feature of the clinical biology of superficial bladder cancer is its idiosyncratic rate of recurrence. Its uniquely high metachronous recurrence rate, distinguishing it from all other organ sites involved by contact carcinogenesis, has served as the basis for a long-standing debate in the urologic literature. Although a number of theories have been proposed to account for this unique feature of superficial bladder cancer, two fundamental theories have received the greatest attention. The concept of urothelial field change following exposure to a urinary carcinogen is both intuitively appealing and supported by multifocality and associated dysplasia in this disease.[1] Nonetheless other contact carcinogen induced tumors should have similar risks and yet fail to have metachronous recurrence rates approximating those associated with superficial bladder neoplasms. For this reason, and given the unique nature of the lower urinary tract, other authors have proposed intraepithelial tumor dissemination and or treatment induced implantation as a phenomenon accounting for the idiosyncrasy of superficial bladder cancer recurrence biology.[73] Anecdotal evidence in support of this concept in addition to the unusual recurrence rate include the temporality of recurrence in relation to surgical removal of a primary lesions and the location of recurrences in relation to the index lesion.[74]

Debate on this issue is traceable to the turn of the century when Albarran first proposed implantation as a mechanism accounting for bladder tumor recurrence.[75] The pendulum swung several times in the ensuing years. In the 1950s, Melicow, and Kaplan clearly demonstrated associated areas of dysplasia and preneoplasia in the urothelium intervening between sites of frank neoplasia.[76,77] However subsequent work by McDonald showed that urothelial malignancies could be implanted into and grow on sites of urothelial trauma even given relatively crude immunosuppression and understanding of transplant rejection in that era.[78] These observations were later expanded on by Soloway[73] and the specific mechanisms involved in tumor implantation delineated by See.

A definitive answer to the issue of the mechanism of bladder tumor recurrence was not provided until early in the 1990s. Using a molecular analysis of X chromosome inactivation in women with multifocal bladder tumors Sidransky and colleagues provided strong evidence to suggest that the multifocal tumors were clonal in origin.[81] Subsequently, Habuchi and colleagues demonstrated that heterotopic urothelial recurrence was associated with identical mutations in P53 at both the upper and lower track sites of occurrence.[82] Most recently this same group did microsatellite analysis on patients with multifocal metachronous tumor recurrence.[83] They found identical microsatellite alterations on multiple chromosomes in 80% of patients with multifocal recurrences. Overall, this combination of data provides virtually conclusive evidence that the majority of superficial bladder recurrences are clonal in their etiology. Nonetheless some minor issues related to the precise mechanism of recurrence remain unresolved. Tsai and colleagues found mosaicism in the human uroepithelium which suggested that clonal heterogeneity within the bladder was more limited than previously thought.[84] Indeed further evidence suggested that the bladder could develop from as few as 200 primordial cells and that the risk of tumor development and recurrence might be a consequence of limited diversity within the progenitor cell population.

While the etiologic debate regarding the mechanism of tumor recurrence has been largely resolved, the molecular mechanisms underlying the ability of superficial bladder tumors to implant and grow at sites different from the primary are largely undefined. See and Chapman outlined the requisite steps necessary for tumor implantation and or intraepithelial tumor dissemination to occur.[85] In the case of implantation, the obvious first step is the presence of free floating tumor cells on the luminal surface of the bladder. These tumor cells must remain viable in the detached state and subsequently be able to adhere to sites on the urothelial surface. Following adherence, the local milieu must be conducive to the ultimate outgrowth of the adherent cell or cells. This would include an ability for the cells to divide, proliferate, and develop a vascular support structure.

Clinical observation and basic science research has provided some insight into factors associated with certain of the aforementioned steps. The mechanism of bladder tumor ablation, that is electrosurgical disruption into a fluid-filled medium, frees tumor cells from their underlying site of origin and effectively disseminates them throughout the luminal surface of the bladder. Surgical injury associated with the process of electrosurgical resection of bladder tumors results in sites of urothelial injury which selectively predisposes to tumor cell adherence via the formation of fibrin clots and effective entrapment/adherence of tumor cells at these sites. Given the central role of cellular adherence to clots at the site of urothelial injury, several studies have suggested that tumor intrinsic pericellular proteolysis through one of several fibrinolytic pathways may be a regulator of tumor cell adherence and ultimate outgrowth.[86–88] However, little work has been done to define whether specific molecular alterations in pericellular proteolysis might account for patterns of recurrence.

Other facets of the implantation process, such as proliferation and neovascularization, have been alluded to in other work. The epidermal growth factor/TGF-α autocrine and paracrine loops have been suggested to predispose to recurrence.[89] Subsequently, cellular production of vascular endothelial growth factor, allowing for the establishment of a vascular support structure, has been suggested as a prognostic feature correlating with recurrence risk.[90] While a number of associated factors have been identified, these studies are at a very preliminary stage. The precise mechanisms responsible for dysregulation of cellular expression of these various proteins remain to be clarified.

MOLECULAR BASIS OF BLADDER CANCER PROGRESSION

Although less common than tumor recurrence, progression of superficial tumors to muscle invasion has profound consequences with respect to prognosis and treatment. In fact, tumor progression encompasses a spectrum of clinical and biological changes in both the tumor and the host from early invasion of the basement membrane to widely metastatic disease.[91] In this section we will focus and highlight the changes occurring when superficial bladder cancers become muscle invasive.

In general, organs are composed of a series of tissue compartments separated from each other by two types of extracellular matrix: basement membranes and interstitial stroma.[92] The extracellular matrix determines tissue architecture, has important biologic functions, and is a mechanical barrier to tumor cell invasion. The nuances of what is meant by invasive and superficial bladder cancer are worth mentioning here, since they are somewhat at odds with the pure definition of tumor invasion which is the penetration of normal tissue barriers such as the basement membrane. In the purest sense only stage Ta and CIS tumors are truly "superficial," thus not penetrating the basement membrane of the bladder wall. Historically, however, urologists have also considered T1 tumors as superficial despite their invasion of the lamina propria. Tumors labeled as "invasive" on the other hand are those penetrating the true muscle of the bladder wall. As a group, most stage T1 lesions are more prone eventually to invade the detrusor during subsequent recurrences than are Ta tumors. Conversely, despite being truly superficial, CIS is more aggressive and behaves more akin to T1 than Ta tumors. This may be the result of the differing genetic lesions that led to its formation compared to those leading to Ta/T1 cancers.[93] Due to the significant drop in the prognosis for a patient with any step in tumor progression, the genetic basis of this phenomenon is therefore a subject of considerable clinical importance. In the current section we will highlight the cytogenetic, molecular genetic, and immunohistochemical evidence supporting the role of specific genetic changes in the progression of bladder cancer to muscle invasive disease.

Cytogenetic Changes associated with TCC progression

Several recent studies have examined the common regions of deletion in human bladder tumors.[53,93] In a recent series, Knowles and associates screened 83 cases of transitional cell carcinoma for LOH on all autosomal chromosome arms.[53] The most frequent losses were monosomies of chromosome 9 (57%), losses on chromosomes 11p (32%), 17p (32%), 8p (23%), 4p (22%), and 13q (15%). This series was composed of a majority of superficial low-grade lesions and thus the incidence of the various losses would be reflective of the genetic alterations specifically present in this cohort of patients. Other groups have focused on identifying the common deletions specifically associated with tumor progression. In these cases, a somewhat different spectrum of abnormalities was observed, involving alterations at chromosomal locations 3p,[94] 4q,[95] 8p,[96] 18q,[97] 10,[98,99] 15,[100,101] and 17p.[57] Some of these changes have also been observed in a recently characterized, highly tumorigenic variant of the T24 human bladder cell line.[102]

Previous studies on predominantly superficial bladder cancer specimens[53] indicated an overall low frequency of chromosome 10 allele losses and deletions in bladder cancer. However when cohorts with significant proportions of invasive tumors were investigated,[99] the incidence of LOH on this chromosome was found in 40% of tumors for at least one locus. Remarkably, LOH on chromosome 10 was observed mainly in muscle-invasive or high-grade tumors, the latter of which were most likely invasive or to have a high chance of future progression to invasive disease. Confirming these findings, Kagan and colleagues[98] found LOH with at least one allele lost on the long arm of chromosome 10 in 9 of 20 (45%) invasive TCCs. Recently, LOH studies have also suggested that human chromosome 15 may harbor a novel putative tumor suppressor gene that appears to play a role during metastasis in breast and bladder cancer.[101] This observation supported other studies where fluorescence in situ hybridization (FISH) for chromosome 15 specific centromeric repeat sequences revealed loss of this chromosome in 67% of specimens from patients with histologically confirmed TCC.[100]

Molecular and Immunohistochemical Changes Associated with TCC Progression

Studies using immunohistochemical techniques (IHC) have suggested that overexpression of *HRAS*-protein (previously discussed),[34] *P53*,[103] and the *EGFR*,[104] in bladder tumors may be related to bladder tumor progression. Loss of *RB*[57] and E-cadherin[105] expression has also been related to this transition. Below, we will discuss the evidence suggesting roles for these genes in bladder cancer progression.

E-Cadherin (CDH1)

The disruption of intercellular contacts, which accompanies cell dissociation and acquisition of motility, is correlated with a redistribution of E-cadherin over the entire cell surface and within the cytoplasm. Normal urothelium expresses E-cadherin, a Ca^{2+}-dependent cell adhesion molecule, located on chromosome 16q22.1 and shown to behave like an invasion suppressor gene in vitro and in vivo in experimental systems.[106] This may explain the inverse relation between expression of E-cadherin and bladder tumor grade.[107] Several investigators further examined E-cadherin expression in bladder cancer samples and sought a correlation with tumor behavior. In an early study on 49 patient specimens (24 superficial and 25 invasive tumors), decreased E-cadherin expression correlated with both increased grade and stage of bladder cancer. More importantly, abnormal E-cadherin expression correlated with shorter patient survival.[108] These relationships to stage and grade were subsequently confirmed by other groups[109,110] whereas those to survival were sometimes[105] but not always[111] shown, despite a correlation with distant metastasis.[112] This latter apparent inconsistency may be due to a lack of statistical power in the various analyses to demonstrate an effect.

Epidermal Growth Factor Receptor

Similar to *H-RAS*, *EGFR* expression levels in bladder cancer have been associated with increasing pathologic grade, stage,[113] and higher rates of recurrence[114] and progression in superficial forms of the disease.[104] As such they may be causally related to the transition from superficial to invasive disease. Most importantly, patients with increased *EGFR* expression on their tumor cells did not survive as long as patients with normal *EGFR* expression. However, when the comparison of survival was limited to patients with invasive bladder cancer, no significant difference was found between patients with high levels of *EGFR* expression and those with low *EGFR* values,[115] suggesting that *EGFR* overexpression might be associated with the phenotypic transition from superficial to invasive forms of disease. Interestingly, gene amplification and gene rearrangement does not appear to be a common mechanism for *EGFR* overexpression in bladder cancer.[116] However, superficial human bladder cancer cells which were engineered to overexpress either mutated or normal *H-RAS* also begin overexpressing *EGFR* at both the mRNA and protein levels, therefore *H-RAS* might also play a role in transcriptional regulation of *EGFR* besides its role in *EGFR* signal transduction.[32,117]

Taken together, these data suggest that regulation of *EGFR* is altered in bladder cancer. In addition, since epidermal growth factor is present in large quantities in urine,[118] with concentrations up to 10-fold greater than those found in blood, this situation is likely to potentiate the consequences of EGFR overexpression since *EGFRs* in bladder cancer are functional.[119] Supporting the notion that *EGFR* overexpression is causally related to tumor progression and not merely an epiphenomenon are a number of in vitro[117,120] studies that have implicated this molecule in several of the steps involved in tumor invasion, such as cell motility.

Retinoblastoma

Deletions of the long arm of chromosome 13, including the *retinoblastoma (RB)* locus on 13q14, were found in 28 of 94 cases, with 26 of these 28 lesions being present in muscle-invasive tumors.[121] *RB* alterations in bladder cancer as a function of stage was studied in 48 primary bladder tumors[122] where a spectrum of altered patterns of expression, from undetectable *RB* levels to heterogeneous expression of *RB*, was observed in 14 patients. Of the 38 patients diagnosed with muscle invasive tumors, 13 were categorized as *RB* altered, while only 1 of the 10 superficial carcinomas had the altered *RB* phenotype. Patient survival was decreased in *RB* altered patients compared with those with normal *RB* expression.

Two recent studies[123,124] have also shown that *RB* and *P53* alterations can further deregulate cell cycle control at the G1 checkpoint and produce tumor cells with reduced response to programmed cell death. The imbalance produced by an enhanced proliferative activity and a decreased apoptotic rate may further enhance the aggressive clinical course of the bladder tumors harboring both *P53* and *RB* alterations. A study focusing on the clinical progression of T1 tumors has demonstrated that patients with normal expression of both proteins have an excellent outcome, with no patient showing disease progression. Patients with abnormal expression of either or both proteins had a significant increase in progression.[125] These data indicate the clinical utility of stratification of T1 bladder cancer patients based on *P53* and *RB* nuclear protein status. They suggest that patients with normal protein expression for both genes may be managed conservatively, whereas patients with alterations in one and particularly both genes may require more aggressive treatment. Conversely, conflicting results have been obtained when *RB* status has been examined in patients with invasive tumors,[126,127] indicating perhaps that this gene may have its primary role in progression from superficial to muscle invasive disease rather than further downstream in the metastatic cascade.

P53

Genetic alterations of the *P53* gene, such as intragenic mutations, homozygous deletions, and structural rearrangements, are frequent events in bladder cancer.[128] Structural alterations of the *P53* gene were investigated using single strand conformation polymorphism (SSCP) in 25 bladder tumors; mutations in 6 of 12 invasive carcinomas were found, whereas only 1 of 13 superficial bladder tumors had such mutations.[129] Moreover, mutations were not identified in any of the 10 grade 1 and 2 lesions, however 8 of 15 grade 3 bladder carcinomas were found to have intragenic mutations. In another study,[130] IHC detectable p53 protein was studied in 42 bladder carcinomas. One out of 11 grade 1 (9%), 12 of 22 grade 2 (55%), and 8 of 9 grade 3 (89%) tumors showed positivity for *P53*. There were significantly more *P53* positive cases in grade 2 and 3 tumors than in grade 1 tumors. There were significantly more *P53* positive cases in stage T2 to T4 tumors than in stage T1 tumors. Another study[131] analyzed 42 specimens of TCC by interphase cytogenetics with a FISH technique and found that *P53* deletion was significantly correlated with grade, stage, S-phase fraction, and DNA ploidy, although *P53* overexpression correlated only with grade. Moch and colleagues[132] studied the overexpression of *P53* by IHC in 179 patients and found that *P53* immunostaining strongly correlated with tumor stage. In addition, this was driven by a marked difference in *P53* expression between pTa (37% positive) and pT1 (71% positive) tumors, although there was no difference between pT1 and pT2 to pT4 tumors. Similarly, a strong overall association between *P53* expression and grade was driven by a marked difference between grade 1 (28%) and grade 2 tumors (71%), and there was no significant difference between grade 2 and grade 3 tumors.

Several groups have investigated the possibility that altered patterns of *P53* expression correlated with tumor progression in patients with T1 bladder cancer.[133,134] Patients with T1 tumors were retrospectively stratified into two groups with either < 20% tumor cells (group A) with positive nuclear staining or > 20% of cells with nuclear immunoreactivity for *P53* (group B).[133] Disease progression rates were 20.5% per year for group B and 2.5% for group A, with patients in group B having significantly shorter progression free intervals. Disease specific survival was also associated with altered patterns of *P53* expression. Another study[134] reported an analysis of T1 tumors using immunohistochemistry and 20% positive nuclear staining as the cutoff value. The mean follow-up time was greater than 10 years. Progression and tumor grade were both significantly related to *P53* nuclear overexpression. However in this last study cited, *P53* expression was not an independent predictor of disease progression.

Other studies have attempted to clarify the role of *P53* as a prognostic marker in muscle-invasive tumors. In one study, *P53* was evaluated in 90 bladder tumors from 111 patients treated with neoadjuvant chemotherapy of methotrexate, vinblastine, Adriamycin [doxorubicin], and cisplatin (MVAC).[135] Patients with *P53* overexpression had a significantly higher proportion of cancer deaths. The long term survival in the *P53* overexpressors was 41% versus 77% in the non-expressors independent of stage and grade. In another study, histologic specimens of stages pTa transitional cell carcinoma of the bladder, to pT4 from 243 patients who were treated by radical cystectomy were examined for the IHC detection of *P53* protein.[48] Nuclear *P53* reactivity was then analyzed in relation to time to recurrence and overall survival. In patients with TCC confined to the bladder, an accumulation of *P53* in the tumor-cell nuclei predicted a significantly increased risk of recurrence and death, independently of tumor grade, stage, and lymph-node status. In a third study, IHC *P53* protein expression analysis was performed on samples from 90 patients with TCC of the urinary bladder.[136] Positive nuclear staining of tumor cells by the antibody to *P53* protein was detected in 32 cases, most of which were invasive and nonpapillary tumors and in high grade tumors. In addition, patients with tumors positive for *P53* staining had a significantly worse survival rate.

Other Genes

Early studies in bladder cancer have indicated a strong association of low level *MYC* (8q24) gains with tumor grade, stage, chromosome polysomy , P53 protein expression, *P53* deletion and tumor cell proliferation as assessed by Ki67 labeling index.[137] These data were consistent with a role of chromosome 8 alterations in bladder cancer progression.[96] However subsequent studies have not found statistical significant correlation between the expression of *MYC* gene and clinical-histopathological parameters,[138] or between the *MYC* methylation pattern and clinical stage.[139] Furthermore, *MYC* overexpression did not correlate with tumor grade or tumor progression.[140] Thus the role of this gene in bladder cancer development or progression is at present unclear.

Amplification and protein overexpression of the *ERBB2* gene located on 17q11.2-q12, has been suggested as a prognostic marker for patients with recurrent progressive bladder tumors.[141,142] However, other studies have failed to link *ERBB2* expression levels as an independent variable predicting disease progression.[143] Other studies have indicated a high level of expression of this gene in malignant as compared to benign bladder epithelium.[143] From these studies it would appear that the role of *ERBB2* as a diagnostic marker may outweigh its usefulness as a prognostic indicator.

The *MDM2* (mouse double minute 2, human homologue of; p53-binding protein) gene is located at 12q13-14 and codes for a 90 kD nuclear protein which is a negative regulator of *P53*. In urinary bladder, a strong statistical association between *MDM2* and *P53* overexpression was found in addition to an association between *MDM2* overexpression and low-stage, low-grade bladder tumors.[144] In addition, the simultaneous assessment of *MDM2* and *P53* was found to be independent factors for both disease progression and survival.[145] However, as with *MYC* and *ERBB2* not all studies have shown assessment of this gene product to be independently related to tumor progression.[146]

CONCLUSION

We have attempted to review the current understanding of both the molecular carcinogenesis and pathogenesis, and the molecular basis for the biology of transitional cell bladder neoplasms. The identification of heritable genetic mutations could possibly allow the early, specific, identification of individuals at risk for certain tumors. The recognition that both the individual genotype and the environment may combine for the ultimate determination of risk may allow patients to adapt their lifestyles for risk modification. For those patients with neoplastic disease, therapy can be tailored to the specific biology of the individual tumor. The ongoing integration of molecular biology with clinical science promises to bring all of this within our reach.

REFERENCES

1. Hunstein W, Rehn K. Tumor-induction through cytostatic agents in man. Dtsch Med Wochenschr 1975;100:155–158.
2. Droller MJ. Treatment of regionally advanced bladder cancer. An overview. Urol Clin North Am 1992;19:685–93.
3. Loeb LA. Mutator phenotype may be required for multistage carcinogenesis. Cancer Res1991;51:3075–9.
4. Hay A. Carcinogenesis. Testing times for the tests [news]. Nature 1991;350:555–6.
5. Melnick RL, Kohn MC, Portier CJ. Implications for risk assess-

ment of suggested nongenotoxic mechanisms of chemical carcinogenesis. Environ Health Perspect 1996;104:123–34.
6. MacLeod MC. A possible role in chemical carcinogenesis for epigenetic, heritable changes in gene expression. Mol Carcinog 1996;15:241–50.
7. Lutz WK. Endogenous genotoxic agents and processes as a basis of spontaneous carcinogenesis. Mutat Res 1990; 238:287–95.
8. Swenberg JA, Richardson FC, Boucheron JA, et al. High- to low-dose extrapolation: critical determinants involved in the dose response of carcinogenic substances. Environ Health Perspect 1987;76:57–63.
9. Lutz WK. Dose-response relationship and low dose extrapolation in chemical carcinogenesis. Carcinogenesis 1990;11:1243–7.
10. Weinstein IB. Mitogenesis is only one factor in carcinogenesis [see comments]. Science1991;251:387–8.
11. Breimer LH. Molecular mechanisms of oxygen radical carcinogenesis and mutagenesis: the role of DNA base damage. Mol Carcinog 1990;3:188–97.
12. Ames BN, Gold LS. Too many rodent carcinogens: mitogenesis increases mutagenesis. Science 1990;249:970–1.
13. Infante PF. Prevention versus chemophobia: a defence of rodent carcinogenicity tests [see comments]. Lancet 1991;337:538–40.
14. Shopland DR, Eyre HJ, Pechacek TF. Smoking-attributable cancer mortality in 1991: is lung cancer now the leading cause of death among smokers in the United States? [see comments]. J Natl Cancer Inst 1991;83:1142–8.
15. Vineis P, Caporaso N. Tobacco and cancer: epidemiology and the laboratory. Environ Health Perspect 1995;103:156–60.
16. Talalay P. Mechanisms of induction of enzymes that protect against chemical carcinogenesis. Adv Enzyme Regul 1989;28:237–50.
17. Wormhoudt LW, Commandeur JN, Vermeulen NP. Genetic polymorphisms of human N-acetyltransferase, cytochrome P450, glutathione-S-transferase, and epoxide hydrolase enzymes: relevance to xenobiotic metabolism and toxicity. Crit Rev Toxicol 1999;29:59–124.
18. Butler MA, Iwasaki M, Guengerich FP, Kadlubar FF. Human cytochrome P-450PA (P-450IA2), the phenacetin O-deethylase, is primarily responsible for the hepatic 3-demethylation of caffeine and N-oxidation of carcinogenic arylamines. Proc Natl Acad Sci U S A 1989;86: 7696–700.
19. Kalow W, Tang BK. Caffeine as a metabolic probe: exploration of the enzyme-inducing effect of cigarette smoking [see comments]. Clin Pharmacol Ther 1991;49:44–8.
20. Kaderlik KR, Kadlubar FF. Metabolic polymorphisms and carcinogen-DNA adduct formation in human populations. Pharmacogenetics 1995;5:S108–17.
21. Bryant MS, Vineis P, Skipper PL, Tannenbaum SR. Hemoglobin adducts of aromatic amines: associations with smoking status and type of tobacco. Proc Natl Acad Sci U S A 1988;85:9788–91.
22. Bell DA, Taylor JA, Butler MA, et al. Genotype/phenotype discordance for human arylamine N-acetyltransferase (NAT2) reveals a new slow-acetylator allele common in African-Americans. Carcinogenesis 1993;14:1689–92.
23. Branch RA, Chern HD, Adedoyin A, et al. The procarcinogen

hypothesis for bladder cancer: activities of individual drug metabolizing enzymes as risk factors. Pharmacogenetics 1995;5:S97–102.

24. Hein DW. Acetylator genotype and arylamine-induced carcinogenesis. Biochim Biophys Acta1988;948:37–66.

25. Risch A, Wallace DM, Bathers S, Sim E. Slow N-acetylation genotype is a susceptibility factor in occupational and smoking related bladder cancer. Hum Mol Genet 1995;4: 231–6.

26. Hayes RB, Bi W, Rothman N, et al. N-acetylation phenotype and genotype and risk of bladder cancer in benzidine-exposed workers. Carcinogenesis 1993;14:675–8.

27. Board P, Coggan M, Johnston P, et al. Genetic heterogeneity of the human glutathione transferases: a complex of gene families. Pharmacol Ther 1990;48:357–69.

28. Bell DA, Taylor JA, Paulson DF, et al. Genetic risk and carcinogen exposure: a common inherited defect of the carcinogen-metabolism gene glutathione S-transferase M1 (GSTM1) that increases susceptibility to bladder cancer. J Natl Cancer Inst 1993;85:1159–64.

29. Foster F. New Zealand Cancer Registry report. Natl Cancer Inst Monogr 1979;4:77–80.

30. Case RA, Hosker ME, McDonald DB, Pearson JT. Tumours of the urinary bladder in workmen engaged in the manufacture and use of certain dyestuff intermediates in the British chemical industry. Part I. The role of aniline, benzidine, alpha-naphthylamine, and beta-naphthylamine. 1954 [classical article]. Br J Ind Med 1993;50:389–411.

31. Yu MC, Skipper PL, Taghizadeh K, et al. Acetylator phenotype, aminobiphenyl-hemoglobin adduct levels, and bladder cancer risk in white, black, and Asian men in Los Angeles, California. J Natl Cancer Inst 1994;86:712–6.

32. Bos JL. All in the family? New insights and questions regarding interconnectivity of Ras, Rap1 and Ral. Embo J 1998;17:6776–82.

33. Parada LF, Tabin CJ, Shih C, Weinberg RA. Human EJ bladder carcinoma oncogene is homologue of Harvey sarcoma virus ras gene. Nature 1982;297:474–8.

34. Fontana D, Bellina M, Scoffone C, et al. Evaluation of c-ras oncogene product (p21) in superficial bladder cancer. Eur Urol 1996;29:470–6.

35. Theodorescu D, Cornil I, Fernandez BJ, Kerbel RS. Overexpression of normal and mutated forms of HRAS induces orthotopic bladder invasion in a human transitional cell carcinoma. Proc Natl Acad Sci U S A 1990;87:9047–51.

36. Pratt CI, Kao CH, Wu SQ, et al. Neoplastic progression by EJ/ras at different steps of transformation in vitro of human uroepithelial cells. Cancer Res 1992;52:688–95.

37. Christian BJ, Kao CH, Wu SQ, et al. EJ/ras neoplastic transformation of simian virus 40-immortalized human uroepithelial cells: a rare event. Cancer Res 1990;50:4779–86.

38. Czerniak B, Cohen GL, Etkind P, et al. Concurrent mutations of coding and regulatory sequences of the Ha-ras gene in urinary bladder carcinomas. Hum Pathol 1992;23: 1199–1204.

39. Czerniak B, Deitch D, Simmons H, et al. Ha-ras gene codon 12 mutation and DNA ploidy in urinary bladder carcinoma. Br J Cancer 1990;62:762–3.

40. Essigmann JM, Wood ML. The relationship between the chemical structures and mutagenic specificities of the DNA lesions formed by chemical and physical mutagens. Toxicol Lett 1993;67:29–39.

41. Dipple A. DNA adducts of chemical carcinogens. Carcinogenesis 1995;16:437–41.

42. Levy DD, Groopman JD, Lim SE, et al. Sequence specificity of aflatoxin B1-induced mutations in a plasmid replicated in xeroderma pigmentosum and DNA repair proficient human cells. Cancer Res 1992;52:5668–73.

43. Loechler EL, Green CL, Essigmann JM. In vivo mutagenesis by O6-methylguanine built into a unique site in a viral genome. Proc Natl Acad Sci U S A 1984;81:6271–5.

44. Marshall CJ, Vousden KH, Phillips DH. Activation of c-Ha-ras-1 proto-oncogene by in vitro modification with a chemical carcinogen, benzo(a)pyrene diol-epoxide. Nature 1984;310:586–9.

45. Ronai ZA, Gradia S, Peterson LA, Hecht SS. G to A transitions and G to T transversions in codon 12 of the Ki-ras oncogene isolated from mouse lung tumors induced by 4-(methylnitrosamino)-1-(3-pyridyl)-1-butanone (NNK) and related DNA methylating and pyridyloxobutylating agents. Carcinogenesis 1993;14:2419–22.

46. Greenblatt MS, Bennett WP, Hollstein M, Harris CC. Mutations in the p53 tumor suppressor gene: clues to cancer etiology and molecular pathogenesis. Cancer Res 1994; 54:4855–78.

47. Simoneau AR, Jones PA. Bladder cancer: the molecular progression to invasive disease. World J Urol 1994;12:89–95.

48. Esrig D, Elmajian D, Groshen S, et al. Accumulation of nuclear p53 and tumor progression in bladder cancer [see comments]. N Engl J Med 1994;331:1259–64.

49. Sidransky D, Von Eschenbach A, Tsai YC, et al. Identification of p53 gene mutations in bladder cancers and urine samples. Science 1991;252:706–9.

50. Habuchi T, Takahashi R, Yamada H, et al. Influence of cigarette smoking and schistosomiasis on p53 gene mutation in urothelial cancer. Cancer Res 1993;53:3795–9.

51. Spruck CHD, Rideout WMD, Olumi AF, et al. Distinct pattern of p53 mutations in bladder cancer: relationship to tobacco usage [published erratum appears in Cancer Res 1993 May 15;53(10 Suppl):2427]. Cancer Res 1993;53:1162–6.

52. Brown JM, Wouters BG. Apoptosis, p53, and tumor cell sensitivity to anticancer agents. Cancer Res 1999;59:1391–9.

53. Knowles MA, Elder PA, Williamson M, et al. Allelotype of human bladder cancer. Cancer Res 1994;54:531–8.

54. Orlow I, Lianes P, Lacombe L, et al. Chromosome 9 allelic losses and microsatellite alterations in human bladder tumors. Cancer Res 1994;54:2848–51.

55. Dalbagni G, Presti JC Jr, Reuter VE, et al. Molecular genetic alterations of chromosome 17 and p53 nuclear overexpression in human bladder cancer. Diagn Mol Pathol 1993;2:4–13.

56. Simoneau AR, Spruck CH 3rd, Gonzalez-Zulueta M, et al. Evidence for two tumor suppressor loci associated with proximal chromosome 9p to q and distal chromosome 9q in bladder cancer and the initial screening for GAS1 and PTC mutations. Cancer Res 1996;56:5039–43.

57. Reznikoff CA, Belair CD, Yeager TR, et al. A molecular genetic model of human bladder cancer pathogenesis. Semin Oncol 1996;23:571–84.

58. Merlo A, Gabrielson E, Mabry M, et al. Homozygous dele-

tion on chromosome 9p and loss of heterozygosity on 9q, 6p, and 6q in primary human small cell lung cancer. Cancer Res 1994;54:2322–6.

59. Schultz DC, Vanderveer L, Buetow KH, et al. Characterization of chromosome 9 in human ovarian neoplasia identifies frequent genetic imbalance on 9q and rare alterations involving 9p, including CDKN2. Cancer Res 1995;55:2150–7.

60. Cairns P, Tokino K, Eby Y, Sidransky D. Localization of tumor suppressor loci on chromosome 9 in primary human renal cell carcinomas. Cancer Res 1995;55:224–7.

61. Cairns P, Shaw ME, Knowles MA. Initiation of bladder cancer may involve deletion of a tumour-suppressor gene on chromosome 9. Oncogene 1993;8:1083–5.

62. Serrano M, Hannon GJ, Beach D. A new regulatory motif in cell-cycle control causing specific inhibition of cyclin D/CDK4 [see comments]. Nature 1993;366:704–7.

63. Gruis NA, Weaver-Feldhaus J, Liu Q, et al. Genetic evidence in melanoma and bladder cancers that p16 and p53 function in separate pathways of tumor suppression. Am J Pathol 1995;146:1199–1206.

64. Choisy-Rossi C, Reisdorf P, Yonish-Rouach E. The p53 tumor suppressor gene: structure, function and mechanism of action. Results Probl Cell Differ 1999;23:145–72.

65. Gonzalez-Zulueta M, Ruppert JM, Tokino K, et al. Microsatellite instability in bladder cancer. Cancer Res 1993;53:5620–3.

66. Kwiatkowski DJ, Henske EP, Weimer K, et al. Construction of a GT polymorphism map of human 9q. Genomics 1992;12:229–40.

67. Weber JL. Informativeness of human (dC-dA)n.(dG-dT)n polymorphisms. Genomics 1990;7:524–30.

68. Peltomaki P, Aaltonen LA, Sistonen P, et al. Genetic mapping of a locus predisposing to human colorectal cancer [see comments]. Science 1993;260:810–2.

69. Leach FS, Nicolaides NC, Papadopoulos N, et al. Mutations of a mutS homolog in hereditary nonpolyposis colorectal cancer. Cell 1993;75:1215–25.

70. Linnenbach AJ, Robbins SL, Seng BA, et al. Urothelial carcinogenesis [letter]. Nature 1994;367:419–20.

71. Schoenberg M, Kiemeney L, Walsh PC, et al. Germline translocation t(5;20)(p15;q11) and familial transitional cell carcinoma. J Urol 1996;155:1035–6.

72. Kiemeney LA, Schoenberg M. Familial transitional cell carcinoma [see comments]. J Urol 1996;156:867–72.

73. Soloway MS, Masters S. Urothelial susceptibility to tumor cell implantation: influence of cauterization. Cancer 1980;46:1158–63.

74. Boyd PJ, Burnand KG. Site of bladder tumor recurrence. Lancet 1974;ii:1290–2.

75. Albarran J, Imbert A. Les Tumeurs de rein. Paris: Masson et cie; 1903. p. 452–9.

76. Melicow MM. Histologic study of vessical urothelium intervening between gross neoplasms in total cystectomy. J Urol 1952;68:261–73.

77. Kaplan JH, McDonald JR, Thompson GJ. Multicentric origin of papillary tumors of the urinary tract. J Urol 1951;66:792–804.

78. McDonald DF, Thomson T. Clinical implications of transplantability of induced bladder tumors to intact transitional epithelium in dogs. J Urol 1956;75:960–4.

79. See WA, Miller JS, Williams RD. Pathophysiology of transitional tumor cell adherence to sites of urothelial injury in rats: mechanisms mediating intravesical recurrence due to implantation. Cancer Res 1989;49:5414–8.

80. See WA, Chapman PH, Williams RD. Kinetics of transitional tumor cell line 4909 adherence to injured urothelial surfaces in F-344 rats. Cancer Res 1990;50:2499–2504.

81. Sidransky D, Frost P, Von Eschenbach A, et al. Clonal origin bladder cancer. N Engl J Med 1992;326:737–40.

82. Habuchi T, Takahashi R, Yamada H, et al. Metachronous multifocal development of urothelial cancers by intraluminal seeding. Lancet 1993;342:1087–8.

83. Takahashi T, Habuchi T, Kakehi Y, et al. Clonal and chronological genetic analysis of multifocal cancers of the bladder and upper urinary tract. Cancer Res 1998;58:5835–41.

84. Tsai YC, Simoneau AR, Spruck CH 3rd, et al. Mosaicism in human epithelium: macroscopic monoclonal patches cover the urothelium. J Urol 1995;153:1697–1700.

85. See WA, Chapman WH. Tumor cell implantation following neodymium-YAG bladder injury: a comparison to electrocautery injury. J Urol 1987;137:1266–9.

86. See WA, Williams RD. Urothelial injury and clotting cascade activation: common denominators in particulate adherence to urothelial surfaces. J Urol 1992;147:541–8.

87. See WA. Plasminogen activators: regulators of tumor cell adherence to sites of lower urinary tract surgical trauma. J Urol 1993;150:1024–9.

88. See WA, Yong X, Crist S, Hedican S. Diversity and modulation of plasminogen activator activity in human transitional carcinoma cell lines. J Urol 1994;151:1691–6.

89. Turkeri LN, Erton ML, Cevik I, Akdas A. Impact of the expression of epidermal growth factor, transforming growth factor alpha, and epidermal growth factor receptor on the prognosis of superficial bladder cancer. Urology 1998;51:645–9.

90. Crew JP, O'Brien T, Bicknell R, et al. Urinary vascular endothelial growth factor and its correlation with bladder cancer recurrence rates. J Urol 1999;161:799–804.

91. Mahadevan V, Hart IR. Metastasis and angiogenesis. Acta Oncol 1990;29:97–103.

92. Bernstein LR, Liotta LA. Molecular mediators of interactions with extracellular matrix components in metastasis and angiogenesis. Curr Opin Oncol 1994;6:106–13.

93. Rosin MP, Cairns P, Epstein JI, et al. Partial allelotype of carcinoma in situ of the human bladder. Cancer Res 1995;55:5213–6.

94. Li M, Zhang ZF, Reuter VE, Cordon-Cardo C. Chromosome 3 allelic losses and microsatellite alterations in transitional cell carcinoma of the urinary bladder. Am J Pathol 1996;149:229–35.

95. Polascik TJ, Cairns P, Chang WY, et al. Distinct regions of allelic loss on chromosome 4 in human primary bladder carcinoma. Cancer Res 1995;55:5396–9.

96. Wagner U, Bubendorf L, Gasser TC, et al. Chromosome 8p deletions are associated with invasive tumor growth in urinary bladder cancer. Am J Pathol 1997;151:753–9.

97. Brewster SF, Gingell JC, Browne S, Brown KW. Loss of heterozygosity on chromosome 18q is associated with muscle-invasive transitional cell carcinoma of the bladder. Br J Cancer 1994;70:697–700.

98. Kagan J, Liu J, Stein JD, et al. Cluster of allele losses within

a 2.5 cM region of chromosome 10 in high-grade invasive bladder cancer. Oncogene 1998;16:909–13.

99. Cappellen D, Gil Diez de Medina S, Chopin D, et al. Frequent loss of heterozygosity on chromosome 10q in muscle-invasive transitional cell carcinomas of the bladder. Oncogene 1997;14:3059–66.

100. Wheeless LL, Reeder JE, Han R, et al. Bladder irrigation specimens assayed by fluorescence in situ hybridization to interphase nuclei. Cytometry 1994;17:319–26.

101. Wick W, Petersen I, Schmutzler RK, et al. Evidence for a novel tumor suppressor gene on chromosome 15 associated with progression to a metastatic stage in breast cancer. Oncogene 1996;12:973–8.

102. Gildea JJ, Golden WL, Harding MA, Theodorescu D. Genetic and phenotypic changes associated with the acquisition of tumorigenicity in human bladder cancer. Genes Chromosomes Cancer 2000;27:252–63.

103. Lacombe L, Dalbagni G, Zhang ZF, et al. Overexpression of p53 protein in a high-risk population of patients with superficial bladder cancer before and after bacillus Calmette-Guerin therapy: correlation to clinical outcome. J Clin Oncol 1996;14:2646–52.

104. Lipponen P, Eskelinen M. Expression of epidermal growth factor receptor in bladder cancer as related to established prognostic factors, oncoprotein (c-erbB-2, p53) expression and long-term prognosis. Br J Cancer 1994;69:1120–5.

105. Schmitz-Drager BJ, Jankevicius F, Ackermann R. Molecular biology of dissemination in bladder cancer—laboratory findings and clinical significance. World J Urol 1996;14:190–6.

106. Mareel M, Boterberg T, Noe V, et al. E-cadherin/catenin/cytoskeleton complex: a regulator of cancer invasion. J Cell Physiol 1997;173:271–4.

107. Syrigos KN, Krausz T, Waxman J, et al. E-cadherin expression in bladder cancer using formalin-fixed, paraffin-embedded tissues: correlation with histopathological grade, tumour stage and survival. Int J Cancer 1995;64:367–70.

108. Bringuier PP, Umbas R, Schaafsma HE, et al. Decreased E-cadherin immunoreactivity correlates with poor survival in patients with bladder tumors. Cancer Res 1993;53:3241–5.

109. Griffiths TR, Brotherick I, Bishop RI, et al. Cell adhesion molecules in bladder cancer: soluble serum E-cadherin correlates with predictors of recurrence. Br J Cancer 1996;74:579–84.

110. Shimazui T, Schalken JA, Giroldi LA, et al. Prognostic value of cadherin-associated molecules (alpha-, beta-, and gamma-catenins and p120cas) in bladder tumors. Cancer Res 1996;56:4154–8.

111. Lipponen PK, Eskelinen MJ. Reduced expression of E-cadherin is related to invasive disease and frequent recurrence in bladder cancer. J Cancer Res Clin Oncol 1995;121:303–8.

112. Mialhe A, Louis J, Montlevier S, et al. Expression of E-cadherin and alpha-, beta- and gamma-catenins in human bladder carcinomas: are they good prognostic factors? Invasion Metastasis 1997;17:124–37.

113. Gorgoulis VG, Barbatis C, Poulias I, Karameris AM. Molecular and immunohistochemical evaluation of epidermal growth factor receptor and c-erb-B-2 gene product in transitional cell carcinomas of the urinary bladder: a study in Greek patients. Mod Pathol 1995;8:758–64.

114. Chow NH, Liu HS, Lee EI, et al. Significance of urinary epidermal growth factor and its receptor expression in human bladder cancer. Anticancer Res 1997;17:1293–6.

115. Nguyen PL, Swanson PE, Jaszcz W, et al. Expression of epidermal growth factor receptor in invasive transitional cell carcinoma of the urinary bladder. A multivariate survival analysis. Am J Clin Pathol 1994;101:166–76.

116. Sauter G, Haley J, Chew K, et al. Epidermal-growth-factor-receptor expression is associated with rapid tumor proliferation in bladder cancer. Int J Cancer 1994;57:508–14.

117. Theodorescu D, Cornil I, Sheehan C, et al. Ha-ras induction of the invasive phenotype results in up-regulation of epidermal growth factor receptors and altered responsiveness to epidermal growth factor in human papillary transitional cell carcinoma cells. Cancer Res 1991;51:4486–91.

118. Chow NH, Tzai TS, Cheng PE, et al. An assessment of immunoreactive epidermal growth factor in urine of patients with urological diseases. Urol Res 1994;22:221–5.

119. Messing EM, Reznikoff CA. Normal and malignant human urothelium: in vitro effects of epidermal growth factor. Cancer Res 1987;47:2230–5.

120. Theodorescu D, Laderoute KR, Gulding KM. Epidermal growth factor receptor-regulated human bladder cancer motility is in part a phosphatidylinositol 3-kinase-mediated process. Cell Growth Differ 1998;9:919–28.

121. Cairns P, Proctor AJ, Knowles MA. Loss of heterozygosity at the RB locus is frequent and correlates with muscle invasion in bladder carcinoma. Oncogene 1991;6:2305–9.

122. Cordon-Cardo C, Wartinger D, Petrylak D, et al. Altered expression of the retinoblastoma gene product: prognostic indicator in bladder cancer [see comments]. J Natl Cancer Inst 1992;84:1251–6.

123. Cordon-Cardo C, Zhang ZF, Dalbagni G, et al. Cooperative effects of p53 and pRB alterations in primary superficial bladder tumors. Cancer Res 1997;57:1217–21.

124. Cote RJ, Dunn MD, Chatterjee SJ, et al. Elevated and absent pRb expression is associated with bladder cancer progression and has cooperative effects with p53. Cancer Res 1998;58:1090–4.

125. Grossman HB, Liebert M, Antelo M, et al. p53 and RB expression predict progression in T1 bladder cancer. Clin Cancer Res 1998;4:829–34.

126. Jahnson S, Karlsson MG. Predictive value of p53 and pRb immunostaining in locally advanced bladder cancer treated with cystectomy. J Urol 1998;160:1291–6.

127. Logothetis CJ, Xu HJ, Ro JY, et al. Altered expression of retinoblastoma protein and known prognostic variables in locally advanced bladder cancer [see comments]. J Natl Cancer Inst 1992;84:1256–61.

128. Cordon-Cardo C, Sheinfeld J, Dalbagni G. Genetic studies and molecular markers of bladder cancer. Semin Surg Oncol 1997;13:319–27.

129. Fujimoto K, Yamada Y, Okajima E, et al. Frequent association of p53 gene mutation in invasive bladder cancer. Cancer Res 1992;52:1393–8.

130. Soini Y, Turpeenniemi-Hujanen T, Kamel D, et al. p53 immunohistochemistry in transitional cell carcinoma and

dysplasia of the urinary bladder correlates with disease progression. Br J Cancer 1993;68:1029–35.

131. Matsuyama H, Pan Y, Mahdy EA, et al. p53 deletion as a genetic marker in urothelial tumor by fluorescence in situ hybridization. Cancer Res 1994;54:6057–60.

132. Moch H, Sauter G, Moore D, et al. p53 and erbB-2 protein overexpression are associated with early invasion and metastasis in bladder cancer. Virchows Arch A Pathol Anat Histopathol 1993;423:329–34.

133. Sarkis AS, Dalbagni G, Cordon-Cardo C, et al. Nuclear over-expression of p53 protein in transitional cell bladder carcinoma: a marker for disease progression. J Natl Cancer Inst 1993;85:53–9.

134. Lipponen PK. Over-expression of p53 nuclear oncoprotein in transitional-cell bladder cancer and its prognostic value. Int J Cancer 1993;53:365–70.

135. Sarkis AS, Bajorin DF, Reuter VE, et al. Prognostic value of p53 nuclear overexpression in patients with invasive bladder cancer treated with neoadjuvant MVAC. J Clin Oncol 1995;13:1384–90.

136. Furihata M, Inoue K, Ohtsuki Y, et al. High-risk human papillomavirus infections and overexpression of p53 protein as prognostic indicators in transitional cell carcinoma of the urinary bladder. Cancer Res 1993;53:4823–7.

137. Sauter G, Moch H, Gasser TC, et al. Heterogeneity of chromosome 17 and erbB-2 gene copy number in primary and metastatic bladder cancer. Cytometry 1995;21:40–6.

138. Sardi I, Dal Canto M, Bartoletti R, et al. Molecular genetic alterations of c-myc oncogene in superficial and locally advanced bladder cancer. Eur Urol 1998;33:424–30.

139. Sardi I, Dal Canto M, Bartoletti R, Montali E. Abnormal c-myc oncogene DNA methylation in human bladder cancer: possible role in tumor progression. Eur Urol 1997;31:224–30.

140. Schmitz-Drager BJ, Schulz WA, Jurgens B, et al. c-myc in bladder cancer. Clinical findings and analysis of mechanism. Urol Res 1997;25:S45–9.

141. Novara R, Coda R, Martone T, Vineis P. Exposure to aromatic amines and ras and c-erbB-2 overexpression in bladder cancer. J Occup Environ Med 1996;38:390–3.

142. Ravery V, Grignon D, Angulo J, et al. Evaluation of epidermal growth factor receptor, transforming growth factor alpha, epidermal growth factor and c-erbB2 in the progression of invasive bladder cancer. Urol Res 1997;25:9–17.

143. Underwood M, Bartlett J, Reeves J, et al. C-erbB-2 gene amplification: a molecular marker in recurrent bladder tumors? Cancer Res 1995;55:2422–30.

144. Lianes P, Orlow I, Zhang ZF, et al. Altered patterns of MDM2 and TP53 expression in human bladder cancer [see comments]. J Natl Cancer Inst 1994;86:1325–30.

145. Shiina H, Igawa M, Shigeno K, et al. Clinical significance of mdm2 and p53 expression in bladder cancer. A comparison with cell proliferation and apoptosis. Oncology 1999;56:239–47.

146. Schmitz-Drager BJ, Kushima M, Goebell P, et al. p53 and MDM2 in the development and progression of bladder cancer. Eur Urol 1997;32:487–93.

4

Molecular Pathogenesis of Proliferative and Progressive (Invasive) Urothelial Cancer Development

PAUL SWEENEY, MD
COLIN P.N. DINNEY, MD

Rapid advances in molecular biology, immunology, and cytogenetics during the last decade have greatly increased our understanding of tumor biology. High-throughput analytical techniques have allowed rapid acquirement of tumor genotypic and phenotypic information.[1] This greater knowledge base has provided an opportunity to identify and evaluate tumor characteristics beyond traditional histopathologic criteria (histological subtype, grade, and stage) and gross deoxyribonucleic acid (DNA) content. The vast amount of information generated by these techniques requires interpretation by bioinformatic and biostatistical means. As a result, there has been a considerable expansion in the number of potential "molecules" that are being evaluated as diagnostic and prognostic markers and potential therapeutic targets in bladder cancer.

Markers for bladder cancer fall into two main groups: diagnostic and prognostic. Considering the natural history of bladder cancer, accurate and reliable diagnostic and prognostic markers are likely to significantly affect the management of transitional cell carcinoma (TCC). The ideal diagnostic marker would identify those patients harboring new or recurrent bladder tumors or identify those patients who are at increased risk of developing tumors in the future and would readily distinguish these patients from those who do not currently have tumors and are at low risk for developing de novo or recurrent TCC. The ideal

prognostic marker would facilitate identification of those patients who are likely to develop recurrent or progressive TCC. An International Bladder Cancer Network was established in 1997 to improve the diagnosis, prevention and treatment of bladder cancer through the application of biologic markers.[2] The group developed the four phases for development and validation of markers for bladder cancer. Phase 1 includes the development of a reliable and reproducible assay that can be applied to clinical specimens. Markers with low prevalence in the at-risk population are unlikely to be clinically useful, and markers with high prevalence may be useful for diagnosis but would have limited capacity to differentiate between tumors with different behavior. Phase 2 development evaluates the utility of the marker in answering a clinical question. The marker is compared with traditional prognostic end points (grade and stage and outcome) to generate a hypothesis regarding clinical utility. Sensitivity, specificity, and appropriate cut-points are determined. In phase 3, clinical utility is tested in appropriately powered studies and in a defined clinical setting (usually within a single institution) using the methodology, cut-off, and sample size determined from phase 2 studies. In phase 4, the phase 3 conclusions are validated in a multicenter setting. Methodology and cut-points of the assay are validated, and inter-institutional and inter-laboratory variability and quality control are assessed.

To date, no marker has replaced the traditional indicators of prognosis—grade and stage. Many molecular marker studies have determined an arbitrary "cut-point" using a retrospective analysis of the relative presence of the marker in the original data set, but few if any markers have been prospectively validated in multicenter clinical studies (phase 4). Furthermore, biomarker studies in bladder cancer need to be designed with sufficient statistical power to detect differences that are considered to be of clinical interest. Many retrospective studies contain too few cases to allow a small but significant difference to be detected, raising the probability of a Type II error.

Some comments regarding the various technologic, methodologic and analytic issues of each diagnostic modality will aid in understanding the relevance and pitfalls of recently published work. Immunohistochemical analysis is the most commonly used technique to determine molecular expression in clinical and/or translational research. The lack of standardization in immunohistochemical methodology leads to difficulties with interpretation of the results. The evaluation of *P53* expression and its relevance as a prognostic marker in bladder cancer illustrates many of the problems associated with immunohistochemistry. Lack of uniformity in the processes of tissue procurement, fixation, and antigen retrieval methods between centers leads to lack of consistency in antigen preservation. A variety of *P53* antibodies and other reagents used in the detection process are available, and variability in the methodology used between centers has led to lack of reliability in results from different laboratories. Furthermore, the determination of cut-points and the definition of positivity have not been standardized and lead to inconsistent results. While these problems are clearly illustrated in the *P53* model, they are prevalent in the evaluation of most molecular markers. Therefore, the methodology, limitations, and potential problems of immunohistochemistry must be clearly understood to allow a critical appraisal of the data in relation to various bladder tumor markers.

Validation of biomarkers would be facilitated by standardization of immunohistochemical techniques. Ideally, all tissues would be procured in accordance with accepted protocols and assayed for the presence of the particular biomarker using standardized methods. Similarly, reliability of results can be achieved through adherence to defined guidelines for interpretation of staining patterns and also through the integration of quality control measures.

Although great efforts have been made to standardize immunohistochemistry, the limitations of this technique must be realized. However, more sophisticated, demanding, and costly techniques, such as single-strand conformational polymorphism, DNA sequencing, polymerase chain reaction (PCR)-based analysis, and newer array-based technologies are also prone to problems arising from lack of standardization, and thus they are unlikely to achieve the accelerated applicability and validation at a multicenter level that may be possible with immunohistochemistry.

The molecular pathogenesis of bladder cancer is a complex area involving the interaction of various growth factors and cytokines and other intracellular regulatory molecules against a background of genetic alterations. This review is not intended to be an exhaustive analysis of the literature but rather an attempt to critically appraise some of the more promising markers and facilitate the appropriate clinical and basic science studies to evaluate and validate these markers further.

E-CADHERIN

The cadherins are a family of homophilic transmembrane glycoproteins that are responsible for calcium-dependent intercellular adhesion in a variety of epithelial tissues (Figure 4–1). Cadherins consist of an extracellular adhesion domain, a transmembrane segment, and a cytoplasmic domain. Structural studies suggest that the extracellular domains from adjacent cells interact to form lateral dimers that exist as zipper-like structures.[3,4] The highly conserved intracellular domain interacts with a group of cytoplasmic proteins, including the alpha-, beta- and gamma- (plakoglabin) catenins that connect cadherins to the actin cytoskeleton. The actin-catenin/cadherin interaction results in a highly organized complex that establishes a direct connection between adjacent cells and their cytoskeltons and is essential for cell–cell adhesion.[5,6] Cadherins control a number of funda-

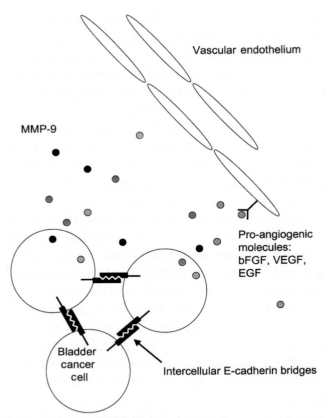

Figure 4–1. Two critical events govern the molecular pathogenesis of bladder cancer as depicted: (1) Invasion and metastasis—the ability of a tumor cell to detach from its neighboring cells and move through the basement membrane (invade) or to distant sites (metastasize) depends on the relative production of proteases (MMPs) and the functional integrity of E-cadherin based intercellular binding. Progression to an invasive phenotype is associated with a shift in the balance towards an excess of protease action over intercellular cohesion and thus the potential for invasion and metastasis is increased. (2) Angiogenesis—the continued growth and metastasis of a tumor necessitates that the tumor acquires the ability to induce a blood supply from the tumor microenvironment. An "angiogenic switch" occurs when tumors produce pro-angiogenic factors VEGF, bFGF, EGF, and IL-8 giving the tumor the ability to induce its own blood supply and thus facilitate further growth and metastasis. These two mechanisms (angiogenesis and invasion/metastasis) do not exist independently and there is considerable overlap between the functions of various molecules. For example proteases such as MMP-9 digest the extracellular matrix (ECM) facilitating the migration of endothelial cells but also allow tumor cells to invade towards the circulation where they can have metastatic potential. bFGF = basic fibroblast growth factor; VEGF = vascular endothelial growth factor; EGF = epidermal growth factor.

mental biologic processes (including cell migration, invasiveness, differentiation, proliferation, and apoptosis) and induce specific molecular responses, including changes in the organization of the cytoskeleton and alteration in the expression of proteases or other cell adhesion receptors. Cadherin-

mediated adhesion is regulated by activation of tyrosine kinases.[7] A number of tyrosine kinases and phosphatases have been shown to interact directly with cadherin/catenin complexes. C-erb-B2 binds to the carboxy terminus of β-catenin. Inhibition of tyrosine phosphatases leads to rapid and reversible loss of cell contacts. Furthermore, many nonreceptor tyrosine kinases are localized to the cadherin-based adherens junctions. Ligand activation of the epidermal growth factor (EGF) or C-met receptor leads to cell dissociation. Thus the cadherins participate in a complex signaling pathway, controlling cellular motility and growth.[8,9] On the basis of these interactions, it appears that tyrosine kinases are mainly negative regulators of cell adhesion and that oncogenic activation of these kinases in tumors contributes to invasion and metastasis by inhibiting E-cadherin function.

In bladder cancer, loss of E-cadherin function can result through several mechanisms: mutation, alteration of transcription, post-translational modification, or changes in the interaction of E-cadherin with the cytoskeleton anchoring proteins (the catenins). The loss of E-cadherin function promotes invasive and metastatic properties in many cancer cells consistent with its function as a tumor suppressor gene.[10] In gastric and breast cancers, the predominant mutation involves the extracellular adhesive domain. The finding of a similar mutation in in situ portions of these tumors indicated that they probably represent an early event in tumorigenesis. The data support the concept that disturbance of E-cadherin-mediated adhesion induced neoplastic growth of the mutated cells. Further support for the role of E-cadherin as a tumor initiator comes from the finding of inherited mutations of the E-cadherin gene in cases of familial gastric cancer.[11] E-cadherin mutations are not believed to be a common cause of gene inactivation in bladder cancer. Methylation has been identified as an important gene inactivating mechanism.[12] Aberrant methylation of the CpG island flanking the 5' transcriptional start site of the E-cadherin gene results in decreased E-cadherin expression in bladder cancer, similar to the relationship described between E-cadherin methylation and gene expression in other types of human cancers. In a study of bladder cancer specimens, significantly diminished levels of E-cadherin expression were observed in 14 (93%) of 15 cases with methylation of the E-cadherin gene. Decreased transcription is a major mechanism leading to decreased E-cadherin expression in tumors.[13]

Support for the role of E-cadherin as a regulator of cell migration and invasiveness in vitro exist in three areas: several groups have reported that levels of E-cadherin detected immunohistochemically are reduced in some bladder cancer cells and transformed epithelial cells compared with normal urothelial cells.[14,15] The loss of E-cadherin in T24 cell lines correlates with a dedifferentiated phenotype and is accompanied by an increase in the invasion and metastatic potential in experimental systems.[16,17] In contrast, normal E-cadherin expression was observed in the weakly tumorigenic, poorly metastatic RT4 cell line.[18] Furthermore, inhibition of E-cadherin function with monoclonal antibodies led to the induction of invasiveness in otherwise noninvasive RT112/84 cells, whereas enforced expression of E-cadherin by cDNA transfection in E-cadherin negative cells abrogated their invasive properties.[19–22]

This work has been extended to in vivo models in which enforced expression of E-cadherin, dominant-negative E-cadherin constructs, and experiments in transgenic mice have confined the anti-invasive, antimetastatic role of E-cadherin.

A small number of studies have evaluated urinary and serum E-cadherin expression as a diagnostic and prognostic marker.[23–26] Overall, these studies have been underpowered and have shown reasonable sensitivity but unacceptable specificity and prospective evaluation is required. A considerable number of studies have evaluated the expression of E-cadherin alone or in combination with other markers in bladder tumor specimens primarily by immunohistochemistry. With most of these studies showing an inverse correlation between E-cadherin expression and tumor grade and stage.[18,27–39] While a few of these studies have suggested that E-cadherin expression may have independent prognostic value in bladder cancer, this conclusion has not been validated prospectively.[31,33-35,37,39,40] For the most part, changes in catenin expression mirror the changes in cadherin expression, but in some instances preservation of cadherin expression but alteration in cell adhesion via absence of one of the catenins was observed.

Roles for other cadherins have been suggested in E-cadherin–deficient cells. It appears that the expression of E-cadherin is coupled to expression of P-cadherin and α-catenin but that in E-cadherin–deficient cells N-cadherin becomes predominantly expressed and can form links with β- or gamma-catenin.[41,42] Similar aberrations in cadherin expression have been described in human bladder tumor specimens but the precise pathologic importance of N- and P-cadherins remains unclear.[43]

MATRIX METALLOPROTEINASES

Matrix metalloproteinases (MMPs) are a family of proteolytic enzymes that degrade the extracellular matrix or components of the basement membrane. Specifically, MMP-9 and MMP-2 are collagenases that degrade type IV collagen, the major constituent of the basement membrane of the urothelium (see Figure 4–1). The type IV collagenase/gelatinases facilitate a variety of biological activities, including invasion, metastasis, and angiogenesis. The ability of tumor cells to degrade the extracellular matrix (ECM) and basement membrane components of connective tissue is an essential prerequisite for invasion and metastasis.[44] Expression of MMP-9 by human TCC of the bladder correlates directly with tumor grade, invasion, and metastasis, and the relative expression of MMP-9 and its endogenous tissue inhibitor TIMP-2 is especially important for predicting the metastatic potential of bladder cancer.

MMPs play a central role in tumor angiogenesis. The proteolytic effect of MMPs facilitates the migration of endothelial cells through the altered ECM toward the source of an angiogenic stimulus; in this manner, MMPs are an integral component of the angiogenesis pathway.[45,46] Synthetic and endogenous MMP inhibitors impede angiogenic responses both in vitro and in vivo.[47] MMP-9 expression is regulated by various factors, including tumor necrosis factor-α,[48] interleukin-1,[49] transforming growth factor-β1,[49,50] EGF,[49,51,52] hepatocyte growth factor,[52] and basic fibroblast growth factor (bFGF).[53]

Increased expression of MMP-2 and MMP-9 has been reported in cell lines with invasive phenotypes.[54,55] Several studies have evaluated MMP-9 and MMP-2 expression in urine and bladder washes and have shown correlation between increased MMP-9 expression and tumor grade, stage, and recurrence. In several studies, elevated MMP-2 and MMP-9 expression in bladder cancer compared with normal urothelium and correlation with tumor stage, grade, or prognosis have been reported.[56–60] Correlation between increased expression of mRNA for MMP-9 and TIMP-2 in patients with bladder cancer and increased risk of recurrence has also been reported.[61] Grignon and colleagues[62] examined the expression of MMP-2 and MMP-9 in a series of cystectomy patients and observed that MMP-2 and MMP-9 expression did not correlate with stage, grade, or outcome.[62] In our laboratory, we used in situ hybridization (ISH) and immunohistochemistry to detect MMP-9 messenger ribonucleic acid (mRNA) and protein in bladder tumors and found that MMP-9 was overexpressed in invasive tumors compared with superficial papillary noninvasive tumors. Thus MMP-9 appears to have a role in the evolution of muscle-invasive TCC.[63]

Tumor growth and metastasis depend upon the balance of the expression of genes that regulate angiogenesis and invasion.[64,65] The process of invasion is regulated within a complex homeostasis by the expression of enzymes such as the MMPs, which are responsible for the degradation of the extracellular matrix and basal membranes[66,67] and the adhesion molecule E-cadherin, that promotes homotypic cellular cohesion (see Figure 4–1). As discussed above, the overexpression of the MMPs, particularly MMP-9, in tissue, serum, and urine of patients with TCC correlates with disease progression and metastasis.[54,56,58–60,62,68–70] Likewise, loss of E-cadherin expression is associated with disease progression.[18,26,33,38,71] Thus, virulent TCC is characterized by a high MMP-9/E-cadherin ratio. Studies in other malignancies have shown that the ratio of the expression levels of MMP-9 to E-cadherin (determined by colorimetric ISH and image analysis) predicted the metastatic potential of colorectal,[72,73] gastric,[74] pancreatic,[75] lung,[76] and prostate carcinomas.[77] In studies in our laboratory, we evaluated the expression of E-cadherin and MMP-9 in 55 patients with muscle-invasive TCC treated with neoadjuvant methotrexate, vinblastine, Adriamycin [doxorubicin], and cisplatin (MVAC) chemotherapy and radical cystectomy and we found that a high expression level of MMP-9 cou-

pled with a low expression level of E-cadherin was associated with early recurrence and death in patients with TCC.[78] It is unlikely that the expression level of either MMP-9 or E-cadherin directly influences chemosensitivity; rather, these levels identify TCC with a propensity to invade and metastasize. This index of the invasive potential of bladder cancer (MMP-9/E-cadherin ratio) was a stronger independent predictor of tumor progression than clinical stage, microvessel density (MVD), or vascular endothelial growth factor (VEGF) expression.

BASIC FIBROBLAST GROWTH FACTOR

Basic fibroblast growth factor, also known as FGF-2, induces proliferation in a wide variety of cells. It is also a potent inducer of angiogenesis via stimulation of endothelial cell proliferation, migration, and proteinase production both in vitro and in vivo (see Figure 4–1). bFGF in the conditioned medium from bladder cancer cells induces endothelial cell migration and corneal neovascularization.[79] Okada-Ban and colleagues[80] demonstrated that enforced expression of bFGF (by transfection) in bladder carcinoma cells increased their tumorigenicity and metastatic capacity. Using sense and antisense bFGF oligonucleotides, Miyake and colleagues[81] have also shown that enforced bFGF expression in the human bladder cancer cell line HT1376 enhances MMP-2 and MMP-9 production and in vitro invasive potential. These findings suggest that FGF-2 plays an important role in the invasive process of human bladder cancer, in part through the regulation of MMP production.[81] Furthermore, Miyake and colleagues[82] have proposed that overexpression of bFGF plays an important role in the acquisition of a chemotherapy-resistant phenotype in bladder cancer.

Previous studies in our laboratory have demonstrated the importance of bFGF in bladder cancer. In a TCC xenograft model, direct intralesional delivery of antisense bFGF cDNA in an adenoviral construct inhibited tumor growth. In this model, the in vivo expression of bFGF and matrix MMP-9 mRNA and protein was reduced, microvessel density was decreased and endothelial cell apoptosis enhanced.[83] We have also evaluated the therapeutic role of interferon in bladder cancer and found that the optimum anti-angiogenic dose of interferon correlates with maximum inhibition of bFGF production in orthotopic bladder cancer xenografts. In these models, decreased bFGF production was accompanied by decreased neovascularization and reduced microvessel density which confirmed the pro-angiogenic role of bFGF and emphasized its role in the pathogenesis and progression of bladder cancer.[84,85]

Increased urinary bFGF has been reported in patients with bladder cancer.[86] Further studies of urinary bFGF as a diagnostic marker for bladder cancer showed low sensitivity and moderate specificity.[87] Increased bFGF has been demonstrated using reverse transcription polymerase chain reaction (RT-PCR) and hybridization analysis in tumors of higher stage, and a correlation with early local relapse has been reported.[88] An interesting observation has been made by O'Brien and colleagues[89] who examined urine and tissue specimens (tumor and normal) from patients with bladder cancer. They noted that these patients had urinary bFGF levels that were as much as 100-fold those of healthy subjects but that these patients failed to show increased bFGF mRNA transcripts or protein expression in their bladder tumors compared with nontumor tissue in the same patients. Given these findings, they suggested two mechanisms of bFGF-induced angiogenesis in bladder cancer. Rarely, neoplastic cells synthesize bFGF, but more commonly bFGF is released by degradation of epithelial basement membranes and detrusor muscle, from where it can diffuse into the tumor microenvironment and bind to blood vessels. Mechanisms of extracellular matrix degradation may be important in bladder cancer angiogenesis and progression and as such are potential therapeutic targets.

In a series of patients receiving neoadjuvant MVAC chemotherapy for muscle-invasive bladder TCC, bFGF expression and microvessel density in the cystectomy specimens after therapy were reported as independent prognostic factors for disease recurrence. Thus high expression of bFGF and increased microvessel density can identify patients with muscle-invasive TCC who are at high risk of developing metastasis after aggressive therapy with systemic MVAC chemotherapy and radical cystectomy.[90] Gazzaniga and colleagues[88] reported increased expression of bFGF mRNA in TCC tumor specimens compared with benign controls and reported a correlation with higher stage and early local relapses. In addition, bFGF was found to be highly expressed in the majority of tumors showing high bcl-2 expression, suggesting that bFGF expression could contribute to the progression of bladder cancer. We evaluated bFGF expression in a series of patients with bladder cancer of various stages of and observed that both muscle-invasive and in situ TCC overexpressed bFGF relative to Ta tumors, suggesting that overexpression of bFGF distinguishes precursor lesions of muscle-invasive TCC from superficial papillary TCC and that upregulation of bFGF occur relatively early in the pathogenesis of muscle-invasive TCC.

These studies on bFGF expression in bladder cancer support the proposed biologic activity of bFGF as a pro-angiogenic molecule and its possible role in facilitating local tumor invasion and subsequent metastasis.

EPIDERMAL GROWTH FACTOR

Epidermal growth factor is a cell-regulating polypeptide that is required for the maintenance and function of some benign tissues and for the transformation and proliferation of certain malignancies. EGF is excreted in urine in high concentrations in a biologically active form. EGF is a potent mitogen and tumor promoter. EGF binds specific receptors on the cell surface and acts via PI3K, STAT and MAPK pathways to regulate gene transcription and control cell cycle progression. Via these pathways EGF controls various cell functions including angiogenesis, metastasis, apoptosis/survival and proliferation (Figure 4–2).

EGF and its receptor (EGFR) can stimulate bladder cancer via three mechanisms: (1) overexpression of ligand; (2) overexpression of EGFR; and (3) mutation of EGFR, leading to a constitutively activated state.

Messing and colleagues[91] reviewed the role of EGF in bladder cancer and described several lines of evidence supporting a role for EGF in TCC development and growth including those that follow: (1) EGF in the normal urine of rats promotes chemically initiated TCC; (2) EGF in normal human urine stimulates the clonal growth of human TCC cells in vitro;

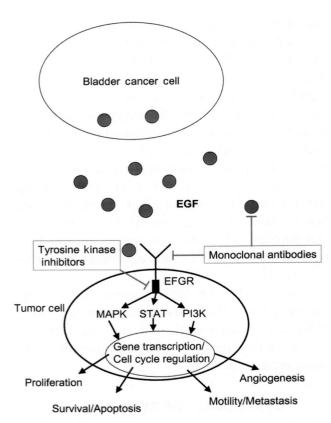

Figure 4–2. EGF binds to specific receptors which may be over-expressed on the tumor cell surface. Multiple signal transduction pathways (PI3K, STAT, and MAPK) lead to an alteration in gene transcription and cell cycle progression to produce specific cellular responses including cellular proliferation, survival/apoptosis, angiogenesis and metastasis. The EGF signaling pathway can be interrupted at several levels and numerous therapeutic strategies can achieve this. Monoclonal antibodies to the EGFR have been developed which interfere with the interaction between EGF ligand and receptor. Tyrosine kinase inhibitors prevent transduction of the EGF signal upon ligand binding and other inhibitors of specific signaling intermediaries (ie, MAPK) have also been developed. EGF = epidermal growth factor; EGFR = epidermal growth factor receptor; MAPK = mitogen activated protein kinase; STAT = signal tranducer and activator of transcription; PI3K = phosphoinositide kinase-3.

(3) EGF stimulates the in vitro growth of human TCC cells but not normal human urothelial cells; (4) the density and distribution of the EGFR on human urothelial tissues permit significant access of premalignant, dysplastic, and malignant cells to EGF; and (5) the concentration of EGF in the voided urine of patients with TCC is reduced, implying that EGF may be "extracted" from urine by the greater number of EGFRs in patients with urothelial malignancy.

Abnormal expression of EGFR and/or altered excretion of EGF may precede overt evidence of TCC and thus may serve as markers of risk or exposure.

Similarly, reversion of EGFR expression or the return of excreted EGF to normal levels may provide a marker of response for preventive and therapeutic strategies. Interference with the EGF/EGFR interaction through dietary or pharmacologic manipulations of the urine, or via targeting strategies employing intravesical administration of conjugated toxins or isotopes is already being employed in experimental and clinical studies. These approaches offer promising new tools in the detection, monitoring, prevention, and management of early-stage bladder cancer.[91]

Various groups have reported reduced urinary concentrations of EGF in patients with bladder cancer.[92,93] Two groups have found that biologically active EGF is excreted in the urine and plays a significant role in the clonal growth of bladder cancer cell lines and in the promotion of bladder carcinogenesis in a rat model.[94–96]

Messing and colleagues[97] reported the mitogenic effects of EGF on human TCC and showed that although normal urothelial cells expressed functional EGFR, stimulation did not produce a mitogenic response. They characterized the expression of EGFR on normal and premalignant urothelium and on invasive bladder tumors. They reported that EGFRs were found only on the basal layer in 95% of normal epithelial cells but that premalignant and invasive lesions had EGFRs richly expressed on the superficial as well as the deeper layers of urothelium. This "malignant" distribution of EGFRs was also found on all specimens of endoscopically normal-appearing urothelium in patients with TCC elsewhere. The density of EGFRs correlated closely with tumor grade on both "premalignant" and frankly neoplastic urothelium. They suggested that the expression of EGFRs on urothelium favors the interaction of premalignant and malignant tissue with urinary EGF.[96,98] Messing and colleagues[97] evaluated the usefulness of urinary EGF as a surrogate diagnostic marker for TCC. EGF concentrations were significantly lower in patients with TCC compared with controls. The reduced concentration of EGF in voided urine supports previous evidence that the urinary EGF/urothelial EGFR interaction is important for TCC development and growth and has the potential to serve as a marker of tumor persistence, recurrence, and therapeutic response.[93]

Perotte and colleagues[99] confirmed the importance of EGF in an orthotopic xenograft model of bladder cancer in nude mice when they successfully induced regression of tumors using a monoclonal antibody to EGFR. Furthermore, they observed that targeting the EGF pathway induced apoptosis in cancer cells and stromal elements within the tumors.[99]

Clinical studies evaluating the significance of EGFR expression in human TCC have shown that greater than 50% of human bladder cancers overexpress EGFR, and that the level of expression directly correlates with tumor grade, stage and survival.[100] In patients with superficial bladder cancer, EGFR expression correlates with multiplicity, time to disease recurrence, and overall recurrence rates.[100] EGFR overexpression also predicts for progression to muscle-invasive or metastatic TCC and was reported, in a multivariate analysis, to be an independent prognostic factor for death. Izawa and colleagues[63] evaluated *EGFR* gene expression in a series of bladder carcinomas and reported that EGFR expression was involved in bladder cancer progression as cells expressing EGFR acquired an invasive phenotype. EGFR expression also has prognostic significance for patients with advanced TCC. Patients with muscle-invasive carcinoma that overexpresses EGFR have a significantly worse cancer-specific survival than those whose tumors do not express EGFRs.[100] These studies establish the importance of EGFR overexpression in the development and progression of human TCC.

Enhanced cellular motility is a prerequisite for invasion. Progression to an invasive phenotype may occur via the acquirement of motility by cells expressing EGF. Data from our group (unpublished) and Theodorescu and colleagues[101] using in vitro invasion models with antisense EGFR have confirmed that cell motility in bladder cancer cells is regulated via the EGF pathway. In support of this concept, using specific pharmacologic inhibition Theodorescu and colleagues[101] reported that PI3K is involved in EGFR motility signaling in this system. Elucidation of the pathways involved in EGF-regulated motility and invasion may lead to development of novel therapies to prevent or retard the progression of aggressive superficial bladder tumors.[101]

EGFR signaling and angiogenesis have been independently evaluated as targets for therapy, but the link between them has only recently been identified.[99,102,103] EGF and transforming growth factor (TGF)-α, which are ligands for the EGFR induce angiogenesis.[104] EGFR activation has also been shown to stimulate VEGF expression in human glioblastoma cells[104] and to regulate tumor invasion by DU-145 prostate cancer cells.[105] Using an orthotopic xenograft model of human TCC, we demonstrated that downregulation of the EGFR signaling pathways inhibited tumor growth by inhibiting tumor mediated angiogenesis, independently of any direct cytostatic effect on tumor growth.[99] We reported regression of established TCC growing in the bladders of nude mice following therapy with a monoclonal antibody to EGFR, that could not be explained solely on the basis of the modest 40% cytostatic effect observed after therapy in culture. The abrogation of tumor growth was accompanied by a reduction in tumor-induced neovascularization attributable to the downregulation of tumor cell expression of the angiogenic factors VEGF, interleukin 8 (IL-8), and bFGF. Endothelial and tumor cell apoptosis was observed, leading to regression of established tumors. Thus, the presence of these proangiogenic factors was necessary to maintain a viable microcirculation and tumor growth. Withdrawal of the angiogenic stimulus by EGFR monoclonal antibodies resulted in regression of tumor neovasculature and contributed to tumor cell death. Similar observations were made following treatment of human squamous cell and pancreatic carcinoma xenografts.[102,103] These observations underline the importance of host-stromal interactions in the progression of bladder cancer. In studies of the variant TCC cell line 253J B-V, which spontaneously metastasizes to lymph nodes and the lungs following established growth in the bladder, we demonstrated that treatment with a monoclonal antibody to EGFR downregulated mRNA expression and activity of MMP-9 in a dose-dependent manner. Following systemic therapy of 253J B-V growing in the bladders of nude mice with EGFR monoclonal antibodies, expression of MMP-9, VEGF, IL-8 and bFGF was significantly reduced compared with controls.[106] The downregulation of these factors preceded endothelial cell apoptosis and involution of blood vessels, suggesting a cause and effect.[99]

Various cytokines and growth factors released by the tumor or microenvironment regulate the level of MMPs secreted by the cell. EGFR activation following EGF or TGF-α ligand binding upregulates the production of proteolytic enzymes[107] and extracellular matrix proteins[108,109] and results in enhanced cell motility[110,111] and invasion through Matrigel membranes.[105] Thus, EGFR specific signal transduction promotes invasion by regulating the levels of MMP-9 and other proteolytic enzymes produced by the tumor cells. In studies with bladder carcinoma cells, in vitro, EGF enhanced anchorage-independent growth in soft agar and increased the number of cells penetrating into a Matrigel membrane. A transient transfection assay revealed that EGF increased the promoter activities of the *MMP-1* and *MMP-9* genes in KU-1 cells.[112]

ANGIOGENESIS IN BLADDER CANCER

Tumor growth and metastasis depend on the ability of a tumor to recruit blood vessels for delivery of oxygen and nutrients.[113] This process, angiogenesis, is driven by various growth factors (VEGF, bFGF, insulin-like growth factor-1 [IGF-1], angiopoietin-1, and EGF), and cytokines (ie, IL-8) and is facilitated by collagenase activity (see Figure 4–1). Antiangiogenic molecules (including thrombospondin, interferons, tissue inhibitors of MMPs, angiopoietin-2, endostatin, and angiostatin) impede angiogenesis. An "angiogenic switch" occurs when the tumor and stroma produce an excess of pro-angiogenic molecules over antiangiogenic factors.[114] This "switch" favors the growth of new blood vessels and thus facilitates proliferation and growth of the tumor. The vascular density of advanced TCC, a histologic surrogate for angiogenesis, correlates with metastases and patient survival.[115] We have reported that MVD in cystectomy specimens was an independent prognostic predictor for patients with invasive TCC treated by neoadjuvant MVAC and radical cystectomy.[90]

VASCULAR ENDOTHELIAL GROWTH FACTOR

VEGF, which is produced by a variety of normal and neoplastic cells, is a potent endothelial cell–specific mitogen that inhibits apoptosis of endothelial cells.[116] It promotes invasion and migration of endothelial cells, and by increasing vascular permeability it facilitates the entry of tumor cells into the circulation allowing them to metastasize to distant sites (Figure 4–3). VEGF is produced in response to hypoxia and is regulated at a transcriptional level by hypoxia-inducible factor 1.[117]

Jeon and colleagues[118] evaluated urinary VEGF levels as a potential marker for TCC. They reported that urinary VEGF concentrations measured by enzyme-linked immunosorbent assay (ELISA) and corrected for creatinine concentration were higher in patients with superficial TCC than in controls, and they found that a higher urinary VEGF level correlated with a greater risk of tumor recurrence. There was no statistical correlation between VEGF levels

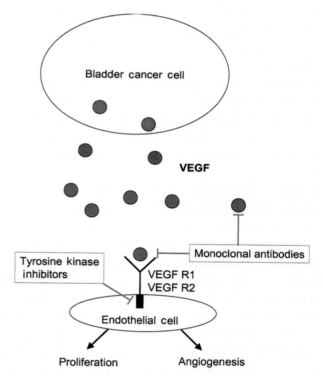

Figure 4–3. VEGF is secreted by bladder cancer cells which circulates to nearby endothelial cells where it binds to specific tyrosine kinase linked receptors on the cell membrane. The activation of these receptors leads to endothelial cell proliferation and angiogenesis. Possible strategies for therapeutic intervention include neutralizing circulating VEGF molecules and interfering with VEGF receptor interaction with monoclonal antibodies or the use of tyrosine kinase inhibitors which inhibit the propagation of the signal within the cells. Such interventions reduce the angiogenic response and these strategies have been successful in in vitro systems and in preclinical models and have shown promise in early clinical studies. VEGF = vascular endothelial growth factor; VEGFR = vascular endothelial growth factor receptor.

and tumor stage (Ta or T1), tumor size, or tumor grade. These results have not been confirmed prospectively. Crew and colleagues[119] also measured urinary VEGF concentration in 153 patients with known bladder cancer and in 108 controls. They reported a weak correlation between urinary VEGF and recurrence in patients with a history of TCC.

Additional studies have used ELISA to evaluate the usefulness of serum VEGF levels as a marker. Serum VEGF levels have shown correlation with tumor stage, grade, vascular invasion, presence of carcinoma in situ, and metastasis. However, on multivariate analysis only stage remained as an independent prognostic factor.[120]

Some reports have suggested that VEGF is differentially expressed in bladder cancer, with high expression in superficial tumors (stage pTa and pT1) contrasting with low expression in muscle-invasive tumors (stage > pT1).[121,122] Others have also evaluated the prognostic significance of VEGF expression in tumor tissue and reported that VEGF expression did not correlate with risk of tumor recurrence or patient survival.[123] In contrast to these findings, Crew and colleagues[124] measured VEGF mRNA and protein in tumor specimens from 55 patients with superficial bladder cancer and reported that high levels of VEGF mRNA and protein were associated with recurrence and progression. They speculate that the relationship between VEGF and early tumor recurrence suggests that seeding via angiogenesis may be a major mechanism in the pathogenesis of recurrence. These studies indicate that VEGF can be predictive of the behavior of superficial bladder tumors and is a therapeutic target for intravesical therapy. We have reported that VEGF expression in precystectomy biopsies was an independent prognostic predictor for survival in patients with invasive TCC treated by neoadjuvant MVAC and radical cystectomy.[90]

INTERLEUKIN-8

IL-8 is a chemoattractant cytokine that is produced by various tissues, neoplasms, and blood components, and it functions locally to attract and activate neutrophils in inflammatory regions of neoplasms.[72–74,125–128] This local chemokine production by tumor cells plays an important role in invasion and metatasis (see Figure 4–1). Koch and colleagues[129] demonstrated that IL-8 is also a pro-angiogenic molecule possessing mitogenic and chemotactic properties for endothelial cells. In bladder cancer, expression of IL-8 follows a pattern similar to that for bFGF, being greater in carcinoma in situ and muscle-invasive tumors than in superficial papillary lesions. IL-8 expression distinguishes between superficial and invasive phenotypes and is a relatively early change in the development of TCC of the bladder.[63]

Studies in human tissue have demonstrated that during the transformation from normal urothelium to carcinoma in situ, up-regulation of IL-8 expression occurs.[63] However, in an analysis of cystectomy specimens following neoadjuvant MVAC chemotherapy, IL-8 in the pretherapy or cystectomy specimens was not predictive of outcome.[90] Studies in our laboratory demonstrated that transfection of tumorigenic 253J B-V cells with IL-8 antisense cDNA diminished tumorigenicity; conversely, IL-8 sense transfection in the nontumorigenic 253J cell line initiated a tumorigenic phenotype. Furthermore, the metastatic potential of the cell line was regulated by IL-8 expression. Additional experiments confirmed that IL-8 expression enhances angiogenic activity through the induction of MMP-9 and subsequently regulates the tumorigenesis and production of spontaneous metastases of human TCC.[44] In further studies in our laboratory, adenoviral mediated antisense IL-8 gene transfer to orthotopic bladder cancer xenografts in nude mice inhibited tumor growth. Adenovirus-IL-8 antisense therapy also decreased the in vivo expression of IL-8 and MMP-9, reduced microvessel density, and enhanced endothelial cell apoptosis.[130] Furthermore, we have shown growth inhibitory effects of a fully humanized anti-IL-8 antibody in orthotopic bladder cancer xenografts (unpublished data). We have evaluated the role of IL-8 in the response to hypoxia stress and acidosis and have reported that IL-8 plays a central role in the host response that is regulated via NF-κB. This concept was confirmed by studies in which NF-κB function was blocked resulting in impairment of tumorigenicity and reduction of metastasis (unpublished data). Thus IL-8 may play a pivotal role in the pathogenesis and progression of bladder cancer and remains a potential therapeutic target for novel treatment.

SUMMARY

Understanding the molecular pathogenesis of bladder cancer remains an area of ongoing research that is facilitated by the recent development of new molecular biological analytical techniques and it is intrinsically linked to the development of novel therapeutic agents. As a greater knowledge of the precise mechanisms involved in the malignant transformation of normal urothelium and the progression of superficial to invasive TCC develops the potential for interventions in these pathways will increase the therapeutic repertoire available to the urologist and oncologist to treat bladder cancer.

REFERENCES

1. Thykjaer T, Workman C, Kruhoffer M, et al. Identification of gene expression patterns in superficial and invasive human bladder cancer. Cancer Res 2001;61:2492–9.
2. Grossman HB. The First and Second International Workshops on Diagnostic and Prognostic Markers in Bladder Cancer. Urol Oncol 2000;5:183–4.
3. Nagar B, Overduin M, Ikura M, Rini JM. Structural basis of calcium-induced E-cadherin rigidification and dimerization. Nature 1996;380:360–4.
4. Shapiro L, Fannon AM, Kwong PD, et al. Structural basis of cell-cell adhesion by cadherins. Nature 1995;374:327–37.
5. Nagafuchi A, Takeichi M. Cell binding function of E-cadherin is regulated by the cytoplasmic domain. EMBO J 1988;7:3679–84.
6. Ozawa M, Ringwald M, Kemler R. Uvomorulin-catenin complex formation is regulated by a specific domain in the cytoplasmic region of the cell adhesion molecule. Proc Natl Acad Sci U S A 1990;87:4246–50.
7. Daniel JM, Reynolds AB. Tyrosine phosphorylation and cadherin/catenin function. Bioessays 1997;19:883–91.
8. Chen H, Paradies NE, Fedor-Chaiken M, Brackenbury R. E-cadherin mediates adhesion and suppresses cell motility via distinct mechanisms. J Cell Sci 1997;110(Pt 3):345–56.
9. Shimoyama Y, Hirohashi S, Hirano S, et al.Cadherin cell-adhesion molecules in human epithelial tissues and carcinomas. Cancer Res 1989;49:2128–33.
10. Takeichi M. Cadherin cell adhesion receptors as a morphogenetic regulator. Science 1991;251:1451–5.
11. Guilford P, Hopkins J, Harraway J, et al. E-cadherin germline mutations in familial gastric cancer. Nature 1998;392: 402–5.
12. Bornman DM, Mathew S, Alsruhe J, et al. Methylation of the E-cadherin gene in bladder neoplasia and in normal urothelial epithelium from elderly individuals. Am J Pathol 2001;159:831–5.
13. Giroldi LA, Bringuier PP, Schalken JA. Defective E-cadherin function in urological cancers: clinical implications and molecular mechanisms [review]. Invasion Metastasis 1994;14:71–81.
14. Ohene-Abuakwa Y, Pignatelli M. Adhesion molecules in cancer biology. Adv Exp Med Biol 2000;465:115–26.
15. Behrens J. Cadherins and catenins: role in signal transduction and tumor progression. Cancer Metastasis Rev 1999;18: 15–30.
16. Bindels EM, Vermey M, De Both NJ, van der Kwast TH. Influence of the microenvironment on invasiveness of human bladder carcinoma cell lines. Virchows Arch 2001;439:552–9.
17. Davies G, Jiang WG, Mason MD. Cell-cell adhesion molecules and their associated proteins in bladder cancer cells and their role in mitogen induced cell-cell dissociation and invasion. Anticancer Res 1999;19:547–52.
18. Wakatsuki S, Watanabe R, Saito K, et al. Loss of human E-cadherin (ECD) correlated with invasiveness of transitional cell cancer in the renal pelvis, ureter and urinary bladder. Cancer Lett 1996;103:11–7.
19. Behrens J, Mareel MM, Van Roy FM, Birchmeier W. Dissecting tumor cell invasion: epithelial cells acquire invasive properties after the loss of uvomorulin-mediated cell-cell adhesion. J Cell Biol 1989;108:2435–47.
20. Frixen UH, Behrens J, Sachs M, et al. E-cadherin-mediated cell-cell adhesion prevents invasiveness of human carcinoma cells. J Cell Biol 1991;113:173–85.
21. Chen WC, Obrink B. Cell-cell contacts mediated by E-cadherin (uvomorulin) restrict invasive behavior of L-cells. J Cell Biol 1991;114:319–27.
22. Vleminckx K, Vakaet LJ, Mareel M, et al. Genetic manipulation of E-cadherin expression by epithelial tumor cells reveals an invasion suppressor role. Cell 1991;66:107–19.
23. Protheroe AS, Banks RE, Mzimba M, et al. Urinary concentrations of the soluble adhesion molecule E-cadherin and total protein in patients with bladder cancer. Br J Cancer 1999;80:273–8.
24. Ross JS, Cheung C, Sheehan C, et al. E-cadherin cell-adhesion molecule expression as a diagnostic adjunct in urothelial cytology. Diagn Cytopathol 1996;14:310–5.
25. Durkan GC, Brotherick I, Mellon JK. The impact of transurethral resection of bladder tumour on serum levels of soluble E-cadherin. BJU Int 1999;83:424–8.
26. Griffiths TR, Brotherick I, Bishop RI, et al. Cell adhesion molecules in bladder cancer: soluble serum E-cadherin correlates with predictors of recurrence. Br J Cancer 1996;74:579–84.
27. Hong RL, Pu YS, Hsieh TS, et al. Expressions of E-cadherin and exon v6-containing isoforms of CD44 and their prognostic values in human transitional cell carcinoma. J Urol 1995;153:2025–8.
28. Ross JS, del Rosario AD, Figge HL, et al. E-cadherin expression in papillary transitional cell carcinoma of the urinary bladder. Hum Pathol 1995;26:940–4.
29. Nakopoulou L, Zervas A, Gakiopoulou-Givalou H, et al. Prognostic value of E-cadherin, beta-catenin, P120ctn in patients with transitional cell bladder cancer. Anticancer Res 2000;20:4571–8.
30. Lipponen PK, Eskelinen MJ. Reduced expression of E-cadherin is related to invasive disease and frequent recurrence in bladder cancer. J Cancer Res Clin Oncol 1995; 121:303–8.
31. Shimazui T, Schalken JA, Giroldi LA, et al. Prognostic value of cadherin-associated molecules (alpha-, beta-, and gamma-catenins and p120cas) in bladder tumors. Cancer Res 1996;56:4154–8.

32. Bringuier PP, Umbas R, Schaafsma HE, et al. Decreased E-cadherin immunoreactivity correlates with poor survival in patients with bladder tumors. Cancer Res 1993;53:3241–5.

33. Syrigos KN, Krausz T, Waxman J, et al. E-cadherin expression in bladder cancer using formalin-fixed, paraffin-embedded tissues: correlation with histopathological grade, tumour stage and survival. Int J Cancer 1995;64:367–70.

34. Syrigos KN, Harrington K, Waxman J, et al. Altered gamma-catenin expression correlates with poor survival in patients with bladder cancer. J Urol 1998;160:1889–93.

35. Byrne RR, Shariat SF, Brown R, et al. E-cadherin immuno-staining of bladder transitional cell carcinoma, carcinoma in situ and lymph node metastases with long-term follow-up. J Urol 2001;165:1473–9.

36. Fujisawa M, Miyazaki J, Takechi Y, et al. The significance of E-cadherin in transitional-cell carcinoma of the human urinary bladder. World J Urol 1996;14 Suppl 1:S12–S15.

37. Garcia del Muro X, Torregrosa A, Munoz J, et al. Prognostic value of the expression of E-cadherin and beta-catenin in bladder cancer. Eur J Cancer 2000;36:357–62.

38. Mialhe A, Louis J, Montlevier S, et al. Expression of E-cadherin and alpha-, beta- and gamma-catenins in human bladder carcinomas: are they good prognostic factors? Invasion Metastasis 1997;17:124–37.

39. Otto T, Birchmeier W, Schmidt U, et al. Inverse relation of E-cadherin and autocrine motility factor receptor expression as a prognostic factor in patients with bladder carcinomas. Cancer Res 1994;54:3120–3.

40. Shariat SF, Pahlavan S, Baseman AG, et al. E-cadherin expression predicts clinical outcome in carcinoma in situ of the urinary bladder. Urology 2001;57:60–5.

41. Mialhe A, Levacher G, Champelovier P, et al. Expression of E-, P-, N-cadherins and catenins in human bladder carcinoma cell lines. J Urol 2000;164:826–35.

42. Giroldi LA, Bringuier PP, Shimazui T, et al. Changes in cadherin-catenin complexes in the progression of human bladder carcinoma. Int J Cancer 1999;82:70–6.

43. Rieger-Christ KM, Cain JW, Braasch JW, et al. Expression of classic cadherins type I in urothelial neoplastic progression. Hum Pathol 2001;32:18–23.

44. Inoue K, Slaton JW, Kim SJ, et al. Interleukin 8 expression regulates tumorigenicity and metastasis in human bladder cancer. Cancer Res 2000;60:2290–9.

45. Karelina TV, Goldberg GI, Eisen AZ. Matrix metalloproteinases in blood vessel development in human fetal skin and in cutaneous tumors. J Invest Dermatol 1995;105:411–7.

46. Fisher C, Gilbertson-Beadling S, Powers EA, et al. Interstitial collagenase is required for angiogenesis in vitro. Dev Biol 1994;162:499–510.

47. Stetler-Stevenson WG. Matrix metalloproteinases in angiogenesis: a moving target for therapeutic intervention. J Clin Invest 1999;103:1237–41.

48. Rao VH, Singh RK, Delimont DC, et al. Transcriptional regulation of MMP-9 expression in stromal cells of human giant cell tumor of bone by tumor necrosis factor-alpha. Int J Oncol 1999;14:291–300.

49. Lyons JG, Birkedal-Hansen B, Pierson MC, et al. Interleukin-1 beta and transforming growth factor-alpha/epidermal growth factor induce expression of M(r) 95,000 type IV collagenase/gelatinase and interstitial fibroblast-type collagenase by rat mucosal keratinocytes. J Biol Chem 1993;268:19143–51.

50. Sehgal I, Thompson TC. Novel regulation of type IV collagenase (matrix metalloproteinase-9 and -2) activities by transforming growth factor-beta1 in human prostate cancer cell lines. Mol Biol Cell 1999;10:407–16.

51. Charvat S, Chignol MC, Souchier C, et al. Cell migration and MMP-9 secretion are increased by epidermal growth factor in HaCaT-ras transfected cells. Exp Dermatol 1998;7:184–90.

52. McCawley LJ, O'Brien P, Hudson LG. Epidermal growth factor (EGF)- and scatter factor/hepatocyte growth factor (SF/HGF)- mediated keratinocyte migration is coincident with induction of matrix metalloproteinase (MMP)-9. J Cell Physiol 1998;176:255–65.

53. Miyake H, Yoshimura K, Hara I, et al. Basic fibroblast growth factor regulates matrix metalloproteinases production and in vitro invasiveness in human bladder cancer cell lines. J Urol 1997;157:2351–5.

54. Furukawa A, Tsuji M, Nishitani M, et al. Role of the matrix metalloproteinase and tissue inhibitors of metalloproteinase families in noninvasive and invasive tumors transplanted in mice with severe combined immunodeficiency. Urology 1998;51:849–53.

55. Kawamata H, Kameyama S, Nan L, et al. Effect of epidermal growth factor and transforming growth factor beta 1 on growth and invasive potentials of newly established rat bladder carcinoma cell lines. Int J Cancer 1993;55:968–73.

56. Bianco FJ Jr, Gervasi DC, Tiguert R, et al. Matrix metallo-proteinase-9 expression in bladder washes from bladder cancer patients predicts pathological stage and grade. Clin Cancer Res 1998;4:3011–6.

57. Margulies IM, Hoyhtya M, Evans C, et al. Urinary type IV collagenase: elevated levels are associated with bladder transitional cell carcinoma. Cancer Epidemiol Biomarkers Prev 1992;1:467–74.

58. Ozdemir E, Kakehi Y, Okuno H, Yoshida O. Role of matrix metalloproteinase-9 in the basement membrane destruction of superficial urothelial carcinomas. J Urol 1999;161:1359–63.

59. Moses MA, Wiederschain D, Loughlin KR, et al. Increased incidence of matrix metalloproteinases in urine of cancer patients. Cancer Res 1998;58:1395–9.

60. Davies B, Waxman J, Wasan H, et al. Levels of matrix metalloproteases in bladder cancer correlate with tumor grade and invasion. Cancer Res 1993;53:5365–9.

61. Hara I, Miyake H, Hara S, et al. Significance of matrix metalloproteinases and tissue inhibitors of metalloproteinase expression in the recurrence of superficial transitional cell carcinoma of the bladder. J Urol 2001;165:1769–72.

62. Grignon DJ, Sakr W, Toth M, et al. High levels of tissue inhibitor of metalloproteinase-2 (TIMP-2) expression are associated with poor outcome in invasive bladder cancer. Cancer Res 1996;56:1654–9.

63. Izawa JI, Slaton JW, Kedar D, et al. Differential expression of progression-related genes in the evolution of superficial to invasive transitional cell carcinoma of the bladder. Oncol Rep 2001;8:9–15.

64. Fidler IJ, Kumar R, Bielenberg DR, Ellis LM. Molecular determinants of angiogenesis in cancer metastasis. Cancer J Sci Am 1998;4 Suppl 1:S58–S66.

65. Kumar R, Fidler IJ. Angiogenic molecules and cancer metastasis. In Vivo 1998;12:27–34.

66. Liotta LA. Tumor invasion and metastases—role of the extracellular matrix: Rhoads Memorial Award lecture. Cancer Res 1986;46:1–7.

67. Welgus HG, Campbell EJ, Cury JD, et al. Neutral metalloproteinases produced by human mononuclear phagocytes. Enzyme profile, regulation, and expression during cellular development. J Clin Invest 1990;86:1496–1502.

68. Hamasaki T, Hattori T, Kimura G, Nakazawa N. Tumor progression and expression of matrix metalloproteinase-2 (MMP-2) mRNA by human urinary bladder cancer cells. Urol Res 1998;26:371–6.

69. Kanayama H, Yokota K, Kurokawa Y, et al. Prognostic values of matrix metalloproteinase-2 and tissue inhibitor of metalloproteinase-2 expression in bladder cancer. Cancer 1998;82:1359–66.

70. Gohji K, Fujimoto N, Ohkawa J, et al. Imbalance between serum matrix metalloproteinase-2 and its inhibitor as a predictor of recurrence of urothelial cancer. Br J Cancer 1998;77:650–5.

71. Imao T, Koshida K, Endo Y, et al. Dominant role of E-cadherin in the progression of bladder cancer. J Urol 1999;161:692–8.

72. Kitadai Y, Ellis LM, Tucker SL, et al. Multiparametric in situ mRNA hybridization analysis to predict disease recurrence in patients with colon carcinoma. Am J Pathol 1996;149:1541–51.

73. Kitadai Y, Ellis LM, Takahashi Y, et al. Multiparametric in situ messenger RNA hybridization analysis to detect metastasis-related genes in surgical specimens of human colon carcinomas. Clin Cancer Res 1995;1:1095–102.

74. Anzai H, Kitadai Y, Bucana CD, et al. Intratumoral heterogeneity and inverse correlation between expression of E-cadherin and collagenase type IV in human gastric carcinomas. Differentiation 1996;60:119–27.

75. Kuniyasu H, Ellis LM, Evans DB, et al. Relative expression of E-cadherin and type IV collagenase genes predicts disease outcome in patients with resectable pancreatic carcinoma. Clin Cancer Res 1999;5:25–33.

76. Herbst RS, Yano S, Kuniyasu H, et al. Differential expression of E-cadherin and type IV collagenase genes predicts outcome in patients with stage I non-small cell lung carcinoma. Clin Cancer Res 2000;6:790–7.

77. Kuniyasu H, Troncoso P, Johnston D, et al. Relative expression of type IV collagenase, E-cadherin, and vascular endothelial growth factor/vascular permeability factor in prostatectomy specimens distinguishes organ-confined from pathologically advanced prostate cancers. Clin Cancer Res 2000;6:2295–308.

78. Slaton JW, Karashima T, Perrotte P, et al. Treatment with low-dose interferon-alpha restores the balance between matrix metalloproteinase-9 and E-cadherin expression in human transitional cell carcinoma of the bladder. Clin Cancer Res 2001;7:2840–53.

79. Campbell SC, Volpert OV, Ivanovich M, Bouck NP. Molecular mediators of angiogenesis in bladder cancer. Cancer Res 1998;58:1298–304.

80. Okada-Ban M, Moens G, Thiery JP, Jouanneau J. Nuclear 24 kD fibroblast growth factor (FGF)-2 confers metastatic properties on rat bladder carcinoma cells. Oncogene 1999;18:6719–24.

81. Miyake H, Yoshimura K, Hara I, et al. Basic fibroblast growth factor regulates matrix metalloproteinases production and in vitro invasiveness in human bladder cancer cell lines. J Urol 1997;157:2351–5.

82. Miyake H, Hara I, Gohji K, et al. Expression of basic fibroblast growth factor is associated with resistance to cisplatin in a human bladder cancer cell line. Cancer Lett 1998;123:121–6.

83. Inoue K, Perrotte P, Wood CG, et al. Gene therapy of human bladder cancer with adenovirus-mediated antisense basic fibroblast growth factor. Clin Cancer Res 2000;6:4422–31.

84. Slaton JW, Perrotte P, Inoue K, et al. Interferon-alpha-mediated down-regulation of angiogenesis-related genes and therapy of bladder cancer are dependent on optimization of biological dose and schedule. Clin Cancer Res 1999;5:2726–34.

85. Dinney CP, Bielenberg DR, Perrotte P, et al. Inhibition of basic fibroblast growth factor expression, angiogenesis, and growth of human bladder carcinoma in mice by systemic interferon-alpha administration. Cancer Res 1998;58:808–14.

86. Nguyen M, Watanabe H, Budson AE, et al. Elevated levels of the angiogenic peptide basic fibroblast growth factor in urine of bladder cancer patients. J Nat Cancer Inst 1993;85:241–2.

87. Chodak GW, Hospelhorn V, Judge SM, et al. Increased levels of fibroblast growth factor-like activity in urine from patients with bladder or kidney cancer. Cancer Res 1988;48:2083–8.

88. Gazzaniga P, Gandini O, Gradilone A, et al. Detection of basic fibroblast growth factor mRNA in urinary bladder cancer: correlation with local relapses. Int J Oncol 1999;14:1123–7.

89. O'Brien T, Cranston D, Fuggle S, et al. Two mechanisms of basic fibroblast growth factor-induced angiogenesis in bladder cancer. Cancer Res 1997;57:136–40.

90. Inoue K, Slaton JW, Karashima T, et al. The prognostic value of angiogenesis factor expression for predicting recurrence and metastasis of bladder cancer after neoadjuvant chemotherapy and radical cystectomy. Clin Cancer Res 2000;6:4866–73.

91. Messing EM, Reznikoff CA. Epidermal growth factor and its receptor: markers of—and targets for—chemoprevention of bladder cancer [review]. J Cell Biochem Suppl 1992;16I:56–62.

92. Kristensen JK, Lose G, Lund F, Nexo E. Epidermal growth factor in urine from patients with urinary bladder tumors. Eur Urol 1988;14:313–4.

93. Messing EM, Murphy-Brooks N. Recovery of epidermal growth factor in voided urine of patients with bladder cancer. Urology 1994;44:502–6.

94. Momose H, Kakinuma H, Shariff SY, et al. Tumor-promoting effect of urinary epidermal growth factor in rat urinary bladder carcinogenesis. Cancer Res 1991;51:5487–90.

95. Kuranami M, Yamaguchi K, Fuchigami M, et al. Effect of urine on clonal growth of human bladder cancer cell lines. Cancer Res 1991;51:4631–5.

96. Smith K, Fennelly JA, Neal DE, et al. Characterization and quantitation of the epidermal growth factor receptor in invasive and superficial bladder tumors. Cancer Res 1989;49:5810–5.

97. Messing EM, Reznikoff CA. Normal and malignant human

urothelium: in vitro effects of epidermal growth factor. Cancer Res 1987;47:2230–5.

98. Messing EM. Clinical implications of the expression of epidermal growth factor receptors in human transitional cell carcinoma. Cancer Res 1990;50:2530–7.

99. Perrotte P, Matsumoto T, Inoue K, et al. Anti-epidermal growth factor receptor antibody C225 inhibits angiogenesis in human transitional cell carcinoma growing orthotopically in nude mice. Clin Cancer Res 1999;5:257–65.

100. Chow NH, Liu HS, Lee EI, et al. Significance of urinary epidermal growth factor and its receptor expression in human bladder cancer. Anticancer Res 1997;17:1293–6.

101. Theodorescu D, Laderoute KR, Gulding KM. Epidermal growth factor receptor-regulated human bladder cancer motility is in part a phosphatidylinositol 3-kinase-mediated process. Cell Growth Differ 1998;9:919–28.

102. Petit AM, Rak J, Hung MC, et al. Neutralizing antibodies against epidermal growth factor and ErbB-2/neu receptor tyrosine kinases down-regulate vascular endothelial growth factor production by tumor cells in vitro and in vivo: angiogenic implications for signal transduction therapy of solid tumors. Am J Pathol 1997;151:1523–30.

103. Bruns CJ, Harbison MT, Davis DW, et al. Epidermal growth factor receptor blockade with C225 plus gemcitabine results in regression of human pancreatic carcinoma growing orthotopically in nude mice by antiangiogenic mechanisms. Clin Cancer Res 2000;6:1936–48.

104. Goldman CK, Kim J, Wong WL, et al. Epidermal growth factor stimulates vascular endothelial growth factor production by human malignant glioma cells: a model of glioblastoma multiforme pathophysiology. Mol Biol Cell 1993;4:121–33.

105. Xie H, Turner T, Wang MH, et al. In vitro invasiveness of DU-145 human prostate carcinoma cells is modulated by EGF receptor-mediated signals. Clin Exp Metastasis 1995;13:407–19.

106. Inoue K, Slaton JW, Perrotte P, et al. Paclitaxel enhances the effects of the anti-epidermal growth factor receptor monoclonal antibody ImClone C225 in mice with metastatic human bladder transitional cell carcinoma. Clin Cancer Res 2000;6:4874–84.

107. Jarrard DF, Blitz BF, Smith RC, et al. Effect of epidermal growth factor on prostate cancer cell line PC3 growth and invasion. Prostate 1994;24:46–53.

108. Thorne HJ, Jose DG, Zhang HY, et al. Epidermal growth factor stimulates the synthesis of cell-attachment proteins in the human breast cancer cell line PMC42. Int J Cancer 1987;40:207–12.

109. Lichtner RB, Wiedemuth M, Noeske-Jungblut C, Schirrmacher V. Rapid effects of EGF on cytoskeletal structures and adhesive properties of highly metastatic rat mammary adenocarcinoma cells. Clin Exp Metastasis 1993;11:113–25.

110. Chen P, Gupta K, Wells A. Cell movement elicited by epidermal growth factor receptor requires kinase and autophosphorylation but is separable from mitogenesis. J Cell Biol 1994;124:547–55.

111. Chen P, Xie H, Sekar MC, et al. Epidermal growth factor receptor-mediated cell motility: phospholipase C activity is required, but mitogen-activated protein kinase activity is not sufficient for induced cell movement. J Cell Biol 1994;127:847–57.

112. Kanno N, Nonomura N, Miki T, et al. Effects of epidermal growth factor on the invasion activity of the bladder cancer cell line. J Urol 1998;159:586–90.

113. Folkman J. Tumor angiogenesis: therapeutic implications. N Engl J Med 1971;285:1182–6.

114. Hanahan D, Folkman J. Patterns and emerging mechanisms of the angiogenic switch during tumorigenesis. Cell 1996;86:353–64.

115. Bochner BH, Cote RJ, Weidner N, et al. Angiogenesis in bladder cancer: relationship between microvessel density and tumor prognosis. J Natl Cancer Inst 1995;87:1603–12.

116. Neufeld G, Cohen T, Gengrinovitch S, Poltorak Z. Vascular endothelial growth factor (VEGF) and its receptors. FASEB J 1999;13:9–22.

117. Levy AP, Levy NS, Wegner S, Goldberg MA. Transcriptional regulation of the rat vascular endothelial growth factor gene by hypoxia. J Biol Chem 1995;270:13333–40.

118. Jeon SH, Lee SJ, Chang SG. Clinical significance of urinary vascular endothelial growth factor in patients with superficial bladder tumors. Oncol Rep 2001;8:1265–7.

119. Crew JP, O'Brien T, Bicknell R, et al. Urinary vascular endothelial growth factor and its correlation with bladder cancer recurrence rates [see comments]. J Urol 1999;161:799–804.

120. Bernardini S, Fauconnet S, Chabannes E, et al. Serum levels of vascular endothelial growth factor as a prognostic factor in bladder cancer. J Urol 2001;166:1275–9.

121. O'Brien T, Cranston D, Fuggle S, et al. Different angiogenic pathways characterize superficial and invasive bladder cancer. Cancer Res 1995;55:510–3.

122. Crew JP, Fuggle S, Bicknell R, et al. Eukaryotic initiation factor-4E in superficial and muscle invasive bladder cancer and its correlation with vascular endothelial growth factor expression and tumour progression. Br J Cancer 2000;82:161–6.

123. Chow NH, Liu HS, Chan SH, et al. Expression of vascular endothelial growth factor in primary superficial bladder cancer. Anticancer Res 1999;19:4593–7.

124. Crew JP, O'Brien T, Bradburn M, et al. Vascular endothelial growth factor is a predictor of relapse and stage progression in superficial bladder cancer. Cancer Res 1997;57:5281–5.

125. Greene GF, Kitadai Y, Pettaway CA, et al. Correlation of metastasis-related gene expression with metastatic potential in human prostate carcinoma cells implanted in nude mice using an in situ messenger RNA hybridization technique. Am J Pathol 1997;150:1571–82.

126. Kitadai Y, Bucana CD, Ellis LM, et al. In situ mRNA hybridization technique for analysis of metastasis-related genes in human colon carcinoma cells. Am J Pathol 1995;147:1238–47.

127. Singh RK, Gutman M, Radinsky R, et al. Expression of interleukin 8 correlates with the metastatic potential of human melanoma cells in nude mice. Cancer Res 1994;54:3242–7.

128. Gutman M, Singh RK, Xie K, et al. Regulation of interleukin-8 expression in human melanoma cells by the organ environment. Cancer Res 1995;55:2470–5.

129. Koch AE, Polverini PJ, Kunkel SL, et al. Interleukin-8 as a macrophage-derived mediator of angiogenesis. Science 1992;258:1798–801.

130. Inoue K, Wood CG, Slaton JW, et al. Adenoviral-mediated gene therapy of human bladder cancer with antisense interleukin-8. Oncol Rep 2001;8:955–64.

5

Clinical Pathogenesis and Staging of Urothelial Bladder Cancer

PETER LAGENSTROER, MD, MS
WILLIAM SEE, MD

Bladder cancer is the second most common urologic malignancy. By virtue of its dichotomous clinical course, it represents a malignancy that is unique in its presentation, staging, and biologic potential. This chapter will summarize the current 2002 American Joint Committee on Cancer (AJCC) staging system,[1] provide a contemporary review of the available staging tools, illustrate the staging algorithm, and address issues concerning clinical presentation as they relate to variable biologic potential. It is important not only to understand the nuances of bladder cancer staging but also to apply them in the contextual framework of biologic potential. The ultimate goal for patient management is selection and application of appropriate therapy. Whereas staging offers a framework for patient management, it is an understanding of the biologic potential at each stage that remains critical. The complex pathogenesis of bladder cancer must be appreciated during the staging process so that the biologic potential at each clinical stage can be translated into tailored patient care.

Identification of a cancerous lesion, whether primary or recurrent, represents a discrete isolated window or "snapshot" of a more dynamic, continuous, and evolving biologic process. The frequent recurrence of bladder cancer affords the clinician the unique opportunity for multiple snapshots and a deeper understanding of the pathogenesis of a particular lesion. However, each episode must be reevaluated for its unique position on the spectrum of each patient's disease process. For example, a Ta low-grade lesion typically has a proliferative expression with minimal potential for progression (2%). If the same lesion is high grade, it is more apt to manifest with a changing phenotype. In this scenario, the recurrences may demonstrate aspects of proliferative, dysplastic, and progressive behavior, represented by papillary, carcinoma in situ (CIS) or sessile lesions, respectively. The genotypic alterations, which dictate biologic potential, are driving this phenotypic presentation. Thus, a snapshot of bladder cancer must be interpreted based not only on the stage but also on the continuum of biologic potential represented clinically by this stage or phenotypic presentation.

OBJECTIVES OF STAGING IN BLADDER CANCER

The most widely employed staging system for carcinoma of the bladder is the tumor - node - metastasis (TNM) International Union Against Cancer (UICC) classification. This staging system and that of the AJCC[1] are identical. Accurate staging provides consistent and reproducible frameworks for study, discussion, and clinical decisions. Staging, in combination with tumor grading and biologic potential, can predict recurrence, progression, prognosis, and outcomes. Moreover, accurate staging is the foundation for research protocols and outcomes analysis. Thus, a thorough understanding of the current staging system is the anchoring step when diagnosing and treating bladder cancer. The staging system described in this review is the current 2002 AJCC system.

BLADDER CANCER STAGING SYSTEM

The basics of the TNM system are reproducible, simple, and generally transferable to other organ systems (Table 5–1). The T characterizes the primary tumor and its local regional involvement. The N and M describe lymph node involvement and distant metastasis. With this basic construct the staging system for bladder cancer is straightforward. As an example, a patient with muscle invasive bladder cancer confined to the deep muscularis propria of the bladder with multiple microscopically positive pelvic lymph nodes and a negative work-up for distant metastasis would be staged T2b, N2, M0.

The three most important levels of staging differentiation are based upon depth of tumor penetration into the bladder wall. Superficial disease (Ta/T1) does not penetrate the muscularis propria. Muscle invasive disease (T2) penetrates through the lamina propria and into the muscularis propria. More advanced extravesical disease has spread through the muscularis propria and into the perivesical fat (T3) and/or adjacent structures (T4). Owing to the

Table 5–1. AJCC 2002 TNM STAGING FOR BLADDER CANCER

Primary Tumor

Tx	Primary tumor cannot be assessed
T0	No evidence of primary tumor
Ta	Noninvasive papillary carcinoma
TIS	Carcinoma in situ
T1	Tumor invades into the subepithelial connective tissue (lamina propria)
T2	Tumor invades into the muscularis propria
	T2a Tumor invades superficial muscularis propria
	T2b Tumor invades deep muscularis propria
T3	Tumor invades into the perivesical tissue
	T3a Microscopic
	T3b Macroscopic
T4	Tumor invades into the adjacent organs
	T4a Tumor invades prostate, uterus or vagina
	T4b Tumor invades pelvic sidewall or abdominal wall

Regional lymph node status

Nx	Regional lymph nodes and cannot be assessed
N0	No regional lymph node metastasis
N1	Metastasis in a single lymph node 2 cm or less in greatest dimension
N2	Metastasis in a single lymph node ≥ 2 cm but not > 5 cm, or multiple lymph nodes not > 5 cm in size
N3	Lymph nodes > 5 cm in size

Distant metastases

Mx	Distant metastases cannot be assessed
M0	No distant metastasis
M1	Presence of distant metastasis

significant and variable pathogenesis and morbidity associated with stage-specific treatment, accurate T staging is paramount.

Superficial disease warrants further description. By definition, superficial disease is not muscularis propria invasive. In this context, muscle invasion refers to the muscularis propria and not the muscularis mucosa. The muscularis mucosa is a component of the subepithelium. This distinction is extremely important and must be clarified with the pathologist.

A Ta designation represents superficial disease that does not violate the lamina propria, whereas T1 disease penetrates into the lamina propria. Muscularis mucosa involvement is T1 disease, whereas muscularis propria involvement is T2 disease.

High-grade T1 disease with or without other negative prognosticators does carry a risk of understaging of up to 40%.[2] In fact, recent studies have attempted to further subcategorize T1 disease by depth of invasion. T1a represents superficial lamina propria invasion, and T1b is deep lamina propria invasion. A few studies have shown that this separation of lamina propria invasion does have prognostic significance.[3–5] The utility of this classification remains controversial,[6] and it is not incorporated into the AJCC system. Because stage and associated pathogenesis drive further therapy ranging from observation to surgical extirpation or systemic chemotherapy, repeat staging resection of the primary lesion may be indicated. A detailed review of the indications for a second staging transurethral resection (TUR) is available but beyond the scope of this chapter.[7]

There are two levels of bladder cancer staging: clinical staging and pathological staging. Clinical staging uses clinical tools such as physical examination, imaging, and endoscopy. Pathological classification (represented by a "p" suffix) is detailed following pathological assessment after extirpation of the surgical specimen. This yields precise information about the extent of local and regional disease. Typically, clinical staging is used for the initial assessment and management whereas the more detailed data from pathological staging dictates long-term management. In the case of multiple or synchronous tumors, a common occurrence with bladder cancer, the tumor with the highest T category is the basis for the stage. Tumor multiplicity, that is, the number of tumors, can be indicated in parentheses, for example T1(5), to improve staging detail. Other modifiers, such as L for lymphatic invasion and V for vascular invasion, may also be used (Table 5–2). When focusing on biologic potential, the additional modifiers will aid in recommending therapy.

In addition to the standard TNM breakdown, the AJCC staging system has additional descriptors that allow for further detailed and precise staging. The descriptors relevant to bladder cancer are listed in Table 5–2. First, the "r" prefix represents recurrent disease. It is used when recurrent tumors are diagnosed following a disease-free interval. The "m" suffix, which is placed in parentheses, indicates the presence of multiple primary tumors of a single site. Both modifiers are apropos because recurrence and multicentricity define the natural history of bladder carcinoma. In addition to the standard TNM classification, the "R" classification describes the presence of residual disease following treatment. It can be used in the clinical setting following TUR or cystectomy.

STAGING SCHEMA FOR UROTHELIAL CANCER (BLADDER)

A schema of the different stages of bladder cancer is useful in providing a framework for the compartmentalization of disease, assessing prognosis of a cancer diathesis at a particular histopathologic "snapshot" in time, determining a course of therapy appropriate in the context of an expected prognosis, and comparing the results of new treatments as applied to specific stages of a cancer. Although schemata such as these imply a sequence of stages through which a given cancer proceeds from the time of its inception through the phase at which it is diag-

nosed and then to its eventual progression to metastasis and patient death. These schemata do not take into account the biologic heterogeneity of cancers within a specific histopathologic stage, their variable responses to particular treatments, and the different developmental pathways that specific cancers within a histopathologic stage may follow in expressing their intrinsic biologic potential (see below and Figure 5–1). Each of these may reflect various genetic and molecular changes responsible for a particular cancer's often-unique behavior. Although staging schemata are useful in categorizing a cancer histopathologically, they can be used more effectively in conjunction with other schemata that portrays various biologic pathways that a cancer with particular characteristics may be likely to follow.

Neoplastic transformation initially leads to CIS, which is the technical designation of cancer cells within the urothelium before a particular pathway is followed in the development of a specific *clinical* form of disease. This should not be confused with the clinical entity CIS, which is a specific diathesis that often pursues a progressive course (see below).

In 70 to 75% of instances, neoplastic transformation leads to the development of papillary tumors that are designated as "superficial" (as distinct from muscle-invasive). "Superficial" tumors comprise those that in the majority (70%) are mucosally confined (stage Ta) and those (30%) that have penetrated the underlying lamina propria (stage T1). Although both are likely to recur (~70%), mucosally confined tumors have a much lesser likelihood of progressing (2–4%) than do those that are superficially invasive (20–30%).

Although grade (the degree of differentiation of cells comprising a tumor) has not been incorporated into standard staging systems, assessment of this characteristic can aid in determination of a tumor's prognosis. High-grade is rarely seen in a truly mucosally confined papillary tumors (2–4%). On the other hand, lamina propria-invasive tumors may be high-grade in 50% of instances, and these may have a 50% likelihood of progression.

For stage Ta tumors that may occur, multiply, and are largely of low-moderate grade, adjacent and intervening mucosa is generally normal histologically. This is not the case for high-grade, lamina pro-

Table 5–2. STAGING MODIFIERS	
(m)	Multiple primary lesions, suffix
r	Recurrence, prefix
c	Clinical staging, prefix
p	Pathologic staging, prefix
R	Residual disease follow treatment
L	Lymphatic invasion
V	Vascular invasion

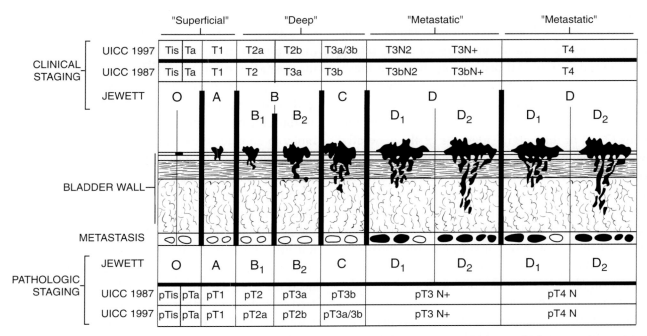

			"Superficial"		"Deep"			"Metastatic"		"Metastatic"	

CLINICAL STAGING

	Tis	Ta	T1	T2a	T2b	T3a/3b	T3N2	T3N+	T4	
UICC 1997	Tis	Ta	T1	T2a	T2b	T3a/3b	T3N2	T3N+	T4	
UICC 1987	Tis	Ta	T1	T2	T3a	T3b	T3bN2	T3bN+	T4	
JEWETT	O	A		B	C		D		D	

Within JEWETT row: B₁, B₂, D₁, D₂, D₁, D₂

BLADDER WALL

METASTASIS

PATHOLOGIC STAGING

	JEWETT	O	A	B₁	B₂	C	D₁	D₂	D₁	D₂
	UICC 1987	pTis	pTa	pT1	pT2	pT3a	pT3b	pT3 N+		pT4 N	
	UICC 1997	pTis	pTa	pT1	pT2a	pT2b	pT3a/3b	pT3 N+		pT4 N	

Figure 5–1. Staging systems for bladder cancer are based on correlations between the layer to which a particular cancer has penetrated the bladder wall, and the prognosis of that type of cancer. The original staging system (developed by Jewett in 1946) suggested distinctions between superficial and muscle-invasive disease. The superficial classification was subsequently divided into tumors confined to the mucosa (stage Ta) and tumors that penetrate the lamina propria (stage T1). Carcinoma in situ undermines the normal urothelium and extends along the plane of the urothelium. Deep bladder tumors penetrate the muscularis propria either superficially (stage T2a) or deeply (stage T2b) or penetrate through the muscularis propria into the perivesical soft tissue either microscopically (stage T3a) or extensively (stage T3b). These distinctions are a recent change in the World Health Organization (WHO) classification system, which now combines all muscle-invasive tumors into one category (stage T2 for superficial invasion and stage T3a for deep muscle invasion). The involvement of lymph nodes is designated by the N category, and involvement of adjacent structures is categorized as stage T4. This format implies a simple pattern of sequential development according to which early cancers appear as lower stages, and then progress to higher stages in sequence. However, this is not necessarily what characterizes the different forms of bladder cancer seen clinically. Rather, a variety of pathways that do not necessarily occur in sequence, but that are possibly interrelated may more accurately reflect the biology of the different forms of bladder cancer. (Reprinted with permission from Droller MJ. Bladder cancer: state of the art care. CA Cancer J Clin 1998;48:269–84.)

pria invasive (stage T1) disease in which the adjacent, intervening, and distant mucosa may be diffusely involved by high-grade malignant cells that may be dispersed through the bladder lining or undermine the normal mucosa.

This entity, so-call CIS, may be focal or diffuse and may extend into the lower ureter or into the prostatic urethra. First described in the setting of muscle-invasive disease, CIS is now recognized as an independent entity that presents a substantial risk of progression in the form of nodular muscle invasion. Although recognized as a distinct entity in the staging of urothelial cancer, its placement in staging schemata has not been fully clarified. CIS is therefore more readily understood in the context of various developmental pathways of urothelial neoplasia.

Stage T1 tumors have been subcategorized as either superficially (stage T1a) or deeply (stage T1b)

invasive, depending upon whether they have penetrated deep to the muscularis mucosa (a variably developed layer of smooth muscle fibers in the lamina propria). Though the extent of lamina propria invasion has been correlated with likelihood of progression, distinctions between stages T1a and T1b have not been formally incorporated into standard staging schemata.

Muscle-invasive (stage T2) cancers have been subcategorized into that have invaded superficially (stage T2a) and those that have invaded deeply (stage T2b). Several accompanying characteristics such as lymphatic or vascular penetration, invasion either in a broad front or with tentacular projections, and presentation in a papillary versus nodular configuration have been associated with aggressiveness of behavior and risk of metastasizing. However, none of these have been incorporated into standard staging systems.

Cancers that have penetrated through the muscularis into the perivesicle soft tissue are staged as T3a for microscopic penetration and T3b for more extensive penetration. Clinical distinctions between these can only be determined if a mass is palpable on bimanual examination under anesthesia.

Those cancers that have involved other pelvic organs (T4a) or the pelvic sidewalls (T4b) generally have a poor prognosis. The exception is when urothelial cancer extends into the prostatic urethra and ducts in the form of CIS, this having a much better prognosis when associated with CIS of "superficial" papillary tumors elsewhere in the bladder than those cancers that have infiltrated the prostatic stroma or those that have involved the prostate by penetration through the bladder wall and into the prostate from the outside.

The different T stages of bladder cancer are associated with an increasing likelihood of metastatic involvement of regional lymph nodes and occurrence of distant metastases with progressive penetration of the bladder wall. In addition, different prognoses may be associated with varying extent of nodal involvement. Standardization of lymph node excision and their pathologic examination is needed to increase the validity of these distinctions.

Although careful delineation of each stage can be used to determine the appropriate approach to therapy, understanding of biologic pathways and placement of a tumor at a given histopathologic stage within this context is important in gauging the implications of a staging schema and characterizing a tumor's potential outcome.

STAGING TOOLS

Radiographic Staging

Excretory Urography

All patients with bladder cancer must have their upper urinary tracts evaluated to assess for concomitant upper-tract urothelial carcinoma. Up to 6% of patients with superficial bladder cancer will have synchronous upper-tract disease.[8] In fact, lower-tract disease may be a manifestation of upper tract seeding. Excretory urography was traditionally performed as the initial work-up for hematuria. Others have used ultrasonography for initial evaluation of the kidneys in hematuria. Regardless of choice, these studies often supersede other studies such as computed tomography (CT) scans.

Our bias remains with the use of a contrast study. To this end, our institution is currently using CT urography to enhance the early diagnostic yield and minimize subsequent staging studies. Using spiral CT scanning and enhanced scanning software, intravenous pyelogram (IVP)–quality kidney, ureter, and bladder (KUB) and contrast images are obtained with the added benefit of full cross-sectional CT abdominal imaging and the potential for three-dimensional reconstruction. More importantly, this eliminates the need for a CT staging if a significant lesion is identified—bladder or otherwise. Our initial experience with the first 230 patients is currently under review.

A KUB is always taken with excretory urography as a scout film. When used alone it has a very limited role in the evaluation of bladder cancer. It may identify the occasional calcification of a bladder carcinoma.[9] Furthermore, it is possible to note osseous metastases on KUB. These lesions will likely present on other follow-up staging studies negating any significant use for a primary KUB.

The intravenous pyelogram remains an excellent test for the evaluation of the upper urinary tract. However, bladder cancer plays a minor role and it cannot directly determine muscle invasive status. The bladder phase of excretory urography will identify only large lesions with a 40% detection rate in a larger earlier series.[9] Small tumors (less than 5 mm), sessile tumors, and CIS are routinely missed. Filling defects, asymmetric filling, and contour irregularities generally represent bladder pathology but are not specific for bladder cancer. Distal ureteral obstruction, present in 8% of patients at the time of diagnosis, can prognosticate muscle invasive disease. Excluding iatrogenic causes, Hatch demonstrated that 92% of patients with bilateral ureteral obstruction would have muscle invasive bladder cancer.[10] Thus, excretory urography is a valuable tool for identifying associated upper-tract disease and can infer muscularis propria invasion, but its role in bladder cancer staging remains limited.

Computed Tomography

Computed tomography is the mainstay of pelvic and intra-abdominal staging for patients with the established diagnosis of muscle invasive bladder cancer. Its primary value is in determining the presence of N+, M+, or regional spread. It is inadequate for determining the depth of muscularis propria invasion or differentiating Ta, T1, or T2 disease. However, it can differentiate T3b and T4 lesions from T3a or less in 80% of patients.[11] The proper technique involves 5 mm sections in the area of interest and triple contrast (oral, rectal, and intravenous). The addition of a radiopaque tampon in the vaginal vault can further delineate the pelvic structures in women. Contemporary literature has not conclusively demonstrated improvement in CT staging when compared with magnetic resonance imaging (MRI) (Table 5–3). The most recent results suggest that accuracy in depicting the appropriate clinical stage ranges from 55 to 95%.[12,13] The best results occurred with air insufflation into the bladder prior to CT scanning.[13] Virtual cystoscopy, involving CT scanning with and without contrast and retrograde CO_2 insufflation, adds minimal information to the mucosal detail and bladder cancer staging.[14] CT-guided transmural core biopsies of bladder tumors have also been reported.[15] However, inadequate sampling and the risk of tumor seeding limit the utility of this technique.

For patients with a high index of suspicion for T2 or greater disease, CT scanning is best performed in the interval between diagnostic cystoscopy and bladder tumor resection. When performed subsequent to the transurethral resection of bladder tumor (TURBT), accurate interpretation of the CT scan can be difficult secondary to perivesical stranding, thickening, and edema as a result of the TUR.

Magnetic Resonance Imaging

Previously, MRI did not offer additional information to bladder cancer staging when compared with CT scanning. However, the past decade has demonstrated an improved accuracy with newer MRI techniques. Primary lesion and nodal staging accuracy has been reported as high as 96% with submillimeter pixel MRI.[16] Other techniques such as fast dynamic first pass MRI, fast low-angle shot images, oblique contrast-enhanced T_1 weight, and rapid gradient echo sequence MRI have all improved staging accuracy (see Table 5–3).[17–19] As with CT scanning, concerns remain with over- and understaging. Despite the improvements in imaging and staging techniques, it is unlikely that many clinical decisions will be based solely on MRI findings. The information gained with lymph node evaluation and extravesical spread will provide the most useful forum for MRI.

Table 5–3. CONTEMPORARY STAGING ACCURACY FOR CT SCANNING AND MRI					
Author	N	Type of staging	CT (%)	MRI (%)	Technique
Herr et al.[51]	105	N stage	42		
Paik et al.[13]	82	T stage	55		
Caterino et al.[14]	65	T stage	95		Intravesical Air
			91		Intravesical Contrast
			87		No instillation
Narnmi et al.[18]	50	T stage		78	Oblique contrast enhanced
				60	Oblique T_2 weighted
Persad et al.[52]	55	T stage		76	
Kim et al.[53]	29	T stage	55		
	36	T stage		75	
Barentsz et al.[19]	28	T stage		78	T_1/T_2 weight spin echo
		N stage		86	T_1/T_2 weight spin echo
		T stage		93	Rapid gradient echo sequence
		N stage		93	Rapid gradient echo sequence
Barentsz et al.[20]	61	T stage		84	Fast low angle shot image
		N stage		93	
Scattoni et al.[54]	48	T stage		58	T_1 weighted
				71	T_2 weighted
				81	Dynamic T_1 weighted
				56	Delayed T_1 weighted

Ultrasonography

The use of ultrasonography (US) in the staging of bladder cancer has been limited. Previously published articles have described various US techniques including transabdominal, transvesical, and transrectal approaches. The global accuracy ranged from 61 to 92%.[20] More recently cystoscopic transurethral ultrasonography has yielded improved staging accuracy. Miniature probes for easier endoscopic US have demonstrated 100% staging accuracy in appropriate selected tumors.[21] Unfortunately, 24% of tumors were too large to accurately stage secondary to lack of tissue penetration and differentiation. As with CT and MRI, limiting factors to US studies are over- and understaging, lesion size, characteristics (lesion contour, calcifications), and operator skill. To date, there are no standardized techniques nor instrumentation for the evaluation of bladder cancer with ultrasound. Thus, further technologic advances are needed before routine use of US staging of bladder cancer becomes accepted.

Bone Scans

The routine staging with bone scans prior to cystectomy in patients with T2 disease remains controversial. The diagnostic yield is limited in the asymptomatic patient.[22] In patients with bone scans highly suspicious for metastatic disease and those with completely negative scans, the accuracy is 63%.[23] The accuracy drops when the bone scan is equivocal. Furthermore, there is no clinically useful correlation between serum alkaline phosphatase and precystectomy bone scan. Thus bone scans should be done judiciously and on an individual basis but may be useful as a baseline for future reference.

Positron Emission Tomography

The value of positron emission tomography (PET) scanning in clinical oncology has been demonstrated in multiple malignancies. The role of PET scanning in bladder cancer remains unclear but has shown some promise and warrants discussion. The two most common radionuclides studied are 18F-2-fluoro-2-deoxy-D-glucose (FDG) and L-(methyl)-11C-methionine (LCM).

Typically, the radionuclides used for PET scanning are primarily glucose derivatives. PET studies exploit the hypermetabolic state of many malignancies when directly compared with normal tissue. Normal and malignant cells, via a glucose transport system, take up deoxyglucose and FDG. Glucose is phosphorylated to glucose-6-phosphate and channeled through the Embden-Meyerhof metabolic pathway. Phosphorylated FDG can neither be metabolized nor leave the cell and should be detectable by PET scanning.

A number of small studies have evaluated FDG-PET scanning in bladder cancer. The sensitivity and specificity for detection ranged from 86 to 100% and 63 to 100%, respectively.[24] Technical considerations limit the use of this radionuclide. Because FDG is renally excreted, continuous irrigation of the bladder is required to allow clear delineation of the bladder wall. Distinguishing the primary tumor from the surrounding artifact can be difficult.

Evaluating lymph node disease and extravesical extension may be best performed with FDG. Lymph node disease was accurately diagnosed in the majority of patients studied. Heicappell demonstrated 2 of 3 patients with histologically confirmed lymph node metastasis had increased FDG uptake.[25] One of the two patients recorded in the study had a 0.9 cm solitary positive lymph node that was noted on PET scanning but regarded as normal on CT scanning. The undetected patient had a 0.5 cm lymph node with micrometastasis that was not detected by CT or PET scanning. In earlier transitional studies, extravesical extension in the pelvis with prior radiation exposure was confirmed by scanning the metabolic activity of the extravesical tissue.[26,27] Low-volume microscopic positivity may then warrant an extended lymph node dissection as proposed by Lerner.[28]

With LCM as the radionuclide, 18 of 23 primary tumors were identified when the bladder was prefilled with saline.[29] Despite this, the diagnostic use and stage specific differentiation are limited, but calculating the specific uptake values for the radiotracer can enhance discrimination among stages T2, T3, and T4. Because LCM uptake in the normal bladder is minimal, depth of tumor invasion cannot be accurately evaluated. A more likely role for this agent is in monitoring responses to neoadjuvant chemotherapy.[30] Regression of metastatic foci or local regional disease may be identified by differentiating residual scar from persistent biologically active disease.

The value of PET scanning in the staging of bladder cancer is not yet fully manifest. Very few studies exist with no clear recommendations for its use. Moreover, most institutions do not have PET scanners available and it may prove cost prohibitive. Further studies are needed to better define the role of PET scanning in bladder cancer staging.

Surgical Staging

Cystoscopy

Cystoscopic examination of the bladder remains the gold standard for identifying suspicious lesions in the lower urinary tract. In most cases, a skilled urologist can recognize bladder cancer by visual inspection; however, a biopsy of the lesions must be performed to establish the diagnosis. Critical to the cystoscopic findings are the phenotypic inferences of biologic potential by evaluating lesion size, location, character, multicentricity, and the association of CIS. Endoscopically, lesions can be grossly categorized as papillary or sessile, terms which are used to subjectively characterize their stage and biologic potential. Thus, cystoscopy alone gives significant clinical impression.

Transurethral Resection

The cornerstone of bladder cancer diagnosis and staging is TUR. TUR is the initial means to establish pathological confirmation of the cystoscopic findings. The TUR specimen must establish the presence of a bladder carcinoma and determine the depth of penetration for appropriate clinical staging. Additional bladder biopsies or cytologies may confirm or exclude the association of CIS. If clear pathologic assessment cannot be established, a repeat TUR should be undertaken. In fact, there are multiple indications for a repeat TUR in patients recently diagnosed with bladder cancer.[7] Of particular concern are patients with high-grade localized T1 lesions. They are at 40% risk for residual disease following the initial resection.[2]

Initial resection is the first opportunity to adequately stage the patient's cancer. Lateral, dome, and bladder neck lesions can pose difficulty with the resection and potentially higher risk for bladder perforation or incomplete resection. However, deep endoscopic resection is needed. If thinning or perforation of the bladder wall is a concern, cold cup biopsies of the resection base can safely provide muscularis propria. Resection should be deep enough to grossly visualize muscular fibers at the resection site. Difficulty can arise when the lesion is sessile and transmural. The entire bladder wall can be replaced with the tumor making it difficult to visualize muscle fibers. Obtaining a frozen section to confirm the presence of muscle and/or muscle invasion may be helpful to avoid overresection and perforation.

Bladder Biopsy

Bladder biopsy plays a minimal role in bladder cancer staging. Unless the lesions are solitary and very small (< 5 mm), simultaneous diagnostic and therapeutic evaluation is unlikely. At the expense of adequate staging, the advantage of performing a simple biopsy rather than a full resection is decreased risk and morbidity. Biopsies can be useful in conjunction with TUR to sample areas of suspected CIS. Additional biopsies of the prostatic urethra are also taken to improve staging information, especially in the setting of positive cytology and negative initial workup. However, as a general rule, simple biopsies of the primary lesion are discouraged when used for tumor staging.

Bimanual Examination

A frequently overlooked aspect of bladder cancer staging is the bimanual examination or examination under anesthesia (EUA). Some physicians have eliminated the EUA in the wake of quality radiographic staging. This is not advisable. The opportunity for performing the EUA is at the time of the initial TUR. Radiographic imaging cannot evaluate tissue mobility, adherence, or pliability.

Interpretation of the bimanual examination requires some experience. It is best performed with the bladder empty. Ideally the bimanual examination should be performed prior to and after completing the TURBT. This will allow the determination of pelvic fixation and tumor size before and after tumor resection. Furthermore, endoscopic correlation of the size of the lesion and bimanual palpation may infer the possibility of extravesical extension, especially in the setting of a completed resection. Coexisting pelvic comorbid states such as prior pelvic surgery, pelvic radiation, and pelvic inflammatory disease will compromise its utility. Despite its inability to predict low-stage disease, when properly performed it can predict high-stage disease with 94% accuracy.[31] Furthermore, it provides significant information concerning surgical resectability. Fixation to the pelvic side wall or anterior abdominal wall may prognosticate surgical unresectability and advanced disease.

Cytology

The role of urinary cytology in staging bladder cancer is limited. Cytologies can neither identify nor differentiate bladder cancer stages. Their utility is in the detection of a urothelial malignancy and/or associated CIS. The presence of an abnormal urinary cytology in the setting of normal radiographic and endoscopic findings mandates further work-up. Thus, information afforded the clinician from urinary cytologies is best directed at further diagnostic and staging studies.

Lymphadenectomy

Lymphadenectomy is a secondary staging tool. It has the potential for both staging and cure. If limited lymph node involvement is documented, a reported therapeutic and diagnostic benefit may be attained.[28] The typical landing sites for lymph node disease in patients with bladder cancer are the prevesical, hypogastric, obturator, external iliac, and presacral lymph nodes. Numerous previous studies have performed lymphangiography and biopsy.[32–34] However, owing to the lack of sensitivity and the quality of modern CT and MRI imaging, lymphangiography has fallen into disfavor.

Diagnostic lymph node staging can be performed in multiple ways. First, enlarged lymph nodes noted on CT scan or MRI can be sampled by a fine needle aspiration. This requires pelvic lymphadenopathy that will allow for percutaneous access for fine needle aspiration. Second, the lymph node sampling is typically performed at the time of definitive surgical management for the muscle invasive bladder cancer. In this setting the need for a second surgical procedure prior to a cystectomy is eliminated. An extended en bloc lymphadenectomy may confer a survival advantage in addition to the diagnostic and staging benefit. If the number of microscopic positive nodes does not exceed five, an overall 18% 5-year survival advantage may be inferred.[28] Finally, if lymph node staging is planned as a separate surgical procedure, a laparoscopic approach can be entertained.

STAGING ALGORITHM

Staging of bladder cancer is significantly more complex than most other urologic malignancies. The algorithm demonstrated in Figure 5–2 is a simplified staging protocol that illustrates a complete and up-to-date medical evaluation for most bladder cancer patients seen in clinical practice. It uses the previous information concerning the appropriate staging tools to function as a simple, cohesive, and usable algorithm for the clinical urologist. As is the case with most all bladder pathology, it begins with the diagnostic cystoscopy to identify the presence of cancerous bladder lesions.

Once lesions are identified, a series of diagnostic tests is required, illustrated by the hexagon configuration on the flow chart in Figure 5–2. Urinary cytology, which is often overlooked, can supplement the information if associated CIS is suspected. Routinely, voided urine cytology is collected at the initial screening visit and at the time of presentation for the cystoscopic evaluation. A confirmatory bladder washing is obtained during the cystoscopy. This method capitulates multiple cytologies without unduly inconveniencing the patient. Identifying an unsuspected CIS in the presence of what would otherwise appear to be a low-grade papillary lesion can have significant prognostic and therapeutic implications. This is an important determinant of biologic potential. Moreover, cytologies can give an indication of upper-tract disease if cystoscopy fails to identify a lesion consistent with the cytologic findings.

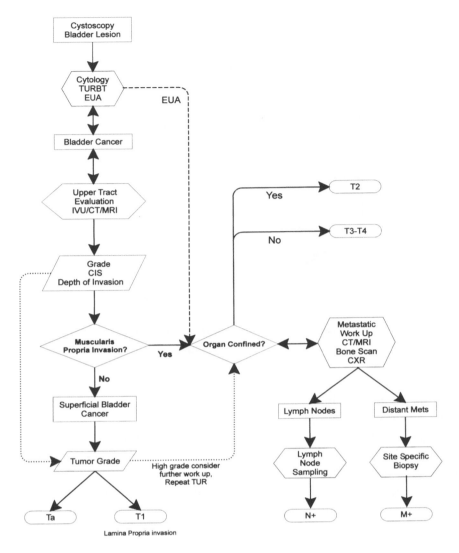

Figure 5–2. Bladder cancer staging algorithm. TURBT = transurethral resection of bladder tumor; EUA = examination under anesthesia; IVU = intravenous urography; CT = computed tomography; MRI = magnetic resonance imaging; CIS = carcinoma in situ; CXR = chest x-ray.

Upper-tract evaluation is always necessary when evaluating new bladder lesions. The CT urogram is ideally suited for the study. It provides IVP-quality anatomic detail of the upper tracts with the added benefit of CT-quality renal parenchymal and local regional pelvic staging. The traditional gold standard was an IVP with standard CT scanning or MRI used as follow-up studies. Ideally, staging studies should be performed prior to the endoscopic surgical staging to avoid staging artifact. An argument can be made for overuse of CT imaging if the lesion is found to be noncancerous or of low malignant potential. Our bias is to obtain a CT urogram prior to the initial diagnostic TUR.

It is important not to overlook the bimanual examination at the time of TUR. As described above, this should be performed before and after the resection. When the diagnosis of bladder cancer is pathologically confirmed, information concerning resectability or T4 disease can be established early in the algorithm. When the results of this examination are combined with the additional findings of the prior CT urogram, the clinical staging is virtually complete.

Up to this point in the algorithm a series of evaluations has been performed in an effort to obtain proactive evaluation of the disease process. The TURBT is the cornerstone of diagnosis and treatment. It must establish the presence of tumor, tumor grade, the presence of CIS, and, most importantly, depth of invasion. Thorough resection with selective deep biopsies of the bladder wall is necessary to

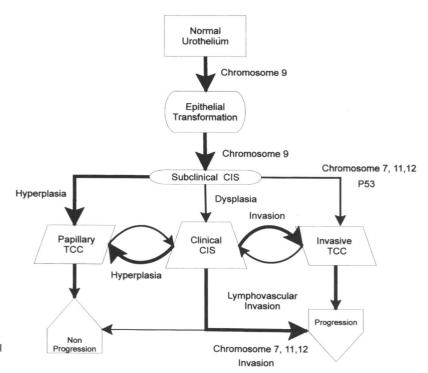

Figure 5–3. Biologic continuum of transitional cell carcinoma (TCC). CIS = carcinoma in situ.

ascertain lamina propria and muscularis propria invasion. Considerable staging errors can occur with inadequate resection. Up to 40% of patients can be inaccurately staged with the initial TURBT.[2]

Regardless of the depth of invasion, the presence of bladder cancer warrants further staging evaluation. The presence of low-grade superficial disease may indicate only an intravenous pyelogram for the study of the upper tracts. The presence of muscle invasion or high-grade disease mandates a more rigorous staging evaluation. At most institutions, the standard of care is a CT scan of the abdomen and pelvis. Again, a word of caution when interpreting the CT scan following the TURBT: perivesical edema, thickening, and stranding can result in overstaging to T3b or T4 disease. The information gleaned from the prior EUA is helpful here in possibly distinguishing between tumor and artifact.

In the absence of upper-tract disease and of muscularis propria invasion, superficial bladder cancer implies Ta or T1 disease. The differentiation at this level is the lamina propria. Lamina propria invasion defines T1 disease. However, a high-grade lesion may be a predictor of understaging, and a repeat TUR is often routinely indicated.[2] Another

indication for repeat TUR is the lack of muscularis propria in the resected specimen. Bladder cancer without associated muscularis propria in the TUR specimen implies either inadequate resection or transmural disease.

T1 lesions are at greater risk for phenotypic alteration and must be managed with more rigor. As the risk factors for progression increase—high grade, multicentricity, large tumor burden, associated CIS, depth of lamina propria invasion (T1a versus T1b), and poor response to local intravesical therapy—reflexive aggressive restaging is needed to understand the phenotypic and genotypic expression that this biologic snapshot is offering.

If the muscularis propria is violated, further staging is mandated. The pathologist must provide clear descriptors differentiating muscularis propria from muscularis mucosa. Muscularis propria invasion defines T2 or greater disease. Occasionally, transmural tumor involvement will completely replace the muscularis propria, making staging difficult. Correlating the findings at endoscopic resection with the pathology can yield the appropriate stage. In the absence of perivesical, intrapelvic, or intra-abdominal disease, T2 is the appropriate clinical stage. Unfortunately radiographic staging cannot differentiate T2b disease from T3a, but based on clinical staging criteria T2 should be assigned. Again, the EUA adds valuable information at this point in the algorithm. Pelvic or abdominal fixation is highly suggestive of T4 disease and unresectability.

Metastatic work-up for T2 or greater disease should include the previously obtained CT scan and a chest x-ray. Additional evaluation with an MRI or bone scan may be selected on an individual patient basis. The presence of large lymph nodes on CT scan should mandate their evaluation. Fine needle aspiration, laparoscopic biopsy, or open surgical sampling at the time of cystectomy are all appropriate modalities. The presence of node positive disease is staged as N+ and portends a much worse prognosis.

A chest CT should follow abnormalities noted on a chest x-ray. Biopsies of pulmonary lesions may be warranted. Symptomatic bone pain should be evaluated with a bone scan and/or plain films of the area involved. The site-specific biopsies of metastatic lesions can be undertaken if indicated. Any lesion found to contain bladder cancer outside of the pelvis is considered M+ disease.

Management of recurrences is based upon the initial diagnostic snapshot. Endoscopically, small, low-grade, superficial Ta lesions have a characteristic papillary appearance. Small recurrences of this same phenotype need not undergo deep resection and can be managed by tumor ablation. However, one must remember that phenotypical alteration, or association of CIS noted endoscopically or by cytology, warrants repeat endoscopic restaging, because this new window into the biologic potential may be expressing a different and more aggressive genotype.

BIOLOGIC SIGNIFICANCE OF THE VARIOUS CLINICAL FORMS OF BLADDER CANCER

The traditional dogma for bladder cancer, initially proposed by Jewett[35] is a chronological continuum of phenotypical bladder cancer sequentially involving a series of cell passages from normal epithelium, to CIS, to frank muscle invasive bladder can-

cer, and ultimately to metastatic disease. However, it is now believed that this continuum is only a phenotypical manifestation of multiple select genetic pathways whereby the genetic makeup of the bladder cancer will likely predetermine its clinical characteristics. Furthermore, the field change concept of bladder cancer has recently been questioned by considerable genetic evidence suggesting bladder cancer is clonal rather than a simultaneous multifocal initiation, promotion, and polyclonal transformation of cells from different locations.[36–38] In some instances polyclonal synchronous lesions may still develop.[38]

Initially all bladder cancer must arise from a normal precursor cell (Figure 5–3). Over time the transitional epithelium becomes susceptible to genetic transformation, especially when exposed to known bladder carcinogens. Following the appropriate sequence of initiation and induction, genetic alterations occur leading to the development of occult bladder cancer. The initiating genetic insult will likely predetermine the clinical characteristics (papillary versus sessile) and biologic significance. Building evidence suggests that the early steps in normal transformation are related to genetic alteration of tumor suppressor genes located on chromosome 9.[39–41] Figure 5–3 demonstrates the relationship with phenotypic expression, driven by genetic makeup. The flow diagram allows for assessment of biologic potential in each clinical setting.

The biologic potential of bladder cancer is defined by its propensity to recur or progress. Recurrence is the development of metachronous tumors with similar phenotypic expression and potential. Progression is recurrence at a more advanced grade or stage.

Low-grade papillary transitional cell carcinoma has a very low propensity to progress (2%) but does have a propensity to recur.[42] In contrast, high-grade transitional cell carcinoma has a much higher propensity to progress.[43] This biphasic phenotypic expression of bladder cancer pathogenesis is attributable to different genetic pathways. Many chromosomal aberrations have been implicated and may mediate the transformation of normal urinary epithelial cells to malignant cells (see Table 5–3). This includes alterations in tumor suppressor genes such as *P53*.[44,45] In a similar fashion the retinoblastoma gene, *Rb*, has been associated with disease recurrence and progression.[45] Chromosomes 7 and 9 typically present in the early setting of epithelial hyperplasia and may lead to noninvasive superficial disease. In fact, these clonal chromosomal abnormalities have been detected in the surrounding normal epithelium indicating an early genetic event. Additional alterations of chromosomes 1, 8, 17, and others may lead to higher grade, higher stage disease and disease progression.[46,47] Table 5–4 presents a summary of some of the genetic alterations studied with the associated clinical manifestations.

Transforming growth factor alpha (TGFα) and epidermal growth factor (EGF) have been studied as to their utility to convey biologic potential. Both factors have demonstrated a correlation with high rates of protein production and disease recurrence.[48] Whereas not clinically apparent, these factors, as well as *P53* and *Rb1,* demonstrate genetic alterations that may drive biologic potential.

The clinical manifestations of bladder cancer frequently present with three different phenotypic pathways: proliferative, progressive, and dysplastic.[49] The three different pathways ultimately manifest as either invasive or noninvasive disease. Figure 5–3 illustrates a summarized version of this theoretical construct. The proliferative pathway leads to the development of low-grade papillary transitional cell carcinoma, whereas the dysplastic pathway usually presents as a high-grade sessile or nodular lesion. The phenotypic presentation of papillary versus sessile helps underscore the biologic potential of each lesion by clinical appearance as seen during the staging process. Thus staging, phenotypic expression, and underlying genetic expression ultimately predict pathogenesis of disease. It is this construct that should drive therapy and predict outcomes.

Once transformation from normal urothelium to subclinical CIS has occurred, the cells can continue to proliferate without dysplasia as an exophytic papillary lesion, continue on as CIS, or undergo further dysplastic change and develop into an invasive form of bladder cancer. However, despite genetic predisposition, this is a dynamic process and, as illustrated, can result in further shifting from one phenotype to another. Some pathways have a higher propensity to interchange and are represented by larger size arrows. Each pathway—papillary, CIS, and invasive—has a unique propensity of progression, mandating that appropriate evaluation and staging is critical.

CONCLUSION

Bladder cancer remains one of the most challenging and interesting cancers for the urologist. Each new lesion and recurrence offers a snapshot of the pathogenesis of the disease state. The understanding of what constitutes this snapshot is a good basis for knowledge and perspective of the staging system, the staging tools, and biologic potential. This will translate into reproducible comprehensive evaluation and state-of-the-art patient management.

Table 5–4. GENETIC LOCALIZATIONS ASSOCIATED WITH BLADDER CANCER		
Author	**Chromosome**	**Bladder Cancer Association**
Berger et al.[54]	9, 18	High grade cytology
Cheng et al.[55]	9, 17	Conserved allelic loss in metastatic disease
Edwards et al.[56]	11, 17	Correlated to higher stage and grade
Eleuteri et al.[39]	9	Tumor progression
	8	Correlated to higher stage and grade
Erbersdobler et al.[57]	8	Correlated to higher stage and grade
Hartman et al.[58]	9	CIS and moderate dysplasia
Langbein et al.[59]	2	High grade
Mahdy et al.[60]	8, 17	Correlated to higher stage and grade
Nemoto et al.[47]	7, 11, 17	Correlated to higher stage and grade
Stadler et al.[40]	9	Early change in cancer development
Tsukamoto et al.[61]	9	Correlated to low grade and stage
	17	Correlated high grade and stage
von Knobloch et al.[62]	5	Correlated to higher stage and grade
Watters et al.[63]	8	Correlated to higher stage and grade

REFERENCES

1. Greene FL, Page DL, Fleming ID, et al. AJCC cancer staging manual. Philadelphia: Springer-Verlag, 2002.

2. Klan R, Loy V, Huland H. Residual tumor discovered in routine second transurethral resection in patients with stage T1 transitional cell carcinoma of the bladder. J Urol 1991;146:316–8.

3. Holmang S, Hedelin H, Anderstrom C, et al. The importance of the depth of invasion in stage T1 bladder carcinoma: a prospective cohort study [comment]. J Urol 1997;157: 800–4.

4. Cheng L, Neumann RM, Weaver AL, et al. Predicting cancer progression in patients with stage T1 bladder carcinoma. J Clin Oncol 1999;17:3182–7.

5. Angulo JC, Lopez JI, Grignon DJ, Sanchez–Chapado M. Muscularis mucosa differentiates two populations with different prognosis in stage T1 bladder cancer. Urology 1995;45:47–53.

6. Platz CE, Cohen MB, Jones MP, et al. Is microstaging of early invasive cancer of the urinary bladder possible or useful? [comment] Mod Pathol 1996;9:1035–9.

7. Langenstroer P, See W. The role of a second transurethral resection for high grade bladder cancer. Current Urology Reports 2000;1:204–207.

8. Walzer Y, Soloway MS. Should the followup of patients with bladder cancer include routine excretory urography? J Urol 1983;130:672–3.

9. Lang EK. The roentgenographic assessment of bladder tumors. A comparison of the diagnostic accuracy of roentgenographic techniques. Cancer 1969;23:717–24.

10. Hatch TR, Barry JM. The value of excretory urography in staging bladder cancer. J Urol 1986;135:49.

11. Barentsz JO, Witjes JA, Ruijs JH. What is new in bladder cancer imaging. Urol Clin North Am 1997;24:583–602.

12. Paik ML, Scolieri MJ, Brown SL, et al. Limitations of computerized tomography in staging invasive bladder cancer before radical cystectomy. J Urol 2000;163:1693–6.

13. Caterino M, Giunta S, Finocchi V, et al. Primary cancer of the urinary bladder: CT evaluation of the T parameter with different techniques. Abdom Imaging 2001;26:433–8.

14. Vining DJ, Zagoria RJ, Liu K, Stelts D. CT cystoscopy: an innovation in bladder imaging. AJR. Am J Roentgenol 1996;166:409–10.

15. Malmstrom PU, Lonnemark M, Busch C, Magnusson A. Staging of bladder carcinoma by computer tomography-guided transmural core biopsy. Scand J Urol Nephrol 1993;27:193–8.

16. Maeda H, Kinukawa T, Hattori R, et al. Detection of muscle layer invasion with submillimeter pixel MR images: staging of bladder carcinoma. Magn Reson Imaging 1995;13:9–19.

17. Narumi Y, Kadota T, Inoue E, et al. Bladder tumors: staging with gadolinium-enhanced oblique MR imaging. Radiology 1993; 187:145–50.

18. Barentsz JO, Jager G, Mugler JP 3rd, et al. Staging urinary bladder cancer: value of T1-weighted three-dimensional magnetization prepared-rapid gradient-echo and two-dimensional spin-echo sequences. AJR Am J Roentgenol 1995;164:109–15.

19. Barentsz JO, Jager GJ, van Vierzen PB, et al. Staging urinary bladder cancer after transurethral biopsy: value of fast dynamic contrast-enhanced MR imaging. Radiology 1996;201:185–93.

20. Rozsahegyi J, Goblyos P, Bohar L, Szule E. Ultrasonography in the diagnosis of bladder tumours. Acta Chirurgica Hungarica 1985;26:235–51.

21. Tomita Y, Kobayashi K, Saito T, et al. Use of miniature ultrasonic probe system for intravesical ultrasonography for transitional cell cancer of the urinary tract. Scand J Urol Nephrol 2000;34:313–6.

22. Hunt MT, Woodhouse CR. Cost-effectiveness of investigations for invasive bladder cancer. J R Soc Med 1987;80: 143–4.

23. Braendengen M, Winderen M, Fossa SD. Clinical significance of routine pre-cystectomy bone scans in patients with muscle-invasive bladder cancer. BJU 1996;77:36–40.

24. Bender H, Schomburg A, Albers P, Ruhlmann J, Biersack HJ. Possible role of FDG-PET in the evaluation of urologic malignancies. Anticancer Res 1997;17:1655–60.

25. Heicappell R, Muller-Mattheis V, Reinhardt M, et al. Staging of pelvic lymph nodes in neoplasms of the bladder and prostate by positron emission tomography with 2-[(18)F]-2-deoxy-D-glucose. Eur Urol 1999;36:582–7.

26. Harney JV, Wahl RL, Liebert M, et al. Uptake of 2-deoxy, 2-(18F) fluoro-D-glucose in bladder cancer: animal localization and initial patient positron emission tomography. J Urol 1991;145:279–83.

27. Kosuda S, Kison PV, Greenough R, et al. Preliminary assessment of fluorine-18 fluorodeoxyglucose positron emission tomography in patients with bladder cancer. Eur J Nucl Med 1997;24:615–20.

28. Lerner SP, Skinner DG, Lieskovsky G, et al. The rationale for en bloc pelvic lymph node dissection for bladder cancer patients with nodal metastases: long-term results. J Urol 1993;149:758–65.

29. Ahlstrom H, Malmstrom PU, Letocha H, et al. Positron emission tomography in the diagnosis and staging of urinary bladder cancer. Acta Radiol 1996;37:180–5.

30. Letocha H, Ahlstrom H, Malmstrom PU, et al. Positron emission tomography with L-methyl-11C-methionine in the monitoring of therapy response in muscle-invasive transitional cell carcinoma of the urinary bladder. BJU 1994; 74:767–74.

31. Jewett HJ. Cancer of the bladder diagnosis and staging. Cancer 1973;32:1072–1074.

32. Boccon Gibod L, Katz M, Cochand B, et al. Lymphography and percutaneous fine needle node aspiration biopsy in the staging of bladder carcinoma. J Urol 1984;132:24–6.

33. Chagnon S, Cochand-Priollet B, Gzaeil M, et al. Pelvic cancers: staging of 139 cases with lymphography and fine-needle aspiration biopsy. Radiology 1989;173:103–6.

34. Gothlin JH, Hoiem L. Percutaneous transperitoneal fine needle biopsy of normal looking lymph nodes and small lesions at lymphography: a preliminary report. Urologic Radiology 1979;1:237–9.

35. Jewett HJ, Strong GH. Infiltrating carcinoma of the bladder: relation of depth of penetration of the bladder wall to incidence of local extension and metastasis. J Urol 1946;55: 366–72.

36. Dalbagni G, Ren ZP, Herr H, et al. Genetic alterations in tp53 in recurrent urothelial cancer: a longitudinal study. Clin Cancer Res 2001;7:2797–801.

37. Vriesema JL, Aben KK, Witjes JA, et al. Superficial and metachronous invasive bladder carcinomas are clonally related. Int J Cancer 2001;93:699–702.

38. Hafner C, Knuechel R, Zanardo L, et al. Evidence for oligo-clonality and tumor spread by intraluminal seeding in multifocal urothelial carcinomas of the upper and lower urinary tract. Oncogene 2001;20:4910–5.

39. Eleuteri P, Grollino MG, Pomponi D, De Vita R. Chromosome 9 aberrations by fluorescence in situ hybridisation in bladder transitional cell carcinoma. Eur J Cancer 2001;37:1496–503.

40. Stadler WM, Steinberg G, Yang X, et al. Alterations of the 9p21 and 9q33 chromosomal bands in clinical bladder cancer specimens by fluorescence in situ hybridization. Clin Cancer Res 2001;7:1676–82.

41. Chow NH, Cairns P, Eisenberger CF, et al. Papillary urothelial hyperplasia is a clonal precursor to papillary transitional cell bladder cancer. Int J Cancer 2000;89:514–8.

42. Heney NM, Nocks BN, Daly JJ, et al. Ta and T1 bladder cancer: location, recurrence and progression. BJU 1982; 54:152–7.

43. Heney NM, Ahmed S, Flanagan MJ, et al. Superficial bladder cancer: progression and recurrence. J Urol 1983; 130:1083–6.

44. Esrig D, Spruck CH 3rd, Nichols PW, et al. p53 nuclear protein accumulation correlates with mutations in the p53 gene, tumor grade, and stage in bladder cancer. Am J Pathol 1993;143:1389–97.

45. Presti JC Jr, Reuter VE, Galan T, et al. Molecular genetic alterations in superficial and locally advanced human bladder cancer. Cancer Res 1991;51:5405–9.

46. Richter J, Jiang F, Gorog JP, et al. Marked genetic differences between stage pTa and stage pT1 papillary bladder cancer detected by comparative genomic hybridization. Cancer Res 1997;57:2860–4.

47. Nemoto R, Nakamura I, Uchida K, Harada M. Numerical chromosome aberrations in bladder cancer detected by in situ hybridization. BJU 1995;75:470–6.

48. Turkeri LN, Erton ML, Cevik I, Akda A. Impact of the expression of epidermal growth factor, transforming growth factor alpha, and epidermal growth factor receptor on the prognosis of superficial bladder cancer. Urology 1998;51:645–9.

49. Baithun SI, Naase M, Blanes A, Diaz-Cano SJ. Molecular and kinetic features of transitional cell carcinomas of the bladder: biological and clinical implications. Virchows Arch 2001;438:289–97.

50. Herr HW. Routine CT scan in cystectomy patients: does it change management? [published erratum appears in Urology 1996;47:785]. Urology 1996;47:324–5.

51. Persad R, Kabala J, Gillatt D, et al. Magnetic resonance imaging in the staging of bladder cancer. BJU 1993; 71:566–73.

52. Kim B, Semelka RC, Ascher SM, et al. Bladder tumor staging: comparison of contrast-enhanced CT, T1- and T2-weighted MR imaging, dynamic gadolinium-enhanced imaging, and late gadolinium-enhanced imaging. Radiology 1994;193:239–45.

53. Scattoni V, Da Pozzo LF, Colombo R, et al. Dynamic gadolinium-enhanced magnetic resonance imaging in staging of superficial bladder cancer. J Urol 1996;155:1594–9.

54. Berger AP, Parson W, Stenzl A, et al. Microsatellite alterations in human bladder cancer: detection of tumor cells in urine sediment and tumor tissue. Eur Urol 2002;41:532–9.

55. Cheng L, Bostwick DG, Li G, et al. Conserved genetic findings in metastatic bladder cancer: a possible utility of allelic loss of chromosomes 9p21 and 17p13 in diagnosis. Arch Pathol Lab Med 2001;125:1197–9.

56. Edwards J, Duncan P, Going JJ, et al. Loss of heterozygosity on chromosomes 11 and 17 are markers of recurrence in TCC of the bladder. Br J Cancer 2001;85:1894–9.

57. Erbersdobler A, Kaiser H, Friedrich MG, Henke RP. Numerical aberrations of chromosome 8 and allelic loss at 8p in non-muscle-invasive urothelial carcinomas of the urinary bladder. Eur Urol 2000;38:590–6.

58. Hartmann A, Schlake G, Zaak D, et al. Occurrence of chromosome 9 and p53 alterations in multifocal dysplasia and carcinoma in situ of human urinary bladder. Cancer Res 2002;62:809–18.

59. Langbein S, Szakacs O, Wilhelm M, et al. Alteration of the LRP1B gene region is associated with high grade of urothelial cancer. Lab Invest 2002;82:639–43.

60. Mahdy E, Pan Y, Wang N, et al. Chromosome 8 numerical aberration and C-MYC copy number gain in bladder cancer are linked to stage and grade. Anticancer Res 2001;21:3167–73.

61. Tsukamoto M, Matsuyama H, Oba K, et al. Numerical aberrations of chromosome 9 in bladder cancer. A possible prognostic marker for early tumor recurrence. Cancer Genet Cytogenet 2002;134:41–5.

62. von Knobloch R, Bugert P, Jauch A, et al. Allelic changes at multiple regions of chromosome 5 are associated with progression of urinary bladder cancer. J Pathol 2000; 190:163–8.

63. Watters AD, Stacey MW, Going JJ, et al. Genetic aberrations of NAT2 and chromosome 8: their association with progression in transitional cell carcinoma of the urinary bladder. Urol Int 2001;67:235–9.

Diagnosis and Diagnostic Pitfalls in Urothelial Bladder Cancer

MARKUS D. SACHS, MD
THERESA CHAN, MD
STEPHEN B. SOLOMON, MD
FRANK KÖNIG, MD
MARK SCHOENBERG, MD

Bladder cancer is usually diagnosed at cystoscopy after the patient presents to the urologist with visible hematuria or dysuria. Very rarely is this disease diagnosed in its preclinical stage and almost never found as an incidental finding on autopsy. Incidences of 10% and 5% of hyperplasia and dysplasia, respectively, and only occasional findings of cancer itself were reported in autopsy studies. Although there may be a long preclinical latency, there is probably a short clinical latency, which makes the early detection and therefore treatment necessary. More importantly, because of the high recurrence rate of up to 80% for superficial disease, early diagnosis of these recurrences is vital as they are connected to tumor progression in 15 to 20% of cases.

CLINICAL APPEARANCE

Hematuria is the most common clinical sign that brings the patient to the urologist and is present in about 75% of cases. Hematuria is often quite intermittent, however, so that a negative result on one or two specimens has little meaning in ruling out the presence of bladder cancer and a thorough investigation is still warranted.[1] It is important to note, that the degree of hematuria is not related to tumor stage or grade. Although there is no disagreement on evaluating gross hematuria for bladder cancer, some argue against full evaluation of all patients with a few erythrocytes in their urine, especially since the prevalence (13%) of microscopic hematuria in the general population is somewhat high, with benign conditions such as stone disease or inflammatory disorders being the main causes. Populations at risk, such as patients over 50 years of age, people with a history of cigarette smoking or previous bladder tumor, and those who were occupationally exposed to certain chemicals should undergo thorough evaluation for any degree of hematuria. For the general population it is agreed that patients with persistently more than 3 to 5 red blood cells per high-powered field on microscopic examination should undergo a diagnostic work-up, even though the results will be unremarkable in most cases.[2]

Other features of bladder tumor include frequency, dysuria and urinary obstruction, partly due to reduced bladder capacity, flank pain from ureteric obstruction, lower extremity edema, and a pelvic mass. Severe frequency, urgency and suprapubic pain ("malignant cystitis") may be present in carcinoma in situ (CIS). However, these symptoms are only occasionally present without microscopic hematuria.[3]

In invasive carcinoma with extension into the paravesical tissues the bladder wall may feel thickened and indurated or the tumor itself may be palpable on bimanual examination.

CYSTOSCOPY AND TRANSURETHRAL RESECTION OF THE BLADDER

Careful cystoscopy and bimanual examination are compulsory in all patients suspected to have bladder tumors. Although still the gold standard in diagnosis and surveillance of bladder cancer, cystoscopy is invasive, costly, operator dependent, and flat lesions can be missed. Patients often experience discomfort and may develop urinary tract infection following the procedure.

Tumors can recur very rapidly and frequent cystoscopic examinations are obligatory, especially in the early stages and up to 5 years or longer.

Retrograde pyelography should be performed if the upper tracts are not adequately visualized on the excretory urogram or if additional disease is suspected in the upper tract (Figure 6–1). If an upper urinary tract lesion is seen, a retrograde ureteropyelogram obtaining urine samples or saline lavages for cytology or brush biopsies should be performed.

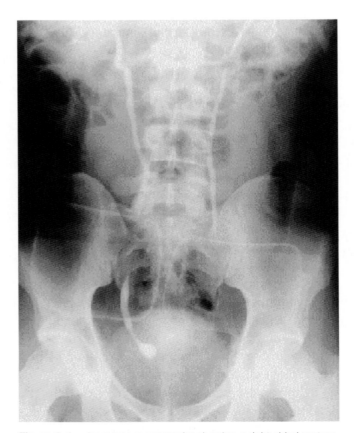

Figure 6–1. Intravenous urography showing a right-sided uretero-cele. Note the round/oval lucent filling defect near the trigone due to the folding of the bladder wall.

Superficial tumors show a fronded appearance with frequent hemorrhage and surrounding clots close to a tumor due to trauma to small vessels in the superficial fronds. Invasive tumors can be small or large enough to fill the whole bladder, they may be round and tufted with short stunted fronds and a broad base. Some show a wide pedicle, that might be difficult to see because of the exuberance of the tufts near the base of the tumor. They can have long fimbrial tissue of up to 2.5 cm in length with avascular ends (Figure 6–2, A–D).

It is not possible to distinguish cystoscopically between muscle and perivesicular invasion of the tumor. Characteristics of infiltrating tumors are superficial hemorrhage and necrosis with surface slough, ulceration, edema, and inflammation of the surrounding tissue. The tumor villi can appear as white, almost transparent tissue. With increasing invasion the lesions tend to be more extensive and ulceration is more common. White areas caused by calcification can be seen (Figure 6–3). Whitish or blueish areas without blood vessels can also be the appearance of leukoplakia. Here, the edge is usually indistinct. The lesion may involve the whole bladder, or only one or more localized areas. It may be present in a diverticulum.

Squamous carcinoma presents as an exophytic or endophytic solid tumor of grey-white color and granular consistence. Ulceration and necrosis are present.

Condyloma acuminatum or Buschke-Löwenstein tumor shows a verrucous form of highly differentiated squamous tumor, which is not considered to be malignant, but may have malignant metaplastic potential.

Adenocarcinoma of the bladder can arise at any site, but most commonly it is seen at the dome. The size of the tumor may vary from small, less than 1 cm in diameter, to very large (10 cm or more). The tumor can be papillary noninfiltrating, papillary infiltrating or most frequently sessile, or nodular and infiltrating. Urachal carcinomas are often extravesical, extending to the anterior abdominal wall.

Cold cup biopsies at cystoscopy can allow the definition of the histological type and grade of the specimen, but do not provide adequate information about the depth of tumor invasion and may not be representative of the entire lesion. Transurethral resection of all visible bladder lesions is the treatment of choice for superficial bladder tumors, but furthermore, this method establishes the pathologic diagnosis for tumor entity, grade and depth of invasion. The pathologic diagnosis and staging represent the cornerstone on which further treatment decisions are based. After complete tumor resection, a separate sampling of the tumor base involving the muscularis propria should be obtained. The tumor base specimen should be sent to the pathologist separately to establish complete tumor resection and to look for muscle invasive disease. After resection, muscle fibers should be visible at the tumor base. Necrotic appearing tissue at the resection base is indicative of muscle invasion.

In patients with extensive, broad-based sessile tumors a complete tumor resection is not always necessary, because these tumors are almost certain to require cystectomy or partial cystectomy, particu-larly if the tumor is located in an area that is difficult to reach with the resectoscope. Furthermore, attempts at complete resection may result in bladder perforation with dissemination of tumor cells. In such cases, it may be more prudent to resect only enough tissue to establish the tumor grade and document muscle invasion.[3]

The whole bladder mucosa should be carefully inspected for other tumors and particularly for changes suggestive of CIS and all suspicious areas should be biopsied. CIS is suspected when a velvety spot, reddish in color, is visible at cystoscopy. On the other hand, diffuse CIS may not be clearly visible. Therefore, some urologists obtain random or selected biopsies (bladder mapping) of normal-appearing mucosa. However, the role of random biopsies is controversial. Some studies indicate that random biopsies

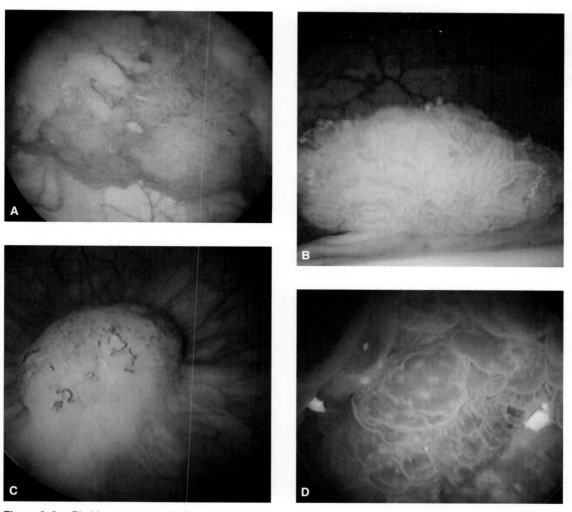

Figure 6–2. Bladder cystoscopy. *A,* T1-tumor; *B,* superficial tumor; *C,* invasive tumor; *D,* inflammation, no tumor.

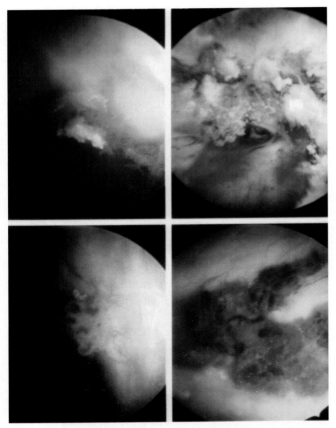

Figure 6–3. Invasive urothelial carcinoma.

are useful for detecting concomitant CIS or dysplasia, permit a better categorization of the tumor and influence the outcome and the decision to administer intravesical therapy.[4] Others argue that biopsies of normal-appearing urothelium in patients with Ta, T1 bladder cancer show no abnormalities in about 90% of cases and performing such biopsies does not contribute to the staging or to the choice of adjuvant therapy after transurethral resection.[5,6] Furthermore, random biopsy may have an effect on the recurrence or the implantation of tumor cells at biopsy sites.[7]

Transurethral prostatic sampling, however, is indicated in patients with bladder tumors that appear to be muscle invasive or in those with suspicion of CIS.

For superficial bladder tumors, although grouped together, a significant variability in biologic behavior and malignant potential has been recognized, which further supports the importance of the initial histopathologic diagnosis. In stage T1 tumors, which invade the subepithelial connective tissue, the heterogeneous biologic behavior is related to tumor grade

and the depth of invasion within the lamina propria. Several histologic subdivisions of T1 bladder cancer have been described, suggesting the clinically relevant prognostic importance of muscularis mucosae invasion in initial biopsy specimens.[8–12] Subdivision of T1 tumors into T1a, defined as invasion superficial to the muscularis mucosae, and stage T1b, defined as extension through the muscularis mucosae, or into T1a (invasion superficial to the muscularis mucosae vascular plexus), T1b (extension within) and T1c (extension beyond this landmark) have been described.[10,12] In summary, the ability of tumor to invade the lamina propria in itself represents an important risk factor for disease progression. Subsequent invasion of the muscularis propria occurs in 30 to 50% of these carcinomas, which clearly influences the treatment, quality of life, and survival of such patients making the treatment of T1 bladder tumors a challenge for the clinician.[13]

After the initial transurethral tumor resection, many patients still have tumor present or develop a tumor recurrence within a short interval. Therefore, a repeated transurethral resection (TUR) after 4 to 6 weeks has been recommended for patients with superficial bladder cancer. Although the rate of histologic findings at the second TUR varies in published reports, a negative second TUR provides important prognostic information and removal of any residual tumor can be achieved early.[14–16] Furthermore, muscle invasive disease was found in up to 29% of cases that were diagnosed as superficial tumors at the first resection.[31] Therefore, the result of a second TUR can change the treatment dramatically, particularly in high-risk tumors, such as multifocal or T1 or poorly differentiated carcinomas.

PHOTODYNAMIC CYSTOSCOPY

Porphyrins and other tetrapyroles are the most commonly employed group of dyes for photodiagnosis (PD) and photodynamic therapy (PDT). The use of hematoporphyrin (Hp) as a fluorophore and photosensitizer was described in 1913.[17] Photofrin®, a purified form of hematoporphyrin derivative (HpD), is approved for PDT in several countries and currently the only approved drug for PDT in the United States. In principle, Photofrin could be used for PD. However, it has the disadvantage of causing skin photosensitization, that can last for several weeks. In contrast, intravesical instillation of aminolevulinic acid (ALA), first described in 1993 by Baumgartner and colleagues, shows no systemic side effects and leads to an increase of protoporphyrin IX (PPIX) in neoplastic bladder lesions.[18] ALA is a precursor of PPIX, which is, in turn, the immediate precursor of heme in the biosynthetic pathway for heme. All mammalian nucleated cells have the capacity to synthesize heme since heme-containing enzymes are required for aerobic energy metabolism. Therefore, PPIX is an endogenous photosensitizer, which fluoresces red under excitation with blue light (Figure 6–4).

The detection system used to capture and to display PPIX-fluorescence images consists of a standard cystoscopy xenon light source with the addition of an internal filter assembly which passes primarily blue light (200–400 mW at 425 nm with a full width at half maximum of ~50 nm) (Figure 6–5).[19]

In 1997 the first clinical study of ALA for detection of bladder carcinoma was performed in the United States.[37] Participating in the study were 55 patients (11 female, 44 male) with suspicion of bladder carcinoma (at initial diagnosis or at tumor follow-up visits). The average patient age was 66 years (range, 31 to 87 yr). An intravesical instillation of 50 mL of a 3% ALA solution (Levulan, DUSA Pharmaceuticals Inc, Tarrytown, NY) was performed in all of these patients prior to cystoscopy.

The solution was freshly prepared immediately prior to instillation by mixing crystalline ALA hydrochloride (molecular weight 167.6) with a bicarbonate buffer (first 19 patients) or, for better stability, with a potassium phosphate buffer (the latter 36 patients). The time interval between intravesical instillation of the drug and cystoscopic procedure ranged from 51 to 710 minutes (mean, 135 minutes). The time of drug exposure, defined as the time between intravesical instillation and drainage of the bladder (voiding or start of cystoscopy), ranged from 30 to 470 minutes (mean, 126 minutes).

There were 63 nonmalignant areas and 67 malignant/dysplastic lesions. In all, ten additional malignant/dysplastic lesions (Table 6–1) were missed during standard white-light cystoscopy but detected under blue light, thus the number of diagnosed lesions was increased by 18%. However, if one considers only dysplasia and CIS, the lesions most readily missed by white-light cystoscopy, the increase is substantially greater (6 with blue light only/12 with white and blue light). Table 6–2 compares the conditions and results of this study with those of earlier studies.

By analyzing the data on all 130 lesions, the sensitivity (87%), specificity (59%), positive predictive value (69%) and negative predictive value (80%) of this method for diagnosis of malignant/dysplastic bladder lesions were found. False-positive results were obtained mainly from inflammatory lesions. Standard

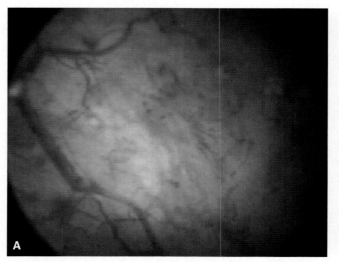
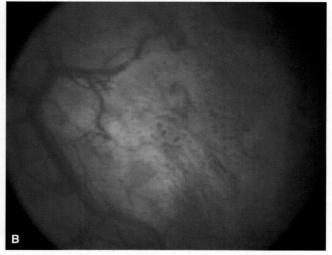

Figure 6–4. White light (*A*) and corresponding blue light image (*B*) of a TaG2 tumor after ALA-instillation. Reprinted from Koenig F, et al,[74] with permission from Elsevier Science.

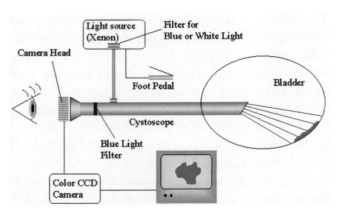

Figure 6–5. Schematic drawing of the technical setup for fluorescence cystoscopy. Reprinted from Koenig F, et al,[74] with permission from Elsevier Science.

white-light cystoscopy had a sensitivity of 84% and 89% for detecting malignant/dysplastic and malignant lesions, respectively. Since most of the lesions that were missed under blue light had a papillary structure or were classified as suspicious under white light, the overall sensitivity (combined white and blue light cystoscopy) was 99%. One mild dysplastic lesion (1%) was detected solely by the random biopsies. No differences in sensitivity or specificity were found by using the two buffer solutions discussed above.

In this first study in the United States as well as in two earlier studies (see Table 6–2) it could be shown that the ALA-induced PPIX fluorescence detection method can improve the diagnosis of bladder cancer by detecting more malignant/dysplastic lesions than with the standard white-light procedure. However, in this study the improvement of 18% is relatively low compared to the results of Kriegmair and colleagues (38%) and Jichlinski and colleagues (76%).[21,22] If the improvement in the detection of only dysplasia and CIS is considered, the study in the United States found a 50% increase.

In the study of Jichlinski and colleagues, the time interval between instillation of the drug and start of fluorescence cystoscopy (mean, 442 min; range, 330–515 min) as well as the time of drug exposure (mean, 239 min; range, 175–285 min) were substantially longer than in the study in the United States (mean, 135 min; range, 51–710 min and mean, 126 min; range, 30–470 min, respectively). Despite the considerably longer intervals, Jichlinski and colleagues have not seen a significantly higher rate of

false positives compared to the study in the United States (43% vs 41%). Comparison of these two studies might suggest that longer time intervals lead to an increase in the number of detected neoplastic lesions per patient (see Table 6–2) during fluorescence cystoscopy. However, recent animal studies by Heil and colleagues using a rat tumor model and 60 minutes of exposure to ALA indicate that optimum tumor/normal contrast is obtained at 60 minutes after the beginning of installation and maximum tumor fluorescence occurs at about 150 minutes after the beginning of installation.[23] While the conditions of the animal and human studies were different the results suggest that the optimum ALA dosing conditions for humans have yet to be determined. Given the differences in results between the three studies discussed here, meaningful results will probably require that the different time regimes be studied by one group while keeping all other conditions constant.

In a more recent publication Zaak and colleagues presented the results of 1,012 fluorescence cystoscopies. Altogether 2,475 specimens were obtained (2.4 biopsies/patient). In 552 endoscopies (54%), neoplastic urothelial lesions had been detected, in 34% only due to their positive fluorescence. Of these additionally detected neoplastic foci, 39% had poorly differentiated histologic features.[24]

Furthermore, Riedl and colleagues could demonstrate that the use of ALA leads to a significant reduction (59%) of residual tumors following the initial resection. In a prospective randomized two-center study, 102 patients underwent TUR of bladder tumor(s) either with white light or ALA-fluores-

Malignant/Dysplastic Lesion (Histopathologic Results)	Number Of Missed Lesions	Total Number
Mild dysplasia	3	7
Moderate dysplasia	1	3
Carcinoma in situ	2	6
TCC-TaG1	2	8
TCC-TaG2	1	25
TCC-T2G3	1	6
Total	10	55

Table 6–1. HISTOPATHOLOGICAL DIAGNOSIS OF 10 LESIONS MISSED DURING WHITE-LIGHT CYSTOSCOPY BUT DETECTED UNDER BLUE LIGHT TOGETHER WITH THE TOTAL NUMBER OF LESIONS OF EACH TYPE

Table 6–2. COMPARISON OF 3 CLINICAL STUDIES OF ALA FOR DETECTION OF BLADDER CARCINOMA			
	Koenig et al.	**Kriegmair et al.[5]**	**Jichlinski et al.[6]**
Drug exposure (time in minutes ALA infusion is retained)*	126 (30–470)	Not reported	239 (175–285)
Time from instillation to cystoscopy (minutes)*	135 (51–710)	145 (10–420)	442 (330–515)
Power of excitation (blue light intensity at end of cystoscope)	220–440 mW (filtered Xenon arc-lamp†)	50–150 mW (Krypton ion laser‡)	10–25 mW (Krypton ion laser) 150–480 mW (filtered Xenon arc-amp)§
Drug dose	1.5g in 50 mL (3%)	1.5g in 50 mL (3%)	1.5g in 50 mL (3%)
Total no. of lesions studied and (per patient)	130 (2.7)	433 (4.2)	215 (6.3)
Random biopsies	12	195	68
Malignant/dysplastic lesions per patient	1.4	1.2	3.2
Dysplasia/CIS per patient	0.4	0.23	1.6
Sensitivity (blue light)	87%	96.9%	89%
Specificity (blue light)	59%	66.6%	57%
Enhanced detection of all malignant/dysplastic lesions	18%	38%	76%
Enhanced detection of dysplasia/CIS	50%	140%	(all dysplasia and CIS were defined as not detectable under white light)

*Mean, (range)
†425 nm with a full width at half maximum of ~ 50 nm
‡407 nm
§Essentially identical results were obtained with both the laser- and lamp-based system
CIS = carcinoma in situ.

cence assisted. A second look TUR with ALA was performed 6 weeks after the initial operation. They found that residual carcinoma was detected in 20 of 51 patients (39%) in the white light group and in only 8 of 51 patients (16%) in the ALA group. The difference was statistically significant ($p = .005$).[25]

In summary, it can be concluded that the ALA-based fluorescence detection system is a safe and simple procedure, which enhances the detection of malignant/dysplastic bladder lesions. However, whether PD could lower the recurrence rate of bladder carcinoma needs to be shown in randomized prospective studies.

RADIOLOGIC IMAGING

Most adults with hematuria or positive urinary cytology require urinary tract imaging. There is some controversy about the choice between ultrasonography and excretory (intravenous) urography (IVU) as the initial imaging study for patients with hematuria. With regard to the rate of diagnosing clinically important lesions it appears that there are only slight differences between the two modalities.[26] An IVU is recom-

mended by the American College of Radiology as the imaging modality of choice in the evaluation of hematuria.[27] Corwin and colleagues, however, argued that IVU does not add significantly to diagnostic accuracy but it does add to cost and morbidity compared to strategies using cystoscopy or ultrasonography as the initial diagnostic test in the work-up of asymptomatic microscopic hematuria.[28] Other studies suggest sonography combined with urine cytology as the routine evaluation for suspicion and follow up of bladder cancer and a combination of IVU and ultrasonography for detecting upper urinary tract malignancies.[29,30]

Intravenous Urography

The pathologic sign to look for on an IVU is a filling defect of contrast medium, which might be irregular and lobulated in the case of a tumor (Figure 6–6). A smooth and regular bladder outline usually indicates the absence of bladder wall penetration.

Other common causes of filling defects include stone disease, blood clot or an enlarged prostate. Uncommon causes of filling defects are focal cystitis (bullous cystitis, cystitis cystica, cystitis glandu-

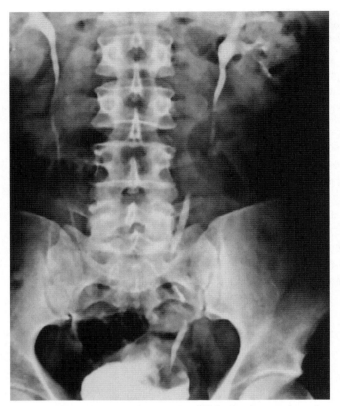

Figure 6–6. Intravenous urography (IVU) showing an irregular, lobulated filling defect of contrast medium on the left bladder wall. Although in this case the diagnosis was confirmed transitional cell cancer of the bladder, other diagnoses based on the IVU should be considered, such as ureterocele or edema from an impacted stone.

laris and malakoplakia), ureterocele, endometriosis, fungus ball, and benign neoplasms, such as leiomyoma (Figures 6–1 and 6–7). The so-called "bunch of grapes" appearance is typical of rhabdomyosarcoma of the bladder (botryoid sarcoma), a nonepithelial tumor that arises from remnants of the urogenital sinus and mesonephric ducts.

An IVU is not a sensitive means of detecting bladder and upper tract tumors, particularly small ones. Sensitivities and specificities have been described between 67 and 75% and 91%.[30] But it is imperative to undertake a careful examination of the ureters and renal pelvis in all cases of bladder tumor, since synchronous tumors of the upper tract occur in 2.3% of patients with bladder cancer.[31] It is also helpful when cystoscopy or biopsy does not confirm a cytologic finding of malignant or high-grade dysplasia cells, as neoplasia may arise from the upper tract. A nonfunctioning or poorly visible kidney can be indicative of obstruction of the ureteral orifice by a

tumor. Bone destruction by tumor may also be seen on IVU. Tumor calcifications may be present as well.

Ultrasonography

Due to the development of high quality ultrasound and the relative widespread availability, the number of patients who have had ultrasound as the first examination in the work-up of hematuria is rising. Sensitivities and specificities have been described between 56 and 90% for the former and 94% for the latter.[30]

On sonogram a bladder neoplasm usually appears as an echogenic structure within the bladder with a mass-like appearance. The most common differential diagnosis is a blood clot. Due to their intimate relationship to the posterior wall of the bladder, inflammatory or neoplastic lesions of the seminal vesicles (rare) or of the prostate could involve the bladder and may be visible on a sonogram. Another diagnostic pitfall might be a stone with reactive edema.

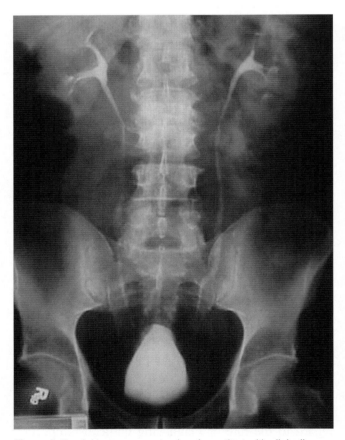

Figure 6–7. Intravenous urography of a patient with clinically suspected bladder cancer. The bladder appears pear-shaped with medial coursing ureters compatible with pelvic lipomatosis.

Ultrasonography should always be done with the patient having a filled bladder. Exophytic tumors are only clearly visible from a certain size (5 mm) and present as a heterogeneous, echogenic area in the surrounding fluid or as a sessile plaque-like tissue mass attached to the bladder wall. An irregular margin might be indicative of wall invasion (Figure 6–8). It has not been possible to achieve the complete diagnostic potential of ultrasonography for bladder scanning. However, it is now possible to introduce a transducer into the bladder through the cystoscope. The transducer head can be rotated through a 360° circle to perform a scan that allows accurate diagnosis of different bladder tumors and can give valuable information about tumor invasion. Koraitim and colleagues assessed the value and limitation of transurethral ultrasonography in the diagnostic evaluation of bladder carcinoma. A total of 115 patients were examined, either at the same time as transurethral resection (*n* = 76) or 2 weeks before radical cystectomy (*n* = 39). They compared the results with the pathologic findings of transurethral and cystectomy specimens and found a correlation between transurethral ultrasonography and pathologic staging of 100% in tumors without muscle invasion (stages Ta and T1), 95.7% and 96.8% in muscle invasive tumors (stages T2 and T3a, respectively), and 70% in tumors with extravesical spread. The authors concluded that transurethral ultrasonography is most valuable in determining the stage of tumor confined to the bladder wall. Also, it is of value in detecting tumors in a diverticulum, and mon-

itoring the success of transurethral resection of disease. The main limitations are the inabilities to discriminate between stages Ta and T1 tumors, and to detect involvement of the pelvic lymph nodes.[32]

Computed Tomography and Magnetic Resonance Imaging

For tumor staging a computed tomographic (CT) or magnetic resonance imaging (MRI) scan are obligatory. They are used mainly to demonstrate extravesical extension of the tumor, and lymph node or distant metastasis. The performance of MRI in the assessment of bladder cancer extension is comparable to that of CT. The advantages of the former include the clearer visualization of the tumor itself, especially in the bladder neck and dome, owing to the exploration in several planes. The sensitivities and specificities vary in different investigations and are described between 58 and 94% and between 42 and 62% respectively for CT and between 44 and 83% and 62 and 100% respectively for MRI. The accuracy for diagnosing the correct tumor stage is between 50 and 80% for CT and between 60 and 85% in the case of MRI.[33–40]

In a contrast filled bladder the normally smooth outline of the bladder can show filling defects (Figure 6–9), generalized or focal wall thickening, and enhancement as an indication of a tumor. Differential diagnoses for filling defects are the same as for IVU, and include blood clot or an enlarged prostate

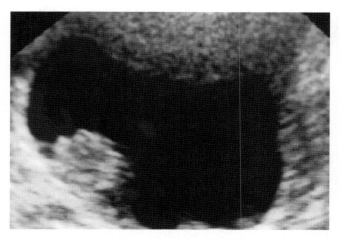

Figure 6–8. Ultrasonogram showing a heterogeneous echogenic area on the mucosal surface of the urinary bladder in the surrounding bladder fluid, highly suspicious of bladder carcinoma.

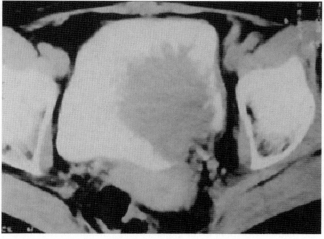

Figure 6–9. Contrast-enhanced CT scan showing a large filling defect in the bladder, which was proven to be bladder cancer.

and rarely focal cystitis, ureterocele, endometriosis, fungus ball, and benign neoplasms. Generalized bladder wall thickening is a nonspecific finding that can also be a sign of nondistention, trabeculation, longstanding bladder outlet obstruction, granulomatous reaction and pancystitis (infection, cytoxan). Uncommon causes of bladder wall thickening are hemorrhage and edema in the bladder wall. Focal bladder wall thickening can be caused by scarring, stone edema, metastasis, or endometrioma (Figures 6–10, 6–11, and 6–12). A contrast enhanced scan may show focally enhancing bladder wall lesions that are highly suggestive of bladder cancer.[41] Pitfalls are inflammation (cystitis, infection), postoperative changes or hemangioma, which can also present with contrast enhancement.

For a complete staging it is necessary to look for pelvic lymphadenopathy, tumor invasion of surrounding tissue and organs, and for distant metastases (Figure 6–13). Invasion of the vagina, for example, could present as a vesicovaginal fistula

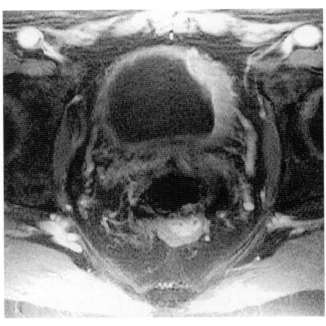

Figure 6–11. Axial contrast T1-weighted pelvic MRI of a patient who presented with clinical signs of bladder tumor. The image shows asymmetric bladder wall thickening on the left compatible with a tumor. Histology revealed a muscle invasive urothelial bladder cancer.

giving rise to air in the bladder. On the other hand, in these cases a primary gynecologic tumor invading the bladder wall must be excluded.

CT and MRI perform well in the detection of bladder tumors but have limited accuracy in staging of patients with invasive bladder carcinoma, which has been described between 35 and 80%, mainly because of its inability to depict microscopic or small volume extravesical tumor extension and lymph node metastases and in some studies did not improve the findings obtained by TUR of the bladder (TURB) alone.[35,42] Despite aggressive attempts over the last three decades to stage muscle invasive disease more accurately, bladder cancer is still staged incorrectly, mostly under-staged in 30 to 50% of patients.[42,43] As a follow-up study, CT and MRI are mainly used in patients with invasive disease. Regular surveillance of superficial tumors consists of cytology, cystoscopy-examination and IVU.

A new and promising technique for the detection of bladder tumor is CT-virtual cystoscopy. The recent development of three-dimensional computer rendering methods with rapid image acquisition and commercially available software has made virtual-reality imaging possible. This allows interac-

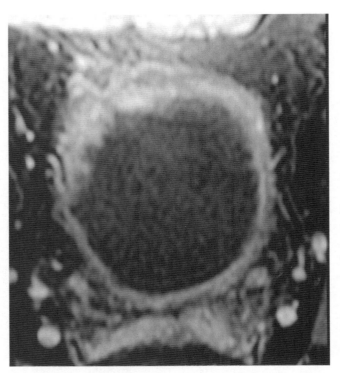

Figure 6–10. Axial contrast T1-weighted pelvic MRI with gadolinium of a patient after cystoscopy and bladder biopsy. This image shows irregular thickening of the anterior-lateral bladder wall, that could be due to post-biopsy changes or tumor recurrence. There is also mild enlargement of the prostate and seminal vesicles. Biopsy revealed a recurrent T1 urothelial tumor of the bladder and intraprostatic ductal carcinoma.

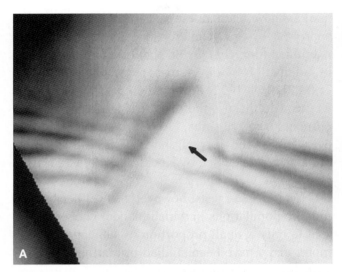

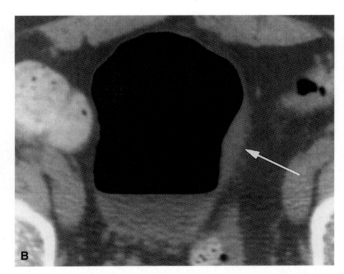

Figure 6–12. (*A*) Virtual cystoscopic and (*B*) transverse CT images reveal an area of wall thickening (*arrow*) involving the left lateral wall of the bladder. Although it is seen on both views, it is more apparent in *B*. The thickening was histologically proved to be scarring from previous biopsy. From Song et al,[61] with permission.

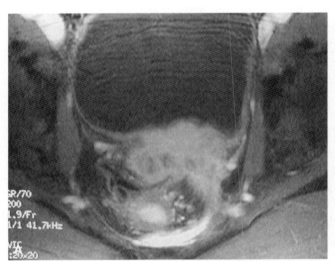

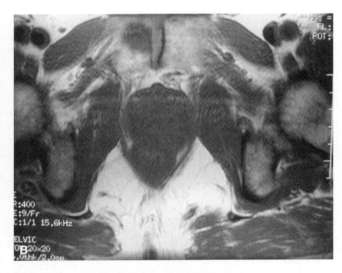

Figure 6–13. Axial contrast-enhanced T1-weighted pelvic MRI of a patient with a history of superficial bladder cancer after multiple transurethral resections. These images show extensive tumor in the base of the bladder extending into the seminal vesicles and extending into and abutting the rectal wall (*A*). A metastatic lesion can be seen in the right pubic symphysis (*B*) and there is hydronephrosis of the left kidney (*C*).

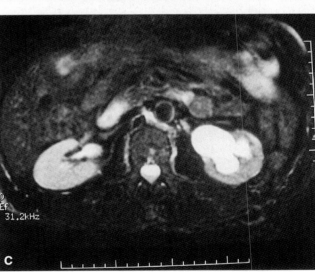

tive intraluminal navigation through any hollow organ to simulate conventional endoscopy. Song and colleagues detected 90% of bladder lesions proved at conventional cystoscopy with a combination of transverse and virtual CT images and concluded that this method is feasible to detect bladder tumors larger than 5 mm. The advantages of this technique are low invasiveness, accurate localization of the lesion due to its wide field of view and depiction of extravesical landmarks. The tumor size is measured objectively and it can be used to monitor treatment response after chemotherapy. As a disadvantage, virtual cystoscopy is not able to detect flat lesions such as carcinoma in situ and the current resolution does not allow reliable visualization of small (< 5 mm) papillary lesions. Most importantly virtual cystoscopy lacks the ability for obtaining tissue samples for histologic analysis[44] (Figures 6–12 and 6–14).

URINE MARKERS

Because of the insufficient sensitivity of urine cytology and the unsatisfying identification of patients who will most benefit from early cystectomy with or without adjuvant treatment, the search for an alternative noninvasive procedure for the diagnosis and follow-up of bladder cancer is one of the major roles in bladder cancer research. Although a lot of new markers have been investigated, only four have been approved by the United States Food and Drug Administration (FDA) for bladder cancer detection in adjunction with cystoscopy: BTA-Stat, BTA-Trak, FDP, NMP22. From the clinical point of view we want to discuss the ones that are being used in clinical trial settings. A more comprehensive overview of the current status of tests for urinary markers are discussed by Koenig and colleagues and Konety and Getzenberg.[45,46]

None of these tests, however, has yet been tested in large populations in which bladder cancer is present in only a small proportion of subjects. Furthermore, many have been studied primarily in patients with high-grade tumors, who are often overrepresented in populations available to academic medical centers. Also, because invasiveness of a diagnostic tool is important, the opinion of the patient should not be left out, and 89% of patients will prefer flexible UCS as the follow-up method, if the sensitivity of a urinary test is lower than 90%.[64]

HISTOPATHOLOGY

Adenocarcinoma

This is a rare lesion, which usually arises from the dome of the bladder and is sometimes palpable as a

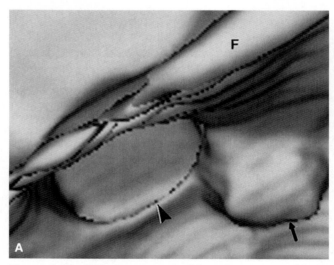
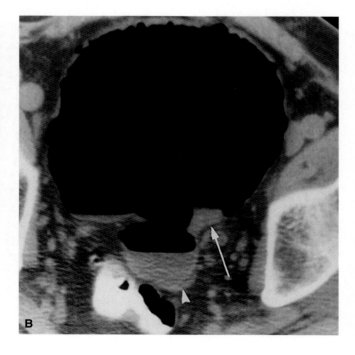

Figure 6–14. Virtual cystoscopic (*A*) and transverse CT (*B*) images show a mass (*arrow*) extending into a bladder diverticulum (*arrowhead*) partially filled with residual urine. A transitional cell carcinoma growing into the diverticulum wall was found at conventional cystoscopy. F = Foley catheter. From Song et al,[61] with permission.

suprapubic mass. Adenocarcinomas of the bladder may appear morphologically similar to those seen in the colon. Therefore, the possibility of a metastatic adenocarcinoma from the colon should be ruled out clinically in cases of pure adenocarcinoma of the bladder. All histologic variants of enteric adenocarcinoma, including signet-ring cell and colloid carcinomas, can occur in the bladder. Most bladder adenocarcinomas are mucin producing.[48] Adenocarcinomas may be papillary or solid. Signet-ring cell carcinomas characteristically produce linitis plastica of the bladder.[49–51] Most adenocarcinomas are poorly differentiated and deeply invasive. When seen in the pure form, they are more commonly associated with cystitis glandularis than with flat urothelial CIS (Figures 6–15, 6–16, 6–17, 6–18, and 6–19).

Squamous Carcinoma

This lesion consists, characteristically, of keratinized islands that contain concentric aggregates of cells and keratin called squamous pearls. They can resemble the prickle cell layer of skin with keratin formation and may show varying degrees of histologic differentiation (Figure 6–20). Squamous cell cancers shed keratinized cells into the urine that sometimes can be detected cytologically. The patho-

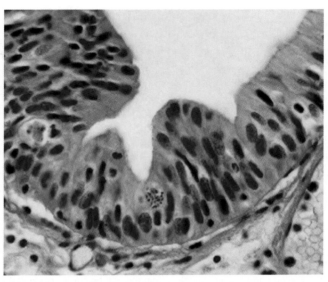

Figure 6–16. A high magnification of in situ adenocarcinoma showing glandular cells with apical cytoplasm, a mitotic figure and apoptosis. (Hematoxylin and eosin stain; original magnification ×600.)

logic diagnosis of squamous carcinoma should be made only when the whole of the tumor is composed of squamous cells, because many TCCs may show squamous metaplasia in some part of the tumor and the transitional cell lining of the bladder easily undergoes squamous metaplasia. These tumors are particularly associated with stones, diverticuli, and bilharzias. The endoscopic and IVU appearances are

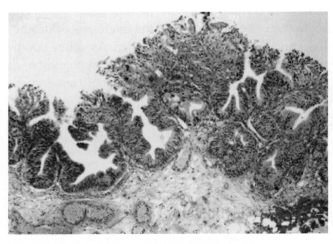

Figure 6–15. An example of in situ adenocarcinoma seen in association with high-grade papillary urothelial (transitional) carcinoma. The high-grade papillary urothelial carcinoma with large pleomorphic cells is seen in the center of the lesion, while in situ adenocarcinoma is seen on either side of the papillary urothelial carcinoma. Note that the in situ adenocarcinoma shows glandular columnar epithelium with apical cytoplasm in contrast to the papillary urothelial (transitional) carcinoma. (Hematoxylin and eosin stain; original magnification ×200.)

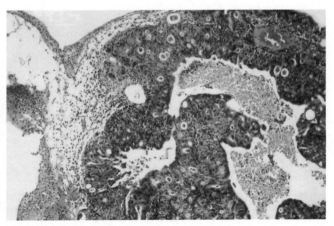

Figure 6–17. Adenocarcinoma: a large nest of malignant cells is seen in the lamina propria. The tumor shows glandular cells with cribriform architecture and an area with central necrosis. The cells show architectural disorganization and loss of polarity. Adenocarcinomas of the bladder may appear morphologically similar to those seen in the colon. Therefore, the possibility of a metastatic adenocarcinoma from the colon should be ruled out clinically in cases of pure adenocarcinoma of the bladder. (Hematoxylin and eosin stain; original magnification ×200.)

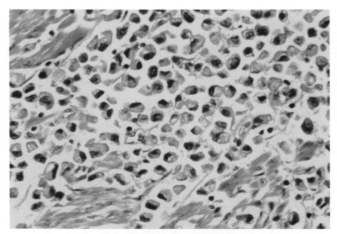

Figure 6–18. Signet-ring cell adenocarcinoma: tumor cells are infiltrating as single cells between the muscle bundles of the muscularis propria. The cells show signet-ring cell features with an eccentric nucleus and mucin vacuole within the cytoplasm. A mucin stain would demonstrate the mucin vacuoles within the cells and a cytokeratin stain would be positive, proving the epithelial nature of the tumor. (Hematoxylin and eosin stain; original magnification ×600.)

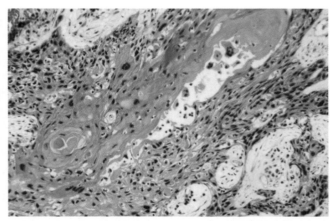

Figure 6–20. Squamous carcinoma: large nests of tumor are seen with an infiltrative pattern. The edges of the nests show jagged, irregular borders. The cells have hyperchromatic pleomorphic nuclei and abundant pink cytoplasm with a glassy dense appearance. In the lower left, a keratin pearl is seen. The presence of keratin pearls and cells with dense glassy eosinophilic cytoplasm are features characteristic of squamous carcinoma. (Hematoxylin and eosin stain; original magnification ×600.)

indistinguishable from advanced TCC. Psoriasin is an 11-kDa calcium binding protein that is only expressed in squamous cell carcinoma (SCC) or TCC with squamous differentiation. It is excreted into the urine and has been suggested as a follow-up marker for patients with SCC.

Other differential diagnoses of transitional cell carcinoma are summarized in Table 6–3 and Figures 6–21 to 6–37.

Summary

Cystoscopy, urinary cytology, transurethral resection, and evaluation of the pathology of histologic section are the mainstays in the diagnosis of urothelial cancer of the urinary bladder. As other conditions may mimic the endoscopic appearance of urothelial malignancies, their pathologic assessment

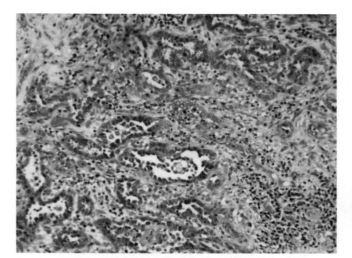

Figure 6–19. Mesonephric adenocarcinoma: the tumor consists of glands lined by large atypical cells with a hob-nail appearance. The term "hob-nail" is used to describe cells with nuclei that protrude into the lumen, and they are best seen in the gland in the center of the image and the gland in the lower left. Another name for this tumor is clear cell adenocarcinoma. This is a subtype of adenocarcinoma and is differentiated from the usual adenocarcinoma with columnar type epithelium because of differences in the clinical presentation. This tumor may be confused with a nephrogenic adenoma, in that hob-nail cells may be seen in both lesions. However, the degree of cytologic atypia and extent of involvement distinguishes the two lesions. (Hematoxylin and eosin stain; original magnification ×400.)

Table 6–3. HISTOLOGIC DIFFERENTIAL DIAGNOSES OF UROTHELIAL CARCINOMA OF THE BLADDER		
	Benign	**Malignant**
Common	Cystitis glandularis cystica follicular nephrogenic adenoma	Adenocarcinoma signet ring urachal mesonephric Squamous carcinoma
Rare	Pseudosarcoma Malakoplakia Amyloid Endometriosis	Malignant melanoma Small cell carcinoma Lymphoma Carcinosarcoma Leiomyosarcoma Pheochromocytoma Rhabdomyosarcoma

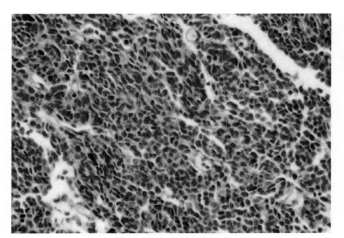

Figure 6–21. An example of small cell carcinoma showing hyperchromatic cells with little cytoplasm. The tumor cells show nuclear molding. The main differential diagnosis is with lymphoma. Immunohistochemical stains may be helpful and small cell carcinomas should show cytokeratin and neuroendocrine expression, in contrast to lymphoma, which would be positive for lymphoid markers. (Hematoxylin and eosin stain; original magnification ×400.)

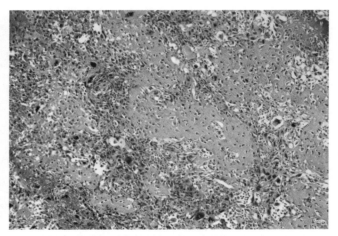

Figure 6–23. Carcinosarcoma 2: in other areas, the tumor shows more pleomorphic cells with large, hyperchromatic nuclei admixed with the spindled component. Some areas show osteoid or bone formation with cells residing in lacunae within an eosinophilic matrix. The pleomorphic appearance along with other areas showing diagnostic carcinoma would argue against a true sarcoma. When a lesion is composed only of the spindled cell component, an immunohistochemical stain for cytokeratin may be helpful to show the epithelial nature of the tumor. (Hematoxylin and eosin stain; original magnification ×200.)

is critical in distinguishing these from urothelial cancers and characterizing the biologic type of cancer that is present. A variety of imaging studies can be brought to bear in the visualizing of the entire urinary tract. These studies are important in assessing the entire urothelium as is the evaluation of a voided urine for abnormal cells (urinary cytology) that can assist in a "pan-urothelial" assessment. All of these

diagnostic modalities, however, may be subject to the pitfalls discussed in this chapter, and need to be noted in approaching an accurate diagnosis of the extent and severity of the disease.

Urinary "markers" (discussed in detail in Chapter 10) have not been sufficiently validated to permit

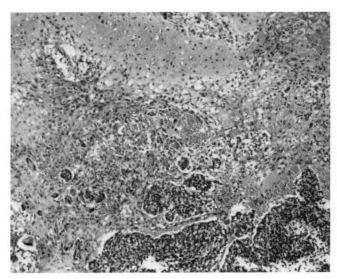

Figure 6–22. Carcinosarcoma 1: extensively infiltrating tumor with pleomorphic appearance. There are areas with cartilaginous differentiation in the upper left. An area of small cell carcinoma is seen in the lower right. The remaining tumor shows spindle cell morphology. (Hematoxylin and eosin stain; original magnification ×200.)

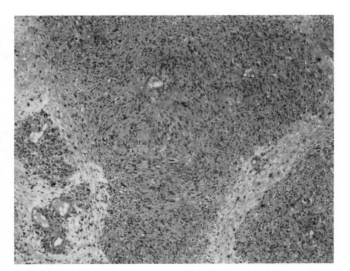

Figure 6–24. Leiomyosarcoma 1: this tumor consists of pleomorphic plump spindle cells with eosinophilic cytoplasm arranged in fascicles. In some areas there is a whorled appearance. When the fascicles are cut in cross section, as seen in the lower right, the cells show perinuclear clearing. (Hematoxylin and eosin stain; original magnification ×200.)

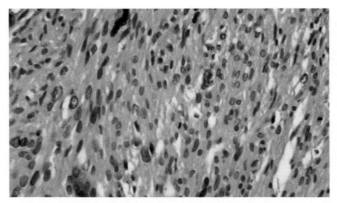

Figure 6–25. Leiomyosarcoma 2: on higher magnification, nuclear pleomorphism and mitotic figures are seen. Immunohistochemical stains for actin are helpful in showing muscle differentiation of the tumor. (Hematoxylin and eosin stain; original magnification ×600.)

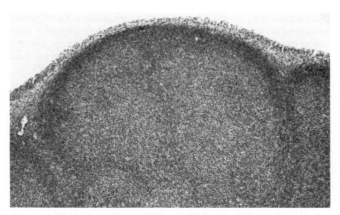

Figure 6–26. Lymphoma: the lamina propria shows a diffuse infiltrate of monotonous lymphoid cells with a vague nodular pattern. The homogeneous population of cells along with the nodular pattern is consistent with a follicular lymphoma. Immunohistochemical stains or flow cytometry from fresh tissue should be performed to show a clonal population of cells and to rule out a reactive process. (Hematoxylin and eosin stain; original magnification ×200.)

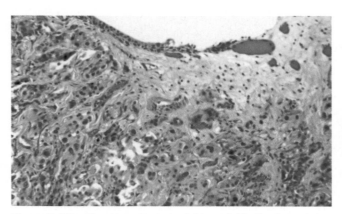

Figure 6–27. Pheochromocytoma 1. Tumor infiltrating in nests are seen in the lamina propria. The tumor cells show some pleomorphism and basophilic cytoplasm. The cell borders are indistinct. (Hematoxylin and eosin stain; original magnification ×200.)

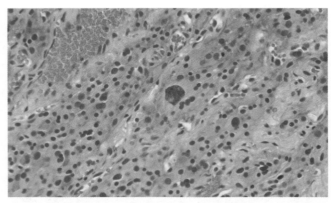

Figure 6–28. Pheochromocytoma 2: A higher magnification shows predominantly cells with round nuclei with occasional cells with large pleomorphic nuclei. The differential diagnosis is with an invasive urothelial carcinoma. Immunohistochemical stains for neuroendocrine markers such as chromogranin, synaptophysin and (NSE) would be positive in a pheochromocytoma and negative in a urothelial carcinoma. In addition an S100 stain would highlight the sustentacular cells around the nests of tumor cells in a pheochromocytoma. (Hematoxylin and eosin stain; original magnification ×600.)

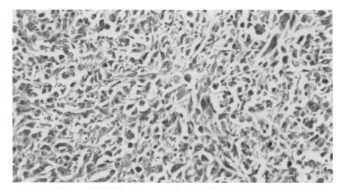

Figure 6–29. Rhabdomyosarcoma: sheet of loosely arranged pleomorphic tumor cells with eosinophilic cytoplasm. Some cells have a round appearance with eccentric pink cytoplasm (cell in center of image). (Hematoxylin and eosin stain; original magnification ×200.)

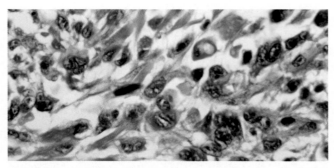

Figure 6–30. Rhabdomyosarcoma 2: on higher magnification, cells show pleomorphic nuclei with prominent nucleoli. The cytoplasm of some cells shows cross striations, indicative of skeletal muscle differentiation; these cells are often referred to as strap cells. Immunohistochemical stains for muscle markers, especially desmin and myogenin would be positive in the tumor cells. (Hematoxylin and eosin stain; original magnification ×600.)

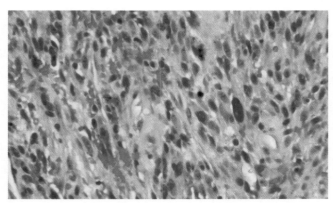

Figure 6–31. Melanoma: the lesion consists of pleomorphic spindle cells. In some areas, cells with prominent nucleoli can be seen. A brown pigment consistent with melanin can be seen in scattered cells. (Hematoxylin and eosin stain; original magnification ×400.)

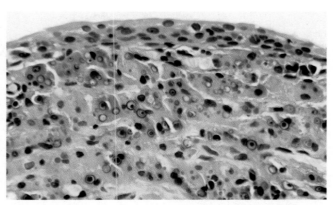

Figure 6–34. Malakoplakia 2: on high magnification, multiple round basophilic structures known as Michaelis-Gutmann bodies are seen. Michaelis-Gutmann bodies are laminated mineralized concretions seen within macrophages and likely represent undigested bacterial material. (Hematoxylin and eosin stain; original magnification ×600.)

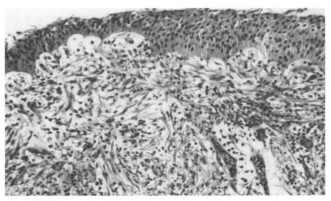

Figure 6–32. Pseudosarcoma: the lesion shows a cellular spindle cell proliferation admixed with hemorrhage and inflammatory cells. High mitotic activity can be seen. The spindle cells do not show significant atypia or pleomorphism. These patients usually have a history of prior instrumentation. The lack of pleomorphism, extravasated red blood cells, mixture of inflammatory cells and history distinguishes this reactive process from a true sarcoma. (Hematoxylin and eosin stain; original magnification ×200.)

Figure 6–35. Amyloid: a diffuse deposit of eosinophilic, amorphous material is seen in the lamina propria. (Hematoxylin and eosin stain; original magnification ×200.)

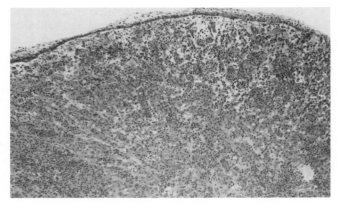

Figure 6–33. Malakoplakia 1: at low magnification, the lamina propria is filled with a cellular infiltrate composed of histiocytes, neutrophils, and lymphocytes. (Hematoxylin and eosin stain; original magnification ×200.)

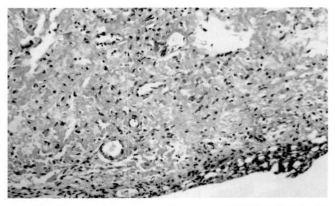

Figure 6–36. Amyloid, congo red: a congo red stain will stain the eosinophilic material dark pink or red. Under polarized light, the amyloid will show apple green birefringence. (Congo red stain; original magnification ×200.)

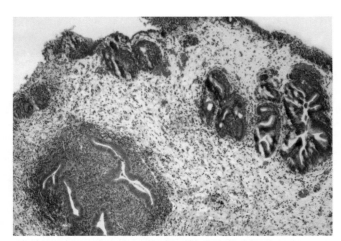

Figure 6–37. Endometriosis: within the lamina propria are glandular structures lined by columnar epithelium with apical cytoplasm, but without mucin vacuoles. Associated with the glands is a cellular stroma; both the glands and stroma are reminiscent of endometrial tissue. Within the cellular stroma, hemosiderin pigment may be seen. The combination of endometrial type glands, stroma, and hemosiderin are diagnostic of endometriosis and would not be confused with an adenocarcinoma. (Hematoxylin and eosin stain; original magnification ×200.)

their routine clinical application, although they may ultimately find use in selected settings. Furthermore, application of various substances that permit flourescent cystoscopy may enhance endoscopic diagnosis of urothelial malignancy. Here too, however, validation of this technique is needed before general clinical application can be achieved. Finally, molecular markers may become increasingly important in diagnosis, as our understanding of the significance of chromosomal and biochemical changes on the biologic potential of a particular tumor diathesis is refined.

REFERENCES

1. Messing EM, Young TB, Hunt VB, et al. The significance of asymptomatic microhematuria in men 50 or more years old: findings of a home screening study using urinary dipsticks. J Urol 1987;137:919–22.
2. Amling CL. Diagnosis and management of superficial bladder cancer. Curr Probl Cancer 2001;25:219–78.
3. Messing EM, Catalona W. Urothelial tumors of the urinary tract. 1998;7:2327–89.
4. Taguchi I, Gohji K, Hara I, et al. Clinical evaluation of random biopsy of urinary bladder in patients with superficial bladder cancer. Int J Urol 1998;5:30–4.
5. Kiemeney LA, Witjes JA, Heijbroek RP, et al. Should random urothelial biopsies be taken from patients with primary superficial bladder cancer? A decision analysis. Members of the Dutch South-East Co-Operative Urological Group. Br J Urol 1994;73:164–71.
6. van der MA, Oosterlinck W, Brausi M, et al. Significance of bladder biopsies in Ta,T1 bladder tumors: a report from the EORTC Genito-Urinary Tract Cancer Cooperative Group. EORTC-GU Group Superficial Bladder Committee. Eur Urol 1999;35:267–71.
7. Yamada Y, Hayashi Y, Kohri K, et al. [Random biopsy and recurrence risk in patients with bladder cancer]. Nippon Hinyokika Gakkai Zasshi 1996;87:61–6.
8. Smits G, Schaafsma E, Kiemeney L, et al. Microstaging of pT1 transitional cell carcinoma of the bladder: identification of subgroups with distinct risks of progression. Urology 1998;52:1009–13.
9. Hermann GG, Horn T, Steven K. The influence of the level of lamina propria invasion and the prevalence of p53 nuclear accumulation on survival in stage T1 transitional cell bladder cancer. J Urol 1998;159:91–4.
10. Angulo JC, Lopez JI, Grignon DJ, Sanchez-Chapado M. Muscularis mucosa differentiates two populations with different prognosis in stage T1 bladder cancer. Urology 1995;45:47–53.
11. Hasui Y, Osada Y, Kitada S, Nishi S. Significance of invasion to the muscularis mucosae on the progression of superficial bladder cancer. Urology 1994;43:782–6.
12. Younes M, Sussman J, True LD. The usefulness of the level of the muscularis mucosae in the staging of invasive transitional cell carcinoma of the urinary bladder. Cancer 1990;66:543–8.
13. Soloway MS, Sofer M, Vaidya A. Contemporary management of stage T1 transitional cell carcinoma of the bladder. J Urol 2002;167:1573–83.
14. Herr HW. The value of a second transurethral resection in evaluating patients with bladder tumors. J Urol 1999;162:74–6.
15. Klan R, Loy V, Huland H. Residual tumor discovered in routine second transurethral resection in patients with stage T1 transitional cell carcinoma of the bladder. J Urol 1991; 146:316–8.
16. Schips L, Augustin H, Zigeuner RE, et al. Is repeated transurethral resection justified in patients with newly diagnosed superficial bladder cancer? Urology 2002;59:220–3.
17. Meyer-Betz F. Untersuchungen über die biologische (photodynamische) Wirkung des Hämatoporphyrins und anderer Derivate des Blut- und Gallenfarbstoffs. Dtsch Arch Klin Med 1913;112:476–476.
18. Baumgartner R, Kriegmair M, Stepp HG, et al. Photodynamic diagnosis following intravesical instillation of aminolevulinic acid (ALA): first clinical experiences in urology. 1993.
19. Koenig F, McGovern FJ. Fluorescence detection of bladder carcinoma. Urology 1997;50:778–9.
20. Koenig F, McGovern FJ, Larne R, et al. Diagnosis of bladder carcinoma using protoporhyrin IX fluorescence induced by 5-aminolaevulinic acid. Br J Urol 1999;83:129–35.
21. Kriegmair M, Baumgartner R, Knuchel R, et al. Detection of early bladder cancer by 5-aminolevulinic acid induced porphyrin fluorescence. J Urol 1996;155:105–9.
22. Jichlinski P, Forrer M, Mizeret J, et al. Clinical evaluation of a method for detecting superficial surgical transitional cell carcinoma of the bladder by light-induced fluorescence of protoporphyrin IX following the topical application of 5-aminolevulinic acid: preliminary results. Lasers Surg Med 1997;20:402–8.

23. Heil P, Stocker S, Sroka R, Baumgartner R. In vivo fluorescence kinetics of porphyrins following intravesical instillation of 5-aminolaevulinic acid in normal and tumour-bearing rat bladders. J Photochem Photobiol B 1997;38:158–63.

24. Zaak D, Kriegmair M, Stepp H, et al. Endoscopic detection of transitional cell carcinoma with 5- aminolevulinic acid: results of 1012 fluorescence endoscopies. Urology 2001; 57:690–4.

25. Riedl CR, Daniltchenko D, Koenig F, et al. Fluorescence endoscopy with 5-aminolevulinic acid reduces early recurrence rate in superficial bladder cancer. J Urol 2001; 165:1121–3.

26. Aslaksen A, Gadeholt G, Gothlin JH. Ultrasonography versus intravenous urography in the evaluation of patients with microscopic haematuria. Br J Urol 1990;66:144–7.

27. American College of Radiology. American College of Radiology appropriateness criteria: urologic imaging—radiologic investigation of patients with hematuria. Available at: http://www.acr.org (accessed Nov 17, 2003).

28. Corwin HL, Silverstein MD. The diagnosis of neoplasia in patients with asymptomatic microscopic hematuria: a decision analysis. J Urol 1988;139:1002–6.

29. Ravi R, Rao RC, Ahlawat R, Berry M. Carcinoma bladder: comparative evaluation of urinary cytology, excretory urography and ultrasonography. Indian J Cancer 1990;27: 55–61.

30. Speelman HR, Kessels AG, Bongaerts AH, et al. Haematuria: intravenous urography, ultrasound or both? Rofo Fortschr Geb Rontgenstr Neuen Bildgeb Verfahr 1996;165:524–8.

31. Wong-You-Cheong JJ, Wagner BJ, Davis CJ Jr. Transitional cell carcinoma of the urinary tract: radiologic-pathologic correlation. Radiographics 1998;18:123–42.

32. Koraitim M, Kamal B, Metwalli N, Zaky Y. Transurethral ultrasonographic assessment of bladder carcinoma: its value and limitation. J Urol 1995;154:375–8.

33. Beer M, Schmidt H, Riedl R. [The clinical value of preoperative staging of bladder and prostatic cancers with nuclear magnetic resonance and computerized tomography]. Urologe A 1989;28:65–9.

34. Buy JN, Moss AA, Guinet C, et al. MR staging of bladder carcinoma: correlation with pathologic findings. Radiology 1988;169:695–700.

35. Husband JE, Olliff JF, Williams MP, et al. Bladder cancer: staging with CT and MR imaging. Radiology 1989;173: 435–40.

36. Kim B, Semelka RC, Ascher SM, et al. Bladder tumor staging: comparison of contrast-enhanced CT, T1- and T2-weighted MR imaging, dynamic gadolinium-enhanced imaging, and late gadolinium-enhanced imaging. Radiology 1994;193:239–45.

37. Koss JC, Arger PH, Coleman BG, et al. CT staging of bladder carcinoma. AJR Am J Roentgenol 1981;137:359–62.

38. Nishimura K, Hida S, Nishio Y, et al. The validity of magnetic resonance imaging (MRI) in the staging of bladder cancer: comparison with computed tomography (CT) and transurethral ultrasonography (US). Jpn J Clin Oncol 1988;18:217–26.

39. Schmidt H, Beer M, Block T, et al. [Value of nuclear magnetic resonance tomography in the staging of tumors of the urinary bladder]. Digitale Bilddiagn 1987;7:104–11.

40. Fisher MR, Hricak H, Tanagho EA. Urinary bladder MR imaging. Part II. Neoplasm. Radiology 1985;157:471–7.

41. Burgener FA, Hamlin DJ. Intravenous contrast enhancement in computed tomography of pelvic malignancies. Rofo Fortschr Geb Rontgenstr Nuklearmed 1981;134:656–61.

42. Paik ML, Scolieri MJ, Brown SL, et al. Limitations of computerized tomography in staging invasive bladder cancer before radical cystectomy. J Urol 2000;163:1693–6.

43. Levy DA, Grossman HB. Staging and prognosis of T3b bladder cancer. Semin Urol Oncol 1996;14:56–61.

44. Song JH, Francis IR, Platt JF, et al. Bladder tumor detection at virtual cystoscopy. Radiology 2001;218:95–100.

45. Koenig F, Jung K, Schnorr D, Loening SA. Urinary markers of malignancy. Clin Chim Acta 2000;297:191–205.

46. Konety BR, Getzenberg RH. Urine based markers of urological malignancy. J Urol 2001;165:600–11.

47. Vriesema JL, Poucki MH, Kiemeney LA, Witjes JA. Patient opinion of urinary tests versus flexible urethrocystoscopy in follow-up examination for superficial bladder cancer: a utility analysis. Urology 2000;56:793–7.

48. Koss LG. Tumors of the urinary bladder. In: Firminger HI, editor. Atlas of Tumor Pathology, 2nd series. Armed Forces Institute of Pathology 1975, Washington (DC); 1.

49. Blute ML, Engen DE, Travis WD, Kvols LK. Primary signet ring cell adenocarcinoma of the bladder. J Urol 1989; 141:17–21.

50. Choi H, Lamb S, Pintar K, Jacobs SC. Primary signet-ring cell carcinoma of the urinary bladder. Cancer 1984;53:1985–90.

51. Sheldon CA, Clayman RV, Gonzalez R, et al. Malignant urachal lesions. J Urol 1984;131:1–8.

7

Pathology of Urothelial Tumors of the Bladder

DAVID G. BOSTWICK, MD, MBA
RODOLFO MONTIRONI, MD, PhD, FRC Path
ANTONIO LOPEZ-BELTRAN, MD
LIANG CHENG, MD

The World Health Organization (WHO) 1973 classification and grading system for bladder tumors has been repeatedly validated and is nearly universally used [1-3] despite introduction of multiple new classification and grading schemes for bladder cancer in the past few years without validation and with little or no input from urologists, oncologists, radiation therapists, or nonpathologists.[4-7] These new grading systems often depart considerably from the popular standard of the 1973 WHO, introducing new terms such as "low malignant potential" and "atypia of uncertain clinical significance" amid controversy. These terms have encountered great resistance among clinician users and nonacademic pathologists, and both were formally abandoned recently.[1]

The main criticism of the WHO 1973 classification has been the imprecise histopathologic diagnostic criteria.[5] In an effort to improve the precision and utility of the WHO 1973 classification, an expanded and refined description of the scheme was introduced as the Ancona (Italy) refinement and is presented herein (Table 7–1). Grading of bladder tumors, particularly papillary tumors, may be difficult owing to intratumoral heterogeneity, and two caveats are recognized. First, grading is based on the highest level of abnormality noted. No formal recommendation has been previously made regarding the amount or extent of a higher grade needed for upgrading, but we require at least one high-power field (40× magnification with additional 20× eyepieces); further study of this suggestion is indicated. Second, tangential cutting of urothelium at the base results in the appearance of fused papillae and sheets of cells with large nuclei and increased number of mitotic figures that may lead to overdiagnosis or overgrading.

This chapter addresses clinically important aspects of pathology of bladder cancer, including contemporary grading of flat and papillary tumors, variants of urothelial cancer, staging and the microscopic criteria that define each stage, pathology of urachal carcinoma, and select cell-based morphologic markers that are now widely used by pathologists to assist with diagnosis in urine samples.

GRADING

FLAT LESIONS

Reactive Changes

Diagnostic Criteria. Reactive changes are almost always associated with acute or chronic inflammation in the lamina propria, and this results from a variety of inciting agents, including bacteria, calculi, trauma, chemicals and toxins, or no apparent cause (idiopathic). In early acute cystitis resulting from bacterial infection, there is vascular dilatation and congestion, erythematous and hemorrhagic mucosa, and moderate to severe edema. With time, polypoid or bullous cystitis may develop, sometimes with ulceration. The urothelium may be hyperplastic or metaplastic and, when ulcerated, is often covered by a fibrinous membrane with neutrophils and bacterial colonies. Stromal edema and chronic inflammation

Table 7–1. THE ANCONA 2001 REFINEMENT OF THE WHO 1973 CLASSIFICATION OF UROTHELIAL TUMORS
Flat lesions
Reactive changes*
Dysplasia
Carcinoma in situ
Papillary lesions
Papilloma
Grade I Carcinoma
Grade II Carcinoma
Grade III Carcinoma

*Although not a "tumor," reactive changes are included here as part of the morphologic continuum of flat urothelial abnormalities.
WHO = World Health Organization.

gradually become more pronounced, particularly in the lamina propria. If the acute inflammation persists, chronic cystitis usually develops, sometimes with prominent mural fibrosis. In chronic cystitis, the mucosa may be thin, hyperplastic, or ulcerated, often with reactive changes (Figure 7–1). Follicular cystitis is an uncommon but distinctive variant of chronic cystitis. Granulation tissue is often conspicuous in the early stages, and may be replaced by dense scarring, particularly in the late healing stages. This process may be transmural and involve perivesicular tissue.

Clinical Significance. Patients with reactive changes are not at increased risk for the development of dysplasia, CIS, or urothelial carcinoma.[8,9] This category of reactive changes now incorporates the WHO/International Society of Urologic Pathology (ISUP) 1998 category of "atypia of unknown clinical significance." Cheng and colleagues studied 35 patients with "atypia of unknown clinical significance" followed for a mean of 3.7 years and found no increased risk for recurrence or progression; they recommended abandoning the term and compressing the category into reactive changes, and we concur.[8]

Dysplasia

Diagnostic Criteria. The cytologic abnormalities in dysplasia are less severe than in CIS and are usually restricted to the basal and intermediate layers (see Figure 7–1). The abnormalities include cell crowding and disorganization with nuclear enlargement, coarsely clumped chromatin, variation in nuclear shape, and scattered notching of chromatinic rims.

Nucleoli are usually small and inconspicuous or rarely enlarged. Mitotic figures are usually absent. The superficial cell layer is intact. Nuclear and architectural features are most useful in distinguishing reactive changes and dysplasia.[10]

Clinical Significance. Urothelial dysplasia is a marker for cancer risk. Cheng and colleagues studied 36 patients with isolated dysplasia of the bladder and found that 19% developed biopsy-proven cancer progression (11% with CIS and 8% with invasive cancer) with a mean follow-up of 8.2 years; three patients developed muscle-invasive cancer.[11] Zuk and colleagues studied 15 patients with dysplasia who were followed for a mean of 4.8 years, and they found that 15% of patients developed CIS.[12] Similarly, Baithun and colleagues found that 14% of patients with dysplasia developed CIS.[13] These results emphasize the need for careful monitoring of patients with dysplasia by endoscopy and cytology; treatments such as intravesical chemotherapy or bacille Calmette-Guérin (BCG) are not currently recommended because the side effects of these agents may outweigh the potential and unknown benefits.

Carcinoma in Situ

Diagnostic Criteria. Urothelial CIS is characterized by flat disordered proliferation of urothelial cells with marked cytologic abnormalities (Figure 7–2). In most cases, CIS is multifocal, appearing cystoscopically as erythematous velvety or granular patches, although it may be visually undetectable.[14] The cells of CIS may form a layer that is only one cell layer thick, of normal thickness (up to seven cells), or the thickness of hyperplasia (greater than seven cells). The diagnosis of CIS requires the presence of severe cytologic atypia (nuclear anaplasia); full thickness change is not essential, although it is usually present. Interobserver agreement with CIS is good to very good.

Prominent architectural disorganization of the urothelium is characteristic, with loss of cell polarity and cohesiveness. Superficial (umbrella) cells may be present except in areas of full thickness abnormality. The tumor cells tend to be large and pleomorphic, with moderate to abundant cytoplasm, although they are sometimes small with a high nucleus-to-cytoplasmic ratio. The chromatin tends to be coarse and clumped. Morphometrically, the cells display increased nuclear area, nuclear perimeter, and maximum nuclear diameter. Nucleoli are usually large and prominent in at least some of the cells, and may be multiple. Mitotic figures are often seen in the uppermost urothelium, and may be atypical. The adjacent mucosa often contains lesser degrees of cytologic abnormality.

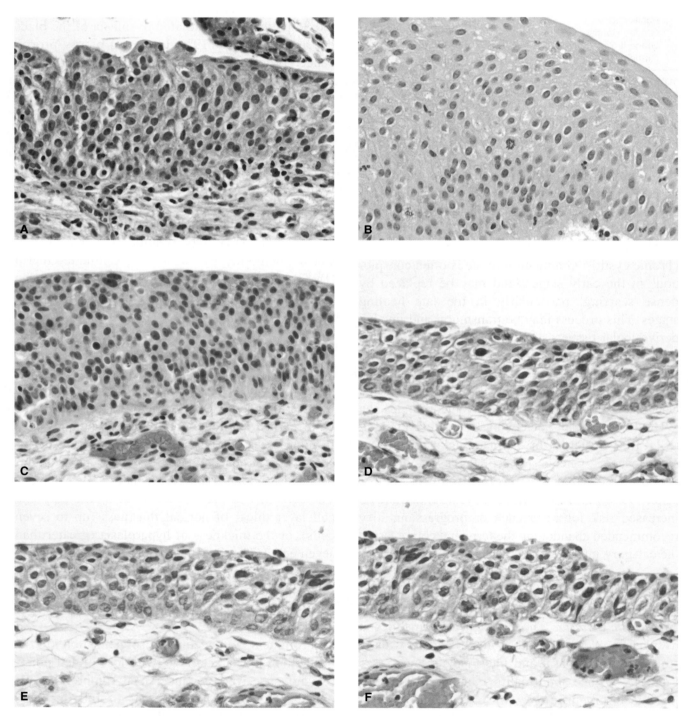

Figure 7–1. *A*: Reactive urothelial changes; *B*: Reactive urothelial changes; *C, D*: urothelial dysplasia; *E, F*: urothelial dysplasia bordering on carcinoma in situ.

The small cell pattern of CIS is usually associated with an increased number of cell layers. In such cases, the cytoplasm is scant and nuclei are enlarged and hyperchromatic, with coarse, unevenly distributed chromatin; scattered prominent nucleoli are distorted and angulated. Mitotic figures are frequently present, often with abnormal forms. The cells are randomly oriented and disorganized, often with striking cellular dyscohesion that, in some cases, results in few or no recognizable epithelial cells on the surface, a condition referred to as denuding cystitis.[9] Careful search of

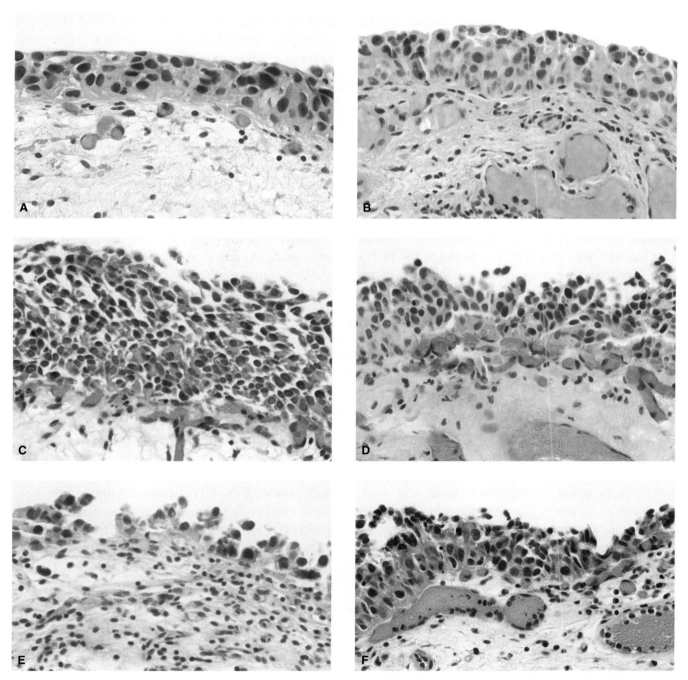

Figure 7–2. *A, B:* Carcinom in situ (CIS) displays disorderly proliferation of malignant urothelial cells with high nuclear cytoplasmic ratio, nuclear pleomorphism, irregular nuclear contours, coarsely granular chromatin, and prominent nucleoli; *C, D:* CIS with early cellular dyscohesion; *E, F:* CIS with denudation.

all residual mucosa is important in biopsies that have little or no mucosa in order to exclude the denuding cystitis of CIS.

CIS is often associated with focal discontinuity of the basement membrane. There may be intense chronic inflammation in the superficial lamina propria in some cases, and vascular ectasia and proliferation of small capillaries is frequent. In denuded areas, residual CIS may involve Von Brunn's nests. Rarely, CIS exhibits pagetoid growth, characterized by large single cells or small clusters of cells within otherwise normal urothelium, in squamous metaplasia, or within prostatic ducts.[15–18] Individual cells showing pagetoid spread have enlarged nuclei with coarse chromatin, single or multiple nucleoli, and abundant pale to eosinophilic cytoplasm that is mucin-negative. Careful search should be made for subepithelial invasion (microinvasion), often appearing as single cells or small nests of cells with retraction artifact. Microinvasion may be masked by chronic inflammation, denuded mucosa, or stromal fibrosis.

Clinical Significance. Urothelial CIS has a high likelihood of progressing to invasive carcinoma if untreated, occurring in up to 83% of cases.[19] Cystectomy reveals foci of microinvasion in 34% of bladders with CIS, and muscle-invasive cancer in up to 9%.[15–17] Patients with CIS treated by radical cystectomy have up to 100% 5-year survival.[20] Intravesicle therapy is also commonly employed, including thiotepa, mitomycin C, and BCG.

Primary CIS has a lower risk of progression (28% versus 59%) and death (7% versus 45%) than secondary CIS.[18] Factors predictive of high risk of progression include multifocality, coexistent bladder neoplasm, prostatic urethral involvement, and recurrence after treatment. Concomitant ureteral CIS is uncommon, present in 8% of patients undergoing radical cystectomy.[21] In a recent study, frozen sections failed to detect CIS of the ureteral margin in 17% of cases but was only rarely associated with local morbidity; the authors questioned the value of frozen section examination of ureteral margins and recommended reliance on urine cytology.[21]

The clinical course of patients with urothelial CIS is variable; up to 83% of patients will develop invasive cancer, and up to 38% of patients will die of bladder cancer.[8,14–18,20–38] Melamed and colleagues first described the natural history of urothelial CIS and found that 9 of 25 patients (36%) developed invasive carcinoma within 5 years after the initial diagnosis; others (16 patients) received cystectomy.[29] Stanisic and colleagues treated 26 patients with intravesical therapy for CIS.[34] At 5 years, 50% of their patients progressed to deeply invasive (muscle or beyond) or metastatic cancer, and 27% died (22). In a study of 62 patients with CIS, Utz and colleagues showed that 60% of patients developed invasive cancer, and 38% died of cancer within a period of 5 years.[37] In detailed mapping studies of 21 cystectomy specimens removed from patients with CIS, invasive cancer was identified in 20% of cases, and extensive mucosal involvement was seen in every case.[37] These results, in conjunction with the findings of Cheng and colleagues,[8,22,37] indicate that urothelial CIS is a significant risk factor for the development of invasive cancer and subsequent death due to cancer.

Isolated urothelial CIS in the absence of papillary urothelial carcinoma is less common. Orozco and colleagues studied 102 patients with urothelial carcinoma in situ and found that 73 patients (72%) had coexistent urothelial carcinoma, including 27 patients with coexistent noninvasive papillary urothelial carcinoma.[18] With less than 5 years of follow-up, 2 of 29 patients with isolated urothelial CIS died of bladder cancer; 33 of 73 patients (45%) with secondary CIS died of bladder cancer. Among 27 patients with coexistent noninvasive papillary urothelial carcinoma, 12 patients (44%) died of bladder cancer (5). Cheng and colleagues found that there was no outcome difference between patients with isolated CIS (80 patients) and those with coexistent papillary noninvasive urothelial carcinoma (58 patients).[22] Fifteen-year cancer-specific survival was 72% for those with isolated CIS compared with 78% for those with coexistent papillary noninvasive urothelial carcinoma ($p = .49$).

Papillary Lesions

Diagnostic Criteria

The World Health Organization in 1973 recommended restrictive criteria for papilloma,[3] and these diagnostic features are now internationally accepted; standardized criteria should eliminate much of the confusion regarding the incidence and diagnosis of this lesion (Table 7–2). The WHO criteria for papilloma include the following five main features: (1) small (less than 2 cm in greatest dimension); (2) usually a solitary papillary lesion with one or more delicate fibrovascular cores; (3) lined by cytologically and architecturally normal urothelium with orderly maturation; (4) an intact superficial (umbrella) cell layer and no mitotic figures; and (5) occurring in patients usually less than 50 years of age.[3] The urothelium is usually of normal thickness, although factitious appearance of thickening may be observed owing to tangential cutting at the base of the papilloma. There is little or no variation in nuclear size, shape, or spacing when compared with normal urothelium, and the chromatin texture is finely granular without nucleolar enlargement (Figure 7–3). Slight deviation from one of these criteria may be acceptable with an otherwise typical papilloma; for example, the presence of mild to moderate cytologic atypia of the superficial cells does not exclude the diagnosis of papilloma, particularly when accompanied by an explanatory inflammatory infiltrate. Papilloma should not be confused with grade I urothelial carcinoma despite the suggestion of a small number of authors to the contrary.[39,40]

Inverted urothelial papilloma shares many features with exophytic papilloma, but is well defined elsewhere. Rare cases have combined features of typical exophytic papilloma and inverted papilloma, and these varied findings should be included in the diagnostic report.

Clinical Significance

Papilloma is uncommon, representing less than 3% of papillary urothelial tumors.[41] Such lesions usually occur in patients less than 50 years of age, but rare cases with otherwise typical features can be seen in patients in their upper fifties. An otherwise typical papilloma occurring in an older patient (well beyond 50 years) is best considered to be grade I urothelial carcinoma.

With the restrictive definition of the WHO 1973 classification, urothelial papilloma has a low recurrence rate and very infrequent association with the development of invasive urothelial carcinoma and cancer death; it does not have the capacity to invade or metastasize.[42,43] However, it is neoplastic, with a small but significant potential for recurrence. Eble and Young reviewed 80 years of published studies of benign and low-grade urothelial neoplasms of the urinary bladder and concluded that urothelial papillomas "are rare tumors somehow fundamentally different from noninvasive low-grade carcinomas."[41] These authors believed that "true papillomas of the bladder that are distinct from grade I papillary carcinoma do occur rarely." Miller and colleagues found that none of 26 patients with papilloma developed recurrence or urothelial carcinoma.[44] Bergkvist and colleagues

Table 7–2.	DIAGNOSTIC FEATURES OF UROTHELIAL PAPILLOMA AND GRADE I CARCINOMA	
	Papilloma	Grade I Carcinoma
Age (y)	Younger (usually < 50)	Older (usually > 50)
Sex (Male: female)	2:1	3:1
Size	Small, usually < 2 cm	Larger
Microscopic findings		
Well-formed papillae	Present	Present
Thickness of urothelium	≤ 7 layers	Usually > 7 layers
Superficial umbrella cells	Present	Usually present
Cytology	Minimal or absent	Mild
Nuclear enlargement	Rare or none	Slight to moderate
Nuclear hyperchromasia	Rare or none	Slight
Chromatin	Fine granular	Slightly coarse or granular
Nucleolar enlargement	Absent	May be present
Mitotic figures	None	Rare
Stromal invasion	Absent	Uncommon

reported no cancer deaths in 12 patients with urothelial papilloma (referred to as grade 0 carcinoma); recurrence rate and the rate of developing urothelial carcinoma were not reported.[45] Buerger believed that "many of the other loosely accepted notions regarding the malignancy of papilloma per se were found to be fallacious."[46]

Cheng and colleagues studied 52 patients with papilloma who were followed for a mean of 9.8 years; 20 patients (38%) had more than 8 years of follow-up.[47] The tumor was solitary in 49 (94%) patients and multiple in 3 (6%) patients. Four (8%) patients developed recurrent papilloma (mean interval from the diagnosis to recurrence, 3.2 years); one developed grade I carcinoma 6 years after the initial diagnosis of papilloma. None of the other patients developed dysplasia, CIS, or urothelial carcinoma, and none died of bladder cancer.

Grade I Urothelial Carcinoma

Diagnostic Criteria

Grade I papillary carcinoma consists of an orderly arrangement of normal urothelial cells lining delicate papillae with minimal architectural abnormalities and minimal nuclear atypia (Figure 7–4). There may be some complexity and fusion of the papillae, but this is usually not prominent. The urothelium is often thickened, with more than seven cell layers, but may be normal; formal counting of the number of cells in thickness in routine practice is discouraged, recognizing that there is no absolute cut point for normal and abnormal. Regardless of thickness, the urothelium displays normal maturation and cohesiveness, with intact superficial cell layer. Nuclei tend to be uniform in

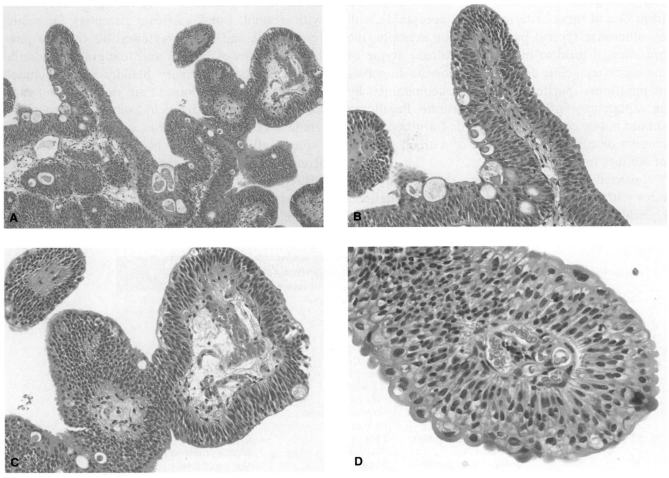

Figure 7–3.   *A, B, C, D*: Papilloma: urothelial papilloma is characterized by a papillary lesion with delicate fibrovascular cores lined by cytologically and architecturally normal urothelium. The papillae are lined by urothelial cells that are less than 7 cell layers in thickness.

shape and spacing, although there may be some enlargement and elongation; the chromatin texture is finely granular, similar to papilloma, without significant nucleolar enlargement. Mitotic figures are rare or absent.

Clinical Significance

Grade I carcinoma appears to have a predilection for the ureteric orifice,[48] referred to as the "typical primary site" by Page and colleagues.[49] Sixty-nine

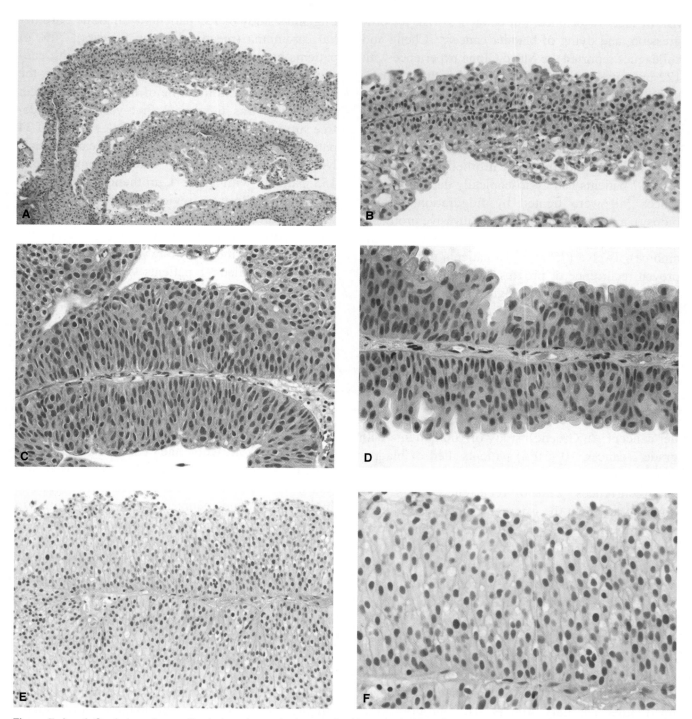

Figure 7–4. *A*: Grade I carcinoma: Grade I carcinoma is characterized by an orderly proliferation of urothelial cells without significant cytologic atypia. The papillae are well formed and are lined by urothelial cells that are usually more than 7 cell layers in thickness; *B*: High-power view of the same tumor; *C, D, E, F*: Grade I carcinoma with mild cytologic atypia.

percent of grade I urothelial carcinomas were centered around the ureteric orifice, and tumor was found in the anterior wall in two patients (1%).[48] The dome appears to be an uncommon location for grade I cancer (3%).

Patients with grade I carcinoma are at significant risk of local recurrence, but of far less risk for progression, and dying of bladder cancer.[42] Cheng and colleagues reported the Mayo Clinic experience with 122 untreated patients with grade I urothelial carcinoma who were followed for a mean of 12.8 years.[50] Thirty-three (29%) patients had recurrence or progression, with mean interval from diagnosis to recurrence or progression of 4.1 years. Twelve patients had biopsy-proven noninvasive urothelial carcinoma (Ta), 17 patients had cystoscopically detected recurrences (all were treated by fulguration without biopsy), and 4 patients developed invasive urothelial carcinoma (including two with muscle-invasive carcinoma). Twelve (75%) of 16 patients with biopsy-proven recurrence or progression had cancer dedifferentiation and resulting higher grade cancer than initial biopsies. Mean interval from initial diagnosis to development of invasive carcinoma was 13.3 years (range, 10 to 14 years). Three patients (3%) died of bladder cancer.

With 20 years of follow-up, Holmang and colleagues found that 14% of patients with noninvasive grade I urothelial carcinoma (pTa GI) died of bladder cancer.[51] In Greene's study of 100 patients with grade I cancer, 10 (10%) patients died of bladder cancer after more than 15 years; of 73 patients who had recurrences, 22% of recurrent cancers were higher grade than the original.[52] The mean interval from initial diagnosis to the development of invasive cancer (10 patients) was 8 years. Malmstrom and colleagues reported that five of 45 (11%) patients with stage pTa grade I urothelial carcinoma developed invasive urothelial carcinoma during a mean follow-up of 6.5 years.[53] Prout and colleagues reviewed a series of 178 patients with pTa grade I bladder cancer for the National Bladder Cancer Study Group and followed them for a median of 4.8 years; they found that 61% subsequently developed other papillary tumors, 16% progressed to higher grade, 4% developed invasive cancer, including three with muscle invasive cancer, and one

patient (0.5%) died of bladder cancer.[54] They concluded that "there are little data to support the use of the term papilloma to describe stage Ta grade I tumors without reservation," and "grade I tumors might best be referred to as Ta, grade I transitional cell tumors" rather than classified as papilloma. In England's study of 135 patients with grade I urothelial carcinoma (mean follow-up 9 years), 70% of patients had recurrence, including seven with cancer progression, and four died of bladder cancer; the mean interval from the time of diagnosis to cancer progression was 6 years.[55] Five-year recurrence-free survival was only 25% in Pocock's report of 34 patients with Ta grade I urothelial carcinoma.[56] Nine (5%) patients died of bladder cancer among 155 patients with grade I urothelial carcinoma.[57] Mufti and colleagues reviewed 198 patients with grade I urothelial carcinoma, and found that only 53% of patients remained cancer-free at 5 years; the actuarial cancer mortality rate was 4%.[48] Jordan and colleagues studied 91 patients with grade I papillary urothelial (transitional cell) tumors and found 40% of patients had recurrence.[43] Twenty percent of patients with recurrences developed high-grade (grade III) cancer, and four patients died of bladder cancer. Long-term follow-up is recommended for patient management. In a recent review of 152 patients with Ta grade I urothelial carcinoma, Leblanc and colleagues found that 83 patients (55%) had tumor recurrence after initial diagnosis, including 37% who had cancer progression. Patients who remained tumor-free for 1 year still had a 43% chance of late recurrence. In light of high risk for late recurrence and the potential to progress into muscle-invasive cancer, the authors concluded that Ta grade I tumor should be considered carcinoma and that lifelong periodic examination is warranted.

Grade II Urothelial Carcinoma

Diagnostic Criteria

Grade II carcinoma retains some of the orderly architectural appearance and maturation of grade I carcinoma, but displays at least focal moderate variation in orderliness, nuclear appearance, and chromatin texture that should be apparent at low magnification (Figure 7–5). Cytologic abnormalities are invariably present in grade II carcinoma, with moderate nuclear crowding, moderate variation in cell polarity, moderate nuclear hyperchromasia, moderate anisonucleosis, and mild nucleolar enlargement. Mitotic figures are usually limited to the lower half of the urothelium, but this is inconstant. Superficial cells are usually present, and the mucosa is predominantly cohesive, although variation may be present. Some tumors may be extremely orderly, reminiscent of grade I carcinoma, with only a small focus of obvious disorder or irregularity in cell spacing; these are considered grade II cancer, recognizing that grade is based on the highest level of abnormality present. Grade II carcinomas represent a wide spectrum of tumors that span the morphologic continuum from grade I to grade III.

Clinical Significance

Most cases of urothelial carcinoma are WHO grade II, and the outcome is significantly worse than those with lower grade papillary cancer. Recurrence risk for patients with noninvasive grade II cancer is 45 to 67%, with invasion occurring in up to 20% and cancer-specific death in 13 to 20% following surgical treatment.[42] Patients with grade II cancer and lamina propria invasion are at even greater risk, with recurrence in 67 to 80% of cases, development of muscle-invasive cancer in 21 to 49%, and cancer-specific death in 17 to 51% of those treated surgically.[42]

In order to improve stratification of the large WHO grade II group, some investigators subdivide these cases into two subgroups based on the degree of nuclear deviation and polarity of cells. In one

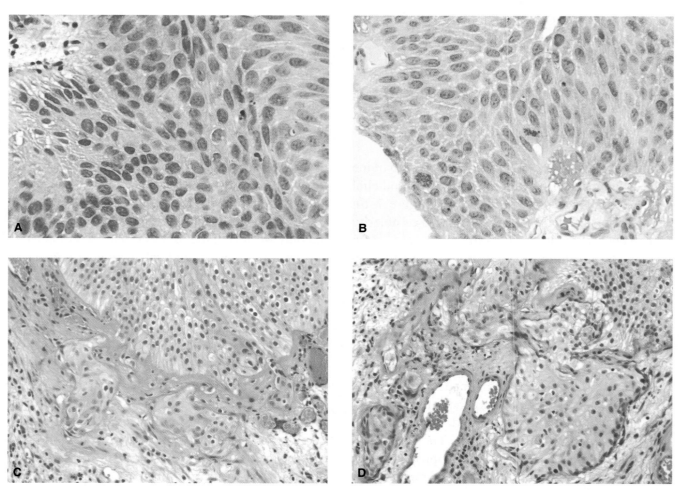

Figure 7–5. *A, B*: Grade II papillary urothelial carcinoma; *C, D*: Early lamina propria invasion with papillary grade II carcinoma (same case).

study, grade IIA consisted of urothelial cancer with slight cellular deviation, some variation in nuclear size, and normal polarity of cells, whereas grade IIB cancer had obvious variability in nuclear size and shape, with some loss of normal polarity.[58] Using this modification, the authors identified tumor progression in 4 and 33% of grade IIa and 2b cancer, respectively (all pTA and pT1).[58] This subdivision of grade II was also of prognostic significance for muscle-invasive cancer.[58,59]

Other investigators considered both nuclear pleomorphism and mitotic count as criteria for subdividing grade II urothelial cancer and were successful in identifying groups of cancers with different outcomes.[60] Grade IIA bladder cancer had a 5-year survival rate of 92 %, similar to grade I cancer, whereas grade IIB cancer was comparable to grade III cancer, with a 5-year survival rate of 43%.[61-63] This subdivision of grading was reproducible, with interobserver agreement of more than 90%.[60] Others found that mitotic index was the single most useful criterion for bladder cancer grading.[64,65]

Grade III Urothelial Carcinoma

Diagnostic Criteria

Grade III carcinoma displays the most extreme nuclear abnormalities among papillary urothelial cancers, similar to those seen in CIS (Figure 7–6). The obvious urothelial disorder and loss of polarity is present at scanning magnification and often includes loss of normal architecture and cell polarity, loss of cell cohesion, and frequent mitotic figures. Cellular anaplasia, characteristic of grade III carcinoma, is defined as increased cellularity, nuclear crowding, disturbance of cellular polarity, absence of differentiation from the base to the mucosal surface, nuclear pleomorphism, irregularity in the size of the cells, variation in nuclear shape and chromatin pattern, increased number of mitotic figures throughout the mucosa, and the occasional presence of neoplastic giant cells.[3] The superficial cell layer is usually partially or completely absent with grade III carcinoma, often accompanied by prominent cellular dyscohesion.

Clinical Significance

Recurrence risk for patients with noninvasive grade III cancer is 65 to 85%, with invasion occurring in 20 to 52% and cancer-specific death in up to 35% following surgical treatment.[42] Patients with grade III cancer and lamina propria invasion recur in 46 to 71% of cases, develop muscle-invasive cancer in 24 to 48%, and cancer-specific death in 25 to 71% of those treated surgically.[42]

VARIANTS OF UROTHELIAL CARCINOMA

There is a variety of unique variants of urothelial carcinoma, including those with mixed differentiation (Table 7–3). Recognition of some of these variants may be prognostically valuable. Two variants with a unique or unexpected immunophenotype are described below; the reader is referred to specialized texts of urologic pathology for details regarding the other variants.[66]

Small Cell Carcinoma (High-grade Neuroendocrine Carcinoma)

Urothelial carcinoma composed partially or completely of small cell undifferentiated carcinoma is rare, with increasing likelihood after therapy such as radiation therapy, similar to prostatic small cell carcinoma. The immunohistochemical findings are typical of small cell carcinoma at other sites, as is the aggressive clinical course (Table 7–4).[67-71]

Immunoreactivity for CD44v6 was absent in 25 of 27 cases of small cell carcinoma, with two showing only weak staining of fewer than 10% of cells; in contrast, all cases of moderately or poorly differentiated urothelial carcinoma displayed moderately intense reactivity in 50 to 100% of cells. CD44v6 immunostaining discriminated cases of poorly differentiated urothelial carcinoma from small cell carcinoma and highlighted the presence of mixed small cell urothelial differentiation when present.[70]

Small cell carcinoma of the bladder has a high number of genomic alterations (mean: 11.3 per tumor).[72] Deletions are most frequent at 10q (7 of 10 tumors deleted), 4q, 5q (5/10 each), and 13q (4/10). These regions may carry tumor suppressor genes with relevance for this particular tumor type. Gains of deoxyribonucleic acid (DNA) sequences were most prevalent at 8q (5/10), 5p, 6p, and 20q (4/10 each). High-level amplifications were found at 1p22-32, 3q26.3, 8q24, and 12q14–21. These loci may pinpoint the localization of oncogenes with relevance for small cell bladder cancer. The analysis of one tumor having areas of both small cell and urothelial carcinoma strongly suggests that small cell carcinoma can develop from urothelial carcinoma through the acquisition of additional genetic alterations.[72]

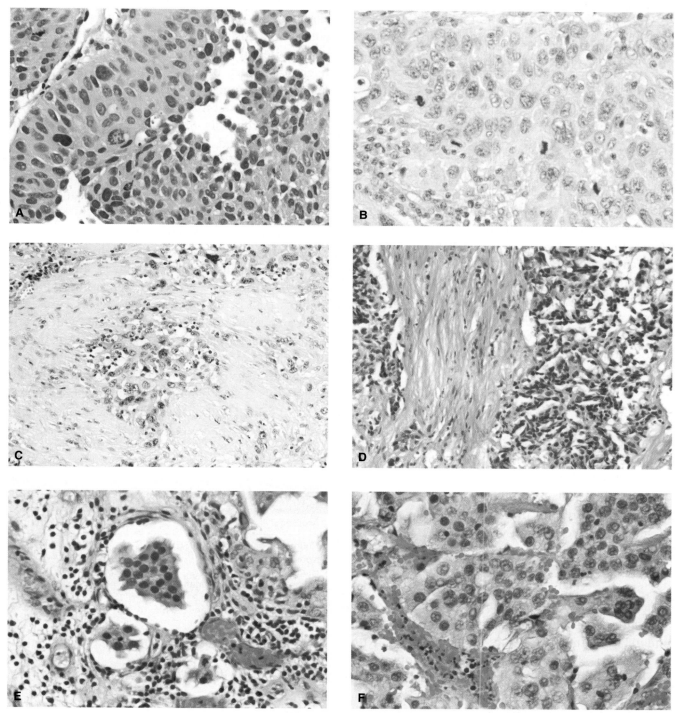

Figure 7–6.   *A, B*: Grade III carcinoma with marked cytologic atypia. *C, D*; Grade III carcinoma with muscularis propria invasion. *E, F*: Grade III carcinoma with vascular invasion.

Table 7–3. VARIANTS OF UROTHELIAL CARCINOMA

Nested
Micropapillary
Microcystic
Lymphoepithelioma-like
Lymphoma-like or plasmacytoma-like
Inverted papilloma-like
Urothelial carcinoma with syncytiotrophoblastic giant cells
Giant cell
Clear cell (glycogen-rich)
Sarcomatoid
Mixed differentiation
Carcinoma with tumor-associated stromal reaction

Urothelial Carcinoma with Syncytiotrophoblastic Giant Cells

Giant cells are present in about 12% of cases of urothelial carcinoma, occasionally producing substantial amounts of immunoreactive beta-human chorionic gonadotrophin (hCG), indicative of syncytiotrophoblastic differentiation.[73] The number of hCG-immunoreactive cells is inversely associated with cancer grade.[74] Secretion of hCG into the serum may be associated with a poor response to radiation therapy.[75] The most important differential diagnostic consideration is choriocarcinoma; most but not all cases previously reported as primary choriocarcinoma of the bladder represent urothelial carcinoma with syncytiotrophoblasts.

STAGING

Pathologic staging of bladder cancer is critical for stratifying patients for therapy and remains the single most important determinant of prognosis.[76,77] The pathologist plays a central role in this determination and, therefore, must have an understanding of staging and terminology (Table 7–5). Currently, the TNM 2002 classification is the main system in practice,[78] and the pathology report should indicate the specific stage as far as possible in bladder biopsy or transurethral resection specimens.[79]

Staging based on biopsies is imperfect, with understaging in up to 46% of cases.[80] Patients with invasion of the lamina propria on biopsy had tumor extending outside the bladder in 15 (27%) of 55 cases at radical cystectomy, and those with invasion of the muscularis propria on biopsy had tumor extending outside the bladder in 47 (49%) of

96 cases, including nodal metastasis in 22 (23%) of 96 cases.[80]

Gross Features of Invasive Carcinoma

Foci of invasion are often single and solid, comprising a variety of growth patterns, including papillary carcinoma. Commonly, there are nests and small clusters of cells that irregularly infiltrate the bladder wall and elicit a stromal fibrous response; alternatively, there may be solid diffuse growth with little intervening stroma. The pattern of growth is clinically important: a broad front of invasion has a more favorable prognosis than tentacular invasion.[17] In small, fragmented, and cauterized specimens, it may be particularly difficult to determine the presence or extent of subepithelial invasion. In such cases, we sometimes employ broad-spectrum antikeratin immunostaining (AE1/AE3) to identify epithelial differentiation in suspicious cells.

Invasive cancer tends to be high grade and is often deeply invasive (pT2 or higher), although rare cases have deceptively benign-appearing cytologic features (see below). In the majority of cases, the stroma contains a lymphocytic infiltrate with a variable number of plasma cells. The inflammation is usually mild to moderate and focal, although it may be severe, dense, and widespread. Neutrophils and eosinophils are rarely prominent unless there is coexistent cystitis. Urothelial carcinoma without inflammation may be more aggressive than inflamed can-

Table 7–4. IMMUNOHISTOCHEMISTRY OF SMALL CELL CARCINOMA OF THE URINARY BLADDER

Antibody	%Cases Staining
Neuron-specific enolase (NSE)	90
Neurofilament	84
Human milk fat globulin	67
Epithelial membrane antigen (EMA)	63
Keratin AE1/AE3; CAM 5.2	61
Carcinoembryonic antigen (CEA)	50
Synaptophysin	46
Leu -M1	43
Chromogranin	41
Serotonin	38
Leu-7	35
S-100 protein	34
Vasoactive intestinal peptide (VIP)	17
Vimentin	17
Adrenocorticotropin hormone (ACTH)	9

Table 7–5. PATHOLOGIC STAGING OF BLADDER CARCINOMA (TNM 2002)	
Noninvasive, papillary	Ta
Noninvasive, flat	TIS
Lamina propria	T1
Superficial muscularis propria	T2a
Deep muscularis propria	T2b
Perivesicle fat	T3
Adjacent structures	T4
Lymph node metastases	N1–3*
Distant metastases	M1

N1 = regional lymph node < 2 cm; N2 = regional lymph nodes 2–5 cm; N3 = regional lymph nodes > 5 cm or other lymph nodes.

cer.[81] Occasionally, mucoid cytoplasmic inclusions may be present, particularly in low-grade carcinoma.

Urothelial carcinoma may arise in a vesical diverticulum, with an incidence of 0.8 to 10%.[82,83] Most are noninvasive and can usually be treated conservatively by local resection and adjuvant intravesical chemotherapy. Regular cystoscopic examination is warranted for patients with diverticulum to exclude the possibility of cancer.

Lamina Propria Invasion

The lamina propria, located beneath the basement membrane, consists of a compact layer of fibrovascular connective tissue. It contains an incomplete muscularis mucosa composed of thin, delicate, smooth-muscle fibers that may be mistaken for muscularis propria in biopsy specimens. The muscularis mucosa is an important diagnostic pitfall in evaluating bladder carcinoma, because the management of cancer invading the muscularis propria is different from that of tumors limited to the lamina propria and surrounding the muscularis mucosa. Therefore, it is important for pathologists to be aware of the existence of delicate muscle bundles within the lamina propria. In biopsy specimens, these smooth-muscle fibers may appear as a continuous layer, a discontinuous or interrupted layer, or as scattered thin bundles of smooth-muscle fibers that do not form an obvious layer. The muscle fibers lie parallel to the mucosal surface, midway between the epithelium and the underlying muscularis propria. Large blood vessels are a constant feature, running parallel to the surface urothelium in close association with the fibers of the muscularis mucosa. To avoid overstag-

ing bladder cancer, it is important for the pathologist to be aware of the existence of fat within the lamina propria and the muscularis propria.[84]

There is a significant difference in outcome between urothelial carcinoma that does not penetrate beyond the basement membrane (pTa) and cancer that invades the lamina propria (pT1). Up to 46% of patients with pT1 cancers progress to muscle invasion.

Recent studies have emphasized the importance of the muscularis mucosa in substaging pT1. Younes and colleagues subdivided the pT1 group into the following: T1a– invasion of connective tissue superficial to the muscularis mucosae; T1b– invasion to the level of the muscularis mucosae; and T1c– invasion through the muscularis mucosae but superficial to the muscularis propria.[85–87] These authors demonstrated that 75% of patients with T1a or T1b cancer survived at least 5 years, whereas only 11% of those with T1c cancer survived.

Absolute depth of invasion may be more important than level of invasion according to the muscularis mucosa. Microinvasive carcinoma of the urinary bladder was defined almost two decades ago as invasion into the lamina propria to a depth of no more than 5 mm from the basement membrane.[17,38] In these classic studies, cystectomy specimens with urothelial CIS were totally embedded, with extensive CIS involving at least 25% of the bladder. Of 70 cases, 24 contained microinvasion, and two patients died of cancer. Recently, the depth of invasion was evaluated in a large series of T1 cancers treated by transurethral resections; researchers found that the depth of invasion when measured by ocular micrometer was predictive of cancer progression with a mean length of follow-up of 5.2 years.[86] The overall 5- and 7-year progression-free survival rates were 82 and 80%, respectively. The depth of invasion in the transurethral resection of bladder tumor (TURB) specimens was associated with cancer progression (hazards ratio, 1.6 for doubling of depth of invasion; 95% confidence interval, 1.03 to 2.4; $p = .037$). The 5-year progression-free survival rate for patients with depth of invasion of $>/= 1.5$ mm was 67%, compared with 93% for those with depth of invasion of less than 1.5 mm ($p = .009$). No other variable, including age, sex, tobacco use, alcohol use, the presence of CIS, histologic grade, lymphocytic infiltration, or muscularis mucosae invasion, was associated with cancer progression.[86]

Vascular/Lymphatic Invasion of the Lamina Propria

The presence of vascular/lymphatic invasion in the lamina propria is predictive of poor outcome, and this finding should be included in the pathology report.[88] Identification of vascular/lymphatic invasion may be difficult and can be confused with artifactual clefting around nests of invasive carcinoma, including perineural invasion.[88] The incidence of vascular/lymphatic invasion is variable, reportedly as high as 7% of cases. Immunohistochemical studies directed against endothelial cells that employ Ulex europaeus lectin, Factor VIII, CD31, or CD34 may be of value in identifying vascular/lymphatic invasion but are rarely used, although less than 40% of cases with vascular/lymphatic invasion by routine light microscopic examination can be confirmed immunohistochemically.[89] Invasion is an important predictor of patient outcome regardless of tumor grade.[88,90]

Muscularis Propria Invasion

The muscle proper of the bladder, the muscularis propria, is moderately thick and consists of an inner longitudinal layer, middle circular layer, and outer longitudinal layer. It spirals around each ureteral orifice and increases in thickness around the internal urethral orifice, forming the internal sphincter of the bladder. The muscularis is surrounded by a coat of fibroelastic connective tissue, the adventitia, and perivesical fat.

One of the most important tasks for staging in bladder biopsies and transurethral resections is determination of whether the muscularis propria has been invaded.[91] Abutment is not considered evidence of invasion, although we document this finding when present to alert the clinician to the possibility of invasion in tissue that is not sampled. Invasion of the muscularis propria is defined as the presence of cancer cells within dense muscle bundles; the delicate muscle fibers of the muscularis mucosa are the single greatest mimic.

Contemporary staging of muscularis propria invasion includes separation of invasion of the superficial half from the deep half; this separation is virtually impossible in biopsy or transurethral resection specimens and is not undertaken in routine practice. In cystectomy specimens, this separation can be attempted, but it is often difficult, and reproducibility has not been tested.

Prostatic Involvement by Urothelial Cancer

Prostatic involvement by urothelial carcinoma is common, with a 52% overall 5-year cancer-specific survival rate.[92–95] In patients with muscle-invasive bladder cancer, the prostate is involved in up to 50% of cases, and the frequency is even higher in those who have multifocal CIS of the bladder.

Prostatic involvement is classified into four TNM staging groups and is the strongest predictor of patient survival: (1) carcinoma confined to the prostatic urethral lining (Tis pu); (2) carcinoma extending into ducts and acini, but confined by the basement membrane (Tis pd); (3) carcinoma invading subepithelial connective tissue (T1); and (4) carcinoma that invades the prostatic stroma (T2). Metastases are most likely with prostatic stromal invasion. The presence of prostatic urethral CIS indicates a high risk for urethral recurrence after radical surgery.[92–95] Prostatic stromal invasion is a strong predictor of poor patient survival.[92–95] Concurrent prostatic adenocarcinoma is present in 8 to 33% of patients.[92]

Prognosis of Urothelial Cancer

The prognosis for patients with invasive urothelial carcinoma is poor, with 5-year survival of less than 50% despite therapy.[88]

Numerous pathologic factors have been shown in select cohorts of patients with bladder cancer to correlate with recurrence, progression, and survival (Tables 7–6 and 7–7). The immune response to the tumor, as measured by immunohistochemical staining for lymphocytes and antigen-presenting dendritic cells, is useful in predicting recurrence.[81] The number of papillary tumors also predicts recurrence but does not appear to be a significant determinant of invasive cancer.[96] Patients with single foci of papillary cancer develop recurrence after transurethral

Table 7–6. FACTORS PREDICTIVE OF RECURRENCE AND PROGRESSION IN UROTHELIAL CARCINOMA WITHOUT MUSCLE INVASION

Number of tumors
Cancer size > 5 cm diameter
Depth of invasion (lamina propria, muscularis mucosae)
Histologic grade
Coexistent dysplasia or carcinoma in situ
Recurrence at 3-month follow-up cystoscopy
Epidermal growth factor receptor expression
Loss of surface blood group antigens
Aneuploidy
*P*53 expression

resection in 45% of cases; however, patients who develop a second tumor have an 84% risk of developing a third tumor. Tumors larger than 5 cm in diameter also increase the risk of muscle invasion.[97,98] Tumor recurrence more than 4 years after resection of the primary tumor is an ominous sign.[99,100] It is important to exclude dysplasia or CIS in the adjacent mucosa or elsewhere in the bladder, as this is a significant factor predictive of recurrence and invasion.[101,102]

Cancer involves regional lymph nodes in 25% of cases in stages pT2 to pT4, and in rare pT1 cases. Implantation metastases after TURB or biopsy and distant metastases in rare locations are more common in high-grade urothelial carcinoma.[103–108]

URACHAL CANCER: PATHOLOGY AND STAGING

Malignancy of the urachus is rare and carries a poor prognosis.[109] The incidence of urachal carcinoma varies from 0.07 to 0.7% of bladder cancers in North America and Europe, but as high as 1.2% in Japan.[110] Most urachal malignancies involve the urinary bladder, creating the difficult problem of classification and separation from primary tumors of the bladder,

Table 7–7. FACTORS PREDICTIVE OF SURVIVAL IN UROTHELIAL CARCINOMA WITH MUSCLE INVASION

Cancer size
Histologic grade
Depth of invasion
Pattern of invasion
Vascular/ lymphatic invasion
Lymph node involvement
*P*53 expression

particularly those at the dome. However, most urachal cancers are adenocarcinoma, in contrast with typical urothelial carcinoma of the bladder.

Criteria for separating adenocarcinoma of the urinary bladder and urachus are summarized in Tables 7–8 and 7–9.[66] Ultimately, advanced cancer in the dome of the bladder may not be distinguishable as vesical or urachal in origin. Unless the evidence of urachal origin is strong for urothelial and squamous cell carcinomas in this area, they are generally assumed to be of bladder mucosal origin. A metachronous urothelial carcinoma of the bladder and urachus has been reported.[111] The staging of urachal carcinoma is similar regardless of histologic subtype (Table 7–10).

Differential diagnostic considerations include metastases or contiguous spread from colorectal adenocarcinoma; this is usually easily distinguished clinically. Unlike colonic adenocarcinoma, urachal and urinary bladder cancers do not produce sulfated acid mucopolysaccharides.

CELL-BASED MORPHOLOGIC FINDINGS IN BLADDER CARCINOMA

Many new biomarkers are now available and routinely used, and some are touted as superior to urine cytology in select patient cohorts.[112–115] Most studies provide sensitivity and specificity data, with low sensitivity indicating numerous false-negative results (undetected cancer) and low specificity indicating numerous false-positive results (presumptive overdiagnosis of cancer, leading to unnecessary investigation such as cystoscopy).[116–122] Different studies

Table 7–8. DIAGNOSTIC CRITERIA FOR URACHAL ORIGIN OF ADENOCARCINOMA

Cancer located in the dome or anterior wall of the bladder
Absence of cystitis cystica or cystitis glandularis in region of dome
Predominant involvement of the muscularis propria by cancer rather than the lamina propria (submucosa). The vesical mucosal surface may be intact or ulcerated
Urachal remnant connected with cancer
Presence of a suprapubic mass
Cancer infiltrating through the bladder wall, with contiguous spread through the space of Retzius in the anterior abdominal wall
Sharp demarcation between the cancer and the overlying urothelium of the bladder dome

Table 7–9.   CRITERIA TO DISTINGUISH URACHAL AND NONURACHAL ADENOCARCINOMA OF THE BLADDER

Location in bladder dome or anterior wall
Cancer is chiefly intramural, with deep ramifications in the
  bladder wall
Absence of intestinal metaplasia in urothelium
Other primary sites excluded

may not be comparable owing to important issues such as patient selection and ascertainment biases, limited number of patients, limited length of follow-up, lack of central pathology review, sampling variation with different techniques, variance in assays,[123] and different thresholds for test result reporting. Decision analysis models by Lotan and Roehrborn indicate that the use of urine-based cancer markers may be cost-effective when alternating with cystoscopy and/or cytology.[124] The discussion herein is limited to commonly employed cytologic tissue findings; elsewhere in this volume is a complete treatise on markers in bladder cancer (see Chapter 10).

Summary

The evolution of a staging system for the classification and grading of urothelial malignancies represents a partnership between urologists and pathologists. Each enhances the other's understanding of the biologic aspects of the various forms of bladder cancer, the intrinsic biologic potential of the forms, the significance of the "snapshot" that the resected specimen provides in assessing the evolution of the malignant diathesis, the prognosis implied by histologic observations, and the treatments that might be considered in view of pathologic findings, implied intrinsic biologic potential, and individual's past history. The most recent consensus conferences have

integrated current clinical and pathologic observations in updating the classification system for these tumors. Undoubtedly, new information on molecular and genetic aspects of the pathogenesis of urothelial cancer will be incorporated into future classification systems as we become better able to refine and obtain greater precision in our understanding of a particular tumor diathesis. The partnership that has enhanced our ability to assess various forms of urothelial cancer, and thereby treat patients with enhanced individualization and greater accuracy, is critical in maintaining our understanding of this intriguing cancer problem.

REFERENCES

1. Oyasu R. World Health Organization and International Society of Urological Pathology classification and two-number grading system of bladder tumors. Cancer 2000;88:1509–12.
2. Sobin LH. The WHO histological classification of urinary bladder tumours. Urol Res 1978;6:193–5.
3. Mostofi FK, Sobin LH. Histologic typing of urinary bladder tumors. Geneva: World Health Organization; 1973.
4. Epstein JI, Amin MB, Reuter VR, Mostofi FK. The World Health Organization/International Society of Urological Pathology consensus classification of urothelial (transitional cell) neoplasms of the urinary bladder. Bladder Consensus Conference Committee. Am J Surg Pathol 1998;22:1435–48.
5. Holmang S, Andius P, Hedelin H, et al. Stage progression in Ta papillary urothelial tumors: relationship to grade, immunohistochemical expression of tumor markers, mitotic frequency and DNA ploidy. J Urol 2001;165:1124–30.
6. Reuter VE, Epstein JI, Amin MB, Mostofi FK. The WHO/ISUP Consensus Classification of Urothelial (Transitional Cell) Neoplasms: continued discussion. Hum Pathol 1999;30:879–80.
7. Mostofi FK, David C, Sesterhenn I. Histologic typing of urinary bladder tumors. World Health Organization. Berlin: Springer-Verlag; 1999.
8. Cheng L, Mostofi FK, David C, Sesterhenn I. Flat intraepithelial lesions of the urinary bladder. Cancer 2000;88:625–31.
9. Elliott GB, Moloney PJ, Anderson GH. "Denuding cystitis" and in situ urothelial carcinoma. Arch Pathol 1973;96:91–4.
10. Murphy WM, Soloway MS. Urothelial dysplasia. J Urol 1982;127:849–54.
11. Cheng L, Cheville JC, Nuemann RM, Bostwick DG. Natural history of urothelial dysplasia of the bladder. Am J Surg Pathol 1999;23:443–7.
12. Zuk RJ, et al. Clinicopathological importance of primary dysplasia of bladder. J Clin Pathol 1988:41:1277–80.
13. Baithun SI, Rogers HS, Martin JE, Zuk RJ. Primary dysplasia of bladder. Lancet 1988;i:483.
14. Zincke H, Utz DC, Farrow GM. Review of Mayo Clinic experience with carcinoma in situ. Urology 1985;26 Suppl 4:39–46.

Table 7–10.   STAGING OF URACHAL ADENOCARCINOMA

Stage I	Carcinoma confined to the urachal mucosa
Stage II	Invasion confined to the urachus
Stage III	Local extension
Stage IIIA	Extension into urinary bladder
III B	Extension into abdominal wall
IIIC	Extension into the peritoneum
IIID	Extension into other viscera
Stage IV	Metastasis
IVA	Metastasis to regional lymph nodes
IVB	Metastasis to distant sites

15. Farrow GM, Utz DC, Rife CC. Clinical observations on sixty-nine cases of in situ carcinoma of the urinary bladder. Cancer Res 1977;37(Pt 2):2794–8.

16. Farrow GM, Barlebo H, Enjoji M, et al. Transitional cell carcinoma in situ. Prog Clin Biol Res 1986;221:85–96.

17. Farrow, GM. Pathology of carcinoma in situ of the urinary bladder and related lesions. J Cell Biochem Suppl 1992; 16:39–43.

18. Orozco RE, Martin AA, Murphy WM. Carcinoma in situ of the urinary bladder. Clues to host involvement in human carcinogenesis. Cancer 1994;74:115–22.

19. Hudson MA, Herr HW. Carcinoma in situ of the bladder. J Urol 1995;153(Pt 1):564–72.

20. Amling CL, Thrasher JB, Frazier HA, et al. Radical cystectomy for stages Ta, Tis and T1 transitional cell carcinoma of the bladder. J Urol 1994;151:31–6.

21. Silver DA, Stroumbakis N, Russo P, et al. Ureteral carcinoma in situ at radical cystectomy: does the margin matter? J Urol 1997;158(Pt 1):768–71.

22. Cheng L, Cheville JC, Neumann RM, et al. Survival of patients with carcinoma in situ of the urinary bladder. Cancer 1999;85:2469–74.

23. Koss LG. Carcinoma of the bladder in situ. JAMA 1969; 207:1919.

24. Koss LG, Tiamson EM, Robbins MA. Mapping cancerous and precancerous bladder changes. A study of the urothelium in ten surgically removed bladders. JAMA 1974;227:281–6.

25. Koss LG, Nakanishi I, Freed SZ. Nonpapillary carcinoma in situ and atypical hyperplasia in cancerous bladders: further studies of surgically removed bladders by mapping. Urology 1977;9:442–55.

26. Koss LG. Evaluation of patients with carcinoma in situ of the bladder. Pathol Annu 1982;17(Pt 2):353–9.

27. Koss LG. Minimal neoplasia as a challenge for early cancer detection. Recent Results Cancer Res 1988;106:1–8.

28. Lamm DL. Carcinoma in situ. Urol Clin North Am 1992;19: 499–508.

29. Melamed MR, Grabstald H, Whitmore WF Jr. Carcinoma in situ of bladder: clinico-pathologic study of case with a suggested approach to detection. J Urol 1966;96:466–71.

30. Melamed MR, Voutsa NG, Grabstald H. Natural history and clinical behavior of in situ carcinoma of the human urinary bladder. 1964. CA Cancer J Clin 1993;43:348–70.

31. Nagy GK, Frable WJ, Murphy WM. Classification of premalignant urothelial abnormalities. A Delphi study of the National Bladder Cancer Collaborative Group A. Pathol Annu 1982;17(Pt 1):219–33.

32. Murphy WM, Busch C, Algaba F. Intraepithelial lesions of urinary bladder: morphologic considerations. Scand J Urol Nephrol Suppl 2000;205:67–81.

33. Riddle PR, Chisholm GD, Trott PA, Pugh RC. Flat carcinoma in situ of bladder. Br J Urol 1975;7:829–33.

34. Stanisic TH, Donovan JM, Lebouton J, Graham AR. 5-year experience with intravesical therapy of carcinoma in situ: an inquiry into the risks of "conservative" management. J Urol 1987;138:1158–61.

35. Utz DC, Hanash KA, Farrow GM. The plight of the patient with carcinoma in situ of the bladder. J Urol 1970;103:160–4.

36. Utz DC, Zincke H. The masquerade of bladder cancer in situ as interstitial cystitis. J Urol 1974;111:160–1.

37. Utz DC, Farrow GM. Management of carcinoma in situ of the bladder: the case for surgical management. Urol Clin North Am 1980;7:533–41.

38. Utz DC, Farrow GM. Carcinoma in situ of the urinary tract. Urol Clin North Am 1984;11:735–40.

39. Murphy WM, Farrow GM, Beckwith B. Renal and bladder tumors. Armed Forces Institute of Pathology Fascile Series. Washington: American Registry of Pathology; 1994.

40. Reuter VE, Melamed MR. The urothelial tract: renal pelvis, ureter, urinary bladder, and urethra. In: Sternberg SS, editor. Diagnostic surgical pathology. 3rd ed. Philadelphia: Lippincott Williams & Wilkins; 1999. p. 1853–1972.

41. Eble JN, Young RH. Benign and low-grade papillary lesions of the urinary bladder: a review of the papilloma-papillary carcinoma controversy, and a report of five typical papillomas. Semin Diagn Pathol 1989;6:351–71.

42. Bostwick DG. Natural history of early bladder cancer. J Cell Biochem Suppl 1992;16:31–8.

43. Jordan AM, Weingarten J, Murphy WM. Transitional cell neoplasms of the urinary bladder. Can biologic potential be predicted from histologic grading? Cancer 1987;60:2766–74.

44. Miller A, Mitchell JP, Brown NJ. The Bristol Bladder Tumour Registry. Br J Urol 1969;41 (Suppl):1–64.

45. Bergkvist A, Ljungqvist A, Moberger G. Classification of bladder tumours based on the cellular pattern. Preliminary report of a clinical-pathological study of 300 cases with a minimum follow-up of eight years. Acta Chir Scand 1965;130:371–8.

46. Buerger L. The pathological diagnosis of tumors of the bladder with particular reference to papilloma and carcinoma. Surg Gynecol Oncol 1915;21:179–98.

47. Cheng L, Darson M, Cheville JC, et al. Urothelial papilloma of the bladder. Clinical and biologic implications. Cancer 1999;86:2098–101.

48. Mufti GR, Virdi JS, Singh M. "Solitary" Ta-T1 G1 bladder tumour—history and long-term prognosis. Eur Urol 1990;18:101–6.

49. Page BH, Levison VB, Curwen MP. The site of recurrence of non-infiltrating bladder tumours. Br J Urol 1978;50: 237–42.

50. Cheng L, Neumann RM, Bostwick DG. Papillary urothelial neoplasms of low malignant potential. Clinical and biologic implications. Cancer 1999;86:2102–8.

51. Holmang S, Hedelin H, Anderstrom C, Johansson SL. The relationship among multiple recurrences, progression and prognosis of patients with stages Ta and T1 transitional cell cancer of the bladder followed for at least 20 years. J Urol 1995:153:1823—7.

52. Greene LF, Hanash KA, Farrow GM. Benign papilloma or papillary carcinoma of the bladder? J Urol 1973;110:205–7.

53. Malmstrom PU, Busch C, Norlen BJ. Recurrence, progression and survival in bladder cancer. A retrospective analysis of 232 patients with greater than or equal to 5-year follow-up. Scand J Urol Nephrol 1987;21:185–95.

54. Prout GR Jr, Barton BA, Griffin PP, Friedell GH. Treated history of noninvasive grade 1 transitional cell carcinoma. The National Bladder Cancer Group. J Urol 1992;148:1413–9.

55. England HR, Paris AM, Blandy JP. The correlation of T1 bladder tumour history with prognosis and follow-up requirements. Br J Urol 1981;53:593–7.

56. Pocock RD, Ponder BA, O'Sullivan JP, et al. Prognostic factors in non-infiltrating carcinoma of the bladder: a preliminary report. Br J Urol 1982;54:711–5.

57. Gilbert HA, Logan JL, Kagan AR, et al. The natural history of papillary transitional cell carcinoma of the bladder and its treatment in an unselected population on the basis of histologic grading. J Urol 1978;119:488–92.

58. Pauwels RP, Schapers RF, Smeets AW, et al. Grading in superficial bladder cancer. (1). Morphological criteria. Br J Urol 1988;61:129–34.

59. Schapers RF, Pauwels RP, Wignen JT, et al. A simplified grading method of transitional cell carcinoma of the urinary bladder: reproducibility, clinical significance and comparison with other prognostic parameters. Br J Urol 1994;73:625–31.

60. Carbin BE, Ekman P, Gustafson H, et al. Grading of human urothelial carcinoma based on nuclear atypia and mitotic frequency. I. Histological description. J Urol 1991;145:968–71.

61. Jakse G, Loidl W, Seeber G, Hofstader F. Stage T1, grade 3 transitional cell carcinoma of the bladder: an unfavorable tumor? J Urol 1987;137:39–43.

62. Kakizoe T, Friedell GH, Soloway MS, et al. Report of the 1991 International Meeting on Fundamental and Clinical Research in Urogenital Cancer. Jpn J Clin Oncol 1992;22:60–5.

63. Takashi M, Sakata T, Murase T, et al. Grade 3 bladder cancer with lamina propria invasion (pT1): characteristics of tumor and clinical course. Nagoya J Med Sci 1991;53:1–8.

64. Lipponen PK, Eskelinen MJ, Kiviranta J, Pesonen E. Prognosis of transitional cell bladder cancer: a multivariate prognostic score for improved prediction. J Urol 1991;146:1535–40.

65. Lipponen PK, Eskelinen MJ, Nordling S. Progression and survival in transitional cell bladder cancer: a comparison of established prognostic factors, S-phase fraction and DNA ploidy. Eur J Cancer 1991;27:877–81.

66. Bostwick DG, Lopez-Beltran A. bladder biopsy interpretation. Glen Allen (VA): United Pathologists Press; 1999.

67. Jones EC, Clement PB, Young RH. Inflammatory pseudotumor of the urinary bladder. A clinicopathological, immunohistochemical, ultrastructural, and flow cytometric study of 13 cases [comment]. Am J Surg Pathol 1993;17:264–74.

68. Yamaguchi T, Imamura Y, Shimamoto T, et al. Small cell carcinoma of the bladder. Two cases diagnosed by urinary cytology. Acta Cytol 2000;44:403–9.

69. Eusebi V, Damiani S, Pasquinelli G, et al. Small cell neuroendocrine carcinoma with skeletal muscle differentiation: report of three cases. Am J Surg Pathol 2000;24:223–30.

70. Iczkowski KA, Shanks JH, Bostwick DG. Loss of CD44 variant 6 expression differentiates small cell carcinoma of urinary bladder from urothelial (transitional cell) carcinoma. Histopathology 1998;32:322–7.

71. Ali SZ, Reuter VE, Zakowski MF. Small cell neuroendocrine carcinoma of the urinary bladder. A clinicopathologic study with emphasis on cytologic features. Cancer 1997;79:356–61.

72. Terracciano L, Richter J, Tornillo L, et al. Chromosomal imbalances in small cell carcinomas of the urinary bladder. J Pathol 1999;189:230–5.

73. Grammatico D, Grignon DJ, Eberwein P, et al. Transitional cell carcinoma of the renal pelvis with choriocarcinomatous differentiation. Immunohistochemical and immuno-electron microscopic assessment of human chorionic gonadotropin production by transitional cell carcinoma of the urinary bladder. Cancer 1993;71:1835–41.

74. Yamase HT, Wurzel RS, Nieh PT, Gondos BY. Immunohistochemical demonstration of human chorionic gonadotropin in tumors of the urinary bladder. Ann Clin Lab Sci 1985;15:414–7.

75. Martin JE, Jenkins BJ, Zuk RJ, et al. Human chorionic gonadotrophin expression and histological findings as predictors of response to radiotherapy in carcinoma of the bladder. Virchows Arch A Pathol Anat Histopathol 1989;414:273–7.

76. Lapham RL, Ro JY, Staerkel GA, Ayala AG. Pathology of transitional cell carcinoma of the bladder and its clinical implications. Semin Surg Oncol 1997;13:307–18.

77. Lapham RL, Grignon D, Ro JY. Pathologic prognostic parameters in bladder urothelial biopsy, transurethral resection, and cystectomy specimens. Semin Diagn Pathol 1997;14:109–22.

78. AJCC Cancer Staging Manual. 6th ed. New York: Springer-Verlag; 2002.

79. Witjes JA, Kiemeney LA, Schaafsma HE, Debruyn FM. The influence of review pathology on study outcome of a randomized multicentre superficial bladder cancer trial. Members of the Dutch South East Cooperative Urological Group. Br J Urol 1994;73:172–6.

80. Chang BS, Kim HL, Yang XJ, Steinberg GD. Correlation between biopsy and radical cystectomy in assessing grade and depth of invasion in bladder urothelial carcinoma. Urology 2001;57:1063–7.

81. Lopez-Beltran A, Morales C, Reymundo C, Toro M. T-zone histiocytes and recurrence of papillary urothelial bladder carcinoma. Urol Int 1989;44:205–9.

82. Shah B, Rodriguez R, Krasnokutsk S, et al. Tumour in a giant bladder diverticulum: a case report and review of literature. Int Urol Nephrol 1997;29:173–9.

83. Baniel J, Vishna T. Primary transitional cell carcinoma in vesical diverticula. Urology 1997;50:697–9.

84. Bochner BH, et al. Angiogenesis in bladder cancer: relationship between microvessel density and tumor prognosis. J Natl Cancer Inst 1995;87:1603–12.

85. Younes M, Sussman T, True LD. The usefulness of the level of the muscularis mucosae in staging of invasive transitional cell carcinoma of the urinary bladder. Cancer 1990;66:542–8.

86. Cheng L, et al. Predicting cancer progression in patients with stage T1 bladder carcinoma. J Clin Oncol 1999;17:3182–7.

87. Diaz-Cano SJ, et al. Molecular evolution and intratumor heterogeneity by topographic compartments in muscle-invasive transitional cell carcinoma of the urinary bladder. Lab Invest 2000;80:279–89.

88. Lopez JI, Angulo JC. The prognostic significance of vascular invasion in stage T1 bladder cancer. Histopathology 1995;27:27–33.

89. Deen S, Ball RY. Basement membrane and extracellular interstitial matrix components in bladder neoplasia—evidence of angiogenesis. Histopathology 1994;25:475–81.

90. Jaeger TM, et al. Tumor angiogenesis correlates with lymph node metastases in invasive bladder cancer. J Urol 1995;154:69–71.

91. Rodriguez V, Sanchez-Martin FM, Redorta JP. Transurethral resection versus transurethral incision in benign prostate hypertrophy—critical assessment. Arch Esp Urol 1994; 47:915–24.

92. Cheville JC, Dundore PA, Bostwick DG, et al. Transitional cell carcinoma of the prostate: clinicopathologic study of 50 cases. Cancer 1998;82:703–7.

93. Sakamoto N, Tsuneyoshi M, Naito S. An adequate sampling of the prostate to identify prostatic involvement by urothelial carcinoma in bladder cancer patients. J Urol 1993;149:318–21.

94. Solsona E, Iborra I, Ricos JV, et al. The prostate involvement as prognostic factor in patients with superficial bladder tumors. J Urol 1995;154:1710–3.

95. Hardeman SW, Perry A, Soloway MS. Transitional cell carcinoma of the prostate following intravesical therapy for transitional cell carcinoma of the bladder. J Urol 1988; 140:289–92.

96. Lutzeyer W, Rubben H, Dahm H. Prognostic parameters in superficial bladder cancer: an analysis of 315 cases. J Urol 1982;127:250–2.

97. Heney NM, Ahmed S, Flanagan MJ, et al. Superficial bladder cancer: progression and recurrence. J Urol 1983;130: 1083–6.

98. Heney NM, Proppe K, Prout GR Jr, et al. Invasive bladder cancer: tumor configuration, lymphatic invasion and survival. J Urol 1983;130:895–7.

99. Holmang S, Hedelin H, Anderstrom C, et al. The importance of the depth of invasion in stage T1 bladder carcinoma: a prospective cohort study. J Urol 1997;157:800–4.

100. Morris SB, Gordon EM, Shearer RJ, Woodhouse CR. Superficial bladder cancer: for how long should a tumour-free patient have check cystoscopies? Br J Urol 1995;75:193–6.

101. Kiemeney LA, Witjes JA, Heijbroek RP, et al. Should random urothelial biopsies be taken from patients with primary superficial bladder cancer? A decision analysis. Members of the Dutch South-East Co-Operative Urological Group. Br J Urol 1994;73:164–71.

102. Kiemeney LA, Witjes JA, Heijbroek RP, et al. Dysplasia in normal-looking urothelium increases the risk of tumour progression in primary superficial bladder cancer. Eur J Cancer 1994;30A:1621–5.

103. Anderson RS, el-Mahdi AM, Kuban DA, Higgins EM. Brain metastases from transitional cell carcinoma of urinary bladder. Urology 1992;39:17–20.

104. Doval DC, Naresh KN, Sabitha KS, et al. Carcinoma of the urinary bladder metastatic to the oral cavity. Indian J Cancer 1994;31:8–11.

105. Mahmoud-Ahmed AS, et al. Brain metastases from bladder carcinoma: presentation, treatment and survival. J Urol 2002;167:2419–22.

106. Adriazola Semino M, Ortiz Cabria R, Garcia Cobo E, et al. Distal bone metastases of transitional-cell carcinoma of the bladder. Apropos of a case. Arch Esp Urol 2002;55: 69–70.

107. Herr HW, Bochner BH, Dalbagni G, et al. Impact of the number of lymph nodes retrieved on outcome in patients with muscle invasive bladder cancer. J Urol 2002;167:1295–8.

108. Wurdinger S, Schutz K, Fuchs D, Kaiser WA. Two cases of metastases to the breast on MR mammography. Eur Radiol 2001;11:802–6.

109. Lane V. Prognosis in carcinoma of the urachus. Eur Urol 1976;2:282–3.

110. Ghazizadeh M, Yamamoto S, Kurokawa K. Clinical features of urachal carcinoma in Japan: review of 157 patients. Urol Res 1983;11:235–8.

111. Satake I, Nakagomi K, Tari K, Kishi K. Metachronous transitional cell carcinoma of the urachus and bladder. Br J Urol 1995;75:244.

112. Tiguert R, Fradet Y. New diagnostic and prognostic tools in bladder cancer. Curr Opin Urol 2002;12:239–43.

113. Tiguert R, Lessard A, So A, Fradet Y. Prognostic markers in muscle invasive bladder cancer. World J Urol 2002;20: 190–5.

114. Kausch I, Ardelt P, Bohle A, Ratliff TL. Immune gene therapy in urology. Curr Urol Rep 2002;3:82–9.

115. Kausch I, Bohle A. Molecular aspects of bladder cancer III. Prognostic markers of bladder cancer. Eur Urol 2002;41: 15–29.

116. Droller MJ. Current concepts of tumor markers in bladder cancer. Urol Clin North Am 2002;29:229–34.

117. Droller MJ. Frequency of positive biopsies after visual disappearance of superficial bladder cancer marker lesions. J Urol 2002;168:2303.

118. Droller MJ. Integrated therapy for locally advanced bladder cancer: final report of a randomized trial of cystectomy plus adjuvant M-VAC versus cystectomy with both preoperative and postoperative M-VAC. J Urol 2002;168: 2307–8.

119. Droller MJ. Plenary debate of randomized phase III trial of neoadjuvant MVAC plus cystectomy versus cystectomy alone in patients with locally advanced bladder cancer. J Urol 2002;168:2308–9.

120. Droller MJ. Prognostic significance of platelet-derived endothelial cell growth factor/thymidine phosphorylase expression in stage pT1 G3 bladder cancer. J Urol 2002; 168:854.

121. Droller MJ. Risk of continued intravesical therapy and delayed cystectomy in the BCG-refractory superficial bladder cancer: an investigational approach. J Urol 2002; 168:858–9.

122. Droller MJ. A study comparing various noninvasive methods of detecting bladder cancer in urine. J Urol 2002;168: 2303–4.

123. Albert PS, McShane LM, Shih JH. Latent class modeling approaches for assessing diagnostic error without a gold standard: with applications to p53 immunohistochemical assays in bladder tumors. Biometrics 2001;57:610–9.

124. Lotan Y, Roehrborn CG. Cost-effectiveness of a modified care protocol substituting bladder tumor markers for cystoscopy for the followup of patients with transitional cell carcinoma of the bladder: a decision analytical approach. J Urol 2002;167:75–9.

8

Urinary Cytology, Cytometry, and New Approaches in the Assessment and Monitoring of Urothelial Cancer

HANS WIJKSTRÖM, MD, PhD
BARBARA Du REITZ, MD
ANNA TOLF, MD

It has been over 100 years since neoplastic cells were first recognized in the urine[1] and well over 50 years since the clinical usefulness of analyzing cytologic smears in patients with urinary tract cancers was described more extensively.[2]

Today pathological consultations based on urinary or bladder wash cytology are used and recommended all over the world as an integral part of the diagnosis and follow-up of urologic tumors.[3–6] The procedure is technically simple, safe, and inexpensive. Its major role is in the detection of high-grade tumors, especially carcinoma in situ (CIS), but it has important limitations with regard to low-grade tumors.

Conventional evaluation of cytologic specimens has recently been challenged, however, by an increasing number of new noninterpretive laboratory tests reflecting a need to develop more precise techniques for noninvasive procedures for diagnosing bladder tumors both initially and during follow-up.[7–12] Nevertheless, there appears to be a consensus that these new urinary markers still need to be tested in large-scale prospective randomized clinical trials in various clinical settings before being introduced into everyday practice. At present, cytology remains the standard against which new tests should be compared. In Table 8–1 the applications for urinary and bladder wash cytology are summarized.

COLLECTION AND LABORATORY PROCESSING OF CYTOLOGIC SAMPLES

By paying careful attention to the available methods and techniques for sampling, many pitfalls encountered in the analysis of cytologic specimens can be avoided. Different types of specimens require different processing procedures, and optimal preparation requires fresh samples. The requisition for cytologic evaluation should always be accompanied by clinical information involving collection, medical history, and endoscopic findings (Table 8–2).

Type of Specimen

Urine

The mode of collection (voiding, catheter, cystoscope), including site of origin, should be specified, because the instrumentation may cause errors in interpretation which are especially important in specimens obtained by retrograde catheterization. Voided urine, which is easily obtained, should always be preferred unless instrumentation is clinically justified. Spontaneously voided urine contains relatively few urothelial cells, but if appropriately collected and processed, it provides reliable infor-

Table 8–1. FIELDS OF APPLICATIONS FOR URINARY AND BLADDER WASH CYTOLOGY
Screening
Risk groups
Diagnosis
High-grade tumors, including CIS
Small lesions and/or inaccessible sites
Follow-up
Monitoring therapy
Instillation therapy
Post-irradiation
Post-cystectomy, urinary diversion, and bladder substitutes
Prognostication
Discriminating between low- and high-grade tumors

mation on the status of the epithelium lining the entire urinary tract (Figure 8–1). Urine is, however, a toxic environment that affects cellular features with resultant difficulties for the interpreter. Both morning urine (which may be enhanced by ingestion of Vitamin C at bedtime) and specimens obtained later are appropriate for analysis. However, although the first morning urine produces the richest yield of cells for evaluation, it may often be contaminated with debris; therefore, the second morning voiding should be recommended. Two or three collections, if clinically practicable, increase the diagnostic accuracy. Fresh voided or catheterized specimens, not infected or mingled with blood, should be processed as soon as possible, but, if necessary, they can be refrigerated overnight without preservatives or additives and still preserve cells adequately for satisfactory interpretation. However, if a delay is anticipated, fixation is recommended and alcohol is usually advocated.

Voided urine is less reliable in the diagnosis of tumors of the ureter and renal pelvis. The poor cellular yield and preservation of cells from the upper tracts need special attention. When the suspicion of tumor is strong, a ureteral catheterization should be performed. This procedure causes scraping of the lining epithelium resulting in a specimen characterized by a population of urothelial cells occurring singly or in aggregates of various sizes (Figure 8–2). Falsely interpreting these cells as originating from a papillary tumor is a common source of diagnostic error.[13] Great care has to be taken to avoid contamination from the contralateral side or the bladder.

Urine from conduits and bladder substitutes can be handled in a similar fashion, but the abundant mucus production from the intestinal graft has to be managed appropriately. The cytologic interpretation may be confounded unless the clinician does not indicate the source of the specimen. However, if the specimen is adequately prepared with good staining, detecting tumor cells should not be too difficult.[13]

Table 8–2. CLINICAL INFORMATION THAT SHOULD ACCOMPANY A CYTOLOGIC CONSULTATION
Type of specimen
Urine or bladder washings
Mode of collection
Voiding, catheterization (indwelling or not) with or without irrigation of the bladder or ureters (separate catheters to avoid contamination; indicate origin left/right), endoscopic sampling with or without any surgical procedure (biopsy, transurethral resection)
Location for sampling
Urethra, bladder, upper tract, conduit, or substitute
Medical history
Earlier or present medication that may confound interpretation; history of previous bladder cancer and treatment: radiotherapy, intravesical instillation therapy, type of earlier surgery
Infection
Treated or not
Symptoms raising suspicions of bladder cancer
Such as dysuria or bleeding
Endoscopy
Exophytic tumor or not, size, single or multiple, configuration, inflammation, areas of erythema, locally aggressive or not, concurrent biopsies or resection

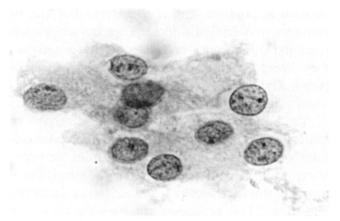

Figure 8–1. Urinary specimen showing a sheet of benign, bland-looking urothelial cells.

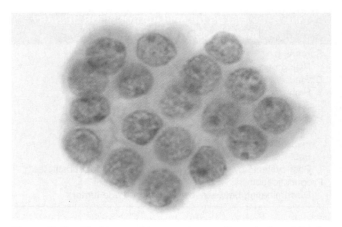

Figure 8–3. Bladder washing specimen with a cluster of benign urothelial cells of polyhedral shape with a central nucleus and evenly distributed finely granular chromatin.

Bladder Washings (Barbotage)

Bladder washings, usually used as an adjunct to cystoscopy, are generally considered to be of superior quality and usually free of contaminants compared to voided urine. Bladder irrigation using isotonic saline should preferably be obtained before any manipulation or bimanual palpation, and the bladder should be fairly vigorously irrigated to obtain an adequate number of cells. All manipulation of the bladder commonly causes detachment of pseudopapillary cell clusters that may lead to a false diagnosis of a highly differentiated transitional cell carcinoma (TCC). However, the nuclei of individual cells in such clusters are usually uniform in size and without hyperchromasia (Figure 8–3). Although

bladder washings are usually considered to be superior to voided urine, similar sensitivities have been reported comparing urine and bladder washings. On the other hand, bladder washings cannot be repeatedly collected with the same ease as voided urine.

Laboratory Processing

The prevention of cell loss and satisfactory preservation of morphologic details are the main goals of the various technical procedures. Specimens may be processed by direct centrifugation and smearing with or without air-drying, cytocentrifugation, or membrane filtration. There are many staining techniques, the most common being Papanicolaou and Giemsa. Regardless of the technique used, it should be standardized and carefully controlled or the cytologic interpretation will be seriously hampered.[14]

CYTOLOGIC INTERPRETATION

Cytologic specimens have to be evaluated in sufficient numbers on a regular basis by trained specialists in close collaboration with the urologist representing a medical consultation requested by one physician from another.[15] Pertinent clinical information, endoscopic findings, and a reference to previously submitted specimens should therefore be given to the cytopathologist (see Table 8–2). If possible, concurrently obtained tissue samples should be analyzed together. Difficulties in interpretation

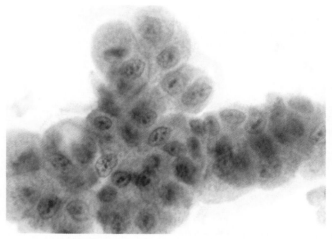

Figure 8–2. Ureteral washing specimen with a pseudopapillary fragment of benign urothelium.

may be caused by overinterpreting normal or reactive changes as malignant, misunderstanding the cytologic effects of intravesical drugs and radiation therapy, or other factors.

Cytologic Findings of the Normal Urinary Sediment

Urothelial cells found in urine are desquamated from the urothelium (normally three to seven layers thick) lining the urinary tract, representing the basal, intermediate, and superficial layers. These cells vary in size (10 to 100 mμ) and shape from the basal layer, consisting of small round cells with scant cytoplasm and single dark round nuclei, to the surface with its layer of large cells with abundant cytoplasm, coarse chromatin, and often more than one nucleus of variable size. These cells, commonly called "umbrella" cells, have typical concave and convex surfaces (Figure 8–4).[14] All these features are normal and should not be mistaken for cancer cells. The umbrella cells should be identified and disregarded when a specimen with suspicion of malignancy is examined. Furthermore, these cells might be preserved on top of an underlying malignancy. Cells from the intermediate and basal layers are cytologically similar (Figure 8–5). The cell borders are well defined and the cytoplasm shows a fine vacuolization. The cell shape can be oval, triangular, or polyhedral. The nucleus is usually central but may be eccentric, and cells may be binucleated. The chromatin is evenly distributed and finely granular. Normally the cells have one or two

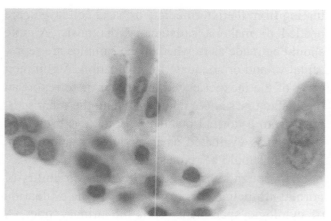

Figure 8–5. Bladder washing specimen. Benign intermediate cells at the left, umbrella cell at the right, and columnar cells in the middle of the figure.

clearly visible nucleoli. It is these subsuperficial urothelial cells, and not the superficial cells, to which comparisons of nuclear characteristics between neoplasia and normal are most appropriately made.[13] Columnar cells are another common finding of the normal urinary sediment but can also be seen in metaplasia and malignancy (Figure 8–6). In addition, benign squamous cells emanating from squamous metaplasia, typically seen in women, may be found.

In the absence of disease, the cellular yield from urine and bladder washings is poor. But the shed cells have distinctive features that are recognizable as normal by an experienced cytologist (Figure 8–1 to 8–6). Usually, cellularity is sufficient to make a cytologic diagnosis of a benign sample. At least five cells in a urine sample, and 15 cells in a bladder washing orig-

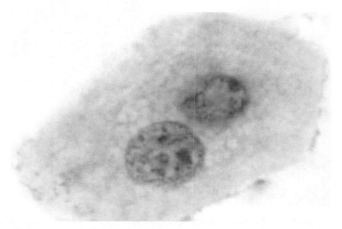

Figure 8–4. Bladder washing specimen showing a normal umbrella cell with abundant cytoplasm, two nuclei, and small nucleoli.

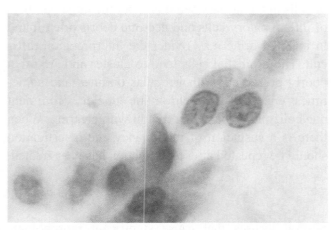

Figure 8–6. Bladder washing specimen. Benign urothelial cells of columnar type with apically elongated cytoplasm.

inating from the intermediate or basal cell layers, are needed to make a satisfactory diagnosis. A note should be made as to whether the samples are representative and/or adequate for evaluation. A common error of the inexperienced interpreter is to report an unsatisfactory sample upon analyzing the scant sediment from a normal bladder.[16] In the event that the specimen is evaluated as inadequate, a subsequent specimen should be requested.

A thorough knowledge of the great variability of normal urothelial cells is necessary in the evaluation of cytologic specimens from the urinary tract. A complete description of the cellular features of the normal and abnormal urinary sediment is found in standard cytology textbooks.[13,14,17,18]

Abnormal Cytology in Noncancerous Conditions

A number of benign conditions of the urinary tract may cause reactive changes mimicking or concealing malignancy (Table 8–3). A knowledge of these changes is of the utmost importance for the interpreting cytopathologist, who must always be aware of the fact that any of these conditions can appear concurrently with a tumor. Furthermore, the clinician must provide the cytologist with appropriate information of the patient's medical history in order to facilitate the interpretation of the findings of the urinary specimen.

Bacteria

Bacterial agents rarely cause significant abnormalities of cells in the urinary sediment, but the large numbers of inflammatory cells and necrotic debris often found in infected urine may render the interpretation difficult. The urothelial cells tend to cluster and are often poorly preserved, with irregular outlines and sometimes enlarged hyperchromatic nuclei, prominent nucleoli, and a coarse chromatin with clearing. When there is a suspicion of malignancy, the investigation should be repeated after the infection has been treated.

Viruses

Several viruses that cause significant morphologic abnormalities in urothelial cells may be mistaken for

Table 8–3. NONCANCEROUS CONDITIONS THAT MAY INTERFERE WITH THE ANALYSIS OF CYTOLOGIC SPECIMENS
Bacteria (known infections should preferably be treated before sending samples for analysis)
Viruses (Herpes, Cytomegalovirus, Human polyomavirus, Human papillomavirus)
Fungi
Parasites
Stones
Radiologic contrast material
Irradiation and laser therapy
Systemic and intravesical chemo- or immunotherapy
Urinary diversion

neoplasia. Human papillomavirus–affected cells are squamous in nature with an irregular nucleus, a perinuclear halo, peripheral keratin condensation, and sometimes binucleation (Figure 8–7). Such abnormal cells may mimic cells of squamous carcinoma. Herpes virus can infect urothelial cells but is usually of limited significance. Induced cellular changes include multinucleation, molding, and margination of chromatin with central ground-glass appearance of the nucleus and with or without nuclear viral inclusions. Human polyomavirus change infected cells dramatically with nuclear enlargement and a huge, round, opaque inclusion. The cytoplasm is sparse and sometimes seen only at one segment of the nuclear periphery (Figure 8–8). Cytomegaloviruses manifest themselves in urine or bladder washings, as infected cells stem from the renal tubuli. Nuclei of infected cells show dark, homogeneous inclusions with a white halo.

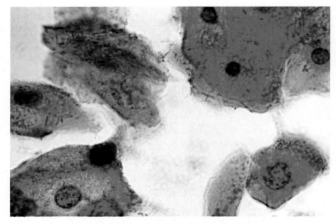

Figure 8–7. Bladder washing specimen with squamous cells affected by human papillomavirus. In the lower left of the figure a cell with a perinuclear halo and peripherally condensed keratin can be seen.

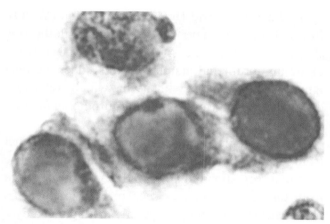

Figure 8–8. Bladder washing specimen. Urothelial cells affected by human polyomavirus. Note the huge opaque intranuclear inclusions.

Fungi

Fungi are readily seen in ordinary Papanicolaou staining, are found together with granulocytes, and do not usually cause any confusion in interpretation.

Parasites (*Schistosoma haematobium*)

There are two important cytologic manifestations of this parasite. First, schistosomal ova can be found in urine. They are readily recognized under polarized light. Second, there is a known and common association of bladder cancer with *S. haematobium* infestation.

Stones

The presence of urolithiasis may not be symptomatic, and the patient may have only hematuria or a filling defect radiologically. The cytologic findings may closely resemble the reactive effects seen after instrumentation of the bladder, causing diagnostic problems (see Figures 8–2 and 8–3). Furthermore, stones increase the cellularity of the specimens and may cause significant atypia. The numerous apoptotic cells found suggest the presence of neoplasia. The nuclei may become enlarged and pleomorphic, leading to an increased nuclear/cytoplasmic (N/C) ratio suggestive of cancer. Columnar cells, mitotic figures, and multinucleated cells can be found. Degenerative cell changes are common, demanding diagnostic caution as a cancer diagnosis should not

be made on poorly preserved cells but ideally only on well-preserved cells. The coexistence of stones and tumors calls for repeated investigations after a stone removal when there is suspicion of malignancy.

Radiologic contrast material alters the morphologic appearance of the cells, mimicking malignancy. A few days after an intravenous pyelogram, a number of abnormalities may be seen in the cytologic specimen which has to be kept in mind as the different investigations of the diagnostic work-up in symptomatic patients may coincide.

Irradiation and Laser Therapy

Pelvic irradiation can cause radiation cystitis and cellular atypia, which may be mistaken for malignancy. As radiation can induce malignancy and also is a therapeutic modality for bladder cancer, the clinical history is essential to diagnosis. Distinguishing radiation effects from cancer can be difficult. The most reliable criterion of radiation effect is marked enlargement of the cell or cytomegaly, that is, macrocytes that may be five times the size of normal urothelial cells.[18] The N/C ratio remains, however, within normal limits. Laser therapy gives rise to striking spindle cell artifacts in the urinary sediment, which may cause trouble in the follow-up after using this therapeutic modality.

Systemic and Intravesical Chemo- or Immunotherapy

Systemic chemotherapy (eg, cyclophosphamide, bisulfan) may become concentrated in urine and remain in contact with the bladder for prolonged periods. In general, drugs administered locally have a lesser effect on the urothelium than those administered systemically.[14] Only a few intravesical agents to which the bladder is exposed cause diagnostic confusion in urinary specimens; among the most common are alkylating agents such as mitomycin C and thiotepa. They mainly affect the umbrella cells, causing an atypical appearance but with a normal N/C ratio. Cyclophosphamide and bisulfan give rise to bizarre nuclear forms often with prominent nucleoli and coarse chromatin. Similar to high-grade tumors, the cytoplasm might become vacuolated. Cyclophosphamide may also induce bladder cancer, which causes additional diagnostic difficulties.

Intravesical bacille Calmette-Guérin (BCG) therapy results in a granulomatous inflammatory reaction with histocytic aggregates with or without multinucleated giant cells, lymphocytes, polymorphs, and macrophages (Figure 8–9). Even the constituent cells of tubercules may be observed in the urinary sediment.[14] However, BCG does not cause cell changes that may be confused with cancer. Transitional cells may show some hyperchromasia but with a smooth nuclear contour and a normal N/C ratio. Therefore the identification of cancer cells in urinary sediments following BCG treatment strongly suggests residual or recurrent disease.

Urinary Diversion

The mucosal fragments are often degenerated and render the search for tumor cells difficult. Cancer cells that usually originate in the renal pelvis differ from those derived from the intestinal interponate, being much larger, with well-demarcated cytoplasm and large, irregular, coarsely granular, hyperchromatic nuclei.

Cytologic Findings in Dysplasia

The incidence of primary dysplasia in the general population is unknown,[19] and the incidence of concurrent dysplasia reported in patients with bladder cancers varies greatly.[20]

In the 1998 World Health Organization (WHO)/International Society of Urological Pathology (ISUP) consensus classification,[3] dysplasia (low-grade intraurothelial neoplasia) falls under the designation of flat lesions with atypia, which are clearly distinct from CIS (high-grade intraurothelial neoplasia) (Figure 8–10, A and B).

The cytologic findings in dysplasia are distinct from reactive changes (Figure 8–11), similar to those seen in a corresponding low-grade TCC, but separate from the cellular changes seen in high-grade TCC. However, one cannot cytologically distinguish a dysplastic or in situ lesion from an exophytic tumor.

There is disagreement as to how to report these findings cytologically, thereby illustrating the diffi-

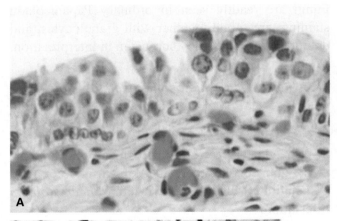

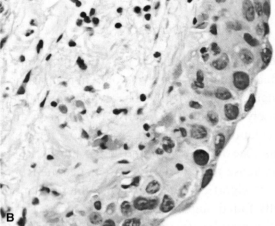

Figure 8–10. *A*, Histologic specimen showing moderate urothelial dysplasia (Hematoxylin and eosin stain; original magnification ×200). The cells are arranged in a somewhat disorderly fashion with enlarged nuclei and prominent nucleoli. *B*, Carcinoma in situ (CIS) for comparison (Hematoxylin and eosin stain; original magnification ×200). The architecture is more disturbed, with a highly atypical urothelium. Note the preserved umbrella cells on the surface of the urothelium.

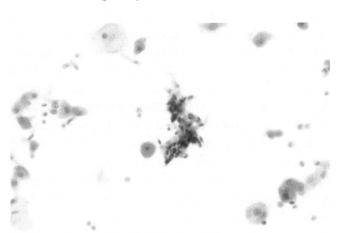

Figure 8–9. Bladder washing specimen from a patient successfully treated with intravesical BCG instillations. There are large cells with very prominent nucleoli but with a normal N/C ratio.

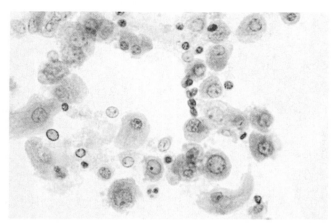

Figure 8–11. Bladder washing specimen showing inflammatory reactive urothelial cells with increased cytoplasm and enlarged and prominent nuclei. There are lymphocytes and polymorphs in the background. No malignant cells are seen.

culties in identifying malignant cells of low grade in cytologic specimens. The term dysplasia can be used for changes distinctive from reactive changes as well as from carcinoma using two categories for atypical cells: atypia of uncertain significance and atypia raising suspicions of malignancy.[21]

The significance of these findings has to be weighed against the medical history, especially a history of bladder cancer, and account has to be taken of how extensive the investigation should be and when it can be terminated.

Cytologic Findings in Cancer

Bladder Cancer

Transitional Cell Carcinoma. TCC constitutes more than 90% of all tumors of the urinary bladder. Approximately 60% of these are moderately (WHO

II) or poorly differentiated (WHO III), or high-grade tumors according to ISUP (Table 8–4).[3,22]

Our ability to detect bladder cancer by cytology depends directly upon which type of cancer is present. Papillary neoplasms of low malignant potential and urothelial carcinoma grade I (both formerly WHO grade 1) cannot be identified reliably by cytology alone. By strictly adhering to defined criteria characterizing neoplasia, it has been stated that "almost all true transitional cell carcinomas (WHO grade II and III) and CIS of the urinary bladder can be detected using urinary cytology."[23] The higher the grade and the more extensive the tumor, the greater is the ability to make a cytologic diagnosis.[18] Important cytologic features of malignancy include enlarged nuclei, an increased N/C ratio, coarse chromatin, and macronucleoli (Table 8–5).[18,23] However, disagreements in interobserver concurrence and the differing quality and experience of cytologists will affect the quality of the diagnosis from center to center.

Low-grade tumors (Figure 8–16), consisting of cells resembling normal urothelium, shed cells into the urine that may be difficult to identify as abnormal in the absence of tissue patterns or to differentiate from effects resulting from instrumentation or stones. The urinary sediment from low-grade neoplasia often contains numerous cells in loose clusters or papillary aggregates. Sometimes a fibrovascular stalk can be seen (diagnostic for papillary TCC, although not required for a malignant diagnosis). The cells are uniform in size and shape with enlarged, eccentric nuclei, a slightly irregular nuclear membrane ("rat-bitten"), and a somewhat increased N/C ratio. They have fine and even chromatin, small or no nucleoli, and a homogeneous cytoplasm.[23]

Table 8–4. CURRENT AND FORMER HISTOLOGIC MALIGNANCY GRADING OF TCC			
	Bergkvist (25–27)	**WHO 1973**	**WHO 1999 (22)**
Papilloma	G 0	Papilloma	Papilloma
	G 1	G 1	PUNLMP (Figure 8–12)
	G 2A	G 1	G I (Figure 8–13)
Low vs. High Grade 3			
	G 2B	G 2	G II (Figure 8–14)
	G 3	G 3	G III (Figure 8–15)

WHO = World Health Organization; PUNLMP = papillary neoplasm of low malignant potential.

Table 8–5.   CYTOLOGIC FEATURES EVALUATED FOR THE DIAGNOSIS OF MALIGNANCY
Arrangement of cells, size, shape, and number
Cytoplasm
Nuclear morphology and size
Nuclear/cytoplasmic ratio (N/C)
Chromatine (coarseness, irregularity)
Nucleoli

These tumors also exfoliate fewer cells than more aggressive tumors. On the other hand, neoplastic cells in a specimen do not necessarily reflect the true grade of the tumor, as superficial parts of a tumor may be more differentiated than its deeper, more invasive components.

The high-grade tumors (Figure 8–17) are composed of cells that differ significantly from normal cells and are readily identified in cytologic specimens with their marked cytoplasmic and nuclear abnormalities. The malignant cells are enlarged and pleomorphic and found isolated or in loose clusters of a variable number. The size of the nucleus is variable with an eccentric position and irregular borders. The chromatin is coarse and uneven with a variable number of nucleoli.[23]

Cytologic Grading of TCC. When tumor cells appear in urinary specimens, they cannot be reliably recognized as distinctive degrees of differentiation for direct correlation with various histologic grading schemes.[23] However, from a clinical standpoint, the identification of low-grade tumors in cytologic smears plays a minor role, whereas

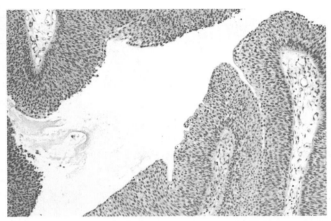

Figure 8–13. Urothelial carcinoma, grade I. Histologic specimen showing slender papillae with a minimal loss of cell polarity and slight variations in nuclear size compared to the features of PUNLMP in Figure 8–12.

identification of tumors of higher grades is of the utmost importance.

In 1972, Esposti, using analysis of exfoliated cells in smears from over 300 patients, showed that it was possible to assess a cytologic grade of malignancy separating transitional cell tumors of low-, moderate, and high-grade atypia.[24] The histologic basis for this cytologic grading was based solely on the degree of cellular atypia in the tissue specimens, with a suggested grading of transitional cell tumors into five grades from 0 to IV according to the severity of cellular deviation from normal transitional epithelium.[25] This histologic classification by Bergkvist, with later modifications, dividing grade II tumors into "A" and

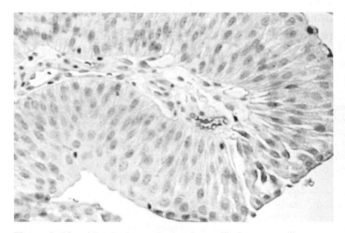

Figure 8–12.   Histologic specimen of a papilla from a papillary neoplasm of low malignant potential (PUNLMP). The cells are slightly and uniformly enlarged without polarity disturbances.

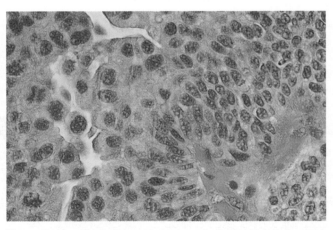

Figure 8–14.   Urothelial carcinoma, grade II. The histologic specimen shows moderately disturbed growth pattern, which is preserved at the base. There is an increased cellular atypia. Note the two mitoses to the left in the figure.

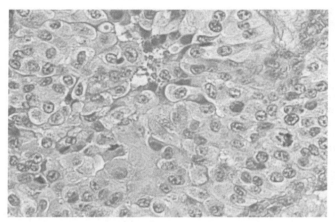

Figure 8–15. Urothelial carcinoma, grade III. The histologic specimen displays a pronounced disorder and cellular atypia with an abnormal mitosis to the right.

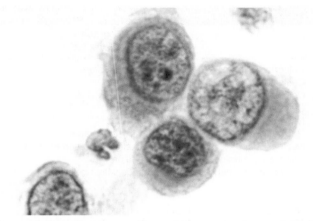

Figure 8–17. Bladder washing specimen showing malignant urothelial cells with poly- and pleomorphous nuclei, consistent with a high-grade tumor. Note the markedly increased N/C ratio.

"B," has been widely used in Scandinavia up to now.[26,27] This separation constitutes an attempt to better define the histologic parameters for the large and heterogeneous group of moderately differentiated tumors. Although the classification was originally designed for categorization of tissue specimens, it was formulated to adapt these parameters to cytology samples, which enables comparison of the two diagnostic modalities. The modified Bergkvist system can further easily be translated into the new 1999 WHO system of malignancy grading.[22]

The cytologic specimen from a TCC grade II (WHO 1999) is usually cellular. The enlarged cells have a high N/C ratio with an eccentrically located nucleus. The cytoplasm is homogeneous, and vac-

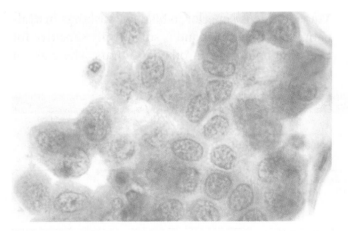

Figure 8–16. Bladder washing specimen showing atypical urothelial cells with suspicion of low-grade malignancy. There is a minor variation in the nuclear contour with some prominent nucleoli.

uolization is found only in degenerated cells, in large amounts. The nuclear membrane is irregular and the chromatin coarse. Nucleoli are clearly visible and vary in size. Mitosis might be observed.

TCC grade III (WHO 1999) tumors usually are solid rather than papillary, and one rarely sees papillary clusters in the cytologic specimens. The cells are pleomorphous, bizarre, and have a markedly increased N/C ratio. The cytoplasm might be vacuolated, and the nuclear membrane is irregular with knots and indentations. Chromatin is irregular, clumped, and dense, or the nucleus might be vacuolated (not to be confused with viral inclusions). The nucleoli are prominent, large, and sometimes multiple.

Table 8–6 summarizes the cellular features for the three WHO grades, enabling a comparison with the Bergkvist grading system.

There have been other efforts to create a grading system of neoplastic cells in cytologic smears into grades I, II, III, corresponding to WHO 1973, to meet the clinical needs of the urologist.[21] The 1973 WHO and Scandinavian systems, although more descriptive, have always been regarded by others as being less reliable for cytologic purposes than other systems that differentiate only between high- and low-grade neoplasms (Table 8–7).[12,14] This is a view that today is strengthened by the new WHO system, although the new grading system still is awaiting general acceptance. Grading of TCC in cytologic specimens, besides the separation into low- and high-grade tumors, is thus today not clinically useful;

Table 8–6. CELLULAR FEATURES OF UROTHELIAL NEOPLASIA ACCORDING TO WHO 1999			
	WHO grade 1 **Bergkvist 2A**	**WHO grade 2** **Bergkvist 2B**	**WHO grade 3** **Bergkvist 3**
Cell arrangement	Papillary, loose clusters	Isolated, loose clusters	Isolated, rarely clusters
Cell size	Enlarged, uniform	Enlarged	Enlarged, pleomorphic
Cell number	Numerous	Increased	Variable
Cytoplasm	Homogeneous	Homogeneous	Variable
N/C ratio	Increased	Increased	Markedly increased
Nuclear size	Enlarged with slight variation	Enlarged with moderate variation	Enlarged with strong variation
Nuclear shape	Round-oval, slight variation in shape	Moderate pleomorphism	Marked pleomorphism
Nuclear membrane	Slightly irregular	Irregular	Very irregular
Nuclear chromatin	Minor variation within cells	Mild variation within and between cells	Marked variation both within and between cells with hyperchromasia
Nucleoli	Usually inconspicuous	Prominent	Multiple, prominent
Mitoses	Occasional	Frequent	Frequent
	Low grade	High grade	High grade

efforts should instead be made to reconcile the differences into one working system.

Squamous Cell Carcinoma

Squamous differentiation is relatively often a component of TCC but constitutes only approximately 5% of all primary bladder tumors when predominantly or completely squamous. The cytologic presentation of well-differentiated as well as poorly differentiated squamous cell carcinomas is usually fairly characteristic and therefore readily identified using urinary cytology (Figures 8–21 and 8–22).[23] In the case of women, a differential diagnosis of cervical cancer must always be kept in mind.

Adenocarcinoma

These are rarely primary in the bladder, accounting for less than 2% of bladder cancers. Mixed TCC with a component of glandular differentiation is more common.[18] Sometimes the tumors are so well differentiated that they cannot be identified as cancers, but their usual appearance is that of high-grade neoplasms (Figures 8–23 and 8–24). Metastatic adenocarcinomas of intestinal or gynecologic origin are more common and do not differ from primary bladder tumors cytologically.[23] Locally advanced tumors of the prostate are sometimes hard to distinguish clinically from bladder cancers and, especially when poorly differentiated, may be mistaken for urothelial cancers cytologically. Figures 8–25 and 8–26 show histology and cytology specimens from a metastasizing malignant melanoma in the bladder.

Cancer of the Upper Tract (Renal Pelvis and Ureters)

Voided urine is superior to bladder washings in evaluating the upper tract and is sufficiently sensitive for detecting high-grade urothelial tumors. There are of

Table 8–7. PROPOSED GRADING SYSTEMS FOR NEOPLASTIC CELLS IN CYTOLOGIC SMEARS OF TCC			
Espostl[24]	**Ooms[21]**	**Murphy[23]**	**Bergkvist[26,27]/WHO 1999[22]**
Low grade atypia	GI*	Negative (LG TCC)	G1
Moderate atypia	GII†	LG TCC	G2A (WHO I, 1999)
Low-grade (LG) vs High-grade (HG)[3]			
Moderate atypia	GII†	HG TCC	G2B (WHO II, 1999)
High grade atypia	GIII‡	HG TCC	G3 (WHO III, 1999)

WHO = World Health Organization
*G I: Grade I carcinoma corresponding to WHO 1, 1973; G II: †Grade II carcinoma corresponding to WHO 2, 1973; ‡G III: Grade III carcinoma corresponding to WHO 3 1973

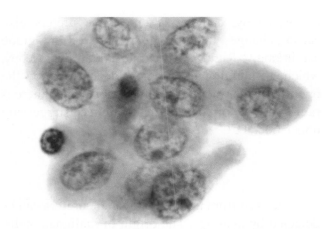

Figure 8–18. Bladder washing specimen. Urothelial atypia of unknown significance, with suspicion of malignancy. The nuclei are somewhat enlarged with quite coarse chromatin and prominent nuclei. Note benign umbrella cells on top. Grade I.

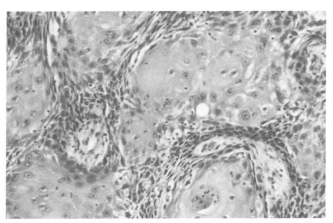

Figure 8–21. Histology specimen. Invasive, well-differentiated squamous cell carcinoma with central keratinization in tumor nests.

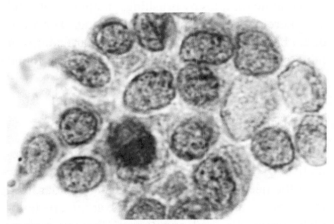

Figure 8–19. Bladder washing specimen. Malignant urothelial cells consistent with urothelial carcinoma, grade II. A cluster of malignant cells with variation in nuclear shape and size and scanty cytoplasm.

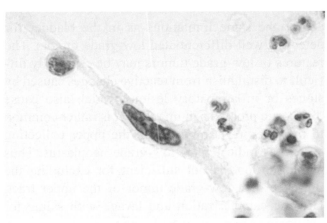

Figure 8–22. Bladder washing specimen. A malignant squamous carcinoma cell ("fiber cell") with a highly disturbed cytoskeleton with cytoplasmic extensions.

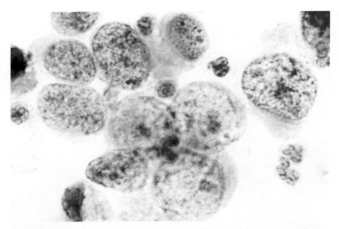

Figure 8–20. Bladder washing specimen. Malignant urothelial cells consistent with urothelial carcinoma, grade III. The cells have a minimal amount of cytoplasm and the nuclear shape varies. There are aptotic cells in the periphery.

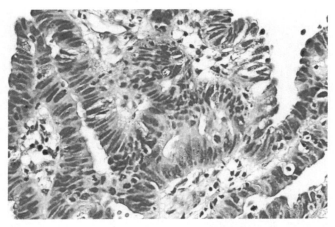

Figure 8–23. Histology specimen with a moderately differentiated adenocarcinoma with cylindrical cells. Lumen formations are seen in the center.

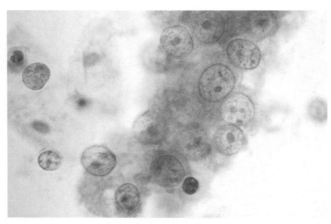

Figure 8–24. Bladder washing specimen with malignant cells from a patient with adenocarcinoma of the prostate. There are malignant glandular cells with scanty cytoplasm, round nuclear contour, and a prominent central nucleolus.

course the same limitations as in the bladder for detecting well-differentiated low-grade tumors. The features of low-grade tumors may be especially difficult to distinguish from reactive changes caused by stones or inflammatory lesions, which also cause diagnostic problems in imaging. It is rather common to overinterpret samples from the upper collecting system as indicative of low-grade neoplasms. Thus cytology alone is not sufficient for excluding the presence of a low-grade tumor of the upper tract. Ureteric catheterization and lavage with saline for cytologic specimens of both upper tracts (+/– retrograde radiographic studies) are warranted in patients with positive urinary cytology or bladder washings in the absence of an obvious tumor in the bladder.

Unfortunately, catheterization of the ureters also causes changes that resemble those of low-grade carcinoma.[14] Rigid and flexible ureteropyeloscopy, which, in addition to visual evidence, provide the opportunity for biopsy, should be done when there is radiographic or cytologic evidence suggesting upper-tract TCC.

Urethral Cancer

Cells derived from tumors of the male urethra can be detected by cytology. The origin of malignant cells, whether in the bladder or urethra, has to be established endoscopically. Cytologic diagnoses from the female urethra have to be made using direct removal of cytologic samples by brushings or applicators and are therefore of minor clinical value. However, direct biopsies are preferred. The cellular features of tumors in the urethra do not differ from those found in the bladder.

TERMINOLOGY AND REPORTING

The cytology report should be descriptive and predictive of histologic findings and in conformity with the needs of the clinician. Using standardized terminology facilitates the dialogue among pathologists, urologists, and oncologists, thereby making cytology an integrated part of therapeutic decision making. Table 8–8 presents the terminology used in our department.

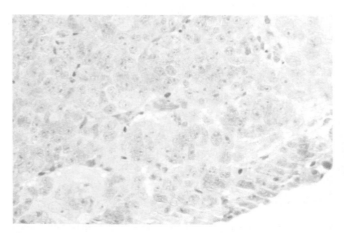

Figure 8–25. Histology specimen from a malignant melanoma metastasizing to the bladder. A thin rim of benign urothelium can be seen on the surface of the specimen.

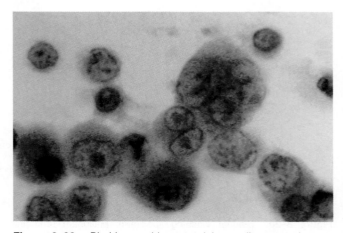

Figure 8–26. Bladder washing containing malignant melanoma cells. There are bizarre pleomorphous nuclei, prominent nucleoli, and a blurred cytoplasm.

Table 8–8. TERMINOLOGY USED AT HUDDINGE UNIVERSITY HOSPITAL, STOCKHOLM, SWEDEN

Transitional cell carcinoma:
  Normal cytology (Figures 8–27 and 8–28)
  1. No cellular material adequate for evaluation.
  2. Benign urothelial cells (Figure 8–27).
     Sparse cellular material with benign urothelial cells.
  3. Benign urothelial cells with an abundant contribution of inflammatory cells.
     Cytologically nonmalignant (Figure 8–28).

  Atypical cells, significance uncertain (Figure 8–29)
  4. Urothelial cells and abundant inflammatory cells. Urothelial cells show minor, probably reactive, changes. Malignant cells not identified.

  Abnormal cells, with suspicion of malignancy (Figure 8–30)
  5. Urothelial cells with indeterminate atypia. The possibility of highly differentiated urothelial cancer cannot be excluded.

  Neoplastic cells present (Figures 8–31–8–33)
  6. Malignant urothelial cells are seen. Consistent with highly differentiated urothelial cancer (WHO grade 1).
  7. Malignant urothelial cells are seen. Consistent with moderately to poorly differentiated urothelial cancer (WHO grade 2).
  8. Malignant urothelial cells are seen. Corresponding to poorly differentiated urothelial cancer (WHO grade 3).

  Squamous cell carcinoma (Figure 8–22)

  Adenocarcinoma (Figure 8–24)

Three types of specimens are recognized: centrifugalized bladder washings, voided urine, or ureteric urine.

In the terminology used, it should be stated whether the samples are representative or not (Table 8–8:1). Benign urothelial cells (Table 8–8: 2 and 3) with or without contribution of inflammatory cells should be described along with a description of the cellular material and a conclusion that the specimen clearly is nonmalignant (Figure 8–27 and 8–28). Reactive changes (atypia of uncertain significance) (Figure 8–29) should be clearly separated from those that raise suspicions of malignancy (Figure 8–30) (Table 8–8: 4 and 5). The description should clearly state either the finding of urothelial cells with minor, probably reactive, changes where malignant cells cannot be identi-

fied, or urothelial cells with intermediate atypia where the possibility of highly differentiated urothelial cancer cannot be excluded.

Whenever neoplastic cells have been identified (Table 8–8: 6 to 8) we still try to grade them, although cells of low-grade papillary tumors (grade 1) usually cannot be distinguished from the normal or reactive specimen. TCC low grade is defined as: Malignant urothelial cells are seen, consistent with highly differentiated urothelial cancer (WHO grade 1 [Figure 8–31]). TCC high grade is defined as: Malignant urothelial cells are seen, consistent with moderately to poorly differentiated

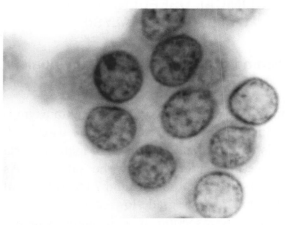

Figure 8–27. Bladder washing with a cluster of normal benign urothelial cells.

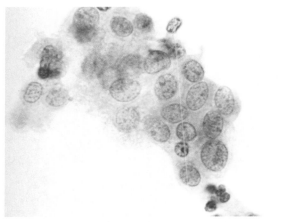

Figure 8–28. Bladder washing showing inflammatory reactive changes. There is a cohesive sheet of uniform, slightly enlarged, bland-looking cells. There are polymorphs at the bottom. No malignant cells are identified.

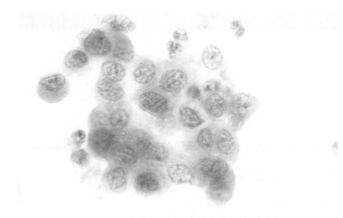

Figure 8–29. Bladder washing specimen showing cells with atypia of unknown significance, which probably is reactive. There is a slight variation in nuclear size and evenly distributed chromatin.

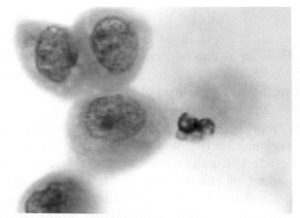

Figure 8–30. Bladder washing specimen with atypical urothelial cells, with suspicion of malignancy. The urothelial cells have eccentric enlarged nuclei. There are umbrella cells in the background.

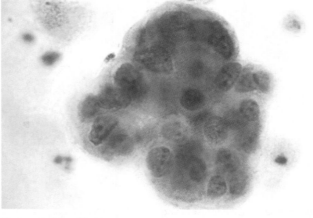

Figure 8–31. Bladder washing with atypical malignant urothelial cells, suggestive of low-grade malignancy, grade I. The cell cluster is causing diagnostic problems with some variation in the nuclear contour.

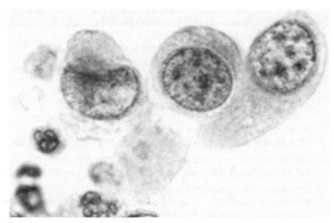

Figure 8–32. Malignant urothelial cells, consistent with urothelial carcinoma grade II. The cells have scanty, unevenly distributed cytoplasm. So called "rat-bitten" cells can be seen to the left.

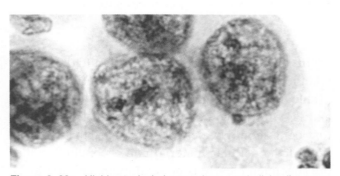

Figure 8–33. Highly atypical pleomorphous urothelial cells, corresponding to urothelial carcinoma grade III.

urothelial cancer (WHO grade 2 [Figure 8–32]), or malignant urothelial cells corresponding to poorly differentiated urothelial cancer (WHO grade 3 [Figure 8–33]) are seen.

CLINICAL USEFULNESS OF CYTOLOGIC ANALYSIS

Screening of Asymptomatic Individuals Including Risk Groups

Screening for bladder cancer, especially in asymptomatic individuals without any of the usual risk factors, is controversial even though many criteria for a successful screening may be satisfied. As most cancers are symptomatic, and 70 to 80% of all new cancers are low grade/low stage and completely cured by resection, it is debatable whether screening is worthwhile for earlier detection in the majority of cancer cases. Urinary cytology, easily obtained without any discomfort to the patient, is not, as earlier pointed out, sensitive enough for low-grade disease. Perhaps new urinary markers with their superior sensitivity in low-grade cancers will prove to be the means needed for early detection through screening.

Whether risk groups (smokers, paraplegics, some industrial workers, etc) with a higher probability of having a cancer should be screened in order to detect an aggressive cancer earlier remains to be decided. A protocol for handling patients exposed to known carcinogens or other risk groups has been proposed comprising a check-up for hematuria, three consecutive voided urinary cytology analyses every 6 months, and cystoscopy, if indicated.[14] Otherwise, information on health risks and general awareness of symptoms indicative of bladder cancer seem at present to be as good as general screening.

Primary Diagnostic Work-up When Symptomatic

Cytology Alone

Patients with symptoms such as hematuria, frequency, nocturia, pain, or mucous discharge should always be fully investigated for occult malignancy, including a freshly voided urine sample (ideally three) for cytologic analysis.[14] A diagnosis of cancer rendered by an experienced cytopathologist on the basis of urine samples can be considered safe. Likewise, a negative cytology report on an adequate specimen is significant because a high-grade lesion can generally be

excluded. Although a voided urinary cytology specimen is regarded by some as the "gold standard" noninvasive test for the detection of urothelial cancer,[8] we are not yet at a point where any noninvasive test for bladder cancer can replace cystoscopy for the primary situation.[9]

The use of urinary cytology alone also reflects the primary care of patients and the access to urologists in different countries. Ideally, there should not be any delay in investigating symptomatic patients. However, with limited resources, patients can be correctly prioritized using the results of a cytologic analysis, that is, low- versus high-grade cytology. Certainly, a negative result of the cytologic analysis should never be an indication for omitting cystoscopy. One should always have a high degree of suspicion in patients with symptoms in order not to not add physician delay to patient delay. In the future, new urinary point-of-care tests may play a more important role in this respect once they have been fully evaluated.

Cytology as an Adjunct to Cystoscopy

Voided urine has the advantage of sampling the entire urinary tract, but bladder wash cytology is usually of superior quality. Therefore, bladder irrigation should also be performed together with cystoscopy in the primary assessment of bladder lesions (Table 8–9).

Visible Lesion and Positive Cytology

Although cystoscopy findings usually correlate well with histology obtained later at resection,[28] a positive

Table 8–9. POSSIBLE COMBINATIONS OF THE DIAGNOSTIC OUTCOME WHEN CYSTOSCOPY AND URINARY OR BLADDER WASH CYTOLOGY ARE USED SYNCHRONOUSLY		
Cytology	Positive	Negative
Endoscopy		
Visible lesion	LG, HG +/– CIS	LG (false negative cytolgy) No cancer (false positive cystoscopy) HG unlikely
No visible lesion	CIS, upper tract tumor, "missed" or inaccessible location	Normal, "missed" LG tumor, does not exclude tumor in bladder or uper tract

LG = low grade; HG = high grade; CIS = carcinoma in situ.

cytology has an additive value for further planning before resection because the need for preoperative imaging or multiple biopsies can be estimated. By identifying lesions of a higher grade at the time of the initial presentation, cytology serves as an indicator, discriminating between neoplasms with a more benign clinical course and those with a poorer prognosis.[29]

Visible Lesion and Negative Cytology

When a tumor is seen at cystoscopy, but the cytology is negative, the lesion is probably low grade and a coexistent high-grade lesion in other parts of the urinary tract is less likely. Although synchronous tumors at sites in the urinary tract other than the bladder may occur at presentation, this is a relatively uncommon occurrence.[30] In conditions mimicking malignancy, such as colovesical fistulas and cystitis glandularis, or in patients with chemical or radiation cystitis, a cytologic examination is highly useful to rule out malignancy.

No Visible Lesion and Positive Cytology

The most evident diagnostic advantage of cytology is its ability to sample inaccessible areas not seen cystoscopically (eg, upper tract, prostatic urethra, diverticula, etc) or areas not of characteristic appearance macroscopically. An unexpected positive cytology, especially of high grade, calls for an aggressive investigation of the entire urinary tract to confirm the origin of malignant cells and especially for CIS, which is generally first detected cytologically and often without visible signs of disease. A tumor of the upper tract must always be excluded when a positive cytology cannot be explained otherwise. The diagnostic sensitivity of cytology is less prominent in upper-tract tumors than in the bladder, but the specificity is the same. Another explanation of a positive cytology may be a missed tumor at the first cystoscopy, a possibility that emphasizes the additional value of cytology. Among other things, a "missed" tumor may also be due to inexperience, bleeding, an immobile patient, a diverticulum, or synchronous infection and inflammation. The possibility of contamination and sample mix-ups also has to be kept in mind. Atypical specimens from patients having conditions such as urinary stones should also be evaluated after treatment, as a simultaneous neoplasm may coexist.

No Visible Lesion and Negative Cytology

A negative cystoscopy complemented by negative bladder wash cytology is a powerful tool to rule out a new or recurrent cancer of high malignant potential.

A distinction must, however, always be made between the normal sample, the inadequate sample, and urinary sediment of unknown significance (see Terminology 1–4). The clinical dilemma is to balance between an extended follow-up and termination of the investigation. Patients having only an indeterminate cytology ("not clearly indicative of malignancy" or "not clearly negative") who are nonsmokers and do not have hematuria or a prior history of urothelial cancer are at low risk of harboring a malignancy.[31,32] An evaluation of every patient who has serious symptoms and negative findings should be performed again because negative examinations do not definitively rule out tumors.

Cytology Findings Compared with Histology

Cytology is complementary to resected tissue samples and, ideally, should be evaluated concurrently with histology. When a tumor is found and the cytology is positive, whether due to TCC or other lesions, there may or may not be agreement between histology and cytology. Concordance will confirm the diagnosis, whereas a discrepancy (ie, low-grade histology/high-grade cytology) indicates a focus of high-grade cancer not initially appreciated. This calls for an extended evaluation.

Multiple Biopsies

Random biopsies are considered by many to be an integral part of the primary evaluation. They should always be considered when there is a discrepancy between the initial histology and cytology. Furthermore, biopsy of the prostatic urethra has also been recommended to rule out TCC in all cases of high-grade positive cytology, even if other bladder foci have been identified.[14] Although the finding of malignancy in the normal-looking mucosa is a very strong prognostic factor, the value of routinely taking biopsy specimens at the time of detection in all patients has been questioned.[33] In fact, cytologic examination serves the same purpose of excluding synchronous malignancy, especially because repeated cytologic evaluations will eventually disclose most high-grade lesions. An alternative to random biopsies is to repeat urinary cytology 2 weeks after resection. This has been reported to have an even better predictive value than random biopsies.[34,35]

Carcinoma In Situ

Although primary CIS classically appears as an area of erythema, it may sometimes be hard to find and prove by biopsy, as the bladder mucosa looks normal. Therefore, cytologic examination of urine or bladder washings is regarded as the single most reliable test for the detection and follow-up of CIS of the bladder.[18]

There are three types of CIS: primary, concomitant, and secondary. There is common agreement that these lesions should be classified as WHO grade III (high-grade intraurothelial neoplasia, including "severe dysplasia" in the 1999 WHO classification). Cytology will be highly positive with severe nuclear atypia corresponding to grade 3, but it cannot be reliably determined whether the disease is in situ or invasive or to localize the lesion by cytologic means. In most published studies, patients with primary CIS are few in number compared with those with secondary or concomitant CIS. Primary CIS accounted for 4% of all newly detected bladder cancers registered in Sweden in 1997.[36]

In a large Nordic study comparing two intravesical instillation schedules in over 300 biopsy-proven CIS patients, malignant, benign, and insufficient cytology were reported in 76, 6, and 18% of patients, respectively. Bladder wash cytology, performed only once, represented routine practice at 29 different centers. However, in specimens considered to be representative, 93% had grade 3 cytology.[37] The high sensitivity in detecting CIS in adequate specimens stresses the importance of repeating an inadequate cytologic analysis.

According to the literature, CIS rarely occurs in association with low-grade lesions but is quite common in association with high-grade or invasive carcinomas.[38] In the Nordic study, 35% of the secondary and concomitant CIS tumors presented initially or synchronously with noninvasive low-grade tumors. This illustrates the importance of cytology at initial detection and tumor resection.

Resection of Bladder Tumors

Histology Shows Papillary Neoplasm of Low Malignant Potential or Low Grade (WHO Grade 1)

Cytology generally fails in the identification of these lesions, but when cytology is negative, biopsies can usually be safely omitted. If there is a discrepancy between histology and cytology, it is an indication of a high-grade lesion elsewhere.

Histology Shows High-Grade (WHO Grades 2–3) Lesion

A positive cytology, which occurs in up to 90% of cases, may reflect shedding from both an exophytic tumor and a concomitant focus of CIS, which may be present in approximately half of such patients.[20] Biopsies therefore have to be performed in all cases with high-grade cytologic findings and should be done at the primary resection if results from a voided urine specimen or a diagnostic cystoscopy are available. Although synchronous tumors at sites in the urinary tract other than the bladder may occur at presentation, this is a relatively uncommon occurrence. Both the upper tracts and the prostatic urethra are candidate sites for such multicentric lesions. Up to 4% of simultaneous bladder cancers with primary renal pelvic tumors and 2% with ureteric tumors have been reported.[39]

A valuable indication for urinary cytology is to repeat the cytologic analysis a few weeks after resection, especially in large or multiple tumors, to determine if the surgical procedure has been complete. This is underlined by reports on residual tumors in surprisingly large numbers (76% in one series) at a second transurethral resection within 6 weeks after the initial resection.[40] This is a fact that has to be considered particularly when choosing between conservative and radical procedures.

Follow-Up

Urinary cytology should be used primarily as an adjunct to cystoscopy in monitoring patients treated for bladder cancer with or without adjuvant instillation therapy. A cytologic evaluation may be used, however, as an extra safety measure between cystoscopies with the possibility of reducing the number of such investigations. A positive or suspicious cytology, which may precede tumor recurrence for a considerable length of time,[18] calls for an earlier cystoscopic investigation. Intravesical chemo- or immunotherapy may cause misinterpretation of the sediment as being malignant despite a complete response to treatment. As a rule, however, changes caused by topical agents can be recognized and are distinguishable from malignancies.[23] Normalization in the status of cytology can be relied on as a good indicator of treatment efficacy.

Carcinoma In Situ

In many reports, the sensitivity of cytology in detecting CIS is almost complete, thus establishing the importance of cytology in this context and making it a useful tool for monitoring this type of bladder cancer and circumventing the need for numerous and repeated biopsies.[41] Close life-long surveillance is mandatory for this group of patients. Further instillation therapy can be instituted on the basis of cytology findings alone. However, a confirming tissue diagnosis is needed before radical treatment is instituted.

Low-Grade, Noninvasive, or Superficially Invasive Tumors

Because urinary cytology has a low sensitivity for detecting low-grade tumors, it is also of minor importance for detecting recurrences or residual low-grade disease after resection. Low-grade tumors generally have a low prospect of progression. However, as many as 50 to 70% of superficial bladder cancer patients have been reported to develop recurrences, with 10 to 20% of these progressing to involve muscle.[42,43] By appreciating well-known prognostic

factors, including the routine use of cytology to rule out high-grade recurrences, the surveillance of these tumors can be tailored for individual patients and trigger the need for repeat cystoscopies.

High-Grade, Noninvasive, or Superficially Invasive Tumors

When a conservative approach has been chosen to monitor these highly unpredictable bladder cancers, cytology has an obvious and important role because it is highly sensitive and specific. A non-radical policy usually requires intravesical immunotherapy with BCG and a meticulous follow-up similar to that for CIS. Most agree that cystoscopies cannot be omitted in these tumors, but the use of cytology is a complement that further improves early detection of recurrences.

In a workshop on initial evaluation and response criteria for patients with high-risk superficial bladder cancer, cystoscopy and cytology were recommended twice during the first 6 months for high-risk patients. However, if the bladder was clear, cystoscopy was recommended at 6-month intervals and cytology at 3-month intervals, replacing cystoscopies. This report also included a detailed description of cytologic technique and criteria.[44]

Muscle-Invasive Tumors, All Grades

Conservative Approach, Including Radiotherapy. In recent years bladder-saving protocols, including chemoradiotherapy[45] or extensive transurethral resections and adjuvant chemotherapy,[46] have gained increasing popularity in carefully selected cases. Monitoring the bladder has, however, proven to be extremely difficult. Cytology may prove to be particularly valuable in detecting residual or early recurrent disease, and a positive cytology may lead the clinician to initiate prompt salvage cystectomy. Cytology specimens may, however, be difficult to evaluate after irradiation, and a positive cytology directly after irradiation may represent both residual disease and/or concomitant CIS that has not responded to irradiation.[23] Positive cytology appearing later on may precede an exophytic recurrence by a long interval or it may represent a secondary CIS.

After Cystectomy

Periodic cytologic examination of urine from patients who have had a cystectomy should be included in the follow-up.[47] It is important to have an optimal collection and that the location of sampling is given so that processing can be done properly. However, even properly handled specimens may contain only a few poorly preserved cancer cells.[23] The purpose of such studies is to monitor both the upper tracts and the urethra for possible recurrences. The ureters are difficult to catheterize through a conduit or a bladder substitute, making retrograde sampling troublesome. In these cases, one has to rely on radiologic techniques to find the focus of malignant cells. Cytology of the remnant urethra after cystectomy is an absolute indication in the follow-up of these patients for evidence of urethral involvement.[13]

Monitoring Ureters and Renal Pelves

Surveillance of the upper tracts after treatment for bladder cancer is particularly important for all patients with a history of high-grade tumors which are more disposed to the development of new tumors in other locations. The poor cell yield from the upper tracts renders the diagnosis difficult, but when malignant cells are found the specificity is high. Screening extravesical sites in high-risk patients should include intravenous pyelograms and urethral catherization and/or biopsy whenever the cytology is positive without evidence of bladder cancer recurrence.[48]

ACCURACY

The diagnostic accuracy of cytology, evaluated in comparison with histology, is affected by a number of factors where the grade and configuration of the tumors define the limitations of detection. Specimens also have to be of optimal quality as the degenerative effects of urine may alter tumor cells so that they seem to be of either a lower or higher grade than they actually are.[23] As in all morphologic techniques, interpretation requires considerable skill and experience to avoid well-known pitfalls, which of

course affect the quality of the diagnosis from one center to another. One always has to consider the prevalence of the disease in a certain situation because it is highly different in a healthy population, in a risk group, or in a group of patients with a history of bladder cancer.

The overall sensitivity (true positives/all with disease) of urine cytology in detecting bladder cancer in low-grade cancers varies considerably with an average figure of 50% being reported,[49] rising to 90% in high-grade lesions.[50] However, it is difficult to compare individual studies because of variable inclusion criteria (different patient populations, different types of tumors, different clinical settings) and variable expertise of the cytologist.

The reported overall specificity (true negatives/all without disease) of cytology in detecting bladder cancer is high, being 90 to 95% in several studies.[49] Increasing the sensitivity by including samples with indeterminate findings instead of requiring unequivocal or highly suspicious samples as positives may lead to a decrease in specificity with a number of false-positive diagnoses.[5] Classifying Papanicolaou class III (suspicious for malignancy) urinary samples as positive has, however, been claimed to improve sensitivity without compromising specificity.[51]

We reviewed our routine practice (bladder washing used systematically) among our outpatients at Huddinge University Hospital, Stockholm, Sweden during the first 6 months of 2001. Cytologic reports from 388 consultations were correlated with clinical follow-ups and pertinent histologic reports. Thirty-four specimens were malignant (two without tumors), 29 raised suspicions of cancer (10 without tumors), and 325 were negative.

In 74 of the 388 consultations, the cytologic specimens could be compared with a tissue-confirmed TCC tumor (Table 8–10). Although a follow-up may prove otherwise, the increased sensitivity attained by considering "abnormal cells, suspicious of malignancy" as positive caused a decrease in specificity.[51]

It is often claimed in many reports comparing cytology and nonmorphologic techniques with new urinary markers that the high diagnostic yield reported from designated centers cannot be repro-

Table 8–10. PERCENTAGE OF MALIGNANT CYTOLOGY SPECIMENS IN 74 CONSULTATIONS WITH A TISSUE-CONFIRMED TCC TUMOR				
Histology	Malignant cytology		Malignant and suspicious cytology	
WHO PUNLMP	1/6	17 %	1/6	17 %
WHO I	10/39	26 %	24/39	62 %
WHO II	5/12	42 %	10/12	83 %
WHO III	16/17	94 %	16/17	94 %
Total	32/74	43 %	51/74	69 %

For comparison, both malignant and those suspicious of malignancy in the same consultations are combined
WHO = World Health Organization; PUNLMP = papillry neoplasm of low malignant potential.

duced in daily practice.[15,52] Much of the criticism that is directed today at cytology is based upon a lack of knowledge of its precise indications and limitations as to what can be achieved by a properly performed evaluation of cytologic sediments in well-trained hands. By careful attention also to details in collection and processing, the interpretation of urinary cytology can be optimized, even in tumors of low malignant potential, and used as an invaluable complement in the clinical management of bladder cancer.

SUMMARY OF THE CLINICAL USEFULNESS OF THE CYTOLOGIC ANALYSIS

- Sample the entire urothelium, including inaccessible and nonvisible sites of the urinary tract, with the principal indication of detection and follow-up of flat cancerous abnormalities of the urothelium.
- Assess grade: low grade versus high grade.
- Sensitivity is low in low-grade tumors.
- False negatives are common in low-grade tumors (reflecting absence of cytologically-recognizable tumor cells).
- Sensitivity is high in high-grade tumors.
- False negatives are infrequent in high-grade tumors.
- The specificity is very high in all types of urothelial tumors when cancer cells are identified.
- Reactive changes may be overinterpreted as low-grade tumors.
- Positive cytology may precede visible recurrences.
- Cannot replace cystoscopy in the initial evaluation but is a powerful complement, which may reduce the number of invasive investigations in the monitoring of bladder cancer.

QUANTITATIVE AND ANALYTICAL TECHNIQUES IN THE ASSESSMENT AND MONITORING OF UROTHELIAL TUMORS

Great efforts have been made to find ancillary methods for improving the sensitivity and reproducibility of the urinary diagnosis in urothelial cancer with a view to minimizing the need for invasive endoscopic examinations and also optimally reducing the increasing workload of routine control investigations. A large variety of novel technologies have been used, including hematuria home testing, marker tests, combining phenotypic antigen expression and/or genetic abnormalities with cytology, multiparameter flow cytometry, and image analysis. Most of these techniques are, however, still awaiting clinical application.

Flow Cytometric DNA Analysis

Automated flow cytometry (FCM) measures the deoxyribonucleic acid (DNA) content of cell nuclei stained with a DNA-binding fluorescent dye. Changes in the gross level of DNA reflect chromosomal abnormalities frequently encountered in cancer cells. FCM of bladder cancer has been used to characterize cell populations at the diagnosis of bladder cancer and to predict progression or response to treatment. In a clinical context, it is one of the best-evaluated methods in molecular biology. Two parameters are particularly useful: cellular DNA content or ploidy and the percentage of cells in the synthetic (S) phase of the cell cycle (proliferation rate). Normal cells are diploid (normal DNA content corresponding to 46 chromosomes) with a small tetraploid (twice the normal DNA content) population of cells currently in division (G_2 and M

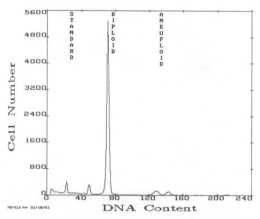

Figure 8–34. DNA histogram from a bladder washing derived from a patient with a histologically noninvasive grade II tumor. The two peaks to the left of the diploid G1 peak (at channel number 70) represent standard cells from chicken and salmon erythrocytes used as internal controls. To the left of the G2 peak at the double channel number (140) from the G1 peak, there is a G1 peak of an aneuploid cell population composed of around 6% of the total cell material. Total G2/M fractions of the diploid populations are 0.9 and 3.3%, respectively. The S-phase fraction of the aneuploid cell population cannot be calculated. The cytologic analysis made from the same specimen was considered to be normal.

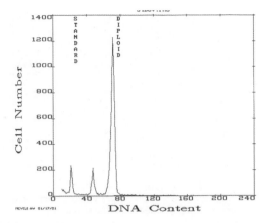

Figure 8–36. DNA histogram from a bladder washing collected during follow-up in a patient who initially had a TaG1 tumor. The DNA histogram, which is contaminated with inflammatory cells, is diploid, and cytology showed high-grade urothelial cancer.

phases). Aneuploidy refers to cell populations deviating from this normal pattern (ie, not an exact multiple of the haploid number of chromosomes) visualized as separate peaks in a DNA histogram.

Tumors can be analyzed by FCM using both urine and bladder washing specimens, as well as cells from tissue biopsies (Figures 8–34 through 8–41).[53,54]

Generally speaking, well-differentiated WHO 1973 grade 1 tumors (papillary neoplasm of low

malignant potential [PUNLMP] and grade I WHO 1999) have a cellular DNA content corresponding to a diploid amount of DNA, whereas poorly differentiated grade 3 tumors are aneuploid. The group of WHO 1973 grade 2 tumors (grade I and II WHO 1999) contain similar numbers of diploid and aneuploid forms.[54,55] This division of tumors in the diploid and aneuploid forms correlates well with the WHO 1999 categorization with a demarcation line between grade I and grade II.[22] By a further subdivision of these tumors into diploid and aneuploid–nontetraploid versus aneuploid forms, a demarcation line can be drawn between those with a good prognosis and those likely to progress to invasive dis-

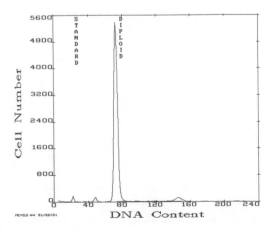

Figure 8–35. DNA histograms from a tumor biopsy taken from the same patient as in Figure 8–34. The histogram shows a diploid cell population with S-phase and G2 fraction of 3.9 and 3.7%, respectively. DNA histograms from three random biopsies were also diploid.

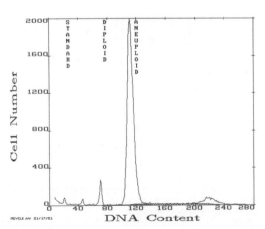

Figure 8–37. The DNA histogram from a random biopsy taken from the same patient as in Figure 8–36 shows an aneuploid cell population with calculated S phase and G2/M fraction of 7.5 and 5.5%, respectively. Histology showed dysplasia corresponding to carcinoma in situ.

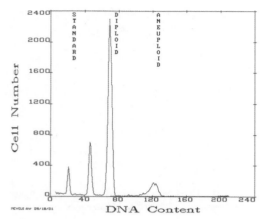

Figure 8–38. DNA histogram from bladder washing coming from a patient previously irradiated for rectal carcinoma. There was no visible lesion in the bladder, cytology was suspicious of malignancy, and biopsies showed only radiation effects without signs of cancer. The DNA histogram shows a G1 peak of an aneuploid cell population amounting to 16% of the total number of cells. The S phase cannot be evaluated.

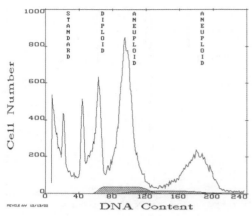

Figure 8–40. Aneuploid DNA histogram from bladder washing heavily contaminated with inflammatory cells and erythrocytes. The high background of debris makes it impossible to calculate the cell cycle composition

ease.[56] A similar shift from diploid to aneuploid is also found with increasing stages of tumors.

It was confirmed in a consensus conference that DNA measurements in superficial bladder cancer provide prognostic information on stage progression to muscle invasive disease and metastases.[57]

Abnormal DNA values have also been linked to CIS and deeply invasive tumors, as synchronous biopsy specimens from seemingly unaffected epithelium showed the same aneuploid pattern as the primary tumor.[58] Aggressive CIS has also been linked to

DNA multiploidy, as CIS with two or more aneuploid peaks in the histogram were more aggressive and more likely to progress to invasive disease.[59]

The proportion of S-phase cells has also been related to grade, stage, and thus progression and has been considered to be equally important as ploidy.[56] However, more recent data[60] and unpublished data from Stockholm (T. Tribukait, personal communication, 2002) show that the proliferation rate provides the most important prognostic information.

Most clinical studies have been done, however, on tissue samplings. Reports on the correspondence between biopsies and bladder washings show some

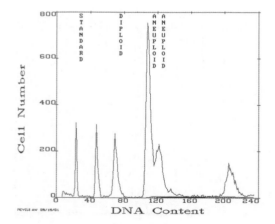

Figure 8–39. The DNA histogram from a biopsy taken from the same patient as in Figure 8–38 shows several aneuploid cell populations not fully evident in bladder washing. The patient later developed a muscle-infiltrating tumor showing the potential of flow cytometry to reveal signs of malignancy in irradiated specimens.

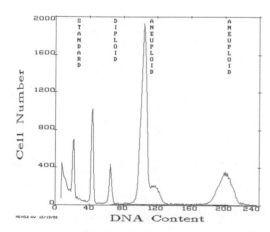

Figure 8–41. The same specimen as in Figure 8–40 after purification with Ficole gradient centrifugation. An additional aneuploid cell population can be identified and the cell cycle composition can be calculated indicating low proliferation of the aneuploid cell populations.

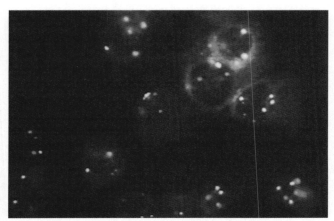

Figure 8–42. Fluorescence in situ hybridization (FISH) of a cytologic sample of bladder cancer cells with a chromosome 9 centromere probe labeled with fluorescen isothiocyanate (FITC) (green) and a chromosome 9q (long arm) probe labeled with tetrarhodamine isothiocyanate (TRITC) (red). Most nuclei contain chromosome 9 with deletion of the long arm.

discrepancy, and the best results have been achieved when both specimens have been used simultaneously. Compared with biopsy material, cell material obtained from bladder washings has proved to be unrepresentative of the tumor in one third of aneuploid superficial exophytic tumors. On the other hand, in deeply invasive tumors, good correspondence was found between biopsy specimens and bladder washings.[56] Flow cytometry of tumor cells from bladder irrigation is usually reported to be more sensitive than that of voided urine because of technical difficulties and poor cell preservation. There are, however, some positive reports showing good results either under routine conditions[61] or using a specialized sedimentation technique for processing voided urine.[62] Developments in the processing of samples have improved the quality of tissue specimens that can be fixed in formalin, whereas urine and bladder washings still have to be processed fresh. The quality of urinary specimens for DNA-FCM down through the years has been consistently inferior to tissue specimens but superior in monitoring intravesical immuno- or chemotherapy and irradiation (T. Tribukait, personal communication, 2002).[56]

Despite shortcomings in quality, FCM on bladder washings has been reported to enhance early detection of bladder cancer, especially CIS,[63] and to be useful for monitoring patients treated with surgery or immunotherapy. An aneuploid pattern was a poor prognostic sign, leading to recurrence and/or progression to invasion.[64] In another study, the combination of urine and bladder washing cytology when one or both displayed neoplastic cells was a better diagnostic and predictive tool than flow cytometry, although specificity was slightly better for FCM with a strict definition of aneuploidy. Inclusion of hyperdiploid specimens within the aneuploid category increased sensitivity but reduced specificity drastically.[65] The final conclusion was, however, that DNA flow cytometry and cytology performed on bladder washing specimens added little information to that obtained from voided urinary cytology. Another study reported that DNA-FCM changes predated cytologic changes and recommended the combined use of urinary cytology and FCM.[66]

The sensitivity of FCM can be increased by various means. New techniques, such as dual-parameter immunoflow cytometry, using monoclonal antibodies or combining FCM with fluorescence in situ hybridization, still need to be evaluated clinically on a larger scale.[67,68]

Digitized Image Analysis

Computer-assisted fluorescent image analysis is an automated cytologic technique analyzing smears of cells quantitatively measuring the DNA content in each cell on a microscopic slide. Various reports have shown good concordance between the two methods.[69,70] As image analysis combines quantitative DNA analysis with visual evaluation of individual cells, it is considered to be more sensitive to rare events than FCM. Thus small subpopulations of aneuploid cells that may remain unnoticed in flow cytometry can be identified. It has therefore been reported to be more sensitive than both conventional cytology and FCM for detecting low-grade tumors, but it is time-consuming.[71] Combining DNA ploidy analysis by image analysis with cytology may add clinical information in cases that are cytologically atypical or dysplastic but not in those with normal or malignant cytologic findings. An abnormal DNA value was reported to be indicative of recurrence.[72]

To evaluate whether FCM could be recommended as a standard clinical procedure for a larger patient population, a specialist committee was set up to study the numerous reports in a clinical setting. They came to the conclusion in 1992 that "it may be a valuable technique but should not be indiscriminately applied and used only in competent laboratories."[73] Although numerous reports have been published evaluating DNA-FCM in the initial work-up of bladder cancer cases, we are still looking for series with a long-term follow-up to establish its clinical value. This may explain the statement in the latest edition of *Campbell's Urology*: "In general, flow cytometry has not been found to be more clinically valuable than conventional cytology."[5]

Fluorescence In Situ Hybridization

Bladder cancer progression is accompanied by chromosomal instability and aneuploidy. Cytogenetic studies of bladder cancer have revealed frequent aberrations including chromosomes 1, 7, 9, 11, 17, and others.[75] FISH techniques allow the identification of individual chromosomes and genetic loci by hybridization with specific fluorescently labeled DNA probes. It is particularly useful in studies in which appropriate probes are used to identify numerical aberrations as well as to map chromosomal deletions numerical aberrations and translocations that cannot be identified by the conventional banding technique.[76] FISH is a rapid, technically easy, and powerful technique for detecting cytogenetic abnormalities in malignant cells regardless of their functional status, thus making the tests reproducible when applied at different institutions. In contrast to conventional cytogenetic technique, FISH techniques can be used on voided urine or bladder irrigation specimens. Detection of specific cytogenetic abnormalities by FISH in voided urine or bladder washing specimens has been suggested to facilitate diagnosis, monitoring, and even for predicting the recurrence of bladder cancer (Figure 8–43).[77]

In one study assessing sensitivity, FISH (using centromere probes for chromosomes 7, 8, 9, and 12) was compared with urinary and bladder washing cytology. In 54 urine and 67 bladder washing specimens from tumors of various grades and stages, the overall sensitivity with FISH was 69% in urine and 63% in bladder washings. The overall sensitivity using conventional cytology was 50% in urine and 77% in bladder washings.[78] In this study, sensitivity and specificity were higher for tumors in stage > pTa and grade 1.

In another study comprising 75 tumors in 265 patients, it was concluded that the sensitivity of FISH for detecting urothelial cancer was superior to cytology, but the specificity was similar. The sensitivity of cytology and FISH, respectively, was 47% and 65% for pTa, 78% and 100% for pTIS, and 60% and 95% for pT1–pT4.[79]

The use of FISH with centromere-specific probes for chromosomes 9 and 17 was more sensitive (85%) in the detection of urothelial cancer than urine cytology (32%) and the original BTA test (64%) in a study of 44 patients with bladder cancer, 20 controls, and 17 patients after complete resection. However, the specificity in this study was inferior to urinary cytololgy (95% versus 100%). Seven out of 13 FISH-positive patients developed tumor recurrences within 27 months versus none of the four FISH-negative patients.[80]

Access to wider diagnostic applications may be opened by commercially available systems. Abbot/UroVysion (Vysis, Downers Grove, IL) is a new multitarget, multicolor FISH assay approved for

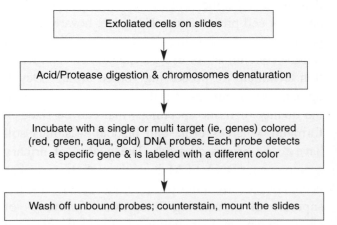

Figure 8–43. A schematic representation of FISH assay. For FISH assay, urine specimens are centrifuged to pellet exfoliated cells. The cells fixed in a methanol + acetic acid solution and placed on slides. The cells are subjected to acid protease digestion to denature chromosomal DNA. The slides are then incubated with various DNA probes, each targeting a different chromosome and labeled with a distinct fluoroprobe. Following hybridization, the slides are washed, counter stained to allow visualization of cells, and then mounted. The slides are observed under fluorescence microscope.[78]

diagnostic purposes. The diagnostic usefulness of UroVysion was studied with a further view on how to optimize the definition of a FISH-positive result because the criteria that define a FISH-positive result are not absolutely clear.[77] FISH was compared to conventional cytology exploring three groups of specimens: (1) group 1, voided urine and bladder washings collected before TURB in 80 cases of bladder tumors; (2) group 2, 17 specimens from patients with a history of bladder cancer but with a negative checkup; and (3) group 3, 38 patients with benign prostatic hyperplasia (BPH). Using new criteria for a FISH-positive result, instead of those suggested by the manufacturer, resulted in highly improved sensitivity and specificity. However, the authors conclude that additional studies on larger series are required to fine tune the definition of FISH-positive specimens. Positive FISH results predicted later recurrences in patients with an initially normal cystoscopy. Patients with a negative urinary FISH result were considered to be at low risk for early recurrence and might be candidates for a reduced frequency of follow-up cystoscopies.

A comparison between BTA stat, hemoglobin dipstick, telomerase, and UroVysion was made in an analysis of samples from 265 patients. UroVysion was reported to be the most sensitive (81% overall in 75 biopsy-proven bladder cancers) and most specific (96%) of the four methods.[81]

With regard to the heterogeneity of urothelial carcinomas and the need for multiple probes to detect disease, it was concluded in a recent review that FISH is "too complex, time-consuming, and expensive for general use in most laboratories."[11]

ImmunoCyt

The ImmunoCyt test (DiagnoCure, Quebec, Canada) is another commerically available test using immunohistochemistry of exfoliated cells from cytologic smears. The three monoclonal antibodies that are used in this assay detect three cellular markers for bladder cancer. Monoclonal antibody 19A 21 labeled with Texas red detects a high molecular form of carcinoma embryonic antigen, and the flourescein labeled–monocolonal antibodies M344 and LDQ10 detects mucins (highly glycosylated cell surface pro-

teins) that are expressed in most bladder cancer cells, but not in normal cells.[83,84] Figure 8–44 shows the key steps involved in the ImmunoCyt test.[85] ImmunoCyt is not a point-of-care test, and has to be done in cytopathology laboratories that have personnel trained in performing immunohistochemistry. An example of exfoliated cells evaluated by the ImmunoCyt test is shown in Figure 8–45.

In a study comprising 264 consecutive patients, 79 having bladder cancer, the sensitivity of ImmunoCyt either alone or together with cytology was evaluated. The overall sensitivity of Immuno-Cyt in this study was 86% with 84 to 90% sensitivity for detecting grade I, grade II, and grade III tumors respectively.[85] Together with cytology, ImmunoCyt had 90% sensitivity and 79% specificity for detecting bladder cancer.

To assess the clinical performance of Immuno-Cyt in the detection of upper urinary tract TCC, a prospective study involving 37 patients, 16 having histology-proven upper tract tumors, was carried out on both voided urine and samples obtained by ureteral catheterization.[86] This preliminary study showed that ImmunoCyt complemented cytology, especially in the detection of low-grade tumors of

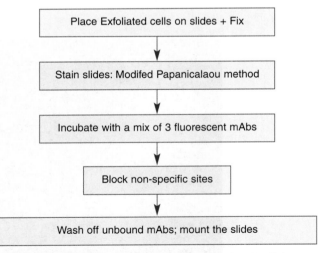

Figure 8–44. A schematic representation of the ImmunoCyt assay. The ImmunoCyt assay involves an immunocytochemisty technique. In this assay, exfoliated cells are collected from about 20 to 40 mL urine by filtration and fixed immediately. The fixed cells are placed on slides and stained using a modified Papanicolaou method. The stained cells are incubated with a blocking solution and then reacted with the three flourescently labeled monoclonal antibodies. Following incubation, the slides are washed, mounted, and observed under a fluorescence microscope.[83]

the upper urinary tract. There is an obvious need for improved diagnosis of low-grade TCC of the upper urinary tract in contrast to low-grade tumors of the urinary bladder.

Although the specificity of ImmunoCyt is high among patients with a history of TCC and in healthy individuals, the test shows 15%, 50%, and 40% false-positive rates among individuals with microhematuria, BPH, and cystitis, respectively.[85,86] Consistent with these observations, another study reported 100% sensitivity almost 70% specificity for ImmunoCyt to detect bladder cancer.[87] The false-positive cases in this study were patients who had either hematuria or inflammation, but normal cystoscopy. In contrast to these studies, however, a Dutch study comprising 104 patients in a follow-up after primary primary superficial bladder tumors (pTa, pT1, and CIS) reported only 50% sensitivity and 73% specificity for ImmunoCyt to detect the recurrences found in 22 of the 104 patients.[88] These authors also noted a high interobserver variation, which might explain why the sensitivity of ImmunoCyt varies in different studies.

ImmunoCyt appears to be a useful adjunct to cytology if used in conjunction with cystoscopy. However, interobserver variability, quality of exfoliated cells, and specificity of the test among benign conditions will have to be improved if this test is to be routinely used together with cytology.

Quanticyt

Quanticyt is an automated, quantitative karyometric cytology system that enables objective interpretation of nuclear features (combining DNA ploidy and nuclear shape analysis) in light microscopic images. The test involves staining of cytospin preparation of ethanol-polyethylene glycol-fixed bladder wash specimens. The nuclear images observed under a light microscope are transferred to a computerized image analysis system. Samples are assessed for mean nuclear shape (MPASS) and DNA content (2c deviation index or 2cD1) parameters using an internal lymphocyte standard.[12,89–93] The procedure takes 2 to 3 hours to carry out. Based on the Quanticyt results, patients can be identified as having low-, intermediate-, or high-risk for the presence or subsequent appearance of bladder cancer.

In two studies, the Quanticyt test had a sensitivity of 59% and 69% respectively, for detecting bladder cancer, and a specificity of 70%[10,93] The test had 57%, 56%, and 85% sensitivity to detect grade I, grade II, and grade III bladder cancer, respectively. In a study done in Nijmegen, the Netherlands, Witjes

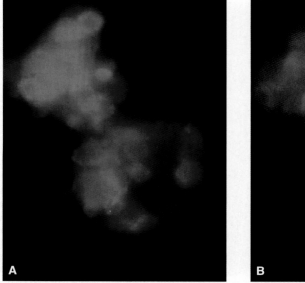

Figure 8–45. ImmunoCyt assay on exfoliated cells. A, red fluorescence shows cells positive for high molecular weight glycosylated carcinomaembryonic antigen. B, green fluorescence shows cells positive for bladder mucin. Adapted from Mian, et al.[83]

and colleagues compared nuclear matrix protein (NMP) 22 and Quanticyt karyometry with regard to diagnosis and recurrence of bladder cancer. The diagnostic negative and positive predictive values of the tests were, respectively, NMP22 91.2% and 56.3%, and karyometry 80% and 33.3%. The prognostic negative and positive predictative values, indicating risk of recurrence, were 77.8% and 27.3%, and 82.6% and 50% for NMP22 and Quanticyt respectively. The authors concluded that NMP22 has a sufficient diagnostic accuracy for being used as a prescreening for cystoscopy, whereas Quanticyt only had a significant positive predictive value with regard to risk of recurrence.[89] In another study, reporting on 105 high-risk patients identified by Quanticyt, malignancy was found in 54 patients.[92] Furthermore, a 2cD1≥2.00 was a significant predictor of CIS, invasive bladder cancer, and progression. Thus, a 2cD1≥2.00 can be used to further stratify high-risk invasive bladder cancer patients.[92] In a retrospective study of 614 patients comprising 5,832 bladder wash specimens, it was suggested that consecutive cytology and Quanticyt analyses of bladder wash specimens improves the rate of detection of high-grade tumors.[90] In that study, however, the risk-score of the first sample was not predictive of recurrence. In five samples, the rate of finding invasive disease was 10% among individuals classified as high-risk from Quanticyt analysis.[90]

Among various studies, it has been indicated that Quanticyt might overestimate the risk of bladder abnormalities, and therefore has a lower specificity than bladder wash cytology and voided urine cytology.[8,10,94] Some samples may also be eliminated because of too few urothelial cells, or if the sample has an abundance of leukocytes and/or erythrocytes.

At present, analysis of cytology specimens with Quanticyt requires sophisticated instrumentation and technical expertise and seems to be too complex and time-consuming to be of clinical use routinely.

CONCLUSIONS

Urine cytology, used in routine clinical practice, has a high specificity and positive predictive value when cancer cells are present, but the well-known weakness in detection of low-grade urothelial neoplasia, representing the bulk of recurrent bladder tumors, continues to be a challenge for cytopathologists.

The refinement of image analysis and the development of a variety of sensitive markers for bladder cancer, using a number of new technologies and biologic principles, can potentially be used in designing follow-up based on individual risks with a view of minimizing the number of invasive diagnostic procedures. No single method or combination of analyses can yet be pointed out to replace cytology in the monitoring of bladder cancer.

Although a large number of ancillary methods, with similar applications as urinary cytology, have been developed and investigated, the clinical usefulness of these new approaches still has to be tested in large and well-characterized series of patients.

ACKNOWLEDGMENTS

Figures 8–34 through 8–41, illustrating DNA flow cytometry analyses of tissue and bladder washing samples from different tumors, have been provided courtesy of Professor Bernhard Tribukait, Karolinska Hospital, Stockholm, Sweden.

Figure 8–42, illustrating FISH, has been provided courtesy of Professor Ulf Bergerheim, Department of Urology, Linköping University Hospital, Linköping, Sweden.

The basis for the text on lmmunoCyt and Quanticyt, including figures, is provided courtesy of Dr. Vinata Lokeshwar, University of Miami School of Medicine, Miami, Florida.

REFERENCES

1. Lambl W. Über Harnblasenkrebs. Ein Betrag zur mikroskopischen Diagnostik am Krankenbette. Prager Vierteljahrschrift für Heilkunde 1856;49:1–15.
2. Papanicolaou GN, Marshal VF. Urine sediment smears: a diagnostic procedure in cancers of the urinary tract. Science 1945;101:519–21.
3. Epstein JI, Amin MB, Reuter VR, Mostofi FK, and the Bladder Consensus Conference Committee. The World Health Organisation/International Society of Urological Pathology Consensus Classification of Urothelial (Transitional Cell) Neoplasms of the Urinary Bladder. Am J Surg Pathol 1998;22:1435–48.
4. Oosterlinck W. The management of superficial bladder cancer. European Urology Update Series 2001. BJU Int 2001; 87:135–40.
5. Messing EM. Urothelial tumors of the urinary tract. In:

Walsh P, Retik, Vaughan, Wein. Campbell's urology. Vol 4. 8th ed. 2002. Elsevier Science; 2002. p. 2732 –84.

6. Skinner DG, Stein JP, Ross R, et al. Cancer of the bladder. Urinary cytology. In: Gillenwater JY, Grayhack JT, Howards SS, Mitchel ME, editors. Adult and pediatric urology. Vol 2. 4th ed. Lippincott, Williams & Wilkins 2002. p. 1318–19.

7. Sarosdy MF, Hudson MA, Ellis WJ, et al. Improved detection of recurrent bladder cancer using the bard BTA stat test. Urology 1997;50:349–53.

8. Wiener HG, Mian C, Haitel A, et al. Can urine bound diagnostic tests replace cystoscopy in the management of bladder cancer? J Urol 1998;159:1876–80.

9. Halachmi S, Linn JF, Amiel GE, et al. Urine cytology, tumour markers and bladder cancer. Br J Urol 1998;82:647–54.

10. Lokeshwar VB, Soloway MS. Current bladder tumor tests: does their projected utility fulfill clinical necessity. J Urol 2001;165:1067–77.

11. Ross JS, Cohen MB. Ancillary methods for detecting of recurrent urothelial neoplasia. Cancer 2000;90:75–86.

12. van der Poel HG, Debrunyne FMJ. Can biological markers replace cystoscopy? An update. Curr Opin Urol 2001;11: 503–9.

13. Murphy WM, editor. Urological pathology. 2nd ed. WB Saunders Company; 1997.

14. Koss LG, editor. Diagnostic cytology of the urinary tract. Lippincott-Raven; 1995.

15. Bastacky S, Ibrahim S, Wilczynski SP, Murphy WM. The accuracy of urinary cytology in daily practice. Cancer 1999;82:118–28.

16. Esposti P-L. Urinary cytology for diagnosis, grading and monitoring response to treatment. In: Oliver RTD, Hendry WF, Bloom HJG, editors. Bladder cancer. Principles of combination therapy. Butterworths; 1981. p. 9–18.

17. Atkinson BF. Urinary cytology. In: Atkinson BF, editor. Atlas of diagnostic cytopathology. WB Saunders; 1992.

18. De May RM. The art & science of cytopathology. Exfoliative cytology. Chicago: ASCP Press; 1996.

19. Cheng L, Cheville JC, Neumann RM, Bostwick DG. Natural history of urothelial dysplasia of the bladder. Am J Surg Pathol 1999;23:443–7.

20. Wolf H, Hojgaard K. Urothelial dysplasia concomitant with bladder tumours as a determinant factor with future new occurrences. Lancet 1983;ii:134–6.

21. Ooms ECM, Veldhuizen RW. Cytological criteria and diagnostic terminology in urinary cytology. Cytopathology 1993;4:51–4.

22. Mostofi FK, Davis CJ, Sesterhenn IA. Histological typing of urinary bladder tumours. International histological classifications of tumours. World Health Organization. Geneva: Springer-Verlag; 1999.

23. Murphy WM. Current status of urinary cytology in the evaluation of bladder neoplasms. Hum Pathol 1990;21:886–96.

24. Esposti P-L, Zajicek J. Grading of transitional cell neoplasms of the urinary bladder from smears of bladder washings. A critical review of 326 tumors. Acta Cytol 1972;16: 529–37.

25. Bergkvist A, Ljungqvist A, Moberger G. Classification of bladder tumours based on the cellular pattern. Preliminary report of a clinical-pathological study of 300 cases with a minimum follow-up of eight years. Acta Chir Scand 1965;130:371–8.

26. Malmström P-U, Busch C, Norlén BJ. Recurrence, progression and survival in bladder cancer. A retrospective analysis of 232 patients with 5-year follow-up. Scand J Urol Nephrol 1987;21:185–95.

27. Carbin B-E, Ekman P, Gustafson H, et al. Grading of human urothelial carcinoma based on nuclear atypia and mitotic frequency. I. Histological description. J Urol 1991;145: 968–71.

28. Herr HW. Does cystoscopy correlate with the histology of recurrent papillary tumours of the bladder? BJU Int 2001;88:683–5.

29. Tut VM, Hildreth AJ, Kumar M, Mellon JK. Does voided urine cytology have biological significance? Br J Urol 1998;82:655–9.

30. Prout GR Jr. Classification and staging of bladder carcinoma. Cancer 1980;45:1832–41.

31. Schwalb DM, Herr HW, Fair WR. The management of clinically unconfirmed positive urinary cytology. J Urol 1993;150:1751–6.

32. Novicki DE, Stern JA, Nemec R, Lidner TK. Cost-effective evaluation of indeterminate urinary cytology. J Urol 1998;160:734–6.

33. Richards B, Parmar MKB, Anderson CK, et al. Interpretation of biopsies of "normal" urothelium in patients with superficial bladder cancer. Br J Urol 1991;67:369–75.

34. Harving N, Wolf H, Melsen F. Positive urinary cytology after tumor resection: an indicator of concomitant carcinoma in situ. J Urol 1988;140:495–7.

35. Zieger K, Wolf H, Olsen PR, Hojgaard K. Long-term survival of patients with bladder tumours: the significance of risk factors. Br J Urol 1998;82:667–72.

36. Statistics – Health and Diseases. Cancer incidence in Sweden 1997. The National Board of Health and Welfare. Centre for Epidemiology. Official Statistics of Sweden. 20 October 1999.

37. Wijkström H, Kasinen E. The Urothelial Cancer Group of the Nordic Association of Urology: a Nordic study comparing intravesical instillations of alternating mitomycin C and BCG with BCG alone in carcinoma in situ of the urinary bladder. J Urol Suppl A:1999;1107, 286.

38. Murphy WM, Busch C, Algaba F. Intraepithelial lesions of urinary bladder: morphologic considerations. Scand J Urol Nephrol 2000;34 Suppl 205:67–81.

39. Hvidi V, Feldt-Rasmussen K. Primary tumours in the renal pelvis and ureter with particular attention to the diagnostic problems. Acta Chir Scand 1973;433 Suppl:91–101.

40. Herr HW. The value of a second transurethral resection in evaluating patients with bladder tumors. J Urol 2000;162: 74–6.

41. Murphy WM, Soloway MS, Jukkola AF, et al. Urinary cytology and bladder cancer. The cellular features of transitional cell neoplasms. Cancer 1984;53:1555–65.

42. Heney NM, Nocks BN, Daly JJ, et al. Ta and T1 bladder cancer: location, recurrence and progression. Br J Urol 1982; 54:152–7.

43. Prout GR Jr, Barton BA, Griffin PP, Friedell GH. Treated history of non-invasive grade 1 transitional cell carcinoma. The National Bladder Cancer Group. J Urol 1992;148:1413–9.

44. Soloway MS, Murphy WM, Johnson DE, et al. Initial evaluation and response criteria for patients with superficial bladder cancer. Report of a workshop. Br J Urol 1990;66:380–5.

45. Shipley WU, Kaufman DS, Zehr E, et al. Selective bladder preservation by combined modality protocol treatment: long-term outcomes of 190 patients with invasive bladder cancer. Urology 2002;60:62–7.

46. Thomas DJ, Roberts JT, Hall RR, Reading J. Radical transurethral resection and chemotherapy in the treatment of muscle-invasive bladder cancer: a long-term follow-up. Br J Urol 1999;83:432–7.

47. Yazdi HM. Genitourinary cytology. Clin Lab Med 1991;11:369–401.

48. Herr HW. Extravesical tumour relapse in patients with superficial bladder tumours. J Clin Oncol 1998;16:1099–102.

49. Cohen MB. Urinary cytology. In: Fitzpatrick JM, Krane RJ, editors. The bladder. Edinburgh: Churchill Livingstone; 1995.

50. Brown FM. Urine cytology. Is it still the gold standard for screening? Urol Clin North Am 2000;27:25–37.

51. Raitanen MP, Aine RAT, Kaasinen ES, et al. Supicious urine cytology (Class III) in patients with bladder cancer: should it be considered as negative or positive? Scand J Urol Nephrol 2002;36:213–7.

52. Malik SN, Murphy WM. Monitoring patients for bladder neoplasms: what can be expected of urinary cytology consultations in clinical practice. Urology 1999;54:62–6.

53. Collste L, Devonec M, Darzynkiewicz Z, et al. Bladder cancer diagnosis by flow cytometry. Correlation between cell samples from biopsies and bladder irrigation fluid. Cancer 1980;45:2389–94

54. Tribukait B. Flow cytometry in surgical pathology and cytology of tumors of the genito-urinary tract. In: Koss LG, Coleman, editors. Advances in clinical cytology. Vol 2. Masson Publishing; 1984. p. 163–89.

55. Tribukait T, Gustafson H, Esposti P-L. Ploidy and proliferation in human bladder tumors as measured by flow cytofluorometric DNA-analysis and its relation to histopathology and cytology. Cancer 1979;43:1742–51.

56. Tribukait B. Flow cytometry in assessing the clinical aggressiveness of genito-urinary neoplasms. World J Urol 1987;5:108–22.

57. Wheeless LL, Badalament RA, de Vere White RW. Consensus review of the clinical utility of DNA cytometry in bladder cancer. Cytometry 1993;14:478–81.

58. Norming U, Nyman CR, Tribukait B. Comparative flow cytometric deoxyribonucleic acid studies on exophytic tumors and random mucosal biopsies in untreated carcinoma of the bladder. J Urol 1989;142:1442–7

59. Norming U, Tribukait B, Gustafson H, et al. Deoxyribonucleic acid profile and tumor progression in primary carcinoma in situ of the bladder. J Urol 1992;147:11–5

60. deVere White RW, Deitch AD, Daneshmand S, et al. The prognostic significance of S-phase analysis in stage Ta/T1 bladder cancer. A Southwest Oncology Group study. Eur Urol 2000;37:595–600.

61. Wijkström H, Lundh B, Tribukait B. Urine or bladder washings in the cytological evaluation of transitional cell carcinoma of the urinary tract. A comparison made under routine conditions supplemented by flow cytometric DNA analysis. Scand J Urol Nephrol 1987;21:119–23.

62. deVere White RW, Deitch A, Baker WC, Strand MA. Urine: a suitable sample for deoxyribonucleic acid flow cytometry studies in patients with bladder cancer. J Urol 1988;139:926–8.

63. Hermansen DK, Badalament RA, Fair WR, et al. Detection of bladder carcinoma in females by flow cytometry and cytology. Cytometry 1989;10:739–42.

64. Klein FA, Herr HW, Soganlt TC. Detection and follow-up of carcinoma of the urinary bladder by flow cytometry. Cancer 1982;50:389–95.

65. Gregoire M, Fradet Y, Meyer F, et al. Diagnostic accuracy of urinary cytology, and deoxyribonucleic acid flow cytometry and cytology on bladder washings during follow-up for bladder tumors. J Urol 1997;157:1160–4.

66. Stricker P, Russel PJ. Analysis of DNA in bladder cancer. In: Fitzpatrick JM, Krane RJ, editors. Tumor markers in bladder cancer. Churchill Livingstone; 1995.

67. Reeder JE, O´Connel MJ, Yang Z, et al. DNA cytometry and chromosome 9 abberations by fluorescence *in situ* hybridization of irrigation specimens from bladder cancer patients. Urology 1998;51:58–61.

68. Eleuteri P, Grollino MG, Pomponi D, De Vita R. Chromosome 9 abberations by fluorescence *in situ* hybridisation in bladder transitional cell carcinoma. Eur J Cancer 2001;37:1496–1503.

69. Bertino B, Knape WA, Pytlinska M, et al. A comparative study of DNA content as measured by flow cytometry and image analysis in 1864 specimens. Anal Cell Pathol 1994;6:377–94.

70. Colombel MC, Pous MF, Abbou CC, et al. Computer assisted image analysis of bladder tumour nuclei for morphonuclear and ploidy assessment. Anal Cell Pathol 1994;6:137–47.

71. Parry WL, Hemstreet GP 3d. Cancer detection by quantitative fluorescence image analysis. J Urol 1988;139:270.

72. Slaton JW, Dinney CPN, Veltri RW, et al. Deoxyribonucleic acid ploidy enhances the cytological prediction of recurrent transitional cell carcinoma of the bladder. J Urol 1997;158:806–11.

73. Aamodt RL, Coon JS, Deitch A, et al. Flow cytometric evaluation of bladder cancer: recommendations of the NCI flow cytometry network for bladder cancer. World J Urol 1992;10:63–7.

74. Sandberg AA, Berger CS. Review of chromosome studies in urological tumors. II. Cytogenetics and molecular genetics of bladder cancer. J Urol 1994;151:545–60.

75. Czerniak B, Hertz F. Molecular biology of common tumors of the urinary tract. In: Koss LG, editor. Diagnostic cytology of the urinary tract. Lippincott–Raven; 1995. p. 345–64.

76. Bubendorf L, Grilli B, Sauter G, et al. Multiprobe FISH for enhanced detection of bladder cancer in voided urine specimens and bladder washings. Am J Clin Pathol 2001;116:79–86.

77. Junker K, Werner W, Mueller C, et al. Interphase cytogenetic diagnosis of bladder cancer on cells from urine and bladder washing. Int J Oncol 1999;14:309–13.

78. Halling KC, King W, Sokolowa IA, et al. A comparison of cytology and fluorescence in situ hybridization for the detection of urothelial carcinoma. J Urol 2000;164:1768–75.

79. Ishiwata S, Takahashi S, Homma Y, et al. Noninvasive detec-

tion and prediction of bladder cancer by fluorescence in situ hybridization analysis of exfoliated urothelial cells in voided urine. Urology 2001;57:811–5.

80. Halling KC, King W, Sokolova IA, et al. A comparison of BTA STAT, hemoglobin dipstick, telomerase and Vysis UroVysion assays for the detection of urothelial carcinoma in urine. J Urol 2002;167:2001–6.

81. Bergeron A, LaRue H, Fradet Y. Biochemical analysis of a bladder cancer-associated mucin: structural features and epitope characterization. Biochem J 1997;321:889–95.

82. Bergeron A, Champetier S, LaRue H, Fradet Y. MAUB is a new mucin antigen associated with bladder cancer. J Biol Chem 1996;271:6933–40.

83. Mian C, Pycha A, Wiener H, et al. ImmunoCyt: a new tool for detecting transitional cell cancer of the urinary tract. J Urol 1999;161:1486–9.

84. Lodde M, Mian C, Wiener H, et al. Detection of upper urinary tract transitional cell carcinoma with ImmunoCyt: a preliminary report. Urology 2001;58:362–6.

85. Olsson H, Zackrisson B. ImmunoCyt: a useful method in the follow-up protocol for patients with urinary bladder carcinoma. Scand J Urol Nephrol 2001;35:280–2.

86. Vriesema JL, Atsma F, Kiemeney LA, et al. Diagnostic effi-cacy of the ImmunoCyt test to detect superficial bladder cancer recurrence. Urology 2001;58:367–71.

87. Witjes JA, van der Poel HG, van Balken MR, et al. Urinary NMP22 and karyometry in the diagnosis and follow-up of patients with superficial bladder cancer. Eur Urol 1998; 33:387–91.

88. van der Poel HG, van Rhijn BW, Peelen P, et al. Consecutive quantitative cytology in bladder cancer. Urology 2000; 56:584–8.

89. Vriesema JL, van der Poel HG, Debruyne FM, et al. Neural network-based digitized cell image diagnosis of bladder wash cytology. Diagn Cytopathol 2000;23:171–9.

90. van Rhijn BW, van der Poel HG, Boon ME, et al. Presence of carcinoma in situ and high 2C-deviation index are the best predictors of invasive transitional cell carcinoma of the bladder in patients with high-risk Quanticyt. Urology 2000;55:363–7.

91. van der Poel HG, van Balken MR, Schamhart DH, et al. Bladder wash cytology, quantitative cytology, and the qualitative BTA test in patients with superficial bladder cancer. Urology 1998;51:44–50.

92. Lokeshwar VB, Block NL. HA-Haase urine test. A sensitive and specific method for detecting bladder cancer and evaluating its grade. Urol Clin North Am 2000;27: 53–61.

9

Quantitative Cell Biomarkers in Transitional Cell Carcinoma of the Bladder

PETER W. HAMILTON, PhD

KATE E. WILLIAMSON, PhD

RODOLFO MONTIRONI, MD, FRCPATH, MCAP(A)

SUBJECTIVITY OF CONVENTIONAL DIAGNOSTIC PRACTICE

The microscopic assessment of tissue biopsies and cytologic smears by pathologists is central to the diagnosis, grading, and staging of urothelial lesions. Biopsies taken at cystoscopy are examined for changes in cell size, nuclear-to-cytoplasmic ratio, nucleolar number, number of mitoses, cell polarity, and presence of umbrella cells. These clues are used to determine the histologic grade of the lesion. This is divided into grades 1, 2, and 3 based on increasing cellular abnormalities and is a feature strongly related to prognosis. Grade 1 tumors show only about 50% recurrence, whereas almost all grade 3 tumors recur. The accurate diagnosis of the flat lesion carcinoma in situ (CIS) is also vital because it has a much poorer prognosis and requires more aggressive therapy. On biopsy, the other job for the pathologist is to stage the lesion by assessing the depth of tumor penetration. This is particularly important in superficial disease (Ta/T1) for predicting progression because only 4% of Ta lesions progress to T2, whereas approximately 30% of T1 lesions progress to T2. Although histologic assessment of tissue histology provides extremely important prognostic clues, it can be extremely subjective. For histologic grading, Ooms and colleagues reported intra- and interobserver rates of between 0.46 and 0.67.[1] This is poor, and some studies have shown that 50% of cases are assigned a different grade on second assessment of exactly the same tissue.[2]

Similarly, the identification of recurrent tumors from urinary cytology or bladder washings is a subjective practice. Again, visual assessment of cellular abnormalities remains the gold standard here, although, again, subjectivity of the technique is high, with sensitivity values as low as 40% with high false-negative rates, particularly for low-grade lesions.[3,4]

Although histologic and cytologic assessment has clear value in the prognostic assessment of patients, there are enormous opportunities to develop new biomarkers that are less subjective and more reproducible and can define tumor aggressiveness (grade) or identify cytologic abnormalities with greater precision.

This chapter focuses on the use of quantitative cytology and histology to define these cellular and tissue abnormalities in a more objective fashion. This involves measuring not only basic changes in cell morphology (size and shape) but also characteristics of the cell that can be specifically labeled, visualized, and measured such as deoxyribonucleic acid (DNA), chromatin, protein expression, and DNA sequences. Many of these latter features can be measured using biochemical techniques, which require dissolution of cells into their molecular components. This chapter, however, concentrates on techniques that allow the in situ analysis of molecular markers, that is, analysis within intact cells or nuclei. Prime among these techniques are computerized image analysis and flow cytometry. These methods have been used in numerous studies to explore the role of quantitative cell data in identifying the onset of disease, grading tumor aggressiveness, predicting disease progression and prognosis, and predicting response to therapy in bladder cancer.

QUANTITATIVE BIOMARKERS IN BLADDER CANCER

In oncology, a biomarker can be defined as a characteristic of cells, tissues, or body fluid, whether biochemical, molecular, or morphologic, that allows the prediction of some future biologic event with clinical significance, whether that is recurrence, progression, metastases, response to treatment, or survival. The term "biomarker" is used extensively in clinical circles and covers a wide spectrum of potential tests and assays that might predict clinical outcome. Many millions of dollars have been invested by government-funded research groups and private industry in the identification and clinical testing of new biomarkers that might provide a more sensitive and specific indicator of clinical outcome. For example, in an attempt to detect recurrent bladder cancer, over 20 different tests have been recently defined.[5] This proliferation in biomarkers and biomarker assays, the lack of a consistent method of statistical comparison of performance, the significant cost associated with the use of these tests, and the frequent lack of evidence of efficacy make the study of biomarkers in bladder cancer a difficult business.[5]

The characteristics of an ideal biomarker are that it should be (1) specific, (2) sensitive, (3) predictive, (4) robust, and (5) additive. In bladder cancer, tumor grade and stage represent tried and tested biomarkers that have been used for many years in the management of patients. As already discussed, they are by no means robust because there is subjectivity in their assessment, and even patients with grade 3 tumors sometimes do very well. This emphasizes the need to explore (1) more objective methods for measuring these existing biomarkers and (2) the identification of other quantitative biomarkers that will either improve on or add predictive value to existing methods.

In this chapter, we concentrate on a specific subset of quantitative biomarkers directly measurable from intact cells or tissues. These biomarkers must be judged using the same criteria as listed above. Nevertheless, as will be seen, direct comparison of biomarker performance in predicting features such as recurrence and progression is difficult to assess owing to differences in sample populations, tissue handling, outcome measures, and technology.

TECHNOLOGY

Object Counting

The simple counting of cells or other morphologic identities within tissue samples can be extremely useful biomarkers. A variety of disease-specific characteristics can be measured in this way, including hyperplasia, mitotic activity, labeling indices (for proteins such as p53, Ki-67, etc), apoptosis, silver-staining nucleolar organizer regions (AgNORs) and microvessel density, all of which have been explored as biomarkers in superficial bladder cancer. Counts like these can be easily achieved by simply counting the number of events within a high-powered microscopic field using a hand counter or a pencil and a piece of paper (Figure 9–1, A). Provided that the microscopic field area is kept constant, then a consistent reference space is maintained. Where the amount of tissue within a microscopic field varies considerably, then alternative approaches to the measurement of the reference tissue area are necessary. More sophisticated approaches include the use of computers (see below), which allow the user to trace the reference area and mark cells on screen (Figure 9–1, B). This measures the reference space, keeps track of counts, and computes the number of objects per unit area. Where labeling indices are being measured, the number of labeled cells (eg, *p53*) needs to be expressed as a percentage of the total cell number (Figure 9–1, C). Again, this can be done by hand but is greatly facilitated through the use of computers and image analysis.

Morphometry and Image Analysis

Simple morphometric measurement of nuclear size and shape offers important quantitative clues in tumor grading. Technically, this can be achieved in

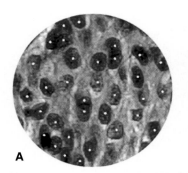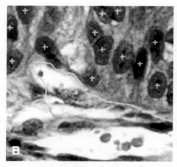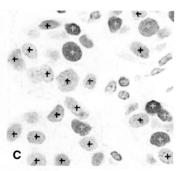

Figure 9–1. *A,* Schematic view of histologic field through eyepiece of a microscope where simple counts can be made. *B,* Using a computer-aided measurement system, regions of interest can be traced, their area calculated, and cell counts made and expressed as number per µm². *C,* Labeling indices require the number of a specific cell type (here p53 positive by D07 immunocytochemistry) to be expressed as a percentage of the total number of epithelial cells (×40 objective magnification).

two ways. The edge of individual nuclei can be individually and manually traced using a mouse or drawing device (Figure 9–2). This profile is then used to compute quantitative features such as area, perimeter, maximum diameter, and shape factor. This represents a convenient, albeit time-consuming and laborious, way to collect quantitative nuclear data, given that approximately 50 nuclei should probably be sampled from each case. The same approach can also be used to measure the dimensions of other tissue structures such as microvessel size and shape.

Alternatively, one can use digital image analysis to automatically identify the nuclear boundaries within an image. This relies on the fact that digital images are composed of pixels, each of which has its own gray value represented by a number between 0 and 255 (Figure 9–3). This numeric information can be used to identify boundaries and regions of homogeneous density within the image using a variety of

image processing and segmentation algorithms (Figure 9–4). This therefore allows the identification of nuclei and other tissue structures.

Although this approach is potentially much more rapid, it is more difficult to achieve owing to the complexities of cytologic and histologic images. The biggest problems arise with overlapping nuclei, which, unless separated, will be measured as a single object. A variety of algorithms are available that can distinguish the boundaries of individual nuclei or allow model-based approaches to image segmentation.[6–8] Automation can also be used for the identification of other morphologic features such as microvessel density.[9] However, owing to the difficulties in fully automated image interpretation, most studies in the bladder have exploited some form of interactive method, even if the images are digitally recorded. Clearly, automation would be the favored approach for routine analysis of clinical material or for the analysis of large numbers of samples in a

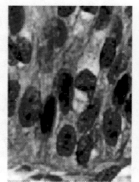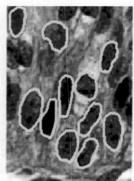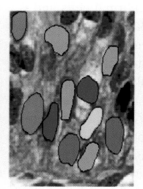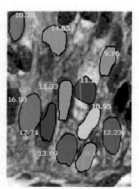

Figure 9–2. Interactive tracing of nuclei using a mouse allows the calculation of the nuclear area and other shape-derived parameters (hematoxylin and eosin, ×60 objective magnification).

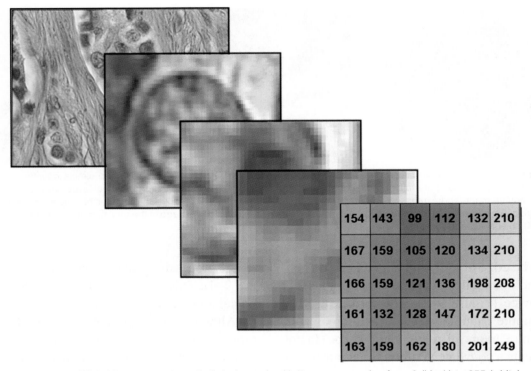

154	143	99	112	132	210
167	159	105	120	134	210
166	159	121	136	198	208
161	132	128	147	172	210
163	159	162	180	201	249

Figure 9–3. Digital images composed of pixels, each with its own gray value from 0 (black) to 255 (white). These numerical data can be stored and used for object identification (see Figure 9–4) and for object measurement, including densitometric and textural features.

research study. There are opportunities, therefore, to develop machine vision methods for the automated analysis of bladder histology and cytology.

DNA Image Cytometry

DNA ploidy describes the complement of DNA within a given cell or cell population. DNA diploid refers to a normal DNA content, which approximates 46 chromosomes. DNA aneuploidy is the term given to an abnormal DNA content, which generally exceeds that observed in normal cells and is typically found in malignant cell populations. There are essentially two approaches to the measurement of DNA content in situ within intact cells. Either one can disaggregate a tissue sample into a single-cell suspension and run it through a flow cytometer (see later) or else one can use DNA image cytometry, which allows measurements to be made using a microscope and tissue sections or cytologic preparations. Nowadays, DNA image cytometry is almost exclusively based around the use of digital images of nuclei that have been specifically stained for DNA.

The most popular staining method used is the Feulgen reaction. This method uses dilute hydrochloric acid to remove the purines in the DNA, thus exposing the aldehyde groups, which are subsequently detected using Schiff's reagent. DNA appears magenta colored. The density of the stain can then be measured using gray values recorded within the boundaries of each nucleus (see Figure 9–3). These gray values need to be converted into optical density units, and care needs to be taken to ensure Feulgen

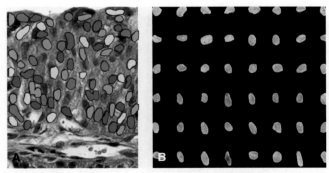

Figure 9–4. A, Using image processing and object identification algorithms, objects such as nuclei can be identified and extracted from the image. B, Extracted nuclei can then be measured for morphometric, DNA, and chromatin texture features.

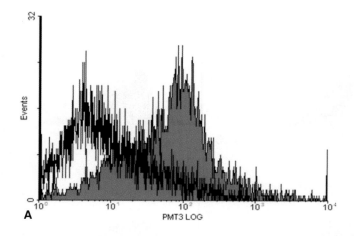

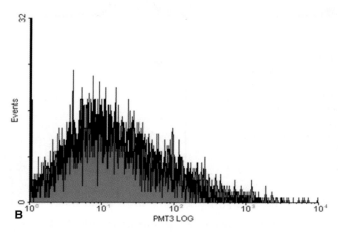

Figure 9–14. Overlay histograms demonstrating bcl2 expression prior to antisense treatment (*A*) and down-regulation of bcl2 protein expression after 1-hour exposure to G3139 bcl2 antisense (*B*). Expression of bcl2 is proportional to the intensity of fluorescence staining (x-axis). The clear histograms represent isotype controls that are subtracted from the corresponding test sample (*red*) to quantitate the level of positive staining.

other proteins could be measured in bladder cell preparations and used to detect protein profile alterations in response to chemotherapy (Figure 9–15).[85] Finally, because most chemo- or radiotherapeutic modalities induce cell death through the process of apoptosis, it is important to be able to objectively measure apoptosis as an indicator of response. This can be achieved using flow cytometry and has been used in studies on antisense and therapy and drug sensitivity.[86,87] Such studies illustrate that the flow cytometric measurement of intracellular proteins has an important role in detecting biomarkers of cancer but may be used to monitor sensitivity and response to therapy.

Decensi and colleagues found that DNA content by flow cytometry was unsuccessful as a surrogate end-point marker for assessing the effect of fenretinide.[88]

Pauwels and colleagues showed a relationship between chromatin texture and sensitivity to the alkylating agent PE1001 and doxorubicin (Adriamycin).[80] Chromatin texture in combination with other parameters such as nuclear morphometry and DNA ploidy has also been used to study the morphologic effects of alkylating agents on bladder tumor cells.[89] These agents appear to induce an increase in cell numbers in the S and G_2 phases of the cell cycle with concomitant changes in the chromatin pattern.

CHEMOPREVENTION AND SURROGATE END-POINT MARKERS

There has been much emphasis placed on chemopreventive therapy in the bladder. Drugs and dietary supplements have been studied as potential effectors in the onset, recurrence, and progression of bladder cancer. Because testing the efficacy of factors such as these primarily relies on long-term measures of clinical outcome, a variety of shorter-term "surrogate end-point" markers have been explored. These markers potentially allow a measure of success or failure of a potential chemopreventive agent over a shorter period and are therefore attractive to the drug industry.

Factors such as DNA ploidy and nuclear texture have been proposed as possible end-point biomarkers of response in the bladder in response to drugs such as dimethylsulfoxide and in risk assessment after exposure to benzidine.[83,90,91]

CONCLUSION

It is clear from the studies outlined above that quantitative methods have strong potential in improving our ability to grade bladder tumors and predict response to therapy and prognosis. However, despite the potential advantages, most centers do not use these techniques routinely. It is advocated that methods for the quantitative analysis of bladder neoplasms need to be better defined, specifically for the routine pathology laboratory, and that standardization and quality control are introduced to ensure comparable results between different laboratories.

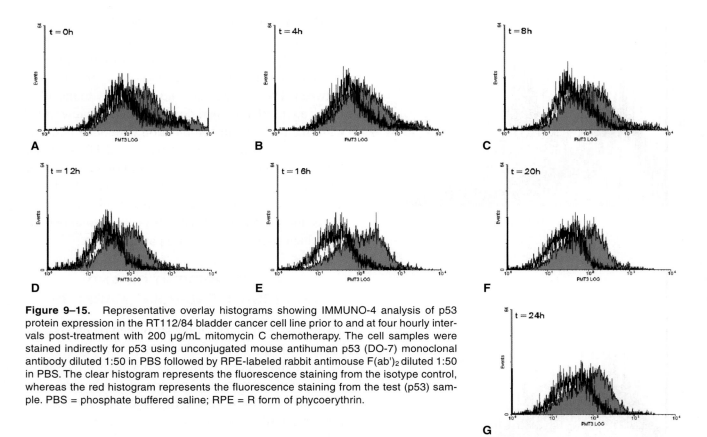

Figure 9–15. Representative overlay histograms showing IMMUNO-4 analysis of p53 protein expression in the RT112/84 bladder cancer cell line prior to and at four hourly intervals post-treatment with 200 µg/mL mitomycin C chemotherapy. The cell samples were stained indirectly for p53 using unconjugated mouse antihuman p53 (DO-7) monoclonal antibody diluted 1:50 in PBS followed by RPE-labeled rabbit antimouse F(ab')₂ diluted 1:50 in PBS. The clear histogram represents the fluorescence staining from the isotype control, whereas the red histogram represents the fluorescence staining from the test (p53) sample. PBS = phosphate buffered saline; RPE = R form of phycoerythrin.

REFERENCES

1. Ooms ECM, Anderson WAD, Alons CL, et al. Analysis of the performance of pathologists in the grading of bladder tumors. Hum Pathol 1983;14:140–3.
2. Sherman AB, Koss LG, Adams SE. Interobserver and intraobserver differences in the diagnosis of urothelial cells—comparison with classification by computer. Anal Quant Cytol Histol 1984;6:112–20.
3. Shenoy UA, Colby TV, Schuman GB. Reliability of urinary cytodiagnosis in urothelial neoplasms. Cancer 1985;56:2041–5.
4. Maier U, Simak R, Neuhold N. The clinical value of urinary cytology: 12 years experience with 615 patients. J Clin Pathol 1995;48:314–7.
5. Ross JS, Cohen MB. Biomarkers for the detection of bladder cancer. Adv Anat Pathol 2001;8:37–45.
6. Demeester U, Young IT, Lindeman J, et al. Towards a quantitative grading of bladder-tumors. Cytometry 1991;12:602–13.
7. Gimenezmas JA, Sanzmoncasi MP, Remon L, et al. Automated textural analysis nuclear chromatin—a mathematical morphology approach. Anal Quant Cytol Histol 1995;17:39–47.
8. Bartels PH, Weber JE, Thompson D, et al. Expert systems in histopathology. In: Hamilton PW, Allen D, editors. Quantitative clinical pathology. London: Blackwell Science; 2002.
9. Wester K, Ranefall P, Bengtsson E, et al. Automatic quantifi-
cation of microvessel density in urinary bladder carcinoma. Br J Cancer 1999;81:1363–70.
10. Hanselaar AGJM, Bocking A, Gundlach H, et al. Summary statement on quantitative cytochemistry (DNA and molecular biology)—Task Force 8. Acta Cytol 2001;45:499–501.
11. Haroske G, Giroud F, Reith A, et al. Part I: basic considerations and recommendations for preparation, measurement and interpretation. Anal Cell Pathol 1998;17:189–200.
12. Puech M, Giroud F. Standardisation of DNA quantitation by image analysis: quality control of instrumentation. Cytometry 1999;36:11–7.
13. Bocking A, Giroud F, Reith A. Consensus report of the European Society for Analytical Cellular Pathology Task Force on Standardization of Diagnostic DNA Image Cytometry. Anal Quant Cytol Histol 1995;17:1–7.
14. Kawamura K, Tanaka T, Ikeda R, et al. DNA ploidy analysis of urinary tract epithelial tumors by laser scanning cytometry. Anal Quant Cytol Histol 2000;22:26–30.
15. Wojcik EM, Saraga SA, Jin JK, et al. Application of laser scanning cytometry for evaluation of DNA ploidy in routine cytologic specimens. Diagn Cytopathol 2001;24:200–5.
16. Dela Roza GL, Hopkovitz A, Caraway NP, et al. DNA image analysis of urinary cytology: prediction of recurrent transitional cell carcinoma. Mod Pathol 1996;9:571–8.
17. van der Poel HG, Witjes JA, van Stratum P, et al. Quanticyt: karyometric analysis of bladder washing for patients with superficial bladder cancer. Urology 1996;48:357–64.
18. Montironi R, Scarpelli M, Sisti S, et al. Prognostic value of

computerized DNA analysis in noninvasive papillary carcinomas of the urinary bladder. Tumori 1987;73:567–74.

19. van der Poel HG, Witjes JA, Schalken JA, et al. Automated image analysis for bladder cancer. Urol Res 1998;26:1–5.

20. Montironi R, Scarpelli M, Braccischi A, et al. Quantitative analysis of nucleolar margination in diagnostic cytopathology. Virchows Arch 1991;419:505–12.

21. Doudkine A, Macauley C, Poulin N, et al. Nuclear texture measurements in image cytometry. Pathologica 1995;87:286–99.

22. Weyn B, Jacob W, da Silva VD, et al. Data representation and reduction for chromatin texture in nuclei from premalignant prostatic, esophageal, and colonic lesions. Cytometry 2000;41:133–8.

23. Bartels PH, Montironi R, Hamilton PW, et al. Nuclear chromatin texture in prostatic lesions II. PIN and malignancy associated changes. Anal Quant Cytol Histol 1998;20:397–406.

24. Williamson KE. Dissaggregation of solid tumours. In: Hamilton PW, Allen D, editor. Quantitative clinical pathology. London: Blackwell Science; 2002.

25. Vandrielkulker AMJ, Eysackers MJ, Dessing MTM, et al. A simple method to select specific tumor areas in paraffin blocks for cytometry using incident fluorescence microscopy. Cytometry 1986;7:601–4.

26. DiFrancesco LM, Murthy SK, Luider J, et al. Laser capture microdissection-guided fluorescence in situ hybridization and flow cytometric cell cycle analysis of purified nuclei from paraffin sections. Mod Pathol 2000;13:705–11.

27. Sanchez-Carbayo M, Ciudad J, Urrutia M, et al. Diagnostic performance of the urinary bladder carcinoma antigen ELISA test and multiparametric DNA/cytokeratin flow cytometry in urine voided samples from patients with bladder carcinoma. Cancer 2001;92:2811–9.

28. Herder A, Bjelkenkrantz K, Grontoft O. Histopathological subgrouping of WHO-II urothelial neoplasms by cytophotometric measurements of nuclear atypia. Acta Pathol Microbiol Immunol Scand 1982;90:405–8.

29. Bjelkenkrantz K, Herder A, Grontoft O, et al. Cytophotometric characterization of the WHO grades of transitional cell neoplasms. Pathol Res Pract 1982;174:68–77.

30. Ooms ECM, Kurver PHJ, Veldhuizen RW, et al. Morphometric grading of bladder tumors in comparison with histologic grading by pathologists. Hum Pathol 1983;14:144–50.

31. Boon ME, Kurver PHJ, Baak JPA, et al. Morphometric differences between urothelial cells in voided urine of patients with grade-I and grade-II bladder-tumors. J Clin Pathol 1981;34:612–5.

32. Schapers RFM, Ploemzaaijer JJ, Pauwels RPE, et al. Image cytometric DNA analysis in transitional-cell carcinoma of the bladder. Cancer 1993;72:182–9.

33. Bol MGW, Baak JPA, de Bruin PC, et al. Improved objectivity of grading of T-A,(1) transitional cell carcinomas of the urinary bladder by quantitative nuclear and proliferation related features. J Clin Pathol 2001;54:854–9.

34. vanderPoel HG, Boon ME, vanStratum P, et al. Conventional bladder wash cytology performed by four experts versus quantitative image analysis. Mod Pathol 1997;10:976–82.

35. Ozer E, Yorukoglu K, Mungan MU, et al. Prognostic significance of nuclear morphometry in superficial bladder cancer. Anal Quant Cytol Histol 2001;23:251–6.

36. Minimo C, Tawfiek ER, Bagley DH, et al. Grading of upper urinary tract transitional cell carcinoma by computed DNA content and p53 expression. Urology 1997;50:869–74.

37. Choi HK, Vasko J, Bengtsson E, et al. Grading of transitional-cell bladder-carcinoma by texture analysis of histological sections. Anal Cell Pathol 1994;6:327–43.

38. Choi HK, Jarkrans T, Bengtsson E, et al. Image analysis based grading of bladder carcinoma. Comparison of object, texture and graph based methods and their reproducibility. Anal Cell Pathol 1997;15:1–18.

39. Lavezzi AM, Biondo B, Cazzullo A, et al. The role of different biomarkers (DNA, PCNA, apoptosis and karyotype) in prognostic evaluation of superficial transitional cell bladder carcinoma. Anticancer Res 2001;21:1279–84.

40. Hamilton PW. Nucleolar organiser regions. In: Hamilton PW, Allen DC, editors. Quantitative clinical pathology. Oxford, UK: Blackwell Science; 1995.

41. Lipponen PK, Eskelinen MJ. Nucleolar organizer regions (nors) in bladder-cancer—relation to histological grade, clinical stage and prognosis. Anticancer Res 1991;11:75–80.

42. Lipponen PK, Eskelinen MJ, Nordling S. Nucleolar organizer regions (AGNORS) as predictors in transitional cell bladder-cancer. Br J Cancer 1991;64:1139–44.

43. Bochner BH, Cote RJ, Weidner N, et al. Angiogenesis in bladder-cancer—relationship between microvessel density and tumor prognosis. J Natl Cancer Inst 1995;87:1603–12.

44. Korkolopoulou P, Konstantinidou AE, Kavantzas N, et al. Morphometric microvascular characteristics predict prognosis in superficial and invasive bladder cancer. Virchows Arch 2001;438:603–11.

45. Pantazopoulos D, IoakimLiossi A, Karakitsos P, et al. DNA content and proliferation activity in superficial transitional cell carcinoma of the bladder. Anticancer Res 1997;17:781–6.

46. Witjes JA, Kiemeney LALM, Wheeless LL, et al. The value of histopathological prognostic factors in superficial bladder cancer: do we need more? Urol Oncol 2000;5:185–90.

47. Kumar NU, Dey P, Mondal AK, et al. DNA flow cytometry and bladder irrigation cytology in detection of bladder carcinoma. Diagn Cytopathol 2001;24:153–6.

48. Kontogeorgos G, Aninos D. Recent aspects in the diagnosis and prognosis of bladder cancer. Tumori 1998;84:301–7.

49. Cianciulli AM, Bovani R, Leonardo F, et al. Interphase cytogenetics of bladder cancer progression: relationship between aneusomy, DNA ploidy pattern, histopathology, and clinical outcome. Int J Clin Lab Res 2000;30:5–11.

50. Eleuteri P, Grollino MG, Pomponi D, et al. Bladder transitional cell carcinomas: a comparative study of washing and tumor bioptic samples by DNA flow cytometry and FISH analyses. Eur Urol 2000;37:275–80.

51. van Velthoven R, Petein M, Oosterlinck W, et al. Identification by quantitative chromatin pattern analysis of patients at risk for recurrence of superficial transitional bladder carcinoma. J Urol 2000;164:2134–7.

52. Colombel M, Delaunoit Y, Bellot J, et al. Prognostic evaluation of morphonuclear parameters in superficial and invasive bladder-cancer. Br J Urol 1995;75:364–9.

53. Gschwendtner A, Hoffmann-Weltin Y, Mikuz G, et al. Quantitative assessment of bladder cancer by nuclear texture analysis using automated high resolution image cytometry. Mod Pathol 1999;12:806–13.

54. van Velthoven R, Petein M, Oosterlinck WJ, et al. The use of digital image-analysis of chromatin texture in Feulgenstained nuclei to predict recurrence of low-grade superficial transitional-cell carcinoma of the bladder. Cancer 1995;75:560–8.

55. van Velthoven R, Petein M, Oosterlinck WJ, et al. The additional predictive value contributed by quantitative chromatin pattern description as compared to DNA ploidy level measurement in 257 superficial bladder transitional cell carcinomas. Eur Urol 1996;29:245–51.

56. Decaestecker C, Petein M, van Velthoven R, et al. The computer-assisted microscope analysis of Feulgen-stained nuclei linked to a supervised learning algorithm as an aid to prognosis assessment in invasive transitional bladder cell carcinomas. Anal Cell Pathol 1996;10:263–80.

57. Veltri RW, Partin AW, Miller MC. Quantitative nuclear grade (QNG): a new image analysis-based biomarker of clinically relevant nuclear structure alterations. J Cell Biochem 2000;(Suppl 35):151–7.

58. Gschwendtner A, Mairinger T. Quantitative assessment of bladder carcinoma by acid labile DNA assay. Cancer 1999;86:105–13.

59. Hamilton PW, Bartels PH, Wilson RH, et al. Nuclear texture measurements in normal colorectal glands. Anal Quant Cytol Histol 1995;17:397–405.

60. Montironi R, Scarpelli M, Mazzucchelli R, et al. Subvisual chromatin changes are detected by karyometry in the histologically normal urothelium in patients with synchronous papillary carcinoma. Hum Pathol 2003 [in press].

61. Desgrippes A, Izadifar V, Assailly J, et al. Diagnosis and prediction of recurrence and progression in superficial bladder cancers with DNA image cytometry and urinary cytology. Br J Urol Int 2000;85:434–6.

62. Mora LB, Nicosia SV, PowSang JM, et al. Ancillary techniques in the followup of transitional cell carcinoma: a comparison of cytology, histology and deoxyribonucleic acid image analysis cytometry in 91 patients. J Urol 1996;156:49–54.

63. Planz B, Synek C, Deix T, et al. Diagnosis of bladder cancer with urinary cytology, immunocytology and DNA-image-cytometry. Anal Cell Pathol 2001;22:103–9.

64. Richman AM, Mayne ST, Jekel JF, et al. Image analysis combined with visual cytology in the early detection of recurrent bladder carcinoma. Cancer 1998;82:1738–48.

65. van der Poel HG, Van Balken MR, Schamhart DHJ, et al. Bladder wash cytology, quantitative cytology, and the qualitative BTA test in patients with superficial bladder cancer. Urology 1998;51:44–50.

66. van Rhijn BWG, van der Poel HG, Boon ME, et al. Presence of carcinoma in situ and high 2c-deviation index are the best predictors of invasive transitional cell carcinoma of the bladder in patients with high-risk Quanticyt. Urology 2000;55:363–7.

67. Slaton JW, Dinney CPN, Veltri RW, et al. Deoxyribonucleic acid ploidy enhances the cytological prediction of recurrent transitional cell carcinoma of the bladder. J Urol 1997;158:806–11.

68. Wiener HG, Remkes GW, Schatzl G, et al. Quick-staining urinary cytology and bladder wash image analysis with an integrated risk classification—a worthwhile improvement in the follow-up of bladder cancer? Cancer Cytopathol 1999;87:263–9.

69. Katz RL, Sinkre PA, Zhang HH, et al. Clinical significance of negative and equivocal urinary bladder cytology alone and in combination with DNA image analysis and cystoscopy. Cancer Cytopathol 1997;81:354–64.

70. Simak R, Wiener H, Foeger A, et al. Cytophotometry in the monitoring of bladder cancer under intravesical chemotherapy. Eur Urol 1996;29:391–8.

71. Bellaoui H, Chefchaouni MC, Lazrak N, et al. Flow cytometric DNA analysis and cytology in diagnosis and prognosis of bladder tumors: preliminary results of a comparative study on bladder washing. Ann D Urol 2002;36:45–52.

72. Tetu B, Katz RL, Kalter SP, et al. Flow-cytometry of transitional cell-carcinoma of the urinary-bladder—influence of prior local therapy. Semin Diagn Pathol 1987;4:243–50.

73. Wheeless LL, Badalament RA, White RWD, et al. Consensus review of the clinical utility of DNA cytometry in bladder-cancer. Cytometry 1993;14:478–81.

74. Duggan BJ, Maxwell P, Kelly JD, et al. The effect of antisense Bcl-2 oligonucleotides on bcl-2 protein expression and apoptosis in human bladder transitional cell carcinoma. J Urol 2001;166:1098–105.

75. Mian C, Pycha A, Wiener H, et al. Immunocyt: a new tool for detecting transitional cell cancer of the urinary tract. J Urol 1997;161:1486–9.

76. Halling KC, King W, Sokolova IA, et al. A comparison of cytology and fluorescence in situ hybridization for the detection of urothelial carcinoma. J Urol 2000;164:1768–75.

77. Sokolova IA, Halling KC, Jenkins RB, et al. The development of a multitarget, multicolor fluorescence in situ hybridization assay for the detection of urothelial carcinoma in urine. J Mol Diagn 2000;2:116–23.

78. Marano A, Pan Y, Li CD, et al. Chromosomal numerical aberrations detected by fluorescence in situ hybridization on bladder washings from patients with bladder cancer. Eur Urol 2000;37:358–65.

79. Hamilton PW, Kelly J, McManus D, et al. Nuclear texture as a predictor of response to MMC in an ex vivo model of superficial bladder cancer. J Pathol 2001;193:45A.

80. Pauwels O, Kiss R. Digital morphonuclear analyses of sensitive versus resistant neoplastic-cells to vinca-alkaloid, alkylating, and intercalating drugs. Cytometry 1991;12:388–97.

81. Shigematsu N, Kawata T, Ihara N, et al. Effect of combined treatment with radiation and low dose etoposide on cell survival. Anticancer Res 2001;21:325–8.

82. Cartsburg O, Kallen C, Hillenkamp J, et al. Topical mitomycin C and radiation induce conjunctival DNA polyploidy. Anal Cell Pathol 2001;23:65–74.

83. Boone CW, Bacus JW, Bacus JV, et al. Properties of intraepithelial neoplasia relevant to the development of cancer chemopreventive agents. J Cell Biochem 1997;(Suppl 28–29):1–20.

84. Duggan BJ, Cotter FE, Kelly JD, et al. Antisense Bcl-2 oligonucleotide uptake in human transitional cell carcinoma. Eur Urol 2001;40:685–95.

85. Canning P. Quantitative assessment of response to mitomycin C chemotherapy in superficial bladder cancer [thesis]. Belfast: Queen's University of Belfast; 2001.

86. Darzynkiewicz Z, Juan G, Li X, et al. Cytometry in cell necrobiology: analysis of apoptosis and accidental cell death (necrosis). Cytometry 1997;27:1–20.

87. Sun HZ, Wu SF, Tu ZH. Knockdown of IGF- I R by antisense oligodeoxynucleotide auguments sensitivity of T24 bladder cancer cells to mitomycin. Acta Pharmacol Sin 2001;22:841–846.

88. Decensi A, Torrisi R, Bruno S, et al. Randomized trial of fenretinide in superficial bladder cancer using DNA flow cytometry as an intermediate end point. Cancer Epidemiol Biomarkers Prev 2000;9:1071–8.

89. Pauwels O, Atassi G, Kiss R. Combination of computerized morphonuclear and multivariate analyses to characterize in vitro the antineoplastic effect of alkylating agents. J Pharmacol Toxicol Methods 1995;33:35–45.

90. Hemstreet GP, Rao JY, Hurst RE, et al. Biomarkers in monitoring for efficacy of immunotherapy and chemoprevention of bladder cancer with dimethylsulfoxide. Cancer Detect Prev 1999;23:163–71.

91. Hemstreet GP, Yin SN, Ma ZZ, et al. Biomarker risk assessment and bladder cancer detection in a cohort exposed to benzidine. J Natl Cancer Inst 2001;93:427–36.

10

Bladder Tumor Markers: Current Concepts and Status

VINATA B. LOKESHWAR, PhD

FRANCISCO CIVANTOS, MD

Management of bladder cancer patients is challenging because bladder tumors frequently recur and show heterogeneity in their ability to invade and metastasize.[1–4] Tumor markers with early detection capabilities, recurrence monitoring abilities, prognostic capabilities and abilities to monitor treatment response should help in detecting bladder tumors before they become invasive, improve surveillance for tumor recurrence, and individualize treatment regimens for each patient. This could result in improved prognosis and a better quality of life for bladder cancer patients.

Unlike prostate cancer, bladder cancer is almost never found as an incidental cancer on autopsy.[1,4] Most bladder cancer patients present with symptoms such as painless hematuria in the absence of any urinary tract infection, and/or irritative voiding.[5–7] This mode of detection may be acceptable for approximately 70% of bladder tumors (ie, transitional cell carcinomas), which are low-grade papillary tumors.[7–10] Most low-grade (ie, grade I) tumors are superficial and remain confined to mucosa, showing little propensity to invade and metastasize (progression rate ~ 2%).[2] However, the majority of patients with high-grade (ie, grade III) bladder cancer, at the time of initial presentation, have tumors that invade the lamina propria (stage T1) and beyond.[2,5,7,10] Muscle invasion by a tumor is ominous, since the majority of patients will develop distant metastasis within 2 years and 60% of the patients will die within 5 years, despite aggressive treatment of the disease.[7]

Detection of tumor in the bladder following treatment of the initial tumor is collectively termed "bladder tumor recurrence." Typically, 30 to 80% of bladder cancer patients will have another tumor within 3 years.[7,11,12] In addition, 30% of the patients with a low-grade tumor will have a higher-grade recurrence.[7,9,13,14] Moreover, tumors may recur as higher stage disease with poorer prognosis.[14] Tumor recurrence may be a result of the "field effect" and/or residual tumor remaining after surgery.[15–26] Whatever the cause of subsequent tumors in the bladder, bladder cancer patients are monitored every 3 to 6 months for recurrence.[7,9]

STANDARD CARE FOR BLADDER CANCER DETECTION AND SURVEILLANCE

The "gold standard" for detecting bladder cancer and monitoring its recurrence is cystoscopy.[5,27,28] Patients presenting with hematuria (either microscopic or gross) or irritative voiding symptoms, absent infection, undergo cystoscopy followed by biopsy of a suspect area. Following treatment of the initial tumor, patients undergo cystoscopy every 3 to 6 months for the first 2 years, and at longer intervals thereafter, depending upon the grade and stage of the resected tumor and frequency of recurrence.[6,7,27] Although a flexible cystoscope reduces discomfort associated with cystoscopy, it is an invasive procedure affecting patients' quality of life since they are subjected to it at multiple times a year. Cystoscopy is also relatively expensive, as the Medicare reimbursement costs range between $200 to $300 ($216.20 at University of Miami).[27] Thus, a non-invasive marker could decrease cost and improve patients' quality of life by reducing the number of surveillance cystoscopies.[29]

The standard non-invasive bladder tumor marker is voided urine cytology.[6,30–34] It is a good marker for detecting high-grade tumors, in particular carcinoma in situ (CIS). However, as discussed below, cytology is not readily available in many parts of the world, its inferences are subjective in nature and it is relatively expensive (average cost $50 to $100).[7,27] Thus, an accurate marker that measures biochemical or genetic changes due to the presence of bladder tumor has a place in diagnosing bladder cancer and monitoring its recurrence.

BLADDER TUMOR MARKERS: WHY DO WE NEED THEM?

A non-invasive and accurate bladder tumor marker may be used for bladder cancer screening, recurrence monitoring and individualized treatment selection.[7,34–36]

Tumor Markers and Bladder Cancer Screening

Cancer screening using tumor marker offers an advantage of early detection of cancer prior to metastasis. Such early detection would result in decreased morbidity associated with metastasis and improved survival. For example, following the acceptance of prostate-specific antigen (PSA) as a screening marker, the majority of prostate tumors that are detected are clinically localized.[37] In the case of bladder cancer, early detection of bladder cancer, prior to becoming invasive (ie, detection at stages ≤ TIb) would result in improved prognosis.[1,3] The prevalence of bladder cancer in the general population is low (0.1001%).[37a] However, Messing et al reported a 1.3% prevalence of bladder cancer in men above the age of 50.[38–40] The incidence of bladder cancer cases is even lower, at 21.2 per 100,000 persons per year.[37a] Given that high-grade bladder tumors account for about 20 to 30% of all bladder

tumors, the prevalence of high-grade bladder tumors in the general population would be even lower. Thus, screening the whole population for bladder cancer, with the possibility of detecting too many false-positives (who will require an expensive work up) will not be cost-effective.

Bladder cancer screening may be cost effective among individuals who are at a higher risk for bladder cancer. Cigarette smoking, occupational exposures to aniline dyes, aromatic amines, benzidine, arsenic, parasitic infections (eg, Schistosoma haematobium), chronic bacterial infections, chronic catheterization, and possibly geographic region (eg, Northeastern United States versus Western United States) have been shown to increase the risk for bladder cancer.[41–57] For example, the risk for bladder cancer among smokers, painters, and workers in industries that deal with arylamines, is two- to eight-fold higher than in normal healthy population after correcting for age, gender, and race.[42,43,47,48,52,54,55,58] The risk for bladder cancer is higher when smoking is combined with exposure to other known bladder carcinogens.[5,43,47] Polymorphisms in N-acetyltransferase–2 (NAT2) (eg, slow acetylator phenotype) and *glutathione-S transferase* (eg, GSTM1 null phenotype) genes, the enzyme products of which are involved in detoxification of bladder carcinogens, are host-related factors that increase the risk for bladder cancer, if the individuals with these phenotypes are exposed to known bladder carcinogens.[58–60] The mean time for the development of bladder cancer, following exposure to bladder carcinogens is 18 years.[1] This time frame allows early detection of bladder cancer prior to the occurrence of invasive disease, if a single or a battery of tumor markers is used for screening the high-risk population.

When using a bladder tumor marker for screening, it is essential that the marker has a low false-positive rate. This will avoid unnecessary anxiety to patients and expensive work up incurred due to false-positive results. One of the possible ways to identify false-positive results would be to have the knowledge of conditions/diseases that give rise to a false-positive result on a particular marker, and then, screening the population for those conditions along with screening for the tumor marker. For example, when screening a population for bladder cancer using hemoglobin dip-stick (detects hematuria), obtaining information on the history of or active episodes of stone disease, urinary tract infection, or cystitis, among other factors, is useful to eliminate false-positive results. In a bladder cancer screening study, involving 401 Department of Energy workers who had a possible exposure to bladder carcinogens, the majority of the positive cases on the BTA-Stat test had an abnormal urine analysis or clinical history (ie, 2+ to 3+ protein on dipstick, microhematuria, presence of leukocytes, history of cystitis, and others). Although there is a possibility that bladder cancer is concomitantly present in these positive individuals, cystoscopy on some of them revealed no evidence of bladder cancer.[61]

In a recent study, Hemstreet and colleagues assessed the risk for the development of bladder cancer, in a cohort of 1,788 Chinese workers who were exposed to benzidine, by developing a biomarker profile.[52] This biomarker profile included the analysis of DNA ploidy, G-actin, and tumor-associated antigen P-300.[52] Although, the biomarker profile placed only 21% of the exposed workers in a high/moderate risk group, 87% of the bladder cancer cases in the entire cohort were found in this group, and all of the tumors were clinically organ confined.[52,53] Of more interest, a positive biomarker profile preceded the clinical detection of bladder cancer by 15 to 33 months. This study suggests that screening a high-risk population using biomarkers may offer an early detection advantage. If early diagnosis translates into detection of tumors prior to progression, clinicians may be able to manage bladder cancer patients with bladder preservation treatments and prolong the time to cystectomy. Lotan and Roehrborn have suggested that the use of bladder tumor markers together with cystoscopy could improve prognosis and reduce medical cost (due to fewer individuals needing cystectomy because of an early detection advantage (average cost of cystectomy, $20,000).[27]

Tumor Markers and Bladder Cancer Recurrence

The management of bladder cancer patients is challenging since bladder tumors frequently recur and often progress to a higher stage. A simple noninva-sive highly sensitive and specific method for detecting bladder cancer would decrease the morbidity associated with cystoscopy, improve patients' quality of life, and decrease costs, since most non-invasive methods are less expensive than cystoscopy.[6,7,13,27,32,62,63] When considering the use of bladder tumor markers, in addition to cost and the quality of life issues, two other issues need consideration. The first issue relates to the accuracy and reliability of a marker to detect bladder cancer recurrence. The advantages of reduced cost and improved quality of life would be less important if a marker misses the recurrence and patients progress to have invasive disease.[12,64] Vriesma and colleagues found that if a marker shows more than a 10% false-negative rate (ie, more than 10% of the recurrences are missed) the patients would not choose switching over from cystoscopy to a noninvasive urine test as the standard mode of surveillance.[65] This trend was more common in women and among patients who are younger than 67 years of age. Currently, several urine markers show less than 90% sensitivity to detect bladder cancer.[7,9,34] Two possible ways or their combinations may be employed to overcome the shortcomings of non-invasive markers in terms of sensitivity.

The first way is to use a combination of two or more markers with comparable performance, in terms of sensitivity and accuracy, for monitoring recurrence. Since different bladder tumor tests detect distinctly different bladder tumor-associated molecules (ie, soluble or cell-associated DNA and protein markers), the possibility that all bladder tumor tests included in the combination will miss a recurrence at the same time, is low. Thus, the sensitivity of the combination for detecting bladder cancer will be higher than the individual tests alone. For example, in a recent study, the HA-HAase test and the BTA-Stat test showed 94% and 61% sensitivity, respectively, for detecting bladder cancer. However, the combination of these two tests had a sensitivity of 98% for detecting bladder cancer recurrence.[61] In another study, Mattioli and colleagues found that combining the inferences of the BTA-TARK and urine cytology increased the sensitivity of detecting bladder tumor recurrence to 91%.[66] The increase in sensitivity of the combination was more impressive for the detection of superficial bladder tumors.[66] Combining two or more invasive tests, however, will increase the number of false-positive results. This is because each test may have its own set of clinical conditions other than bladder cancer that give rise to a false-positive result. However, if the objective of bladder cancer surveillance is to detect each and every episode of recurrence, then even if there is some increase in false-positive cases, a combination of non-invasive tests with > 95% sensitivity, will improve patients' quality of life and reduce medical cost while detecting most recurrences. It is also noteworthy that a combination of non-invasive markers (eg, HA-HAase and BTA-Stat or BTA-TARK and cytology) will be less expensive when compared to cystoscopy. For example, in a recent study from the authors' laboratory, the combination of HA-HAase and BTA-Stat tests cost less than $50.[61]

For a bladder tumor marker, the false-positive results are defined as the absence of tumor in bladder upon cystoscopic observation. However, most non-invasive tests detect biochemical (eg, protein detection by a dipstick or enzyme-linked immunosorbent assay [ELISA]), or genetic (eg, detection of mRNA expression by RT-PCR, loss of heterozygosity [LOH], or microsatellite analysis) changes in individual tumor cells and/or in tumor-associated stroma.[6,7,9,13,14,16,28,31,32,34–36,63] Since most biochemical and genetic changes precede tumor growth, which is cystoscopically visible, and the sensitivity of diagnostic tests for detecting such changes is high. Various tests can detect tumor before it becomes cystoscopically visible. This is exemplified in many recent studies involving microsatellite DNA analysis, HA-HAase test, fluorescence in situ hybridization (FISH), and the biomarker profile described in the study by Hemstreet and colleagues.[52,61,67–69] These studies would tend to suggest that tumor markers can detect bladder cancer recurrence early. However, it remains to be established whether such early detection of recurrence translates into better prognosis and/or improved quality of life.

The second way to overcome the shortcomings of a non-invasive marker due to low sensitivity, would be to combine the use of markers and cystoscopy in a surveillance protocol. Recently, Lotan and Roehrborn showed that alternating between cys-toscopy plus cytology and tumor markers, such that there is a 6-month interval between consecutive cystoscopies will allow detection of recurrence prior to progression.[27] Assuming that the average cost of a marker test is ~ $20, it would yield a net saving of more than $17,335,000 for the 53,000 new bladder cancer patients detected each year in the United States.[27] Using combinations of markers, rather than a single marker in the modified protocol, could further improve the probability of detecting each and every case of recurrence prior to progression. As suggested by Lotan and Roehrborn, the modified protocol should be evaluated in a prospective randomized trial to determine whether the benefits of this outweigh potential drawbacks.[27]

Tumor Markers and Individualized Treatment Selection

Multiple forms of bladder tumors such as superficial papillary (low-grade, low-stage), high-grade superficial, and high-grade tumors (either invasive or superficial) associated with CIS, arise from different biochemical and genetic pathways, each requiring distinct clinical management.[1,15,17,70] Patients who have superficial tumors that have a high metastatic potential will benefit from aggressive treatment; whereas those patients whose tumors have a lower metastatic potential can enjoy a better quality of life by receiving a less aggressive treatment. Tumor markers that can distinguish the invasive potential of individual bladder tumors of the same histologic grade and stage predict the frequency of recurrence for individual tumors, and evaluate response to treatment will help in making individualized treatment selection that is suited for each patients' need.[71,72] Among several prognostic indicators, immunostaining of *P53* and *P53* mutations as predictors of prognosis is well studied. For example, p53 status in bladder tumors may predict response to Bacille-Calmette-Guerin (BCG) therapy and radiation therapy, and distinguish pT1G3 tumors that are more aggressive and more likely to recur from those that are less aggressive.[73,74] However, other studies show that p53 is not a predictor of treatment response.[75] Other prognostic markers that may also predict treatment response include,

Ki67, chromosomal alterations, and apoptosis index.[74–76] The usefulness of these markers in making treatment decisions or predicting treatment response will be discussed later in this chapter.

As genetic alterations and the protein products of the expression of these altered genes that regulate the development of various types of bladder cancers are understood, our knowledge of how such information can be used in an integrated fashion to predict treatment response will improve. However, before tumor markers could be used in making treatment decisions, clinical trials using a single marker or a combination of markers will be necessary.

IDEAL TUMOR MARKER

An ideal tumor marker should be technically easy to assay, and easy to interpret the results. It should have low inter- and intra-assay variability. Most importantly, the marker should have high accuracy, which is a reflection of high sensitivity and specificity.[7,12,77]

Bladder Tumor Markers and Technical Simplicity of Detection

It is relatively easy to design non-invasive tests/markers for bladder cancer. Since urine comes in contact with bladder tumors while it is stored in the bladder, many tumor-associated molecules are secreted in urine. These molecules can be assayed by designing urine tests.[7] Tumor cells are also shed in urine, and thus allow design of markers/tests that detecte tumor-cell associated molecules. Many bladder cancer tests such as, BTA-Stat/TARK, NMP22, FDP/Accu-Dx, HA-HAase, BLCA-4, survivin, UBC, urinary cytokeratin 19 (CYFRA 21-1) detect soluble tumor markers present in urine.[7,9] Other bladder cancer markers/tests such as ImmunoCyt, cytokeratin-20, telomerase, Quanticyt-nuclear karyometry, FISH, and microsatellite DNA analysis require exfoliated cells in voided urine or bladder wash specimens as the starting material.[7,9,67,68]

Tests such as the BTA-Stat, Accu-Dx, newer version of the NMP22 test (not yet marketed), and UBC-rapid are point-of-care office-based tests (product inserts). Other tests such as, BTA-TARK, NMP22, HA-HAase, BLCA-4, survivin, UBC, CYFRA 21-1

are ELISAs.[7,9] Telomerase, cytokeratin-20, microsatellite DNA analysis are polymaerase chain reaction (PCR)–based assays; whereas FISH, Quanticyt karyometry, and ImmunoCyt require microscopy and image analysis.[7,9,67,68] For performing ELISAs, PCR assays, or fluorescence microscopy and imaging, urine samples have to be shipped to a central laboratory for analysis. This should not pose a problem for either office-based or academic urology practices, since these practices routinely ship sera to reference laboratories for PSA measurement and urine for cytology evaluation.[7] Thus, a point-of-care bladder cancer test is desirable but not a necessity.

Inter- and Intra-Assay Variability

A diagnostic test that measures quantitative changes in the concentration of a bladder tumor marker among bladder cancer patients and healthy individuals or among various grades and stages of bladder tumors, should have low inter- and intra-assay variability.[7,12] As evident from the term, intra-assay variability for a tumor marker is computed by assaying the same sample at multiple times in a single experiment, and then computing the intra-class correlation by using one-way analysis of variance.[78,79] Intra-class correlation approaching 1.0 indicates low intra-assay variability. Inter-assay variability is calculated by assaying the same sample in different experiments. The inter-assay variability is calculated from the data of different experiments using Pearson's correlation analysis. The Pearson's correlation coefficient approaching 1.0 indicates low inter-assay variability.[78,79]

Statistical Parameters for Evaluating Marker Efficiency

Efficacy of a marker is analyzed by 2×2 analysis. A 2×2 table [ie, a contingency table is set up as 2 columns representing tumor positive and tumor negative and 2 rows representing test (or marker) positive and test (or marker) negative (Figure 10–1)].[79] Each individual in the study population is placed in one of the four cells of the contingency table. True-positives (TP) are individuals who have the tumor and are positive on the test. False-negative

Equations: % Sensitivity: TP ÷ (TP + FN) × 100

% False-negative rate: FN ÷ (TP + FN) × 100

% Specificity: TN ÷ (TN + FP)/ × 100

% False-positive rate: FN ÷ (TN + FP)/ × 100

% Accuracy: (TP + TN) ÷ (TP + TN + FN + FP) × 100

% PPV: TP ÷ (TP + FP)/ × 100

% NPV: TN ÷ (TN + FN) × 100

Figure 10–1. Contigency table. FN = false-negative; FP = false positive; TP = true-positive.

(FN) individuals have the tumor but are negative on the test. False-positive (FP) individuals do not have the tumor but are positive on the test. True negative individuals are those who do not have the tumor and are negative on the test. The contingency table can also be set up for assessing the risk of developing the disease (eg, bladder cancer) following exposure to a particular risk factor (eg, smoking or exposure to arylamines, benzidine, pelvic radiation, and arsenic). In such studies the presence or absence of the risk factor replaces the term for test/marker.

The contingency tables are used to evaluate the statistical significance in a cross-sectional, retrospective, or a prospective study. An example of a cross-sectional study would be, assessing the association between current use of cigarette smoking and current presence of bladder cancer in a population. A retrospective study, for example, would be assessing the association between presence of a marker/test in archival specimens and the presence of disease progression, prognosis, or survival among patients. An example of a prospective study would be that the study individuals are examined for the presence of a marker/test and then followed for a specific period of time, to detect disease recurrence, progression, or survival.

Sensitivity and False-Negative Rate

Sensitivity of a test/marker is defined as the percent of patients with the disease (eg, bladder cancer) for whom the test is positive.[7,79] It is calculated from the contingency table as (TP/(TP + FN)) × 100. The false-

negative rate is defined as the percent of patients with the disease in whom the test is negative. It is calculated as (FN/(TP + FN)) × 100. For an ideal tumor marker/test, the sensitivity and the false-negative rate should approach 100% and 0%, respectively.[7,79] A higher false-negative rate for a non-invasive tumor marker will increase the risk for disease progression, and hence for poor prognosis, is due to missed tumor.[7,12] This may be particularly important, if the marker/test is used for monitoring bladder cancer recurrence, because ~ 30% of low-grade tumors recur as high-grade tumors and the high-grade tumors frequently recur as well as progress in stage. When evaluating the sensitivity of a marker/test, it is important to keep in mind that the reported sensitivity of that marker/test is valid only for the study population in which it was evaluated. For example, most bladder tumor markers/tests will have high sensitivity for detecting high-grade, large volume, and advanced tumors.[7] A large volume tumor will ensure the secretion of high levels of tumor-associated molecules, as well as exfoliated cells in urine. Thus, many non-invasive tests that detect either soluble tumor-associated molecules or exfoliated cells will be positive if a large volume tumor is present. Therefore, in order to assess how a marker will perform in a heterogeneous community setting, field testing that includes patients with low-grade, low-stage, as well as high-grade, high-stage tumors is essential.[7]

Specificity and False-Positive Rate

The specificity of a marker/test is defined as the percent of individuals without the disease in whom the test is negative.[7,79] Specificity is calculated from the contingency table as (TN/(TN + FP)) × 100.[7,79] The false-positive rate of a test/marker is defined as the percent of individuals without the disease in whom the test is positive. The false-positive rate is calculated as (FP/(TN + FP)) × 100). For an ideal tumor marker, the specificity and false-positive rate should approach 100% and 0%, respectively. Higher specificity of a marker is particularly desirable if the marker is being used for screening.[7] Since the prevalence of bladder cancer, even in a high-risk population, is low (eg, ~ 1%) a marker with high specificity and reasonable sensitivity will reduce anxiety and medical cost due to unnecessary work-up, caused by too many false-positive results.[7,12,38,52] As we discussed in an earlier review article, the reported specificity of a marker/test is determined by the composition of the study population.[7] For example, many bladder cancer markers have > 90% specificity among healthy individuals but have poor specificity among patients with hematuria, or other genitourinary conditions.[7]

Accuracy

Accuracy of a tumor/marker is dependent upon both the sensitivity and specificity of that marker/test in a given study population. The accuracy of a marker/test is calculated as (TP + TN)/(TP + TN + FN + FP)) × 100.[7,79] Since both sensitivity and specificity of a marker/test are valid only for the study population in which they were tested, accuracy of that marker/test is also dependent on the composition of the study population.

Positive and Negative Predictive Values

The contingency table is also used to calculate the positive predictive value (PPV) and negative predictive value (NPV) of a marker/test.[7,79] Both PPV and NPV are dependent upon the prevalence of the disease in the study population.[7,79] The PPV is defined as the percent of individuals in whom the test/marker is positive and the disease is present. PPV is calculated as (TP/(TP + FP)) × 100.[7,79] The NPV is defined as the percent of individuals in whom the test is negative and the disease is not present. NPV is calculated as, (TN/(TN + FN)) × 100.[79] Since the PPV and NPV are dependent on the prevalence of the disease in the population, these values can be either low or high in different study populations, even if a marker/test has the same sensitivity and specificity in those different populations.[7,79] Let us study some examples to understand this concept.

In the study by Hemstreet and colleagues, the total incidence of bladder cancer among workers who were either exposed or not exposed to benzidine is 1.4%.[52] In another study, Messing and colleagues reported an incidence of bladder cancer among asymptomatic men above the age of 50 years at 1.3% (21 bladder cancer cases among 1,575 individuals).[38] Assuming an incidence of 1.4%, a marker with 90% sensitivity and 90% specificity will have a PPV of 11.3% and an NPV of 99.8%. A PPV of 11.3% means that close to 90% of the test/marker-positive individuals are false-positives. Thus, a screening program for bladder cancer in the general population, using any bladder tumor marker/test, regardless of its accuracy, will be costly.

The risk for bladder cancer, as determined by incidence rate (IR = (number of new cases/period of time per number of individuals in the risk group) risk ratio and odds ratio (as defined later in text), among smokers, painters and industry workers exposed to arylamines is two- to eight-fold higher than in normal unexposed healthy individuals.[41-57] The risk is even higher if smoking is combined with other risk factors.[42,43,45,52,54,55,58] In the study by Hemstreet and colleagues, the total incidence of bladder cancer among high/moderate-risk groups (as defined by the biomarker profile) was 5.8% (26 cancers in 447 individuals).[52] Thus in the second example, assuming an incidence rate of 3%, a marker with 90% sensitivity and 90% specificity will have 21.8% PPV and 99.7% NPV. The lessons learned from widespread acceptance of prostate-specific antigen (PSA) screening for prostate cancer may suggest that screening a population at higher risk for bladder cancer with reasonably high sensitivity (> 80%) and specificity (> 80%) may help for early detection of bladder cancer with economic feasibility.[7,80-83] Many bladder tumor markers that are currently available have higher sensitivity and specificity than that reported for PSA. Thus, bladder cancer screening in high-risk population may become more of an acceptability issue than of a feasibility issue, among clinicians and patients alike.[7,29] Studies have shown that the prevalence of bladder cancer among patients with a history of bladder cancer ranges between 26 to 70%.[27] In the third example, assuming the prevalence of bladder cancer at 30%, a marker with 90% sensitivity and 90% specificity, will have 79.4% PPV and 95.5% NPV. Thus, a non-invasive marker test with high sensitivity and reasonably good specificity has a place in the management of recurrent bladder cancer.

In summary, the usefulness of a marker very much depends upon the population in which it is applied. If a marker is planned for bladder screening, the marker should have high specificity and high PPV to avoid unnecessary work-up. If a marker is to be used for monitoring bladder cancer recurrence, the marker should have high sensitivity and high NPV in order not to miss any tumor recurrence episode.

Biochemical Markers and Evaluation of Early Detection

As discussed above, since biochemical markers can detect tumor-associated molecules at nano- or pico-molar concentrations, and molecular biology techniques have the capability to detect even a single tumor cell in a milliliter of serum or urine, most diagnostic tests can potentially detect the presence of bladder tumor before it becomes cystoscopically visible. If such markers are used in the clinical practice for monitoring bladder cancer recurrence, a false-positive result would create a dilemma for physicians. This would be, whether to impose treatment in the absence of a positive cystoscopy or allow the tumor to become clinically visible that by then may have progressed in its grade and stage.[12] The significance of false-positive results in predicting recurrence within a specific time period can be statistically evaluated by performing the *chi-squared* analysis and calculating the risk ratio and odds ratio.

Chi-squared (χ^2) Analysis

The chi-squared analysis for statistical significance is calculated using a contingency table. The formulae to calculate the chi-square are algebraically the same for the cross-sectional, retrospective, and prospective studies.[79] In the chi-squared analysis, a χ^2 value of greater than or equal to 3.84 (or a "Z" value of 1.96) is considered statistically significant, at $p \leq .05$.[79] Thus, if there is a statistically significant association between a false-positive result on a specific marker/test, and the occurrence of bladder tumor in the specified time, the χ^2 value will be ≥ 3.84 and $p = \leq .05$.

Fisher's exact test is used in place of the *chi-squared* analysis when the sample size is small. The sample size is considered small, when the expected value of either one or more cells in the contingency table is less than 5.

Risk Ratio (RR) and Odds Ratio (OR):

The ability of a marker to predict bladder cancer recurrence can be further assessed by calculating RR and OR. The RR is defined as the ratio of risk of developing the disease if the factor is present and the risk of developing the disease if the factor is absent (Figure 10-1). The OR is a surrogate measure of the RR and is defined as, the ratio of the odds of having been exposed to a risk factor among individuals with the disease and the odds of having been exposed when the disease is not present.

In the study by Hemstreet and colleagues, the risk of developing bladder cancer among biomarker positive individuals was high, with RR for various markers ranging between 16 to 38 and OR ranging between 40 and 46.[52] The biomarker profile in that study predicted the presence of bladder cancer 15 to 33 months before the clinical detection of the disease. In another study, where the risk of bladder cancer recurrence was evaluated using the HA-HAase test, a false-positive inference of the test carried a 3.5- to 10-fold risk for bladder tumor recurrence within 5 months.[61] The false-positive results on microsatellite DNA analysis, as well as FISH, have also been shown to predict future recurrences before the clinical documentation of the disease, in a statistically significant manner.[67,68] The ability of bladder tumor markers to allow detection of recurrence before the detection of the tumor by cystoscopy suggests that evaluating the performance of a marker/test based solely on cystoscopy observations may be inaccurate.[61,84] Thus, the overall acceptance of tumor markers in general, will not only depend upon the accuracy of the specific markers for diagnosis and surveillance of bladder cancer, but it will also depend upon the willingness of urologists and patients to accept the usefulness of the marker in clinical practice.[7]

URINE CYTOLOGY: THE STANDARD NON-INVASIVE MARKER

Voided urine cytology is the standard non-invasive marker used mainly for monitoring bladder cancer recurrence.[30] Urine cytology is highly tumor specific (> 90–95% specificity in most studies) but the sensitivity reported in various studies is from 11 to 76% (average 40%).[85–100] Several factors can influence the sensitivity of cytology and include type of specimen (low sensitivity if the specimen has low number of cells or is degenerated), type of tumor (low sensitivity for low-grade tumors), use of different classification systems, and the expertise of the pathologist.[7,30,94] In addition, although cytology has the potential for being rapid and office-based, at most offices in North America, urine is sent to a regional or national reference/specialty laboratory for evaluation. The variability of voided urine cytology, due to specimen quality, is improved by concentrating exfoliated cells (by centrifugation or filtration) or by obtaining bladder wash (ie, barbotage) specimens.[88,92,96,99] Although the barbotage specimens improve the yield of exfoliated cells, the procedure is invasive, which can introduce some instrument artifacts such as curling of the instrument-detached fragments of urothelium which results in a nested or a pseudo-papillary pattern. A trained pathologist would in most cases be able to recognize such instrument artifacts. For example, a trained pathologist would diagnose a papillary/nested fragment in voided urine as suspicious for papillary neoplasia, but would disregard the same pattern in a bladder wash specimen as an instrument artifact. In a study by Walsh and colleagues, the sensitivity of barbotage cytology (48%) was better than that for voided urine cytology (11%).[88] However, in other studies, the sensitivity of cytology was not different among bladder wash specimens and voided urine specimens.[88,92,96] These results raise questions regarding the labor involved in obtaining the barbotage specimens, procedure-associated morbidity and of the cost involved for obtaining barbotage specimens. Mungan and colleagues also tested the possibility of improving the sensitivity of cytology by collecting first, mid, and terminal streams of voided urine and by collecting first, mid, and last portions of bladder wash specimens.[96] In their study, the sensitivity was 34.6%, 38.5%, and 38.5% for the first, mid, and terminal stream of voided urine cytology and 34.6%, 38.5%, and 34.6% for the first, mid, and last portions of bladder wash cytology, respectively. Thus, there was no significant difference in different portions of urine/bladder wash specimens with respect to the presence of bladder tumor cells. The sensitivity of urine cytology may be improved if three consecutive samples are obtained on three separate days. Casetta and colleagues showed that urine cytology performed on three samples has higher sensitivity (59.3%) than both BTA-TARK (sensitivity 57%) and NMP22 (sensitivity 56%). The sensitivity of cytology in this study was even higher (73.3%), when "dubious inferences" were considered as positive.[101]

The overall low sensitivity of cytology to detect bladder cancer is almost exclusively due to its unreliability in detecting low-grade bladder cancer (sensitivity 15–20%).[85,96,97,100,102] Since the low-grade bladder tumor cells resemble normal urothelial cells, cytopathologists often document the results as "atypical cells" and at most, suggestive of low-grade cancer.[30,93] Some of the cytopathologic features that are used to identify low-grade bladder tumor cells include increased nuclear/cytoplasmic ratio, nuclear membrane irregularities, and coarsely granular chromatin.[30] Figure 10–2 panels A to C represent examples of "atypical cytology" and corresponding biopsy specimens.

Urine cytology has the highest sensitivity (60–90%) in detecting high-grade tumors.[88,97,98,100] Malignant tumor cells have larger nuclei than normal urothelial cells and have higher nuclear to cytoplasmic ratio, more frequent mitotic figures, individual nuclei with irregular membranes, and prominent nucleoli.[30] Figure 10–2 panels D to F show examples of high-grade malignant urothelial cells observed in cytology and in a corresponding biopsy specimen showing grade 3 bladder cancer. It is sometimes assumed that observation of a cluster of malignant urothelial cells in cytology indicates invasive carcinoma, whereas, if the cells occur singly, it indicates CIS. However, this notion is not accurate, note that the cluster of malignant urothelial cells in Figure 10–2 (D) originated from CIS, as revealed in the biopsy specimen. Nonetheless, due to its high sensitivity in detecting CIS and high tumor specificity, cytology remains as a useful adjunct to cytoscopy.[6,7]

Overall, urine cytology is highly specific for bladder cancer detection. However, it has low sensitivity for detecting low-grade bladder tumors and requires a skilled cytopathologist for interpreting

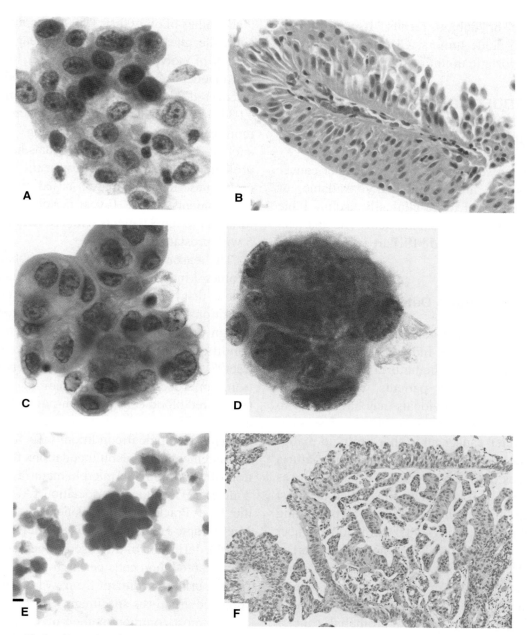

Figure 10–2. Examples of cytology and corresponding biopsy specimens of transitional cell carcinomas of the bladder. *A*, Cytology specimen showing atypical cells. Note the large nucleoli and abundant cytoplasm. Cytologic appearance may be due to reactive processes such as, inflammation, prior radiation, or intravesical chemotherapy, and it cannot be distinguished cytologically from low-grade urothelial carcinoma. *B*, Biopsy specimen obtained subsequently to the cytology specimen shown in *A*. Note that the polarity and order in the superficial cell layer are preserved. There are no mitotic figures present in the nuclei; however, nuclei of different sizes are present. According to the World Health Organization/International Society of Urological Pathology classification, this specimen is classified as urothelial neoplasia of low malignant potential.[93] *C*, A large cluster of very atypical cells. Cells have large nucleoli, increased nucleus/cytoplasmic ratio, and irregular nuclear membranes. The diagnosis would be atypical cytology, suspicious but not diagnostic for low-grade papillary carinoma or papillary neoplasia of low malignant potential; cystoscopy to be clinically considered.[93] *D*, High-grade malignant urothelial cells, showing little cytoplasm and large nuclei with darker and clumped areas of chromatin. The diagnosis will be malignant urothelial cells present, to be followed by cystoscopy and biopsy. In subsequent biopsy, the patient had CIS and in some areas there was papillary carcinoma with invasion of muscularis propria. *E*, Clump of malignant urothelial cells showing large nuclei and very little cytoplasm. The diagnosis will be malignant urothelial cells present, requiring biopsy. *F*, Biopsy specimen subsequent to obtaining the cytology specimen in *E*. The specimen is high-grade transitional cell carcinoma. This micropapillary variant initially described by Amin and colleagues, is a very aggressive and usually advanced carcinoma.[94] Although cytology detects it as malignant urothelial cells, it does not distinguish the degree of aggressiveness.

"atypical cells" or "dubious results." Its major role is to detect high-grade tumors; CIS, in particular, in the bladder, prostatic urethra, and upper tract.

BLADDER TUMOR MARKERS FOR DIAGNOSIS AND MONITORING RECURRENCE

In the following section, we discuss bladder cancer markers/tests that are commercially available, or have shown potential to be clinically useful. Table 10–1 lists all of these tests/markers. The markers Immunocyt, Quanticyt, and FISH are included in the chapter on cytology.

Hematuria Detection

Microscopic hematuria is common among asymptomatic adults. About 4% of individuals in the general population may have hematuria.[103–105] Among asymptomatic hematuria patients, approximately 42% and 17% of the individuals may have minor to serious urologic diseases, respectively. The incidence of bladder cancer and other urologic malignancies among asymptomatic microhematuria patients ranges between 0.5 and 3%, and can be as high as 11%.[103–107] It is clear, however, that the most common finding among individuals representing urinary tract malignancies (~ 85% of bladder cancer patients and 40% of renal carcinoma patients) is hematuria.[7,108] Asymptomatic hematuria may be present, as the sole sign or manifestation, 5 to 6 years before the clinical diagnosis of urothelial malignancy.[106–107] Hematuria due to urothelial cancers may be grossly visible or only visible on microscopic examination, and is independent of tumor grade and/or stage.[38–40,108]

Several studies have been conducted to test the usefulness of hematuria screening for detecting bladder cancer in the general population. Wakui and Shigai screened a total of 21,372 adults for hematuria. Of the 912 individuals positive for hematuria, 1 case of bladder cancer was detected.[108] Messing and colleagues have suggested repeated testing of urine for occult blood (home screening) in the high-risk adult population over the age of 50 years of age, because hematuria originating from tumor is intermittent.[38] In

their studies of more than 1,500 individuals, Messing and colleagues and Britton and colleagues found 21 to 24% of individuals with hematuria, but only 0.7% had bladder cancer.[109,110] Murakami and colleagues discovered 24 cases of urinary tract cancers among 1,034 individuals positive for microhematuria and 4 more cases within 3 years of testing.[111] In this and another study, 22% of the individuals had significant urologic diseases requiring treatment.[103,111] Mohr and colleagues, in a population-based study, followed 781 residents over a 10-year period for microhematuria and found 8 patients with urothelial cancers and 5 with prostate cancer.[105]

The reason for low prevalence of bladder cancer, or other urinary tract cancers, in patients with hematuria is that hematuria may arise from inflammatory conditions, urinary tract infection, stone disease, benign prostatic hyperplasia (BPH), and any other condition that produces blood in the urinary tract.[103–107] When evaluated in the general population, microscopic appearance of blood cells (< 3–5 red blood cells per high-power field) may be evident in many individuals without any underlying clinical/pathological condition.[12] To formulate policy statements and recommendations for the evaluation of asymptomatic microhematuria in adults, the American Urological Association (AUA) convened the Best Practice Policy Panel on Asymptomatic Microscopic Hematuria.[112] The panel recommended that the definition of microscopic hematuria is, three or more red blood cells per high-power microscopic field in urinary sediment from two of three properly collected urinalysis specimens.

The most common method of screening patients for hematuria is hemoglobin dipstick (Hemastix; Bayer Corp). The test is available over the counter in any pharmacy and costs about 60 cents per test. The test may be performed at home or in a physician's office. A sample is recorded as positive when any hemoglobin is present (trace, small, moderate, or large). Considering that hematuria screening may also detect other serious diseases, the cost of detecting a true positive case through such screening would be approximately $1,300.[109] To reduce unnecessary cost and morbidity associated with further work-up, evaluation of red cell morphology by phase contrast microscopy has been suggested.[108,113]

Table 10–1. CURRENT BLADDER TUMOR MARKERS FOR DIAGNOSIS AND SURVEILLANCE

Test/marker	Marker detected	Specimen	Assay type	Marker type	Manufacturer	Sensitivity (%)	Specificity (%)	References
Cytology	Tumor cells	Voided urine Barbotage specimen	Microscopy	Cell morphology	Diagnostic Reference Laboratories	11-76	> 90	30, 85-102
Hematuria detection	A: Hemoglobin B: Red cells	A: Voided urine B: Voided urine	A: Dipstick B: Interference-contrast microscopy or Red cell analyzer	A: Soluble protein B: Red cell morphology	A: Bayer Corp. B:—	A: ~ 90 B: ~ 100	A: Low B: ~ 100	A: 103-111 B: 108, 113, 114
BTA-Stat	Complement factor H-related protein (and also Complement factor H)	Voided urine	Dipstick immunoassay	Soluble antigen	Bard/Bion Diagnostics	36–89 Low sensitivity for low-grade tumors, low-tumor volume	50–70 Low specificity among benign urologic conditions	67, 85, 86, 88–91, 117–125
BTA-TRAK	Complement factor H-related protein (and also Complement factor H)	Voided urine	Sandwich ELISA	Soluble antigen	Bard/Bion Diagnostics	57–83 Sensitivity value depends on cut-off limit selection	~50 in benign urologic conditions; ~ 90% healthy individuals	66, 87, 116, 126–129
NMP22	Nuclear mitotic apparatus protein	Voided urine	Sandwich ELISA (Newer version: A point-of-care device)	Soluble antigen	Matritech, Inc.	47–100 Sensitivity value depends on cut-off limit selection, tumor volume, and patient population	55–80 Specificity depends on presence of benign urologic conditions	97, 100, 101, 117, 118–120, 134–147
BLCA-4	Nuclear matrix protein	Voided urine	ELISA (using a rabbit polyclonal antibody)	Soluble antigen	Eichrom Technologies	96.4	100 in healthy individuals; 81 in other urologic conditions	148,149
Survivin	A member of inhibitors of apoptosis gene family	Voided urine	Bio-dot test (dot blot assay using a rabbit polyclonal antibody)	Soluble antigen	–	100	87–100	150, 151
UBC	Cytokeratin 8 and 18 (cytoskeletal proteins)	Voided urine	Sandwich ELISA or a point-of-care test	Soluble antigen	IDL Biotech.	65–80 May be low to detect Ta, T1 tumors	88–92; may be low in benign urologic conditions	118, 120, 139, 154–156
Cytokeratin 20	Cytoskeletal protein	Exfoliated cells*	RT-PCR or immunocytology	mRNA or cell-associated protein	–	82–87	55–70 Low in benign urologic conditions	159–163, 165, 166
CYFRA 21-1	Cytokeratin 19 (a cytoskeletal protein)	Voided urine	Immunoradiometric assay or electrochemiluminescent immunoassay	Soluble antigen	Bio International; Roche Diagnostics	75–97; ~55 to detect G1 tumors	67–71; low for urolithiasis, stenosis, BPH and UTI	138, 139, 167, 168

*Isolated by urine centrifugation or bladder wash specimens.

Continued

Table 10–1. CONTINUED

Test/marker	Marker detected	Specimen	Assay	Marker type	Manufacturer	Sensitivity (%)	Specificity (%)	References
Accu-DX	Fibrin degradation products (and also fibrin and fibrinogen)	Voided urine	Point-of-care immunoassay	Soluble antigen	Formerly Mentor Urology	52–81; low for detecting tumor recurrence (47%)	68–80; low for hematuria patients	98, 172–174
Telomerase (TRAP assay)	Enzyme activity	Exfoliated cells*	TRAP assay	Cell-associated enzyme	Intergen, Oncor?	70–80; but as low as 7–46 (enzyme unstable in urine)	60–70; low if UTI, urolithiasis, or inflammation present	128, 174, 182–189
Telomerase (hTERT)	hTERT	Exfoliated cells*	RT-PCR (conventional or real-time)	mRNA for hTERT	—	83–95 but as low as 24	60–70; low if UTI, urolithiasis, or inflammation present	193–195, 197–199
Microsatellite DNA test	Microsatellite markers on chromosomes	Exfoliated cells	Genomic DNA PCR	Genomic DNA	—	72–97	> 95% in healthy individuals; false positive results if BPH or cystitis present	199–207
Urovysion	Alterations in chromosomes 3, 7, 17 and 9p21	Exfoliated cells	Multi-colored, multi-probe FISH	Denatured chromosomal DNA	Vysis	81–84; low for low-grade tumors?	> 90	208–210
ImmunoCyt	Carcinomaembryonic antigen, 2 bladder tumor cell–associated mucins	Exfoliated cells	Immunocytochemistry	Cell-surface antigen	DiagnoCure, Inc.	50–100; low for low-grade tumors, and recurrent tumors?	73–80; low if microhematuria, BPH, or cystitis present	102, 213–215
Quanticyt	Mean nuclear shape and DNA content	Exfoliated cells	Computerized analysis of light microscopy images	Nucleus, DNA	—	59–70; detection of high-risk patients and prediction regarding progression	~ 70	6, 147, 216–220
HA-HAase	Hyaluronic acid and hyaluronidase	Voided urine	ELISA-like assays using a biotinylated HA-binding protein	2 Soluble matrix components	—	90–94	Overall 84; 63–71 in recurrent tumors: 60 false positive results become true positive in 5 months	61, 78, 227–230

BPH = benign prostatic hyperplasia; UTI = urinary tract infection; FISH = fluorescence in situ hybridization.
*Isolated by urine centrifugation or bladder wash specimens.

Schramek and colleagues separated individuals with asymptomatic hematuria based on red cell morphology, which was examined by an interference-contrast microscope.[113] The authors found that in the dysmorphic cell group (193 individuals) with a median follow-up of 42 months, no cases of urologic malignancies were found. However, in the eumorphic/mixed cell group (123 individuals), 13 cases of urologic malignancies were found. Wakui and Shigai used red cell volume distribution curves (RDC) generated by an automated blood cell analyzer to divide 912 subjects with a positive hemoglobin dipstick into two groups.[108] Group 1 consisted of 38 individuals who showed normocytic or mixed cell pattern, which is a predictor of a high-risk for urinary tract cancer. Among group 1 individuals, immediate evaluation found a single case of bladder cancer (1 in 38; prevalence rate 2.6%). However, among group 2 individuals (*n* = 869) who showed a microcytic pattern on RDC, no bladder cancer cases were detected during three years of clinical follow-up. The microcytic pattern probably arises due to urinary tract infection or glomelular disorder. Thus, the RDC method appears to reduce total work-up cost by 93.8% when compared to a conventional setting that involves a full evaluation of all cases of hematuria.[108] Georgopoulos and colleagues suggested that the assessment of the erythrocyte morphology, and distinguishing them as either dysmorphic or eumorphic cells, should be carried out at pH < 7.0, and at osmolarity ≥ 700 mOsmol/kg. Under these conditions, if > 90% of cells are dysmorphic, the blood pressure is normal and there is no proteinuria; then hematuria is most likely reno-paranchymal, requiring only routine check-up twice a year. However, if > 90% cells are eumorphic, microhematuria is most likely post-renal and requires a full work-up.[114]

Overall, hematuria screening for detection of bladder cancer and other urologic malignancies has high sensitivity (~ 90%) and may detect high-grade bladder cancer before it becomes invasive. However, hematuria detection has low positive predictive value due to low prevalence of urologic malignancies among hematuria patients. Newer techniques that help to distinguish between hematuria originating from malignancy or other disorders/infections should help to improve specificity without changing sensitivity.

BTA-Stat and BTA-TARK

Bard/Bion Diagnostics has been manufacturing Bladder Tumor Antigen (BTA) tests for the last several years. The original BTA test detected a basement membrane protein antigen released into the urine of bladder cancer patients (BTA product insert).[7,9] The current BTA-Stat and BTA-TRAK tests detect a human complement factor H–related protein (product insert BTA-Stat/BTA-TRAK). In addition to being present in the urine of bladder cancer patients, this complement factor H–related protein is produced and secreted by several bladder and renal cancer cell lines.[115,116] The difference between BTA-Stat and BTA-TRAK tests is that the BTA-Stat is a qualitative point-of-care test, whereas, BTA-TRAK is quantitative requiring testing in a diagnostic laboratory.

BTA-Stat is an immunoassay that uses two monoclonal antibodies. These antibodies detect two different epitopes on the complement factor H–related protein (BTA-Stat product insert). The complement factor H–related protein has almost, if not the same, amino acid composition and function as the human complement factor H protein.[115,116] Therefore, complement factor H that is present in normal human serum at high levels (0.5 mg/mL; BTA-Stat product insert) can react with both monoclonal antibodies that are used in the BTA-Stat test.[116] The BTA-Stat test is performed by placing 5 drops of urine in the sample well of the test device and allowing it to react for exactly 5 minutes. A visible red line in the sample window (however faint) indicates a positive result, while a line in the control window shows that the test is working correctly. The test is distributed in a package of 30 tests, costing $289 per package and can be purchased from Polymedco, Inc., New York, New York, and Mentor Urology.

The sensitivity of the BTA-Stat reported in several studies ranges from as low as 36% to as high as 89%.[67, 85,86,88–91,117–120] In most studies the overall sensitivity of the BTA-Stat test ranges between 55% to 64%.[67,117,85,86,89–91] The sensitivity of the BTA-Stat test to detect low-grade tumors is low, ranging between 13% and 55%.[118,119,121] The sensitivity of the BTA-Stat test to detect G2 and G3 bladder tumors varies between 36% and 67%, and 63% and 90%, respectively.[85,85,118,88–91,118,122] The specificity of the BTA-Stat test is high among healthy individuals (> 90%). However, the BTA-Stat test has low specificity (~ 50%) among patients with benign urologic conditions such as, hematuria, 2+ to 3+ protein in urine on dipstick, infection, renal disease, genitourinary trauma, cystitis, renal or bladder calculi, nephritis and renal stones.[61,121–123] The specificity of the BTA-Stat test is also low among patients receiving intravesical chemotherapy.[122] The BTA-Stat product insert states that the test should not be used if the above mentioned urologic conditions are present. In a study, Nasuti and colleagues found an 84% false-positive rate for BTA-Stat test results among patients with symptoms of dysuria, incontinence, and hematuria.[124] Recently Oge and colleagues showed that the specificity of the BTA-Stat test decreases from 100% in normal urine to 80% and 24% respectively, if microscopic or gross hematuria is present. Thus, the BTA-Stat is not a reliable test in the presence of hematuria.[123] The low specificity of the BTA-Stat test among patients with hematuria is due to the fact that the test detects complement factor H protein, which is abundantly present in blood (BTA-Stat product insert).

Some studies have explored the use of BTA-Stat as a prognostic test. Raitanen and colleagues reported that disease-free survival is shorter among bladder cancer patients with a positive result for the BTA-Stat test.[125] Among G2 patients those positive for the BTA-Stat had a 68.6% risk of recurrence within the first year compared to a 42.9% risk for those with a negative test result.[125] However, the same group in another study showed that only 16% of the false-positive cases on the BTA-Stat test have a tumor recurrence in the near future and the majority of the false-positive cases on the BTA-Stat test are due to intravesical therapy or infection.[89] In that study, the authors concluded that the predictive value of the BTA-Stat test to predict recurrence is low. Similarly, van Rhijn and colleagues showed that a positive BTA-Stat test did not predict recurrence in cystoscopy and biopsy negative cases.[67] We recently found that a false-positive BTA-Stat result does not carry any significant risk (RR = 1.4, OR = 1.5) for recurrence within 5 months.[61] Thus, in most studies, the potential of the BTA-Stat test result to predict recurrence is low.

BTA-TRAK is a standard sandwich enzyme-linked immunosorbent assay (ELISA). Figure 10–3 shows a schematic of a standard sandwich ELISA. In the BTA-TRAK test, an anti-human complement factor H–related protein monoclonal antibody, coated on the 96-well microtiter plate captures the complement H–related protein (as well as complement factor H) present in patient urine. The antigen bound to the microtiter wells is detected by a second reporter anti-human complement factor H monoclonal antibody. The assay utilizes the alkaline phosphatase color detection system (BTA-TARK product insert; 7,116). The amount of complement factor H–related protein (as well as complement factor H) is calculated using a calibration curve and expressed as units/mL, where 1 unit corresponds to 4.5 ng of complement factor H–related protein. The list price of the BTA-TRAK test is $650 per microtiter plate (distributed by Polymedco Inc. and Mentor Urology)

In various studies, the sensitivity of BTA-TARK ranges between 57% and 83%.[66,87,116] Chautard and colleagues showed that there is a statistically significant increase in the median BTA-TRAK level with increasing tumor grade (G1, 6.9 U/mL; G2, 13.1 U/mL; and G3, 235 U/mL) and stage (pTa, 11.9 U/mL; pT1, 57 U/mL; pT2/T3, 391 U/mL).[126] Consistent with these observations, Thomas and colleagues reported a 48%, 59%, and 77% sensitivity of BTA-TARK for detecting G1, G2, and G3 tumors, respectively.[127] The sensitivity of BTA-TARK varies significantly depending upon the cut-off limit. At 14 U/mL, which is the cut-off limit recommended by the manufacturer, the sensitivity of BTA-TARK varies between 58% and 77% with specificity varying between 54% and 75%.[126–128] The sensitivity and specificity of the BTA-TARK test do not change if the cut-off limit is raised to 40 U/mL or 60 U/mL.[101,128] In fact, Khaled and colleagues reported a 94% sensitivity of the BTA-TARK to detect bilharzia-related bladder cancer at 60 U/mL.[129] However, at 1,300 U/mL the test has excellent specificity (ie, 95%) when tested among individuals with benign urologic conditions, but has very low sensitivity (13%).[128]

As is the case with the BTA-Stat test. The specificity of the BTA-TARK is low (~ 50%) among patients with benign urologic conditions. Priolo and

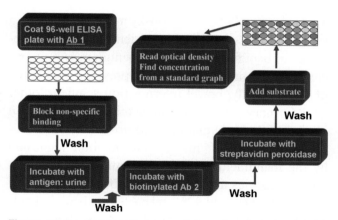

Figure 10–3. Schematic representation of a typical sandwich ELISA (Enzyme-Linked Immuno-Sorbent Assay). In a sandwich ELISA, the antigen (eg, tumor marker) is "sandwiched" between two antibodies, which detect two different epitopes on the antigen. In the first step, 96-well microtiter wells are coated with antibody 1 (eg, IgG fraction of monoclonal antibody 1). Following blocking of non-specific binding sites, the microtiter wells are incubated with aliquots of samples containing the antigen (eg, urine specimens from bladder cancer patients), in an assay buffer. Following washing-off the unbound material, the wells are incubated with the antibody 2 (eg, IgG fraction of monoclonal antibody 2) which is usually biotinylated. Following washing-off the unbound antibody 2, the wells are incubated with streptavidin-conjugated peroxidase (or streptavidin-conjugated alkaline phosphatase). Following washing-off the unbound material, a colorless substrate (eg, ABTS, if using streptavidin-conjugated peroxidase) is added to the wells. The optical density of the colored product (green, if ABTS substrate is used) is measured in a microplate reader, at appropriate wavelength. The amount of antigen present in the sample is calculated from a standard graph. The standard graph is prepared by analyzing the known amount of antigen (eg, ng/mL) by the ELISA and plotting antigen concentration (ng/mL) versus optical density.

colleagues noted that the BTA-TARK values are elevated in patients with non-neoplastic urothelial diseases and mucosal abnormalities.[87] BTA-TARK values of > 72 U/mL are often obtained when microscopic hematuria is present.[87] The lower specificity of the BTA-TARK among patients with benign urologic conditions when compared to healthy individuals can be expected, since the BTA-TARK also detects complement factor H protein that is abundantly present in blood. Thus, when hematuria is present, regardless of whether bladder cancer is present, the BTA-TARK test most likely will be positive. Considering these possibilities, the manufacturer recommends that the BTA-TARK test should be used only with information available from the clinical evaluation of the patient and other diagnostic procedures. The test should not be used as a screening test (BTA-TARK product insert).

Based on the published reports discussed above, the BTA-Stat and BTA-TARK tests may be more useful as surveillance tests for monitoring bladder cancer recurrence than as diagnostic tests for detecting bladder cancer among symptomatic patients (eg, patients with hematuria). According to the BTA product inserts, the United States Food and Drug Administration (FDA) has approved these tests for use as an aid in the management of bladder cancer in combination with cystoscopy.

NMP22

The NMP22 test detects a 240 kD nuclear mitotic apparatus protein (NMP22) that is an abundant component of the nuclear matrix.[7,9,130–132] Nuclear matrix is a nonchromatin structure that regulates nuclear shape and DNA organization, and is required for DNA replication, RNA processing, and transcription.[132] NMP22 is distributed during interphase and localizes within spindle poles during mitosis. In tumor cells, NMP22 levels are elevated and the protein is released from the cells most likely following apoptosis.[133] The NMP22 test is designed to measure NMP22 levels in patient urine by a quantitative sandwich ELISA that uses two monoclonal antibodies. Each of these monoclonal antibodies detects a different epitope on NMP22. The amount of NMP22 present in urine is calculated using the naturally occurring nuclear mitotic apparatus as a standard (NMP22 product insert). Matritech Inc., Newton, MA, manufactures the NMP22 test and Fisher Scientific distributes it. A single NMP22 kit costs $967.50, and a urine stabilizer kit (required to stabilize urine before shipping it to a reference laboratory for NMP22 testing) costs $108. Forty unknown samples can be assayed in one NMP22 kit. One stabilizer kit is sufficient for 100 urine specimens. Urologists may ship urine samples to several reference laboratories including Labcor, Smith Kline, and Quest for NMP22 testing.

The sensitivity and specificity of the NMP22 test have been evaluated in many studies. Although, the manufacturer recommends a cut-off limit of 10 U/mL, in many studies cut-off limits from 3.6 U/mL to 12 U/mL have been used to determine the sensitivity and specificity of the NMP22 test. In these studies a wide range of sensitivity (47–100%) has been reported for the NMP22 test to detect bladder cancer.[85,97,100,101,117,118–120,122,134–140] It is expected that lowering the cut-off limit of the NMP22 test from what is recommended by the manufacturer will increase the sensitivity of the test and decrease the specificity.[7] However, different studies have reported different results regarding sensitivity and specificity, regardless of the cut-off limit used. For example, Chahal and colleagues used a 4.75 U/mL cut-off for the NMP22 test and reported 42.4% sensitivity and 85% specificity for detecting bladder cancer among patients with hematuria, irritative voiding symptoms, or a history of bladder cancer.[134] Using similar cut-off limit (4 U/mL), Boman and colleagues reported 65% sensitivity for detecting new tumors and 45% sensitivity for detecting recurrent tumor.[117] Gutier-rez-Banos and colleagues, reported higher sensitivity (6 U/mL, 84.2%; 10 U/mL, 76.3%) but comparable specificity (6 U/mL 86.5%; 10 U/mL 90.4%) when using cut-off limits as indicated.[85] In many studies, the sensitivity and specificity of the NMP22 test are between 50 and 70%, and 55 and 80%, respectively, at the 10 U/mL cut-off limit.[97,100,101,117,120,122,135–140]

In studies that have compared the sensitivity of NMP22 according to tumor grade, the test appears to have lower sensitivity to detect low-grade tumors.[85,97,113,118,129,140,141] For example, at the 10 U/mL cut-off limit, the sensitivity of the NMP22 test for detecting G1 tumors varies between 30% and 50%. However, in most studies the sensitivity of the NMP22 test for detecting G2 and G3 tumors varies between 50 and 70% and 70 and 100%, respectively.[85,97,113,118,129,140,141] A possible reason for the increased sensitivity of this test for detecting higher-grade tumors may be that the urinary NMP22 levels increase with tumor grade. For example, Paoluzzi and colleagues have reported that the median urinary NMP22 levels in CIS, G1, G2, and G3 patients are 102 U/mL, 30 U/mL, 66 U/mL and 54 U/mL, respectively.[141]

The specificity of the NMP22 test in various studies is reported at 60 to 80%, although in one study the specificity is reported at 90%. The NMP22 test has been shown to have higher false-positive rates (33–50%) among patients with urolithiasis, inflammation, benign prostatic hyperplasia, and urinary tract infection.[97,119,137–138] Ponsky and colleagues, in a study of 608 symptomatic patients, found 6 categories of benign conditions (ie, benign inflammatory conditions, renal bladder calculi, presence or absence of foreign body, bowel interposition segment, other genitourinary cancer, instrumentation, and no known clinical pathology) that increase urinary NMP22 levels well above 10 U/mL, the cut-off limit suggested by the manufacturer.[142] In their study, exclusion of these categories improved the specificity and PPV of NMP22 to 99% and 92%, respectively. Ishii and colleagues found that the NMP22 has 42 to 100% false-positive rate among patients with urinary diversions of different kinds, whereas, Oge and colleagues found that the NMP22 levels increase following transurethral resection of the bladder tumor.[119,143] In the later case it is possible that during tumor resection, many tumor cells are dislodged and die, releasing NMP22 into urine. Atsu and colleagues studied the effect of the degree of hematuria and pyuria on NMP22 levels.[144] Their results show that the median NMP22 levels of normal individuals are 4 U/mL. However, these levels surpass the levels present in bladder cancer patients if more than 2 ml blood per L of urine or ~ 1,039 red blood cells (range 278 to 1,438) are present per high-power field. The presence of leukocytes also affected NMP22 levels in urine.[144] These results suggest that inflammation, urinary tract infections, and hematuria may negatively influence the specificity of the NMP22 test.

Some studies of the NMP22 test also give an idea regarding how much reduction in medical cost might be achieved if a tumor marker is used to monitor bladder cancer recurrence. For example, Lachaine and colleagues showed that the NMP22 monitoring modality (cost $257/6 months) saved $55 per patient during the first 6 months of follow-up over the standard surveillance protocol. The trade-off using NMP22 in this study was that in some patients there was a delay of 3 months before diagnosis of recurrence.[145] In similar cost evaluation studies, Zippe and colleagues have suggested that the NMP22 test may save $17,000 to $43,331 per evaluation per 100 symptomatic patients.[146] However, due to its low sensitivity and low specificity to detect low-grade tumors, others have suggested that the NMP22 test cannot be adopted as a routine tool for surveillance following bladder preservation treatments.[112,147]

To evaluate the usefulness of the NMP22 test for monitoring bladder tumor recurrence and in screening a symptomatic population, a consensus among researchers regarding the cut-off limit on this test is necessary.[7] However, more than the cut-off limit used in each study, the knowledge of tumor size, benign urologic conditions concurrently present at the time of testing, and tumor grade may be essential when considering clinical utility of this marker. The FDA has cleared the NMP22 test for use as an aid in the diagnosis of patients at risk for or with symptoms of bladder cancer.

BLCA-4

BLCA-4 is another example of a nuclear matrix protein that like the NMP22 is expressed in bladder tumor tissues.[9,47] BLCA-4 is released in urine from bladder cancer cells, most likely due to apoptosis.[9,148] An ELISA has been developed to measure BLCA-4 levels in the urine of bladder cancer patients.[147] The assay involves precipitation of total protein from urine specimens and coating it on a 96-well microtiter plate. The presence of BLCA-4 on the microtiter wells, is detected using a rabbit polyclonal anti-BLCA-4 peptide antibody. Using 13 O.D. units/mg protein as the cut-off limit, Konety and colleagues reported a sensitivity of 96.4% for detecting bladder cancer.[149] In a study that involved 55 bladder cancer patients, bladder cancer was detected using BLCA-4 regardless of tumor grade and stage. In the same study the specificity of the BLCA-4 was 100% among normal individuals ($n = 51$) and 81% among individuals with spinal cord injuries ($n = 202$).[149] The early results of this test, manufactured by Eichrom Technologies, Inc, Darien, IL, are encouraging. It remains to be determined how the BLCA-4 test compares with the more established NMP22 test, in a side-by-side comparison of both tests. The test in its present format requires special laboratory techniques and trained personnel for doing the assay.

Survivin

Survivin is a member of the inhibitors of apoptosis gene family that modulates cell death and viability

balance in tumor cells.[150] Survivin is almost undetectable in normal adult tissues; however, it is highly over-expressed in human cancers.[150] Its expression correlates with unfavorable prognosis. The survivin test is a "Bio-dot-test" where the urine samples are blotted as dots on nitrocellulose membranes using a Bio-dot filtration apparatus. Survivin present in the samples is detected using a rabbit polyclonal anti-survivin antibody and the standard dot-blot detection reagents.[151,152] In a small study involving 46 bladder cancer patients, the survivin dot-blot assay had 100% sensitivity.[151] Its specificity among normal volunteers and patients with a history of bladder cancer and patients with benign urologic conditions was 100%, 91%, and 87%, respectively.[151,152] The assay in its current format requires specialized equipment and trained personnel. Simplification of this assay to a sandwich ELISA that utilizes monoclonal anti-survivin antibodies will improve technical ease, specificity (due to the use of monoclonal versus a rabbit polyclonal antibodies) and help in the assessment of this marker in a larger study.

Cytokeratins

Cytokeratins are intermediate filament type cytoskeletal proteins that have been tested as bladder tumor markers in many studies. In human cells, a total of 20 cytokeratins have been identified and their expression reflects the type and differentiation state of the epithelial cells.[153] Since cytokeratins are intracellular proteins, the detection of these proteins in urine by ELISA type techniques is possible only when they are released in urine following cell death. In addition, RT-PCR to detect the expression of various cytokeratins at the mRNA level can be performed on exfoliated cells in urine or bladder wash specimens. As discussed below, in various studies, the marker potential of cytokeratins 7, 8, 18, 19, 20 has been studied.

The Ideal Monoclonal UBC ELISA Test

This is a 2-hour urine test that detects the presence of cytokeratins 8 and 18 in the urine of patients with urothelial tumors.[139,154] UBC assay is a sandwich ELISA test manufactured by IDL Biotech, Borlänger, Sweden. Alternatively, a point-of-care UBC-rapid test is also available.[155] In four studies the overall sensitivity of UBC to detect bladder cancer is 65 to 66% with 88 to 92% specificity.[118,139,154,155] The sensitivity of the UBC to detect G1, G2, and G3 bladder tumors is 44 to 60%, 67 to 79%, and 69 to 75%, respectively.[118,154,155] Mian and colleagues have suggested that the UBC is a better marker than the BTA-Stat and NMP22 tests.[118,154] However, Mungan and colleagues, in a study of 100 patients, observed that the sensitivity of the UBC test to detect superficial bladder cancer (ie, pTa, T1 and CIS) is only 21% and concluded that the UBC has insufficient diagnostic value for detecting superficial bladder cancer.[155] Recently, Sanchez-Carbayo and colleagues have suggested a combined use of DNA and cytokeratin 8 and 18 flow cytometry on exfoliated cells and measurement of cytokeratin 8 and 18 levels by UBC for detecting recurrent bladder cancer. This technique increased the sensitivity of UBC from 77% when used alone, to 89% when used in combination with DNA analysis. However, the authors caution that the combination has a higher false-positive rate among individuals with benign urologic diseases and persons undergoing intravesical therapy.[156] Thus, more studies are needed to assess the diagnostic value of this marker. In addition, since cytokeratin markers show a high false-positive rate among individuals with a wide range of clinical disorders, the specificity of this marker may also need to be rigorously tested.

Cytokeratin 20

The expression of cytokeratin 20 is restricted to superficial and occasionally intermediate cells of the normal urothelium.[153] Aberrant cytokeratin 20 expression is present in bladder cells and in other urothelial cancer cells.[153] Harnden and colleagues initially observed that cytokeratin 20 expression examined by immunohistochemistry, could be used to distinguish between noninvasive papillary urothelial tumors which recur, and those which do not.[157] In this study, patients with tumors showing a normal cytokeratin 20 expression did not recur (median follow-up 18 months), whereas those with abnormal cytokeratin 20 expression recurred (median time to

recurrence 6 months).[157] McKenney and colleagues have suggested the use of cytokeratin 20 along with p53 as an immunohistochemical marker for distinguishing CIS from reactive atypia.[158]

In several studies, cytokeratin 20 expression in bladder cancer patients has been studied using an RT-PCR assay.[159–163] Figure 10–4 shows a schematic representation of the steps involved in a generic RT-PCR assay. Buchumensky and colleagues initially studied the expression of cytokeratin 20 in exfoliated cells from 192 individuals, using the RT-PCR assay. There is no cytokeratin 20 expression in normal individuals, however, a 370 bp PCR fragment is amplified from the exfoliated cells in the urine of bladder cancer patients which indicates cytokeratin 20 expression.[161] Studies that examined the cytokeratin 20 RT-PCR have demonstrated 82 to 87% sensitivity in detecting bladder cancer.[159–163] Furthermore, a strong correlation was found between tumor grade and cytokeratin 20–positive tumor cells in urine.[159–163] In addition, Rotem and colleagues reported that 44% of the false-positive cases on the cytokeratin 20 RT-PCR assay recurred within 6 months.[159] The cytokeratin 20 RT-PCR assay is found to detect as low as 2 cancerous bladder cells per milliliter of blood and has been suggested as a promising approach for the early detection of systemic progression of bladder cancer.[162] However, Gazzaniga and colleagues found that blood samples from only 17% of bladder cancer patients were positive for cytokeratin 20 RT-PCR.[163] In addition, the lessons learned from the possible use of prostate-specific antigen (PSA) RT-PCR to predict prostate cancer progression suggest that the high sensitivity of any RT-PCR assay technique is associated with low specificity.[164] Consistent with this argument are the observations of Cassel and colleagues who demonstrated an 82% sensitivity for the cytokeratin 20 RT-PCR to detect bladder cancer.[160] However in this study, among control individuals with various clinical conditions other than bladder cancer, the specificity of the cytokeratin 20 RT-PCR assay was 55%.

Immunocytochemical staining of exfoliated cells using anti-cytokeratin 20 antibody has been suggested to help in the identification of bladder cancer among atypical cytology cases. For example, Lin and colleagues reported an overall 94.4% sensitivity

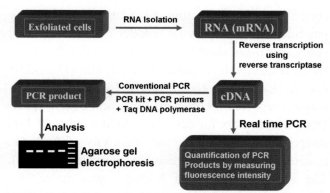

Figure 10–4. Schematic representation of a typical RT-PCR assay. In an RT-PCR (reverse transcriptase-polymerase chain reaction) assay, total RNA is isolated from exfoliated cells present in urine sediments, using a commercially available RNA isolation kit. The messenger RNA (mRNA) is reverse transcribed to first strand complementary DNA (cDNA) using a commercially available reverse transcription kit that contains a retroviral reverse transcriptase (eg, AMV-reverse transcriptase). The first-strand cDNA is amplified in a conventional PCR machine using PCR reagents, Taq DNA polymerase and forward and reverse complementary PCR primers (short oligonucleotide sequences, ~ 20-mers) that specifically amplify the cDNA of interest (eg, cytokeratin 20). The PCR product is analyzed by agarose gel electrophoresis and ethidium bromide staining to visualize the PCR product. Alternatively, the first-strand cDNA is amplified using a real-time PCR apparatus and a specialized PCR kit to quantify the mRNA expression in various samples.

and 80.5% specificity, respectively, for cytokeratin 20 immunocytochemical staining to detect bladder cancer.[165] Golijanin and colleagues also reported a high sensitivity (ie, 82%) and specificity (ie, 76%) for detecting bladder cancer using a cytokeratin 20 immunocytology technique.[166] However, in this study the sensitivity to detect bladder cancer according to tumor grade was 56.5%, 93%, and 92% for G1, G2, and G3 bladder tumors, respectively.[166] Thus, although cytokeratin 20 immunocytology improves the overall sensitivity of cytology, this technique still misses 43% of low-grade bladder tumors. Since the sensitivity of cytology to detect high-grade tumors is high, an added value of cytokeratin 20 immunocytology may be justified only if it can improve the sensitivity of cytology for detecting G1 bladder tumors.

Overall, cytokeratin 20 detection (ie, RT-PCR assay, immunocytology, and immunohistochemistry) appears to be a useful marker to detect bladder cancer. Identification of benign conditions that cause aberrant expression of cytokeratin 20 may help to improve the clinical applicability of this marker in detecting bladder cancer.

CYFRA 21-1

Cytokeratin 19 is expressed in normal urothelium. Since urothelial cells exfoliate, lysed cells release cytokeratin 19 in urine.[153] CYFRA 21-1 is a soluble fragment of cytokeratin 19 that is measured either by a solid phase sandwich immunoradiometric assay (Cis Bio International, Gif-sur-Yvette, France) or an electrochemiluminescent immunoassay with the Elec sys 2010 system (Roche Diagnostics).[138,139] The levels of cytokeratin 19 are normalized to urinary creatinine. Pariente and colleagues initially found that CYFRA 21-1 levels in bladder cancer patients, patients with other urologic conditions, and normal controls are 123.5 ng/mL, 11.9 ng/mL, and 2.3 ng/mL, respectively.[167] Based on this study, they used a cut-off value of 4 ng/mL to calculate the sensitivity and specificity of CYFRA 21-1 assay to detect bladder cancer. More recently using the immunoradiometric assay for measuring CYFRA 21-1, they observed 96.9% sensitivity and 67.2% specificity for detecting bladder cancer.[168] In this study, patients with urolithiaisis and urinary tract infection had high urinary levels of cytokeratin 19. In another study Sanchez-Carbayo and colleagues reported a 75.5% sensitivity and 71% specificity for detecting bladder cancer, using the electrochemiluminescent assay for measuring CYFRA 21-1 levels.[138] In that study, the sensitivity of the CYFRA 21-1 test to detect G1, G2, and G3 tumor was 54.5%, 66.7%, and 88.2%, respectively. However, in various urologic conditions such as, urolithiasis, stenosis, benign prostatic hyperplasia, and urinary tract infections the false-positive rate is approximately 33%.

Overall, cytokeratins are epithelial differentiation markers but their expression is not bladder tumor specific. The detection of various cytokeratin proteins in urine depends on the amount of exfoliated cells in urine and subsequent lysis of these cells to release cytokeratins into the urine. As a result, the sensitivity of any assay to detect the cytokeratins is subjected to variation. The sensitivity of various cytokeratins to detect low-grade bladder tumors is also < 60%.[138,166] In addition, clinical conditions such as, infection, inflammation, and urolithiasis cause false-positive results on cytokeratin assays.[137–139,160] Thus, the utility of cytokeratin markers for detecting bladder cancer will depend upon improving sensitivity of these markers to detect low-grade tumors and reducing the high false-positive rate among several urologic conditions other than bladder cancer.

Fibrin and Fibrinogen Degradation Products (FDP)

Reports as early as 1975 have suggested the potential of fibrin and fibrinogen degradation products in the detection of bladder cancer.[169] The vessel wall permeability is increased in tumor vasculature and leads to leakage of blood proteins including plasminogen, fibrinogen, and clotting factors into extravascular space.[170,171] When fibrinogen is converted to fibrin, it binds to plasminogen and converts it into plasmin. Plasmin is a proteolytic enzyme that degrades fibrinogen and fibrin into FDP.[169–171]

To detect FDP, earlier studies used a heagglutination immunoinhibition assay, latex agglutination assay or an ELISA involving a monoclonal antibody. In these studies, FDP results had a sensitivity ranging from 27 to 100% and specificity varying from 0 to 98%.[170,171] In the last 5 years, Accu-Dx, a one-step point-of-care qualitative assay has been used to detect FDP in urine.[98,172–174] However, the monoclonal antibodies used in this sandwich immunoassay also react with fibrinogen and fibrin, which are present at high concentration in human serum (Accu-Dx product insert). In this test, samples containing fibrin, fibrinogen, or FDP bind antibody-labeled particles to capture the antibodies in a sandwich type reaction, producing a purple red dot in the test window within 7 minutes (Accu-Dx product insert).[7] Mentor Urology, Santa Barbara, CA, distributed this test previously; however, the company has discontinued carrying this product.

Schmetter and colleagues initially showed that Accu-Dx has a sensitivity of 68% and a specificity of 80% to detect bladder cancer.[173] In this study the sensitivity of Accu-Dx to detect G1, G2, G3, and grade not assigned bladder cancer was 61.5%, 63.9%, 86.4%, and 50%, respectively. Johnston and colleagues reported an overall sensitivity of 81% and a specificity of 75% for detecting bladder cancer.[172] Ramakumar and colleagues in a study of 186 patients reported that Accu-Dx has 52% sensitivity and 91%

specificity for detecting bladder cancer among patients with a history of bladder cancer.[174] In that study, Accu-Dx showed 25%, 46%, and 92% sensitivity, respectively, to detect G1, G2, and G3 bladder cancer. In a more recent study Topsakal and colleagues reported 69.6% sensitivity and 67.9% specificity of Accu-Dx for detecting bladder cancer.[98] It is interesting, in this study, the sensitivity of Accu-Dx to detect bladder cancer recurrence was low (47.3%). The lower sensitivity of Accu-Dx was mainly for detecting low-grade, low-stage tumors (about 30%). In the same study, some patients with benign conditions such as, chronic inflammation, stone disease, urogenital tuberculosis, and cystitis were false positive on the Accu-Dx test. When assessing the utility of Accu-Dx for detecting bladder cancer, it is necessary to note that the test detects fibrinogen at concentrations as low as 33 ng/mL[7] (Accu-Dx product insert). Since fibrinogen is abundant in blood, any tests that are designed to detect FDP may yield false-positive results among hematuria patients.

Telomerase

The sequences that cap the end of the eukaryotic chromosomes called telomeres play a critical role in chromosome replication and protecting chromosomes from degradation.[175,176] Telomeres are repeats of a single-sequence DNA. In humans, the sequence of the telomeric repeat is TTAGGG.[175] These sequences are repeated hundreds or thousands of times, thus spanning several kilobases. During DNA replication, the leading strand (5' → 3') of the parent DNA is synthesized in a continuous manner. However, the lagging strand (3' → 5') is synthesized discontinuously as short DNA fragments (called Okazaki fragments) using short RNA primers. However, the synthesis of Okazaki fragments requires the presence of some DNA ahead of the sequence to be copied to serve as the template for an RNA primer. Since there cannot be a template for the last few nucleotides of a liner DNA molecule, during each DNA replication 50 to 200 nucleotides are lost during the lagging strand synthesis. Since telomeres are present at the end of the chromosome, their lengths progressively decrease during multiple rounds of DNA replication.[175,177–182] If the cells continue to lose telomeres during each cycle of DNA replication, they can undergo only finite numbers of replications before significant sequences from chromosomes begin to be lost during replication. This will lead to chromosomal instability and cell death.[180] Telomerase is a ribonucleoprotein complex, which contains a reverse transcriptase activity that adds repetitive telomeric sequences at the end of the lagging strand using the RNA template present in the ribonucleoprotein complex.[175,178,180] Thus, telomerase can reset the molecular clock and allow cells to proliferate indefinitely.[181] Telomerase is normally found in germ cells and proliferative cells. However in cancer cells, telomerase levels are elevated, resetting the molecular clock to immortality.[178–182]

Since telomerase is not present in normal somatic cells, such as the normal urothelium, its detection in exfoliated cells has been suggested as a sensitive marker for detecting bladder cancer.[176,177] A common technique used to measure the telomerase activity in biological samples (eg, urine) is the TRAP (Telomeric Repeat Amplification Protocol) assay. It involves PCR amplification of a telomere template by the telomerase present in clinical samples.[7,9,176] PCR products are analyzed using real-time quantitative PCR, by agarose gel electrophoresis, or by the telomerase PCR ELISA kit. Thus, the TRAP assay requires sophisticated instruments (ie, a thermocycler or a real-time PCR instrument and a microplate reader) and trained personnel. TRAP assay reagents are marketed by Intergen or Oncor, Gaithersberg, MD.

In several studies, the sensitivity of the TRAP assay to detect bladder cancer varies between 70% and 86%.[128,174,182–189] A sensitivity of up to 95% is achieved if voided urine specimens are combined with bladder wash specimens.[182,188] Kavaler and colleagues reported that the TRAP assay has 79%, 84%, and 87.5% sensitivity to detect G1, G2, and G3 bladder tumors, respectively.[186] Similar sensitivity for different grades of tumors has been reported in other studies.[128,174,182,187,189] However, some studies have reported extremely low sensitivity, ranging from 7 to 46%, for detecting bladder cancer.[190–195] This low sensitivity cannot be explained by differences in the timing of sampling such as the first voided sample versus the second voided sample. de Kok and colleagues recently reported that the sensitivity of the TRAP

assay to detect bladder cancer is low, regardless whether the specimen is a first void (sensitivity 38%) or a second void (sensitivity 31%) specimen.[191,192] The low sensitivity of telomerase in many studies is due to degradation of telomerase in the harsh urine environment.[7,176,193–195] Wu and colleagues also observed high intra- and inter-assay variation with the TRAP assay, attributed primarily to high cell number in samples and the presence of non-tumor cells or interfering substances in patient specimens.[196]

To improve the sensitivity of telomerase as a marker for bladder cancer, several investigators have used RT-PCR to amplify the mRNA of human telomerase reverse transcriptase (hTERT) from exfoliated cells.[95,193–195,197–198] Using this method, sensitivity between 83% and 95% is achieved for detecting bladder cancer. However, in contrast to their earlier studies, de Kok and colleagues recently reported only 24% sensitivity using the real-time hTERT RT-PCR assay. This low sensitivity may be due to lysis of exfoliated cells followed by rapid mRNA degradation.[191,192,198]

The specificity of the TRAP assay in various studies is often between 60% and 70% (range, 60 to 90%).[128,174,182–189] The majority of benign conditions that cause a false-positive result on the TRAP assay include urinary tract infection, chronic and severe inflammation, and urolithiasis.[157] This is not surprising, since telomerase is expressed in proliferating cells such as lymphocytes.[7] The specificity of the hTERT PCR assay is also in the similar range.[95,193–195,197,198] Since an RT-PCR assay can detect even a single positive cell among 10 cells and given the fact that telomerase is expressed in proliferating cells, even mild inflammatory conditions or urinary tract infections may give rise to false-positive results on the hTERT assay.[7]

Overall, telomerase enzyme is active in tumor cells. Many studies have shown that the TRAP and hTERT RT-PCR assays show high sensitivity and reasonable specificity to detect bladder cancer. However, the results of different studies will differ due to instability of telomerase in urine.

Microsatellite DNA Analysis

Microsatellites are short, highly polymorphic tandem repeats (eg, [GTGT…]n or [CACA…]n) that are found throughout the human genome.[175] The number of each repeat at any two chromosome locations is different in each person. In addition, the two copies of a chromosome (ie, paternal and maternal alleles) in somatic cells of an individual will have the same microsatellite sequence but different numbers of it, at any given locus. As a result, PCR amplification of a chromosomal DNA (ie, genomic DNA) region that contains a particular microsatellite, will give rise to two PCR products, one representing the maternal and the other representing the paternal allele. Figure 10–5 shows a schematic representation of the microsatellite DNA analysis used to detect bladder cancer.

In bladder cancer, loss of heterozygosity (LOH) has been demonstrated in chromosomes 4p, 8p, 9p, 9q, 11p, 13p, 16q, 17p, as well as in others.[76,199–203] Several microsatellite markers have been identified to demonstrate LOH in bladder cancer cells or exfoliated cells (eg, locus 4q28, marker FGA; locus 17p17, marker TP53).[67,202–208] van Rhijn and colleagues used microsatellite DNA analysis to detect bladder cancer. They used 19 microsatellite markers to detect LOH and microsatellite instability in DNA isolated from exfoliated cells of 93 bladder cancer patients and 8 age-matched patients with benign urologic diseases.[67] In that study, the microsatellite DNA analysis had 74% sensitivity to detect bladder cancer.

In various other studies, the sensitivity of the microsatellite DNA analysis varies between 72% and 97% to detect bladder cancer recurrence.[199–205] Schneider and colleagues reported 79%, 82%, and 96% sensitivity for detecting G1, G2, and G3 bladder cancer, respectively.[204] In a study by Sengelov and colleagues, microsatellite markers for chromosomes 1p, 8p, 10p, 13q, and 17p did not predict response to chemotherapy and outcome.[199] However, in the study by van Rhijn and colleagues, although microsatellite analysis missed all 11 TaG1 tumors that were small; 55.5% of the false-positive cases (as opposed to only 12% of the true-negative cases) recurred clinically within 6 months.[67] This result suggests that the microsatellite DNA analysis may have some predictive capabilities. In another study, Hafner and colleagues reported that microsatellite analysis found chromosome 9 deletions in 73% of the tumors tested and deletions in chromosome 9q21

correlated with invasive tumor growth.[18] Furthermore in a study involving 45 patients, Uchida and colleagues showed that patients with LOH at 18q21.1 and 9p 21-22 exhibited poor prognosis and higher death rate.[205] Taken together, microsatellite DNA analysis may have prognostic capapbilities.

The specificity of the microsatellite DNA analysis among a healthy population is high at > 95%. However, Christensen and colleagues observed that patients with benign prostatic hyperplasia and cystitis show LOH, as well as microsatellite instability.[206] These alterations are more pronounced when both benign conditions are present at the same time. Based on these results Christensen and colleagues concluded that microsatellite alterations in urine are indicators of not only malignancy but also of inflammatory conditions.[206]

Overall, the microsatellite DNA analysis appears to have high sensitivity for detecting bladder cancer. However, in different studies different microsatellite

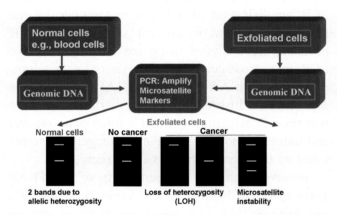

Figure 10–5. A schematic representation of microsatellite DNA analysis. Microsatellite DNA analysis involves a pair-wise comparison between normal somatic cells and tumor cells regarding the microsatellite allelic pattern, present at a specified chromosomal location that is known to undergo genetic alteration during tumor initiation or progression. The analysis begins by isolating genomic DNA from normal somatic cells (ie, blood cells) and tumor cells (eg, exfoliated cells). To identify chromosomal alterations, PCR amplification is performed using PCR primers that specifically amplify specific microsatellite markers known to be present in the chromosomal regions that undergo alterations. The PCR products are analyzed by agarose gel electrophoresis. The PCR analysis from normal somatic cells will generate two PCR products each amplified from either the maternal or paternal allele. The size of these products will depend on the length of the microsatellite (ie, number of copies of the tandem repeats). Any changes in the pattern of PCR products that is generated from the genomic DNA of exfoliated cells, when compared to that generated from genomic DNA of normal cells indicate cancer. These changes may be loss of heterozygosity or microsatellite instability.

markers are used. Therefore, a direct comparison of the results of various studies is difficult. In addition, the specificity of microsatellite DNA analysis needs be tested among various benign urologic conditions, which also show LOH and microsatellite instability. New microsatellite markers that are specific for bladder cancer will improve the specificity of this assay. At this point it is unclear whether there might be technical issues related to sample preparation that could affect the integrity of exfoliated cells, stability of chromosomal DNA, or other parameters. A semi-automated microsatellite analysis of urine sediments that allows the analysis of 18 samples using 15 microsatellite markers in a day may help to resolve some of the technical issues.[207]

HA-HAase Test

This test measures urinary levels of hyaluronic acid (HA) and hyaluronidase (HAase) using two very similar ELISA-like assays.[61,78,209] A schematic of HA and HAase tests is shown in Figure 10–6. HA is a glycosaminoglycan, that is a component of the extracellular matrix. HA plays a structural role in maintaining the hydration status and osmotic balance in tissues. In addition, HA regulates cell adhesion, migration, and proliferation.[210,211] HA concentrations are elevated in several tumors including colon, esophagus, breast, prostate, and bladder.[78,211,212] In tumor tissues, HA promotes tumor metastasis and protects tumor cells from immune surveillance.[211] Small fragments of HA stimulate angiogenesis in vivo and stimulate endothelial cell proliferation, migration, and capillary formation in vitro.[213,214] HAase is an enzyme that degrades HA into small angiogenic HA fragments and such fragments are detected in the urine of bladder cancer patients with high-grade tumors.[215,216] HYAL1 type HAase has been shown to be the major HAase expressed in bladder and prostate tumor cells.[212,217]

In an initial study, urinary HA, measured using the HA test, was found to be elevated 2.5- to 6.5-fold in patients with bladder cancer, regardless of tumor grade.[215] The HAase levels measured using the HAase test, however, were preferentially elevated 3- to 7-fold in the urine of patients with G2 and G3 bladder cancer.[216] In a study of 504 individuals that

included 261 bladder cancer patients and 243 control individuals, the HA test had 83.1% sensitivity and 90.1% specificity to detect bladder cancer regardless of the tumor grade.[78] In the same study, the HAase test had 81.5% sensitivity and 83.8% specificity for detecting G2 and G3 bladder cancer. Combining these 2 tests into the HA-HAase test, resulted in the detection of bladder cancer with higher overall sensitivity (91.9%); with 86.4%, 95.7%, and 93.3% sensitivity to detect G1, G2, and G3 bladder tumors, respectively.[78] The HA-HAase test also detected both superficial (stages Ta, T1 and CIS) and invasive (stages ≥ T2) tumors with 87% to 100% sensitivity, respectively. The HA-HAase test also detected metastasis of tumors of other origin (ie, melanoma, colon cancer, ovarian, and cervical),

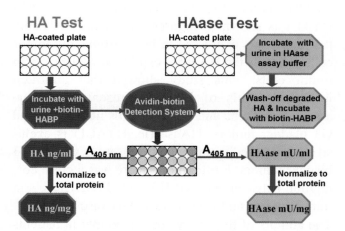

Figure 10–6. A schematic of HA and HAase tests. The HA and HAase tests involve two very similar ELISA-like assays. These are called ELISA-like assays (and not ELISA), because these assays do not use an antibody for detection. Instead, these assays use a bovine nasal cartilage HA-binding protein for detection.[78] The HA test is based on a competitive binding principle, in which HA present in samples (eg, urine) competes with HA that is coated on the microtiter wells, to bind to the biotinylated HA-binding protein. The HA-binding protein bound to the microtiter wells is detected using an avidin-biotin color detection system. The HA levels (ng/mL) present in the sample are calculated using a standard graph, prepared by plotting $A_{405 nm}$ versus HA concentration (ng/mL). The HA levels are then normalized to total urinary protein (mg/mL) and expressed as ng HA/mg protein (ng/mg). Normalization to protein is performed to eliminate the influence of the hydration status patients on the test's results. In the HAase test, HAase present in the sample degrades HA that is coated on the microtiter wells. Following incubation, HA remaining on the microtiter wells is detected using the same biotinylated HA-binding protein and the avidin-biotin color detection system. The HAase levels (mU/mL) present in the sample are calculated using a standard graph, prepared by plotting $A_{405 nm}$ versus HAase concentration (mU/mL). The HAase levels are then normalized to total urinary protein (mg/mL) and expressed as mU HAase/mg protein (mU/mg).[7,78,222]

although the number of such patients included in the study was small. The overall specificity of the HA-HAase test in this study was 84%.[78] The control population included normal healthy individuals, patients with genitourinary conditions such as, stone disease, BPH, microhematuria, urinary tract infection, and cystitis and patients with a history of bladder cancer but no evidence of disease at the time of testing.

In another study involving 83 bladder tissues and 34 urine specimens, Hautmann and colleagues investigated the correlation between tissue expression of HA and HAase and inferences on the HA-HAase test.[218] The tissue localization of HA and HYAL1 was studied using an immunohistochemistry technique. A schematic representation of the steps involved in a typical immunohistochemistry assay is shown in Figure 10–7. Immunostaining of bladder tissues for the localization of HA and HYAL1 is shown in Figures 10–8 and 10–9; note that the HA is expressed in both stroma and tumor cells, whereas the HAase is expressed exclusively in tumor cells. This study showed that although increased levels of HA are present in tumor-associated stroma and in tumor cells in G1, G2, and G3 bladder tumors, HAase (ie, HYAL1) is exclusively expressed in tumor cells present in G2 and G3 bladder tumors. Furthermore, there was a close correlation between elevated HA and HYAL1 levels in tumor tissues and a positive HA-HAase urine test. The authors of that study concluded that in patients with bladder cancer, tumor-associated HA and HYAL1 are secreted in urine, which results in a positive HA-HAase test.[218]

More recently, the ability of the HA-HAase to monitor bladder cancer recurrence was evaluated in a study of 70 patients with recurrent bladder cancer.[61] In that cohort, the HA-HAase test had 91% sensitivity, 70% specificity, 87% accuracy, 92% PPV, and 67% NPV. Of more interest is that of the 14 false-positive cases, 6 recurred within 5 months, whereas, only 4 out of the 33 true-negative cases recurred during the same period. Thus, a false-positive HA-HAase test carried a relative risk of 3.5 (RR = 3.5) for tumor recurrence within 5 months.[61] The comparison of the HA-HAase and the BTA-Stat tests for bladder cancer surveillance and screening is discussed in the next section.

Overall, the HA-HAase test appears to be a promising method for detecting the new onset and recurrent bladder tumor. This test may also be useful in screening a high-risk population for bladder cancer. The accuracy of this test is currently being evaluated in a multicenter trial.

COMPARATIVE ANALYSIS OF BLADDER TUMOR MARKERS (2000–2002)

Several studies have compared sensitivity and specificity of a variety of markers with each other and with cytology. Most of the markers have significantly higher sensitivity than cytology to detect bladder cancer. However, none of the markers is as tumor specific as cytology.[30] Many markers show lower specificity among patients with benign urologic conditions such as, cystitis, urinary tract infection, hematuria, urolithiasis, and BPH. Table 10–1 summarizes some of the comparative studies that improve our understanding of the performance of different markers evaluated in the same study population. Of the many comparative studies summarized in Table 10-1, studies by Ramakumar and colleagues, Wiener and colleagues, Sharma and colleagues, Sözen and colleagues, Del Nero and col-

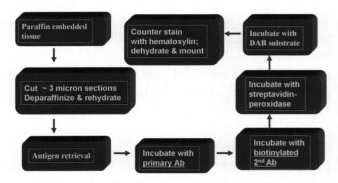

Figure 10–7. A schematic representation of immunohistochemistry technique. Paraffin-embedded fixed tissues are cut into approximately 3-micron sections and placed on positively charged slides. The tissues are deparaffinized and rehydrated. The tissues are then subjected to an antigen-retrieval step, which improves the binding of antibodies to various antigens present in tissues. Following the blocking of non-specific binding sites, the slides are sequentially incubated with a primary antibody and a secondary antibody, which is usually biotinylated. The slides are then sequentially incubated with Streptavidin-peroxidase and the DAB (3,3'-diaminobenzidine) substrate. The slides are then counter stained with hematoxylin, dehydrated, and mounted.[230]

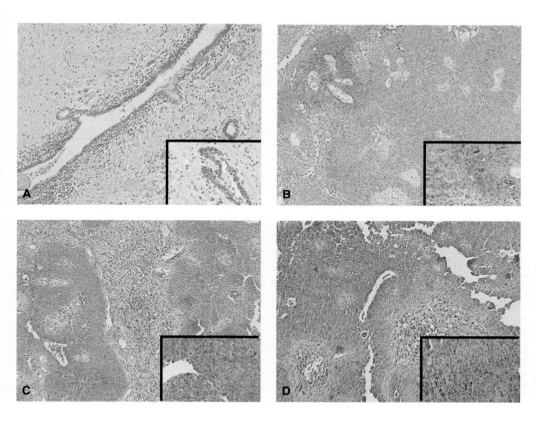

Figure 10–8. Immunohisto-chemical localization of HA in bladder tissues. *A*, normal tissue. *B*, grade 1 bladder tumor. *C*, grade 2 bladder tumor. *D*, grade 3 bladder tumor. Inset: ×400 original magnification. HA was localized using the biotinylated HA-binding protein Reprinted with permission from Hautmann et al.[218]

leagues, Landman and colleagues, Johnston and colleagues, Abbate and colleagues, and Schmetter and colleagues will not be discussed in the text because we have previously discussed these studies in detail in a recent review.[7,100,172–174,219–222]

Giannopoulos and colleagues, in a study of 213 patients, compared the efficacies of the urinary UBC, NMP22 and BTA-Stat tests.[120] For the NMP22 test, the authors used 8 U/mL as the cut-off limit, which is lower than the cut-off limit suggested by the manufacturer (ie, 10 U/mL). The overall sensitivity and specificity were 72.9%, and 64.6% for the BTA-Stat, 63.5% and 75% for the NMP22 and 80.5% and 80.2% for the UBC test, respectively. The UBC test also detected low-grade and low-stage bladder cancer with higher sensitivity and specificity than the NMP22 and BTA-Stat tests. Based on these results, the authors concluded that UBC may be a better diagnostic marker for bladder cancer than the NMP22 and BTA-Stat tests.

Mian and colleagues compared the accuracy of the UBC test with BTA-Stat and NMP22 in two separate studies.[118,154] In the first study involving 183 patients with a history of bladder cancer, the BTA-Stat and UBC had 52.8% and 66% sensitivity, respectively, for detecting bladder cancer.[154] It should be noted that the UBC test used in this study was a "rapid point-of-care" test that requires no specialized techniques. The sensitivity of both the UBC and BTA-Stat tests to detect low-grade tumors was low, at 38.8% for the BTA-Stat test and 44.4% for UBC test, respectively. The specificity of the BTA-Stat and UBC tests was 70% and 90%, respectively.

In the second study, when comparing the performances of the UBC and the NMP22 tests among patients with symptoms suggestive of bladder cancer, Mian and colleagues used 10 U/mL cut-off value for the NMP22 test and 12 mg/L cut-off value for the UBC ELISA test.[118] The UBC test had a slightly higher sensitivity (64.8%) than the NMP22 test (55.5%) in detecting bladder cancer. For detecting G1, G2, and G3 bladder tumors, the sensitivity was 50%, 50%, and 68.7% for the NMP22 test and 66.6%, 60%, and 68.7% for the UBC test, respectively. The UBC test had higher sensitivity (ie, 80%) to detect muscle invasive tumors when compared to Ta (62.1%) and T1 (53.8%) tumors. The specificity of both tests was 79% and 92%, respectively. However, both tests had a

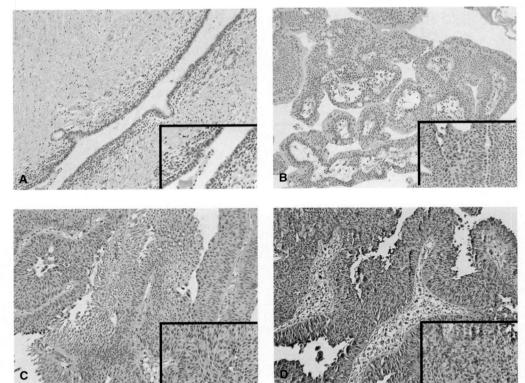

Figure 10–9. Immunohistochemical localization of HYAL1 type HAase in bladder tissues. *A*, normal tissue. *B*, grade 1 bladder tumor. *C*, grade 2 bladder tumor. *D*, grade 3 bladder tumor. Inset: ×400 original magnification. HYAL1 was localized using an anti-HYAL1 antibody Reprinted with permission from Hautmann et al.[218]

higher positive rate among patients with cystitis or benign lesions of the urinary tract. Based on both studies, Mian and colleagues concluded that although the UBC test is superior to both, the BTA-Stat and the NMP22 tests, all three tests can be used only to lower the number of cystoscopies while monitoring recurrence but cannot replace it completely.[118,154]

Sánchez-Carbayo and colleagues compared the diagnostic potential of the UBC, NMP22, and CYFRA 21-1 tests with cytology and microhematuria detection in 112 patients with symptomatic bladder cancer and 75 with benign urologic conditions.[138] In that study the authors also compared the diagnostic characteristics of urinary tumor markers with or without normalization to urinary creatinine. In the absence of normalization, the UBC, CYFRA 21-1, and NMP22 tests had a sensitivity of 69.4%, 67.3%, and 61.2% and a specificity of 91.3%, 88.4%, and 89.9%, respectively. Normalization to creatinine increased the sensitivity of the CYFRA 21-1 (75.5%) and NMP22 (73.5%) tests; however, it decreased the specificity significantly (NMP22, 68.1% and CYFRA 21-1, 71%). All three markers had significantly higher sensitivity than cytology (35.4%) and

microhematuria (55.1%). However, the majority of the false-negatives were among G1-tumor patients and those with superficial bladder cancer. The sensitivity of all three markers for detecting G1 tumors varied between 27% and 54% either with or without normalization to creatinine. The false-positive rate for all three markers among patients with benign genitourinary conditions (ie, BPH, urinary tract infection, stenosis, and lithiasis) was between 23% and 39%, either with or without normalization to urinary creatinine. Therefore, although the combination of the NMP22, UBC, and BTA-Stat tests will improve sensitivity of bladder cancer detection, it will significantly impact the specificity and the positive predictive value of the combination.

Boman and colleagues compared the performances of the BTA-Stat, NMP22, and UBC tests with cytology in detecting new tumors and tumor recurrence among a total of 250 study patients.[117] One of the important salient features of this study is that, it documents that there is a large difference in size between new tumors (median size, 15 mm) and recurrent tumor (median size, 6.5 mm) and that new tumors tend to have higher grade and stage than

Table 10-2. COMPARATIVE ANALYSIS OF BLADDER TUMOR MARKERS/TESTS (2000–2002)*

Study	Cytology	BTA-Stat	BTA-TARK	NMP22	UBC	FDP	HA-HAase	CYFRA 21-1	Telomerase	hTERT	Microsatellite DNA	FISH	Cytokeratin-20
Giannopoulos et al[120]	—	72.9/64.6	—	63.5/75	80.5/80.2	—	—	—	—	—	—	—	—
Mian et al[118,154]	—	52.8/70	—	55.5/79	66/90	—	—	—	—	—	—	—	—
Sanchez-Carbayo et al[138]	35.4/97.2												
A: no normalization to creatinine		—	—	A: 61.2/89.9	A: 69.4/91.3	—	—	A: 67.3/88.4	—	—	—	—	—
B: normalization to creatinine				B: 73.5/68.1	B: 69.4/87			B: 75.5/71					
Boman et al[117]	41/94	75P; 55R/54	—	65P; 45R/64	60P; 40R/72	—	—	—	—	—	—	—	—
Gutierrez-Banos et al[85]	69.7/93.2	72.3/89.2	—	84.2/86.5 @ 6 U/mL; 76.3/90.5 @ 10 U/mL	—	—	—	—	—	—	—	—	—
Oge et al[119]	—	89/78.7	—	66.6/69.6	—	—	—	—	—	—	—	—	—
Casella et al[140]	52/89	52/89	—	51/83	—	—	—	—	—	—	—	—	—
Serretta[122]	—	57/62	62/79	74/55	—	—	—	—	—	—	—	—	—
Topsakal[98]	45/96.4	—	—	—	—	69.9 (P: 97; R: 47.3/67.9	—	—	—	—	—	—	—
Bialkowska-Hobrzanska et al[190]	61.9/100	—	—	—	—	—	—	—	48.6/92	94.3/100	—	—	—
Cassel[160]	—	—	—	—	—	—	—	—	84.1/24.1	—	—	—	81.8/55.2
Halling et al[222]	58/96	—	—	—	—	—	—	—	—	—	—	81/98	—
Ishiwata et al[224]	32/100	64/80	—	—	—	—	—	—	—	—	—	85/95	—
Lokeshwar et al[61]	61/74	—	—	—	—	—	94/63†	—	—	—	—	—	—
Van Rhijn et al[67]	22/95	56/79	—	—	—	—	—	—	—	—	74/82‡	—	—

*the table shows % sensitivity / % specificity of each marker

† = corrected: 81%.

‡ = corrected: 94

P = primary tumors; R = recurrent tumors.

recurrent tumors. The sensitivity of all three markers for detecting new tumors was higher (NMP22, 65%; BTA-Stat, 75%; and UBC, 60%) than that for detecting recurrent tumors (NMP22, 45%; BTA-Stat, 55%; and UBC, 40%). The sensitivity of cytology for detecting both new and recurrent tumors was 41 to 45%. The difference in the sensitivity of the three markers for detecting new and recurrent tumors disappeared when the tumors in both categories were differentiated with respect to size, grade, and stage. Thus, all three markers had a lower sensitivity for detecting smaller superficial tumors. Based on this study, the authors concluded that these three tumor markers or any combination of them cannot replace follow-up cystoscopy, mainly because most recurrent tumors are small. Another point to consider is that if the purpose of noninvasive tumor markers is to detect bladder tumors prior to them becoming invasive, the tumor markers should have a reasonably high sensitivity for detecting small, superficial tumors.

Gutierrez-Banos and colleagues, and Oge and colleagues compared the efficacies of the NMP22 and BTA-Stat tests and cytology among symptomatic patients.[85,119] Gutierrez-Banos and colleagues in a study of 150 patients found a sensitivity of 84.2% at 6 U/mL cut-off and 76.3% sensitivity at 10 U/mL cut-off, respectively, for the NMP22 test.[85] The sensitivity of the NMP22 test to detect G1, G2, and G3 bladder tumors was 68.7%, 75.9%, and 100%, respectively at a 6 U/mL cut-off value and 50%, 69%, and 96.8%, respectively at a 10 U/mL cut-off value. The sensitivity of the BTA-Stat test and cytology for detecting bladder cancer was 72.3% and 69.7%, respectively. The sensitivity for detecting G1, G2, and G3 tumors was 56.2%, 62.1%, and 90.3%, respectively, for the BTA-Stat test and 43.8%, 62.1%, and 90.3%, respectively, for cytology. The specificity of the BTA-Stat (89.2%) and NMP22 (86.5%, 6 U/mL, and 90.5%, 10 U/mL) tests and cytology (93.2%) was comparable. Based on these results the authors suggested using 6 U/mL as a cut-off for the NMP22 test. However, this conclusion should not be generalized because in the study by Boman and colleagues, the NMP22 test had low sensitivity (ie, 65% for detecting new tumors and 45% for detecting recurrent tumors) even when a cut-off value of 4 U/mL was used.[117] Since in the Gutierrez-Banos study, all tests including cytology had a

higher sensitivity for detecting bladder cancer when compared with other studies, it is possible that the study patients may have had larger sized tumors that are more readily detected by the markers than the smaller size tumors.[85–100]

In the study by Oge and colleagues, the BTA-Stat significantly outperformed the NMP22 test, in fact this is the only study in which the BTA-Stat test has shown such a high sensitivity and specificity.[67, 85,86,88–91,117–120] The NMP22 and BTA-Stat tests had 66.6% and 89% sensitivity, and 69.6% and 78.7% specificity, respectively. However, the sensitivity of both tests to detect low-grade tumors was low, 55.5% for the BTA-Stat and 33.3% for the NMP22 test, respectively.

Casella and colleagues compared the performance of the NMP22 test with bladder wash cytology in a study of 200 patients and found that the sensitivity of the NMP22 test (51%) was very similar to the sensitivity of cytology (52%) for detecting bladder cancer.[140] The NMP22 test sensitivity was 36% for superficial tumors and 73% for invasive tumors. Bladder wash cytology was slightly better than the NMP22 test with 38% sensitivity for superficial tumors and 83% for invasive tumors. The NMP22 test and bladder wash cytology again had a similar sensitivity for detecting G1 and G2 tumors; however, the bladder wash cytology was significantly better (sensitivity 91%) than the NMP22 test (sensitivity 69%) in detecting G3 tumors. Based on these results the authors concluded that with a 49% false-negative rate, the danger of missing NMP22 negative tumors (many of which are high-grade tumors), is too high to rely on its results in an individual patient.[140]

Casetta and colleagues compared the usefulness of the BTA-TARK and NMP22 tests with urine cytology (performed on three consecutive samples) to detect bladder cancer. This is the only study where the sensitivity of cytology was the higher than the tumor makers under study.[101] The study was conducted on two groups of patients, group 1 included 94 patients with symptoms highly suspicious of bladder cancer and group 2 had 102 patients who were being monitored for bladder cancer recurrence. The overall sensitivity of the NMP22 (cut-off 11 U/mL), BTA-TARK (cut-off 60 U/mL), and cytology testing was 56%, 57%, and 59.3%, respectively. When "dubious results" on cytology were considered as positive cases, the sensitivity of cytology increased to 73.3%. The sensitivity of the two tumor markers was not different in the two groups and it did not improve by lowering the cut-off values on both tests. Based on these results, the authors concluded that urine cytology performed on three samples outperforms the NMP22 and BTA-Stat tests. The authors also observed that the diagnostic advantage of cytology over the two urine tests was maintained even when the patients were stratified according to tumor grade.

Serretta and colleagues compared the efficacy of the NMP22, BTA-Stat, and BTA-TARK among 170 patients, who were being followed for recurrent superficial bladder tumors.[122] The NMP22, BTA-Stat, and BTA-TARK tests had a sensitivity of 55%, 62%, and 79%, respectively, for detecting bladder cancer recurrence. In this study approximately 52% of patients were receiving adjuvant intravesical chemotherapy. All three tests showed a higher false-positive rate among these patients. This is not surprising, since during the course of chemotherapy there will be cell death (releasing NMP22 in urine), as well as inflammatory reaction (possibly causing the BTA-Stat/TARK tests to be positive), which will lead to a positive NMP22 and/or BTA-Stat/TARK tests. The authors of this study concluded that bladder cancer monitoring using certain non-invasive test should not be carried out during intravesical treatment.

Topsakal and colleagues compared the efficacy of the Accu-Dx test with cytology in detecting bladder cancer, in a study of 97 patients.[98] The overall sensitivity and specificity of Accu-Dx were 69.6% and 67.9%, respectively, whereas the cytology had 45% sensitivity and 96.4% specificity for detecting bladder cancer. As observed in the study by Boman and colleagues, it is interesting to note that whereas the tumor markers such as, the NMP22, BTA-Stat, and UBC had a higher sensitivity to detect new tumors, the Accu-Dx test was more sensitive to detect new primary tumors (sensitivity 97%) than it was for detecting recurrent tumors (sensitivity 47.3%).[117] This difference among new and recurrent tumors was most evident among low-grade and low-stage tumors. For example, the Accu-Dx test had 90.9% and 85.7% sensitivity, respectively, for detecting primary G1 and Ta tumors. However, among recurrent tumors, the Accu-Dx had only 28.5% and 33.3% sensitivity to detect G1 and Ta tumors, respectively.[98] The specificity of Accu-Dx among patients with inflammatory conditions, cystitis, and stone disease was 68%. Based on these results, the authors concluded that Accu-Dx due to its low accuracy and specificity rates may be inadequate to replace conventional cystoscopy. In addition, due to its low sensitivity for detecting tumor recurrence, Accu-Dx may be used only as an adjunct to cystoscopy.

As discussed in the earlier section, an RT-PCR assay that amplifies the human telomerase reverse transcriptase (hTERT) may be a better alternative to the TRAP assay for detecting bladder cancer. Bialkowska-Hobrzanska and colleagues directly compared the TRAP assay and hTERT/GAPDH RT-PCR to detect bladder cancer in a study of 35 patients.[190] In the hTERT/GAPDH RT-PCR assay, the hTERT message amplification is normalized to the amplification of GAPDH (a housekeeping gene), which eliminates disparity in results due to different amounts of exfoliated cells in different samples, differences in RNA extraction, and other variables. In this study the hTERT/GAPDH RT-PCR outperformed the TRAP assay by almost 2-fold, in terms of sensitivity (94.3% for hTERT/GAPDH versus 48.6% for TRAP assay, $p < .001$). The sensitivity of urine cytology in this study was 61.9%. The hTERT/GAPDH had a significantly higher sensitivity (90%) in detecting G1 and G2 tumors than the TRAP assay (25%) and urine cytology (58.3%). The overall specificity of the hTERT/GAPDH RT-PCR (92%), TRAP assay (100%) and urine cytology (100%) was comparable. Thus, in this small study the hTERT/GAPDH RT-PCR was significantly better than the TRAP assay for detecting bladder cancer.

In contrast to the Bialkowska-Hobrzanska study, de Kok and colleagues found that the sensitivity of the TRAP assay (29%) and hTERT real-time (ie, quantitative) RT-PCR (24%) was poor.[191] The authors concluded that several variables including inter-laboratory differences in sample storage and processing and the presence of occult blood may lead to poor reproducibility of the TRAP assay and hTERT RT-PCR. In their study only patients with bladder cancer were studied, and hence, evaluation of specificity was not performed.

Cassel and colleagues evaluated the performance of TRAP-ELISA and cytokeratin-20 RT-PCR to detect bladder cancer, in a study of 44 bladder cancer patients and 26 age-matched controls with a wide variety of clinical disorders.[160] The clinical disorders included BPH, perichondritis, renal colic, bilateral inguinal hernia, epilepsy, prostatectomy, impotence, and bowel obstruction. In this study the telomerase activity and cytokeratin-20 RT-PCR had 84.1% and 81.8% sensitivity, respectively, for detecting bladder cancer. However, among the urologic and non-urologic cases, the specificity of telomerase activity (24.1%) and cytokeratin-20 (55.2%) was low. These results demonstrate that telomerase activity and cytokeratin-20 expression are not specific for malignancy and may be detected in many non-malignant cases. Therefore, the use of these molecules, as potential markers for bladder cancer needs to be carefully evaluated.

Halling and colleagues demonstrated the sensitivity and specificity of multicolored, multiprobe FISH assay with cytology in a study of 150 patients with and 115 patients without a history of bladder cancer.[223] For FISH analysis, labeled probes to the peri-centromeric regions of chromosomes 3, 7, and 17 and to chromosome 9p21 locus were used. In this study, FISH assay was more sensitive (81%) than cytology (58%) in detecting bladder cancer. The sensitivity to detect G1, G2, and G3 bladder cancer was 36%, 76%, and 97% for FISH assay and 27%, 54%, and 71%, for cytology, respectively. The difference in the sensitivity of FISH and cytology for detecting low-grade (36% versus 27%) and low-stage (65% versus 47%) tumors was not statistically significant. The specificity of FISH and cytology among healthy individuals and patients with genitourinary conditions other than bladder cancer, was 98% and 96%, respectively. Based on these results the authors concluded that the FISH assay is superior to cytology in detecting bladder cancer. However, FISH appears to be only slightly better than cytology in detecting low-grade and low-stage tumors.

Ishiwata and colleagues compared the clinical utility of multiprobe FISH, BTA-Stat and cytology for detecting bladder cancer and monitoring its recurrence.[223] In this study, for FISH analysis, the authors used centromere-specific probes for chromosomes 9

and 17. The overall sensitivity of FISH, cytology, and the BTA-Stat test was 85%, 32%, and 64%, respectively. In contrast to the Halling and colleagues study, the FISH had 81% sensitivity to detect G1 and G2 tumors and 100% sensitivity for detecting G3 tumors. For each tumor grade and stage category, FISH was superior to cytology and the BTA-Stat test. Of the 17 patients, who were being monitored for recurrence, 13 had false-positive results on the FISH assay. Of these 13 patients, 7 recurred within 27 months, whereas none of the patients with true-negative results recurred during the same time. Given the fact that the time interval between surveillance cystoscopies is usually 3 to 6 months, it remains to be determined, whether recurrence within 27 months among patients with positive results on the FISH assay has any clinical significance.

Lokeshwar and colleagues compared the performance of the HA-HAase test with the BTA-Stat test in 26 patients with a history of bladder cancer (111 urine specimens).[61] These patients were monitored over a course of 4 years. The HA-HAase and BTA-Stat tests had 94% and 61% sensitivity, 63% and 74% specificity and 87% and 64% accuracy, respectively. The HA-HAase and the BTA-Stat tests had 89% and 88% PPV and 77% and 38% NPV, for detecting bladder cancer. The HA-HAase test had 91%, 100%, and 92.3% sensitivity for detecting G1, G2, and G3 bladder tumors, respectively. The BTA-Stat test showed 73%, 52%, and 62% sensitivity for detecting G1, G2, and G3 bladder tumors. In this study, 60% of the false-positive cases on the HA-HAase test recurred within 4.7 months. However, during the same time period, only 12% of the true-negative cases recurred. Thus, a false-positive HA-HAase test carried a 10-fold risk of recurrence within 4.7 months (RR = 10.2; OR = 24; p = .004). In contrast, a false-positive result on the BTA-Stat test did not carry any significant risk of recurrence within 4.7 months (RR = 1.4; OR = 1.5; p = .756). This study concluded that the HA-HAase test is superior to the BTA-Stat test in monitoring and in predicting future bladder cancer recurrence. In the same study a comparison between the performance of the HA-HAase and BTA-Stat tests was conducted, for screening of 401 former Department of Energy workers who had a possible exposure to bladder carcinogens for at least 1 year. The HA-HAase and BTA-Stat tests were positive among 14% and 17% of the individuals, respectively. Sixty-three percent of the positive results on the BTA-Stat test compared to only 25% of the positives on the HA-HAase test had abnormal urine analysis or benign urologic conditions. It should be noted that even after a rigorous follow-up, only 29 individuals who were positive on either one or both of the HA-HAase and BTA-Stat tests underwent cystoscopy and only 20, who were negative for bladder cancer, reported their results. This study suggests that non-invasive tests with low-false positive rates could be used for bladder cancer screening. But more importantly, it also reveals some of the challenges in terms of patient follow-up, when conducting screening trials involving biomarkers.

van Rhijn and colleagues compared the efficacy of microsatellite DNA test with the BTA-Stat test and voided urine cytology in 93 patients.[67] The microsatellite DNA test, BTA-Stat test, and cytology had 74%, 56%, and 22% sensitivity and 82%, 79%, and 95% specificity, respectively. Although the microsatellite DNA analysis missed all 11 TaG1 tumors, 55% of the false-positive cases on the microsatellite DNA test recurred within 6 months. In contrast, only 11.6% of the true-negative cases recurred during that time. Thus, the corrected specificity of the test is 94%. It should be noted, however, that 14 patients were eliminated from the study either due to insufficient DNA quality or abundance of leukocytes, both of which render the results of microsatellite test unreliable. Based on these results, the authors concluded that microsatellite analysis, a DNA test in urine, reliably signals the presence of recurrent bladder cancer, sometimes even before cystoscopic evidence of disease.[67]

Comparative studies show that non-invasive tests are more sensitive than cytology. Some of these tests can also detect bladder cancer recurrence before it can be detected clinically. Thus, non-invasive tests with a high sensitivity and reasonable specificity can be used in a surveillance setting to reduce the number of cytoscopies performed each year for monitoring bladder tumor recurrence. The use of non-invasive tests for screening a high-risk population can be made economically sound by choosing non-invasive tests that have high specificity and rea-

sonable sensitivity. Furthermore, by concurrently performing urine analysis on each specimen and having knowledge about clinical history of patients, will reveal conditions that might render a false-positive result on the non-invasive tests.

PROGNOSTIC MARKERS FOR BLADDER CANCER

Tumor grade and stage are the primary parameters used to predict the prognosis of bladder cancer. However, tumor grade is pathologist-dependent and a significant number of bladder tumors are under-staged.[70–76] Since tumors with the same grade and/or stage differ in recurrence and progression rates, many investigations are directed towards finding molecular markers that can accurately predict prognosis (ie, recurrence, progression, and survival) and response to treatment. Such markers would allow individualation of treatment based on the molecular characteristics of each tumor that determine its ability to recur, metastasize, and respond to treatment. Several cell-associated molecules that have been tested as prognostic indicators can be classified into following groups:

1. Tumor suppressors (eg, *p53*, *Rb*, *p16*),
2. Proto-oncogenes (eg, epidermal growth factor (EGF)–receptor, HER-2/neu, c-myc, H-ras),
3. Proliferation-associated markers (eg, Ki67 (MIB1), p27, Kip1, p21WAF1/CIP1, PCNA, cyclin D1),
4. Apoptosis-related markers (eg, bcl-2, bax),
5. Metastasis-associated markers (eg, matrix metalloproteinases, tissue inhibitors of metalloproteinases [TIMPs]),
6. Cell-associated markers (eg, E-cadherin, uroplakin),
7. Cytoskeletal proteins (eg, beta-catenin, cytokeratin 20),
8. Miscellaneous markers (eg, thymidylate synthase, glutathione S-transferase).[70–73]

Rather than discussing each marker separately, in this section we will discuss how the potential of these markers as prognostic indicators and treatment response indicators has been evaluated in various studies. The molecular functions of these markers and their role in bladder cancer have been discussed in many reviews.[70–73]

Markers for Predicting Recurrence, Progression, and Disease-Specific Survival

Plastiras and colleagues evaluated the prognostic significance of p53, bcl-2, and PCNA among patients with high-risk superficial and invasive bladder cancer by immunohistochemical staining of archival bladder tumor tissues.[225] The median follow-up of patients was 52 months. Among superficial tumors, both p53 and PCNA were significant predictors of disease specific death compared to tumor grade, size, and multiplicity. However, for muscle invasive tumors, none of the markers offered prognositic information.

In contrast to the study of Plastrias and colleagues study, Liukkonen and colleagues in a prospective randomized study, found that while tumor grade was an independent predictor of recurrence, MIB1 and papillary status were independent predictors of cancer specific survival.[226] This study involved immunohistochemical analysis of p53, MIB1 (is a monoclonal antibody that detects Ki-67), mitotic index, and EGF-receptor expression in surperficial (ie, Ta, T1) bladder cancer. However, no independent prognostic significance could be established for p53 and EGF-receptor expression. The cell cycle markers including p53, mdm2, p21 and Ki67 were also found not to be predictive of recurrence in a study by Pfister and colleagues.[227] In this study, which involved immunostaining of 249 specimens with cell-cycle markers, only clinicopathologic index (ie, tumor grade, tumor stage, multifocality, and tumor diameter) was found to predict recurrence.

Prognostic significance of p53 mutations was evaluated in two studies. Gao and colleagues compared immunostaining of p53 with presence of p53 mutations in bladder tumor specimens.[228] Since mutant p53 protein is more stable than the wild type p53, it is generally assumed that over-expression of p53 in tumor tissues suggests the presence of p53 mutations. Contrary to this assumption, Gao and colleagues found that about 50% tumors in which high p53 staining was observed did not show the presence of p53 mutations. Furthermore, neither

p53 over-expression nor p53 mutations were superior to staging as prognostic markers. Friedrich and colleagues investigated the relevance of p53 mutations and loss of heterozygosity (LOH) for tumor recurrence. In this study, neither disease-free survival nor recurrence, correlated with p53 mutations, p53 LOH, or their combination. However, a positive p53 staining was significantly associated with short disease free survival.[229]

The comparison between the prognostic capability of Ki67 and p53 immunostaining has been done in several studies. Wolf and colleagues compared the prognostic value of p53 and Ki-67 along with p21/WAF1, bcl-2, bax and bak in T1G3 bladder tumors, using immunohistochemistry and antibodies that specifically detect respective tissue markers.[230] In this study p53 and bcl-2 were found to be significant predictors of tumor-free survival. For example, T1G3 patients with p53-positive tumors had shorter survival (mean = 3 months) when compared to patients with p53-negative tumors (mean = 82 months). Based on these results, the authors concluded that p53 and bcl-2 immunoreactivity identifies most aggressive T1G3 carcinomas.

In contrast to T1G3 tumors or muscle invasive tumors, Ki-67 appears to be a prognostic marker for superficial (Ta–T1) low-grade tumors.[231–234] Gonetero and colleagues observed that Ki67 and multifocality but not p53 were independent prognostic indicators for recurrence. Furthermore, a > 20% Ki67 index in a single Ta–T1 G1/G2 tumor predicted recurrence within 1 year.[231] Wu and colleagues also reported similar findings related to p53, bcl-2, and Ki67.[233] In their study, Ki67 was found to be the only independent predictor of recurrence for primary superficial low-grade bladder cancers. Furthermore, Ki67 was found to differentiate G2 tumor patients into those who have and those who do not have a favorable prognosis. Oosterhuis and colleagues studied the prognostic significance of Ki67 among 301 patients using MIB1. The comparison of MIB1 staining among low-grade and high-grade bladder tumors is shown in Figure 10–10. Based on the immunohistochemical analysis of Ki67, Oosterhuis and colleagues found that Ki67 proliferation index is an independent predictor of recurrence-free survival among patients with Ta and T1 tumors.[234]

The prognostic significance of p53 to predict recurrence and survival has also been compared with other markers such as, E-cadherin, EGF-receptor, c-erbB-2, p21/WAF1, p16, mdm-2, Rb, bcl-x, bak, and uroplakin among squamous cell carcinoma and transitional cell carcinoma of the bladder.[235–247] Korkolopoulou and colleagues compared the prognostic capability of p53, pRb, p16 and cell proliferation markers (ie, PCNA and Ki67) immunostaining in advanced stage and superficial bladder cancer.[235] Based on the immunostaining results, Korkolopoulou and colleagues found that while aberrant p16 expression was an adverse prognostic indicator in advanced stage bladder cancer (ie, T3 and T4 tumors), double negative p16/Rb and p53/p16 phenotypes predicted a reduced overall and disease-free survival. The p53/p16 abnormal expression was also an independent predictor for poor prognosis in mus-

cle invasive tumors. However, as has been reported in other studies, only proliferation markers had independent prognostic significance for superficial tumors (stage Ta and T1).[235]

The expression of Ki67 appears to correlate with decreased expression of p27/Kip1 and low staining of cyclin E. Kamai and colleagues observed that low cyclin E and p27 levels, and high Ki67 index correlate with poorly differentiated grade, muscle invasion, lymph node metastasis, and shorter overall survival.[234] In addition, low p27 and high Ki67 expressions are indicators of shortened disease-free survival and early recurrence. In this study, Ki67 expression correlated with the recurrence of superficial tumors.

Another marker that may have some prognostic significance is PCNA. Lavezzi and colleagues observed that PCNA labeling index is an independent prognostic indicator for patient survival among

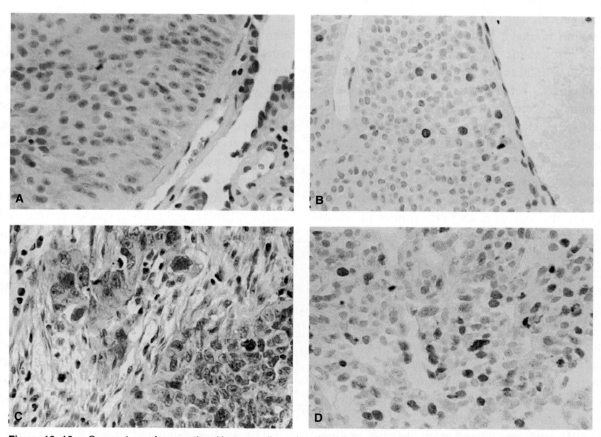

Figure 10–10. Comparison of conventional hematoxylin and eosin staining of transitional cell carcinoma with MIB-1-stained specimen. Panels 1 and 2: Grade 2a/low-grade transitional cell carcinoma. Panels 3 and 4: Grade 3/high-grade transitional cell carcinoma. Panels 1 and 3 show hematoxylin and eosin staining. Panels 2 and 4 show MIB-1 stained specimens. Note the low proliferative activity in panel 1 and high proliferative activity in panel 4. (Adopted from: Oosterhuis et al. Figure 1. Cancer 2001;88:2598–2605.).

patients with superficial (stage T1) bladder cancer.[237] However, cyclin D1 may not be an independent prognostic indicator. Takagi and colleagues, in a study of 102 patients, examined immunostaining for cyclin D1 in bladder cancer specimens. Based on this immunostaining pattern, Takagi and colleagues reported that cyclin D1 immunostaining in bladder tumors inversely correlates with tumor stage (superficial tumors with higher staining than muscle invasive tumors) and it is not an independent predictor of survival.[238] Sgambato and colleagues recently showed that in superficial tumors (Ta, T1) cyclin D1 overexpression correlates with p53 mutations and high cyclin D1 expression correlated with longer disease-free survival, and low-risk of recurrence.[239] These reports suggest that to test the potential of cyclin D1 as an "independent predictor of survival and recurrence" stratification of data with respect to tumor grade and stage may be necessary.

The expression of E-cadherin also, plausibly, has some prognositic capabilities. In contrast to the cell proliferation markers, however, E-cadherin appears to be a prognostic indicator for invasive disease.[240–242] Garcia and colleagues and Nakopoulou and colleagues, reported that loss of E-cadherin expression, as examined by immunohistochemistry, is an independent predictor of survival and this association was stronger among patients with muscle invasive disease.[240,241] In addition to E-cadherin, loss of beta-catenin also appears to be a strong predictor of poor survival.[240,241] Similar to E-cadherin protein expression, the loss of E-cadherin transcript, examined by semi-quantitative RT-PCR analysis, is also a predictor of poor survival. Byrne and colleagues determined association of abnormal expression of E-cadherin and lymph node metastasis using immunhistochemistry.[242] Figure 10–11 shows the expression of E-cadherin in normal urothelium and in non-invasive and invasive bladder tumors. Based on their analysis, Byrne and colleagues demonstrated that decreased or loss of E-cadherin expression associates with muscle invasion by a bladder tumor and lymph node metastasis. E-cadherin expression was also significantly associated with disease progression and bladder cancer specific survival.

Uroplakin II appears to be another marker that is associated with high-stage disease and lymph node metastases.[243,244] The expression of uroplakin II is confined to urothelial and bladder tumor cells. Li and colleagues showed that detection of uroplakin II mRNA in peripheral blood by RT-PCR is indicative of metastatic spread of bladder tumor cells.[244] This RT-PCR assay has sensitivity to detect even 1 circulating bladder cancer cell in 5 mL of blood. Xu and colleagues tested the diagnostic value of uroplakin immunostaining of fine needle aspiration.[243] This method detected 93% of metastatic transitional cell carcinoma cases suggesting that uroplakin may be a marker for detecting and predicting metastasis of pathologically organ-confined bladder tumors. Seraj and colleagues recently confirmed these findings using an RT-PCR assay for uroplakin II expression and concluded that uroplakin may be a marker for predicting perivesical and lymph node metastases.[245]

The EGF-receptor family and their ligands may also offer some prognostic information regarding bladder cancer.[246,247] Thogersen and colleagues evaluated the expression of EGF, epiregulin, TGF-α, amphiregulin, HB-EGF, betacellulin, and two EGF receptors (HER1 and HER2) mRNA in 73 bladder tumor biopsies.[255] The study showed that the expression of epiregulin, TGF-α, amphiregulin and HB-EGF correlated with survival and the expression was increased in T2–T4 tumors more than in Ta tumors. Chow and colleagues evaluated the prognostic significance of coexpression of various EGF-receptor family members by immunohistochemistry.[247] The study demonstrated that tumor staging, levels of EGF-receptor, ErbB2, and ErbB3 expression were indictors for survival. Furthermore, in a subset of G2 tumors co-expression of all 3 EGF-receptors predicted development of a second recurrence. Thus, expression of both the ligands and the receptors of the EGF family may have some prognostic significance.

In addition to the above markers, thymidylate synthase, dihydropyrimidine dehydrogenase, cytokeratin 20 (and possibly cytokeratin 7) and matrix metalloproteinases assayed by RT-PCR have also been shown to have some prognostic potential to predict invasiveness and recurrence of bladder cancer.[248–253]

The studies discussed above help us to draw a coherent picture about the molecular heterogeneity among superficial and invasive bladder tumors. Furthermore, they address how this heterogeneity can be

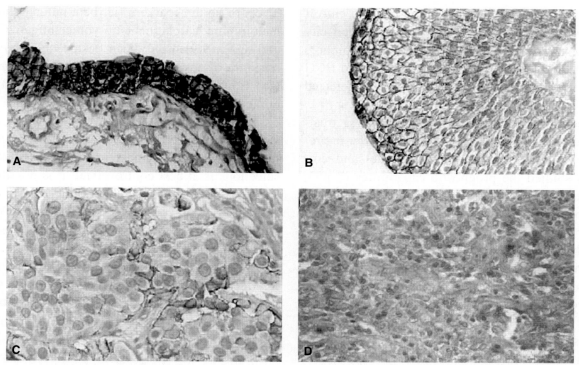

Figure 10–11. Immunohistochemical analysis of E-cadherin expression in bladder tumors. *A*, 100% preserved E-cadherin expression in normal urothelium. *B*, E-cadherin expression in G1Ta transitional cell carcinoma, 90–100% preserved expression. *C*, Heterogeneous E-cadherin expression in G3P3bN2 with lymphovascular invasion (10% to 49% positive). *D*, E-cadherin expression in G4p3b (note the lack of expression). (Original magnification, ×400). (Adopted from: Byrne et al. Figure 1. J Urol 2001;165:14739.).

exploited to identify prognostic markers that can predict recurrence, progression, and survival of patients with superficial or invasive bladder cancer. For example, p53, E-cadherin, beta-catenin, uproplakin, and Rb appear to be prognostic indicators for invasive bladder cancer. However, proliferation markers (eg, Ki67 and mitotic index) appear to predict tumor recurrence and survival among patients with superficial bladder cancer. This heterogeneity may explain why different studies report seemingly opposite results regarding the same markers.[230,233–235] The performance of prognostic indicators also depends upon the quality of fixed antigens, detection reagents, cut-off limits set for deciding positive and negative predictive inferences, and subjectivity in scoring. For example, *P53* mutations are known to increase protein stability and hence can be detected by immunostaining. However, the staining may be positive in the absence of mutations or mutations may prematurely terminate the p53 protein, resulting in the loss of an epitope that is recognized by the antibodies used in immunohistochemistry.[73] In addition, RT-PCR assays that detect even one tumor cell in circulating blood may be too sensitive for predicting clinical outcome. This is because metastasis is an inefficient and a multi-step process and, therefore, presence of a small number of tumor cells in blood does not necessarily offer prognostic indication regarding metastasis or survival.

Markers for Predicting Treatment Response

Several studies have examined the prognostic capabilities of p53, Ki67, p27, and other markers to predict the response to BCG or radiation. Zlotta and colleagues evaluated the ability of p53, Ki67, and p21 immunostaining in bladder tissues to predict response to intravesical BCG therapy.[75] However, the study found no independent prognostic significance for any of the markers to predict a treatment response. In contrast, Lebret and colleagues found that Ki67 (MIB1) predicted response to BCG in high-risk T1G3 patients. All study patients whose tumor tissues showed Ki67 staining below a cut-off limit responded to BCG.[254] However, the specificity of the test was low, at 44%. Therefore, the authors concluded that Ki67 cannot predict failure to BCG therapy and, hence, patients should not be selected to have cystectomy based on Ki67 staining.

In contrast to failure in predicting BCG treatment response, prognostic markers are better in predicting response to radiotherapy. Rodel and colleagues studied the prognostic capabilities of p53, apoptotic index, Ki67, and bcl-2 to predict response to radiotherapy following transurethral resection of bladder tumor. In this study, a high apoptosis index and a high Ki67 index correlated with and were independent predictors of the initial and complete response as well as of local control of the disease with preserved bladder 5-years or more after treatment.[74] However, p53 and bcl-2 expression had no prognostic significance for predicting response to radiochemotherapy. Consistent with this report, Rotterud and colleagues reported that p53 overexpression in immunostaining studies, which is believed to represent mutant p53, in fact correlated with longer overall survival and cancer-specific survival among patients with T2 to T4 bladder cancer, who received radiotherapy before and after cystectomy. Thus, p53 expression is not related to response to radiotherapy.[255] In this study, both p21 and mdm2 also did not have any prognostic significance. Lara and colleagues reported that low Ki67 index correlated with a better local control of the disease, 5 years following radical radiation therapy (66 Gy/6–7 weeks), suggesting that Ki67 has prognostic capabilities to predict response to radiation.[256]

In contrast to the studies discussed above, Moonen and colleagues reported that among patients receiving external beam radiation for invasive bladder cancer, the tumors which expressed wild type p53 and higher apoptotic index, had better local control. Although tumors with high Ki67 index showed shorter time for distant metastases, both Ki67 index and cyclin D1 expression were not predictive of treatment response.[257] It should be noted that in this study, none of the markers predicted survival.

In addition to cell proliferation markers and tumor suppressors, chromosomal alterations (eg, LOH at 1p, 8p, 10p, 13q, and 17q) or change in the levels of serum markers (ie, beta-human choriogonadotrophin, carcinoma embryonic antigen, CA125, and CA 19.9) have been tested to predict the response of advanced bladder cancer to chemotherapy. However, these changes did not predict either clinical response or survival.[70,76,258]

The studies discussed above suggest that, at present, the role of prognostic markers to predict treatment response and to make individualized treatment selections is at best controversial. It is possible that specific markers are useful in predicting treatment response only in certain groups of patients. A better understanding of the markers and conditions under which they are expressed will improve the use of their prognostic potential, in terms of predicting treatment response. Furthermore, technical aspects such as, when and how the specimen was obtained, reagents used for detecting the marker, and interpretation of results are also critical when assessing the usefulness of various prognostic markers in predicting response to treatment.

In addition to tumor detection, monitoring treatment response and making predictions regarding prognosis, tumor markers may help in identifying rare urothelial tumors such as, nested variant of urothelial carcinoma.[259] This is a muscle invasive high-grade tumor; however cytology tends to miss it as being benign and on biopsy it resembles atypical Brunns epithelial nests.[259] In immunohistochemical studies, the loss of p27 appears to be a frequent event in the progression of nested variant of urothelial carcinoma.[260] Similarly, tumor markers such as cytokeratin 20, p53, and MIB1 may act as indicators of dysplastic changes in the urothelial mucosa and may help to confirm the diagnosis of CIS.[261]

SUMMARY

Heterogeneity of bladder tumors to invade and metastasize and their frequent recurrence pose a challenge for the physicians who treat patients with bladder cancer and for the researchers who work on bladder cancer diagnosis, recurrence, and treatment-related areas. For the majority of new bladder cancer cases, investigation begins when patients are symptomatic (ie, hematuria or irritative voiding). This mode of detection is often inadequate for nearly

30% of these new cases that have high-grade bladder cancer and the tumor is already in the invasive stage at the time of diagnosis. Bladder cancer patients are on a mandatory 3- to 6-month surveillance schedule, since bladder tumors frequently recur. The current mode of detecting bladder cancer involves cystoscopy, which is an invasive and relatively expensive procedure. Voided urine cytology, the standard non-invasive marker, is highly tumor specific and has good sensitivity to detect high-grade tumors. However, the sensitivity to detect low-grade tumors is low, the accuracy depends upon the expertiseof the pathologist, and this testing is not readily available in all countries.

Non-invasive tests that detect tumor-associated molecules (ie, enzymes, sugar polymers, and tumor cell–associated proteins), altered gene expression, or chromosomal alterations would be useful for detecting bladder cancer, evaluating its grade, monitoring recurrence, and predicting prognosis.

Due to low prevalence of bladder cancer, screening of the general population for bladder cancer using non-invasive tests is not cost-effective. However, non-invasive tests may be effective in screening and in early detection of bladder cancer among high-risk individuals. The most practical use of non-invasive tests would be for monitoring bladder cancer recurrence and cutting down the number of surveillance cystoscopies performed each year. Tumor markers that evaluate the metastatic potential of bladder tumors before they become metastatic, predict tumor recurrence and response to therapy can help clinicians in making individualized treatment selections and predicting prognosis of patients.

For a non-invasive test to become clinically useful it should be easy to perform, have low intra- and inter-assay variability, minimum requirements for sample handling and preparation, and should be reliable. A non-invasive test should have high sensitivity and specificity in order to minimize the false-negative and false-positive cases, respectively. Due to highly sensitive detection methods, many non-invasive tests can detect a bladder tumor before it becomes clinically visible. The risk ratio and the odds ratio calculated for the false-positive results on a non-invasive test should help physicians in making treatment decisions based on positive test results in the absence of clinical evidence of bladder cancer.

Several tumor markers and tests such as, hemoglobin dipstick, BTA-Stat, BTA-TARK, NMP22, HA-HAase, BLCA-4, cytokeratins (18, 19, and 20), ImmunoCyt, survivin, Quanticyt, microsatellite analysis, telomerase (TRAP assay and hTERT RT-PCR), and FISH have been tested for their clinical usefulness. Some of these markers have also been compared with each other and/or with cytology. Most of these markers have significantly higher sensitivity than cytology, and some also have the ability to detect bladder tumor recurrence before it becomes clinically visible. However, cytology is superior to all of the markers in terms of specificity. As we learn more about these markers through clinical trails, and have a better understanding of the conditions that cause false-positive or false-negative results, it should be possible to select a single marker or a combination of markers that can accurately detect bladder cancer.

Several proliferation and metastasis-associated molecules such as, p53, Ki67, Rb, EGF-receptors, E-cadherin, cyclins, p21/WAF1, Kip1, and apoptosis-related molecules have shown potential to be useful in providing prognostic information related to metastasis, recurrence, and overall survival, and cancer-specific survival. However, the results of many studies are contradictory and there is no accurate marker as yet. The ability to predict prognosis will improve as our understanding of the biology of bladder cancer, and of the basis of molecular heterogeneity among bladder tumors of the same histologic grade and stage, improves. Development of reliable and accurate detecting methods will also improve the acceptability of prognostic markers among physicians.

The field of non-invasive bladder tumor markers and prognostic indicators is rapidly expanding. Although, none of the non-invasive markers or tests can replace cystoscopy at the present time, certainly many markers together with cystoscopy can improve the current practice of managing bladder cancer patients. Ultimately, it will be the willingness of both the physicians and patients to accept the utility of tumor markers/tests in screening a high-risk population for bladder cancer, being an adjunct to cystoscopy for monitoring tumor recurrence and for predicting prognosis will decide whether any of the current, or yet to be discovered, markers will be a "PSA for bladder cancer."[29]

ACKNOWLEDGEMENTS

Vinata Lokeshwar would like to dedicate this article to her biostatistics mentor, Dr. Robert C Duncan, Professor, Department of Epidemiology, University of Miami School of Medicine, Miami, Florida, who spent many hours teaching her how biostatistics relates to urology. She would also like to thank her chairman, Dr. Mark Soloway, Department of Urology, for his enthusiastic support in identifying "a PSA for bladder cancer," and Dr. Michael Droller, Department of Urology, Mount Sinai School of Medicine, New York, New York, for critically reviewing of many of her works. This work was supported by the NIH grant R01 CA 72821-A06, Sylvester Comprehensive Cancer Center and Department of Urology, University of Miami School of Medicine, Miami, Florida.

REFERENCES

1. Lee R, Droller MJ. The natural history of bladder cancer. Implications for therapy. Urol Clin North Am 2000;27:1–13.
2. Heney NM. Natural history of superficial bladder cancer. Prognostic features and long-term disease course. Urol Clin North Am 1992;19:429–33.
3. Droller MJ. Cancer heterogeneity and its biologic implications in the grading of urothelial carcinoma. J Urol 2001;165:696–7.
4. Hassen W, Droller MJ. Current concepts in assessment and treatment of bladder cancer. Curr Opin Urol 2000;10:291–9.
5. Amling CL. Diagnosis and management of superficial bladder cancer. Curr Probl Cancer 2000;25:219–78.
6. van der Poel HG, Debruyne FM. Can biological markers replace cystoscopy? An update. Curr Opin Urol 2001;11:503–9.
7. Lokeshwar VB, Soloway MS. Current bladder tumor tests: does their projected utility fulfill clinical necessity? J Urol 2001;165:1067–77.
8. Saad A, Hanbury DC, McNicholas TA, et al. The early detection and diagnosis of bladder cancer: a critical review of the options. Eur Urol 2001;39:619–33.
9. Konety BR, Getzenberg RH. Urine-based markers of urological malignancy. J Urol 2001;165:600–11.
10. Van Der Meijden A, Sylvester R, Collette L, et al. The role and impact of pathology review on stage and grade assessment of stages Ta and T1 bladder tumors: a combined analysis of 5 European Organization for Research and Treatment of Cancer Trials. J Urol 2000;164:1533–7.
11. Millan-Rodriguez F, Chechile-Toniolo G, Salvador-Bayarri J, et al. Primary superficial bladder cancer risk groups according to progression, mortality and recurrence. J Urol 2000;164:680–4.
12. Droller, MJ. Bladder cancer: State-of-the-art-care. CA Cancer J Clin 1998;48:269–84.
13. Zaher A, Sheridan T. Tumor markers in the detection of recurrent transitional cell carcinoma of the bladder: a brief review. Acta Cytol 2001;45:575–81.
14. Fradet Y, Lacombe L. Can biological markers predict recurrence and progression of superficial bladder cancer? Curr Opin Urol 2000;10:441–5.
15. Orntoft TF, Wolf, H. Molecular alterations in bladder cancer. Urol Res 1998;26:223–33.
16. Brandau S, Bohle A. Bladder cancer. Molecular and genetic basis of carcinogenesis. Eur Urol 2001;39:491–7.
17. Knowles MA. What we could do now: molecular pathology of bladder cancer. Mol Pathol 2001;54:215–21.
18. Hafner C, Knuechel R, Zanardo L, et al. Evidence for oligo-clonality and tumor spread by intraluminal seeding in multifocal urothelial carcinomas of the upper and lower urinary tract. Oncogene 2001;20:4910–5.
19. Louhelainen J, Wijkstrom H, Hemminki K. Multiple regions with allelic loss at chromosome 3 in superficial multifocal bladder tumors. Int J Oncol 2001;18:203–10.
20. Gonzalgo ML, Schoenberg MP, Rodriguez R. Biological pathways to bladder carcinogenesis. Semin Urol Oncol 2000;18:256–63.
21. Louhelainen J, Wijkstrom H, Hemminki K. Allelic losses demonstrate monoclonality of multifocal bladder tumors. Int J Cancer 2000;87:522–7.
22. Chern HD, Becich MJ, Persad RA, et al. Clonal analysis of human recurrent superficial bladder cancer by immuno-histochemistry of P53 and retinoblastoma proteins. J Urol 1996.156:1846–9.
23. Vriesema JL, Aben KK, Witjes JA, et al. Superficial and metachronous invasive bladder carcinomas are clonally related. Int J Cancer 2001;93:699-702.
24. Hoglund M, Sall T, Heim S, et al. Identification of cytogenetic subgroups and karyotypic pathways in transitional cell carcinoma. Cancer Res 2001;61:8241–6.
25. Fadl-Elmula I, Gorunova L, Mandahl N, et al. Karyotypic characterization of urinary bladder transitional cell carcinomas. Genes Chromosomes Cancer 2000;29:256–65.
26. Fadl-Elmula I, Gorunova L, Mandahl N, et al. Cytogenetic monoclonality in multifocal uroepithelial carcinomas: evidence of intraluminal tumour seeding. Br J Cancer 1999;81:6–12.
27. Lotan Y, Roehrborn CG. Cost-effectiveness of a modified care protocol substituting bladder tumor markers for cystoscopy for the followup of patients with transitional cell carcinoma of the bladder: a decision analytical approach. J Urol 2002;167:75–9.
28. Han M, Schoenberg MP. The use of molecular diagnostics in bladder cancer. Urol Oncol 2000;5:87–92.
29. Soloway MS. Do we have a prostate specific antigen for bladder cancer? [editorial] J Urol 1999;161:447–8.

30. Brown FM. Urine cytology. It is still the gold standard for screening? Urol Clin North Am 2000;27:25–37.

31. Han KR, Pantuck AJ, Belldegrun AS, Rao JY. Tumor markers for the early detection of bladder cancer. Front Biosci 2002;7:19–26.

32. Kausch I, Bohle A. Bladder cancer. II. Molecular aspects and diagnosis. Eur Urol 2001;39:498–506.

33. Ozen H, Hall MC. Bladder cancer. Curr Opin Oncol 2000; 12:255–9.

34. Burchardt M, Burchardt T, et al. Current concepts in biomarker technology for bladder cancers. Clin Chem 2000; 46:595–605.

35. Ross JS, Cohen MB. Biomarkers for the detection of bladder cancer. Adv Anat Pathol 2001;8:37–45.

36. Grossman HB, Schmitz-Drager B, Fradet Y, Tribukait B. Use of markers in defining urothelial premalignant and malignant conditions. Scand J Urol Nephrol Suppl 2000;205:94–104.

37. Partin AW, Mangold LA, Lamm DM, et al. Contemporary update of prostate cancer staging nomograms (Partin Tables) for the new millennium. Urology 2001;58:843–8.

37a. Ries LAG, Eisner MP, Kosary CL, et al (eds). SEER Cancer Statistics Review, 1975–2001, National Cancer Institute. Bethesda, Maryland, http://seer.cancer.gov/csr/1975_2001/, 2004.

38. Messing EM, Young TB, Hunt VB, et al. Comparison of bladder cancer outcome in men undergoing hematuria home screening versus those with standard clinical presentations. Urology 1995;45:387–96.

39. Messing EM, Young TB, Hunt VB, et al. Urinary tract cancers found by homescreening with hematuria dipsticks in healthy men over 50 years of age. Cancer 1989;64:2361–7.

40. Messing EM, Young TB, Hunt VB, et al. Hematuria home screening: repeat testing results. J Urol 1995;154:5761.

41. Hodder SL, Mahmoud AA, Sorenson K, et al. Predisposition to urinary tract epithelial metaplasia in Schistosoma haematobium infection. Am J Trop Med Hyg 2000;63: 133–8.

42. Brauers A, Jakse G. Epidemiology and biology of human urinary bladder cancer. J Cancer Res Clin Oncol 2000; 126:575–83.

43. Vineis P, Marinelli D, Autrup H, et al. Current smoking, occupation, N-acetyltransferase-2 and bladder cancer: a pooled analysis of genotype-based studies. Cancer Epidemiol Biomarkers Prev 2001;10:1249–52.

44. Michaud DS, Clinton SK, Rimm EB, et al. Risk of bladder cancer by geographic region in a U.S. cohort of male health professionals. Epidemiology 2001;12:719–26.

45. Brennan P, Bogillot O, Greiser E, et al. The contribution of cigarette smoking to bladder cancer in women (pooled European data). Cancer Causes Control 2001;12:411–7.

46. Pitard A, Brennan P, Clavel J, et al. Cigar, pipe, and cigarette smoking and bladder cancer risk in European men. Cancer Causes Control 2001;12:551–6.

47. Zeegers MP, Swaen GM, Kant I, et al. Occupational risk factors for male bladder cancer: results from a population based case cohort study in the Netherlands. Occup Environ Med 2001;58:590–6.

48. Castelao JE, Yuan JM, Skipper PL, et al. Gender- and smoking-related bladder cancer risk. J Natl Cancer Inst 2001;93: 538–45.

49. Gago-Dominguez M, Castelao JE, Yuan JM, et al. Use of permanent hair dyes and bladder-cancer risk. Int J Cancer 2001;91:575–9.

50. Rothman N, Talaska G, Hayes RB, et al. Acidic urine pH is associated with elevated levels of free urinary benzidine and N-acetyl-benzidine and urothelial cell DNA adducts in exposed workers. Cancer Epidemiol Biomarkers Prev 1997;6:1039–42.

51. Rothman N, Hayes RB, Zenser TV, et al. The glutathione S-transferase M1 (GSTM1) null genotype and benzidine-associated bladder cancer, urine mutagenicity, and exfoliated urothelial cell DNA adducts. Cancer Epidemiol Biomarkers Prev 1996;5:979–83.

52. Hemstreet GP, Yin S, Ma Z, et al. Biomarker risk assessment and bladder cancer detection in a cohort exposed to benzidine. J Natl Cancer Inst 2001;93:427–36.

53. Gazdar AF, Czerniak B. Filling the void: urinary markers for bladder cancer risk and diagnosis. J Natl Cancer Inst 2001;93:413–5.

54. Vineis P, Pirastu R. Aromatic amines and cancer. Cancer Causes Control 1997;8:346–55.

55. Fortuny J, Kogevinas M, Chang-Claude J, et al. Tobacco, occupation and non-transitional-cell carcinoma of the bladder: an international case-control study. Int J Cancer 1999;80:44–6.

56. West DA, Cummings JM, Longo WE, et al. Role of chronic catheterization in the development of bladder cancer in patients with spinal cord injury. Urology 1999;53:292–7.

57. Warren JW. Catheter-associated urinary tract infections. Infect Dis Clin North Am 1997;11:609–22.

58. Golka K, Reckwitz T, Kempkes M, et al. N-Acetyltransferase 2 (NAT2) and glutathione S-transferase micro (GSTM1) in bladder-cancer patients in a highly industrialized area. Int J Occup Environ Health 1997;3:105–10.

59. Golka K, Prior V, Blaszkewicz M, Bolt HM. The enhanced bladder cancer susceptibility of NAT2 slow acetylators towards aromatic amines: a review considering ethnic differences. Toxicol Lett 2002;128:229–41.

60. Kontani K, Kawakami M, Nakajima T, Katsuyama T. Tobacco use and occupational exposure to carcinogens, but not N-acetyltransferase 2 genotypes are major risk factors for bladder cancer in the Japanese. Urol Res 2001;29:199–204.

61. Lokeshwar VB, Schroeder GL, Selzer GS, et al. Bladder tumor markers for monitoring recurrence and screening: comparison of HA-HAase and BTA-Stat tests. Cancer 2001 [in press].

62. Grossman HB. Biomarkers for transitional cell carcinoma-pro. Urology 2001;57:847–8.

63. Koenig F, Jung K, Schnorr D, Loening SA. Urinary markers of malignancy. Clin Chim Acta 2000;297:191–205.

64. Schoenberg M. Biomarkers for transitional cell carcinoma-con. Urology 2001;57:849–51.

65. Vriesema JL, Poucki MH, Kiemeney LA, Witjes JA. Patient opinion of urinary tests versus flexible urethrocystoscopy in follow-up examination for superficial bladder cancer: a utility analysis. Urology 2000;56:793–7.

66. Mattioli S, Seregni E, Caperna L, et al. BTA-TRAK combined with urinary cytology is a reliable urinary indicator of recurrent transitional cell carcinoma (TCC) of the bladder. Int J Biol Markers 2000;15:219–25.

67. van Rhijn BW, Lurkin I, Kirkels WJ, et al. Microsatellite analysis—DNA test in urine competes with cystoscopy in follow-up of superficial bladder carcinoma: a phase II trial. Cancer 2001;92:768–75.

68. Bubendorf L, Grilli B, Sauter G, et al. Multiprobe FISH for enhanced detection of bladder cancer in voided urine specimens and bladder washings. Am J Clin Pathol 2001;116:79–86.

69. Cianciulli AM, Bovani R, Leonardo C, et al. DNA aberrations in urinary bladder cancer detected by flow cytometry and FISH: prognostic implications. Eur J Histochem 2001;45:65–71.

70. Cordon-Cardo C, Cote RJ, Sauter G. Genetic and molecular markers of urothelial premalignancy and malignancy. Scand J Urol Nephrol 2000;205 Suppl:82–93.

71. Stein JP, Grossfeld GD, Ginsberg DA,et al. Prognostic markers in bladder cancer: a contemporary review of the literature. J Urol 1998;160:645–59.

72. Zlotta AR, Schulman CC. Biological markers in superficial bladder tumors and their prognostic significance. Urol Clin North Am 2000;27:179–89.

73. Olumi AF. A critical analysis of the use of p53 as a marker for management of bladder cancer. Urol Clin North Am 2000;27:75–82.

74. Rodel C, Grabenbauer GG, Rodel F, et al. Apoptosis, p53, bcl-2, and Ki-67 in invasive bladder carcinoma: possible predictors for response to radiochemotherapy and successful bladder preservation. Int J Radiat Oncol Biol Phys 2000;46:1213–21.

75. Zlotta AR, Noel JC, Fayt I, et al. Correlation and prognostic significance of p53, p21WAF1/CIP1 and Ki-67 expression in patients with superficial bladder tumors treated with bacillus Calmette-Guerin intravesical therapy. J Urol 1999;161:792–8.

76. Sengelov L, Christensen M, von der Maase HD, et al. Loss of heterozygosity at 1p, 8p, 10p, 13q, and 17p in advanced urothelial cancer and lack of relation to chemotherapy response and outcome. Cancer Genet Cytogenet 2000; 123:109–13.

77. Tsihlias J, Grossman HB. The utility of fibrin/fibrinogen degradation products in superficial bladder cancer. Urol Clin North Am 2000;27:3946.

78. Lokeshwar VB, Obek C, Pham HT, et al. Urinary hyaluronic acid and hyaluronidase: markers for bladder cancer detection and evaluation of grade. J Urol 2000;163:348–56.

79. Duncan RC, Cnapp RG, Miller MC III. Introductory biostatistics for the health sciences. 2nd ed. New York; John Wiley and Sons; 1983.

80. Sarma AV, Schottenfeld D. Prostate cancer incidence, mortality, and survival trends in the United States: 1981-2001. Semin Urol Oncol 2002;20:39.

81. de Koning HJ, Auvinen A, Berenguer Sanchez A, et al. Large-scale randomized prostate cancer screening trials: program performances in the European Randomized Screening for Prostate Cancer trial and the Prostate, Lung, Colorectal and Ovary cancer trial. Int J Cancer 2002;97:237–44.

82. Jani AB, Vaida F, Hanks G, et al. Changing face and different countenances of prostate cancer: racial and geographic differences in prostate-specific antigen (PSA), stage, and grade trends in the PSA era. Int J Cancer 2001;96:363–71.

83. Bunting PS. Screening for prostate cancer with prostate-specific antigen: beware the biases. Clin Chim Acta 2002; 15:719–7.

84. Blumenstein BA, Ellis WJ, Ishak LM. The relationship between serial measurements of the level of a bladder tumor associated antigen and the potential for recurrence. J Urol 1999;161:57–60.

85. Gutierrez Banos JL, Rebollo Rodrigo MH, Antolin Juarez FM, Martin Garcia B. NMP22, BTA stat test, and cytology in the diagnosis of bladder cancer: a comparative study. Urol Int 2001;66:185–90.

86. Gutierrez Banos JL, Del Henar Rebollo Rodrigo M, Antolin Juarez FM, Garcia BM. Usefulness of the BTA STAT Test for the diagnosis of bladder cancer. Urology 2001; 57:685–9.

87. Priolo G, Gontero P, Martinasso G, et al. Bladder tumor antigen assay as compared to voided urine cytology in the diagnosis of bladder cancer. Clin Chim Acta 2001;305:47–53.

88. Walsh IK, Keane PF, Ishak LM, Flessland KA. The BTA stat test: a tumor marker for the detection of upper tract transitional cell carcinoma. Urology 2001;58:532–5.

89. Raitanen MP, Kaasinen E, Lukkarinen O, et al. Analysis of false-positive BTA STAT test results in patients followed up for bladder cancer. Urology 2001;57:680–4.

90. Raitanen MP, Marttila T, Nurmi M, et al. Human complement factor H related protein test for monitoring bladder cancer. J Urol 2001;165:374–7.

91. Raitanen MP, Marttila T, Kaasinen E, et al. Sensitivity of human complement factor H related protein (BTA stat) test and voided urine cytology in the diagnosis of bladder cancer. J Urol 2000;163:1689–92.

92. Wiener HG, Mian C, Haitel A, et al. Can urine bound diagnostic tests replace cystoscopy in the management of bladder cancer? J Urol 1998;159:1876–80.

93. Epstein JI, Amin MB, Reuter VR, Mostofi FK. The World Health Organization/International Society of Urological Pathology consensus classification of urothelial (transitional cell) neoplasms of the urinary bladder. Bladder Consensus Conference Committee. Am J Surg Pathol 1998;22:1435–48.

94. Amin MB, Ro JY, el-Sharkawy T, et al. Micropapillary variant of transitional cell carcinoma of the urinary bladder. Histologic pattern resembling ovarian papillary serous carcinoma. Am J Surg Pathol 1994;18:1224–32.

95. Neves M, Ciofu C, Larousserie F, et al. Prospective evaluation of genetic abnormalities and telomerase expression in exfoliated urinary cells for bladder cancer detection. J Urol 2002;167:1276–81.

96. Mungan NA, Kulacoglu S, Basar M, et al. Can sensitivity of voided urinary cytology or bladder wash cytology be improved by the use of different urinary portions? Urol Int 1999;62:209–12.

97. Lahme S, Bichler KH, Feil G, Krause S. Comparison of cytology and nuclear matrix protein 22 for the detection and follow-up of bladder cancer. Urol Int 2001;66:72–7.

98. Topsakal M, Karadeniz T, Anac M, et al. Assessment of fibrin-fibrinogen degradation products (Accu-Dx) test in bladder cancer patients. Eur Urol 2001;39:287–91.

99. Olsson H, Zackrisson B. ImmunoCyt a useful method in the follow-up protocol for patients with urinary bladder carcinoma. Scand J Urol Nephrol 2001;35:280–2.

100. Del Nero A, Esposito N, Curro A, et al. Evaluation of urinary level of NMP22 as a diagnostic marker for stage pTa-pT1 bladder cancer: comparison with urinary cytology and BTA test. Eur Urol 1999;35:93–7.

101. Casetta G, Gontero P, Zitella A, et al. BTA quantitative assay and NMP22 testing compared with urine cytology in the detection of transitional cell carcinoma of the bladder. Urol Int 2000;65:100–5.

102. Lodde M, Mian C, Wiener H, et al. Detection of upper urinary tract transitional cell carcinoma with ImmunoCyt: a preliminary report. Urology 2001;58:362–6.

103. Thompson IM. The evaluation of microscopic hematuria: a population-based study. J Urol 1987;138:1189–90.

104. Froom P, Froom J, Ribak J. Asymptomatic microscopic hematuria—is investigation necessary? J Clin Epidemiol 1997;50:1197–200.

105. Mohr DN, Offord KP, Melton LJ. Isolated asymptomatic microhematuria: a cross-sectional analysis of test-positive and test-negative patients. J Gen Intern Med 1987;2:318–24.

106. Friedman GD, Carroll PR, Cattolica EV, Hiatt RA. Can hematuria be a predictor as well as a symptom or sign of bladder cancer? Cancer Epidemiol Biomarkers Prev 1996;5:9936.

107. Hiatt RA, Ordonez JD. Dipstick urinalysis screening, asymptomatic microhematuria, and subsequent urological cancers in a population-based sample. Cancer Epidemiol Biomarkers Prev 1994;3:439–43.

108. Wakui M, Shiigai T. Urinary tract cancer screening through analysis of urinary red blood cell volume distribution. Int J Urol 2000;7:248–53.

109. Messing EM, Young TB, Hunt VB, et al. Hematuria home screening: repeat testing results. J Urol 1995;154:57–61.

110. Britton JP, Dowell AC, Whelan P, Harris CM. A community study of bladder cancer screening by the detection of occult urinary bleeding. J Urol 1992;148:788–90.

111. Murakami S, Igarashi T, Hara S, Shimazaki J. Strategies for asymptomatic microscopic hematuria: a prospective study of 1,034 patients. J Urol 1990;144:99–101.

112. Grossfeld GD, Wolf JS Jr, Litwan MS, et al. Asymptomatic microscopic hematuria in adults: summary of the AUA best practice policy recommendations. Am Fam Physician 2001;63:1145–54.

113. Schramek P, Schuster FX, Georgopoulos M, et al. Value of urinary erythrocyte morphology in assessment of symptomless microhaematuria. Lancet 1989;2:1316–9.

114. Georgopoulos M, Schuster FX, Porpaczy P, Schramek P. Evaluation of asymptomatic microscopic haematuria—influence and clinical relevance of osmolality and pH on urinary erythrocyte morphology. Br J Urol 1996;78:192–6.

115. Kinders R, Jones T, Root R, et al. Complement factor H or a related protein is a marker for transitional cell cancer of the bladder. Clin Cancer Res 1998;4:2511–20.

116. Malkowicz SB. The application of human complement factor H-related protein (BTA TRAK) in monitoring patients with bladder cancer. Urol Clin North Am 2000;27:63–73.

117. Boman H, Hedelin H, Holmang S. Four bladder tumor markers have a disappointingly low sensitivity for small size and low grade recurrence. J Urol 2002;167:80–3.

118. Mian C, Lodde M, Haitel A, et al. Comparison of two qualitative assays, the UBC rapid test and the BTA stat test, in the diagnosis of urothelial cell carcinoma of the bladder. Urology 2000;56:228–31.

119. Oge O, Atsu N, Sahin A, Ozen H. Comparison of BTA stat and NMP22 tests in the detection of bladder cancer. Scand J Urol Nephrol 2000;34:349–51.

120. Giannopoulos A, Manousakas T, Gounari A, et al. Comparative evaluation of the diagnostic performance of the BTA stat test, NMP22 and urinary bladder cancer antigen for primary and recurrent bladder tumors. J Urol 2001;166:470–5.

121. Heicappell R, Muller M, Fimmers R, Miller K. Qualitative determination of urinary human complement factor H-related protein (hcfHrp) in patients with bladder cancer, healthy controls, and patients with benign urologic disease. Urol Int 2000;65:181–4.

122. Serretta V, Pomara G, Rizzo I, Esposito E. Urinary BTA-stat, BTA-trak and NMP22 in surveillance after TUR of recurrent superficial transitional cell carcinoma of the bladder. Eur Urol 2000;38:419–25.

123. Oge O, Kozaci D, Gemalmaz H. The BTA stat test is nonspecific for hematuria: an experimental hematuria model. J Urol 2002;167:1318–9.

124. Nasuti JF, Gomella LG, Ismial M, Bibbo M. Utility of the BTA stat test kit for bladder cancer screening. Diagn Cytopathol 1999;21:27–9.

125. Raitanen MP, Kaasinen E, Rintala E, et al. Prognostic utility of human complement factor H related protein test (the BTA-stat Test). Br J Cancer 2001;85:552–6.

126. Chautard D, Daver A, Bocquillon V, et al. Comparison of the Bard TARK test with voided urine cytology in the diagnosis and follow-up of bladder tumors. Eur Urol 2000;38:686–90.

127. Thomas L, Leyh H, Marberger M, et al. Multicenter trial of the quantitative BTA TRAK assay in the detection of bladder cancer. Clin Chem 1999;45:472–7.

128. Mahnert B, Tauber S, Kriegmair M, et al. BTA-TRAK—a useful diagnostic tool in urinary bladder cancer? Anticancer Res 1999;19:2615–9.

129. Khaled HM, Abdel-Salam I, Abdel-Gawad M, et al. Evaluation of the BTA tests for the detection of bilharzial related bladder cancer: the Cairo experience. Eur Urol 2001;39:91–4.

130. Grocela JA, McDougal WS. Utility of nuclear matrix protein (NMP22) in the detection of recurrent bladder cancer. Urol Clin North Am 2000;27:47–51.

131. Ib Z. On the history of nuclear matrix manifestation. Cell Res 1998;8:99–103.

132. Getzenberg RH, Pienta KJ, Ward WS, Coffey DS. Nuclear structure and the three dimensional organization of DNA. J Cell Biochem 1991;47:289–99.

133. Shelfo SW, Soloway MS. The role of nuclear matrix protein 22 in the detection of persistent or recurrent transitional-cell cancer of the bladder. World J Urol 1997;15:107–11.

134. Chahal R, Darshane A, Browning AJ, Sundaram SK. Evaluation of the clinical value of urinary NMP22 as a marker in the screening and surveillance of transitional cell carcinoma of the urinary bladder. Eur Urol 2001;40:415–20.

135. Miyanaga N, Akaza H, Tsukamoto T, et al. Urinary nuclear matrix protein 22 as a new marker for the screening of urothelial cancer in patients with microscopic hematuria. Int J Urol 1999;6:173–7.

136. Giannopoulos A, Manousakas T, Mitropoulos D, et al. Comparative evaluation of the BTAstat test, NMP22, and voided urine cytology in the detection of primary and recurrent bladder tumors. Urology 2000;55:871–5.

137. Sanchez-Carbayo M, Urrutia M, Gonzalez de Buitrago JM, Navajo JA. Utility of serial urinary tumor markers to individualize intervals between cystoscopies in the monitoring of patients with bladder carcinoma. Cancer 2001;92:2820–8.

138. Sanchez-Carbayo M, Urrutia M, Silva JM, et al. Comparative predictive values of urinary cytology, urinary bladder cancer antigen, CYFRA 21-1 and NMP22 for evaluating symptomatic patients at risk for bladder cancer. J Urol 2001;165:1462–7.

139. Sanchez-Carbayo M, Herrero E, Megias J, et al. Comparative sensitivity of urinary CYFRA 21-1, urinary bladder cancer antigen, tissue polypeptide antigen, tissue polypeptide antigen and NMP22 to detect bladder cancer. J Urol 1999;162:1951–6.

140. Casella R, Huber P, Blochlinger A, et al. Urinary level of nuclear matrix protein 22 in the diagnosis of bladder cancer: experience with 130 patients with biopsy confirmed tumor. J Urol 2000;164:1926–8.

141. Paoluzzi M, Cuttano MG, Mugnaini P, et al. Urinary dosage of nuclear matrix protein 22 (NMP22) like biologic marker of transitional cell carcinoma (TCC): a study on patients with hematuria [abstract in English]. Arch Ital Urol Androl 1999;71:13–8.

142. Ponsky LE, Sharma S, Pandrangi L, et al. Screening and monitoring for bladder cancer: refining the use of NMP22. J Urol 2001;166:75–8.

143. Ishii T, Okadome A, Takeuchi F, Hiratsuka Y. Urinary levels of nuclear matrix protein 22 in patients with urinary diversion. Urology 2001;58:940-2.

144. Atsu N, Ekici S, Oge OO, et al. False-positive results of the NMP22 test due to hematuria. J Urol 2002;167:555–8.

145. Lachaine J, Valiquette L, Crott R. Economic evaluation of NMP22 in the management of bladder cancer. Can J Urol 2000;7:974–80.

146. Zippe C, Pandrangi L, Potts JM, et al. NMP22: a sensitive, cost effective test in patients at risk for bladder cancer. Anticancer Res 1999;19:2621–3.

147. Witjes JA, van der Poel HG, van Balken MR, et al. Urinary NMP22 and karyometry in the diagnosis and follow-up of patients with superficial bladder cancer. Eur Urol 1998;33:387–91.

148. Konety BR, Nguyen TS, Dhir R, et al. Detection of bladder cancer using a novel nuclear matrix protein, BLCA-4. Clin Cancer Res 2000;6:2618–25.

149. Konety BR, Nguyen TS, Brenes G, et al. Clinical usefulness of the novel marker BLCA-4 for the detection of bladder cancer. J Urol 2000;164:634–9.

150. Altieri DC. The molecular basis and potential role of survivin in cancer diagnosis and therapy. Trends Mol Med 2001;7:542–7.

151. Smith SD, Wheeler MA, Plescia J, et al. Urine detection of survivin and diagnosis of bladder cancer. JAMA 2001;285:324–8.

152. Sharp JD, Hausladen DA, Maher MG, et al. Bladder cancer detection with urinary survivin, an inhibitor of apoptosis. Front Biosci 2002;7:36–41.

153. Southgate J, Harnden P, Trejdosiewicz LK. Cytokeratin expression patterns in normal and malignant urothelium: a review of the biological and diagnostic implications. Histol Histopathol 1999;14:657–64.

154. Mian C, Lodde M, Haitel A, et al. Comparison of the monoclonal UBC-ELISA test and the NMP22 ELISA test for the detection of urothelial cell carcinoma of the bladder. Urology 2000;55:223–6.

155. Mungan NA, Vriesema JL, Thomas CM, et al. Urinary bladder cancer test: a new urinary tumor marker in the follow-up of superficial bladder cancer. Urology 2000;56:787–92.

156. Sanchez-Carbayo M, Ciudad J, Urrutia M, Navajo JA, Orfao A. Diagnostic performance of the urinary bladder carcinoma antigen ELISA test and multiparametric DNA/cytokeratin flow cytometry in urine voided samples from patients with bladder carcinoma. Cancer 2001;92:2811–19.

157. Harnden P, Mahmood N, Southgate J. Expression of cytokeratin 20 redefines urothelial papillomas of the bladder. Lancet 1999;353:974–7.

158. McKenney JK, Desai S, Cohen C, Amin MB. Discriminatory immunohistochemical staining of urothelial carcinoma in situ and non-neoplastic urothelium: an analysis of cytokeratin 20, p53, and CD44 antigens. Am J Surg Pathol 2001;25:1074–8.

159. Rotem D, Cassel A, Lindenfeld N, et al. Urinary cytokeratin 20 as a marker for transitional cell carcinoma. Eur Urol 2000;37:601–4.

160. Cassel A, Rahat MA, Lahat N, et al. Telomerase activity and cytokeratin 20 as markers for the detection and followup of transitional cell carcinoma: an unfulfilled promise. J Urol 2001;166:841–4.

161. Buchumensky V, Klein A, Zemer R, et al. Cytokeratin 20: a new marker for early detection of bladder cell carcinoma? J Urol 1998;160:1971–4.

162. Retz M, Lehmann J, Roder C, et al. Cytokeratin-20 reverse-transcriptase polymerase chain reaction as a new tool for the detection of circulating tumor cells in peripheral blood and bone marrow of bladder cancer patients. Eur Urol 2001;39:507–15.

163. Gazzaniga P, Gandini O, Giuliani L, et al. Detection of epidermal growth factor receptor mRNA in peripheral blood: a new marker of circulating neoplastic cells in bladder cancer patients. Clin Cancer Res 2001;7:577–83.

164. Hara N, Kasahara T, Kawasaki T, et al. Frequency of PSA-mRNA-bearing cells in the peripheral blood of patients after prostate biopsy. Br J Cancer 2001;85:557–62.

165. Lin S, Hirschowitz SL, Williams C, et al. Cytokeratin 20 as an immunocytochemical marker for detection of urothelial carcinoma in atypical cytology: preliminary retrospective study on archived urine slides. Cancer Detect Prev 2001;25:202–9.

166. Golijanin D, Shapiro A, Pode D. Immunostaining of cytokeratin 20 in cells from voided urine for detection of bladder cancer. J Urol 2000;164:1922–25.

167. Pariente JL, Bordenave L, Michel P, et al. Initial evaluation of CYFRA 21-1 diagnostic performances as a urinary marker in bladder transitional cell carcinoma. J Urol 1997;158:338–41.

168. Pariente JL, Bordenave L, Jacob F, et al. Analytical and prospective evaluation of urinary cytokeratin 19 fragment in bladder cancer. J Urol 2000;163:1116–69.

169. Tsihlias J, Grossman HB. The utility of fibrin/fibrinogen degradation products in superficial bladder cancer. Urol Clin North Am 2000;27:39–46.

170. Wajsman Z, Merrin CE, Chu TM, et al. Evaluation of biological markers in bladder cancer. J Urol 1975;114:879–93.

171. Martinez-Pineiro JA, Pertusa C, Maganto E, et al. Urinary fibrinogen degradation products (FDP) in bladder cancer. Eur Urol 1978;4:348–50.

172. Johnston B, Morales A, Emerson L, Lundie M. Rapid detection of bladder cancer: a comparative study of point of care tests. J Urol 1997;158:2098–101.

173. Schmetter BS, Habicht KK, Lamm DL, et al. A multicenter trial evaluation of the fibrin/fibrinogen degradation products test for detection and monitoring of bladder cancer. J Urol 1997;158:801–5.

174. Ramakumar S, Bhuiyan J, Besse JA, et al. Comparison of screening methods in the detection of bladder cancer. J Urol 1999;161:388–94.

175. Alberts B, Bray D, Lewis J, et al. Molecular biology of the cell. 3rd ed. New York, Garland Publishing 1994. p. 338,364,365.

176. Liu BC, Loughlin KR. Telomerase in human bladder cancer. Urol Clin North Am 2000;27:115–23.

177. Muller M. Telomerase: Its clinical relevance in the diagnosis of bladder cancer. Oncogene 2000;21:650–5.

178. Hiyama E, Hiyama K. Clinical utility of telomerase in cancer. Oncogene 2002;21:643–9.

179. Hackett JA, Greider CW. Balancing instability: dual roles for telomerase and telomere dysfunction in tumorigenesis. Oncogene 2002;21:619–26.

180. Collins K, Mitchell JR. Telomerase in the human organism. Oncogene 2002;21:564–79.

181. Stewart SA, Weinberg RA. Senescence: does it all happen at the ends? Oncogene 2002;21:627–30.

182. Wu WJ, Liu LT, Huang CN, et al. The clinical implications of telomerase activity in upper tract urothelial cancer and washings. BJU Int 2000;86:213–9.

183. Rahat MA, Lahat N, Gazawi H, et al. Telomerase activity in patients with transitional cell carcinoma: a preliminary study. Cancer 1999;85:919–24.

184. Dalbagni G, Han W, Zhang ZF, et al. Evaluation of the telomeric repeat amplification protocol (TRAP) assay for telomerase as a diagnostic modality in recurrent bladder cancer. Clin Cancer Res 1997;3:1593–8.

185. Landman J, Chang Y, Kavaler E, et al. Sensitivity and specificity of NMP-22, telomerase, and BTA in the detection of human bladder cancer. Urology 1998;52:398–402.

186. Kavaler E, Landman J, Chang Y, et al. Detecting human bladder carcinoma cells in voided urine samples by assaying for the presence of telomerase activity. Cancer 1998;82:708–14.

187. Kinoshita H, Ogawa O, Kakehi Y,et al. Detection of telomerase activity in exfoliated cells in urine from patients with bladder cancer. J Natl Cancer Inst 1997;89:724–30.

188. Lee DH, Yang SC, Hong SJ, et al. Telomerase: a potential marker of bladder transitional cell carcinoma in bladder washes. Clin Cancer Res 1998;4:535–8.

189. Yokota K, Kanda K, Inoue Y, et al. Semi-quantitative analysis of telomerase activity in exfoliated human urothelial cells and bladder transitional cell carcinoma. Br J Urol 1998;82:727–32.

190. Bialkowska-Hobrzanska H, Bowles L, Bukala B, et al. Comparison of human telomerase reverse transcriptase messenger RNA and telomerase activity as urine markers for diagnosis of bladder carcinoma. Mol Diag 2000;5:267–77.

191. de Kok JB, van Balken MR, Ruers TJ, et al. Detection of telomerase activity in urine as a tool for noninvasive detection of recurrent bladder tumors is poor and cannot be improved by timing of sampling. Clin Chem 2000;46:2014–5.

192. de Kok JB, van Balken MR, Roelofs RW, et al. Quantification of hTERT mRNA and telomerase activity in bladder washings of patients with recurrent urothelial cell carcinomas. Clin Chem 2000;46:2003–7.

193. Ito H, Kyo S, Kanaya T, et al. Detection of human telomerase reverse transcriptase messenger RNA in voided urine samples as a useful diagnostic tool for bladder cancer. Clin Cancer Res 1998;4:2807–10.

194. Muller M, Krause H, Heicappell R, et al. Comparison of human telomerase RNA and telomerase activity in urine for diagnosis of bladder cancer. Clin Cancer Res 1998;4:1949–54.

195. Ito H, Kyo S, Kanaya T, et al. Expression of human telomerase subunits and correlation with telomerase activity in urothelial cancer. Clin Cancer Res 1998;4:1603–8.

196. Wu YY, Hruszkewycz AM, Delgado RM, et al. Limitations on the quantitative determination of telomerase activity by the electrophoretic and ELISA based TRAP assays. Clin Chim Acta 2000;293:199–212.

197. Fukui T, Nonomura N, Tokizane T, et al. Clinical evaluation of human telomerase catalytic subunit in bladder washings from patients with bladder cancer. Mol Urol 2001;5:19–23.

198. de Kok JB, Schalken JA, Aalders TW, et al. Quantitative measurement of telomerase reverse transcriptase (hTERT) mRNA in urothelial cell carcinomas. Int J Cancer 2000; 87:217–20.

199. Sengelov L, Horn T, Steven K. p53 nuclear immunoreactivity as a predictor of response and outcome following chemotherapy for metastatic bladder cancer. J Cancer Res Clin Oncol 1997;123:565–70.

200. Utting M, Werner W, Dahse R, et al. Microsatellite analysis of free tumor DNA in urine, serum, and plasma of patients: a minimally invasive method for the detection of bladder cancer. Clin Cancer Res 2002;8:35–40.

201. Seripa D, Parrella P, Gallucci M, et al. Sensitive detection of transitional cell carcinoma of the bladder by microsatellite analysis of cells exfoliated in urine. Int J Cancer 2001;95:364–9.

202. von Knobloch R, Hegele A, Brandt H, et al. Serum DNA and urine DNA alterations of urinary transitional cell bladder carcinoma detected by fluorescent microsatellite analysis. Int J Cancer 2001;94:67–72.

203. Zhang J, Fan Z, Gao Y, et al. Detecting bladder cancer in the Chinese by microsatellite analysis: ethnic and etiologic considerations. J Natl Cancer Inst 2001;93:45–50.

204. Schneider A, Borgnat S, Lang H, et al. Evaluation of microsatellite analysis in urine sediment for diagnosis of bladder cancer. Cancer Res 2000;60:4617–22.

205. Uchida A, Tachibana M, Miyakawa A, et al. Microsatellite analysis in multiple chromosomal regions as a prognostic indicator of primary bladder cancer. Urol Res 2000;28:297–303.

206. Christensen M, Wolf H, Orntoft TF. Microsatellite alterations in urinary sediments from patients with cystitis and bladder cancer. Int J Cancer 2000;85:614–7.

207. Baron A, Mastroeni F, Moore PS, et al. Detection of bladder cancer by semi-automated microsatellite analysis of urine sediment. Adv Clin Pathol 2000;4:19–24.

208. Sokolova IA, Halling KC, Jenkins RB, et al. The development of a multitarget, multicolor fluorescence in situ hybridization assay for the detection of urothelial carcinoma in urine. J Mol Diagn 2000;2:116–23.

209. Lokeshwar VB, Block NL. HA-HAase urine test. A sensitive and specific method for detecting bladdercancer and evaluating its grade. Urol Clin North Am 2000;27:53–61.

210. Lee JY, Spicer AP. Hyaluronan: a multifunctional, megaDalton, stealth molecule. Curr Opin Cell Biol 2000;12:581–6.

211. Delpech B, Girard N, Bertrand P, et al. Hyaluronan: fundamental principles and applications in cancer. J Intern Med 1997;242:41–8.

212. Lokeshwar VB, Rubinowicz D, Schroeder GL, et al. Stromal and epithelial expression of tumor markers hyaluronic acid and HYAL1 hyaluronidase in prostate cancer. J Biol Chem 2001;276:11922–32.

213. West DC, Kumar S. Hyaluronan and angiogenesis. Ciba Found Symp 1989;143:187–201.

214. Lokeshwar VB, Selzer MG. Differences in hyaluronic acid-mediated functions and signaling in arterial, microvessel, and vein-derived human endothelial cells. J Biol Chem 2000;275:27641–9.

215. Lokeshwar VB, Obek C, Soloway MS, Block NL. Tumor-associated hyaluronic acid: a new sensitive and specific urine marker for bladder cancer. Cancer Res 1997;57:773–7.

216. Pham HT, Block NL, Lokeshwar VB. Tumor-derived hyaluronidase: a diagnostic urine marker for high-grade bladder cancer. Cancer Res 1997;57:778–83.

217. Lokeshwar VB, Young MJ, Goudarzi G, et al. Identification of bladder tumor-derived hyaluronidase: its similarity to HYAL1. Cancer Res 1999;59:4464–70.

218. Hautmann SH, Lokeshwar VB, Schroeder GL, et al. Elevated tissue expression of hyaluronic acid and hyaluronidase validates the HA-HAase urine test for bladder cancer. J Urol 2001;165:2068–74.

219. Wiener HG, Mian C, Haitel A, et al. Can urine bound diagnostic tests replace cystoscopy in the management of bladder cancer? J Urol 1998;159:1876–80.

220. Sharma S, Zippe CD, Pandrangi L, et al. Exclusion criteria enhance the specificity and positive predictive value of NMP22 and BTA stat. J Urol 1999;162:53–7.

221. Sozen S, Biri H, Sinik Z, et al. Comparison of the nuclear matrix protein 22 with voided urine cytology and BTA-stat test in the diagnosis of transitional cell carcinoma of the bladder. Eur Urol 1999;36:225–9.

222. Abbate I, D'Introno A, Cardo G, et al. Comparison of nuclear matrix protein 22 and bladder tumor antigen in urine of patients with bladder cancer. Anticancer Res 1998; 18:3803–5.

223. Halling KC, King W, Sokolova IA, et al. A comparison of cytology and fluorescence in situ hybridization for the detection of urothelial carcinoma. J Urol 2000;164: 1768–75.

224. Ishiwata S, Takahashi S, Homma Y, et al. Noninvasive detection and prediction of bladder cancer by fluorescence in situ hybridization analysis of exfoliated urothelial cells in voided urine. Urology 2001;57:811–5.

225. Plastiras D, Moutzouris G, Barbatis C, et al. Can p53 nuclear over-expression, Bcl-2 accumulation and PCNA status be of prognostic significance in high-risk superficial and invasive bladder tumours? Eur J Surg Oncol 1999;25:61–5.

226. Liukkonen T, Lipponen P, Raitanen M, et al. Evaluation of p21WAF1/CIP1 and cyclin D1 expression in the progression of superficial bladder cancer. Finbladder Group. Urol Res 2000;28:285–92.

227. Pfister C, Larue H, Moore L, et al. Tumorigenic pathways in low-stage bladder cancer based on p53, MDM2, and p21 phenotypes. Int J Cancer 2000;89:100–4.

228. Gao JP, Uchida T, Wang C, et al. Relationship between p53 gene mutation and protein expression: clinical significance in transitional cell carcinoma of the bladder. Int J Oncol 2000;16:469–75.

229. Friedrich MG, Riethdorf S, Erbersdobler A, et al. Relevance of p53 gene alterations for tumor recurrence in patients with superficial transitional cell carcinoma of the bladder. Eur Urol 2001;39:159–66.

230. Wolf HK, Stober C, Hohenfellner R, Leissner J. Prognostic value of p53, p21/WAF1, Bcl-2, Bax, Bak and Ki-67 immunoreactivity in pT1 G3 urothelial bladder carcinomas. Tumour Biol 2001;22:328–36.

231. Gontero P, Casetta G, Zitella A, et al. Evaluation of P53 protein overexpression, Ki67 proliferative activity and mitotic index as markers of tumour recurrence in superficial transitional cell carcinoma of the bladder. Eur Urol 2000;38:287–96.

232. Stavropoulos NE, Ioachim E, Charchanti A, et al. Tumor markers in stage P1 bladder cancer. Anticancer Res 2001;21:1495–8.

233. Wu TT, Chen JH, Lee YH, Huang JK. The role of bcl-2, p53, and ki-67 index in predicting tumor recurrence for low grade superficial transitional cell bladder carcinoma. J Urol 2000;163:758–60.

234. Oosterhuis JW, Schapers RF, Janssen-Heijnen ML, et al. MIB-1 as a proliferative marker in transitional cell carcinoma of the bladder: clinical significance and comparison with other prognostic factors. Cancer 2000;88:2598–605.

235. Korkolopoulou P, Christodoulou P, Lazaris A, et al. Prognostic implications of aberrations in p16/pRb pathway in urothelial bladder carcinomas: a multivariate analysis including p53 expression and proliferation markers. Eur Urol 2001;39:167–77.

236. Kamai T, Takagi K, Asami H, et al. Decreasing of p27(Kip1) and cyclin E protein levels is associated with progression from superficial into invasive bladder cancer. Br J Cancer 2001;84:1242–51.

237. Lavezzi AM, Biondo B, Cazzullo A, et al. The role of different biomarkers (DNA, PCNA, apoptosis and karyotype) in prognostic evaluation of superficial transitional cell bladder carcinoma. Anticancer Res 2001;21:1279–84.

238. Takagi Y, Takashi M, Koshikawa T, et al. Immunohistochemical demonstration of cyclin D1 in bladder cancers as an inverse indicator of invasiveness but not an independent prognostic factor. Int J Urol 2000;7:366–72.

239. Sgambato A, Migaldi M, Faraglia B, et al. Cyclin D1 expression in papillary superficial bladder cancer: its association with other cell cycle-associated proteins, cell proliferation and clinical outcome. Int J Cancer 2002;97:671–8.

240. Garcia del Muro X, Torregrosa A, Munoz J, et al. Prognostic value of the expression of E-cadherin and beta-catenin in bladder cancer. Eur J Cancer 2000;36:357–62.

241. Nakopoulou L, Zervas A, Gakiopoulou-Givalou H, et al. Prognostic value of E-cadherin, beta-catenin, P120ctn in patients with transitional cell bladder cancer. Anticancer Res 2000;20:4571–8.

242. Byrne RR, Shariat SF, Brown R, et al. E-cadherin immunostaining of bladder transitional cell carcinoma, carcinoma in situ and lymph node metastases with long-term followup. J Urol 2001;165:1473–9.

243. Xu X, Sun TT, Gupta PK, et al. Uroplakin as a marker for typing metastatic transitional cell carcinoma on fine-needle aspiration specimens. Cancer 2001;93:216–21.

244. Li SM, Zhang ZT, Chan S, et al. Detection of circulating uroplakin-positive cells in patients with transitional cell carcinoma of the bladder. J Urol 1999;162:931–5.

245. Seraj MJ, Thomas AR, Chin JL, Theodorescu D. Molecular determination of perivesical and lymph node metastasis after radical cystectomy for urothelial carcinoma of the bladder. Clin Cancer Res 20017:1516–22.

246. Thogersen VB, Sorensen BS, Poulsen SS, et al. A subclass of HER1 ligands are prognostic markers for survival in bladder cancer patients. Cancer Res 2001;61:6227–33.

247. Chow NH, Chan SH, Tzai TS, et al. Expression profiles of ErbB family receptors and prognosis in primary transitional cell carcinoma of the urinary bladder. Clin Cancer Res 2001;7:1957–62.

248. Mizutani Y, Wada H, Yoshida O, et al. Prognostic significance of a combination of thymidylate synthase and dihydropyrimidine dehydrogenase activities in grades 1 and 2 superficial bladder cancer. Oncol Rep 2002;9:289–92.

249. Mizutani Y, Wada H, Ogawa O, et al. Prognostic significance of thymidylate synthase activity in bladder carcinoma. Cancer 2001;92:510–8.

250. Jiang J, Ulbright TM, Younger C, et al. Cytokeratin 7 and cytokeratin 20 in primary urinary bladder carcinoma and matched lymph node metastasis. Arch Pathol Lab Med 2001;125:921–3.

251. Durkan GC, Nutt JE, Rajjayabun PH, et al. Prognostic significance of matrix metalloproteinase-1 and tissue inhibitor of metalloproteinase-1 in voided urine samples from patients with transitional cell carcinoma of the bladder. Clin Cancer Res 2001;7:3450–6.

252. Nakopoulou L, Gakiopoulou H, Zervas A, et al. MMP-3 mRNA and MMP-3 and MMP-1 proteins in bladder cancer: a comparison with clinicopathologic features and survival. Appl Immunohistochem Mol Morphol 2001;9:130–7.

253. Hara I, Miyake H, Hara S, et al. Significance of matrix metalloproteinases and tissue inhibitors of metalloproteinase expression in the recurrence of superficial transitional cell carcinoma of the bladder. J Urol 2001;165: 1769–72.

254. Lebret T, Becette V, Herve JM, et al. Prognostic value of MIB-1 antibody labeling index to predict response to Bacillus Calmette-Guerin therapy in a high-risk selected population of patients with stage T1 grade G3 bladder cancer. Eur Urol 2000;37:654–9.

255. Rotterud R, Berner A, Holm R, et al. p53, p21 and mdm2 expression vs the response to radiotherapy in transitional cell carcinoma of the bladder. BJU Int 2001;88:202–8.

256. Lara PC, Rey A, Santana C, et al. The role of Ki67 proliferation assessment in predicting local control in bladder cancer patients treated by radical radiation therapy. Radiother Oncol 1998;49:163–7.

257. Moonen L, Ong F, Gallee M, et al. Apoptosis, proliferation and p53, cyclin D1, and retinoblastoma gene expression in relation to radiation response in transitional cell carcinoma of the bladder. Int J Radiat Oncol Biol Phys 2001;49:1305–10.

258. Cook AM, Huddart RA, Jay G, et al. The utility of tumour markers in assessing the response to chemotherapy in advanced bladder cancer. Br J Cancer 2000;82:1952–7.

259. Drew PA, Furman J, Civantos F, Murphy WM. The nested variant of transitional cell carcinoma: an aggressive neoplasm with innocuous histology. Mod Pathol 1996;9:989–94.

260. Lin O, Cardillo M, Linkov I, et al. Immunohistochemical expression of p21, p27, p53, EGF-R, bcl-2, and MIB-1 in the nested variant of urothelial carcinoma [abstract]. Mod Pathol 2002;5:170.

261. Castillo M, Mallotre C, Palactin A, Cardesa A. Immunohistochemical expression of CK-20, p-53 and Ki-67 as objective markers for urothelial dysplasia [abstract]. Mod Pathol 2002;5:170.

11

Intravesical Chemotherapy in Approaches to Treatment and Prophylaxis

GREGORY L. ALBERTS, MD

SAM S. CHANG, MD

JOSEPH A. SMITH JR, MD

Non–muscle invasive urothelial carcinoma, often referred to as superficial bladder cancer, is defined as stage Ta, T1, and/or Tis and is the most common bladder tumor type at initial presentation (Figure 11–1). Cystoscopy with transurethral resection of the tumor remains the initial diagnostic and therapeutic intervention of choice. There is a wide range of tumor biology observed among superficial transitional cell carcinoma (TCC) with variation in the rates of recurrence and progression. For example, only a small percentage of stage Ta tumors progress to muscle invasive disease, while 50 to 70% of patients will have a recurrence if treated only with transurethral resection.[1] However, those patients with high grade T1 lesions and/or carcinoma in situ (CIS) are not only at significant risk for recurrence, but also have a substantial risk for stage progression.[2] It is this inherent heterogeneous nature of superficial bladder cancer that compounds the difficulty in comparing therapeutic efficacy of different treatment modalities and establishing treatment recommendations.

Adjuvant intravesical chemotherapy is often used in patients at higher risk for recurrence. Patients are classified as high risk based on the presence of multiple tumors, recurrent tumors, high-grade tumors, CIS, pathologic stage T1 tumors, or initially large tumors.[3] The rationale behind adjuvant therapy often encompasses the goals of prophylactic therapy and primary completion therapy.

At this time, there is no single agent that clearly demonstrates superiority in the treatment of superficial, high risk tumors. Efficacy, cost, possible complications, and the urologist's familiarity with a particular agent are factors that must be considered when selecting an agent for intravesical therapy. In addition, variable treatment schedules and dosing regimens must be factored into the physician's decision. Often there is not a universally accepted method of administering these agents. Determination of the different dosing regimens has often been empirically derived, contributing to variations among these treatment schedules.

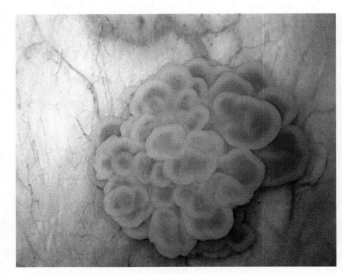

Figure 11–1. Superficial bladder tumor at cystoscopy.

Intravesical drug concentration during treatment is determined by several factors: dose, volume of diluent, volume of residual urine before treatment, urine production during treatment, and drug absorption across the mucosa.[4] Basic treatment guidelines for all intravesical therapies include: immediate emptying of the bladder prior to instillation, urinalysis prior to chemotherapy to rule out an infection, aseptic and atraumatic placement of urethral catheter, avoidance of excessive fluid intake during the treatment session, and retaining the agent for 1 to 2 hours. Efforts to optimize drug delivery include fluid restriction 8 hours before and during treatment session, administration of sodium bicarbonate to alkalinize the urine, and drainage of any post-void residual urine. These techniques, which are often underutilized, can significantly improve treatment efficacy.[4]

This chapter describes the mechanism of action, dosing, efficacy, and side effects of different intravesical chemotherapy agents employed as adjuvant therapy after transurethral resection in selected patients with superficial bladder cancer. The use of Bacille Calmette-Guérin (BCG) and other immunotherapeutic agents will be explored elsewhere, but comparisons of these agents with BCG will be discussed.

THIOTEPA

Mechanism of Action

First used in 1960, thiotepa was the first intravesically administered chemotherapeutic agent used with success in the treatment of superficial TCC.[5] Thiotepa is a lipophilic alkylating agent, chemically related to nitrogen mustard compounds, possessing a molecular weight of 189kD. This agent exerts its cytotoxic effect by the cross linking of deoxyribonucleic acid (DNA) and riboncleic acid (RNA) through the formation of covalent bonds with nucleic acids leading to interference with cellular protein synthesis. Thiotepa targets rapidly dividing cells of urothelial tumors but is not cell cycle specific.[6]

As a result of the low molecular weight of thiotepa, it can easily permeate the bladder mucosa resulting in systemic absorption. Approximately 19% of a 1 mg/mL dose is absorbed in patients with an intact urothelium. Absorption is greatly increased in those patients with cystitis, multiple papillary tumors, or damaged mucosa secondary to transurethral resection.[7,8] Its absorption is also influenced by dose, temperature of solution, retention time, and frequency of instillation.[9]

Dosing

As with other intravesical agents, the optimal dosing schedule for thiotepa has not been clearly established. The usual protocol is 30 to 60 milligrams of thiotepa delivered in 20 to 100 milliliters of distilled water, with resulting drug concentrations in the range of 0.5–2.0 mg/mL.[5] A study by Koontz and the National Collaborative Bladder Cancer Group A evaluated recurrence rate in patients receiving 30 mg/30 mL versus 60 mg/60 mL of thiotepa as prophylaxis. Recurrence rates for patients in the treatment arm were significantly better than control patients, with 50% of patients remaining disease free at 12 months compared to only 31% of the controls. No significant difference in recurrence rate or time to recurrence was noted between the two dosing regimens.[10] A recent study has shown that increasing the concentration of drug during intravesical instillation to 2.0 mg/mL is effective in increasing drug delivery to the tumor without significant increases in systemic absorption and side effects.[11]

Thiotepa is most commonly delivered as weekly instillations over a 4 to 8 week period followed by monthly instillations for 1 year.[6] To minimize the risk of thiotepa associated toxicity it is recommended that the practitioner use 30 mg of thiotepa reconstituted in 30 mL saline during each treatment session, administer one dose each week and not more frequently than every 4 days, and discontinue use after 1 year if patient is tumor free. Studies have also reported treatment with a single dose of thiotepa, the success of which has been inconsistent.[9,12,13] As with other agents, if tumors persist, alternative treatments should be pursued.

Efficacy

Historically, thiotepa was used in the treatment of residual superficial tumors and/or CIS, and also as a prophylactic agent to prevent recurrence and progression of disease. Heney and colleagues, in a phase III prospective randomized study, compared the efficacy of thiotepa and mitomycin C in the ablation of unresected Tis, Ta and T1 lesions. All patients were treated with 8 weekly instillations of thiotepa 30 mg/30 mL or mitomycin 40 mg/40 mL followed by cystoscopy. Thiotepa was inferior to mitomycin C in the ablation of low grade/stage lesions. Importantly, however, neither agent demonstrated a significant complete response rate in those patients enrolled in the study.[14]

A review of initial results using thiotepa as definitive therapy for superficial TCC in 321 patients demonstrated an overall complete response rate of 38% and a partial response rate of 24%. Complete responses were defined as disappearance of tumor on follow-up cystoscopic examination and biopsy and partial responses were defined as apparent shrinkage of initial lesion based on cystoscopic examination.[5]

In studying the effect of thiotepa on recurrence rate, the results vary (Table 11–1). In a randomized prospective study the prophylactic effect of BCG, doxorubicin, and thiotepa were evaluated. After 36 months the rate of recurrence was 35.7% for the thiotepa group, 43.3% for the Adriamycin group, and 13.4% for the BCG group. In comparing patients with Ta versus T1 tumors the recurrence rate for thiotepa was 39% and 33%, respectively. In patients treated with Adriamycin the recurrence rate was 19% (Ta) versus 60% (T1) and patients treated with BCG demonstrated a recurrence rate of 17% (Ta) and 12% (T1). In those patients with associated Tis, recurrence rates were 100% for the Adriamycin group, 40% for the thiotepa group, and 33% for the BCG group. The overall progression rate was 1.5% for the BCG group, 3.6% for the thiotepa group, and 7.5% for the Adriamycin group.[15] Lamm reviewed recurrence rates in patients receiving thiotepa compared to control patients. In those 1,007 patients, a 44% recurrence rate was noted in the treatment arms compared to a 56% recurrence rate in control patients, representing a 12% advantage using thiotepa. It should be noted that four of these studies did not demonstrate a statistical difference.[16]

The Medical Research Council Working Party on Urological Cancer evaluated the effect of intravesical thiotepa on tumor recurrence after endoscopic ablation of newly diagnosed superficial bladder cancer. This trial provided long-term follow-up in 417 patients treated either with resection alone, a single instillation of thiotepa at time of resection, or a single instillation at the time of resection followed by 4 instillations delivered every 3 months for 1 year. After a median follow-up of almost 9 years, analysis failed to show a difference between the groups with respect to time to first recurrence, recurrence rates or failure free interval.[12]

Thiotepa is not effective in preventing progression of disease.[15,17] In a comprehensive review examining progression rates, a rate of 4.5% was noted in the thiotepa treatment group compared to a rate of 6% in the control group.[18]

Side Effects

Myelosuppression is the most significant side effect of thiotepa administration, occurring in 15 to 20% of patients. The risk of such myelosuppressive effects is greatest with frequent (every 1–4 days) and/or higher

Study, Year (Reference)	Recurrence in Control Patients— TUR Alone (%)	Recurrence in Treatment Patients— TUR and Thiotepa (%)	Difference (%)
Burnand, 1976[86]	97	58	39
Byar, 1977[87]	60	47	13
Zincke, 1983[13]	71	30	41
Prout, 1983[88]	76	64	12
Medical Research Council, 1985[89]	37	40	-3
Medical Research Council, 1994[12]	51	40	11

Table 11–1. RESULTS OF THIOTEPA PROPHYLACTIC ADMINISTRATION IN 6 CONTROLLED CLINICAL TRIALS IN TERMS OF TUMOR RECURRENCE

TUR = transurethral resection.

doses (60–120 mg). Leukopenia (< 3,000/mm^3) has been reported to occur in 9 to 54% and thrombocytopenia (< 100,000/mm^3) in 3 to 31% of patients.[19] It is recommended that a complete blood count be checked prior to each instillation to prevent unidentified significant myelosuppression.

Irritative bladder symptoms occur in 12 to 69% of patients. Although bothersome, these symptoms rarely lead to discontinuation of therapy. Patients may also experience urinary tract infection, fever, nausea/vomiting, dermatitis, and stomatitis. The variability in frequency of side effects is related to variable dosing schedules, concentration of drug administered, and variable time between drug instillation and previous resection.[19,20] Other potential side effects include infertility, eosinophilic cystitis, hemorrhagic cystitis, unanticipated vesicoureteral reflux, and occurrence of acute nonlymphocytic leukemia.[21–25]

MITOMYCIN C

Mechanism of Action

Mitomycin C (MMC) is an antimicrobial and anticancer agent initially isolated from the fermentation fluid culture medium of *Streptomyces caespitosus* in 1958.[26] It is a bioreductive alkylating agent, with a molecular weight of 334 kD. It is this larger size that limits its systemic absorption. This agent possesses a different molecular structure from other alkylating agents, with three active side groups: a quinone, a urethane, and an aziridine ring.[19] MMC requires enzymatic bioactivation, via metabolic pathways for one and two-electron reduction, leading to the generation of cytotoxic species. Enzymes involved in drug activation include NADPH cytochrome P-450 reductase and NAD(P)H:quinone oxidoreductase.[27]

Acting as an intracellular agent, MMC demonstrates activity against bladder carcinoma and other solid tumors.[28] This agent is technically cell cycle–nonspecific; however, cell lines show increased susceptibility during late G1 and early S phase of the cell cycle.[29] MMC exerts its effect primarily through creation of DNA-DNA cross-links leading to protein synthesis inhibition and strand breakage. It has also been shown to exert antitumor effect through superoxide free radical formation.[19]

Certain tumor cell lines have demonstrated resistance to this particular chemotherapeutic agent. Mechanisms of impaired drug activation include down-regulation of activating enzymes, reduced intracellular accumulation of drug, repair of MMC-induced DNA cross-links and enhanced glutathione S transferase mediated drug inactivation. Interestingly, cells developing resistance to MMC demonstrate resistance to other compounds such as paclitaxil.[28] Insensitivity of tumor cells to MMC may also be related to inadequate drug delivery, specifically in regards to the inability of MMC to penetrate deep muscle and instability of the drug at an acid pH.[4]

Appealingly, MMC has limited systemic absorption secondary to its higher molecular weight.[19] Increased absorption, however, may be noted in the setting of damaged bladder mucosa, recent transurethral resection, and previous radiation therapy.[30] In these settings, possible systemic absorption should be carefully monitored.

Dosing

The intravesical dose of drug ranges from 20 mg to 60 mg in most series, however most recent studies employ a dose of 30–40 mg diluted in 40 to 50 mL of water.[5,6,31–36] The concentration of drug ranges from 0.5 to 2.0 mg/mL depending on the amount of diluent. Bladder dwell time ranges from 1 to 2 hours.

Typically treatment regimens include weekly instillations beginning immediately after transurethral resection and continuing for 6 to 8 weeks, followed by monthly maintenance doses for 1 year.[37] Investigators have evaluated the benefit of a single instillation following transurethral resection and successfully demonstrated a decreased rate of early recurrence; however, there was no demonstrable benefit in terms of long-term recurrence or progression of disease.[32]

Au and colleagues carried out a randomized, multi-institutional phase III trial to evaluate whether enhancing the concentration of the drug in urine would improve efficacy. Patients were randomized to an optimized treatment arm and a standard treatment arm. Patients in the optimized arm received MMC 40 mg/20 mL, underwent complete bladder emptying, were placed on fluid restriction 8 hours prior to treatment and were administered three doses of oral sodium bicarbonate (1.3g). Patients in the standard treatment group received MMC 20 mg/mL, underwent a single catheterization and were instructed to refrain from drinking fluids. There were minimal differences between the two arms in terms of hematologic and nonhematologic toxicity. Dysuria was the only side effect that was statistically significant in the optimized arm; however, the ability to tolerate the regimen was similar in both arms. It was also noted that patients in the optimized arm had a statistically significant longer time to recurrence and a higher recurrence-free interval compared to patients in the standard arm. The overall percentage of patients who were recurrence free at 5 years was 24.6% in the standard treatment arm and 41.0% in the optimized arm. Recurrence rates were similar for both Ta and T1 tumors.[4]

Efficacy

The Bladder Cancer Clinical Guidelines Panel Summary Report from the American Urological Association has concluded that MMC has been shown to be more effective than other intravesical chemotherapeutic agents including thiotepa and Adriamycin.[38] Reduction in the rate of recurrence of superficial transitional carcinoma with adjuvant, intravesical MMC versus transurethral resection (TUR) alone is approximately 5 to 20% (Table 11–2). A review of 5 studies demonstrated that the recurrence rate for control patients was 52% compared to a 37% recurrence rate for those patients undergoing transurethral resection and MMC instillation.[18] In this review, however, only two of the cited studies demonstrated a statistically significant benefit of MMC and follow-up

tended to be short. Traynelis and Lamm analyzed data from 23 controlled clinical trials and found an average net benefit of intravesical MMC compared to transurethral resection alone of 14% at 1 and 3 years.[39] One study evaluated the efficacy of monthly MMC for 12 months following an 8 week induction course. Tumor recurrence rates were 45% after 12 months and 58% after 48 months in controls versus, 29% and 44%, respectively, in those patients receiving MMC.[40] Further investigation regarding maintenance therapy may help to further clarify its role in the treatment of superficial bladder cancer.

Lundholm and colleagues evaluated the efficacy and toxicity of long-term MMC versus BCG instillation in patients at high risk for recurrence. Intravesical therapy was administered weekly for the first 6 weeks, monthly during year 1, and every 3 months during year 2. After a median of 39 months follow-up, 49% of patients receiving BCG and 34% of patients receiving MMC were free of disease. Median time to recurrence was longer in those treated with BCG.[36]

Tolley and colleagues was able to show a 34 to 50% decreased risk of subsequent recurrence in patients receiving a single instillation or five instillations.[31] Two European Organisation for Research and Treatment of Cancer (EORTC) genitourinary group phase III trials investigated the potential benefit of early versus delayed administration of intravesical MMC after transurethral resection. Early administration seemed to be slightly superior in terms of recurrence in patients with superficial, low-grade lesions. The recurrence rate was higher, although not statistically significant, for those patients undergoing delayed treatment without maintenance.[34] Recently, Solsona and colleagues

	Recurrence in Control Patients—	Recurrence in Treatment Patients—	Difference
Study, Year (Reference)	TUR Only (%)	TUR and MMC (%)	(%)
Huland, 1984[41]	52	10	42
Niijima, 1983[90]	62	57	5
Kim, 1989[91]	82	81	1
Tolley, 1988[42]	60	41	19
Rubben, 1988[92]	42	35	7
Krege, 1996[93]	46	27	19
Solsona, 1999[32]	54	40	14
Akaza, 1992[43]	33	24	9

Table 11–2. EFFICACY OF PROPHYLACTIC MMC IN CONTROLLED SERIES

examined the recurrence rate, at 24 months follow-up, with a single immediate instillation of MMC (30 mg in 50 mL) after transurethral resection of bladder tumor (TURBT) versus TURBT alone in low-risk superficial disease. There was a significant difference in disease recurrence during this time period, 15.8% versus 34%. However, importantly, there was no difference in recurrence rate (22.8% versus 21.8%) with longer follow-up.[32]

Independent from the issue of recurrence is tumor progression. Initially, it was suggested that intravesical MMC therapy reduced the risk of tumor progression. Huland and colleagues demonstrated a progression rate of 26% in patients treated with TUR only versus 2% in patients treated with MMC following TURBT, but due to small numbers, this was not statistically significant.[41] Witjes and colleagues in an evaluation of 361 patients comparing MMC to BCG, also demonstrated an apparent benefit of MMC over BCG in terms of tumor progression ($p = .006$).[33]

The majority of studies, however, do not show a clear impact on tumor progression with MMC instillation. Tolley and colleagues demonstrated a rate of disease progression of 2.4% in patients receiving MMC versus 5% in control patients.[42] The Japanese Urological Cancer Research Group conducted a controlled study that demonstrated a progression rate of 14.6% in patients receiving MMC versus 19.4% in controls.[43] In addition, a recent meta-analysis of available literature confirmed the lack of effect of MMC on tumor progression.[38]

Side Effects

Chemical cystitis and irritative voiding symptoms are the most frequently encountered side effect occurring in 10 to 42% of patients. Treatment may also be associated with bacterial cystitis (20%) and hematuria (16%). Systemic side effects included arthralgia (9%), fever or chills (3%), flu-like symptoms (20%), nausea/vomiting (9%), skin rash (13%), and myelosuppression (2%).[38]

Contact dermatitis is noted to occur in 5 to 12% of patients.[44–46] Several investigators have noted palmar desquamation associated with eczema after intravesical administration of MMC. Some reports state that the reaction is secondary to contact dermatitis related to inadvertent handling of the agent and recommend careful cleansing of the hands and perineum to prevent this type of reaction.[44] Colver and colleagues have postulated that this reaction may be secondary to a delayed hypersensitivity reaction to the drug. This group has demonstrated that bladder biopsies after MMC instillation demonstrated marked numbers of eosinophils. Importantly, skin reactions were noted only in conjunction with the second instillation, not after the first MMC treatment. In support of these findings, skin patch tests were strongly positive in those patients previously exposed to the agent in contrast to control volunteers.[47]

Witjes and colleagues in a long-term follow-up of an EORTC randomized prospective trial evaluated side effects associated with MMC compared to BCG. Bacterial cystitis, drug-induced cystitis, and allergic reactions were noted most frequently in those patients receiving MMC. Interestingly, systemic side effects were more frequent and severe in those patients receiving BCG. In this study toxicity led to discontinuation of treatment in 2% of patients receiving MMC.[33]

Necrosis of soft tissue related to extravasation of MMC following traumatic catheterization has been reported. Neulander and colleagues reported a case of necrosis of the glans penis and Brady and colleagues reported a case of urethral slough following MMC administration.[48,49] Other less frequent complications include bladder wall calcification, severe bladder contracture, renal failure, aplastic anemia, and development of bilateral ureteral stricture associated with reduced bladder capacity and vesicoureteral reflux.[50–55]

ADRIAMYCIN

Mechanism of Action

Adriamycin is an anthracycline antibiotic, originally isolated by aerobic fermentation of *Streptomyces peucetius caesius*.[56] Its molecular weight of 580 kD limits the systemic absorption after intravesical instillation.[57,58] Another important factor limiting the systemic absorption is the integrity of the bladder wall at the time of administration. In addition, decreased systemic levels of drug with each successive treatment session have been demonstrated in previous studies.[59,60]

This agent exerts its antitumor effect through binding of DNA base pairs, intercalation into base pairs, inhibition of topoisomerase II and production of oxygen free radicals. It has also been demonstrated that Adriamycin exhibits a direct cytotoxic effect through interaction with the cell wall. Adriamycin is typically classified as a non–cell cycle specific agent; however, primary cytotoxic activity occurs during the S phase of the cell cycle.[6]

Several investigators have attempted to increase the effectiveness of intravesical Adriamycin by the concomitant administration of additional agents. For example, the fluoroquinolone antibiotics, ciprofloxacin and ofloxacin, exhibit significant time- and dose-dependent cytotoxicity against TCC cells and significantly enhance the cytotoxic effects of intravesical Adriamycin. Kamat and colleagues compared cell kill rates between doxorubicin alone and in combination with ciprofloxacin or ofloxacin. Cytotoxicity increased from 35.1 to 78.5% when combined with ciprofloxacin (25 μg/mL) and from 26.6 to 81.8% when combined with ofloxacin (50 μg/mL). It should be noted that these concentrations are achievable in urine after oral administration. This suggests that quinolones might be useful as an adjunct to intravesical chemotherapy and might reduce the seeding of tumor cells after transurethral resection of bladder tumors.[61] Other investigators have evaluated the potential efficacy of concomitant intravesical administration of calcium channel blockers. The reponse rate, defined as complete disappearance of tumor of 50% reduction in the side of the tumor, was 61% in patients receiving Adriamycin only and 48% in patients receiving Adriamycin and verapamil.[62] An additional study by Tsushima and colleagues was unable to demonstrate increased efficacy in the treatment of superficial tumors when combining Adriamycin with verapamil.[62] Further investigation is necessary in this area.

Dosing

Doses range from 30 to 100 mg, usually at a concentration of 1 mg/mL (0.5–2.0 mg/dL). Schedules are variable, usually ranging from weekly to every 3 week administration. Bladder dwell time ranges from 1 to 2 hours.[6] There are many maintenance schedules for the administration of Adriamycin. Maintenance schedules up to 2 years have been described.[63] Some argue against maintenance therapy based on the assertion that cytotoxic chemotherapy is only effective against rapidly dividing cells, chemotherapeutic agents are only effective in the presence of tumor cells, and chemotherapy is mutagenic and potentially carcinogenic. In addition, various studies have shown no benefit for mitomycin C and doxorubicin in terms of maintenance therapy.[18]

Efficacy

When used as definitive therapy the response rate of papillary tumors varies from 28 to 56% with an average response rate of 38%.[64] In the setting of CIS the complete response rate has been shown to be approximately 34% with a mean time to failure of 5 months.[65] In this study complete responses were defined by complete disappearance of disease documented by normal cystoscopic examination, normal findings on random bladder biopsy and normal cystology. Treatment failures were defined as the termination of treatment due to persistence, recurrence, or progression of disease.

Studies have demonstrated a beneficial effect of intravesical Adriamycin for treatment of superficial, papillary tumors (Ta or T1) in terms of recurrence rate and time to first recurrence when compared to TUR-only control patients (Table 11–3). Like other intravesical agents, however, Adriamycin has not been as effective as BCG in preventing recurrence in superficial disease. Lamm and colleagues showed that patients with superficial, papillary lesions demonstrated a recurrence rate of 80.9% in patients treated with Adriamycin versus 65.1% in patients treated with BCG. Likewise, the median time to treatment failure was 10.4 months in patients receiving Adriamycin and 22.5 months in patients treated with BCG. This study also analyzed the response of patients with CIS. In patients receiving Adriamycin the complete response rate was 34% versus 70% in patients receiving BCG. The median time to treatment failure for patients receiving Adriamycin was 5.1 months and for those receiving BCG was 39.0 months.[66]

Table 11–3. EFFICACY OF PROPHYLACTIC ADRIAMYCIN IN CONTROLLED SERIES			
Study, Year (Reference)	Recurrence in Control Patients— TUR Only (%)	Recurrence in Treatment Patients— TUR and Adriamycin (%)	Difference (%)
Niijima, 1983[90]	45	30	15
Zincke, 1983[13]	71	32	39
Rubben, 1988[3]	61	56	5
Akaza, 1987[94]	33	25	8
Kurth, 1997[95]	64	52	12
Ali-el-Dein, 1997[67]	65	37	29

In addition, there is no convincing evidence that Adriamycin significantly impacts tumor progression (Table 11–3).[6] This is similar to other intravesical chemotherapy agents. This ineffectiveness may also be uniquely due in part to the development of specific resistance of tumor cells to this drug.[62]

Side Effects

Systemic reactions secondary to intravesical administration range from 1.2 to 5.1%.[19] These reactions include systemic allergic responses noted in 0.3% of patients, fever in 0.8% of patients, and gastrointestinal side effects noted to occur in approximately 1.7% of patients. Local side effects relate mainly to irritative side effects of doxorubicin. Chemical cystitis was noted in 4 to 56% of patients, bacterial cystitis and hematuria may also be noted. Reduced bladder capacity is a rarely encountered complication.[66] Simple cessation of intravesical administration leads to cessation of symptoms with few long-term sequelae reported in the literature.

EPIRUBICIN

Mechanism of Action and Dosing

A derivative of Adriamycin, 4'epidoxorubicin, possesses a similar mechanism of action. Secondary to its unique structure, however, this agent possesses a more favorable toxicity profile when compared to Adriamycin. The dosing of epirubicin ranges from 50 to 80 mg per instillation delivered at a concentration of 1.0 to 1.6 mg/mL. Treatment is often initiated 1 to 2 weeks after transurethral resection. Dwell time as with most agents ranges from 1 to 2 hours. Treatment schedules involve 8 weekly instillations and if maintenance is selected, monthly for the remainder of the year.[6,67]

Efficacy

Epirubicin demonstrates similar efficacy when compared to Adriamycin. A phase II study evaluating the efficacy in intravesical epirubicin demonstrated a recurrence rate of 30.1%. This is similar to recurrence rates in patients treated with intravesical Adriamycin that range from 21 to 34% with varying follow-up. Evaluation was stratified based on primary cases and recurrent cases, and a significant increase in recurrence rate was noted in patients with recurrence tumors, 19.7% versus 61.9%.[68,69] Ali-el-Dein and colleagues demonstrated increased efficacy of epirubicin when compared to Adriamycin or TUR alone.[67] In that study no recurrences in Ta patients treated with chemotherapy, epirubicin, or Adriamycin were noted. In those patients with T1 tumors 22% of patients treated with epirubicin experience recurrence compared to 39% of patients receiving Adriamycin and 70% of patients treated by TUR only. A comparison was also made between epirubicin doses of 50 mg/50 mL and 80 mg/50 mL and no differences in tumor recurrence or progression were noted. It is also interesting to note that in their study there was no significant difference in terms of progression between treatment and control arms. Masters and colleagues evaluated the potential benefit of increasing the dose concentration of epirubicin but was unable to demonstrate benefit in the high dose group.[70] As with MMC, a single dose instillation following TUR has been studied. An EORTC study using 80 mg immediately after TURBT demonstrated a reduction in the early recurrence rate.[71]

In an evaluation of epirubicin versus BCG in the treatment of superficial Ta and T1 disease, Melekos and colleagues failed to demonstrate an overall difference in recurrence rate. The recurrence rate was 40% in patients receiving epirubicin, 32% in patients receiving BCG, and 59% in control patients. Sixty percent of patients treated with eprubicin and 68% of patients treated with BCG remained free of recurrence at a mean follow-up of 32.9 months. However, there was a significant benefit of BCG treatment in those patients with higher risk tumors (stage T1 grade 3).[72]

As noted previously with other agents, epirubicin demonstrates little impact on overall disease progression compared to resection alone.[38,67]

Side Effects

The impetus for the intravesical use of epirubicin arose from the observation that with systemic administration of the drug, few hematologic and cardiac side effects were noted. The major local side effects include frequency/dysuria (26%), chemical cystitis (6.8–15%), and allergy (0.9%)[73,74] A subsequent evaluation by Eto and colleagues noted occurrence of micturitional pain in 10%, urinary frequency in 15%, and hematuria in 5%.[75] Bacterial cystitis is another potential complication of therapy occurring in approximately 10% of patients, as defined by bacterial growth on routine urine culture.[76] Allergic reactions are noted in less than 1% of patients and bladder contraction has been noted in 2.4% of patients. Often these local side effects can be alleviated with temporary cessation of therapy.

VALRUBICIN

Mechanism of Action and Dosing

Valrubicin is a new semisynthetic, lipid soluble derivative of the anthracycline antibiotic doxorubicin. The chemical structure of valrubicin is, N-trifluoro-acetyl Adriamycin-14-valerate. Valrubicin rapidly traverses the cell membrane, accumulating in the cytoplasm, while minimal absorption is noted across the bladder wall.[77] The drug is delivered as

Valstar™, each vial containing 200 mg/5 mL. The dose of agent is 800 mg per instillation with a range of 400 to 800 mg. Prior to instillation, 4 vials are diluted in 75 mL of normal saline. Instillation time is approximately 90 minutes (1–2 hours). In initial studies most patients are able successfully to retain the drug for a full treatment session.[77] Steinberg and colleagues demonstrated that approximately 99% of the valrubicin dose is recovered after 24 hours, with minimal metabolism.[78]

Efficacy

Valrubicin has been licensed as an intravesical therapy for BCG-refractory CIS of the urinary bladder in patients for whom immediate cystectomy would be associated with unacceptable morbidity or mortality. In an open label clinical trial, 90 patients with BCG-refractory CIS were treated with valrubicin at a dosage of 800 mg/week for 6 weeks. In this study 99% of patients had received two or more treatments prior to failure. Complete responses with valrubicin therapy were 44% at 3 months and 21% at 6 months. At the end of 2 years, 77% patients who had failed valrubicin treatment had undergone additional therapy.[78] Further study is needed and is ongoing.

Side Effects

Valrubicin has a favorable side effect profile, with few systemic side effects, similar to Adriamycin. The most frequently noted side effects are urinary frequency (66%), dysuria (60%), urgency (63%), and hematuria.[78] Other less frequently reported side effects include bladder spasm, pelvic pain, urethral burning/pain, incontinence, cystitis, and nocturia. Systemic reactions are few and have included one case each of neutropenia and contact dermatitis following instillation.[77]

CONCLUSION

Current management of superficial bladder cancer includes a variety of chemotherapeutic agents, and more agents such as intravesical ethoglucid,[79] cisplatin,[80] mitoxantrone,[81] and gemcitabine have been and continue to be studied. Most urologists

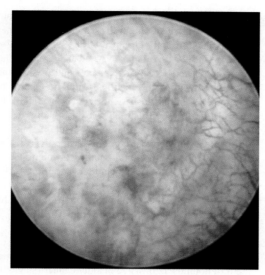

Figure 11–2. Carcinoma in situ at cystoscopy.

agree upon the short-term effectiveness of induction intravesical adjuvant chemotherapy in preventing tumor recurrence. In fact, a recent meta-analysis of eight randomized studies examined the effect of chemotherapy on recurrent tumors and concluded that intravesical therapy does decrease recurrence at 1, 2, and 3 years post-TURBT by 30 to 80%.[82] Although there do not seem to be large differences in the efficacy of various agents, evidence suggests that MMC may offer better tumor control when compared to thiotepa, Adriamycin or epirubicin. Currently, intravesical instillation of BCG or MMC is recommended for the treatment of CIS and after endoscopic removal of T1 lesions and high grade Ta tumors.[38]

The real concern, however, is long term prophylaxis and the prevention of disease progression. Studies do not clearly show a significant long-term beneficial effect of intravesical chemotherapy.[83–85] Although this treatment technique is clearly appealing, none of the agents thus far have been proven to prevent progression or improve overall prognosis in patients with superficial disease.[38] In addition, these agents, especially in the setting of CIS, appear less effective than BCG immunotherapy.[38] Multiple factors, however, must be considered prior to choosing to use intravesical therapy and then the specific agent and regimen to be used. Clearly, the specific intravesical therapy chosen for patients with superficial TCC must be individualized.

REFERENCES

1. Batts CN. Adjuvant intravesical therapy for superficial bladder cancer. Ann Pharmacother 1992;26:1270–9.
2. Herr HW, Laudone VP, Whitmore WF Jr. An overview of intravesical therapy for superficial bladder tumors. J Urol 1987;138:1363–8.
3. Rubben H, Lutzeyer W, Fischer N, et al. Natural history and treatment of low and high risk superficial bladder tumors. J Urol 1988;139:283–7.
4. Au JL, Badalament RA, Wientjes MG, et al. Methods to improve efficacy of intravesical mitomycin C: results of a randomized phase III trial. J Natl Cancer Inst 2001;93:597–604.
5. Richie JP. Intravesical chemotherapy. Treatment selection, techniques, and results. Urol Clin North Am 1992;19:521–7.
6. Duque JL, Loughlin KR. An overview of the treatment of superficial bladder cancer. Intravesical chemotherapy. Urol Clin North Am 2000;27:125–35.
7. Lunglmayr G, Czech K. Absorption studies on intraluminal thio-tepa for topical cytostatic treatment of low-stage bladder tumors. J Urol 1971;106:72–4.
8. Veenema RJ, Dean AL Jr, Uson AC, et al. Thiotepa bladder instillations: therapy and prophylaxis for superficial bladder tumors. J Urol 1969;101:711–5.
9. Sarosdy MF. Principles of intravesical chemotherapy and immunotherapy. Urol Clin North Am 1992;19:509–19.
10. Koontz WW Jr, Prout GR Jr, Smith W, et al. The use of intravesical thio-tepa in the management of non-invasive carcinoma of the bladder. J Urol 1981;125:307–12.
11. Masters JR, McDermott BJ, Harland S, et al. ThioTEPA pharmacokinetics during intravesical chemotherapy: the influence of dose and volume of instillate on systemic uptake and dose rate to the tumour. Cancer Chemother Pharmacol 1996;38:59–64.
12. The effect of intravesical thiotepa on tumour recurrence after endoscopic treatment of newly diagnosed superficial bladder cancer. A further report with long-term follow-up of a Medical Research Council randomized trial. Medical Research Council Working Party on Urological Cancer, Subgroup on Superficial Bladder Cancer. Br J Urol 1994;73:632–8.
13. Zincke H, Utz DC, Taylor WF, et al. Influence of thiotepa and doxorubicin instillation at time of transurethral surgical treatment of bladder cancer on tumor recurrence: a prospective, randomized, double-blind, controlled trial. J Urol 1983;129:505–9.
14. Heney NM, Koontz WW, Barton B, et al. Intravesical thiotepa versus mitomycin C in patients with Ta, T1 and TIS transitional cell carcinoma of the bladder: a phase III prospective randomized study. J Urol 1988;140:1390–3.
15. Martinez-Pineiro JA, Jimenez Leon J, Martinez-Pineiro L Jr, et al. Bacillus Calmette-Guerin versus doxorubicin versus thiotepa: a randomized prospective study in 202 patients with superficial bladder cancer. J Urol 1990;143:502–6.
16. Lamm DL. Urologic cancer. In: Ernstoff M, Heaney JA, Peschel RE, editors. Boston: Blackwell Science, 1997. p. 72–86.
17. Novak R, Kern J, Fister H, et al. Effects of local chemotherapy and immunotherapy on the recurrence and progres-

sion of superficial bladder cancer. Eur Urol 1988;14: 367–70.

18. Lamm DL. Long-term results of intravesical therapy for superficial bladder cancer. Urol Clin North Am 1992;19:573–80.

19. Thrasher JB, Crawford ED. Complications of intravesical chemotherapy. Urol Clin North Am 1992;19:529–39.

20. Soloway MS, Ford KS. Thiotepa-induced myelosuppression: review of 670 bladder instillations. J Urol 1983;130: 889–91.

21. Silberberg JM, Zarrabi MH. Acute nonlymphocytic leukemia after thiotepa instillation into the bladder: report of 2 cases and review of the literature. J Urol 1987;138:402–3.

22. Mukamel E, Glanz I, Nissenkorn I, et al. Unanticipated vesicoureteral reflux: a possible sequela of long-term thiotepa instillations to the bladder. J Urol 1982;127:245–6.

23. Treible DP, Skinner D, Kasimain D, et al. Intractable bladder hemorrhage requiring cystectomy after use of intravesical thiotepa. Urology 1987;30:568–70.

24. Homonnai TZ, Paz G, Servadio C. Sterilisation following instillation of thiotepa into the urinary bladder. Br J Urol 1982;54:60.

25. Choe JM, Kirkemo AK, Sirls LT. Intravesical thiotepa-induced eosinophilic cystitis. Urology 1995;46:729–31.

26. Paroni R, Arcelloni C, De Vecchi E, et al. Plasma mitomycin C concentrations determined by HPLC coupled to solid-phase extraction. Clin Chem 1997;43:615–8.

27. Xu BH, Gupta V, Singh SV. Mechanism of differential sensitivity of human bladder cancer cells to mitomycin C and its analogue. Br J Cancer 1994;69:242–6.

28. Bleicher RJ, Xia H, Zaren HA, Singh SV. Biochemical mechanism of cross-resistance to paclitaxel in a mitomycin c-resistant human bladder cancer cell line. Cancer Lett 2000;150:129–35.

29. Badalament RA, Farah RN. Treatment of superficial bladder cancer with intravesical chemotherapy. Semin Surg Oncol 1997;13:335–41.

30. Wajsman Z, Dhafir RA, Pfeffer M, et al. Studies of mitomycin C absorption after intravesical treatment of superficial bladder tumors. J Urol 1984;132:30–3.

31. Tolley DA, Parmar MK, Grigor KM, et al. The effect of intravesical mitomycin C on recurrence of newly diagnosed superficial bladder cancer: a further report with 7 years of follow up. J Urol 1996;155:1233–8.

32. Solsona E, Iborra I, Ricos JV, et al. Effectiveness of a single immediate mitomycin C instillation in patients with low risk superficial bladder cancer: short and long-term follow-up. J Urol 1999;161:1120–3.

33. Witjes JA, v d Meijden AP, Sylvester LC, et al. Long-term follow-up of an EORTC randomized prospective trial comparing intravesical bacille Calmette-Guerin-RIVM and mitomycin C in superficial bladder cancer. EORTC GU Group and the Dutch South East Cooperative Urological Group. European Organisation for Research and Treatment of Cancer Genito-Urinary Tract Cancer Collaborative Group. Urology 1998;52:403–10.

34. Bouffioux C, Kurth KH, Bono A, et al. Intravesical adjuvant chemotherapy for superficial transitional cell bladder carcinoma: results of 2 European Organization for Research and Treatment of Cancer randomized trials with mitomycin C and doxorubicin comparing early versus delayed

instillations and short-term versus long-term treatment. European Organization for Research and Treatment of Cancer Genitourinary Group. J Urol 1995;153:934–41.

35. Witjes JA, Caris CT, Mungan NA, et al. Results of a randomized phase III trial of sequential intravesical therapy with mitomycin C and bacillus Calmette-Guerin versus mitomycin C alone in patients with superficial bladder cancer. J Urol 1998;160:1668–71; discussion 1671–2.

36. Lundholm C, Norlen BJ, Ekman P, et al. A randomized prospective study comparing long-term intravesical instillations of mitomycin C and bacillus Calmette-Guerin in patients with superficial bladder carcinoma. J Urol 1996;156:372–6.

37. Huben RP. Intravesical chemotherapy versus immunotherapy for superficial bladder cancer. Semin Urol Oncol 1996; 14:17–22.

38. Smith JA Jr, Labasky RF, Cockett AT, et al. Bladder cancer clinical guidelines panel summary report on the management of nonmuscle invasive bladder cancer (stages Ta, T1 and TIS). The American Urological Association. J Urol 1999;162:1697–701.

39. Traynelis CL, Lamm DL. Current status of intravesical therapy for bladder cancer. In: Rous SN, editor. Urology Annual. Vol 8. New York: WW Norton and Company; 1994. p. 56–62.

40. Minervini R, Felipetto R, Vigano L, et al. Recurrences and progression of superficial bladder cancer following long-term intravesical prophylactic therapy with mitomycin C: 48-month follow-up. Urol Int 1996;56:234–7.

41. Huland H, Otto U, Droese M, Kloppel G. Long-term mitomycin C instillation after transurethral resection of superficial bladder carcinoma: influence on recurrence, progression and survival. J Urol 1984;132:27–9.

42. Tolley DA, Hargreave TB, Smith PH, et al. Effect of intravesical mitomycin C on recurrence of newly diagnosed superficial bladder cancer: interim report from the Medical Research Council Subgroup on Superficial Bladder Cancer (Urological Cancer Working Party). Br Med J (Clin Res Ed) 1988;296:1759–61.

43. Akaza H, Koiso K, Kotake T, et al. Long-term results of intravesical chemoprophylaxis of superficial bladder cancer: experience of the Japanese Urological Cancer Research Group for Adriamycin. Cancer Chemother Pharmacol 1992; 30 Suppl:S15–20.

44. Nissenkorn I, Herrod H, Soloway MS. Side effects associated with intravesical mitomycin. J Urol 1981;126:596–7.

45. Issell BF, Prout GR Jr, Soloway MS, et al. Mitomycin C intravesical therapy in noninvasive bladder cancer after failure on thiotepa. Cancer 1984;53:1025–8.

46. DeFuria MD, Bracken RB, Johnson DE, et al. Phase I-II study of mitomycin C topical therapy for low-grade, low stage transitional cell carcinoma of the bladder: an interim report. Cancer Treat Rep 1980;64:225–30.

47. Colver GB, Inglis JA, McVittie E, et al. Dermatitis due to intravesical mitomycin C: a delayed-type hypersensitivity reaction? Br J Dermatol 1990;122:217–24.

48. Brady JD, Assimos DG, Jordan GH. Urethral slough: a rare and previously unreported complication of intravesical mitomycin. J Urol 2000;164:1305.

49. Neulander EZ, Lismer L, Kaneti J. Necrosis of the glans

penis: a rare complication of intravesical therapy with mitomycin c. J Urol 2000;164:1306.

50. Baker WC, Russo MA, deVere White RW. Severe bladder contracture in patient receiving intravesical mitomycin C for superficial bladder cancer. Urology 1987;30:357–8.

51. Farha AJ, Krauss DJ. Renal failure after intravesical mitomycin C. Urology 1989;34:216–7.

52. Zein TA, Friedberg N, Kim H. Bone marrow suppression after intravesical mitomycin C treatment. J Urol 1986; 136:459–60.

53. Alter AJ, Malek GH. Bladder wall calcification after topical mitomycin C. J Urol 1987;138:1239–40.

54. Wass AR, Lawson TR, Urwin GH. Bilateral ureteric strictures after intravesical mitomycin C. Br J Urol 1993; 72:661–2.

55. Inglis JA, Tolley DA, Grigor KM. Allergy to mitomycin C complicating topical administration for urothelial cancer. Br J Urol 1987;59:547–9.

56. Carter SK. Adriamycin—a review. J Natl Cancer Inst 1975; 55:1265–74.

57. Jauhiainen K, Eksborg S, Kangas L, et al. The absorption of doxorubicin and mitomycin C in perioperative instillation. An experimental and clinical study. Eur Urol 1985; 11:269–72.

58. Lundbeck F, Mogensen P, Jeppesen N. Intravesical therapy of noninvasive bladder tumors (stage Ta) with doxorubicin and urokinase. J Urol 1983;130:1087–9.

59. Witjes WP, Witjes JA, Oosterhof GO, Debruyne MJ. Update on the Dutch Cooperative Trial: mitomycin versus bacillus Calmette-Guerin-Tice versus bacillus Calmette-Guerin RIVM in the treatment of patients with pTA-pT1 papillary carcinoma and carcinoma in situ of the urinary bladder. Dutch South East Cooperative Urological Group. Semin Urol Oncol 1996;14:10–6.

60. Highley MS, van Oosterom AT, Maes RA, De Bruijn EA. Intravesical drug delivery. Pharmacokinetic and clinical considerations. Clin Pharmacokinet 1999;37:59–73.

61. Kamat AM, DeHaven JI, Lamm DL. Quinolone antibiotics: a potential adjunct to intravesical chemotherapy for bladder cancer. Urology 1999;54:56–61.

62. Tsushima T, Ohmori H, Ohi Y, et al. Intravesical instillation chemotherapy of Adriamycin with or without verapamil for the treatment of superficial bladder cancer: the final results of a collaborative randomized trial. Cancer Chemother Pharmacol 1994;35 Suppl:S69–75.

63. Flamm J. Long-term versus short-term doxorubicin hydrochloride instillation after transurethral resection of superficial bladder cancer. Eur Urol 1990;17:119–24.

64. Bouffioux C, van der Meijden A, Kurth KH, et al. Objective response of superficial bladder tumors to intravesical treatment (including review of response of marker lesions). Prog Clin Biol Res 1992;378:29–42.

65. Wientjes JA, Debruyne FM. Intravesical chemotherapy. In: Volgelzang N, Scardino P, Shipley W, Coffey D, editors. Comprehensive textbook of genitourinary oncology. Vol. 2nd ed. Philadelphia, PA: Lippincott, Williams & Wilkins; 2000. p. 394–405.

66. Lamm DL, Blumenstein BA, Crawford ED, et al. A randomized trial of intravesical doxorubicin and immunotherapy with bacille Calmette-Guerin for transitional-cell carcinoma of the bladder. N Engl J Med 1991;325:1205–9.

67. Ali-el-Dein B, el-Baz M, Aly AN, et al. Intravesical epirubicin versus doxorubicin for superficial bladder tumors (stages pTa and pT1): a randomized prospective study. J Urol 1997;158:68–73; discussion 73–4.

68. Ryoji O, Toma H, Nakazawa H, et al. A phase II study of prophylactic intravesical chemotherapy with epirubicin in the treatment of superficial bladder cancer. Tokyo Women's Medical College Bladder Cancer Collaborating Group. Cancer Chemother Pharmacol 1994;35 Suppl:S60–4.

69. Okamura K, Murase T, Obata K, et al. A randomized trial of early intravesical instillation of epirubicin in superficial bladder cancer. The Nagoya University Urological Oncology Group. Cancer Chemother Pharmacol 1994;35 Suppl:S31–5.

70. Masters JR, Popert RJ, Thompson PM, et al. Intravesical chemotherapy with epirubicin: a dose response study. J Urol 1999;161:1490–3.

71. Oosterlinck W, Kurth K, Schroder FH, et al. A prospective European Organization for Research and Treatment of Cancer Genitourinary group randomized trial comparing transurethral resection followed by a single intravesical instillation of epirubicin or water in single Ta, T1 papillary carcinoma of the bladder. J Urol 1993;149:749–52.

72. Melekos MD, Chionis HS, Paranychianakis GS, Dauaher HH. Intravesical 4'-epidoxorubicin (epirubicin) versus bacillus Calmette-Guerin. A controlled prospective study on the prophylaxis of superficial bladder cancer. Cancer 1993;72:1749–55.

73. Matsumura Y, Tsushima T, Ozaki Y, et al. Intravesical chemotherapy with 4'-epiAdriamycin in patients with superficial bladder tumors. Cancer Chemother Pharmacol 1986;16:176–7.

74. Burk K, Kurth KH, Newling D. Epirubicin in treatment and recurrence prophylaxis of patients with superficial bladder cancer. Prog Clin Biol Res 1989;303:423–34.

75. Eto H, Oka Y, Ueno K, et al. Comparison of the prophylactic usefulness of epirubicin and doxorubicin in the treatment of superficial bladder cancer by intravesical instillation: a multicenter randomized trial. Kobe University Urological Oncology Group. Cancer Chemother Pharmacol 1994;35 Suppl:S46–51.

76. Whelan P, Cumming JA, Garvie WH, et al. Multi-centre phase II study of low dose intravesical epirubicin in the treatment of superficial bladder cancer. Yorkshire and Scottish Urological Cancer Research Groups. Br J Urol 1991;67:600–2.

77. Marchetti A, Wang L, Magar R, et al. Management of patients with bacilli Calmette-Guerin-refractory carcinoma in situ of the urinary bladder: cost implications of a clinical trial for valrubicin. Clin Ther 2000;22:422–38.

78. Steinberg G, Bahnson R, Brosman S, et al. Efficacy and safety of valrubicin for the treatment of bacillus Calmette-Guerin refractory carcinoma in situ of the bladder. The Valrubicin Study Group. J Urol 2000;163:761–7.

79. Robinson MR, Shelty MB, Richards B, et al. Intravesical Epodyl in the management of bladder tumours: combined experience of the Yorkshire Urological Cancer Research Group. J Urol 1997;118:972–3.

80. Bouffioux C, Denis L, Oosterlinck W, et al. Adjuvant chemotherapy of recurrent superficial transitional cell

carcinoma: results of an European Organization for Research on Treatment of Cancer randomized trial comparing intravesical instillations of thiotepa, doxorubicin, and cisplatin. J Urol 1992;148:297–301.

81. Stewart DJ, Green R, Futter N, et al. Phase I and pharmacology study of intravesical mitoxantrone for recurrent superficial bladder tumors. J Urol 1990;143:714–6.

82. Huncharek M, McGarry R, Kupelnick B. Impact of intravesical chemotherapy on recurrence rate of recurrent superficial transitional cell carcinoma of the bladder: results of a meta-analysis. Anticancer Res 2001;21:765–9.

83. Lamm DL, Riggs DR, Traynelis CL, et al. Apparent failure of current intravesical chemotherapy prophylaxis to influence the long-term course of superficial transitional cell carcinoma of the bladder. J Urol 1995;153:1444.

84. Baselli EC, Greenberg RE. Intravesical therapy for superficial bladder cancer. Oncology (Hunting) 2000;14:719–29; discussion 729–31, 734, 737.

85. El-Gabry EA, Strup SE, Gomella LG. Superficial bladder cancer current treatment modalities and future directions, Part II. AUA Updates 2000;19:154–160.

86. Burnand KG, Boyd PJ, Mayo ME, et al. Single dose intravesical thiotepa as an adjuvant to cystodiathermy in the treatment of transitional cell bladder carcinoma. Br J Urol 1976;48:55–9.

87. Byar D, Blackard C. Comparisons of placebo, pyridoxine, and topical thiotepa in preventing recurrence of stage I bladder cancer. Urology 1977;10:556–61.

88. Prout GR Jr, Koontz WW Jr, Coombs LJ, et al. Long-term fate of 90 patients with superficial bladder cancer randomly assigned to receive or not to receive thiotepa. J Urol 1983;130:677–80.

89. The effect of intravesical thiotepa on the recurrence rate of newly diagnosed superficial bladder cancer. An MRC Study. MRC Working Party on Urological Cancer. Br J Urol 1985;57:680–5.

90. Niijima T, Koiso K, Akaza H. Randomized clinical trial on chemoprophylaxis of recurrence in cases of superficial bladder cancer. Cancer Chemother Pharmacol 1983;11 Suppl:S79–82.

91. Kim HH, Lee C. Intravesical mitomycin C instillation as a prophylactic treatment of superficial bladder tumor. J Urol 1989;141:1337–9; discussion 1339–40.

92. Rubben H. Superficial bladder cancer. In: Debruyne F, Denis L, Van Der Meijden APM, editors. NY: Alan R. Liss; 1989. p. 145–50.

93. Krege S, Giani G, Meyer R, et al. A randomized multicenter trial of adjuvant therapy in superficial bladder cancer: transurethral resection only versus transurethral resection plus mitomycin C versus transurethral resection plus bacillus Calmette-Guerin. Participating clinics. J Urol 1996;156:962–6.

94. Akaza H, Isaka S, Koiso K, et al. Comparative analysis of short-term and long-term prophylactic intravesical chemotherapy of superficial bladder cancer. Prospective, randomized, controlled studies of the Japanese Urological Cancer Research Group. Cancer Chemother Pharmacol 1987;20:S91–6.

95. Kurth K, Tunn U, Ay R, et al. Adjuvant chemotherapy for superficial transitional cell bladder carcinoma: long-term results of a European Organization for Research and Treatment of Cancer randomized trial comparing doxorubicin, ethoglucid and transurethral resection alone. J Urol 1997;158:378–84.

12

Intravesical Bacille Calmette-Guérin in the Treatment and Prophylaxis of Urothelial Bladder Cancer

MICHAEL A. O'DONNELL, MD
JENNIFER A. BURNS, MD

INTRODUCTION

Formulating a Disease-Risk Analysis

Following transurethral ablative surgery for superficial bladder cancer, there are two major unfavorable outcomes that one wishes to avoid. The cancer may recur/persist or it may progress to invasive disease. Although recurrence and persistence are quite bothersome to the patient, ultimately, only progression is life threatening. Thus, before any adjuvant therapy can be decided on, an independent risk assessment for tumor recurrence and progression must be determined to decide if it is even worthwhile to begin additional therapy. This decision is guided by an appreciation of the risk factors associated with the presenting tumor histology (grade, stage, architecture, field effects, size, multifocality), previous tumor history (recurrence rate/year, cumulative years of tumor, recurrence types, prior therapy), and, most recently, biochemical and/or genetic markers, many of which are not yet used in routine clinical practice (eg, ploidy, Ki-67/ MIB-1, *P53*, retinoblastoma, *P21*, E-cadherin). To date, there is no algorithm that can accurately define the risk for any single individual, but the confluence of these multiple parameters can help guide the appropriateness and aggressiveness of therapy. From a large (> 1,500) cohort of primary (first time) tumors in the Spanish tumor registry, the most predictive variables in order of importance (by odds ratio) for recurrence were multiplicity (2.0), size > 3 cm (1.65), and coincident carcinoma in situ (CIS; 1.6).[1] For progression, the predictive variables were grade 3 (19.9), coincident CIS (2.1), multiplicity (1.9), and size > 3 cm (1.7). Disease-specific mortality was most heavily influenced by grade 3 (14) and CIS (3.0).

Idealized Goals of Intravesical Therapy

Ideally, intravesical therapy should safely eradicate residual bladder cancer and prevent tumor recurrence, thus averting the consequences of muscle invasion and metastasis. There is a wide array of topical chemotherapeutic and immunotherapeutic drugs; however, the perfect agent is not yet available. Although intravesical chemotherapy results in reasonable short-term cancer response rates, the durable net benefit for tumor recurrence is marginal.[2,3] Furthermore, multiple well-designed intravesical chemotherapy studies have not shown a favorable alteration in tumor progression rate or survival.[4] The immunotherapeutic agent bacille Calmette-Guérin (BCG) comes closest to meeting the ideal therapy with high early and durable complete response (CR) rates and a decrease in disease progression. However, conclusive evidence of a survival advantage with BCG has not yet been demonstrated. Additionally, the toxicity associated with BCG is significant enough to impact patient selection. Ultimately, the physician must balance the risk of the disease and perceived benefit of the contemplated adjuvant therapy with the toxicity, expense, and inconvenience of intravesical therapy.

HISTORY OF BCG

In response to the successful development and application of bacterial and antiviral vaccines such as vaccinia for smallpox at the turn of the nineteenth century, coworkers Albert Calmette and Camille Guérin in 1921 at the Pasteur Institute in France succeeded in attenuating the cow tuberculosis bacillus *Mycobacterium bovis*.[5] Despite the loss of much of its virulence, this bacillus retained enough strong antigenicity to become an effective vaccine for the prevention of human tuberculosis.[6] Seed lots from the Pasteur Institute form the basis for most of the clinical substrains of BCG in use today, but genetic drift and differences in culture conditions have resulted in subtle differences between substrains. The clinical significance of these differences is not entirely clear.[7] What is known is that an estimated 2.5 billion people have now been vaccinated with BCG, primarily in Asia, Europe, South America, and the Pacific Rim. The United States and Canada have consciously opted against a program of mass vaccination.

The idea that BCG might have potential as a therapeutic agent against cancer probably emerged out of the combined observations by Coley, who demonstrated that bacterial products had anticancer activity, as well as the report by Pearl, which stated that patients with a history of tuberculosis had lower cancer rates.[8,9] However, it was not until 1969, when Mathe and Hadsiev showed a significant antitumor effect of BCG in acute leukemia and bronchial carcinoma, that its potential clinical usefulness began to be realized.[10,11] The following year, Morton and colleagues reported good results with direct injection of BCG into melanoma nodules.[12] Then Coe and Feldman explored the potential for BCG to be used in the treatment of bladder cancer.[13] They showed that the bladder was an immunocompetent organ responsive to topical BCG. Zbar and colleagues then observed that close contact between BCG and a limited tumor volume in immunocompetent animals was required for

efficacy.[14] In 1976, Morales and colleagues reported on the first successful treatment in seven of nine patients with recurrent superficial stage Ta/T1 transitional cell carcinoma (TCC) using 6 weeks of sequential intravesical BCG plus simultaneous intradermal inoculation.[15] It is noteworthy to realize, however, that the choice of dose, interval, dwell time, and number of treatments was arbitrary without the benefit of phase I or II studies. In the early 1980s, both the Southwest Oncology Group (SWOG) and Memorial Sloan-Kettering Cancer Center verified the efficacy of the Morales and colleagues regimen against TCC, which led to the clinical acceptance of this treatment scheme during the ensuing two decades.[16,17] The only unquestioned modification was the elimination of coincident intradermal injection.[18–21]

BASIC SCIENCE OF BCG

BCG Is a Pleiotropic Immune Stimulator Oriented toward Cellular Immunity

Mycobacteria have long been known to be potent stimulators of the immune response. BCG has been shown to activate macrophages, natural killer (NK) cells, B cells, and various T cells (CD4+, CD8+ and γδ-T cells) in vitro and in vivo.[22–31] T helper type 1 (Th1) cells, which are restrictive for cell-mediated immunity, appear to be more accessible to BCG than Th2 cells that are restrictive for humoral/allergic immunity.[32,33] This is not surprising because BCG is an obligate intracellular pathogen and can be effectively cleared only by a cell-mediated immune process similar to that occurring during viral infection. Analysis of potent immune mediators, cytokines, produced from murine splenocyte cultures, human peripheral blood mononuclear cell (PBMC) cultures, and human urine during BCG treatment has demonstrated that BCG can stimulate the expression of interleukins (IL) -1, -2, -4, -6, -8, -10, -12, -15, and -18, as well as tumor necrosis factor (TNF)-α, granulocyte-macrophage colony-stimulating factor, interferon (IFN)-inducible protein 10 (IP)-10, and IFN-γ.[34–51] Of these, IFN-γ appears to be a critical mediator of antimycobacterial immunity as both mice and humans with defective IFN-γ production or IFN-γ receptors are susceptible to overwhelming mycobacterial infection.[52,53] Furthermore, the state of Th1/Th2 balance, although not only directly responsible for effective pathogen elimination, may actually determine important aspects of the disease itself.[33]

BCG Antitumor Therapy Appears to Depend on a Cell-Mediated Th1 Immune Response

Although the exact mechanism of BCG action in bladder cancer remains incompletely understood, it appears to rely on cell-mediated immunity. Within 4 to 6 hours of a typical late-induction cycle BCG instillation, there is massive pyuria containing neutrophils and mononuclear cells, often appreciated by patients as passage of cloudy urine or "tissue" representing white blood cell "clots."[24,27,54,55] Parallel with this cellular exudate, Th1 cytokines (IL-2, IFN-γ, and TNF-α) appear in the patient's urine at the time when bladder cancer cytology reverts from malignant to nonmalignant.[56,57] Typical delayed-type hypersensitivity response in the bladder can be histologically observed after clinical BCG instillation, showing a mononuclear cell infiltration into the superficial layers of the bladder associated with edema and granuloma formation.[24,35,54,58–60] Immunohistologically, the major types of infiltration cells can be identified to be CD4+ (helper) and CD8+ (cytotoxic) T cells, macrophages, and a few natural killer (NK) cells.[24,25,60–64] A phenomenon of elevated expression of major histocompatibility complex (MHC) class I and II antigens on the urothelium is also apparent, which persists for 3 to 6 months after BCG treatment.[25,64,65] Augmented peripheral blood lymphocyte responses to BCG persist for a similar period of time before eventually waning.[66]

The relationship between measured cytokines and tumor responses in patients receiving BCG remains incompletely defined but suggests a benefit to Th1 over Th2 orientation. Patients with high urinary IL-2 expression are more likely to have durable bladder cancer responses.[34,43,67–71] Likewise, elevations of serum IL-2 are associated with a favorable clinical outcome.[72] In contrast, bladder cancer patients whose PBMCs during active BCG therapy show a depressed ability to make IL-2 messenger

ribonucleic acid (mRNA) have much lower clinical cancer responses.[73] IL-2 production is strongly linked to IFN-γ production in vitro and in vivo, and both tend to rise in parallel in the urine during initial induction therapy.[36,42,43,74] The clinical utility of urinary IFN-γ levels, however, has been controversial, possibly owing to the inherent instability of this molecule in acidic urine, but generally higher levels have been associated with a better prognosis.[36,38,50,69,70,75] The early expression of IL-8 and IL-18 has also correlated with a better clinical response, possibly reflecting the appropriate initiation of a nonspecific inflammatory component, without which maturation into a more directed Th1 response is not possible.[51] On the other hand, patients with elevations in serum antibody to BCG or elevated urinary IL-6, typical of Th2 immune responses, are less likely to be cured of their bladder cancer by BCG.[76,77] Moreover, the potent Th1-suppressing cytokine IL-10 is readily assayable in the urine of patients after BCG treatment, typically rising after the peak of IFN-γ and IL-2, suggesting that it may play a role in shutting down the Th1 response.[70,78] A genetic basis for differential responses to mycobacteria in humans has been linked to polymorphisms in the natural resistance–associated macrophage protein 1 gene.[79] Similarly, many polymorphisms in cytokine genes or receptors, including IFN-γ, have been identified.[80] Their role in the anticancer activity to BCG remains largely unexplored.

Although BCG induces multiple cytokines, direct antitumor effects have been linked primarily to IFN-γ and TNF-α. Both inhibit bladder tumor proliferation as well as up-regulate the expression of MHC class I and II antigens and adhesion molecules on bladder cancer cells.[25,81–86] This change in surface phenotype increases the likelihood that tumor cells will be recognized by CD4+ T cells or CD8+ cytotoxic T lymphocytes (CTLs).[2,87–90] TNF-α and IFN-γ also induce Fas receptor (a homologue to the TNF receptor) on bladder cancer cells, providing a mechanism for apoptotic destruction by Fas ligand+-activated T cells and NK cells that are not MHC restricted but are usually associated with a Th1 response.[91–93] BCG-activated killer (BAK) cells, a unique subpopulation of IFN-γ-dependent killer cells, are also expanded by BCG stimulation and exhibit cytotoxicity against

NK-resistant bladder cancer cells via a perforin mechanism.[94-96] It has even been found that BCG induces a hostile environment for endothelial cell proliferation through its induction of IFN-γ, TNF-α, and the antiangiogenic chemokine IP-10.[48,97]

Studies on animal bladder tumor models have further reinforced the requirement of Th1 cells for BCG anticancer efficacy. In these models, the ability to either prevent or retard the outgrowth of tumor with BCG has been shown to be T cell dependent.[98,99] Similarly, immunocompetent mice lose the capacity to reject bladder tumors after BCG treatment if they are first depleted in vivo of either CD4+ or CD8+ T cells.[53] IFN-γ and IL-2 mRNA are up-regulated in the bladder tissue of mice treated with intravesical BCG[100] and potentiated in genetically altered IL-10 knockout mice, suggesting that IL-10 is a functional Th1 inhibitor.[101-103] The role of NK cells has been more difficult to establish. Although they are clearly activated by BCG, initially, it was reported that they were not necessary for BCG antitumor activity in the mouse bladder (MB)T2 mouse model.[98] However, in the MB49 orthotopic mouse model, they were found to be essential.[104] The most plausible explanation is that as one of the first leukocyte subsets in the innate immune system to respond to BCG, depending on the model, NK cells may play a key role in initiating a cytokine cascade that leads to the production of the global "type 1" cytokine response, which can then be reinforced by specific T-cell subsets. Depending on their degree of activation, these NK cells may also be effective participants in the cytotoxic process (Figure 12-1).

Step 1: Invasion

BCG must infect the bladder by attachment and internalization. Binding of BCG to the urothelium is mediated via fibronectin.[105] Once attached, BCG is internalized into both malignant and normal urothelial cells via integrin receptors, resulting by itself in decreased proliferation, reduced telomerase expression, increased surface protein expression, and cytokine secretion.[86,91,106-108] This process is impaired in nonviable BCG preparations, possibly explaining the requirement for live BCG for clinical effi-

cacy. Live BCG persists, likely intracellularly, for weeks to months.[109]

Step 2: Danger Signal Generated

According to a new paradigm, immune responses require an inciting, threatening, or damaging event that acts as a signal for immune cell recruitment and activation.[110] With regard to BCG, there is evidence that the early production of chemokines such as IL-8 and IP-10 by urothelial cells may be among the first signals to recruit submucosal monocytic and T-cell infiltration.[86,111] Other chemokines, such as macrophage inhibitory protein-1 (MIP-1), monocyte chemotactic protein-1 (MCP-1), and regulated on activation normal T expressed and secreted (RANTES), may also be involved.[112]

Step 3: Recruitment of Leukocytes into the Bladder

The net effect of chemokine signals is an escalating increase in monocytic and granulocytic leukocytes into the bladder with each successive weekly BCG instillation. Acutely, neutrophils are recruited, but, eventually, T cells predominate within the submucosa and may even form granulomas.[24-28,54,56,58]

Step 4: Activation of Recruited Leukocytes

It is felt that the resident CD1a+ dendritic cells of the bladder, a monocyte macrophage that acts as an antigen-presenting cell (APC), are likely crucial in T-cell activation.[113] These APCs can display BCG antigens on surface MHC I and II molecules while providing necessary costimulatory signals and important cytokine coactivators such as IL-12, IL-15, IL-18, and TNF-α.[114,115] To some extent, urothelial cells themselves may even act as professional APCs after BCG exposure.[85-87,108] IFN-γ can potentiate APC activity, which sets off a Th1 cascade, which elaborates IL-2, which synergizes with IL-12 and TNF-α to make more IFN-γ, which activates APCs to make more IL-12, thus continuing this self-stimulating cycle. This, in part, is responsible for the escalation of symptoms with sequential weekly BCG therapy. Simultaneous to this cycle is the potential for NK

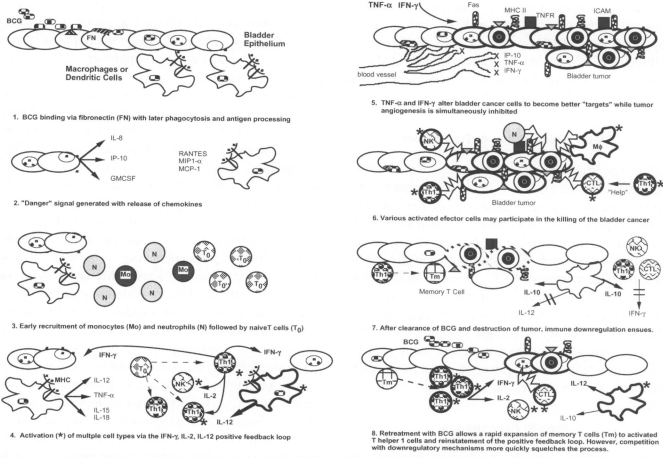

Figure 12–1. Mechanism of action for bacille Calmette-Guérin (BCG). CTL = cytotoxic T lymphocyte; GM-CSF = granulocyte-macrophage colony-stimulating factor; ICAM = intercellular adhesion molecule; IFN = interferon; IL = interleukin; IP = inducible protein; MHC = major histocompatibility complex; MIP = macrophage inhibatory protein; NK = natural killer; RANTES = regulated on activation normal T expressed and secreted; Th = T helper; TNF = tumor necrosis factor; TNF-R = TNF-receptor.

and T-cell activation by IL-2 and IL-12, Fas ligand induction by CD4+ and CD8+ cells by BCG antigens with T-cell receptors, BAK cell induction, and nonspecific activation of macrophages and neutrophils by IFN-γ and TNF-α.

Step 5: Alteration of Local Cancer Phenotype by the Cytokine Milieu to Make Better Targets for Immune Elimination

Bioactive cytokines released into the urine that bathe the tumor contribute substantially to the prolonged elevation of MHC I and II, intracellular adhesion molecules (ICAMs), and apoptotic receptors that are seen on the urothelium after BCG therapy. Additionally, it is known that IFN-γ, TNF-α, and IP-10 directly inhibit bladder cancer proliferation and/or

angiogenesis.[48] In theory, these changes should make the tumor a better target for immune recognition and elimination.

Step 6: Effector Cell Killing of Malignant Cells

This is the least understood process, and, in fact, the actual effector cell(s) responsible for tumor killing is unknown. Although there is strong evidence for a T-cell–dependent process, there is no direct evidence for generation of classic tumor-specific CTLs that show memory and an ability to seek out and destroy similar tumor cells elsewhere in the body. Possible effector mechanisms include the following: (1) direct killing of BCG-infected bladder cancer cells by BCG-specific CTLs; (2) direct killing by MHC nonrestricted NK cells, $\gamma\delta$- T cells, or the BAK cell subset; (3) direct killing by tumoricidal macrophages; (4) bystander killing of Fas+ bladder cancer by Fas ligand+ BCG-specific T cells; or (5) direct killing of ICAM-1+ bladder cancer by activated neutrophils expressing the cognate leukocyte function antigen-1 (LFA-1) receptor.[116]

Step 7: Restoration or Repression

After the initial immune effect, there are at least two different outcomes that may occur within the urothelium. One possibility is clearance of the infection with dispersement/elimination of activated white blood cells and repopulation of the urothelium from a normal basal layer. A second outcome may occur if there is an excessive BCG infection. In this case, a self-protective down-modulatory state of unresponsiveness or anergy may occur that resembles the Th2 state in leprosy or anergic tuberculosis.[117] This anergic state can be demonstrated in many patients receiving "excessive" retreatment during BCG maintenance or reinduction.[42,70,118]

Step 8: Rechallenge

During maintenance or reinduction therapy, the entire immune process is accelerated, likely owing to reactivation and recruitment of resident and systemic memory T cells that specifically recall BCG and its antigens. Clinical responses in terms of symptoms and urinary Th1 cytokines are stronger and more rapid; however, the down-modulatory process is also more likely.[117,118]

CLINICAL SCIENCE OF BCG

Considerations in Interpreting Intravesical Therapy Trials

There are three specific therapeutic modalities in which BCG may be used: (1) prophylaxis after definitive resection of papillary bladder tumors (stages Ta and T1), (2) adjuvant therapy to eliminate nonresectable residual papillary transitional cell carcinoma (pTCC), and (3) primary therapy to eradicate CIS. Owing to its diffuse and macroscopically indistinct appearance, CIS is presumed to be unre-

sectable by surgery alone. Although many of the early reports on BCG efficacy grouped these categories together, differences in the state of the disease at study entry make direct comparisons difficult and potentially erroneous.[119]

To compare the literature, there must be a clear definition of terminology regarding outcomes. Thus, the term complete response (CR) is appropriate only when evaluating ablation of residual disease after transurethral resection (TUR) (pTCC and CIS). In contrast, recurrence rate (percentage of patients with any recurrence by a given time), recurrence index (number of recurrence episodes per 100 patient-months), and time to first recurrence are only meaningful in the prophylactic setting or after a CR has already been achieved. Kaplan-Meier analysis is often used in these different treatment groups to provide estimates of percent freedom from disease or percent disease-free survival over time. This is more accurate than reporting the "overall" or "simple" event rate that may be overly optimistic if there are a significant number of patients with short-term minimum follow-up. However, even though the Kaplan-Meier technique does compensate for dropouts (censoring) and differential time of follow-up, caution must also be exercised in interpreting projections well beyond the median follow-up where few numerical study subjects may exist.

Because all of these outcome determinations depend heavily on time, it is vital to know the degree of follow-up. Defining the start and end points can also be problematic. For prophylactic treatment, the appropriate start time is the time of definitive TUR, whereas the start time in the adjuvant or primary therapy setting may be assigned to the first evaluable point or to the midpoint between start of therapy and first evaluation. End points for failure may be similarly ambiguous: does one choose the time of documented failure, the last point of no evidence of disease, or some point between? Freedom from disease progression (≥ stage T2 or metastasis) and survival (preferably disease specific) are clinically meaningful end points for all treatment groups and may be appropriately compared. However, because these are relatively rare events, usually only very large studies, those with long range follow-up, or those with very high-risk subjects are able to provide this information. Recently, the concept of worsening free survival has emerged as a surrogate end point to reflect the clinical decision to definitively alter therapy even without clear pathologic evidence of disease progression.[120] Thus, time to cystectomy, radiation therapy, and/or systemic chemotherapy might all be counted as appropriate "worsening" events in addition to true disease progression.

Intravesical BCG for Prophylaxis after Transurethral Resection of Bladder

Multiple clinical trials directly comparing transurethral resection of bladder (TURB) alone to BCG plus TURB for tumor prophylaxis (ie, no CIS or obvious residual disease) have demonstrated a statistically significant benefit in the reduction of bladder cancer recurrence rate, ranging between 20 and 57% at median follow-ups of 2 to 7 years.[121–128] In aggregate, this amounts to an estimated net benefit of about 32% versus surgery alone, an amount over twice that reported for intravesical chemotherapy by Lamm and colleagues using a similar comparison technique.[4] Relative risk for recurrence was found to be reduced to 0.3 using the large Spanish primary bladder tumor registry[1] and 0.3 at 12 months in an even larger British meta-analysis.[129] Interestingly, the greatest clinical benefits appear to be derived by those patients with more recurrent or aggressive disease, including prior chemotherapy failures.[21,121,122] The median duration of disease freedom is 2 to 4 years, over twice that expected for surgery alone, along with a three- to fourfold reduction in recurrence index. Reduction in true disease progression has been more difficult to demonstrate in any single trial, although the Spanish registry showed a reduction in relative risk of progression to 0.3 with BCG therapy. Likewise, Solsona and colleagues reported a statistically significant reduction in progression rate of 12% for BCG versus 29% for chemotherapy in the composite analysis of two randomized high-risk adjuvant intravesical therapy trials.[130] An even larger meta-analysis involving 4,863 patients in 24 trials found a 27% reduction in the odds of progression for patients receiving BCG at a mean follow-up of 2.5 years (9.8% versus 13.8%).[131]

BCG for Residual Disease

One of the most demonstrable examples of intravesical BCG's anticancer activity is its ability to ablate existing bladder tumors either following incomplete TURB (residual tumor) or in place of TURB as primary therapy.[132–141] Although the ablative effect of one course of BCG on residual papillary tumors varies between 15 and 70%, a significant and consistent total CR rate of approximately 60% is found if at least one additional course of therapy is included. By comparison, similar intravesical chemotherapy trials have reported CR rates for residual disease of between 30 and 50%.[142] Those BCG studies providing 1- to 3-year follow-up show only a marginal dropoff over time, but this is difficult to interpret given the tendency to institute various regimens of maintenance therapy. Results from these trials also suggest that it is prudent to (1) perform debulking TURB whenever possible, especially if tumor burden exceeds 3 cm; (2) institute therapy soon after TURB (within 3 weeks); and (3) use caution when treating residual T1 grade 2 to 3 disease because these tumors appear to be less responsive to BCG ablation alone and are often clinically understaged.[143]

BCG for CIS

With its high progression rate and inaccessibility to complete surgical resection, CIS represents the prototype disease for intravesical therapy. Numerous BCG therapy trials for CIS have been reported previously and demonstrate aggregate CR rates between 70 and 75% if up to two induction cycles are used.[144] In one study, the ultimate CR of CIS to BCG followed a delayed time course, whereby the 6-month CR was 20% above that of the 3-month CR even in the absence of additional therapy.[145] High CR rates have been reported with multiple different BCG strains worldwide and exceed those reported for chemotherapy trials, which range between 38% for thiotepa and 53% for mitomycin C.[146] These results make BCG the therapy of choice for primary CIS, secondary CIS, and concomitant CIS.[147] Over half of complete responders remain disease free over 5 years from the start of therapy, resulting in a substantial reduction in the need for alternative therapy, primarily cystectomy.[148–150]

Comparative Clinical Trials of BCG versus Chemotherapy

Most studies suggest that BCG is superior to chemotherapy for tumor prophylaxis after TURB for pTCC.[123,125,126,150–160] However, controversy remains regarding mitomycin C, with some trials favoring BCG and others showing no significant difference between BCG and mitomycin. Two independent Dutch trials suggest equivalence if not superiority for mitomycin over BCG for recurrent tumors in the absence of CIS.[157,158] The reason for this discrepancy is not entirely clear. Patient selection was more biased toward lower-risk patients in the Dutch studies, where the superiority of BCG may not be so clear. BCG was administered as a single 6-week induction course, a regimen now considered suboptimal. In a meta-analysis of contemporary BCG versus mitomycin C trials, BCG superiority was found when at least 1 year of maintenance BCG was provided (Boehle, personal communication 2003). Not at controversy was the observation that fewer and less severe side effects were found in the mitomycin treatment arms.

With regard to CIS, there are few comparative trials of BCG versus chemotherapy, but almost all strongly support BCG as first-line therapy. The SWOG study comparing BCG to doxorubicin (Adriamycin) showed initial CR rates of 70% versus 34%, respectively, that decreased to 45% and 18% by 5 years ($p < .001$).[150] Similarly, Malmstrom and colleagues reported 55% freedom from disease at 5 years for BCG versus 26% for mitomycin C ($p = .04$).[159]

Long-Term Results with BCG on Tumor Recurrence, Progression, and Survival

With several independent clinical BCG trials maturing since the early to mid 1980s, it is now possible to provide reliable 5-, 10-, and even 15-year data on the fate of patients treated with BCG.[139,148–150,157–159,161–165] It is clear that the greatest number of recurrences occur within the first year, often at the time of the first cystoscopic evaluation, despite various retreatment and maintenance schedules. Among medium- to high-risk patients with recurrent or aggressive disease, this amounts to an initial failure rate of 30 to 35%. By 5 years, roughly half of all of the originally treated patients have relapsed. Beyond 5 years, there appears to be continued dropouts, albeit at a slower rate, of less than 4% per year. The longest study to date, by Herr and colleagues, suggests that the recurrence rate levels off between 10 and 15 years.[166] Roughly one-third of their patients were free of disease, whereas half experienced disease progression. The updated results from the Washington University group show that, in general, the earlier the relapse, the more likely the disease is to be life threatening.[149] This is especially true for relapses within the first 3 to 6 months that are accompanied by positive cytology or stage/grade progression.[162] Indeed, such features portend an ominous prognosis with unrecognized muscle invasion, metastasis, and reduced survival.[166] This increased risk of progressive bladder cancer persists even up to 5 years from the onset of successful BCG therapy, whereas recurrences beyond 5 years tend to be more manageable, although, occasionally, these, too, can be significant.[149] For tumors with accompanying multifocal CIS, 20% of cases may have disease outside the bladder, such as the upper tracts and prostatic ducts.[167] These collective observations substantiate the need for close surveillance of both the upper and lower tracts during the first 5 to 10 years and a policy of treating aggressively any recurrences displaying high-grade features.

Whether BCG decreases tumor progression in the long term or merely delays the inevitable, failure cannot be determined with complete confidence from the studies to date. Small numbers, low intrinsic progression rates, and insufficient follow-up may be responsible. It is noteworthy that even in several of the aforementioned larger comparative BCG/TURB/chemotherapy trials, no absolute differences, let alone statistical differences, have been observed in progression to muscle-invasive disease. Where apparent improvements in progression have been reported, statistical significance was either not achieved[153,155,156] or follow-up was too short.[122] The SWOG study randomizing patients to either BCG, or to doxorubicin did not show a difference in progression or survival, but three times as many patients underwent cystectomy in the doxorubicin group, suggesting a practical benefit in reducing "disease worsening."[150] The strongest published evidence has come from the aforementioned study performed by Herr and colleagues in a randomized series of 86 patients with aggressive superficial bladder cancers, 57% of which had coincident CIS.[163] In this very high-risk group, BCG therapy delayed tumor progression and prolonged short-term survival. At 6 years, progression to muscle invasion/metastasis was significantly improved from 95% in the TURB controls to 53% in the BCG-treated patients. Cystectomy was performed in 42% of the control patients versus 26% of the BCG-treated patients at a median of 8 and 24 months, respectively. Survival was also superior—64% versus 84%, respectively. Unfortunately, these benefits were ultimately lost owing to later recurrence and/or progression occurring over the next 10 years of follow-up, often outside the bladder vault.[164,165] Two recent Spanish reports have emerged to support BCG as positively altering the natural history of TCC; however, neither conclusion was based on prospectively randomized studies but rather on large databases of pooled results.[1,130]

Role of BCG Maintenance Therapy

Many modern BCG treatment programs incorporate some form of time-limited continuous retreatment with BCG for patients in whom no demonstrable disease is present with the implicit assumption that this will help maintain a tumor-free status. This practice probably finds its origin from (1) the historical use of maintenance intravesical chemotherapy (incidentally not proven to be effective), (2) the recognized benefit of additional courses of BCG reinduction therapy, (3) the steady relapse rate of initial complete responders over time, and (4) the uncertainty in knowing whether all disease is eliminated or simply at a subclinical level of detection.[4,122,134,136,139,167] With many uncontrolled trials showing good overall results with this strategy, there has been little impetus for change. However, until recently, there has not been any clear proof that such a policy has any real clinical benefit.

Two early randomized controlled studies using either one dose of BCG every 3 months or one dose monthly for 2 years failed to demonstrate a statistical advantage to this approach.[168,169] In the former case, 42 evaluable patients split between maintenance and no maintenance had essentially identical Kaplan-Meier disease-free survival curves when followed over 2 years. In the latter case, 93 randomized patients had the same mean number of tumors per month, equivalent disease-free recurrence rates at 2 years, and equivalent progression rates. Furthermore, in both trials, additional local toxicity attributable to BCG was found. Studies from other countries have been equally disappointing. Tachibana and colleagues reported on 44 patients randomized to no maintenance, 12 monthly treatments, or ≥ 18 monthly treatments and did see favorable results in the maintenance groups, but statistical significance was not achieved.[152] Interestingly, Akaza could not demonstrate any advantage to 12 monthly maintenance treatments for patients achieving a complete ablative response to BCG, but a statistically significant difference of 37% at 1 year and 41% at 3 years was seen for patients having only a partial response requiring completion TURB.[141] Palou and colleagues, in a large, randomized Spanish trial, reported an 11% overall benefit to routine 6-week courses every 6 months for 2 years in patients with no evidence of disease 6 months after TUR and induction BCG, but this difference did not reach statistical significance in this underpowered trial.[170] The exclusion of early relapsers within 6 months might also have diminished the impact of additional therapy.

Recently, the results of the SWOG 8507 trial specifically intended to answer the maintenance question have been released, indicating that an alternative schedule is useful (Figure 12–2).[145] Using three weekly miniseries treatments administered at 3, 6, and 12 months, then biannually to 3 years, there was a statistically significant difference in favor of maintenance therapy over a 10-year follow-up. For 233 randomized patients with CIS, 84% ultimately achieved a CR with maintenance versus 68% without ($p = .004$), with durable benefits beyond 5 years. Patients not free of disease at the first 3-month evaluation appeared to benefit most, demonstrating that this schedule also possesses ablative activity. For 254 patients with papillary disease and complete resection at the time of randomization, 87% were disease free at 2 years in the

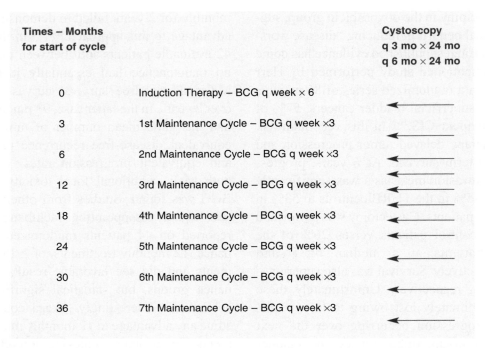

Times – Months for start of cycle		Cystoscopy q 3 mo × 24 mo q 6 mo × 24 mo
0	Induction Therapy – BCG q week × 6	←
3	1st Maintenance Cycle – BCG q week ×3	←
6	2nd Maintenance Cycle – BCG q week ×3	←
12	3rd Maintenance Cycle – BCG q week ×3	← ←
18	4th Maintenance Cycle – BCG q week ×3	← ←
24	5th Maintenance Cycle – BCG q week ×3	←
30	6th Maintenance Cycle – BCG q week ×3	←
36	7th Maintenance Cycle – BCG q week ×3	←

Figure 12–2. Southwest Oncology Group 8507 bacille Calmette-Guérin (BCG) maintenance plan.

maintenance arm compared with 57% without maintenance. At least a 20% differential persisted up to 5 years. This differential was gradually lost by 10 years, partly as a result of death from other causes that were not censored in this analysis. For combined CIS plus papillary groups, median recurrence-free survival was roughly doubled from 36 to 77 months, whereas worsening free survival was reduced by 6% even at the 10-year mark ($p = .04$). An overall 5% survival differential favoring maintenance therapy approached but did not reach statistical significance ($p = .08$). Not surprisingly, maintenance therapy did not come without a price. One-quarter of patients on maintenance experienced significant grade 3 toxicity and less than half completed more than three cycles, with only 16% completing all seven planned cycles. On the basis of these results, it has been argued that even more extended treatments should be given, perhaps indefinitely, to prevent the inexorable dropoff in response with time. Alternatively, the maintenance group as a whole benefited even without most patients completing a full 3 years of therapy, suggesting that maximum benefit may have been achieved earlier. These results have been reproduced in a smaller, nonrandomized study, with only 19% completing the entire mainte-

nance schedule.[171] Although the authors attempted to identify parameters that would guide improved tolerability of the regimen, no definitive parameters were found. At this time, one can say only that this schedule should be regarded as the new benchmark with which other maintenance schedules should be compared.

Treating the High-Risk Superficial Bladder Cancer Patient with BCG

The worst thing that can happen to a patient with bladder cancer is that he or she progresses to an unresectable stage during the time in which intravesical therapy or observation is under way. Patients at greatest risk of progression include those with stage T1 disease, any grade 3 disease, and multifocal CIS with or without associated pTCC. Grade 3 disease and CIS are the most important pretreatment variables for progression and disease-specific mortality, but other factors, such as multiplicity and tumor size > 3 cm, also influence progression.[1]

Are there patients with superficial bladder cancer for whom up-front cystectomy is the most appropriate treatment? Given the very aggressive nature of stage T1 grade 3 bladder cancer that progresses to muscle-invasive disease or metastatic disease at a rate of up to 50% in 3 to 5 years, it has been argued that this particular group may best be served by early cystectomy.[172–175] Although no large, randomized trials to immediate cystectomy versus transurethral resection of bladder tumor (TURBT) plus BCG have been undertaken, multiple retrospective and prospective studies with BCG therapy have indicated that over two-thirds of patients may achieve long-term progression-free survival with their bladders intact.[176–183] Furthermore, total disease-specific survival for such patients (including delayed cystectomy when appropriate) is as high as that reported with up-front cystectomy series. One key stipulation is that accurate staging be performed from the onset as several investigators have reported unrecognized residual T1 disease or even muscle-invasive disease in 30 to 40% of cases.[184,185] Unfortunately, there does not appear to be any clinical or genetic feature that predicts the likelihood of response to BCG.[166] Even positive p53 protein immunostaining, which has been associated with more aggressive disease, has not proven to be a reliable discriminator prior to the initiation of BCG.[186–189] Neither has T1 substaging been shown to be predictive of BCG success or failure.[190] A front-line trial of BCG immunotherapy thus appears justified in most cases of high-grade stage T1 bladder cancer without putting the patient at excess risk. However, up-front cystectomy still remains a viable option.

Patients with prostatic TCC represent a special risk category owing to the anatomy and logistics of therapy. Prostatic involvement may take four distinct forms: (1) superficial mucosal disease (often CIS), (2) ductal or acinar disease, (3) frank stromal invasion, or (4) contiguous growth from a deeply invasive primary tumor in the bladder (stage 4a).[191] Stromal and/or contiguous invasions are not amenable to local therapy, and most require radical cystoprostatectomy. However, mucosal and ductal/acinar disease will usually respond to BCG. In the former case, BCG may be applied even without formal transurethral prostatectomy (TURP) for prostatic CIS with the expectation of a 70 to 80% initial CR and local progression rate of 10 to 12% by 2 to 3 years.[192,193] For visible disease and/or suspected duc-

tal or acinar disease originating in the prostatic urethra, a two-part specimen TUR (complete mucosal resection followed by deeper stromal resection) may be necessary to eliminate and/or accurately stage the depth of disease. CR rates remain relatively high (63%) from two small series.[194–196] However, given the reduced 5-year survival of 42% noted in historical series of acinar/ductal TCC, vigorous follow-up is recommended.[197] The use of repeat induction and/or maintenance has been advocated but not formally studied in a comparative trial setting.[198]

BCG TOXICITY

The toxic effects of BCG may occur both locally and systemically. The vast majority of patients experience a self-limited cystitis associated with marked frequency, urgency, and dysuria that escalates with later treatments.[199–202] Symptoms usually begin 2 to 4 hours after instillation, peak between 6 and 10 hours, and resolve rapidly over the next 24 to 48 hours. Microscopic hematuria and pyuria are common, whereas occasional gross hematuria occurs in about one-third. Systemic manifestations of the inflammatory response follow a similar time course and include fevers, chills, a flu-like malaise, and occasional arthralgias. During reinduction or maintenance cycles, all of these symptoms tend to be more intense, occur sooner after the instillation, and reach the highest level by the second or third treatment. Most symptoms can be controlled with the appropriate use of acetaminophen, nonsteroidal anti-inflammatory drugs (NSAIDs), urinary analgesics, and antispasmodics (Table 12–1). The practice of routinely administering antibiotics with catheterization is to be discouraged. If clinically indicated for non-BCG infection, penicillins, cephalosporins, trimethoprim/sulfa, and nitrofurantoin are preferred, whereas fluoroquinolones, clarithromycin, and doxycycline are to be avoided because they are cidal to BCG and could affect efficacy.[203,204] In two controlled studies, short courses of the anti-BCG–specific antibiotic isoniazid (INH) were not shown to diminish the incidence of serious BCG infection, although a modest reduction of local side effects was seen in one.[160,205] However, neither study showed impairment in anticancer effi-

Table 12–1. RECOMMENDATIONS FOR TREATMENT OF BACILLE CALMETTE-GUÉRIN (BCG) TOXICITY

Sign/Symptom	Intensity and Description	Therapeutic Response
Cystitis: dysuria, urgency, frequency	0 = none 1 = mild, transient < 48 h 2 = moderate, < 5 d 3 = moderate-severe, > 5 d 4 = severe, persistent > 10 d	0, 1 = no treatment 2 = antispasmodics, urinary analgesics, and NSAIDs PRN 3 = delay and/or reduce BCG dose; check for UTI and treat 4 = cancel further BCG this cycle; start fluoroquinolone 3–6 wk; sandwich in 2-week oral steroid taper if symptoms continue > 2 wk
Hematuria (gross)	0 = none or microhematuria only 1 = mild, transient < 48 h 2 = moderate, < 5 d 3 = moderate-severe, > 5 d 4 = severe with clots or obstruction or > 10 d	0, 1 = no treatment 2 = push fluids 3 = delay and/or reduce BCG dose 4 = cancel further treatment this cycle
Fever and chills	0 = none 1 = mild < 100.5, < 24 h 2 = moderate < 101.5, < 24 h 3 = moderate-severe < 102.5, < 48 h 4 = severe > 102.5, > 48 h, rigors; relapsing nighttime fevers, or associated hypotension. Onset of symptoms often within 2 h of BCG treatment. Often associated with traumatic (bloody) catheterization.	0, 1 = no treatment or acetaminophen 2 = pretreatment with NSAIDs (eg, ibuprofen 600 mg) 3 = delay and/or reduce BCG dose; check for UTI and treat; consider truncating further treatment this cycle 4 = start fluoroquinolone pending U C and S; cancel all further BCG this cycle. For fevers > 24 h, start INH/rifampin. For suspected sepsis, hospitalize and add steroids.
Flu-like symptoms: myalgia, malaise, arthalgias, headache	0 = none 1 = mild 2 = moderate 3 = moderate-severe 4 = severe	0, 1 = no treatment 2 = NSAIDs 3 = delay and/or reduce BCG dose 4 = cancel further BCG this cycle
Other adverse events	0 = none 1 = mild 2 = moderate 3 = severe 4 = life threatening	0, 1 = no treatment 2 = delay and/or reduce BCG dose until condition clears 3 = cancel further BCG this cycle 4 = cancel all future BCG

INH = isoniazid; NSAIDs = nonsteroidal anti-inflammatory drugs; PRN = as needed; UC and S = urine culture and sensitivity; UTI = urinary tract infection. Antibiotic guidelines: (1) Routine use of prophylactic antibiotics is discouraged in the absence of documented bacterial cystitis except when the patient has a prosthetic device such as a heart valve or orthopedic hardware. When antibiotics are indicated, a nonquinolone antibiotic is recommended, preferably a penicillin, cephalosporin, sulfa, or nitrofurantoin. (2) Fluoroquinolone antibiotics are cidal to BCG and may be useful for treating early grade 3 toxicity. A minimum of 5 days is probably necessary. (3) INH (300 mg/day) plus rifampin (600 mg/day) should be considered for refractory grade 3 toxicity. Vitamin B6 (50 mg/day) should accompany prolonged treatment. Grade 4 toxicity may require a third drug such as ethambutal (1,200 mg/day). BCG is uniformly resistant to cycloserine and this agent should NOT be used. Early systemic steroids (eg, prednisone 40 mg/day) may be lifesaving in cases of frank BCG sepsis.

cacy. Studies are now under way in Europe to test the less toxic fluoroquinolones. Importantly, despite most patients experiencing some temporary toxicity from BCG therapy, two studies have shown that this does not adversely affect their overall long-term quality of life.[206,207]

Clinical signs of a more serious process, such as BCG intravasation into the bloodstream (BCGosis), include exaggerated manifestations of the above systemic effects, particularly if they occur early during the initial course of induction therapy, within 2 hours after BCG instillation, or in the setting of traumatic catheterization. In the extreme case, a picture resembling gram-negative sepsis may emerge with the rapid and sequential appearance of chills, rigors, high temperatures (often over 103°F), and hypotension likely as a result of high levels of bioactive inflammatory mediators, cytokines, released directly into the bloodstream (systemic hypersensitivity reaction). The incidence for this life-threatening event was 0.4% in a cumulative yet early report on BCG toxicity.[208] More recent estimates suggest that this septic reaction occurs in about 1 of 15,000 treated patients.[209] Prompt fluid resuscitation measures should be instituted, as well as antipyretics, antituberculosis antibiotics, and systemic steroids, which have been shown to be lifesaving in such instances.[210–212] An animal model of BCG sepsis also strongly backs the benefit of high-dose systemic steroids with coincident fluoroquinolones, an approach that has now been substantiated in clinical case reports.[213,214]

Although any fever over 102.5°F associated with chills or rigors is cause for concern, this, in itself, is not a definite sign of BCGosis, especially if it occurs at the expected peak time of 6 to 10 hours and resolves within 24 hours. This may represent a leak or spillover of bioactive cytokines from the bladder into the systemic circulation. In fact, it has been reported that such patients have higher therapeutic responses.[20] These patients may be treated with NSAID or cyclooxygenase-2 inhibitor prophylaxis (ie, ibuprofen 600 mg every 6 hours up to 3 times or rofecoxib 25 mg up to 1 time, beginning 2 hours prior to therapy) and receive a reduced dose of BCG (M. A. O'Donnell, unpublished data, 2002). Conversely, fevers that begin after 24 hours, persist more than 48 hours, or relapse in a diurnal pattern (usually in the early evening) are more indicative of an established BCG infection (BCGitis). The diurnal variation is thought to be secondary to the endogenous cortisol cycle. Organ-specific manifestations may be present, suggesting epididymal orchitis, pneumonitis, and hepatitis that occur with a cumulative incidence of 2 to 3%.[215] Computed tomographic scans may show a pattern typical of miliary spread in the liver or lung. These patients usually require hospitalization and the administration of double- or triple-drug therapy such as INH (300 mg/day), rifampin (600 mg/day), and, alternatively, ethambutol (1,200 mg/day). A second- or third-generation fluoroquinolone may be added or substituted because it covers most gram-negative infections and has moderate activity against BCG. BCG is resistant to both pyrizidimide and cycloserine. It is reasonably sensitive to amikacin but less sensitive to gentamicin or tobramycin.[204] Failure to improve on such therapy within a week or any significant clinical deterioration should prompt institution of systemic steroids (ie, prednisone 40 mg/day tapered over 2 to 6 weeks).[216] Antituberculosis drugs should be continued for 3, 6, or 12 months depending on the severity of the presenting illness. Liver enzyme monitoring is required for INH and rifampin therapy.

Prolonged symptomatic BCG cystitis and/or prostatitis (often associated with granulomas) can become a troubling problem during therapy and in the post-BCG observation period. This is particularly more likely to occur during retreatment or prolonged maintenance therapy. This situation is best avoided by withholding BCG treatment until all significant symptoms from the prior instillation have subsided. It may also be heralded by significant sterile pyuria (> 5 white blood cells per high-power field of unspun urine).[55] A 1- to 2-week delay has not been shown to reduce BCG efficacy in such a setting.[121,151,217] Reinstitution of BCG at a lower dose or premature termination of further treatment for that cycle may also be appropriate. If localized severe cystitis does occur and conservative symptomatic treatment measures fail, this condition can be treated with oral fluoroquinolones (3 to 12 weeks) or oral INH. A short 2- to 3-week oral steroid taper sandwiched between antibiotic coverage has also been shown to be helpful in refractory cases.[218] The incidence of permanent bladder contracture after BCG is estimated as under 2%.[199,208] Other very rare events include a noninfectious hypersensitivity, Reiter's-type syndrome (urethritis, arthritis, conjunctivitis), frank inflammatory arthritis, and allergic or anaphylactic reactions.[219,220] These require immediate and usually permanent cessation of further therapy.

NEW PROSPECTIVES FOR BCG

Dose-Reduction Strategies

Efforts to decrease BCG toxicity while maintaining or enhancing efficacy are currently under study for all subgroups of patients treated with BCG. Several recent clinical trials have shown that decreasing the dose of BCG to half or one-third in the induction phase will lower the local toxicity by a 20 to 30% differential, but controversy exists as to whether efficacy is sacrificed, especially in multifocal and in the more high-risk CIS and stage T1/grade 3 patients (Table 12–2).[122,176,221–234] In certain studies, cancer results were worse, but, in other cases, they were actually better. In addition to intrinsic tumor risk factors, some of this discrepancy may be attributable to the differences in BCG sensitivity of various patient populations, either genetically or from prior BCG immunization. For example, US and

Table 12–2. BCG DOSE REDUCTION TRIALS

Authors (Year)	Patients	Follow-up (mo)	Tumor Type	BCG Strain	Dose Reduced	Results (NED) Control	Toxicity	Regimen
Uncontrolled trials								
Rintala et al[222] (1989)	36	26	Ta, T1	Pasteur	75 mg (1/2)	7× decrease recur rate	Dropout 19% no BCGitis	qwk × 4; qmo × 2 yr
Blumenstein et al[223] (1990)	136	65	CIS	Connaught	120 mg	40% CR for CIS 45% at 5 yr	Not specified	qwk × 6; q3mo × 2; q6mo × 2 yr
Pagano et al[122] (1991)	70	21 12 44	Ta, T1 T1 CIS	Pasteur	75 mg (1/2)	74% vs 17% TUR 33% 64%	Severe cystitis 5% Temp > 102°F 17% No BCGitis	qwk × 6; repeat if NR qmo × 1 yr
Rivera et al[224] (1993)	108	37	T1, grade 2–3	Japanese	1 mg (1/80th)	81%	None severe	qwk × 4; q2wk × 4; qmo × 1 yr
Mack[180] (1995)	25	31	Ta, T1	Connaught	27 mg (1/3)	84%	No systemic toxicity; rare, severe, local	qwk × 6; qmo × 1 yr
Hurle et al[227] (1996)	51	33	T1, grade 3	Pasteur	75 mg (1/2)	55%	Severe cystitis 4% Fever 14% No BCGitis	qwk × 6; repeat if NR qmo × 1 yr
Lebret et al[176] (1998)	35	45	T1, grade 3	Pasteur	75 mg (1/2)	57%	Not specified	qwk × 6; repeat if NR
Losa et al[228] (2000)	70	69	CIS ± pTCC	Pasteur	75 mg (1/2)	71%	26% cystitis, 8.5% hematuria 11% fever	qwk × 6; repeat if NR qmo × 1 yr
Lebret[221] (2000)	32	58	Ta, grade 3	Pasteur	75 mg (1/2)	28%	37% minor; 17% moderate cystitis	qwk × 6; repeat if NR
Mack et al[225] (2001)	44	3	Ta, T1 marker	Connaught	30 mg (1/4)	61%	54% dysuria; 39% hematuria	qwk × 6

Table 12–2. CONTINUED

Authors (Year)	Patients	Follow-up (mo)	Tumor Type	BCG Strain	Dose Reduced	Results (NED) Reduced	Results (NED) Control	Toxicity	Regimen
Controlled trials									
Morales et al[229] (1992)	97	21	Ta, T1, CIS	Armand-Frappier	60 mg (1/2)	67%	37%	Toxicity 33% vs 12%	qwk × 6
Takashi et al[230] (1995)	74	NS	Ta, T1	Tokyo 172	40 mg (1/2)		Ta, T1: control better	Decreased toxicity	qwk × 8
Martinez-Pineiro et al[231] (1995)	381	19 33	Ta, T1	Connaught	27 mg (1/3)	Ta, T1: 82% CIS Prog: 2.4%	Ta, T1: 80% CIS: 92% Prog: 4.8%	Severe, local 23% vs 4% CIS: 69% Pulm 2.3% vs 0.4%	qwk × 6; q2wk × 6 Fever 27% vs 13%
Pagano et al[233]/ Bassi et al[234] (1995/99)	210	59	Ta, T1, CIS	Pasteur	75 mg (1/2)	Ta: 58% T1: 44% CIS: 30% Prog: equal	Ta: 56% T1: 53% CIS: 62% Prog: equal	Cystitis 57% vs 32% Fever 33% vs 18% Hematuria 26% vs 13%	qwk × 6; repeat of NR qmo × 2 yr
Martinez-Pineiro et al[232] (2002)	500	69	Ta, T1, CIS	Connaught	27 mg (1/3)	70.5% Prog: 11.5% BLCA death 7.5%	70.4% Better for ≥ 3 tumors Prog: 13.3% BLCA death 7.3%	Grade 3/4 local 17.5% vs 6.5% Grade 3/4 systemic 3.6% vs 4.4% Withdrawal 9.1% vs 4% Delay 16.8% vs 8.8%	qwk × 6; q2wk × 6

BCG = bacille Calmette-Guérin; BLCA = bladder cancer; CIS = carcinoma in situ; CR = complete response; NR = no response; NS = not significant; Prog = progression; pTCC = papillary transitional cell carcinoma; Pulm = pulmonary; TUR = transurethral resection.

Canadian populations are rarely vaccinated with BCG, whereas this practice had been or still is commonly used throughout much of the world. The routine use of reinduction courses and extended maintenance regimens may also make up for a weaker induction course. However, until this controversy is resolved, a more sensible approach may be to reduce the dose during the maintenance phase to increase treatment tolerability, an option that has shown efficacy in combined BCG plus IFN trials.[235,236] Finally, there is at least one preliminary report that every-other-week BCG dosing for low- to intermediate-risk patients may be as effective as the conventional every-week dosing scheme but with reduced side effects.[237]

Regimen Modifications

The conventional BCG treatment regimen has come under increased scrutiny with the emerging knowledge about BCG's effect on the human immune system during clinical therapy. Realizing that the original six weekly induction therapy by Morales and colleagues from over 25 years ago was completely arbitrary (but nonetheless clearly successful), several rational modifications are likely to be explored in the near future.[15] Additionally, if a good surrogate marker of the appropriate immune response in the bladder can be found, it may be possible to eventually individualize therapy on a real-time basis. Studies monitoring lymphoproliferative responses to BCG antigens, for instance, suggest that preimmunized patients may peak after just four induction treatments, whereas nonimmunized patients may require more than six.[66] Likewise, with reinduction cycles, plateau urinary IL-2 is reached by treatment three, whereas during maintenance therapy, peaks occur most commonly with the second treatment.[70,118] Formal studies to prospectively investigate such strategies are in development.

Intravesical Combination Therapy Strategies

There have been several recent investigations into the use of combined intravesical chemotherapy plus BCG therapy for superficial bladder cancer using various regimens of sequential or alternating treatments.[238–248] The results of these various regimens are difficult to interpret; therefore, no definitive conclusions can be drawn. What do appear encouraging, however, are the data on perioperative intravesical chemotherapy followed by an adequate course of BCG stimulation. There is strong clinical evidence to suggest that a single perioperative dose of chemotherapy is at least comparable to and, perhaps, more effective than a longer chemotherapy course initiated 2 to 3 weeks postoperatively.[249–251] It is postulated that the single dose immediately following TURB reduces tumor seeding, which thereby reduces recurrence within the first 12 months. There is also good experimental evidence that chemotherapy can increase fibronectin expression on the bladder surface, facilitating BCG adherence.[238] However, a randomized, controlled trial to test this specific hypothesis has not yet been performed.

The possibility of combining BCG plus IFN-α as up-front therapy has also received much attention. In vitro studies have revealed that BCG and IFN-α are synergistic via direct antiproliferative effects against bladder cancer cell lines.[30,252] IFN-α will also cooperate with BCG-induced cytokines IFN-γ and TNF-α to induce potentially important phenotypic changes in bladder cancer cells such as increased expression of HLA antigens and apoptotic cell surface receptors.[253,254] Most importantly, IFN-α has been shown to clearly potentiate and polarize in vitro human PBMC Th1 responses to BCG by at least an order of magnitude, predominantly by reducing IL-10 production.[117] As a single agent, intravesical IFN-α has been shown to have moderate (~ 40%) dose-dependent (better for doses at or above 80 MU) clinical activity against papillary bladder cancer both in post-TURBT (prophylactic) and in marker lesion (ablative) settings.[255,256] As a combination therapy, BCG plus IFN-α-2b has been proven to be pharmacologically biocompatible.[257] The clinical trials of this combination therapy began with assessing tolerability of the regimen while reducing the dose of BCG. Two trials, with a limited number of patients, demonstrated improved tolerability and at least equivalent efficacy to BCG alone.[258,259] Another small study of 80 patients randomized to full-dose BCG, reduced-dose BCG, and reduced-dose BCG plus IFN-α-2b showed 50%, 30%, and 10% recurrence rates, respectively, at 19 months follow-up. They also noted significantly reduced local side effects with the reduced-dose regimens.[260] Small single-institution studies have yielded a disease-free rate between 60 and 68% at 1 to 2 years.[235] A large multicenter phase II trial including BCG-naive patients demonstrated a 58% disease-free rate at 24 months among intermediate- to high-risk patients (M. A. O'Donnell, unpublished data, 2003). A multicenter phase III trial looking at BCG-naive patients randomized to BCG versus BCG plus IFN-α-2b is currently ongoing. It is not yet known if combination therapy will provide a substantial benefit vis-à-vis the increased cost when applied in this up-front schedule.

Use of Megadose Vitamins Following BCG Therapy

Deficiency of vitamin A produces increased susceptibility to chemical carcinogenesis.[261] The vitamin A analog etritinate has reduced tumor occurrence in superficial bladder cancer but is associated with moderate toxicity.[262,263] Pyridoxine (vitamin B$_6$) was found to be as effective as thiotepa in reducing superficial bladder cancer recurrence.[264] The antioxidant vitamins C and E have not been specifically studied in bladder cancer but have been shown to reduce colon cancer and prostate cancer, respectively.[265,266] Vitamin E has also been shown to increase the skin test responsiveness to the BCG purified protein derivative and protect against potential vitamin A toxicity.[267] With this in mind, a 65-patient, randomized, double-blind study comparing standard Recommended Dietary Allowance (RDA) vitamins to a megadose antioxidant formulation (primarily vitamins A, B$_6$, C, and E) plus zinc for papillary superficial bladder cancer recurrence after BCG was performed.[19] Overall recurrence was 80% for RDA versus 40% ($p = .001$) for megavitamins, with benefits first apparent after 1 year of therapy but that persisted throughout the study period. These potentially exciting results also await independent verification and are currently being addressed in a phase III trial.

BCG FAILURES

Many, if not most, patients eventually fail BCG.[149] The decision of how to handle these patients must be individualized based on the intrinsic tumor risk, pattern of failure, comorbidity, and patient preference. For patients with intrinsically aggressive tumors such as those with multifocal stage T1/grade 3 tumors that fail immediately after one cycle of BCG, the radical treatment option must be considered early because up to one-third have unsuspected muscle-invasive disease for which topical therapy is not effective.[268] The progression rate for these tumors has been reported to be as high as 70% by the end of 1 year following BCG failure.[166] The progression rate for CIS after one BCG failure cycle is considerably slower, but after two immediate BCG failures, it may be up to 100% by 6 months.[269] Furthermore, between 5 and 10% of patients with CIS may silently metastasize without a forewarning visible invasive local recurrence.[166] Conversely, a patient with recurrences of stage Ta/grade 1 to 2 tumors may explore many other conservative options without great fear of jeopardizing his/her survival, at least in the short term. An analysis of the type of BCG failure is also important. Patients who never achieve a disease-free state of greater than 6 months duration or who fail on active maintenance have a higher risk of progression and are unlikely to benefit from additional BCG alone, whereas those that relapse a few years later can be retreated with a reasonably high expectation of success.[270] Similarly, relapsers with tumors that have increased in stage, grade, positive cytology, or are p53-positive deserve more aggressive action.[149,166,173] Other dynamic parameters, such as shortened interval to first recurrence and high recurrence index, have also been linked to an increased progression risk.[130,271] A positive cytology in the absence of a bladder lesion should additionally prompt a search for disease in the upper tract or prostate that occurs in up to 20% of patients if followed long enough.[268,272] Unfortunately, some patients with locally advanced superficial disease are not candidates for radical surgery owing to comorbid medical illnesses. Others frankly refuse to consider losing their bladders even after extended discussions of risk. For all of these circumstances, alternative conservative measures may be appropriate.

Therapies available to salvage BCG failures are limited. Intravesical chemotherapy has been attempted with mitomycin and valrubicin, an anthracycline derivative of doxorubicin with higher lipid solubility. Mitomycin showed limited success in one small series of 21 patients failing one course of BCG in which only four (19%) were disease free at 3 years.[159] Limited efficacy was also seen in the pivotal trial of valrubicin, which led to the only US Food and Drug Administration (FDA)-approved therapy for BCG failures.[273] The study consisted of 90 patients, all with CIS, who had received at least two prior courses of intravesical therapy, including at least one course of BCG. The patients received one 6-week course of valrubicin, but only 19 of the 90 patients (21%) remained disease free at 6 months. The responders ultimately had a mean follow-up of 18 months, with only 7 (8%) remaining disease free and 4 going on to cystectomy. Of the 79 patients who ultimately recurred after therapy, 44 (56%) went on to cystectomy, with no apparent risk to disease progression owing to delay in surgery. Another study took the valrubicin trial data and did an interesting analysis of the cost implications.[274] This study showed that the expected costs of valrubicin therapy were $19,912 for the first year and $23,496 for the second year, lower than would otherwise have been the case had up-front cystectomy been undertaken on every patient.

Alternate immunotherapy regimens have also been investigated. Catalona and colleagues noted in a series of eleven patients that a third course of BCG was effective only in 20% of patients.[275] IFN-α-2b monotherapy, usually 100 million units per week over 8 weeks, has been studied in a few small series. One study showed that two of nine patients (22%) were disease free at a limited follow-up of 6 months.[276,277] Another series with 34 patients having CIS showed that 13 patients (38%) were disease free at 3 months, which dropped to 5 (15%) at 12 months but leveled at 4 (12%) at 33 months.[276,278] An interesting finding was that patients who relapsed after successful BCG therapy or were intolerant to BCG responded much better than patients who were completely BCG refractory, 21% versus 0%, respectively, at 12 months. One of the most intriguing prospects for the immediate future is investigations looking into the clinical application of low-dose BCG plus IFN-α-2b in patients who are BCG failures. The results of a single-institution study are very provocative.[235] In 40 patients, 78% of whom had either CIS or T1 disease and who had failed at least one previous cycle of BCG, 63% and 53% were disease free at 12 and 24 months, respectively. Two other small single-institution studies have confirmed these results without apparently jeopardizing risk for metastasis at the time of delayed cystectomy.[236,279] Preliminary data from a large multicenter phase II trial currently under way demonstrate a 42% freedom from disease rate at 24 months (M. A. O'Donnell, unpublished data, 2003). The expected efficacy results for these conservative options are summarized in Table 12–3. The clinically tested protocol schema for combination intravesical BCG plus IFN-α use is provided in Figure 12–3.

Table 12–3. COMPARATIVE EFFICACY OF CONVENTIONAL AGENTS AFTER BACILLE CALMETTE GUÉRIN (BCG) FAILURE

Authors	Agent	Patient Group (n)	2-Year NED (%)
Catalona et al[275]	BCG (third)	Mixed (11)	20
Williams et al[278]	IFN-α	CIS—pure (34)	12
Malmstrom et al[159]	MMC*	Mixed (19)	23
Steinberg et al[273]	Valrubicin†	CIS (90)	8
O'Donnell et al[235]	BCG + IFN-α‡	Mixed (40)	53
O'Donnell§	BCG + IFN-α‖	Mixed (320)	42

CIS = carcinoma in situ; IFN = interferon; MMC = mitomycin C.
*For BCG failures × 1; crossover.
†All concurrent papillary transitional cell carcinoma resected.
‡Up to two induction courses plus maintenance; results same for BCG failures × 1 and × 2+.
§Unpublished data.
‖One induction course plus maintenance; results same for BCG failures × 1 and × 2+.

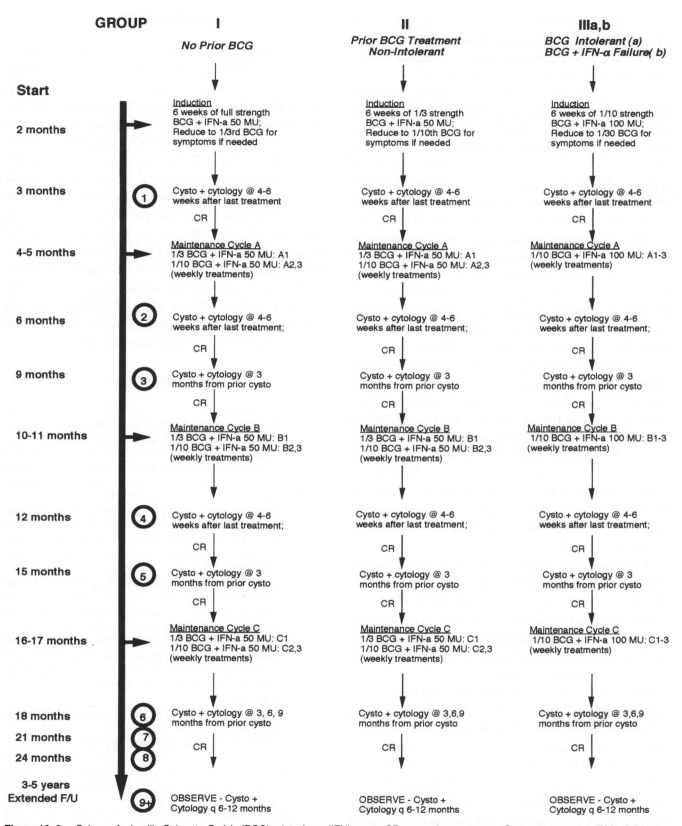

Figure 12–3. Schema for bacille Calmette-Guérin (BCG) + interferon (IFN)-α use. CR = complete response; Cysto = cystoscopy; F/U = follow-up.

Other investigational strategies include keyhole limpet hemocyanin (KLH), photodynamic therapy (PDT), and new chemotherapeutics. KLH is a powerful, nonspecific immune response modifier. The limited data in the literature using KLH as a first-line therapy for superficial bladder cancer reveal that KLH is inferior to BCG.[280,281] Little information is available regarding its use for BCG failures. PDT has been used with some success in patients who fail BCG. One study of 36 patients with CIS who failed BCG showed a response rate of 58% at 3 months, which was durable to 31% at 12 months.[282] A more recent study, with follow-up at 36 months in 24 patients, shows 60% response (3 of 5) for CIS and 21% response (4 of 19) for papillary tumors.[283] There are significant limitations to this therapy, however, that include generalized cutaneous photosensitivity, severe local irritative voiding symptoms, and occasional bladder contractures. As with KLH, this therapy is currently available only at a few select research centers. At one point, the oral IFN-inducing agent bropiramine appeared to show promise for CIS patients previously failing BCG.[284] Unfortunately, this drug did not gain FDA approval and is no longer available. A preliminary report of intravesical gemcitabine, a chemotherapeutic agent used successfully intravenously against metastatic TCC, shows evidence of activity against aggressive BCG-refractory tumors but with as yet unknown durability.[285]

External beam radiation therapy is rarely appropriate for the treatment of superficial bladder cancer because it may cause significant local morbidity while displaying limited efficacy. CIS is particularly resistant, and low-grade papillary disease responds more poorly than higher-grade disease. The combination of aggressive TURB and radiochemotherapy, however, may incur some benefit for patients with stage T1 grade 3 disease.[286,287] A recent study with 74 patients showed an 84% CR at 3 months and 47% continuous disease-free status to a median of 57 months. The overall 5-year survival rate was 72%.[287] The data on trimodality treatment for muscle-invasive disease would also suggest that there is benefit from this regimen. Shipley and colleagues reviewed the literature and found about 50 to 60% disease-specific survival at 5 years.[288]

CONCLUSION

BCG remains the most powerful weapon in the arsenal of topical therapeutics against superficial bladder cancer, especially for aggressive cases. The early use of BCG can provide long-term periods that are free of meaningful disease worsening. With newer refinements in regimen optimization, there is reasonable hope that even better results can be obtained in the future, both in improved efficacy and reduced toxicity. However, in all cases, constant vigilance is required because progression to more advanced disease can occur insidiously, sometimes outside the bladder vault. Superficial bladder cancer is often a lifelong disease, but it must not necessarily be a life-shortening or debilitating one as long as conservative and radical options are applied in a rational manner using evidence-based considerations of risk versus benefit for the individualized patient.

REFERENCES

1. Millan-Rodriguez F, Chechile-Toniolo G, Salvador-Bayarri J, et al. Multivariate analysis of the prognostic factors of primary superficial bladder cancer. J Urol 2000;163:73–8.
2. Pawinski A, Sylvester R, Kurth KH, et al. A combined analysis of European Organization for Research and Treatment of Cancer, and Medical Research Council randomized clinical trials for the prophylactic treatment of stage TaT1 bladder cancer. European Organization for Research and Treatment of Cancer Genitourinary Tract Cancer Cooperative Group and the Medical Research Council Working Party on Superficial Bladder Cancer. J Urol 1996;156:1934–40; discussion 1940–1.
3. Nilsson S, Ranhammar P, Glimelius B, Nygren P, SBU-Group. Swedish Council of Technology Assessment in Health Care. A systematic overview of chemotherapy effects in urothelial bladder cancer. Acta Oncol 2001;40:371–90.
4. Lamm DL, Riggs DR, Traynelis CL, Nseyo UO. Apparent failure of current intravesical chemotherapy prophylaxis to influence the long-term course of superficial transitional cell carcinoma of the bladder. J Urol 1995;153:1444–50.
5. Crispen R. History of BCG and its substrains. Prog Clin Biol Res 1989;310:35–50.
6. Luelmo F. BCG vaccination. Am Rev Respir Dis 1982;125:70–2.
7. Behr MA, Wilson MA, Gill WP, et al. Comparative genomics of BCG vaccines by whole-genome DNA microarray. Science 1999;284:1520–3.
8. van der Meijden AP, Debruyne FM, Steerenberg PA, de Jong WH. Aspects of non-specific immunotherapy with BCG in superficial bladder cancer: an overview. Prog Clin Biol Res 1989;310:11–33.

9   Pearl R. Cancer and tuberculosis. Am J Hygiene 1929;9: 97–159.

10. Mathe G, Amiel JL, Schwarzenberg L, et al. Active immuno-therapy for acute lymphoblastic leukaemia. Lancet 1969; 1:697–9.

11. Hadziev S, Kavaklieva-Dimitrova J. [Use of BCG in human cancer.] Folia Med (Plovdiv) 1969;11:8–14.

12. Morton D, Eilber FR, Malmgren RA, Wood WC. Immuno-logical factors which influence response to immunother-apy in malignant melanoma. Surgery 1970;68:158–63; discussion 163–4.

13. Coe JE, Feldman JD. Extracutaneous delayed hypersensitiv-ity, particularly in the guinea-pig bladder, Immunology 1966;10:127–36.

14. Zbar B, Bernstein ID, Bartlett GL, et al. Immunotherapy of cancer: regression of intradermal tumors and prevention of growth of lymph node metastases after intralesional injection of living *Mycobacterium bovis*. J Natl Cancer Inst 1972;49:119–30.

15. Morales A, Eidinger D, Bruce AW. Intracavitary bacillus Cal-mette-Guérin in the treatment of superficial bladder tumors. J Urol 1976;116:180–3.

16. Lamm DL, Thor DE, Harris SC, et al. Bacillus Calmette-Guérin immunotherapy of superficial bladder cancer. J Urol 1980;124:38–40.

17. Pinsky CM, Camacho FJ, Kerr D, et al. Intravesical adminis-tration of bacillus Calmette-Guérin in patients with recur-rent superficial carcinoma of the urinary bladder: report of a prospective, randomized trial. Cancer Treat Rep 1985;69:47–53.

18. Herr HW, Pinsky CM, Whitmore WF Jr, et al. Long-term effect of intravesical bacillus Calmette-Guérin on flat car-cinoma in situ of the bladder. J Urol 1986;135:265–7.

19. Lamm DL, Riggs DR, Shriver JS, et al. Megadose vitamins in bladder cancer: a double-blind clinical trial. J Urol 1994;151:21–6.

20. Luftenegger W, Ackermann DK, Futterlieb A, et al. Intraves-ical versus intravesical plus intradermal bacillus Cal-mette- Guérin: a prospective randomized study in patients with recurrent superficial bladder tumors. J Urol 1996;155:483–7.

21. Witjes JA, Fransen MP, van der Meijden AP, et al. Use of maintenance intravesical bacillus Calmette-Guérin (BCG), with or without intradermal BCG, in patients with recurrent superficial bladder cancer. Long-term follow-up of a randomized phase 2 study. Urol Int 1993;51:67–72.

22. Wang MH, Chen YQ, Gercken J, Ernst M, et al. Specific acti-vation of human peripheral blood gamma/delta[+] T lym-phocytes by sonicated antigens of *Mycobacterium tuber-culosis*: role in vitro in killing human bladder carcinoma cell lines. Scand J Immunol 1993;38:239–46.

23. Thanhauser A, Bohle A, Flad HD, et al. Induction of bacillus Calmette-Guérin activated killer cells from human peripheral blood mononuclear cells against human blad-der carcinoma cell lines in vitro. Cancer Immunol Immunother 1993;37:105–11.

24. Peuchmaur M, Benoit G, Vieillefond A, et al. Analysis of mucosal bladder leucocyte subpopulations in patients treated with intravesical bacillus Calmette-Guérin. Urol Res 1989;17:299–303.

25. Prescott S, James K, Hargreave TB, et al. Intravesical Evans strain BCG therapy: quantitative immunohistochemical analysis of the immune response within the bladder wall. J Urol 1992;147:1636–42.

26. Inoue T, Yoshikai Y, Matsuzaki G, Nomoto K. Early appear-ing T cells during infection with Calmette-Guérin bacil-lus. J Immunol 1991;146:2754–62.

27. De Boer EC, DeJong WH, Van der Meijden AP, et al. Pres-ence of activated lymphocytes in the urine of patients with superficial bladder cancer after intravesical immunother-apy with bacillus Calmette-Guérin. Cancer Immunol Immunother 1991;33:411–6.

28. Bruno S, Machi AM, Semino C, et al. Phenotypic, functional and molecular analysis of lymphocytes associated with bladder cancer. Cancer Immunol Immunother 1996;42: 47–54.

29. Adams DO, Marino PA. Evidence for a multistep mechanism of cytolysis by BCG-activated macrophages: the interre-lationship between the capacity for cytolysis, target bind-ing, and secretion of cytolytic factor. J Immunol 1992; 126:981–7.

30. Pryor K, Stricker P, Russell P, et al. Antiproliferative effects of bacillus Calmette-Guérin and interferon alpha 2b on human bladder cancer cells in vitro. Cancer Immunol Immunother 1995;41:309–16.

31. Wolfe SA, Tracey DE, Henney CS. Induction of "natural killer" cells by BCG. Nature 1976;262:584–6.

32. Yamamura M, Wang XH, Ohmen JD, et al. Cytokine patterns of immunologically mediated tissue damage. J Immunol 1992;149:1470–5.

33. Orme IM. Immunity to mycobacteria. Curr Opin Immunol 1993;5:497–502.

34. Fleischmann JD, Toossi Z, Ellner JJ, et al. Urinary inter-leukins in patients receiving intravesical bacillus Cal-mette-Guérin therapy for superficial bladder cancer. Can-cer 1989;64:1447–54.

35. Schamhart DHJ, Kurth KH, deReijke TM, Vleeming R. BCG treatment and the importance of inflammatory response. Urol Res 1992;20:199–203.

36. Prescott S, James K, Hargreave TB, et al. Radioimmunoassay detection of interferon-gamma in urine after intravesical Evans BCG therapy. J Urol 1990;144:1248–51.

37. Huygen K, Abramowicz D, Vandenbussche P, et al. Spleen cell cytokine secretion in *Mycobacterium bovis* BCG-infected mice. Infect Immun 1992;60:2880–6.

38. DeBoer EC, DeJong WH, Steerenberg PA, et al. Induction of urinary interleukin-1 (IL-1), IL-2, IL-6 and tumor necro-sis factor during intravesical immunotherapy with bacil-lus Calmette-Guérin in superficial bladder cancer. Cancer Immunol Immunother 1992;34:306–12.

39. Bohle A, Nowc C, Ulmer AJ, et al. Detection of urinary TNF, IL-1, and IL-2 after local BCG immunotherapy for blad-der carcinoma. Cytokine 1990;2:175–81.

40. Murray PJ, Aldovini A, Young RA. Manipulation and poten-tiation of antimycobacterial immunity using recombinant bacille Calmette-Guérin strains that secrete cytokines. Proc Natl Acad Sci U S A 1996;93:934–9.

41. Shin JS, Park JH, Kim JD, et al. Induction of tumour necro-sis factor-alpha (TNF-alpha) mRNA in bladders and spleens of mice after intravesical administration of bacil-

lus Calmette-Guérin. Clin Exp Immunol 1995;100: 26–31.

42. O'Donnell MA, Chen X, DeWolf WC. Maturation of the cytokine immune response to BCG in the bladder: implications for treatment schedules [abstract]. J Urol 1996;155:1030A.

43. De Reijke TM, De Boer EC, Kurth KH, Schamhart DH. Urinary cytokines during intravesical bacillus Calmette-Guérin therapy for superficial bladder cancer: processing, stability and prognostic value. J Urol 1996;155:477–82.

44. Thalmann GN, Dewald B, Baggiolini M, Studer UE. Interleukin-8 expression in the urine after BCG therapy: a potential predictor of tumor recurrence and progression [abstract]. J Urol 1996;155:34A.

45. Wallis RS, Amir-Tahmasseb M, Ellner JJ. Induction of interleukin 1 and tumor necrosis factor by mycobacterial proteins: the monocyte Western blot. Proc Natl Acad Sci U S A 1990;87:3348–52.

46. O'Donnell MA, Aldovini A, Duda RB, et al. Recombinant *Mycobacterium bovis* BCG secreting functional interleukin-2 enhances gamma interferon production by splenocytes. Infect Immun 1994;62:2508–14.

47. DeJong WH, DeBoer EC, Van Der Meijden APM. Presence of interleukin-2 in urine of superficial bladder cancer patients after intravesical treatment with bacillus Calmette-Guérin. Cancer Immunol Immunother 1990;31:182–6.

48. Poppas DP, Folkman J, Pavlovich CP, et al. Intravesical bacillus Calmette-Guérin (BCG) induces the anti-angiogenic chemokine IP-10. Urology 1998;52:268–76.

49. Ikemoto S, Kishimoto T, Wada S. Clinical studies on cell-mediated immunity in patients with bladder carcinoma: blastogenic response, interleukin-2 production and interferon-gamma production of lymphocytes. Br J Urol 1990; 65:333–8.

50. Jackson AM, Ivshina AV, Senko O, et al. Prognosis of intravesical bacillus Calmette-Guérin therapy for superficial bladder cancer by immunological urinary measurements: statistically weighted syndromes analysis. J Urol 1998; 159:1054–63.

51. Thalmann GN, Sermier A, Rentsch C, et al. Urinary interleukin-8 and 18 predict the response of superficial bladder cancer to intravesical therapy with bacillus Calmette-Guérin. J Urol 2000;164:2129–33.

52. Flynn JL, Chan J, Triebold KJ, et al. An essential role for interferon-γ in resistance to *Mycobacterium tuberculosis* infection. J Exp Med 1993;178:2249–54.

53. Newport MJ, Kuxley CM, Huston S, et al. A mutation in the interferon-γ-receptor gene and susceptibility to mycobacterial infections. N Engl J Med 1996;335:1941–9.

54. De Boer EC, De Reijke TM, Vos PC, et al. Immunostimulation in the urinary bladder by local application of *Nocardia rubra* cell-wall skeletons (rubratin) and bacillus Calmette-Guérin as therapy for superficial bladder cancer: a comparative study. Clin Infect Dis 2000;31 Suppl 3: S109–14.

55. Saint F, Patard JJ, Irani J, et al. Leukocyturia as a predictor of tolerance and efficacy of intravesical BCG maintenance therapy for superficial bladder cancer. Urology 2001; 57:617–21.

56. Shapiro A, Lijovetzky G, Pode D. Changes of the mucosal

57. Satoh E, Arai H, Gotoh T, et al. Intravesical bacillus Calmette-Guérin instillation therapy for carcinoma in situ of the urinary bladder and prediction of effects by urinary cytologic examination. Nippon Hinyokika Gakkai Zasshi 1999;90:901–5.

58. Pagano F, Bassi P, Milani C. Pathologic and structural changes in the bladder after BCG intravesical therapy in men. Prog Clin Biol Res 1989;310:81–91.

59. Ratliff TL, Ritchey JK, Yuan JJ, et al. T-cell subsets required for intravesical BCG immunotherapy for bladder cancer. J Urol 1993;150:1018–23.

60. Bohle A, Gerdes J, Ulmer AJ, et al. Effects of local BCG therapy in patients with bladder carcinoma on immunocompetent cells of the bladder wall. J Urol 1990;144:53–58.

61. Cornel EB, Van Moorselaar RJ, Van Stratum P, et al. Antitumor effects of bacillus Calmette-Guérin in a syngeneic rat bladder tumor model system, RBT323. J Urol 1993;149: 179–82.

62. Boccafoschi C, Montefiore F, Pavesi M. Immunophenotypic characterization of the bladder mucosa infiltrating lymphocytes after intravesical BCG treatment for superficial bladder carcinoma. Eur Urol 1992;21:304–8.

63. Chang SG, Lee SJ, Huh JS, Lee JH. Changes in mucosal immune cells of bladder tumor patient after BCG intravesical immunotherapy. Oncol Rep 2001;8:257–61.

64. Saint F, Patard JJ, Groux Muscatelli B, et al. Evaluation of cellular tumour rejection mechanism in the peritumoral bladder wall after bacillus Calmette-Guérin treatment. BJU Int 2001;88:602–10.

65. Stefanini FF, Bercovich E, Mazzeo V, et al. Class I and Class II HLA antigen expression by transitional cell carcinoma of the bladder: correlation with T cell infiltration and BCG treatment. J Urol 1989;141:1449–53.

66. Zlotta AR, Van Vooren JP, Huygen K, et al. What is the optimal regimen for intravesical BCG therapy: are six weekly instillations necessary? Eur Urol 2000;37:470–7.

67. Haaff EO, Catalona WJ, Ratliff TL. Detection of interleukin-2 in the urine of patients with superficial bladder tumors after treatment with intravesical BCG. J Urol 1986;136:970–4.

68. Scamhart DH, De Boer EC, De Reijke TM, Kurth K. Urinary cytokines reflecting the immunological response in the urinary bladder to biological response modifiers: their practical use. Eur Urol 2000;37:16–23.

69. Sanchez-Carbayo M, Urrutia M, Romani R, et al. Serial urinary IL-2, IL-6, IL-8, TNF-alpha, UBC, CYFRA 21-1 and NMP22 during follow-up of patients with bladder cancer receiving intravesical BCG. Anticancer Res 2001;4B:3041–7.

70. Saint F, Patard JJ, Maille P, et al. T helper 1/2 lymphocyte urinary cytokine profiles in responding and nonresponding patients after 1 and 2 courses of bacillus Calmette-Guérin for superficial bladder cancer. J Urol 2001;166:2142–7.

71. Saint F, Patard JJ, Maille P, et al. Prognostic value of a T helper 1 urinary cytkine response after intravesical bacillus Calmette-Guérin treatment for superficial bladder cancer. J Urol 2002;167:364–7.

72. Magno C, Melloni D, Gali A, et al. The anti-tumor activity of bacillus Calmette-Guérin in bladder cancer is associated

with an increase in the circulating level of interleukin-2. Immunol Lett 2002;81:235–8.

73. Kaempfer R, Gerez L, Farbstein H, et al. Prediction of response to treatment in superficial bladder carcinoma through pattern of interleukin-2 gene expression. J Clin Oncol 1996;14:1778–86.

74. Patard JJ, Guille F, Lobel B, et al. [Current state of knowledge concerning the mechanisms of action of BCG.] Prog Urol 1998;8:415–21.

75. Patard J-J, Muscatelli-Groux F, Saint Z, et al. Evaluation of local immune response after intravesical bacille Calmette-Guérin treatment for superficial bladder cancer. Br J Urol 1996;78:709–14.

76. Esuvaranathan K, Alexandroff AB, McIntyre M, et al. Interleukin-6 production by bladder tumors is upregulated by BCG immunotherapy. J Urol 1995;154:572–5.

77. Zlotta AR, Drowart A, Huygen K, et al. Humoral response against heat shock proteins and other mycobacterial antigens after intravesical treatment with bacille Calmette-Guérin in patients with superficial bladder cancer. Clin Exp Immunol 1997;109:157–65.

78. O'Donnell MA, Luo Y, Chen X, et al. Role of IL-12 in the induction and potentiation of IFN-γ in response to bacillus Calmette-Guérin. J Immunol 1999;163:4246–52.

79. Buu N, Sanchez F, Schurr E. The *Bcg* host-resistance gene. Clin Infect Dis 2000;31 Suppl 3:S81–5.

80. Hoffmann SC, Stanley EM, Darrin Cox E, et al. Association of cytokine polymorphic inheritance and in vitro cytokine production in anti-CD3/CD28-stimulated peripheral blood lymphocytes. Transplantation 2001;72:1444–50.

81. Kurisu H, Matsuyama H, Ohmoto Y, et al. Cytokine-mediated antitumor effect of bacillus Calmette-Guérin on tumor cells in vitro. Cancer Immunol Immunother 1994;39:249–53.

82. Campbell SC, Tanabe K, Alexander JP, et al. Intercellular adhesion molecule-1 expression by bladder cancer cells: functional effects. J Urol 1994;151:1385–90.

83. Hawkyard SJ, Jackson AM, James K, et al. The inhibitory effects of interferon gamma on the growth of bladder cancer cells. J Urol 1992;147:1399–1403.

84. Jackson AM, Alexandrov AB, Prescott S, et al. Expression of adhesion molecules by bladder cancer cells: modulation by interferon-gamma and tumour necrosis factor-alpha. J Urol 1996;148:1583–6.

85. Pryor K, Goddard J, Goldstein D, et al. Bacillus Calmette-Guérin (BCG) enhances monocyte- and lymphocyte-mediated bladder tumor cell killing. Br J Cancer 1995;71:801–7.

86. Prescott S, Jackson AM, Hawkyard SJ, et al. Mechanisms of action of intravesical bacille Calmette-Guérin: local immune mechanisms. Clin Infect Dis 2000;31 Suppl 3:S91–3.

87. Lattime EC, Gomella LG, McCue PA. Murine bladder carcinoma cells present antigen to BCG specific CD4+ T-cells. Cancer Res 1992;52:4286–90.

88. Ratliff TL. Role of the immune response in BCG for bladder cancer. Eur Urol 1992;21(Suppl 2):17–21.

89. Ratliff TL. Mechanisms of action of intravesical BCG for bladder cancer. Prog Clin Biol Res 1989;310:107–22.

90. Paul WE, Seder RA. Lymphocyte responses and cytokines. Cell 1994;76:241–51.

91. Luo Y, Szilvasi A, Chen X, et al. A novel method for monitoring *Mycobacterium bovis* BCG trafficking using

recombinant BCG expressing green fluorescent protein. Clin Diag Lab Immunol 1996;3:761–8.

92. O'Donnell MA, Szilvasi A, Luo Y, DeWolf WC. Fas mediated killing of transitional cell carcinoma (TCC). J Urol 1996;155:567A.

93. Klein LT, Miller MI, Ikeguchi E, et al. Anti-fas antibody mediated apoptosis in bladder tumor cells: a potential intravesical therapeutic agent. Proc Annu Meet Am Assoc Cancer Res 1996;37:A103.

94. Bohle A, Thanhauser A, Ulmer A, et al. Dissecting the immunobiological effects of bacillus Calmette-Guérin (BCG) in vitro: evidence of a distinct BCG-activated killer (BAK) cell phenomenon. J Urol 1993;150:1932.

95. Brandau S, Bohle A, Thanhauser A, et al. In vitro generation of bacillus Calmette-Guérin-activated killer cells. Clin Infect Dis 2000;31 Suppl 3:S94–100.

96. Brandau S, Suttmann H, Riemensberer J, et al. Perforin-mediated lysis of tumor cells by *Mycobacerium bovis* bacillus Calmette-Guérin-activated killer cells. Clin Cancer Res 2000;6:3729–38.

97. Pavlovich CP, Kraling BM, Stewart RJ, et al. BCG-induced urinary cytokines inhibit microvascular endothelial cell proliferation. J Urol 2000;163:2014–21.

98. Ratliff TL, Shapiro A, Catalona WJ. Inhibition of murine bladder tumor growth by bacillus Calmette-Guérin: lack of a role of natural killer cells. Clin Immunol Immunopathol 1986;41:108.

99. Ratliff TL, Gillen D, Catalona WJ. Requirement of a thymus dependent immune response for BCG-mediated antitumor activity. J Urol 1987;137:155.

100. Nadler RB, Ritchey JK, Day ML, Ratliff TL. Cytokine patterns in BCG treated mouse bladders. J Urol 1994;151:515A.

101. Halak BK, Maguire HC Jr, Lattime EC. Tumor-induced interleukin-10 inhibits type 1 immune responses directed at a tumor antigen as well as a non-tumor antigen present at the tumor site. Cancer Res 1999;59:911–7.

102. Ratliff TL. Role of animal models in understanding intravesical therapy with bacille Calmette-Guérin. Clin Infect Dis 2000;31 Suppl 3:S106–8.

103. Riemensberger J, Bohle A, Brandau S. IFN-gamma and IL-12 but not IL-10 are required for local tumour surveillance in a syngeneic model of orthotopic bladder cancer. Clin Exp Immunol 2002;127:20–6.

104. Braundau S, Riemensberger J, Jacobsen M, et al. NK cells are essential for effective BCG immunotherapy. Int J Cancer 2001;92:697–702.

105. Kavoussi LR, Brown EJ, Ritchey JK, Ratliff TL. Fibronectin-mediated Calmette-Guérin bacillus attachment to murine bladder mucosa. Requirement for the expression of an antitumor response. J Clin Invest 1990;85:62–7.

106. Becich MJ, Carroll S, Ratliff TL. Internalization of bacille Calmette-Guérin by bladder tumor cells. J Urol 1991; 145:1316–24.

107. Saitoh H, Mori K, Kudoh S, et al. BCG effects on telomerase activity in bladder cancer cell lines. Int J Clin Oncol 2002;7:165–70.

108. Ikeda N, Toida I, Iwasaki A, et al. Surface antigen expression on bladder tumor cells induced by bacillus Calmette-Guérin (BCG): a role of BCG internalization into tumor cells. Int J Urol 2002;9:29–35.

109. Durek C, Richter E, Basteck A, et al. The fate of bacillus Calmette-Guérin afer intravesical instillation. J Urol 2001;165:1765–8.

110. Matzinger P. Tolerance, danger, and the extended family. Annu Rev Immunol 1994;12:991–1045.

111. Chen X, Luo Y, Yamada H, O'Donnell MA. BCG potentiates human chemokine induction in vivo and in vitro [abstract]. J Urol Suppl 2001;165(5 Suppl 1):114, no. 465.

112. Reale M, Intorno R, Tenaglia R, et al. Production of MCP-1 and RANTES in bladder cancer patients after bacillus Calmette-Guérin immunotherapy. Cancer Immunol Immunother 2002;51:91–8.

113. Troy AJ, Davidson JT, Atkinson CH, Hart DNJ. C1A dendritic cells predominate in transitional cell carcinoma of bladder and kidney but are minimally activated. J Urol 1999;161:1962–7.

114. Stoll S, Jonuleit H, Schmitt E, et al. Production of functional IL-18 by different subtypes of murine and human dendritic cells (DC): DC-derived IL-18 enhances IL-12-dependent Th1 development. Eur J Immunol 1998;28:3231–9.

115. Kuniyoshi JS, Kuniyoshi CJ, Lim AM, et al. Dendritic cell secretion of IL-15 is induced by recombinant huCD40LT and augments the stimulation of antigen-specific cytolytic T cells. Cell Immunol 1999;193:48–58.

116. Alexandroff AB, Jackson AM, O'Donnell MA, James K. BCG immunotherapy of bladder cancer: 20 years on. Lancet 1999;353:1689–94.

117. Luo Y, Chen X, Downs TM, et al. IFN-alpha 2B enhances Th1 cytokine responses in bladder cancer patients receiving *Mycobacterium bovis* bacillus Calmette-Guérin immunotherapy. J Immunol 1999;162:2399–405.

118. DeReijke TM, DeBoer EC, Kurth KH, Schamhart DH. Urinary interleukin-2 monitoring during prolonged bacillus Calmette-Guérin treatment: can it predict the optimal number of instillations? J Urol. 1999;161:67–71.

119. Blumenstein BA. Clinical trial design and analysis. Monograph: update on diagnosis and treatment of superficial bladder cancer. Parsippany: MPE Communications, Inc.; 1998.

120. Lamm DL, Blumenstein B, Sarosdy M, et al. Significant long-term patient benefit with BCG maintenance therapy. J Urol Suppl 1997;157:213.

121. Lamm DL. Bacillus Calmette-Guérin immunotherapy for bladder cancer. J Urol 1985;134:40–7.

122. Pagano F, Bassi P, Milani C, et al. A low dose bacillus Calmette-Guérin regimen in superficial bladder cancer therapy: is it effective? J Urol 1991;146:32–5.

123. Melekos MD, Chionis H, Pantazakos A, et al. Intravesical bacillus Calmette-Guérin immunoprophylaxis of superficial bladder cancer: results of a controlled prospective trial with modified treatment schedule. J Urol 1993;149:744–8.

124. Yang DA, Li SQ, Li XT. [Prophylactic effects of zhuling and BCG on postoperative recurrence of bladder cancer.] Chung Hua Wai Ko Tsa Chih 1994;32:433–4.

125. Zhang S, Li H, Cheng H. [The preventive recurrent results of postoperative intravesical instillation therapy in bladder cancer.] Chung Hua Wai Ko Tsa Chih 1995;33:304–6.

126. Krege S, Giani G, Meyer R, et al. A randomized multicenter trial of adjuvant therapy in superficial bladder cancer: transurethral resection only versus transurethral resection plus mitomycin C versus transurethral resection plus bacillus Calmette-Guérin. Participating clinics. J Urol 1996;156:962–6.

127. Tkachuk VN, al-Shukri A, al-Khani F. [The use of BCG vaccine for preventing recurrences of superficial bladder cancer.] Urol Nefrol (Mosk) 1996;2:23–5.

128. Iantorno R, Nicolai M, Mastroprimiano G, et al. Randomized prospective study comparing long-term intravesical instillation of BCG after transurethral resection alone in patients with superficial bladder cancer. J Urol Suppl 1999;161:284.

129. Shelley MD, Court JB, Kynston H, et al. Intravesical bacillus Calmette-Guérin in Ta and T1 bladder cancer. Cochrane Database Syst Rev 2000;4:CD001986.

130. Solsona E, Iborra I, Dumont R, et al. The 3-month clinical response to intravesical therapy as a predictive factor for progression in patients with high risk superficial bladder cancer. J Urol 2000;164:685–9.

131. Sylvester RJ, Van der Meijden APM, Lamm DL. Intravesical bacillus Calmette-Guérin reduces the risk of progression in patients with superficial bladder cancer: a meta-analysis of the published results of randomized clinical trials. J Urol 2002;168:1964–70.

132. Douville Y, Pelouze G, Roy R, et al. Recurrent bladder papillomata treated with bacillus Calmette-Guérin: a preliminary report (phase I trial). Cancer Treat Rep 1978;62:551–2.

133. Morales A, Ottenhof P, Emerson L. Treatment of residual, non-infiltrating bladder cancer with bacillus Calmette-Guérin. J Urol 1981;125:649–51.

134. Brosman SA. BCG in the management of superficial bladder cancer. Urology 1984;23:82–7.

135. deKernion JB, Huang MY, Lindner A, et al. The management of superficial bladder tumors and carcinoma in situ with intravesical bacillus Calmette-Guérin. J Urol 1985;133:598–601.

136. Heney NM, Koontz WW, Weinstein R, Barton B. BCG in superficial bladder cancer. J Urol Suppl 1986;135:184A.

137. Schellhammer PF, Ladaga LE, Fillion MB. Bacillus Calmette-Guérin for superficial transitional cell carcinoma of the bladder. J Urol 1986;135:261–4.

138. Pansadoro V, De Paula F. Intravesical bacillus Calmette-Guérin in the treatment of superficial transitional cell carcinoma of the bladder. J Urol 1987;138:299–301.

139. Kavoussi LR, Torrence RJ, Gillen DP, et al. Results of 6 weekly intravesical bacillus Calmette-Guérin instillations on the treatment of superficial bladder tumors. J Urol 1988;139:935–40.

140. Khanna OP, Son DL, Mazer H, et al. Multicenter study of superficial bladder cancer treated with intravesical bacillus Calmette-Guérin or Adriamycin. Urology 1990;35:101–8.

141. Akaza H. BCG treatment of existing Ta, T1 tumours or carcinoma in situ of the bladder. Eur Urol 1995;27 Suppl 1:9–12.

142. Witjes JA, Oosterhof GO, DeBruyne FM. Management of superficial bladder cancer Ta/T1/TIS: intravesical chemotherapy. In: Vogelzang NJ, Scardino PT, Shipley WU, Coffey DS, editors. Comprehensive textbook of genitourinary oncology. Baltimore: Williams & Wilkins; 1996. p. 416–27.

143. Ozen H, Ekici S, Uygur MC, et al. Repeated transurethral

resection and intravesical BCG for extensive superficial bladder tumors. J Endourol 2001;15:863–7.

144. Hudson MA. Carcinoma in situ of the bladder. J Urol 1995; 153:564–72.

145. Lamm DL, Blumenstein BA, Crissman JD, et al. Maintenance BCG immunotherapy in recurrent Ta, T1 and carcinoma in situ transitional cell carcinoma: a randomized Southwest Oncology Group study. J Urol 2000;163:1124–9.

146. Lamm DL. Carcinoma in situ. Urol Clin North Am 1992; 19:499–508.

147. Jakse G. Intravesical instillation of BCG in carcinoma in situ of the urinary bladder. EORTC protocol 30861. EORTC-GU Group. Prog Clin Biol Res 1989;310:187–92.

148. Herr HW, Wartinger DD, Fair WR, Oettgen HF. Bacillus Calmette-Guérin therapy for superficial bladder cancer: a 10-year followup. J Urol 1992;147:1020–3.

149. Nadler RB, Catalona WJ, Hudson MA, Ratliff TL. Durability of the tumor-free response for intravesical bacillus Calmette-Guérin therapy. J Urol 1994;152:367–73.

150. Lamm DL, Blumenstein BA, Crawford ED, et al. A randomized trial of intravesical doxorubicin and immunotherapy with bacille Calmette-Guérin for transitional-cell carcinoma of the bladder. N Engl J Med 1991;325:1205–9.

151. Brosman SA. Experience with bacillus Calmette-Guérin in patients with superficial bladder carcinoma. J Urol 1982; 128:27–30.

152. Tachibana M, Jitsukawa S, Iigaya T, et al. [Comparative study on prophylactic intravesical instillation of bacillus Calmette-Guerin (BCG) and Adriamycin for superficial bladder cancers.] Nippon Hinyokika Gakkai Zasshi 1989;80: 1459–65.

153. Martinez-Pineiro JA, Jimenez Leon J, Martinez-Pineiro L Jr, et al. Bacillus Calmette-Guérin versus doxorubicin versus thiotepa: a randomized prospective study in 202 patients with superficial bladder cancer. J Urol 1990;143:502–6.

154. Rintala E, Jauhiainen K, Alfthan O, et al. Intravesical chemotherapy (mitomycin C) versus immunotherapy (bacillus Calmette-Guérin) in superficial bladder cancer Eur Urol 1991;20:19–25.

155. Lamm DL, Blumenstein B, Crawford ED, et al. Randomized intergroup comparison of bacillus Calmette Guérin immunotherapy and mitomycin C chemotherapy prophylaxis in superficial transitional cell carcinoma of the bladder. Urol Oncol 1995;1:119–26.

156. Melekos MD, Zarakovitis I, Dandinis K, et al. BCG versus epirubicin in the prophylaxis of multiple superficial bladder tumours: results of a prospective randomized study using modified treatment schemes. Int Urol Nephrol 1996;28:499–509.

157. Vegt PD, Witjes JA, Witjes WP, et al. A randomized study of intravesical mitomycin C, bacillus Calmette-Guérin Tice and bacillus Calmette-Guérin RIVM treatment in pTa-pT1 papillary carcinoma and carcinoma in situ of the bladder. J Urol 1995;153:929–33.

158. Witjes JA, van der Meijden AP, Sylvester LC, et al. Long-term follow-up of an EORTC randomized prospective trial comparing intravesical bacille Calmette-Guérin-RIVM and mitomycin C in superficial bladder cancer. EORTC GU Group and the Dutch South East Cooperative Urological Group. European Organisation for Research and Treatment of Cancer Genito-Urinary Tract Cancer Collaborative Group. Urology 1998;52:403–10.

159. Malmstrom PU, Wijkstrom H, Lundholm C, et al. 5-year followup of a randomized prospective study comparing mitomycin C and bacillus Calmette-Guérin in patients with superficial bladder carcinoma. Swedish-Norwegian Bladder Cancer Study Group. J Urol 1999;161:1124–7.

160. van der Meijden APM, Brausi M, Zambon V, et al, and Members of the EORTC Genito-Urinary Group. Intravesical instillation of epirubicin, bacillus Calmette-Guérin, and bacillus Calmette-Guérin plus isoniazid for intermediate and high risk Ta, T1 papillary carcinoma of the bladder: a European Organization for Research and Treatment of Cancer Genito-urinary Group randomized phase III trial. J Urol 2001;166:476–81.

161. DeJager R, Guinan P, Lamm D, et al. Long-term complete remission in bladder carcinoma in situ with intravesical Tice bacillus Calmette Guérin. Urology 1991;38:507–13.

162. Coplen DE, Marcus MD, Myers JA, et al. Long-term followup of patients treated with 1 or 2, 6-week courses of intravesical bacillus Calmette-Guérin: analysis of possible predictors of response free of tumor. J Urol 1990;144:652–7.

163. Herr HW, Laudone VP, Badalament RA, et al. Bacillus Calmette-Guérin therapy alters the progression of superficial bladder cancer. J Clin Oncol 1988;6:1450–5.

164. Herr HW, Schwalb DM, Zhang ZF, et al. Intravesical bacillus Calmette-Guérin therapy prevents tumor progression and death from superficial bladder cancer: ten-year follow-up of a prospective randomized trial. J Clin Oncol 1995; 13:1404–8.

165. Cookson MS, Herr HW, Zhang ZF, et al. The treated natural history of high risk superficial bladder cancer: 15-year outcome. J Urol 1997;158:62–7.

166. Herr HW, Badalament RA, Amato DA, et al. Superficial bladder cancer treated with bacillus Calmette-Guérin: a multivariate analysis of factors affecting tumor progression. J Urol 1989;141:22–9.

167. Okamura T, Tozawa K, Yamada Y, et al. Clinicopathological evaluation of repeated courses of intravesical bacillus Calmette-Guérin instillation for preventing recurrence of initially resistant superficial bladder cancer. J Urol 1996;156:967–71.

168. Hudson MA, Ratliff TL, Gillen DP, et al. Single course versus maintenance bacillus Calmette-Guérin therapy for superficial bladder tumors: a prospective, randomized trial. J Urol 1987;138:295–8.

169. Badalament RA, Herr HW, Wong GY, et al. A prospective randomized trial of maintenance versus nonmaintenance intravesical bacillus Calmette-Guérin therapy of superficial bladder cancer. J Clin Oncol 1987;5:441–9.

170. Palou J, Laguna P, Millan-Rodriguez F, et al. Control group and maintenance treatment with bacillus Calmette-Guérin for carcinoma in situ and/or high grade bladder tumors. J Urol 2001;165:1488–91.

171. Saint F, Irnai J, Jacques J, et al. Tolerability of bacille Calmette-Guérin maintenance therapy for superficial bladder cancer. Urology 2001;57:883–8.

172. Heney NM, Ahmed S, Flanagan MJ, et al. Superficial bladder cancer: progression and recurrence. J Urol 1983; 130:1083–6.

173. Kaubisch S, Lum BL, Reese J, et al. Stage T1 bladder cancer: grade is the primary determinant for risk of muscle invasion. J Urol 1991;146:28–31.

174. Stockle M, Alken P, Engelmann U, et al. Radical cystectomy—often too late? Eur Urol 1987;13:361–7.

175. Esrig D, Freeman JA, Stein JP, Skinner DG. Early cystectomy for clinical stage T1 transitional cell carcinoma of the bladder. Semin Urol Oncol 1997;15:154–60.

176. Lebret T, Gaudez F, Herve JM, et al. Low-dose BCG instillations in the treatment of stage T1 grade 3 bladder tumours: recurrence, progression and success. Eur Urol 1998;34:67–72.

177. Pansadoro V, Emiliozzi P, Defidio L, et al. Bacillus Calmette-Guérin in the treatment of stage T1 grade 3 transitional cell carcinoma of the bladder: long-term results. J Urol 1995;154:2054–8.

178. Pansadoro V, Emiliozzi P, de Paula F, et al. Long-term follow-up pf G3T1 transitional cell carcinoma of the bladder treated with intravesical bacille Calmette-Guérin: 18-year experience. Urology 2002;59:227–31.

179. Cookson MS, Sarosdy MF. Management of stage T1 superficial bladder cancer with intravesical bacillus Calmette-Guérin therapy. J Urol 1992;148:797–801.

180. Baniel J, Grauss D, Engelstein D, Sella A. Intravesical bacillus Calmette-Guérin treatment for stage T1 grade 3 transitional cell carcinoma of the bladder. Urology 1998;52:785–9.

181. Hurle R, Losa A, Manzetti A, Lembo A. Intravesical bacille Calmette-Guérin in stage T1 grade 3 bladder cancer therapy: a 7-year follow-up. Urology 1999;54:258–63.

182. Davis JW, Sheth SI, Doviak MJ, Schellhammer PF. Superficial bladder carcinoma treated with bacillus Calmette-Guérin: progression-free and disease specific survival with minimum 10-year follow-up. J Urol 2002;167:494–500.

183. Brake M, Loertzer H, Horsch R, Keller H. Recurrence and progression of stage T1, grade 3 transitional cell carcinoma of the bladder following intravesical immunotherapy with bacillus Calmette-Guérin. J Urol 2000;163:1697–701.

184. Klan R, Loy V, Huland H. Residual tumor discovered in routine second transurethral resection in patients with stage T1 transitional cell carcinoma of the bladder. J Urol 1991;146:316–8.

185. Herr HW. The value of a second transurethral resection in evaluating patients with bladder tumors. J Urol 1999;162:74–6.

186. Lacombe L, Dalbagni G, Zhang ZF, et al. Overexpression of p53 protein in a high-risk population of patients with superficial bladder cancer before and after bacillus Calmette-Guérin therapy: correlation to clinical outcome. J Clin Oncol 1996;14:2646–52.

187. Zlotta AR, Noel JC, Fayt I, et al. Correlation and prognostic significance of p53, p21WAF1/CIP1 and Ki-67 expression in patients with superficial bladder tumors treated with bacillus Calmette-Guérin intravesical therapy. J Urol 1999;161:792–8.

188. Lebret T, Becette V, Barbagelatta M, et al. Correlation between p53 over expression and response to bacillus Calmette-Guérin therapy in a high risk select population of patients with T1G3 bladder cancer. J Urol 1998;159:788–91.

189. Pages F, Flam TA, Vieillefond A, et al. P53 status does not predict initial clinical response to bacillus Calmette-Guérin intravesical therapy in T1 bladder tumors. J Urol 1998;159:1079–84.

190. Kondylis FI, Demirci S, Ladaga L, et al. Outcomes after intravesical bacillis Calmette-Guérin are not affected by substaging of high grade T1 transitional cell carcinoma. J Urol 2000;163:1120–3.

191. Pagano F, Bassi P, Ferrante GL, et al. Is pT4a (D1) stage reliable in assessing transitional cell carcinoma of the prostate in patients with concurrent bladder cancer? A necessary distinction for contiguous and noncontiguous involvement. J Urol 1996;155:244–7.

192. Hillyard RW, Ladaga L, Schellhammer PE. Superficial transitional cell carcinoma of the bladder associated with mucosal involvement of the prostatic urethra: results of treatment with intravesical bacillus Calmette-Guérin. J Urol 1988;139:290–3.

193. Bretton PR, Herr HW, Whitemore WF, et al. Intravesical bacillus Calmette-Guérin therapy for in situ transitional cell carcinoma involving the prostatic urethra. J Urol 1989;141:853–6.

194. Palou J, Xavier B, Laguana B, et al. In situ transitional cell carcinoma of the prostatic urethra: bacillus Calmette-Guérin therapy without previous transurethral resection of the prostate. Urology 1996;47:482–4.

195. Oversen H, Poulsen AL, Steven K. Intravesical bacillus Calmette-Guérin with the Danish strain for the treatment of carcinoma in situ of the bladder. Br J Urol 1993;72:744–8.

196. Schellhammer PF, Ladaga LE, Moriarty RP. Intravesical bacillus Calmette-Guérin for treatment of superficial transitional cell carcinoma of prostatic urethra in association with carcinoma of the bladder. J Urol 1995;153:53–6.

197. Hardeman SW, Soloway MS. Transitional cell carcinoma of the prostate: diagnosis, staging and management. World J Urol 1988;6:170–4.

198. Bassi PF. BCG (bacillus Calmette-Guérin) therapy of high-risk superficial bladder cancer. Surg Oncol 2002;11:77–83.

199. Orihuela E, Herr HW, Pinsky CM, Whitmore WF Jr. Toxicity of intravesical BCG and its management in patients with superficial bladder tumors. Cancer 1987;60:326–33.

200. van der Meijden AP. Practical approaches to the prevention and treatment of adverse reactions to BCG. Eur Urol 1995;27 Suppl 1:23–8.

201. Steg A, Adjiman S, Debre B. BCG therapy in superficial bladder tumours—complications and precautions. Eur Urol 1992;21 Suppl 2:35–40.

202. Berry DL, Blumenstein BA, Magyary DL, et al. Local toxicity patterns associated with intravesical bacillus Calmette-Guérin: a Southwest Oncology Group Study. Int J Urol 1996;3:98–100; discussion 101.

203. van der Meijden PM, van Klingeren B, Steerenberg PA, et al. The possible influence of antibiotics on results of bacillus Calmette-Guérin intravesical therapy for superficial bladder cancer. J Urol 1991;146:444–6.

204. Durek C, Rusch-Gerdes S, Joacham D, Bohle A. Sensitivity of BCG to modern antibiotics. Eur Urol 2000;37 Suppl 1:21–5.

205. Al Khalifa M, Elfving P, Mansson W, et al. The effect of isoniazid on BCG-induced toxicity in patients with superficial bladder cancer. Eur Urol 2000;37 Suppl 1:26–30.

206. Bohle A, Balck F, von Weitersheim J, Jocham D. The quality of life during intravesical bacillus Calmette-Guérin therapy. J Urol 1996;155:1221–6.

207. Mack D, Frick J. Quality of life in patients undergoing bacille Calmette-Guérin therapy for superficial bladder cancer. Br J Urol 1996;78:369–71.

208. Lamm DL, Steg A, Boccon-Gibod L, et al. Complications of bacillus Calmette-Guérin immunotherapy: review of 2602 patients and comparison of chemotherapy complications. Prog Clin Biol Res 1989;310:335–55.

209. Lamm DL. Efficacy and safety of bacille Calmette-Guérin immunotherapy in superficial bladder cancer. Clin Infect Dis 2000;31:S86–90.

210. Steg A, Leleu C, Debre B, et al. Systemic bacillus Calmette-Guérin infection in patients treated by intravesical BCG therapy for superficial bladder cancer. Prog Clin Biol Res 1989;310:325–34.

211. DeHaven JI, Traynellis C, Riggs DR, et al. Antibiotic and steroid therapy of massive systemic bacillus Calmette-Guérin toxicity. J Urol 1992;147:738–42.

212. Shimasaki N, Yamasaki I, Kamada M, Syuin T. Two cases of successful treatment with steroid for local and systemic hypersensitivity reaction following inravesical instillation of bacillus Calmette-Guérin. Hinyokika Kiyo 2001;47:281–4.

213. Durek C, Jurczok A, Werner H, et al. Optimal treatment of systemic bacillus Calmette-Guérin infection: investigations in an animal model. J Urol 2002;168:826–31.

214. Andres E, Gaunard A, Blickle JF, et al. Systemic reactions after inravesical BCG instillation for bladder cancer. Q J Med 2001;94:719.

215. Lamm DL, van der Meijden PM, Morales A, et al. Incidence and treatment of complications of bacillus Calmette-Guérin intravesical therapy in superficial bladder cancer. J Urol 1992;147:596–600.

216. Case records of the Massachusetts General Hospital. Weekly clinicopathological exercises. Case 29-1998. A 57-year-old man with fever and jaundice after intravesical instillation of bacille Calmette-Guérin for bladder cancer [clinical conference]. N Engl J Med 1998;339:831–7.

217. Bassi P, Spinadin R, Crando R, et al. Modified induction course: a solution to side-effects? Eur Urol 2000;37 Suppl 1: 31–2.

218. Wittes R, Klotz L, Kosecka U. Severe bacillus Calmette-Guérin cystitis responds to systemic steroids when antituberculous drugs and local steroids fail. J Urol 1999;161:1568–9.

219. Saporta L, Gumus E, Karadag H, et al. Reiter syndrome following intracavitary BCG administration. Scand J Urol Nephrol 1997;31:211–2.

220. Shoenfeld Y, Aron-Maor A, Tanai A, Ehrenfeld M. BCG and autoimmunity: another two-edged sword. J Autoimmun 2001;16:235–40.

221. Lebret T, Bohin D, Kassardjian Z, et al. Recurrence, progression and success in stage Ta grade 3 bladder tumors treated with low dose bacillus Calmette-Guérin instillations. J Urol 2000;163:63–7.

222. Rintala E, Jauhiainen K, Alfthan O. Mitomycin-C and BCG in intravesical chemotherapy and immunotherapy of superficial bladder cancer. Finnbladder Research Group. Prog Clin Biol Res 1989;310:271–4.

223. Blumenstein BA, Lamm D, Jewett MA. Effect of colony-forming unit dose of Connaught BCG on outcome to immunotherapy in superficial bladder cancer. J Urol Suppl 1990;143:340A.

224. Rivera P, Caffarena E, Cornejo H, et al. [Microdoses of BCG vaccine for prophylaxis in bladder cancer stage T1.] Actas Urol Esp 1993;17:243–6.

225. Mack D, Frick J. Low-dose bacille Calmette-Guérin (BCG) therapy in superficial high-risk bladder cancer: a phase II study with the BCG strain Connaught Canada. Br J Urol 1995;75:185–7.

226. Mack D, Holtl W, Bassi P, et al, of the EORTC. The ablative effect of quarter dose bacillus Calmette-Guérin on a papillary marker lesion of the bladder. J Urol 2001;165:401–3.

227. Hurle R, Losa A, Ranieri A, et al. Low dose Pasteur bacillus Calmette-Guérin regimen in stage T1, grade 3 bladder cancer therapy. J Urol 1996;156:1602–5.

228. Losa A, Hurle R, Lembo A. Low dose bacillus Calmette-Guérin for carcinoma in situ of the bladder: long-term results. J Urol 2000;163:68–72.

229. Morales A, Nickel JC, Wilson JW. Dose-response of bacillus Calmette-Guérin in the treatment of superficial bladder cancer. J Urol 1992;147:1256–8.

230. Takashi M, Wakai K, Ohno Y, et al. Evaluation of a low-dose intravesical bacillus Calmette-Guérin (Tokyo strain) therapy for superficial bladder cancer. Int Urol Nephrol 1995;27:723–33.

231. Martinez-Pineiro JA, Solsona E, Flores N, Isorna S. Improving the safety of BCG immunotherapy by dose reduction. Cooperative Group CUETO. Eur Urol 1995;27 Suppl 1: 13–8.

232. Martinez-Pineiro JA, Flores N, Isorna S, et al, of CUETO. Long-term follow-up of prospective trial comparing a standard 81 mg dose of intravesical bacille Calmette-Guérin with a reduced dose of 27 mg in superficial bladder cancer. BJU Int 2002;89:671–80.

233. Pagano F, Bassi P, Piazza N, et al. Improving the efficacy of BCG immunotherapy by dose reduction. Eur Urol 1995;27 Suppl 1:19–22.

234. Bassi P, Pappagallo GL, Piazza N, et al. Low dose vs. standard dose BCG therapy of superficial bladder cancer: final results of a phase III randomized trial. J Urol Suppl 1999;161:285.

235. O'Donnell MA, Krohn J, DeWolf WC. Salvage intravesical therapy with interferon-α2b plus low dose bacillus Calmette-Guérin is effective in patients with superficial bladder cancer in whom bacillus Calmette-Guérin alone previously failed. J Urol 2001;166:1300–5.

236. Luciani LG, Neulander E, Murphy WM, Wajsman Z. Risk of continued intravesical therapy and delayed cystectomy in BCG-refractory superficial bladder cancer: an investigational approach. Urology 2001;58:376–9.

237. Bassi P, Spinadin R, Carando R, et al. Modified induction course: a solution to side-effects? Eur Urol 2000;37 Suppl 1:31–2.

238. Coplen DE, Ratliff TL, Kavoussi LR, et al. Combination of Adriamycin and BCG in the treatment of superficial bladder cancer. J Urol Suppl 1990;143:341A.

239. Gelabert-Mas A, Arango Toro O, Bielsa Gali O, Llado Carbonell C. [A prospective and randomized study of the complete response, index of recurrences and progression

in superficial bladder carcinoma treated with mitomycin C alone versus mitomycin C and BCG alternatively.] Arch Esp Urol 1993;46:379–82.

240. Erol A, Ozgur S, Basar M, Cetin S. Trial with bacillus Calmette-Guérin and epirubicin combination in the prophylaxis of superficial bladder cancer. Urol Int 1994;52:69–72.

241. Uekado Y, Hirano A, Shinka T, Ohkawa T. The effects of intravesical chemoimmunotherapy with epirubicin and bacillus Calmette-Guérin for prophylaxis of recurrence of superficial bladder cancer: a preliminary report. Cancer Chemother Pharmacol 1994;35 Suppl:S65–8.

242. Rintala E, Jauhiainen K, Rajala P, et al. Alternating mitomycin C and bacillus Calmette-Guérin instillation therapy for carcinoma in situ of the bladder. The Finnbladder Group. J Urol 1995;154:2050–3.

243. Rintala E, Jauhiainen K, Kaasinen E, et al. Alternating mitomycin C and bacillus Calmette-Guérin instillation prophylaxis for recurrent papillary (stages Ta to T1) superficial bladder cancer. Finnbladder Group. J Urol 1996;156:56–9; discussion 59–60.

244. Van der Meijden AP, Hall RR, Macaluso MP, et al. Marker tumour responses to the sequential combination of intravesical therapy with mitomycin-C and BCG-RIVM in multiple superficial bladder tumours. Report from the European Organisation for Research and Treatment on Cancer-Genitourinary Group (EORTC 30897). Eur Urol 1996;29:199–203.

245. Witjes JA, Caris CT, Mungan NA, et al. Results of a randomized phase III trial of sequential intravesical therapy with mitomycin C and bacillus Calmette-Guérin versus mitomycin C alone in patients with superficial bladder cancer. J Urol 1998;160:1668–71.

246. Wijkstrom H, Kassinen E, Malmstrom P, et al. A nordic study comparing intravesical instillations of alternating mitomycin C and BCG with BCG alone in carcinoma in situ of the urinary bladder. J Urol Suppl 1999;161:286.

247. Ali-El-Dein B, Nabeeh A, Ismail EH, Ghoneim MA. Sequential bacillus Calmette-Guérin and epirubicin versus bacillus Calmette-Guérin alone for superficial bladder tumors: a randomized prospective study. J Urol 1999;162:339–42.

248. Kassinen E, Rintala E, Anna-Kaisa P, et al, and the Finnbladder Group. Weekly mitomycin C followed by monthly bacillus Calmette-Guérin or alternating monthly interferon-α2b and bacillus Calmette-Guérin for prophylaxis or recurrent papillary superficial bladder cancer. J Urol 2000;164:47–52.

249. Oosterlinck W, Kurth KH, Schroder F, et al. A prospective European Organization for Research and Treatment of Cancer Genitourinary Group randomized trial comparing transurethral resection followed by a single intravesical instillation of epirubicin or water in single stage Ta, T1 papillary carcinoma of the bladder. J Urol 1993;149:749–52.

250. Tolley DA, Parmar MK, Grigor KM, et al. The effect of intravesical mitomycin C on recurrence of newly diagnosed superficial bladder cancer: a further report with 7 years of follow up. J Urol 1996;155:1233–8.

251. Solsona E, Iborra I, Ricos JV, et al. Effectiveness of a single immediate mitomycin C instillation in patients with low risk superficial bladder cancer: short and long- term followup. J Urol 1999;161:1120–3.

252. Zhang Y, Khoo HE, Esuvaranathan K. Effects of bacillus Calmette-Guérin and interferon alpha-2B on cytokine production in human bladder cancer cell lines. J Urol 1999;161:977–83.

253. Hawkyard SJ, Jackson AM, Prescott S, et al. The effect of recombinant cytokines on bladder cancer cells in vitro. J Urol 1993;150:514–8.

254. Bandyopadhyay S, Fazeli-Matin S, Rackley R, et al. Interferon-resistant transitional cell carcinomas (TCC) have defective signal transduction factors: a clinical basis for interferon combination therapy. J Urol Suppl 1999;161:113.

255. Giannakopoulos S, Gekas A, Aivizatos G, et al. Efficacy of escalating doses of intravesical interferon alpha-2b in reducing recurrence rate and progression in superficial transitional cell carcinoma. Br J Urol 1998;82:829–34.

256. Malmstrom PU. A randomized comparative dose-ranging study of interferon-alpha and mitomycin-C as an internal control in primary or recurrent superficial transitional cell carcinoma. BJU Int 2002;89:681–6.

257. Downs TM, Szilvasi A, O'Donnell MA. Pharmacological biocompatibility between intravesical preparations of BCG and interferon-alpha 2B. J Urol 1997;158:2311–5.

258. Stricker P, Pryor K, Nicolson T, et al. Bacillus Calmette-Guérin plus intravesical interferon alpha-2b in patients with superficial bladder cancer. Urology 1996;48:957–62.

259. Bercovich E, Deriu M, Manferrari F, Irianni G. BCG vs. BCG plus recombinant alpha-interferon 2b in superficial tumors of the bladder. Arch Ital Urol Androl 1995;67:257–60.

260. Esuvaranathan K, Kamaraj R, Mohan RS, et al. A phase IIB trial of BCG combined with interferon alpha for bladder cancer. J Urol Suppl 2000;163:152.

261. Harris CC, Kaufman DG, Sporn MB, Staffiotti U. Histogenesis of squamous metaplasia and squamous cell carcinoma of the respiratory epithelium in an animal model. Cancer Chemother Rep 1973;4:43–7.

262. Alfthan O, Tarkkanen J, Grohn P, et al. Tigason (etretinate) in prevention of recurrence of superficial bladder tumors. A double-blind clinical trial. Eur Urol 1983;9:6–9.

263. Studer UE, Biedermann C, Chollet D, et al. Prevention of recurrent superficial bladder tumors by oral etretinate: preliminary results of a randomized, double blind multicenter trial in Switzerland. J Urol 1984;131:47–9.

264. Byar D, Blackard C. Comparisons of placebo, pyridoxine, and topical thiotepa in preventing recurrence of stage I bladder cancer. Urology 1977;10:556–61.

265. Bussey HJ, DeCosse JJ, Deschner EE, et al. A randomized trial of ascorbic acid in polyposis coli. Cancer 1982;50:1434–9.

266. Heinonen OP, Albanes D, Virtamo J, et al. Prostate cancer and supplementation with alpha-tocopherol and beta-carotene: incidence and mortality in a controlled trial. J Natl Cancer Inst 1998;90:440–6.

267. Meydani SN, Meydani M, Blumberg JB, et al. Vitamin E supplementation and in vivo immune response in healthy elderly subjects. A randomized controlled trial. JAMA 1997;277:1380–6.

268. Merz VW, Marth D, Kraft R, et al. Analysis of early failures after intravesical instillation therapy with bacille Cal-

mette-Guérin for carcinoma in situ of the bladder. Br J Urol 1995;75:180–4.

269. Orsola A, Palou J, Xavier B, et al. Primary bladder carcinoma in situ: assessment of early BCG response as a prognostic factor. Eur Urol 1998;33:457–63.

270. Bui TT, Schellhammer PF. Additional bacillus Calmette-Guérin therapy for recurrent transitional cell carcinoma after an initial complete response. Urology 1997;49:687–90; discussion 690–1.

271. Bassi P, Iafrate M, Spinadin R, et al. Superficial bladder neoplasia unresponsive to endocavitary treatment: when should the treatment approach be changed? Arch Ital Urol Androl 2001;73:181–6.

272. Schwalb MD, Herr HW, Sogani PC, et al. Positive urinary cytology following a complete response to intravesical bacillus Calmette-Guérin therapy: pattern of recurrence. J Urol 1994;152:382–7.

273. Steinberg G, Bahnson R, Brosman S, et al, and the Valrubicin Study Group. Efficacy and safety of valrubicin for the treatment of bacillus Calmette-Guérin refractory carcinoma in situ of the bladder. J Urol 2000;163:761–7.

274. Marchetti A, Wang L, Magar R, et al. Management of patients with bacilli Calmette-Guérin refractory carcinoma in situ of the urinary bladder: cost implications of a clinical trial of valrubicin. Clin Ther 2000;22:422–38.

275. Catalona WJ, Hudson MA, Gillen DP, et al. Risks and benefits of repeated courses of intravesical bacillus Calmette-Guérin therapy for superficial bladder cancer. J Urol 1987;137:220–4.

276. Belldegrun AS, Franklin JR, O'Donnell MA, et al. Superficial bladder cancer: the role of interferon-alpha. J Urol 1998;159:1793–801.

277. Glashan RW. A randomized controlled study of intravesical α-2b-interferon in carcinoma in situ of the bladder. J Urol 1980;144:658.

278. Williams RD, Gleason DM, Smith AY, et al. Pilot study of intravesical alfa-2b interferon for treatment of bladder carcinoma in situ following BCG failure. J Urol Suppl 1996;155:494A.

279. Lam JS, Benson MC, O'Donnell MA, et al. Bacillus Calmette-Guérin plus interferon alfa 2B intravesical therapy maintains an extended treatment plan for superficial bladder cancer with minimal toxicity. J Urol Suppl 2002;167:190.

280. Jurincic-Winkler CD, Metz KA, Beuth J, Klippel KF. Keyhole limpet hemocyanin for carcinoma in situ of the bladder: a long term follow-up study. Eur Urol 2000;37 Suppl 3:45–9.

281. Lamm DL, Dehaven JI, Riggs DR. Keyhole limpet hemocyanin immunotherapy of bladder cancer: laboratory and clinical studies. Eur Urol 2000;37 Suppl 3:41–4.

282. Nseyo UO, Shumaker B, Klein EA, Sutherland K. Photodynamic therapy using porfimer sodium as an alternative to cystectomy in patients with refractory transitional cell carcinoma in situ of the bladder. Bladder Photofrin Study Group. J Urol 1998;160:39–44.

283. Weidelich R, Stepp H, Baumgartner R, et al. Clinical experience with 5-aminolevulinic acid and photodynamic therapy for refractory superficial bladder cancer. J Urol 2001;165:1904–7.

284. Sarosdy MF, Manyak MJ, Sagalowsky AI, et al. Oral bropirmine immunotherapy of bladder carcinoma in situ after prior intravesical bacille Calmette-Guérin. Urology 1998;51:226–31.

285. Dalbagni G, Russo P, Sheinfeld J, et al. Phase I trial of intravesical gemcitabine in bacillus Calmette-Guérin-refractory transitional cell carcinoma of the bladder. J Clin Oncol 2002;20:3193–8.

286. Quilty PM, Duncan W. Treatment of superficial (T1) tumours of the bladder by radical radiotherapy. Br J Urol 1986;58:147–52.

287. Robel C, Dunst J, Grabenbauer GG, et al. Radiotherapy is an effective treatment for high-risk T1 bladder cancer. Strahlenther Onkol 2001;177:82–8.

288. Shipley WU, Kaufman DS, Heney NM, et al. An update of combined modality therapy for patients with muscle invading bladder cancer using selective bladder preservation or cystectomy. J Urol 1999;162:445–50; discussion 450–1.

13

Outcomes and Quality of Life Issues Following Radical Cystectomy and Urinary Diversion

ERIN E. KATZ
R. COREY O'CONNOR
GARY D. STEINBERG

Bladder carcinoma is the second most common genitourinary tumor, accounting for approximately 4% of all cancers. Each year in the United States more than 60,200 patients are diagnosed with and more than 12,700 patients die from bladder cancer.[1,2,3] Radical cystectomy with urinary diversion continues to be the standard treatment of invasive bladder cancer. The morbidity and mortality rates of continent and incontinent urinary diversions are no longer statistically different.[4] As a result, assessing the quality of life after urinary tract reconstruction has become increasingly important. Historically, however, it has been difficult to measure urinary, bowel and sexual function as well as overall patient satisfaction with the ileal conduit, continent urinary reservoir and orthotopic neobladder. This is primarily due to a paucity of quality of life (QOL) studies comparing various urinary diversions that use validated, reliable questionnaires. Additionally, it is unclear whether the presently available QOL questionnaires and instruments are relevant to cystectomy and urinary diversion. Thus, it is difficult to prove the relative psychosocial benefits of various types of urinary tract reconstruction. In this chapter we will review the published literature regarding different types of urinary diversions, outcomes, and QOL issues following radical cystectomy.

TYPES OF URINARY DIVERSION, OUTCOMES, AND BLADDER PRESERVATION

Various types of urinary diversions have become standard surgical techniques worldwide. Currently, in most centers patients can now be offered a noncontinent cutaneous diversion, a continent cutaneous diversion, or an orthotopic neobladder with comparable morbidity rates.[5] Although some urinary diversions are performed for nonmalignant conditions, invasive bladder cancer is the most common indication for diversion.

Bladder preservation using single modality therapy such as transurethral resection of bladder tumor (TURBT), partial cystectomy, external beam radiation therapy or combination therapy with TURBT, cisplatin based chemotherapy and external beam radiation are treatment options for invasive bladder cancer in select patients. Patients undergoing TURBT or partial cystectomy as single modality therapy must have a newly diagnosed solitary tumor, with low volume. The advantages to this treatment include sparing bladder function, urinary continence and potency; however, there is a high likelihood of recurrent bladder cancer.[3] Patients treated with combination therapy (ie, TURBT, chemotherapy and external beam radiation to the bladder and pelvic lymph nodes) require lifelong surveillance of the bladder, upper urinary tracts and urethra. Up to 50% of this population will require salvage cystectomy due to recurrent or refractory bladder cancer. Approximately 25 to 40% of patients are clinically free of cancer with an intact bladder at 5 years after treatment.[6] Advocates of organ preservation argue that patients with an intact, normally functioning bladder have greater self-esteem, sexual function, bladder function, and overall improved activities of daily living compared to patients with orthotopic or "artificial bladders."[7] To our knowledge, no validated quality of life study has been performed to compare radical cystectomy versus bladder preservation for the treatment of bladder cancer.

Ileal Conduit

The ileal conduit is the simplest and most common form of urinary diversion (Figure 13–1). The non-continent diversion is created by connecting both ureters into the proximal end of an isolated 15 cm

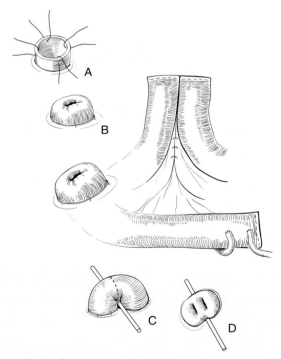

Figure 13–1. Operative technique of ileal/colon conduit. *A*, A short intestinal segment (15–20 cm) is brought out through the anterior abdominal wall, and *B*, creation of an end "rosebud" stoma. *C* and *D*, creation of a Turnbull loop stoma. Adapted from Rowland, RG, Krupp, BP. Evolution of the Indiana continent urinary reservoir. J Urol 1994;152:2247–51.

segment of ileum at least 15 cm proximal to the ileo-cecal valve. The distal end of the intestinal conduit is secured to the anterior abdominal wall as a stoma. The ileum is commonly used although jejunum, colon, or stomach may also be used.[8,9]

At our institution ileal conduits are generally performed on patients with diminished renal function (creatinine > 2.0 mg/dL), bulky extravesical or nodal disease, the inability to care for a continent reservoir or significant other co-morbidities. Advantages of the ileal conduit over continent diversions include that it is technically easier to perform, may take less operative time, and may be associated with the fewest number of perioperative and postoperative complications, especially when performed by surgeons with limited experience with continent reconstruction. Disadvantages are related to the need for an external urine collection device, and potential feelings of decreased sociability and sexuality.

Stoma Care

Advances in stoma care have improved the quality of life in patients with incontinent urinary diversions. Selection of the stoma site is one of the most critical considerations in avoiding complications. The stoma should *not* be placed in an abdominal crease, at the belt line, or over any pre-existing scars because an ill fitting external collection device will likely result. A poorly fitted appliance can lead to urinary leakage, skin breakdown, dermatitis, and an overall sense of helplessness and depression.

Hart and colleagues reported that 62% of all the patients who underwent radical cystectomy reported at least one diversion related problem, with urinary leakage and odor being the most common. The study also reported that 30% of the patients had frequent problems with skin irritation, and 57% had difficulty managing the collecting device.[10] Other stomal complications include parastomal hernias, stomal stenosis, and retraction of the stoma.

The stoma must be measured often during the first few weeks after surgery secondary to change in size due to subsiding edema. If an appliance is cut too large, the stomal effluent will make contact with the skin, causing irritation and blistering. Avoidance of straining and heavy lifting in the first 3 months after surgery will help to prevent parastomal hernias and prolapse. A properly fitting stoma and meticulous stoma care is essential for patients undergoing a non-continent urinary diversion. Neglect of the stoma, poor hygiene, and the inability to care for the stoma site can contribute to the overall decrease of quality of life. Family members, visiting nurses and enterostomal therapists play an important role in maintaining the stoma and minimizing complications. Patients undergoing diversions with stomas will more readily adapt to their new body image if they receive professional input preoperatively and throughout the hospital stay. Some patients have difficulties postoperatively with day-to-day living due to physical weakness, lethargy, feelings of insecurity, and fear of responsibility for stomal care. Physicians must have the ability to communicate understanding to patients and provide reassurance to help decrease their anxiety.

Indiana Pouch

The Indiana pouch, a continent cutaneous urinary diversion, is an alternative to the ileal conduit (Figure 13–2). Isolating the distal most 10 cm of ileum and most proximal 25 cm of ascending/transverse colon creates this catheterizable reservoir. The colonic segment is detubularized along the antimesenteric border and folded in the shape of the letter "U". The ureters are connected to the colonic pouch in a non-antirefluxing manner. Next, the 10 cm segment of terminal ileum is tapered to 12 to 14 French diameter and brought to the anterior abdominal wall or umbilicus as a catheterizable stoma. The detubularized colonic segment (which creates a low pressure reservoir) and the ileocecal valve function as continence mechanisms.

In our experience, Indiana pouches are best created for patients with unhealthy or radiated urethras or cancer at the bladder neck/prostatic urethra, both conditions which are unsuitable for anastomosis with a neobladder. Patients must demonstrate adequate manual dexterity to self-catheterize to be eligible for an Indiana pouch. Advantages of the Indiana pouch urinary diversion are related to a 94 to 97% continence rate and, unlike the ileal conduit, there is no need for an external urine collection device.[11–13]

Patients have the ability to stay dry for at least 4 hours without having to catheterize the stoma and many patients can remain continent during the normal sleep interval without requiring catheterization. Rowland and colleagues reviewed the outcomes of 81 patients treated with an Indiana pouch following cystectomy.

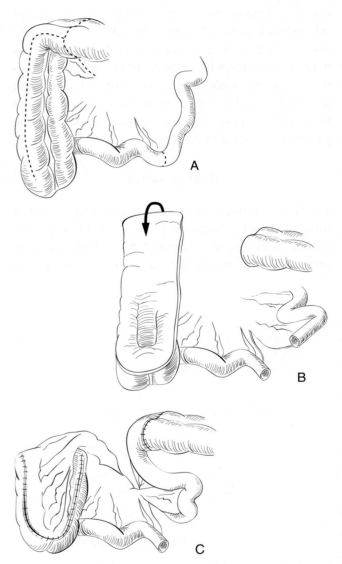

Figure 13–2. Indiana Pouch. *A*, The dotted lines show the margins of resection used to create an ileocecal segment reservoir. The incision along the antimesenteric border is used to detubularize the colonic segment. *B*, The arrow indicates the direction in which the detubularized colon will be folded to create the reservoir. The dotted line on the distal segment of the ileum, which will remain in the fecal stream, indicates the area to be spatulated to compensate for the size discrepancy between the ileum and the colon. *C*, The reservoir has been closed transversely in a Heinecke-Mikulicz type of reconfiguration. The end-to-end ileocolostomy has been completed. As an alternative, an end-to-side stapled anastomosis can be performed. Adapted from Rowland, RG, Krupp, BP. Evolution of the Indiana continent urinary reservoir. J Urol 1994;152:2247–51.

Early complications included bowel obstruction, difficulty with catheterization, pouch leak and infection. Late complications included urinary incontinence, stomal stenosis, parastomal hernias, pyelonephritis, and pouch stone formation. Pouch calculi are usually related to poor patient compliance with intermittent catheterization schedules. Reoperation rates for early and late complications were 3% and 15%, respectively.[11] Blute and colleagues reported on 194 females who underwent an Indiana pouch cutaneous diversion. The continence rate was found to be 90%. The reoperation rate was 15% and late complications occurred in 17%, including pouch calculi, stomal stenosis, incontinence, stomal hernia, small bowel obstruction, and renal insufficiency.[14] Other studies also report an 11% risk of metabolic acidosis and 7.5% occurrence of uretero–Indiana pouch strictures.[15,16] Traditionally, Indiana pouches were the continent diversion of choice for women. However, the worldwide experience with orthotopic diversion in women is increasing.[17] The benefits of orthotopic diversion versus Indiana pouch in this population are currently not well defined.

Orthotopic Neobladder

The orthotopic neobladder offers patients the option of continent urinary diversion that does not require an external stoma or routine clean intermittent catheterization. There are several techniques using ileum including the Studer, Hautmann, chimney modification of the Hautmann, and the "T" pouch as well as ileocolonic and sigmoid neobladder (see Figures 13–3, 13–4, 13–5). Presently, the neobladder is constructed by isolating a 60 cm segment of terminal ileum 15 cm proximal to the cecum. The bowel is fashioned in the shape of a "W," detubularized, and sewn in the shape of a sphere. The most proximal 8 to 10 cm are not detubularized (the chimney). The ureters are connected in a non-antirefluxing manner into the chimney. Finally, a 6 mm window is cut in the most dependant portion of the pouch to create a neobladder neck and anastomosed to the urethra.[9,18,19]

Candidates for orthotopic urinary diversion include patients with serum creatinine < 2.0 mg/dL, a healthy urethra with no evidence of cancer involving the urethra or bladder neck in women, or prosta-

tic stromal involvement in men, and a healthy gastrointestinal tract. Relative contraindications include bulky extravesical or nodal disease and previous pelvic or abdominal radiation. We do not believe that age or superficial involvement of the prostatic urethra is a contraindication to orthotopic urinary diversion. Advantages of the orthotopic ileal neobladder over other types of diversions include the avoidance of an external stoma and preservation of near-normal volitional control of micturition. Continence rates exceed 93% (daytime) and 86% (nighttime).[20] Complications are similar to those seen with the Indiana pouch. Hautmann and colleagues described the

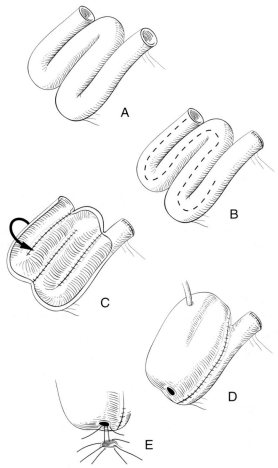

Figure 13–3. Operative technique of Hautmann neobladder with chimney modification. *A*, The neobladder is contructed by removing an ileal segment 68 cm in length, and orienting it into the shape of a "W" with four equal limbs, each 15 cm in length. *B*, The most proximal 8–12 cm of the ileal segment is not detubularized, and the remaining 60 cm of bowel is opened along the antimesenteric border. *C*, The posterior plate of the "W" is sewn together *D*, and the pouch is closed. *E*, Ileal urethral anastomosis. Adapted from Rowland, RG, Krupp, BP. Evolution of the Indiana continent urinary reservoir. J Urol 1994;152:2247–51.

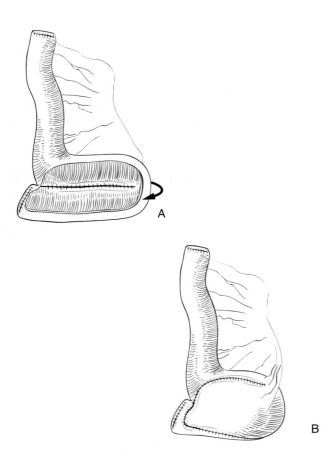

Figure 13–4. Operative technique of Studer ileal neobladder. A 60–65 cm ileal segment is excluded from bowel continuity. *A*, The distal 40 cm are detubularized and oriented into the shape of a "U". Both ureters are anastomosed end-to-side to the remaining 25 cm isoperistaltic limb. *B*, closure of the anterior wall of the pouch. Adapted from Rowland, RG, Krupp, BP. Evolution of the Indiana continent urinary reservoir. J Urol 1994;152:2247–51.

11-year results of 363 patients followed up after cystectomy and ileal neobladder surgery. Early and late neobladder-related complications occurred in 15.4% and 23.4%, respectively. The reoperation rate for neobladder related complications was 0.3% (early) and 4.4% (late).[19] Complications included ureteral to neobladder strictures, bladder neck contractures, and urinary retention. Many of these problems can be managed endoscopically.[21]

QUALITY OF LIFE ISSUES

Currently, major medical centers are reporting similar complication rates for continent and non-continent urinary diversions in appropriately selected patients.[4,21,22,23] As a result, surgeons must carefully consider an individual's desires and needs when plan-

ning therapy. It is important to tailor treatment to each individual, and to educate the patient by providing maximal information on outcomes for various treatment modalities. In addition to cure and survival, urologists must also try to identify predictors of therapeutic success with respect to QOL after cystectomy. As one would expect, cystectomy has been shown to adversely affect most aspects of life.[24] Since urinary leakage has proven to negatively impact QOL, one would assume that a continent urinary diversion would improve lifestyle and health related satisfaction when compared to non-continent diversion.[25] Currently, there are few measurements of postoperative QOL and the impact the type of urinary diversion has on patients after cystectomy. Surgical technique, physical well being and general health, sexuality, social functioning, coping strategies and social support may all play a role in determining a patient's degree of satisfaction following treatment. Many studies on health related QOL following cystectomy

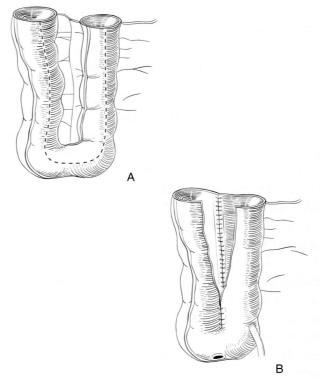

Figure 13–5. Operative technique of the Sigmoid pouch. *A*, a 30 cm segment of Sigmoid colon is excluded from bowel continuity, detubularization, and oriented into the shape of a "U". *B*, After closing the lower half of the anterior pouch wall, anastomosis of the most dependent portion of the pouch to the membranous urethra is performed. Adapted from Rowland, RG, Krupp, BP. Evolution of the Indiana continent urinary reservoir. J Urol 1994;152:2247–51.

and urinary diversion are flawed by design. There has been no general consensus on how QOL should be measured and what tool is best to accurately assess it. Older studies use non-validated questionnaires, whereas many of the more recent publications used either portions of validated forms combined with other validated or nonvalidated supplements. It is unclear to what extent these combinations alter the reliability of the questionnaire and the results.

Currently, several validated questionnaires have been used to quantify a patient's QOL after radical cystectomy and urinary diversion. The SF-36 Quality of Life survey is a generic, reliable, health-related survey used to evaluate the outcomes of a multitude of medical conditions. It contains diagnostic descriptions of illnesses that can be used to evaluate the impact of the illness or condition on the individual, social network, and society. This short form survey contains 36 questions assessing aspects of general health, physical and mental functioning, and vitality. Each question is given a score of 0 to 100 with a higher score indicating a better result.[26] The QLQ-C30 is a validated, reliable cancer-specific quality-of-life questionnaire developed by the European Organization for Research and Treatment of Cancer (EORTC). The self-assessed questionnaire is composed of 30 questions covering 9 categories—five functional items (physical, social, cognitive, emotional, and role functioning), three symptom items (pain, fatigue, nausea), global health and overall QOL scale, and several single-item measures (quality of sleep, gastrointestinal (GI) symptoms, financial impact of disease, and others). A higher score for the functional and QOL items indicates a higher level of functioning; whereas higher scores on the scale questions measuring symptoms indicate a reduced QOL.[27] In previous studies using this questionnaire for men with prostate cancer, there was weak to moderate correlation with clinical data.[28] The Functional Assessment of Cancer Therapy general score (FACT-G) is a validated, cancer-specific 28-item questionnaire divided into social, physical, functional, and emotional well-being categories. This questionnaire is a measure of difficulties and symptoms related to having cancer and its associated treatment.[29] The Sickness Impact Profile (SIP) consists of 136 questions divided into 12 categories representing behavioral changes related to generic illness; higher scores indicated poorer quality of life.[30] A new bladder cancer–specific module has become available.[31] It is not known if studies using questionnaires more specific to bladder cancer will demonstrate different results than past studies.

Dutta and colleagues recently reported a trend toward improved health related QOL scores for patients with orthotopic neobladders as compared to patients with ileal conduits. Emotional and functional well-being was improved with a neobladder but both groups appeared to be satisfied with their type of diversion.[32]

Published reports on the validity of the notion that continent diversions are "better" than ileal or colon conduits have been inconclusive (Table 13–1). Hara and colleagues reported the results of 85 patients who underwent cystectomy and urinary diversion with either an ileal conduit ($n = 37$) or an orthotopic neobladder ($n = 48$). Health related and overall QOL as measured by the SF-36 validated questionnaire showed no significant difference between the two groups.[33] Similarly, Fugisawa and colleagues found no difference in overall QOL in 56 cystectomy patients diverted with either a conduit ($n = 20$) or neobladder ($n = 36$) using the same SF-36 questionnaire.[34] Hart and colleagues using portions of four validated questionnaires to study 224 patients following radical cystectomy also confirmed these findings. The study reported that 95% of the patients rated QOL as good to excellent regardless of the type of urinary diversion. However, 28% of the patients who underwent a radical cystectomy and cutaneous Kock pouch surgery diversion had frequent problems with stomal catheterization.[10]

Conversely, Hobisch and colleagues reviewed the outcomes of 102 patients after either cystectomy and urinary diversion with orthotopic neobladder ($n = 69$) or ileal conduit ($n = 33$). QOL was objectively measured using the EORTC QLQ-C30 validated questionnaire and an additional supplement. They reported that patients with neobladders demonstrated a significantly higher QOL than patients with ileal conduits. Furthermore, 97% of neobladder patients would recommend the same urinary diversion to other patients needing a cystectomy whereas only 36% of conduit patients would do the same.[4]

Table 13–1. COMPARISON OF DIVERSIONS

Authors, Reference (Year)	No. Pts.	No. Patients per Type of Diversion (n)	Questionnaire Type	QOL Results
Hara et al,[33] (2002)	85	IC – (37) NB – (48)	SF-36	NB = IC
Dutta et al,[32] (2002)	72	IC – (23) NB – (49)	SF-36 FACT-G	NB > IC NS
Hobisch et al,[4] (2000)	102	IC – (33) NB – (69)	EORTC QLQ-C30 and supplement	NB > IC S
Fujisawa et al,[34] (2000)	56	IC – 20 NB – 36	SF-36	NB = IC
McGuire et al,[53] (2000)	92	IC – (38) CR – (16) NB – (38)	SF-36	NB = CR > IC S
Hart et al,[10] (1999)	221	IC – (25) CR – (93) NB – (103)	4 adapted, validated questionnaires	NB > CR > IC S
Kitamura et al,[54] (1999)	79	IC – (36) CR – (22) NB – (21)	Non-validated questionnaire	NB = CR = IC
Weijerman et al,[55] (1998)	56	CR – (23) NB – (33)	Sickness impact profile + supplement	NB > CR NS
Sullivan et al,[25] (1998)	55	CR – 10 NB – 45	Non-validated questionnaire	NB = CR
Gerharz et al,[50] (1997)	192	IC – 131 CR – 61	Non-validated questionnaire	CR > IC NS
Bjerre et al,[51] (1994)	76	IC – 50 CR – 26	Non-validated questionnaire	CR > IC S
Mansson et al,[56] (1988)	60	IC or CC – 40 CR – 20	Non-validated questionnaire	CR > IC S
Boyd et al,[52] (1987)	172	IC – 87 NB or CR – 85	4 adapted, validated questionnaires	NB > IC NS

IC = ileal conduit; CC = colon conduit; CR = catheterizable (cutaneous) reservoir; NB = neobladder; NS = not significant; S = significant.

Patients need to understand and accept certain potential risks associated with surgery. Cystectomy and any type of urinary diversion can have complications. An important question arises—is a patient with an orthotopic neobladder who had a difficult postoperative recovery as happy as a patient with an ileal conduit who had a routine postoperative recovery? Or, is a patient who receives an uncomplicated neobladder happier than a patient who has a properly functioning ileal conduit? Further comparative studies need to be performed to answer these questions.

URINARY CONTINENCE AND FUNCTION

Urinary sphincter control and volitional voiding are considered basic components of human socialization. Continent urinary diversions were developed, in part, to diminish the potentially embarrassing and detrimental effects associated with the loss of these functions. The inability to volitionally control urine may change one's body image, and cause general uneasiness and anxiety from fear of stomal leakage and odor. These issues can deter patients from various activities of daily living, leading to feelings of isolation and depression. Continuous improvement in the external appliances, surgical technique, and the aide of enterostomal therapy has decreased stoma-related complications. The most common complaint made by patients with incontinent urinary diversions is leakage. Large leaks from loose fitting bags, or "flush," or poorly positioned stomas can cause episodes of soaked clothes. Nocturnal leakage resulting in bed-wetting and disrupted sleep causes an additional high level of distress. Patients with continent reservoirs may also experience incontinence; however, these episodes are usually con-

Table 13–2. URINARY TRACT SYMPTOMS AFTER ILEAL NEOBLADDER*

Symptom	Neobladder (% of Patients)	Control (% of Patients)
Daytime/nightime urinary frequency		
Diurnal	3	3
Nocturnal	15	13
Urinary leakage	18	5
Use of pads		
Day	31	2
Night	69	0
Calculi formation	39	—
Urinary tract infection	14	6
Distress from urinary symptoms	15	5
Intermittent self catheterization	26	—
Anxiety level with CIC	50	—
Anxiety level with straining to empty	7	—
Depression in patients requiring CIC	50	—
Depression in patients who strain to empty	0	—

CIC = clean intermittent catheterization.
*Henningsohn et al.[35]

trolled by wearing protective pads. Patients with continent cutaneous urinary diversions also may experience distressful episodes of urinary leakage or difficulty with catheterization. A recent study performed by Henningsohn and colleagues assessed distressful urinary symptoms in 101 patients who underwent an ileal neobladder procedure compared to a control group without bladder cancer (Table 13–2). Anxiety and depression were significantly higher in patients with the ileal neobladder who performed clean intermittent catheterization compared to those who emptied their neobladders volitionally by valsalva. However, well-being and subjective QOL were similar in the two groups.[35]

Intestinal segments used in urinary diversion continue to produce mucus to varying degrees depending on the type of intestine used, hydration, and the type of operation performed. Mucus accumulation can obstruct the urethra, impair bladder or pouch emptying, and can lead to the formation of calculi which can ultimately contribute to decreased quality of life. In time, it is thought that the mucus production will decrease, especially with small bowel segments. In a study by N'Dow and colleagues 53% of patients who underwent neobladder reconstruction experienced intermittent obstruction of the urinary stream by mucus.[36] The incidence of

mucus blockage in the neobladder and ileal conduit was 17 to 30% and 0 to 20%, respectively. Interestingly, the SF-36 QOL questionnaire did not demonstrate a significant difference in scores between patients receiving the neobladder versus the ileal conduit. However, patients regretting having undergone surgery as a consequence of mucus production problems were 13% for the neobladder, and 0% for the ileal conduit.[36] In the experience of the authors of this chapter, predominantly using ileal neobladders, the mucus production greatly decreases with time and is actually felt to be responsible for signaling patients with the sensation to void. When a drop of mucus enters the proximal urethra, this creates a sensation of urgency. It has been infrequent that patients have had urinary retention secondary to mucus plugs.

SEXUAL FUNCTION

Sexuality after urinary diversion is a significant patient concern. After cystectomy there is an overall decrease in sexual desire, interaction with one's partner, and sexual activities. As sexual activities are limited there is a change in the patient–partner relationship that can result in a decrease in self-esteem.

Sexuality is unique to the individual. It is a combination of sexual intercourse, human contact, comfort, security, and self-worth. The embarrassment of wearing an appliance during sexual intercourse can inhibit patients, often leading to a decrease or cessation of sexual activity. Changes in physical appearance and the possibility of permanent sexual dysfunction should be discussed prior to surgery. However, proper preoperative and postoperative counseling can often diminish these fears.

Hart and colleagues found that concerns with sexual functioning were one of the most common complaints after any type of urinary diversion. The study reported that 47% of patients indicated a moderate to severe level of sexual dissatisfaction, as compared to 16% prior to surgery. It was also found that women experienced significantly less sexual desire after radical cystectomy and urinary diversion than men. The results also indicated that men who received penile implants after radical cystectomy and urinary diversion showed a statistically significant improvement in sexual function and satisfaction.[10] This study confirms the idea that it is reasonable and just for physicians to discuss the various treatment options for erectile dysfunction prior to performing a radical cystectomy and urinary diversion.

Surgery for bladder cancer may lead to erectile dysfunction due to injury to the autonomic nerves from the sacral parasympathetic plexus to the corpora cavernosa. Henningsohn and colleagues reported that 94% of male patients reported some degree of erectile dysfunction following cystectomy and neobladder diversion as compared to 48% in age matched controls. In addition, 68% of men who underwent the procedure did not engage in sexual intercourse during the 6 months preceding the study, versus 48% of control patients.[35] Schlegel and colleagues first described nerve-sparing cystoprostatectomy in 1987, with a follow-up series published from Johns Hopkins in 1990 and 1996.[37–39] Restoration of sexual function is dependent on the age of the patient, size and location of the tumor, and surgical technique. Erectile function satisfactory for intercourse may be recovered in up to 70% of patients with or without the drug sildenafil. Unfortunately, many urologic surgeons do not perform cystoprostatectomy using the nerve sparing technique.

Anterior pelvic exenteration in women can cause vaginal scarring, decreased vault size, and reduced vaginal lubrication that can result in painful intercourse and sexual dysfunction. Loss of a functional vagina can be managed with the creation of a "neovagina" using myocutaneous muscle flaps or intestine. Women of childbearing age with an ileal conduit must be informed that there is a decrease in the absorption of oral birth control pills, thus other forms of contraception are recommended. Furthermore, the displacement of the stoma by the enlarging uterus can occur, causing difficulty in managing the stoma.

SATISFACTION WITH BODY IMAGE

Body image is defined as the way we see ourselves. After cystectomy, patients are presented with permanent changes to their accepted body image and lifestyle. It is important for patients and their families to receive information and emotional support

Table 13–3. SEXUAL FUNCTION AND BODY IMAGE*		
	Neobladder (% of Patients)	Control (% of Patients)
Men		
Erectile dysfunction (ED)	94	48
Dissatisfaction with sex life	48	—
Distress from erectile dysfunction	58	32
Felt less attractive	13	7
General distress	19	8
Women		
Dissatisfaction with sex life	43	40
Felt less attractive	0	0

*Henningsohn et al.[35]

preoperatively according to their needs (Table 13–4). Physicians should provide educational literature that is specific to the type of diversion planned, and reinforces information already discussed. Patients usually experience psychological symptoms postoperatively, including anxiety and depression with the adjustment to their new body image. Urinary stomas can have a profound effect on a patient's self-perception, resulting in feelings of insecurity and embarrassment. Fortunately, it has been reported that most patients adapt well to a stoma in terms of overall satisfaction with body image.[10]

DIVERSION IN FEMALE PATIENTS

Orthotopic neobladder reconstruction following cystectomy was, until recently, performed solely in male patients. It is now a viable option for women due to the better understanding of female pelvic anatomy and the continence mechanism in women. Traditionally, women underwent an anterior pelvic exenteration including total urethrectomy for treatment of bladder cancer. Using strict patient selection criteria, including absence of bladder neck involvement with carcinoma and negative urethral margin on frozen section, orthotopic reconstruction has been demonstrated to be a viable technique with regards to both oncologic and functional outcomes (Table 13–4).[39–41] Stein and colleagues reported the results of 33 women following cystectomy with orthotopic neobladder reconstruction.[41] With a median follow up of 30 months, no patients were found to have urethral recurrence. Day and nighttime continence was 88% and 82%, respectively. "Hyper-

Table 13–4. ORTHOTOPIC BLADDER RECONSTRUCTION IN WOMEN: CONTINENCE RESULTS				
Authors	No. Patients	Continence – diurnal (%)	Continence – nocturnal (%)	CIC (%)
Jarolim et al,[57] (2000)	41	28 (68)	–	14 (34)
Mills and Studer,[17] (2000)	15	15 (100)	12 (80)	1 (7)
Ali-el-Dein et al,[42] (1999)	43	40 (93)	32 (74)	6 (14)
Arai et al,[58] (1999)	12	10 (83)	6 (50)	3 (25)
Stein et al,[41] (1997)	33	29 (88)	27 (82)	5 (15)
Univ. of Chicago (unpublished)	25	21 (84)	20 (80)	5 (20)

CIC = clean intermittent catheterization.

continence" requiring clean intermittent catheterization was required by 5%. A number of centers as well as the authors' have noted excellent urinary continence after female orthotopic reconstruction. However, we have found that approximately 20 to 25% of women who undergo radical cystectomy and orthotopic neobladder at our institution are "hypercontinent," and require clean intermittent catheterization. Other surgeons have reported this as well (see Table 13–4). The etiology of the hypercontinence may be multifactorial. Ali-el-Dein believe that the retention is mechanical in nature due to the pouch prolapsing posteriorly resulting in acute angulation at the urethral pouch junction.[42] Using omental interposition and ventral suspension of the dome of the neobladder as well as increased vaginal support may prevent this. Some investigators believe that "nerve sparing" of the autonomic innervation of the corpora cavernosum of the clitoris is important, however, others believe that division of autonomic nerves will decrease voiding dyssynergia.[43,44]

Micturition via the urethra and urinary continence after a radical cystectomy and orthotopic neobladder for bladder cancer may provide a better QOL for women. However, patients must be appropriately selected for this type of diversion. All patients must be marked preoperatively for a stoma site and instructed on how to catheterize the urethra if necessary postoperatively. All patients should undergo preoperative cystourethroscopy with evaluation of the bladder neck and urethra. The female urethra may be preserved in cases of invasive bladder cancer that does not involve the bladder neck. In multiple pathologic studies, only female patients with cancer involvement of the bladder neck had urethral involvement as well. However, this does not predict subsequent future urethral recurrence with transitional cell carcinoma. Preoperative urodynamics to examine the anatomic and functional integrity of the urethra may also be considered. Finally, all patients should have intraoperative frozen section of the bladder neck taken, and if positive result obtained an alternative form of diversion should be performed.

The continence mechanism in women is thought to be a combination of anterior vaginal and urethral support, the rhabdosphincter mechanism (in the distal two-thirds of the urethra), and pubourethral ligaments. It is critical to avoid injury to the urethra with minimal anterior dissection in the region of the proximal urethra and anterior vaginal support. The pubourethral suspensory ligaments should be left in place to provide support and to help maintain the intrapelvic neobladder position. This also may contribute to the continence mechanism in women.[45] Dissection between the anterior vaginal wall and bladder up to the vesico-urethral junction will aid in maintaining a functional vagina. An intact anterior vaginal wall provides additional support to the proximal urethra. Finally, a well-vascularized omental pedicle graft should be interposed between the reconstructed neobladder and the vagina to prevent fistula formation.

In the postoperative period, voiding re-education is of paramount importance, with the instruction on pelvic floor relaxation, timed voiding to prevent over distention, and regular follow-up. With strict selection criteria, female orthotopic neobladder substitution provides excellent long-term functional results.

DIVERSION IN ELDERLY PATIENTS

There is a growing need for bladder substitution in elderly patients. In the past, patients in their mid seventies and older were believed to be poor surgical candidates. In fact, today many patients well into their 80's safely undergo radical cystectomy.[46–49] However, the majority of these patients receive ileal conduits. Chronological age alone should not be a contraindication to continent diversion, especially an orthotopic urinary diversion. Data supports aggressive surgical management of bladder cancer in many elderly patients, mainly due to advances in surgical technique, anesthesia and postoperative care. Patient selection is important when considering an orthotopic neobladder or an Indiana pouch, because the patient must have the manual dexterity and cognitive skills to perform self-catheterization and irrigation of the pouch if needed. A detailed medical history, physical examination, especially cardiovascular and pulmonary, and metabolic and nutritional status must be obtained. The most common early complications in the elderly population were pyelonephritis, disorientation, pneumonia, and prolonged ileus. The most common late complications include ureteroileal anastamotic stenosis, and hernia.[46] The major concern is the ability of the elderly to tolerate major cardiovascular, pulmonary, or infectious complications (Table 13–5).

CONCLUSION

QOL is increasingly recognized as an important outcome measure after treatment for bladder cancer. The perceived issues such as activity of daily living, satisfaction with body image, and social interaction must be recognized as important post radical cystectomy outcome measures. Continent urinary diversion is intuitively the first choice for most patients. Hart and colleagues noted a strong preference before surgery for an orthotopic urinary diversion for both men and women. The study, however, did not demonstrate QOL advantages of any type of diversion over another.[10] Moreover, continent diversion is advantageous with respect to all the issues directly related to stomas, however initial reports comparing the QOL in these two groups of patients (continent and incontinent diversion) typically have demonstrated mixed results in all other aspects of quality of life issues. Gerharz and colleagues reported a significantly better score on the global assessment QOL as a single item in patients who underwent an orthotopic neobladder procedure. This study also demonstrated that continent diversions are significantly better with regard to all aspects related to the stoma.[50] Bjerre and colleagues confirmed the finding that leakage episodes cause significant distress among patients who received ileal conduits versus orthotopic neobladders. Also, patients who were converted from ileal conduits to orthotopic neobladders were the most satisfied following the second surgery.[51] The orthotopic neobladder patients in this series had similar complication rates compared to the ileal conduit patients, which is not the case for the neobladder patients in the studies of Mansson et al[24] and Boyd et al.[52] It is difficult to directly compare patient groups because in the past, patients who received ileal conduits tended to be older, and sicker. However, Dutta et al found that using the SF-36 and FACT-G suggested that patients with an orthotopic neobladder had only marginal QOL advantages over those with ileal conduits.[32] Further review of the literature on health related QOL and analysis of the data raises the question of whether generic QOL instruments are sensitive enough to even measure and validate differences in QOL of these specific patient groups.

Disease related social support and family support play an important role and may be more important

| | | Median | Mean | Median | | | |
Authors	No. Patients	Age (yr)	O.R. Time (hr)	Hospital Stay (d)	Complication Rate	Perioperative Mortality (%)	Type of Diversion
Soulie et al,[46] (2002)	73	79	4.5	34	47% early, 17% late	3	IC – 39 CR – 12 NB – 22
Chang et al,[47] (2001)	44	78	—	7	36% minor, 5% major	0	IC
Stroumbakis et al,[48] (1997)	44	81	6.5	14	22% surgical, 43% medical	5	IC
Navon et al,[49] (1995)	25	79	—	12	28% early, 16% late	8	CR

Table 13–5. RADICAL CYSTECTOMY AND URINARY DIVERSION IN THE ELDERLY POPULATION

IC = ileal conduit; CR = catheterizable reservoir; NB = neobladder.

than the treatment modality itself. There are few existing studies that use validated QOL surveys to evaluate and measure the differences in patients who have undergone an ileal conduit versus an orthotopic neobladder reconstruction. Therefore, comparative studies measuring QOL after lower urinary tract reconstruction remains controversial. Disease specific and procedure specific QOL questionnaires will need to be more fully developed to address these issues. In addition, valid comparisons between radical cystectomy, urinary tract reconstruction and bladder sparing treatments are necessary to identify patients best suited for various treatment modalities.

REFERENCES

1. Montie JE, Smith DC, Sandler HM. Carcinoma of the bladder. In: Abeloff MD, editor. Clinical oncology, 2nd ed. London: Churchill Livingstone; 2000. p. 1800–18.
2. Jemal A, Tiwari RC, Murray T, et al. Cancer Statistics, 2004. CA Cancer J Clin 2004;54:8–29.
3. O'Connor RC, Alsikafi NJ, Steinberg GD. Therapeutic options and treatment of muscle invasive bladder cancer. Expert Rev Anticancer Ther 2001;1:511–22.
4. Hobisch A, Tosun K, Kinzl J, et al. Quality of life after cystectomy and orthotopic neobladder versus ileal conduit urinary diversion. World J Urol 2000;18:338–44.
5. Hollowell CMP, Steinberg GD, Rowland RG. Current concepts of urinary diversion in men. In: Droller MJ, editor. Current clinical urology: bladder cancer: current diagnosis and treatment. Humanna Press; p. 343–66.
6. Shipley WU, Winter KA, Kaufman DS, et al. Phase III trial of neoadjuvant chemotherapy in patients with invasive bladder cancer treated with selective bladder preservation by combined radiation therapy and chemotherapy: initial results of radiation therapy oncology group 89-03. J Clin Oncol 1998;16:3576.
7. Raghavan D. Bladder preservation in patients with bladder cancer–quality versus quantity of life? [editorial] J Urol 1998;160:1678–9.
8. Bricker E. Bladder substitution after pelvic evisceration. Surg Clin North Am 1950;30:1511.
9. Hollowell CMP, Christiano AP, Steinberg GD. Technique of Hautmann ileal neobladder with chimney modification: interim results in 50 patients. J Urol 2000;163:47–51.
10. Hart S, Skinner E, Meyerowitz B, et al. Quality of life after radical cystectomy for bladder cancer in patients with an ileal conduit, or cutaneous or urethral Kock pouch. J Urol 1999;162:77–81.
11. Rowland RG, Kropp BP. Evolution of the Indiana continent urinary reservoir. J Urol 1994;152:2247–51.
12. Bihrle R. The Indiana pouch continent urinary reservoir. Urol Clin North Am 1997;24:773–9.
13. Bales GT, Kim H, Steinberg GD. Surgical therapy for locally advanced bladder cancer. Semin Oncol 1996;23:605–13.
14. Steinberg GD, Rinker-Schaeffer CW, Sokoloff MH, Brendler

CB. Highlights of the Urologic Oncology Meeting; 2001 June 2. J Urol 2002;168:653–9.
15. Gutierrez Godinez F, Reyna Perez R, Espinoza Valverde R, et al. Use of the Indiana type continent reservoir: review of our series. Arch Esp Urol 1999;52:851–5.
16. Pantuck AJ, Han KR, Perrotti M, et al. Ureteroenteric anastomosis in continent urinary diversion: long term results and complications of direct versus nonrefluxing techniques. J Urol 2000;163:450–5.
17. Mills RD, Studer UE. Female orthotopic bladder substitution: a good operation in the right circumstance. J Urol 2000;163:1501–4.
18. Madersbacher S, Mohrle K, Burkhard F, Studer UE. Long-term voiding pattern with ileal orthotopic bladder substitutes. J Urol 2002;167:2052–7.
19. Hautmann RE, De Petriconi R, Gottfried H, et al. The ileal neobladder: complications and functional results in 363 patients after 11 years of followup. J Urol 1999; 161:427–8.
20. Parekh DJ, Gilbert WB, Smith JA Jr. Functional lower urinary tract voiding outcomes after cystectomy and orthotopic neobladder. J Urol 2000;163:58–9.
21. Laven BA, O'Connor RC, Steinberg GS, Gerber GS. Long-term results of antegrade endoureterotomy using the holmium laser in patients with ureterointestinal strictures. J Urol 2001;58:924–9.
22. Gburek B, Lieber M, Blute M. Comparison of Studer ileal neobladder and ileal conduit urinary diversion with respect to perioperative outcome and late complications. J Urol 1998;160:721–3.
23. Carlin BI, Rutchik SD, Resnick MI. Comparison of the ileal conduit to the continent cutaneous diversion and orthotopic neobladder in patients undergoing cystectomy: a critical analysis and review of the literature. Semin Urol Oncol 1997;15:189–92.
24. Mansson A, Caruso A, Capovilla S, et al. Quality of life after radical cystectomy and orthotopic bladder substitution: a comparison between Italian and Swedish men. BJU Int 2000;85:26–31.
25. Sullivan LD, Chow VDW, Ko DSC, et al. An evaluation of quality of life in patients with continent urinary diversions after cystectomy. Br J Urol 1998;81:699–704.
26. Ware JE. SF-36 Health Status Questionnaire-Boston. Quality Quest Inc. 1989.
27. Aaronson NK, Ahmedzai S, Bergman B, et al. The European Organization for Research and Treatment of Cancer QLQ–C30: a quality-of-life instrument for use in international clinical trials in oncology. J Natl Cancer Inst 1993;85(5):365–76.
28. Da Silva FC, Fossa SD, Aaronson NK, et al. The quality of life of patients with newly diagnosed M1 prostate cancer: experience with EORTC clinical trial 30853 [abstract]. Eur J Cancer 1996;32:72–7.
29. Cella DF, Tulsky DS, Gray G, et al. The Functional Assessment of Cancer Therapy Scale development and validation of the general measure. J Clin Oncol 1993;11:570–9.
30. Bergner M, Bobbitt RA, Carter WB, et al. The Sickness Impact Profile: development and final revision of a health status measure. Med Care 1981;19:787–805.

31. Mansson A, Mansson W. When the bladder is gone: quality of life following different types of urinary diversion. World J Urol 1999;17:211–8.

32. Dutta SA, Chang SS, Coffey CS, et al. Health related quality of life assessment after radical cystectomy: comparison of ileal conduit with continent orthotopic neobladder. J Urol 2002;168:164–7.

33. Hara I, Miyake H, Hara S, et al. Health-related quality of life after radical cystectomy for bladder cancer: a comparison of ileal conduit and orthotopic bladder replacement. BJU Int 2002;89:10–3.

34. Fugisawa M, Isotani S, Gotoh A, et al. Health-related quality of life with orthotopic neobladder versus ileal conduit according to the SF-36 survey. Urology 2000;55:862–5.

35. Henningsohn L, Steven K, Kallestrup EL, Steineck G. Distressful symptoms and well-being after radical cystectomy and orthotopic bladder substitution compared with a matched control population. J Urol 2002;168:168–75.

36. N'Dow J, Robson CN, Matthews JN, et al. Reducing mucus production after urinary reconstruction: a prospective randomized trial. J Urol 2001;165(5):1433–40.

37. Schlegel PN, Walsh PC. Neuroanatomical approach to radical cystoprostatectomy with preservation of sexual function. J Urol 1987;138:1402–6.

38. Brendler CB, Steinberg GD, Marshall FF, et al. Local recurrence and survival following nerve sparing radical cystoprostatectomy. J Urol 1990;144(5):1137–40.

39. Schoenberg MP, Walsh PC, Breazeale DR, et al. Local recurrence and survival following nerve sparing radical cystoprostatectomy for bladder cancer. J Urol 1996;155:490–4.

41. Stein JP, Grossfield GD, Freeman JA, et al. Orthotopic lower urinary tract reconstruction in women using the Koch ileal neobladder: updated experience in 34 patients. J Urol 1997;158:406–7.

42. Ali-El Dein B, Gomha M, Ghoneim MA. Critical evaluation of the problem of chronic urinary retention after orthotopic bladder substitution in women. J Urol 2002;168:587–92.

43. Schoenberg M, Hortopan S, Schlossberg L, Marshall FF. Anatomical anterior exenteration with urethral and vaginal preservation: illustrated surgical method. J Urol 1999;161:569–72.

44. Stenzl A, Colleselli K, Poisel S, et al. Rationale and technique of nerve sparing radical cystectomy before an orthotopic neobladder procedure in women. J Urol 1995;154:2044–9.

45. Cancrini A, De Carli P, Fattahi H, et al. Bladder cancer: orthotopic ileal neobladder in female patients after radical cystectomy: 2-year experience [original articles]. J Urol 1995;153:956–8

46. Soulie M, Straub M, Game X, et al. Multicenter study of the morbidity of radical cystectomy in select elderly patients with bladder cancer. J Urol 2002;167(3):1325–8.

47. Chang SS, Alberts G, Cookson MS, Smith JA Jr. Radical cystectomy is safe in elderly patients at high risk. J Urol 2001;166:938–41.

48. Stroumbakis N, Herr HW, Cookson MS, Fair WR. Radical cystectomy is safe in the octogenarian, J Urol 1997;158(6):2113–7.

49. Navon JD, Wong AK, Weinberg, AC, Ahlering TE. Comparative study of postoperative complications associated with modified Indiana pouch in elderly versus younger patients. J Urol 1995;154:1325–8.

50. Gerharz E, Weingartner K, Dopatka K, et al. Quality of life after cystectomy and urinary diversion: results of a retrospective interdisciplinary study. J Urol 1997;158(3):778–85.

51. Bjerre BD, Johansen C, Steven K. Health-related quality of life after urinary diversion: continent diversion with Kock pouch compared with ileal conduit. A questionnaire study. Scand J Urol Nephol 1994;157 (Suppl):113–8.

52. Boyd SD, Feinberg SM, Skinner DG, et al. Quality of life survey of urinary diversion patients: comparison of ileal conduits versus continent Kock ileal reservoirs. J Urol 1987;138:1386–9.

53. McGuire MS, Grimaldi G, Grotas J, Russo P. The type of urinary diversion after radical cystectomy significantly impacts on the patient's quality of life. Ann Surg Oncol 2000;7:4–8.

54. Kitamura H, Miyao N, Yanase M, et al. Quality of life in patients having an ileal conduit, continent reservoir or orthotopic neobladder after cystectomy for bladder carcinoma. Int J Urol 1999;6:393–9.

55. Weijerman PC, Schurmans JR, Hop WC, et al. Morbidity and quality of life in patients with orthotopic and heterotropic continent urinary diversion. Urology 1998;51:51–6.

56. Mansson A, Johnson G, Mansson W. Quality of life after cystectomy. Comparison between patients with conduit and those with continent caecal reservoir urinary diversions. Br J Urol 1988;62:240–5.

57. Jarolim L, Babjuk M, Peecher SM, et al. Causes and treatment of residual urine volume after orthotopic bladder replacement in women. Eur Urol 2000;38:748–52.

58. Arai Y, Okubo K, Konami T, et al. Voiding function of orthotopic ileal neobladder in women. Urology 1999;54:44–9.

14

Neoadjuvant and Adjunctive Systemic Chemotherapy in the Treatment of Invasive Urothelial Cancer of the Bladder

AMNON VAZINA, MD

DEREK RAGHAVAN, MD, PhD

SETH P. LERNER, MD

Approximately 11,000 cases of muscle invasive bladder cancer are diagnosed in the United States each year, representing about 20% of new cases of urinary tract malignancy.[1] Results from contemporary radical cystectomy and pelvic lymph node dissection for T2–4NxM0 transitional cell carcinoma (TCC) of the bladder indicate that this operation is safe, with a surgical mortality rate of 0.5 to 3%.[2] Radical cystectomy accomplishes excellent, durable, local control of the primary tumor; provides accurate pathologic staging of the primary tumor and lymph nodes; and, due to increasing expertise with continent urinary diversion, affords preservation of quality of life. Despite these advances, the 5-year survival rate for all patients with pathological stage (pT)2 tumors is 50 to 80%, with patients with negative lymph nodes having 64 to 86% 5-year survival. The 5-year survival rates for regionally advanced cancers, pT3 and pT4, in contemporary series range from 22 to 58%. Among patients with pathologically proven lymph node metastasis, the 5-year survival probability following radical cystectomy is only 29%.[3] The 5-year survival rate is 50% for patients with nodal metastases and tumors confined to the muscularis propria, whereas with more advanced primary tumors, the survival rate drops significantly to 18% or less.[2]

CHEMOTHERAPY

The rationale for adding systemic chemotherapy to definitive local therapy requires evidence of efficacy of chemotherapy for patients with measurable metastatic disease. The early clinical trials of chemotherapy for bladder cancer showed that several single agents have activity, including cyclophosphamide, the vinca alkaloids, methotrexate, mitomycin C, 5-fluorouracil, doxorubicin, and cisplatin.[4] More recently, ifosfamide, gallium nitrate, paclitaxel, docetaxel, and gemcitabine have been shown in a series of phase I–II clinical trials to have substantial antitumor effect against TCC of the urinary tract.[5–11]

In the early development of chemotherapy for bladder cancer, combination chemotherapy regimens produced higher objective response rates than single agents but did not improve survival.[12,13] The first randomized trial to demonstrate a survival benefit from combination chemotherapy was reported from an international group (United States, Canada, Australia) and showed that the combination of methotrexate, vinblastine, Adriamycin (doxorubicin), and cisplatin (MVAC regimen) yielded a significantly increased response rate and progression-free and total survival compared with a single agent, cisplatin.[14,15] A randomized study from the M.D.

Anderson Cancer Institute confirmed this result by demonstrating a statistically improved survival from the MVAC regimen compared with the combination of cyclophosphamide, doxorubicin, and cisplatin.[16] Although MVAC remains a standard treatment for patients with metastatic disease, the cure fraction is low, and new treatments are urgently required.[17]

Several of the novel compounds listed above are currently under evaluation in combination chemotherapy regimens. Paclitaxel has been incorporated into combination regimens with carboplatin, cisplatin, ifosfamide plus cisplatin, and methotrexate plus cisplatin.[18–22] Objective response rates in the range of 30 to 70% have been documented, but in many instances, the median survival has been shorter than would be expected from the MVAC regimen.

The combination of gemcitabine with cisplatin increases the objective response rate to nearly 70%, with a median survival greater than 12 months, and trials in progress are also assessing its use in association with carboplatin, paclitaxel, and ifosfamide.[23–25]

These agents are particularly important as they appear to be much less toxic than some of the earlier agents (eg, the MVAC regimen) and hence may be more easily introduced into combined-modality regimens. A recently published randomized trial comparing the MVAC regimen against the gemcitabine and cisplatin combination suggested that these two regimens were associated with equivalent response rates, with less toxicity for patients treated with gemcitabine and cisplatin.[26] Finally, paclitaxel and gemcitabine are radiosensitizers. Thus, they may have a role in improving local control in combination with radiotherapy and may potentially be important in the control of systemic disease.

NEOADJUVANT CHEMOTHERAPY

Invasive bladder cancer is now considered to be a systemic disease. As many as half of the presenting cases will eventually relapse with distant metastases, presumably because micrometastases are present early in the course of the disease.[27] Systemic chemotherapy has been added to locoregional treatment in an attempt to improve cure rates by downstaging the primary tumor, reducing and potentially eliminating micrometastases, and, in some instances, functioning as a radiosensitizer.[28]

Neoadjuvant chemotherapy implies treatment prior to definitive local therapy that is based on the clinical stage of the cancer defined by transurethral resection of the bladder tumor (TURBT) and bimanual examination under anesthesia. The advantages are the presence of measurable disease to assess response, introduction of chemotherapy with the smallest potential volume of metastatic disease, and the opportunity for downstaging of "unresectable" tumors, making them "resectable." In contrast, the possible drawbacks of this strategy include the risk of using an ineffective initial treatment, thus delaying potentially definitive treatment approaches (such as radiotherapy or surgery) and the use of systemic treatment to control a localized tumor, exposing the patient to the risk of side effects without benefit. The results of randomized trials of neoadjuvant chemotherapy are summarized in Table 14–1.

The initial, nonrandomized, single-agent trials were very promising as they demonstrated substantial tumor downstaging and apparently improved tumor resection rates.[29–33] However, randomized clinical trials that tested single-agent chemotherapy plus local treatment versus local treatment alone did not show any benefit from this strategy.[34–36] Similarly, the use of combination chemotherapy regimens, such as cisplatin, methotrexate, and vinblastine (CMV) or MVAC, as neoadjuvant treatment initially appeared to be highly effective, but late follow-up studies did not indicate any apparent long-term benefit.[37–42] Also of relevance, Kaye and colleagues demonstrated an apparent absence of objective response when using the combination of cyclophosphamide, methotrexate, and 5-fluorouracil prior to radiotherapy for T3 tumors.[43] The median survival was 27 months, with a 3-year survival probability of 26%, which was comparable to contemporary results with radiotherapy alone, suggesting that this was an ineffective chemotherapy regimen and that the noninvasive assessment of clinical tumor stage within the bladder might be flawed.

By contrast, the Nordic Cooperative Bladder Cancer Study Group reported that two cycles of neoadjuvant cisplatin and doxorubicin conferred a reduced death rate in patients with T3 and T4a bladder cancer who were treated by cystectomy and preoperative

Table 14–1. RESULTS OF RANDOMIZED TRIALS OF NEOADJUVANT CHEMOTHERAPY AND RADICAL CYSTECTOMY

Series	Regimen	Progression		Survival		
		No. of Patients	Median	Median	5 Year (%)	Survival Benefit?
Australia/United Kingdom[35]	Cis/RT	255 total		24	39 (3 yr)	No
	RT			22	39 (3 yr)	
CUETO[36]	Cis	60	30.3	37.5	50	No
	Observation	62	13.1	35	50	
Nordic I[44]	Cis/A/RT	151	23		59	Yes[7]
	RT	160	14		51	For T3–4
Nordic I[45]	MTX/Cis	316 total			50	No
	Observation				50	
Canada/NCI[65]	Cis/RT or Cis/RT/Cyst	51			47 (3 yr)	No
	RT or RT/Cyst	48			33 (3 yr)	
Abol-Eneim[49]	Carboplatin, MTX, V	94			59.1	Yes
	Observation	100			41.6%	
GUONE[48]	MVAC	102			55%	No
	Observation	104			54%	
EORTC/ MRC[46]	CMV/RT or CMV/Cyst	491		44	55.5 (3 yr)	No
	RT or Cyst	485				
SWOG[51]	MVAC	153		74.7	57.2	Yes
	Observation	154		43.2	42.1	

A = adriamycin; Cis = cisplatin; CMV = cisplatin, methotrexate, vinblastine; CUETO = Spanish Oncology Group; Cyst = cystectomy; EORTC = European Organization for the Research and Treatment of Cancer; GUONE = North Eastern Uro Oncological Group; MTX = methotrexate; MVAC = methotrexate, vinblastine, Adriamycin (doxorubicin), cisplatin; NCI = National Cancer Institute; RT = radiotherapy; SWOG = Southwestern Oncology Group; V = vinblastine.

short-course pelvic irradiation.[44] This study, however, had only a modest statistical power because of the patient numbers. In a second study by the same group, 316 patients with T2–4aNxM0 tumors were randomized to three cycles of cisplatin and methotrexate followed by cystectomy versus cystectomy alone.[45] Cystectomy was performed in 90% of the patients, and lymph node metastases were identified in 17% and 21%, respectively. Neoadjuvant chemotherapy conferred a P0 rate of 26% versus 9% for cystectomy alone. Despite these differences, the crude 5-year survival rate was 50% in each arm.

An International Intergroup (Medical Research Council/European Organization for the Research and Treatment of Cancer [EORTC]) Trial, in which 976 patients were randomly allocated to three cycles of neoadjuvant CMV plus local treatment or local treatment alone, was well executed, with a high compliance to protocol design, but suffered from a lack of central pathology review.[46] Planned local treatment was cystectomy (42.5%), radiotherapy (49.7%), or both (7.8%). The trial was powered to detect a 10% absolute difference in survival, but despite significant downstaging of tumors treated by neoadju-

vant chemotherapy, the 3-year survival probability was 55.5% in the chemotherapy arm compared with 50% in the no-chemotherapy arm ($p = .075$).

Similar results have been produced by the recent Radiation Therapy Oncology Group (RTOG) study, in which patients were randomly allocated to receive definitive chemoradiation (incorporating cisplatin and radical dose radiotherapy) or two cycles of neoadjuvant CMV chemotherapy, followed by an identical schedule of chemoradiation.[47] This study reported 5-year survival rates of 48% and 49%, clearly showing an absence of survival benefit with the use of neoadjuvant chemotherapy.

The North Eastern Uro Oncological Group (GUONE) from Italy has completed a study in which 206 patients were randomized to either four cycles of MVAC followed by cystectomy or cystectomy alone. The study was powered to detect an improvement in overall 3-year survival from 45 to 60%.[48] The 3-year survival probability was 62% in the chemotherapy arm versus 68% in the cystectomy alone arm and 55% versus 54% at 5 years, respectively. In contrast, preliminary data from a randomized trial conducted in Egypt in 196 patients with bladder TCC, demonstrated 5-year survival estimates of 59%, with two cycles of neoadjuvant carboplatin, methotrexate, and vinblastine compared with 42% for patients treated with cystectomy alone ($p \leq .044$).[49]

The long-awaited North American Intergroup trial (Southwestern Oncology Group [SWOG] 8710, Intergroup 0080) was reported at the American Urological Association and American Society of Clinical Oncology meetings in 2001.[50,51] A total of 317 patients were randomized to three cycles of MVAC followed by cystectomy or cystectomy alone. The median follow-up was 7.1 years and the estimated median survival rates were 6.2 years and 3.8 years for the MVAC and no-MVAC arms, respectively. The 5-year survival estimates were 57% and 42%, respectively. This advantage was translated by the authors into a hazard ratio of 0.74 (95% confidence interval [CI]= 0.55 to 0.99; p = .027) in favor of the chemotherapy arm. Much has been debated about the use of a one-sided test of significance in this trial. In planning the study, the investigators felt that only an improvement in survival associated with the chemotherapy would change medical practice. A two-sided test also considers the possibility that chemotherapy may be harmful and requires more events to achieve the same level of significance as a one-sided test. With two-sided testing,

the revised hazard ratio was 0.78 (95% CI = 0.58 to 1.04; p = .088), suggesting the absence of statistically significant benefit to three cycles of neoadjuvant MVAC chemotherapy.[52]

An updated meta-analysis was recently reported that includes the SWOG and GUONE studies (Figure 14–1).[52] A total of 2,524 patients from 10 studies were reviewed, including 4 trials that used single-agent cisplatin. The hazard ratio was 0.9 (95% CI = 0.81 to 1.00), suggesting borderline results in favor of chemotherapy. A meta-analysis using individual patient data from all randomized trials has been undertaken by the United Kingdom's Medical Research Council.

PERIOPERATIVE CHEMOTHERAPY

Chemotherapy has also been administered before and after definitive locoregional treatment for bladder cancer. Shearer and colleagues studied the role of methotrexate in this context in a randomized trial that predominantly assessed the impact of neoadjuvant chemotherapy but also had a component of adjuvant therapy after completion of definitive treatment.[34] No survival gain was noted compared with standard treatment.

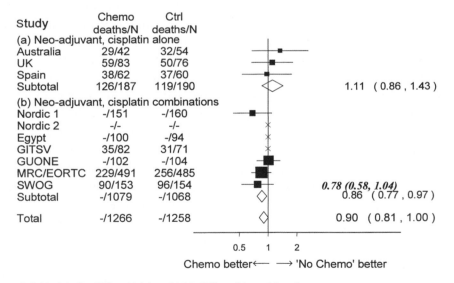

Figure 14–1.   Mortality in randomized studies of neoadjuvant treatment with cisplatin in patients with locally advanced bladder cancer. Reprinted with permission from Sternberg CN and Parmar MK.[52] EORTC = European Organization for the Research and Treatment of Cancer; GITSV = Gruppo Italiano per lo studio dei Tumori della Vescica; GUONE = North Eastern Uro Oncological Group; MRC = Medical Research Council; SWOG = Southwestern Oncology Group.

In a pilot study conducted by the Eastern Cooperative Oncology Group, two cycles of MVAC were administered before cystectomy, followed by another two cycles postoperatively.[53] Seventeen patients had T3 disease and one had a stage T2 tumor. Nearly half of the cases showed downstaging in response to MVAC, but at a median follow-up time of 23 months, 50% had died. Logothetis and colleagues tested a similar strategy and reported an interim analysis of a trial in which 100 patients were randomized to receive either two cycles of MVAC followed by cystectomy and then three adjuvant cycles of MVAC or initial cystectomy followed by five cycles of adjuvant MVAC.[54] There was no statistically significant difference between the survival results in the two arms, despite the significant level of downstaging after neoadjuvant chemotherapy. The final results were recently reported, and 58% (81/140) patients remained free of disease at a median follow-up of 6.8 years.[55] The perioperative complication rates were similar for the two arms.[56] Both trials revealed an unexpectedly high rate of deaths from vascular complications, again demonstrating the importance of randomized trials in the assessment of these novel strategies of management.[57]

NEOADJUVANT CHEMOTHERAPY: CONCLUSIONS

Until recently, the conclusions from randomized trials suggested that there was no clear rationale to support neoadjuvant chemotherapy outside a clinical trial for patients who were at high risk for relapse. The recent release of data from the SWOG and M.D. Anderson trials provides a stronger sense that the combination of chemotherapy and cystectomy is safe and may provide better overall survival probability compared with cystectomy alone. There are, however, many unresolved issues, including (1) the accuracy of clinical staging and the risk of overtreating patients, (2) the optimum chemotherapy regimen, (3) molecular determinants of response to therapy, and (4) relative benefit for patients with node-negative versus node-positive disease. Future studies must include molecular as well as pathologic staging of response to chemotherapy and be adequately powered.

Patients who have unresectable disease, either because of fixation to the pelvic side wall or pathologically proven pelvic lymph nodes above the bifurcation of the common iliac artery, may benefit with respect to disease-free survival from initial chemotherapy followed by cystectomy if there is a significant response to chemotherapy. This approach may reduce complications and morbidity from local progression of cancer, although this has not been formally evaluated in prospective studies. An overall survival benefit has not been demonstrated, however, for neoadjuvant chemotherapy even in this context.

ADJUVANT CHEMOTHERAPY

When cystectomy is performed as initial definitive therapy, complete pathologic staging becomes available, and patients are selected for adjuvant chemotherapy who are at increased risk for occult metastatic disease and therefore most likely to benefit from it. The disadvantages are the absence of measurable tumor to determine objective response to therapy, delay in treatment of micrometastatic disease, and that patients who are debilitated after cystectomy may eventually not receive chemotherapy at all. There are four published randomized trials of radical cystectomy with or without adjuvant chemotherapy (Table 14–2). Three trials comparing combined neoadjuvant and adjuvant chemotherapy versus adjuvant therapy are discussed in the perioperative chemotherapy section earlier in this chapter.

The first contemporary randomized trial of adjuvant chemotherapy following cystectomy was performed at the University of Southern California (USC).[58] This trial accrued 100 patients (91 evaluable) from a group of 160 who were eligible over 8 years. Patients were randomized to four courses of adjuvant PAC (or CISCA: cisplatin 100 mg/m^2, cyclophosphamide 600 mg/m^2, and Adriamycin [doxorubicin] 60 mg/m^2) or observation following radical cystectomy and bilateral pelvic and iliac lymphadenectomy. Eligible patients had pathologic stage pT3, pT4, N0 or N+, M0 bladder TCC. Although the target accrual goal was to enrol 75 patients in each arm, only 100 patients total were enrolled. At 3 years, the probability of disease recurrence was 30 ± 8% for the chemotherapy arm and 54 ± 8% for the observa-

Table 14–2. RESULTS OF RANDOMIZED TRIALS OF ADJUVANT CHEMOTHERAPY AND RADICAL CYSTECTOMY

Series	Regimen	No. of Patients Randomized	Progression		Survival		Survival Benefit?
			Median	5 Year*	Median	5 Year*	
USC[58]	CISCA	44	6.58 yr	51%	4.25 yr	39%	No
	Observation	47	1.92 yr	34%	2.41 yr	44%	
Mainz[61]	MVA(E)C†	26	not reached	63% 3 yr	—	—	Not evaluated
	Observation	23	16 mo	0% 3 yr	—	—	
Mainz[62]	MVA(E)C‡	26	Not reached	64% 3 yr	38 mo	54%‡	Yes
	Observation	23	16 mo	14% 3 yr	17 mo	14%	
SAKK[64]	Cisplatin	37	—	—	Not reached	57%	No
	Observation	40	—	—	Not reached	54%	
Stanford[66]	CMV§	25	37 mo	50%	63 mo	55%	No
	Observation	25	12 mo	22%	36 mo	35%	

CISCA = cisplatin, cyclophosphamide, and Adriamycin (doxorubicin); CMV = cisplatin, methotrexate, and vinblastine; MVA(E)C = methotrexate, vinblastine, Adriamycin (doxorubicin)/(epirubicin), and cisplatin; SAKK = Swiss Group for Clinical Cancer Research; USC = University of Southern California.
*Kaplan-Meier estimates.
†Survival data not reported.
‡Follow-up report from original series; event-free survival (event defined as progression- or tumor-unrelated death) at 36 months estimated from Kaplan-Meier plots.
§Results estimated from Kaplan-Meier plots.

tion arm. The probability of cancer death at 3 years was $29 \pm 8\%$ and $50 \pm 8\%$, respectively. This benefit persisted with additional follow-up, but when analyzed for the subsets of node-negative and node-positive patients, it was significant only for patients with no nodes or one positive node only. This study has several methodologic flaws common to many of the subsequent studies described in this chapter. Only 63% of the eligible patients were enrolled. Of the 44 patients randomized to chemotherapy, 11 refused treatment and several more were not treated with the protocol chemotherapy regimen. The initial statistical analysis used the Wilcoxon test, which emphasizes early differences in outcome measures. Subsequent analysis using the log rank test showed a statistically significant benefit for chemotherapy regarding the end point of time to recurrence but not survival.[59,60] Whether a prolongation of the time to recurrence is perceived as beneficial has not been formally addressed in quality of life studies.

A subsequent study from Mainz, Germany, randomized patients to three courses of MVAC/MVEC (substituting epirubicin for doxorubicin) in patients with pT3b, pT4, pN0 or pN1, pN2 TCC of the bladder.[61] Lymph node metastases were proven pathologically in 59% of patients. The trial design called for 100 randomized patients and was powered to detect an improvement in freedom from disease recurrence

from 20% in the observation arm to 55% in the chemotherapy arm. Of the 60 eligible patients encountered over 32 years, 49 patients were randomized: 26 to the chemotherapy arm and 23 to the observation arm. Eight patients randomized to chemotherapy were not treated with MVAC or MVEC. The trial did not permit chemotherapy at the time of relapse in the observation arm. Documented tumor progression occurred in 7 of 26 patients randomized to chemotherapy and in 18 of 23 patients in the observation arm ($p = .0015$). Chemotherapy ($p = .0007$) and the number of involved lymph nodes ($p = .0028$) were significant risk factors for recurrence in a Cox proportional hazards model that also included gender, age, and pT stage. The study was closed early because an interim analysis showed a significant advantage for the chemotherapy arm. No survival benefit could be determined owing to the short follow-up (median follow-up for those alive was 21 to 24 months).

Subsequent to this, the authors began offering adjuvant chemotherapy to patients with pathologically proven non–organ-confined cancer and updated their experience in 1995.[62] With longer follow-up of the original patients in the randomized trial, there was a significant benefit attributed to adjuvant chemotherapy for both time to progression and event-free survival (defined as no progression and tumor-unrelated death) ($p = .0005$ and $p = .0055$, respectively). Among patients with lymph node metastases treated with cystectomy and pelvic lymphadenectomy, adjuvant chemotherapy was associated with a decreased probability of tumor progression for patients with positive nodes.[63] The potential for selection bias given the small numbers of patients in this trial and unplanned subset analysis clearly confounds the results and makes these data difficult to interpret in valid statistical terms. Nonrandomized patients were then added to the randomized study and a survival benefit was reported, further confounding the statistical analysis of this study.

In 1994, these investigators initiated a new multicenter German trial with similar entry criteria to compare three cycles of MVAC and three cycles of cisplatin and methotrexate. The study design calls for enrolling 320 patients and will test for equivalence, which they define as lowering the progression rate by no more than 15%. Accrual was completed in October 2000 and the results are pending (J. Lehmann, personal communication, 2002). A third German trial initiated in 2000 will evaluate immediate versus deferred single-agent gemcitabine in patients with pT3–T4N0 or any N+ cancers that are not able to be treated with cisplatin.

A Swiss Group for Clinical Reseach (SAKK) study evaluated three courses of adjuvant, single-agent cisplatin (90 mg/m^2) following cystectomy versus cystectomy alone.[64] Patients with multifocal recurrent T1 cancer and patients with muscle-invasive cancers (T2–T4a) were eligible. A total of 80 patients were enrolled of 168 who met the pathologic entry criteria. Reasons for exclusion included ureteral obstruction, radiographic evidence of nodal metastases, impaired renal function, or decreased performance status. Only 7 of 80 (9%) patients had pathologic nodal metastases and only 35 of 80 (44%) had pT3b or pT4 tumors. Only 65% of patients received the three cycles of chemotherapy; 7 patients refused chemotherapy altogether and 6 had fewer than three courses. The study was closed early after a planned interim analysis on 80 patients failed to show a significant difference in 5-year survival rates.

The Stanford trial evaluated total cystectomy and pelvic lymph node dissection plus adjuvant chemotherapy with four courses of CMV versus cystectomy and node dissection alone.[66] All but one eligible patient evaluated at the institution were enrolled in the trial. A total of 55 patients with pT3b and pT4 cancers with or without nodal metastases were randomized, with 88% of the 27 patients randomized to chemotherapy completing treatment (64% had positive nodes). At a median follow-up of 62 months, the median time to progression was 12 months versus 37 months for the observation and chemotherapy arms, respectively, and the relapse rates were 80% and 52%, respectively. Despite this improvement in time to progression, there was no survival benefit with adjuvant chemotherapy. This may be attributable to the very small numbers of cases entered or to the fact that the study was designed prospectively to treat all patients in the observation arm with CMV chemotherapy at the time of relapse. A total of 19 of 25 patients treated with cystectomy alone relapsed and 15 of 19 did receive chemotherapy (one to six cycles of CMV). Three patients (16%) were without disease at 50, 75, and 77 months after cystectomy. The toxicity was acceptable, yet one patient died of neutropenia and sepsis following cycle one of chemotherapy.

Despite the similar survival probabilities in the chemotherapy and observation arms, the authors argue that adjuvant chemotherapy in a high-risk group of patients is preferable to chemotherapy at relapse, which requires more chemotherapy in a frequently debilitated patient with 2-year survival probabilities of 10 to 15%. This study was criticized for small sample size, the long interval for accrual (7 years), and early termination, which the authors state was done because the end point of freedom from progression had been reached with fewer than anticipated patients.

ADJUVANT CHEMOTHERAPY: CONCLUSIONS

The data reported from randomized trials to date are insufficient to conclusively determine the efficacy of adjuvant chemotherapy following radical cystectomy for pT3b, pT4 node-negative or node-positive (any pT) TCC. The total number of patients (267) is small, and 70 of these patients were treated with single-agent cisplatin, which is inferior to combination chemotherapy for patients with measurable disease.[14] The percentage of patients randomized to chemotherapy who did not receive any chemotherapy ranges from 4 to 31%. These data should be accounted for when designing future studies, as an increase in sample size will be required to maintain the power of the study. In addition to pathologic tumor stage and nodal metastases, the use of histologic features (eg, lymphatic or vascular invasion) and molecular markers to identify a high-risk group that may benefit from adjuvant chemotherapy should be evaluated prospectively in clinical trials.

Several other trials are under way that will help clarify the role of adjuvant chemotherapy and explore novel drug combinations and dose intensity (Table 14–3). The largest of these was initiated in the EORTC, and several North American cooperative groups are participating. This trial will randomize 1,344 patients following radical cystectomy with pT3–4N0 or any N+ to four cycles of adjuvant chemotherapy versus deferred chemotherapy (six cycles) at relapse. Three regimens will be used at the discretion of the participating institution and includes standard or high-dose MVAC and gemcitabine and cisplatin. The Spanish Oncology Genitourinary Group (SOGUG) has initiated a trial that will randomize 380 patients following radical cystectomy to paclitaxel, cisplatin, and gemcitabine versus observation. A trial under way at Memorial Sloan-Kettering Cancer Center with entry criteria similar to those of the EORTC trial randomizes patients to four cycles of gemcitabine and cisplatin versus a dose-dense strategy of four cycles of doxorubicin and gemcitabine administered every 14 days followed by four cycles of paclitaxel and cisplatin administered every 14 days.

Investigators at USC and Baylor have initiated a National Cancer Institute–funded multicenter, multinational clinical trial to evaluate *P53* and other markers in patients treated with radical cystectomy for cancers pathologically confined to the muscularis propria or lamina propria. This study will test two hypotheses: (1) *P53* alterations in organ-confined bladder TCC significantly increase the risk of recurrence and death and (2) three cycles of adjuvant MVAC chemotherapy may improve survival in patients with *P53* alterations. This study will also create a repository of archival tissue for the examination of other markers including *RB* and cell-cycle regulatory proteins including p16 and p21 (Lerner SP, principal investigator).

SUMMARY

After more than 25 years of research, the true role of combined-modality treatment for locally advanced bladder cancer remains controversial. The encouraging data from the SWOG neoadjuvant trial and now a plethora of both neoadjuvant and adjuvant studies that are in progress should help clarify what up until now has been a very cloudy picture regarding the integration of chemotherapy and radical cystectomy or radia-

Table 14–3. CURRENT PHASE III ADJUVANT RANDOMIZED STUDIES WITH CYSTECTOMY AS A LOCAL TREATMENT					
Group	Phase	No. of patients	Arm I	Arm II	Status
SOGUG	III	380	Paclitaxel/cisplatin/gemcitabine	Observation	Activated
P53-MVAC trial	III	190*	MVAC	Observation	Activated
ECOG 1897	III	490	Carboplatin/paclitaxel	MVAC	Activated
German GU group AUO 05/95	III	320	MVEC	Cisplatin/MTX	Closed 10/00; results pending
German GU group AUO 22/00	III	178 unfit for cisplatin	Immediate gemcitabine	Deferred gemcitabine	Activated
EORTC 30994	III	1344	Immediate cisplatin/gemcitabine or MVAC	Deferred cisplatin/gemcitabine or MVAC	Activated

ECOG = Eastern Cooperative Oncology Group; EORTC = European Organization for the Research and Treatment of Cancer; GU = German Genitourinary Group; MVAC = methotrexate, vinblastine, Adriamycin (doxorubicin), and cisplatin; MVEC = methotrexate, vinblastine, epirubicin, and cisplatin; SOGUG = Spanish Oncology Genitourinary Group.
*190 *P53*-positive randomized patients

tion therapy. Although an emerging sense is that such combination therapy is better that monotherapy, this can be proven only in the context of adequately powered randomized trials. It is our belief that the improved tools of molecular prognostication will allow us to design randomized trials more precisely and to identify the true utility of adjuvant chemotherapy strategies. In addition, with the advent of novel, less toxic chemotherapy regimens, it may be possible to introduce earlier, or more intensive, adjuvant regimens in an effort to improve outcome. The urologic community has an obligation to its patients to support these studies so that these critical questions can be answered. Where no relevant trials are open, recommendations for neoadjuvant or adjuvant chemotherapy should be made in the context of a complete informed consent describing the risks of chemotherapy and the limitations of the studies conducted to date.

REFERENCES

1. Jemal A, Thomas A, Murray T, et al. Cancer statistics, 2002. CA Cancer J Clin 2002;52:23–47.

2. Lerner SP, Skinner DG. Radical cystectomy for bladder cancer. In: Vogelzang J, Shipley WU, Scardino PT, et al, editors. Comprehensive textbook of genitourinary oncology. 2nd ed. Philadelphia: Lippincott Williams and Wilkins; 1999. p. 425–47.

3. Lerner SP, Skinner DG, Lieskovsky G, et al. The rationale for en bloc pelvic lymph node dissection for bladder cancer patients with nodal metastases: long-term results. J Urol 1993;149:758–65.

4. Loehrer PJ S, DeMulder PP. Management of metastatic bladder cancer. In: Raghavan HI, Scher S, Leibel SA, et al, editors. Principles and practice of genitourinary oncology. Philadelphia: Lippincott-Raven; 1997. p. 299–305.

5. Witte RS, Elson P, Bono B, et al. Eastern Cooperative Oncology Group phase II trial of ifosfamide in the treatment of previously treated advanced urothelial carcinoma. J Clin Oncol 1997;15:589–93.

6. Seligman PA, Crawford ED. Treatment of advanced transitional cell carcinoma of the bladder with continuous-infusion gallium nitrate. J Natl Cancer Inst 1991;83: 1582–4.

7. Roth BJ, Dreicer R, Einhorn LH, et al. Significant activity of paclitaxel in advanced transitional-cell carcinoma of the urothelium: a phase II trial of the Eastern Cooperative Oncology Group. J Clin Oncol 1994;12:2264–70.

8. McCaffrey JA, Hilton S, Mazumdar M, et al. Phase II trial of docetaxel in patients with advanced or metastatic transitional-cell carcinoma. J Clin Oncol 1997;15:1853–7.

9. Pollera CF, Ceribelli A, Crecco M, et al. Weekly gemcitabine in advanced bladder cancer: a preliminary report. Ann Oncol 1994;5:132–4.

10. Stadler W, Kuzel T, Roth B, et al. Phase II study of single-agent gemcitabine in previously untreated patients with metastatic urothelial cancer. J Clin Oncol 1997;15: 3394–8.

11. Moore MJ, Tannock IF, Ernst DS, et al. Gemcitabine: a promising new agent in the treatment of advanced urothelial cancer. J Clin Oncol 1997;15:3441–5.

12. Soloway MS, Einstein A, Corder MP, et al. A comparison of cisplatin and the combination of cisplatin and cyclophosphamide in advanced urothelial cancer. A National Bladder Cancer Collaborative Group A study. Cancer 1983; 52:767–72.

13. Hillcoat BL, Raghavan D, Matthews J, et al. A randomized trial of cisplatin versus cisplatin plus methotrexate in advanced cancer of the urothelial tract. J Clin Oncol 1989;7:706–9.

14. Loehrer PJ Sr, Einhorn LH, Elson PJ, et al. A randomized comparison of cisplatin alone or in combination with methotrexate, vinblastine, and doxorubicin in patients with metastatic urothelial carcinoma: a cooperative group study. J Clin Oncol 1992;10:1066–73.

15. Saxman SB, Propert KJ, Einhorn LH, et al. Long-term follow-up of a phase III intergroup study of cisplatin alone or in combination with methotrexate, vinblastine, and doxorubicin in patients with metastatic urothelial carcinoma: a cooperative group study. J Clin Oncol 1997;15:2564–9.

16. Logothetis CJ, Dexeus FH, Finn L, et al. A prospective randomized trial comparing MVAC and CISCA chemotherapy for patients with metastatic urothelial tumors. J Clin Oncol 1990;8:1050–5.

17. Levine EG, Raghavan D. MVAC for bladder cancer: time to move forward again. J Clin Oncol 1993;11:387–9.

18. Vaughn DJ, Malkowicz SB, Zoltick B, et al. Paclitaxel plus carboplatin in advanced carcinoma of the urothelium: an active and tolerable outpatient regimen. J Clin Oncol 1998;16:255–60.

19. Redman BG, Smith DC, Flaherty L, et al. Phase II trial of paclitaxel and carboplatin in the treatment of advanced urothelial carcinoma. J Clin Oncol 1998;16:1844–8.

20. Murphy BA, Johnson DR, Smith J, et al. Phase II trial of paclitaxel (P) and cisplatin (C) for metastatic or locally unresectable urothelial cancer [abstract]. Proc Am Soc Clin Oncol 1996;15:245.

21. McCaffrey J, Hilton S, Mazumdar M, et al. A phase II trial of ifosfamide, paclitaxel and cisplatin (ITP) in patients (pts) with advanced urothelial tract tumors [abstract]. Proc Am Soc Clin Oncol 1996;15:251.

22. Tu SM, Hossan E, Amato R, et al. Paclitaxel, cisplatin and methotrexate combination chemotherapy is active in the treatment of refractory urothelial malignancies. J Urol 1995;154:1719–22.

23. Kaufman D, Stadler W, Carducci M, et al. Gemcitabine (GEM) plus cisplatin (CDDP) in metastatic transitional cell carcinoma (TCC): final results of a phase II study [abstract]. Proc Am Soc Clin Oncol 1998;17:320a.

24. Vaishampayan U, Smith D, Redman B, et al. Phase II evaluation of carboplatin, paclitaxel and gemcitabine in advanced urothelial carcinoma [abstract]. Proc Am Soc Clin Oncol 1999;18:333a.

25. Bellmunt J, Guillem V, Paz-Ares L, et al. A phase II trial of

paclitaxel, cisplatin and gemcitabine (TCG) in patients (pts) with advanced transitional cell carcinoma (TCC) of the urothelium [abstract]. Proc Am Soc Clin Oncol 1999;18:332a.

26. von der Maase H, Hansen SW, Roberts JT, et al. Gemcitabine and cisplatin versus methotrexate, vinblastine, doxorubicin, and cisplatin in advanced or metastatic bladder cancer: results of a large, randomized, multinational, multicenter, phase III study. J Clin Oncol 2000;18:3068–77.

27. Raghavan D, Shipley W, Garnick M, et al. Biology and management of bladder cancer. N Engl J Med 1990;322:1129–38.

28. Raghavan D. Pre-emptive (neo-adjuvant) intravenous chemotherapy for invasive bladder cancer. Br J Urol 1988;61:1–8.

29. Herr HW. Preoperative irradiation with and without chemotherapy as adjunct to radical cystectomy. Urology 1985;25:127–34.

30. Soloway MS, Ikard M, Ford K. Cis-diamminedichloroplatinum (II) in locally advanced and metastatic urothelial cancer. Cancer 1981;47:476–80.

31. Fagg SL, Dawson-Edwards P, Hughes MA, et al. Cisdiamminedichloroplatinum (DDP) as initial treatment of invasive bladder cancer. Br J Urol 1984;56:296–300.

32. Raghavan D, Pearson B, Duval P, et al. Initial intravenous cisplatinum therapy: improved management for invasive high risk bladder cancer? J Urol 1985;133:399–402.

33. Pearson BS, Raghavan D. First-line intravenous cisplatin for deeply invasive bladder cancer: update on 70 cases. Br J Urol 1985;57:690–3.

34. Shearer RJ, Chilvers CF, Bloom HJ, et al. Adjuvant chemotherapy in T3 carcinoma of the bladder. A prospective trial: preliminary report. Br J Urol 1988;62:558–64.

35. Wallace DM, Raghavan D, Kelly KA, et al. Neo-adjuvant (pre-emptive) cisplatin therapy in invasive transitional cell carcinoma of the bladder. Br J Urol 1991;67:608–15.

36. Martinez-Pineiro JA, Gonzalez Martin M, Arocena F, et al. Neoadjuvant cisplatin chemotherapy before radical cystectomy in invasive transitional cell carcinoma of the bladder: a prospective randomized phase III study. J Urol 1995;153:964–73.

37. Meyers FJ, Palmer JM, Freiha FS, et al. The fate of the bladder in patients with metastatic bladder cancer treated with cisplatin, methotrexate and vinblastine: a Northern California Oncology Group study. J Urol 1985;134:1118–21.

38. Vogelzang NJ, Moormeier JA, Awan AM, et al. Methotrexate, vinblastine, doxorubicin and cisplatin followed by radiotherapy or surgery for muscle invasive bladder cancer: the University of Chicago experience. J Urol 1993;149:753–7.

39. Scattoni V, Bolognesi A, Cozzarini C, et al. Neoadjuvant CMV chemotherapy plus radical cystectomy in locally advanced bladder cancer: the impact of pathologic response on long-term results. Tumori 1996;82:463–9.

40. Scher H, Herr H, Sternberg C, et al. Neo-adjuvant chemotherapy for invasive bladder cancer. Experience with the M-VAC regimen. Br J Urol 1989;64:250–6.

41. Zincke H, Sen SE, Hahn RG, et al. Neoadjuvant chemotherapy for locally advanced transitional cell carcinoma of the bladder: do local findings suggest a potential for salvage of the bladder? Mayo Clin Proc 1988;63:16–22.

42. Schultz PK, Herr HW, Zhang ZF, et al. Neoadjuvant chemotherapy for invasive bladder cancer: prognostic factors for survival of patients treated with M-VAC with 5-year follow-up. J Clin Oncol 1994;12:1394–1401.

43. Kaye SB, MacFarlane JR, McHattie I, et al. Chemotherapy before radiotherapy for T3 bladder cancer. A pilot study. Br J Urol 1985;57:434–7.

44. Malmstrom PU, Rintala E, Wahlqvist R, et al. Five-year followup of a prospective trial of radical cystectomy and neoadjuvant chemotherapy: Nordic Cystectomy Trial I. The Nordic Cooperative Bladder Cancer Study Group. J Urol 1996;155:1903–6.

45. Malmstrom P.-U, Erkki R, Rolf W, et al. Neoadjuvant cisplatin-methotrexate chemotherapy of invasive bladder cancer. Nordic Cystectomy Trial 2 [abstract]. Eur Urol 1999;35 (Suppl 2):60.

46. Neoadjuvant cisplatin, methotrexate, and vinblastine chemotherapy for muscle-invasive bladder cancer: a randomised controlled trial. International collaboration of trialists. Lancet 1999;354:533–40.

47. Shipley WU, Winter KA, Kaufman DS, et al. Phase III trial of neoadjuvant chemotherapy in patients with invasive bladder cancer treated with selective bladder preservation by combined radiation therapy and chemotherapy: initial results of Radiation Therapy Oncology Group 89-03. J Clin Oncol 1998;16:3576–83.

48. Bassi P, Pagano F, Pappagallo G, et al. Neoadjuvant M-VAC chemotherapy of invasive bladder cancer: the G.U.O.N.E. multicenter phase III trial [abstract]. Eur Urol 1998;33 (Suppl 1):142.

49. Abol-Enein H, El-Mekresh M, El-Baz M, et al. Neo adjuvant chemotherapy in treatment of invasive transitional bladder cancer: a controlled prospective randomized study [abstract]. Br J Urol 1997;80 (Suppl 2):49.

50. Natale R, Grossman HB, Blumenstein B, et al. SWOG 8710 (int-0080): randomized phase II trial of neoadjuvant M-VAC + cystectomy versus cystectomy alone in patients with locally advanced bladder cancer. Proc Am Soc Clin Oncol 2001;20:3.

51. Crawford D, Denver C, Barton G, et al. SWOG 8710 (int-0080): randomized phase II trial of neoadjuvant M-VAC + cystectomy versus cystectomy alone in patients with locally advanced bladder cancer. J Urol 2001;165:1069.

52. Sternberg CN, Parmar MK. Neoadjuvant chemotherapy is not (yet) standard treatment for muscle-invasive bladder cancer. J Clin Oncol 2001;19 Suppl 18:21S–6S.

53. Dreicer R, Messing EM, Loehrer PJ, et al. Perioperative methotrexate, vinblastine, doxorubicin and cisplatin (M-VAC) for poor risk transitional cell carcinoma of the bladder: an Eastern Cooperative Oncology Group pilot study. J Urol 1990;144:1123–6.

54. Logothetis C, Swanson D, Amato R, et al. Optimal delivery of perioperative chemotherapy: preliminary results of a randomized, prospective, comparative trial of preoperative and postoperative chemotherapy for invasive bladder carcinoma. J Urol 1996;155:1241–5.

55. Millikan R, Dinney C, Swanson D, et al. Integrated therapy for locally advanced bladder cancer: final report of a randomized trial of cystectomy plus adjuvant M-VAC versus cystectomy with both preoperative and postoperative M-VAC. J Clin Oncol 2001;19:4005–13.

56. Hall MC, Swanson DA, Dinney CP. Complications of radical cystectomy: impact of the timing of perioperative chemotherapy. Urology 1996;47:826–30.

57. Raghavan D. Perioperative chemotherapy for invasive bladder cancer—what should we tell our patients [editorial]? J Urol 1996;155:1246–7.

58. Skinner DG, Daniels JR, Russell CA, et al. The role of adjuvant chemotherapy following cystectomy for invasive bladder cancer: a prospective comparative trial. J Urol 1991;145:459–64.

59. Raghavan D. Editorial comment re: Skinner DG, Daniels JR, Russell CA, Lieskovsky G, Boyd SD, Nichols P, Kern W, Sakamoto J, Krailo M, Groshen S: The role of adjuvant chemotherapy following cystectomy for invasive bladder cancer: a prospective comparative trial. J Urol 1991; 145:465–6.

60. Droller MJ. Editorial comment re: Skinner DG, Daniels JR, Russell CA, Lieskovsky G, Boyd SD, Nichols P, Kern W, Sakamoto J, Krailo M, Groshen S: The role of adjuvant chemotherapy following cystectomy for invasive bladder cancer: a prospective comparative trial. J Urol 1991; 145:465.

61. Stockle M, Meyenburg W, Wellek S, et al. Advanced bladder cancer (stages pT3b, pT4a, pN1 and pN2): improved survival after radical cystectomy and 3 adjuvant cycles of chemotherapy. Results of a controlled prospective study. J Urol 1992;148:302–6.

62. Stockle M, Meyenburg W, Wellek S, et al. Adjuvant polychemotherapy of nonorgan-confined bladder cancer after radical cystectomy revisited: long-term results of a controlled prospective study and further clinical experience. J Urol 1995;153:47–52.

63. Stockle M, Wellek S, Meyenburg W, et al. Radical cystectomy with or without adjuvant polychemotherapy for nonorgan-confined transitional cell carcinoma of the urinary bladder: prognostic impact of lymph node involvement. Urology 1996;48:868–75.

64. Studer UE, Bacchi M, Biedermann C, et al. Adjuvant cisplatin chemotherapy following cystectomy for bladder cancer: results of a prospective randomized trial. J Urol 1994;152:81–4.

65. Coppin CM, Gospodarowicz MK, James K, et al. Improved local control of invasive bladder cancer by concurrent cisplatin and preoperative or definitive radiation. The National Cancer Institute of Canada Clinical Trials Group. J Clin Oncol 1996;14:2901–7.

66. Freiha F, Reese J, Torti FM. A randomized trial of radical cystectomy versus radical cystectomy plus cisplatin, vinblastine and methotrexate chemotherapy for muscle invasive bladder cancer. J Urol 1996;155:495–9.

15

Cystectomy in the Elderly

PETER E. CLARK, MD
JOHN P. STEIN, MD

With advances in medicine and technology, the population of the United States has progressively aged as people's life expectancy has increased.[1,2] The proportion of the US population over the age of 65 years is expected to increase from approximately 12% in 1987 (or 29 million people) to 23% by the year 2050.[3–5]

Transitional cell carcinoma (TCC) of the bladder generally affects older patients, with a peak incidence in the seventh decade of life.[6] As a consequence, of the 53,200 estimated new cases of TCC diagnosed in 2000, approximately 40% occurred in patients at least 70 years of age.[7,8] The issue of managing TCC in the elderly has and will become increasingly important.

Approximately 25% of all new cases of TCC will present with muscle-invasive disease. The standard of care in the United States for muscle-invasive TCC has been and remains radical cystectomy.[9–15] When contemplating radical cystectomy in the elderly patient, a number of unique challenges must be anticipated and considered. The purpose of this chapter is to outline these issues and review the results of major series involving radical cystectomy in the elderly for TCC.

MOLECULAR BIOLOGY OF AGING

The physiologic changes seen in the human body as one ages have their roots in more fundamental changes at the cellular and molecular levels. Scientists have actively studied these changes in the hope of understanding and impacting on the process of aging, or more properly senescence, in much the same way as for cancer and other disease processes. Although scientists have been pursuing answers to the process of aging for years, remarkably little is known about most mechanisms that regulate the aging process.

A number of theories as to the cause of aging have been proposed. They can be divided into two categories: stochastic theories and developmental-genetic theories.[16,17] The stochastic theories suggest that there is progressive accumulation of random damage to the vital mechanisms of the cell or organism that ultimately leads to the physiologic decline of aging. Perhaps the most prominent example is the somatic mutation theory, which states that damage owing to radiation, free radicals, mutational interactions, transposable elements, or epimutations, such as DNA methylation status, accumulate and ultimately lead to malfunction and ultimately death.[18–23]

The most widely accepted of these theories is the free radical theory of aging, also known as the oxidative stress theory.[23,24] This theory holds that as organisms age, their cellular components, such as DNA, lipids, and protein, are damaged by free radicals in the body. Initially, these free radicals were thought to be generated from exogenous sources such as ionizing radiation. Although this may be true in some cases, most free radical damage is now thought to be attributable to endogenous sources of free radicals in the form of reactive oxygen species generated through the body's own use of oxygen to generate energy via phosphorylation in the mitochondria (Figures 15–1 and 15–2). Many of the other stochastic theories of aging are now explained via the free radical theory in that the wear and tear damage they describe are felt to be secondary to free radicals.[24]

The free radical theory of aging is supported by a number of lines of evidence. It has been shown that

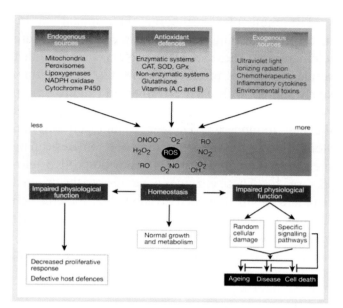

Figure 15–1. The sources and cellular responses to reactive oxygen species (ROS). Oxidants are generated as a result of normal intracellular metabolism in mitochondria and peroxisomes, as well as from a variety of cytosolic enzyme systems. In addition, a number of external agents can trigger ROS production. A sophisticated enzymatic and nonenzymatic antioxidant defense system including catalase (CAT), superoxide dismutase (SOD), and glutathione peroxidase (GPx) counteracts and regulates overall ROS levels to maintain physiologic homeostasis. Lowering ROS levels below the homeostatic set point may interrupt the physiologic role of oxidants in cellular proliferation and host defense. Similarly, increased ROS may also be detrimental and lead to cell death or to an acceleration in aging and age-related diseases. Traditionally, the impairment caused by increased ROS is thought to result from random damage to proteins, lipids, and DNA. In addition to these effects, a rise in ROS levels may also constitute a stress signal that activates specific redox-sensitive signaling pathways. Once activated, these diverse signaling pathways may have either damaging or potentially protective functions. NADPH = reduced nicotinamide adenine dinucleotide phosphate. Reproduced with permission from Finkel and Holbrook.[23]

the amount of oxidative damage to DNA, lipids, and proteins within cells increases as animals age.[25] This may be attributable to increased generation of free radicals with age, a decline in antioxidant defenses, a decline in the efficiency of repair mechanisms, or a combination of the above.[24] Also supporting the free radical theory is the observation that caloric intake restriction, but not malnutrition, can increase the life span of rodents while increasing the oxidative defense mechanisms and decreasing oxidative damage (Figure 15–3).[26] It has been shown that the tissue from species with longer life spans is less susceptible to oxidative damage than that from shorter-lived species.[27] In a similar vein, those species with a higher metabolic rate, and therefore presumably a

higher rate of free radical generation, generally have a shorter life span than species with a slower metabolic rate.[28] Finally, it has also been demonstrated that by genetically engineering improved antioxidant defense mechanisms, it is possible to increase the life span of the fruit fly *Drosophila melanogaster*.[29]

The second broad category is the developmental-genetic theories. In general, these theories hold that aging is part of the genetically programmed progression of the organism through development, maturation, aging, and death. These theories hold that the aging process is governed by a biologic "clock(s)" that tracks time and controls the aging process.[30]

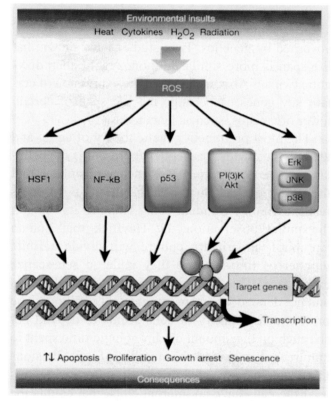

Figure 15–2. Major signaling pathways activated in response to oxidative stress. Reactive oxygen species (ROS) can originate outside the cell, or may be generated intracellularly in response to external stimuli. Heat-shock transcription factor 1 (HSF1), nuclear factor (NF)κB, and p53 are themselves transcription factors, whereas the PI(3)K/Akt and MAPK pathways regulate transcription factors through phosphorylation. The degree to which a given pathway is activated is highly dependent on the nature and duration of the stress, as well as the cell type. The consequences of the response vary widely, with the ultimate outcome being dependent on the balance between these stress-activated pathways. HSF1 is responsible for activation of the heat-shock response. Factors depicted in pink represent those pathways whose activities are altered with aging. Reproduced with permission from Finkel and Holbrook.[23]

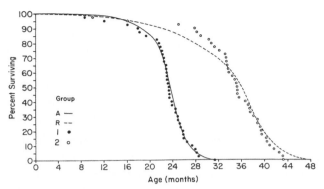

Figure 15–3. Survival curves of Fischer 344 rats fed an ad libitum diet (groups A and 1) or a 60% caloric restricted diet beginning at age 6 weeks (groups R and 2). Curves from groups A and R represent 115 rats each; groups 1 and 2 represent 40 rats each. Caloric restriction results in dramatically prolonged median survival. Reproduced with permission from Yu et al.[26]

There is some evidence that aging is, at least in part, governed by genetics. Twin studies have shown that life span is more similar in monozygotic than dizygotic twins.[18] Also, a change in the expression of certain key genes can change the life span of certain lower organisms, such as nematodes.[31]

The most prominent genetic theory of aging and the one most widely accepted at present is the cellular senescence theory.[24] This theory postulates that the biologic clock that governs the aging process resides within individual cells. This has its roots in the initial observations by Hayflick that human fibroblasts in primary culture will divide a finite number of times before they undergo senescence and die.[32,33] This is apparently intrinsic to the cells and not dependent on environmental conditions. The proliferative capacity of cells seems to depend not so much on the amount of chronologic time spent in culture but rather on the number of cell divisions that the cells have undergone.[34] In other words, it is as if the cells have an internal clock that counts the number of divisions and at the prescribed number of divisions initiates a process leading to cell senescence. This phenomenon is related to the age of the donor, such that cells from an older donor reach senescence faster than cells from a younger donor of the same species.[35] In addition, the life span of primary cell cultures is directly proportional to the life span of the donor species.[36] Thus, cells from longer-lived species (such as humans) live longer in culture than cells from shorter-lived species (eg, a mouse).

The molecular structures that appear to be involved in keeping track of these cell divisions are telomeres.[37,38] These are DNA-protein complexes that reside on the tips of chromosomes that get progressively shorter with each cell division (Figure 15–4). At a critical length, this telomere shortening signals the cell to undergo senescence, and cell division stops. The progressive shortening of telomeres can be prevented through a group of enzymes called telomerases.[37,39] These enzymes act to restore the original telomere length after each division, thus allowing cell division to continue (Figure 15–5). The finding that telomerases are abnormally expressed in many human malignancies has led to extensive and exciting

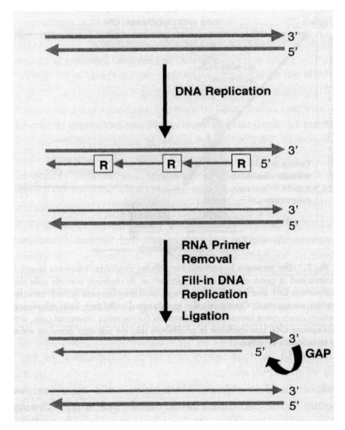

Figure 15–4. The end-replication problem during DNA replication by DNA-dependent DNA polymerases. Parental DNA strands are shown in red, with newly synthesized strands in green. Because a ribonucleic acid (RNA) primer (R) primes synthesis of the lagging strand, removal of the RNA primer leaves a gap at one of the two newly synthesized chromosome ends. The ends of chromosomes have telomeric DNA repeats, which are capped by telomeres to help solve this end-replication problem. The telomeric DNA repeats are reconstituted after DNA replication by telomerases. Reproduced with permission from Meyerson M. Role of telomerase in normal and cancer cells. J Clin Oncol 2000;18:2626–34.

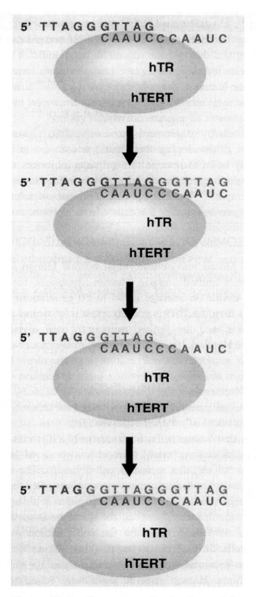

Figure 15–5. De novo synthesis of new telomeres by telomerase. The telomerase catalytic subunit, hTERT, synthesizes new telomeric DNA repeats, GGTTAG, complementary to the sequence CCCUAA in the telomerase ribonucleic acid (RNA) subunit hTR. Existing telomeric DNA is shown in blue, newly synthesized telomeric DNA in green, and the template portion of the RNA subunit in red. Reproduced with permission from Meyerson M. Role of telomerase in normal and cancer cells. J Clin Oncol 2000;18:2626–34.

research into their role in carcinogenesis as well as the possibility of using telomerase as a target for therapeutic or preventive treatment strategies.[24,40,41]

Although, at present, the cell senescence theory and the free radical theory of aging are the most widely favored, the search for a unified theory of aging continues.[24] Intensive and meticulous effort investigating the biology of aging and its relationship to oncogenesis and other disease processes is ongoing.

At the cellular level, there are numerous changes that can be demonstrated as cells age. Specific changes can be demonstrated in senescent versus nonsenescent cells in culture. For instance, a more labile form of the epidermal growth factor receptor (EGFR) is made by senescent cells that are not made by younger cells, and there are changes in the tyrosine kinase activity of the EGFR as cells age.[42,43] In addition, there have been changes demonstrated in the downstream transduction pathway in senescent cells for both arachidonic acid and prostaglandin metabolism.[44] Senescent cells have an impaired ability to respond to mitogenic stimuli, as evidenced by a decreased ability to respond to extracellular calcium, alterations in calmodulin function, and a decreased ability to translocate protein kinase C to the cell membrane.[45–47] A series of other molecular changes in senescent cells have also been demonstrated (Table 15–1). Collectively, these changes reflect a progressively decreased ability of cultured cells to respond to their environment and to external stresses as they age, which parallels the same phenomenon noted at the physiologic level in a variety of organ systems, as discussed later in the chapter.

Intensive efforts to better elucidate the process of aging at the molecular and cellular levels continue. The changes delineated in these studies are reflected in the physiologic changes noted by the clinician. A better understanding of the molecular engine driving these changes may ultimately help the clinician to better diagnose and treat disease processes in the elderly. An exhaustive review of the literature regarding the molecular biology of aging is ultimately beyond the scope of this chapter; however, the interested reader can pursue the subject further through a number of recent reviews.[1,11,24,40,41,48]

AGING AND TUMOR BIOLOGY

The question of whether age has an influence on the biology and behavior of bladder cancer remains controversial. Several studies have suggested that the elderly present with more advanced stages of blad-

Table 15–1. MOLECULAR CHANGES IN CULTURED CELLS UNDERGOING SENESCENCE

Gene/Molecule	Description	Young Cells	Senescent Cells
c-fos	Early cell cycle regulated gene	NI	Reduced[132]
AP-1 complex	Formation important in cell cycle regulation	NI	Severely reduced[133]
Retinoblastoma (Rb)	Tumor suppressor	Phosphorylated normally	Poor phosphorylation[134]
Proliferating cell nuclear antigen	A cofactor of DNA polymerase (DNA replication)	NI	Not expressed[135]
Heat shock protein expression	Expressed in response to stress (eg, hyperthermia)	NI	Reduced[136,137]
Replication-dependent histones	Proteins associated with DNA in the nucleus	NI	Reduced[132]

der cancer than younger patients.[7,49,50] Autopsy series, however, suggest that TCC, as well as other malignancies, metastasizes less frequently in the elderly.[51–54] These discrepancies may reflect a difference in the biology of the tumor or a delay in diagnosis owing to a variety of factors, including access to health care or physician delay.[7]

Age as a predictor of survival after radical cystectomy is also controversial. Thrasher and colleagues reviewed 531 patients with TCC undergoing radical cystectomy and urinary diversion from 1969 to 1990 and evaluated predictors of cancer-specific survival.[55] Age (defined as less than or greater than 65 years old) was an independent predictor of survival on multivariate analysis, second only to the pathologic stage. Similarly, Takashi and colleagues performed a multivariate analysis on 264 patients and found that age less than or greater than 70 years old was an independent predictor of survival, although this was less important than stage, size of the tumor, and the presence of irritative voiding symptoms.[56] Narayana and associates found that in patients with a prior history of bladder cancer, age was also an independent predictor of prognosis after cystectomy ($p = .047$).[57] However, when all patients were considered, including those without a prior history of bladder cancer, the association with increasing age and worse prognosis was weak ($p = .083$).

A study by Skinner and colleagues found no association between age and survival at 36 months after cystectomy among 286 patients.[58] Similarly, Lipponen and colleagues evaluated 265 bladder cancer patients and found that stage was the most important independent predictor of survival, whereas age was not found to be an independent predictor of outcome.[59]

The data are clearly contradictory and subject to confounding factors such as possible delay in proceeding with cystectomy owing to age and comorbidities, delay in diagnosis, or less aggressive therapy owing to age.[7] None of the studies listed above analyzed the role of patient selection in choice of treatment and its possible influence on outcomes. A recent review of 1,054 cystectomy patients at the University of Southern California (USC) has shown an apparent association between age over 80 years old and worsening recurrence-free survival (Clark and colleagues, unpublished observation). It was postulated that these results may have been attributable to a lower probability of older patients undergoing adjuvant chemotherapy despite being more likely to have extravesical disease; however, this did not reach statistical significance.

The data on age, as a predictor of outcome among patients receiving chemotherapy, also yield conflicting results. One study evaluating neoadjuvant chemotherapy did not find that age was an independent prognostic variable; whereas a randomized study looking at adjuvant chemotherapy for TCC by Skinner and colleagues suggested that patients over the age of 65 did better than younger patients.[60,61] Similarly, a trial from Memorial Sloan-Kettering Cancer Center studying Methotrexate, vinblastine, Adriamycin (doxorubicin), and cisplatin (MVAC) chemotherapy for metastatic disease found that patients over the age of 60 had an improved survival.[62] A cooperative group trial studying cisplatinum versus MVAC for metastatic TCC showed an association between increased age and an improved response rate, although this was not statistically significant.[63] It must be emphasized that all of the aforementioned studies can be criticized and have the potential confounding effect of performance status and comorbidities determining who will be treated with chemotherapy.[7] It is possible that in older patients, physicians may be more selective in administering chemotherapy and/or deciding who was eligible for the trial, thus potentially biasing the results in favor of the elderly patients.

Because of the many potential confounding variables discussed, the relationship between age and tumor biology remains largely unknown. Studies examining the influence of age on outcome after either cystectomy or chemotherapy for TCC have yielded conflicting results. Most of the differences between studies can be accounted for by factors such as patient selection, delay or differences in therapy, and differing access to health care. As a consequence, the fundamental question, whether tumors in older patients are more aggressive, remains unanswered and awaits further study.

PHYSIOLOGY OF AGING

Starting at approximately the age of 30, a series of progressive physiologic changes occur as a person ages.[5] The rate at which these changes occurs is subject to individual variation and is influenced by many social and environmental factors such as toxins (tobacco, alcohol, intravenous drug use, etc), socioeconomic status, exercise levels, and occupational exposures. Nevertheless, a series of physiologic changes occur that can be quantified, resulting in a generalized decline in the patient's "physiologic reserve."[64] As patients age, they function reasonably well at baseline but demonstrate a progressive decline in their ability to respond to and maintain homeostasis in the face of major environmental stresses, such as surgery.

The first physiologic trend is the predictable alterations in body composition as a person ages. In general, men will increase their body weight by about 25% by the time they are 60 years old, whereas for women, this figure is approximately 18%.[65] After age 60, this slowly decreases, reaching

the weight from young adulthood, and then continues to decline beyond this as the person gets older. From young adulthood to the age of 80, a 40% decline in muscle mass is observed, accompanied by an 18 to 36% increase in fat among men and a 33 to 48% increase among women.[66,67] This effect increases the relative volume of distribution for lipid-soluble medications in elderly patients, thus prolonging their effects. Conversely, a decrease in total body water occurs as people age, thus lowering the volume of distribution of water-soluble medications.[68–70] Furthermore, an approximately 20% drop in the mean serum albumin levels occurs with aging, thus increasing the unbound concentration of drugs that are normally protein bound and potentially increasing their effects.[70]

In the central and peripheral nervous systems, there is a progressive loss of neurons as people age.[65,70] This decline is accompanied by a progressive decrease in cerebral blood flow and a gradual decrease in cerebral metabolic demand. At the molecular level, there is a decreased number of neurotransmitter receptor sites as people age. These changes overall lead to an increased sensitivity of patients to drugs that have activity on the central nervous system, such as sedatives and narcotics.[70] This may also explain why there is a gradual rise in the rates of clinically apparent cognitive dysfunction as people age, from 2% in those 75 to 79 years of age to 13% of those over the age of 85.[71]

A progressive, measurable decline in pulmonary function also occurs with age (Figure 15–6). As people age, there is a gradual decrease in the elasticity of the lung and an increase in the rigidity of the thoracic cage.[5,72] This leads to an increase in the residual volume and the functional residual capacity. In addition, there is a decrease in both the forced expiratory volume in 1 second and the forced vital capacity as people age, as well as parenchymal changes that lead to an increased tendency toward small airway closure and ventilation-perfusion mismatches.[65,70] Collectively, these changes predispose the elderly to a relative hypoxia. For example, the ability of the elderly to respond to hypercapnia or hypoxemia is decreased by about half compared with younger patients.[70] There is also an increased risk for atelectasis, accompanied by a decrease in both the ciliary function of the lung

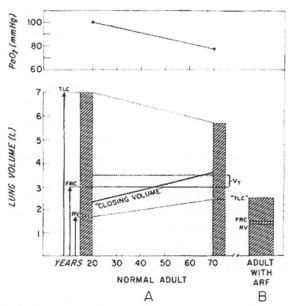

Figure 15–6. Changes in PaO$_2$ and lung volumes with age in normal adults in the supine position (A) and typical values for functional residual capacity (FRC) and vital capacity (B) in an adult patient with acute respiratory failure (ARF). RV = residual volume; TLC = total lung capacity. The horizontal band represents normal tidal breathing range (V$_T$). Vital capacity (TLC-RV) falls progressively with age. "Closing volume" increases linearly with age and in the supine position exceeds FRC at age 44 years. The PaO$_2$ line was drawn from data obtained in supine subjects by Sorbini et al. TLC, RV, and FRC are taken from the table of predicted normal values for a male, 175 cm tall, of Bates et al. FRC has been reduced 20% below predicted to account for the fall occurring with change from sitting to supine position. The line indicating closing volume was drawn from data by Leblanc et al. Reproduced with permission from Pontoppidan H, Geffin B, Lowenstein E. Acute respiratory failure in the adult (first of three parts). N Engl J Med 1972;287:690–8.

epithelium and a general decline in the immune system, making the elderly much more prone to the development of pneumonia.[5,70]

As people age, there is a generalized decrease in the ability of the cardiovascular system to respond to autonomic stimulation and as a consequence to external stress. Anatomically, this is manifested by ventricular wall hypertrophy, thickening and calcification of the heart valves, and loss of elasticity and stiffening of the major arteries.[73,74] Physiologically, this decreased reserve is also reflected by a decrease in the maximum achievable heart rate in the elderly.[68,75] Although basal cardiac output is generally well maintained (at least in healthy individuals), the maximum achievable cardiac output is reduced.[5,68,76] This is attributable, at least in part, to the fact that younger patients increase their cardiac output mainly by

increasing their heart rate, whereas older patients rely more on increasing their stroke volume, predominantly by increasing their end-diastolic volume. Consequently, elderly patients are more dependent on preload to increase their cardiac output than younger patients, so volume depletion is not as well tolerated in the elderly.[67,77] Elderly patients also are at increased risk of cardiac conduction abnormalities and dysrhythmias.[68,76] Given these cardiac changes, it is not surprising that nearly 50% of postoperative deaths in the elderly are secondary to cardiovascular events.[78] Careful attention to the cardiovascular history and physical examination is, therefore, particularly important in predicting outcome after surgery. A study by Gerson and colleagues demonstrated that exercise tolerance was a major predictor of outcome after surgery, as judged by the ability to perform at least 2 minutes of supine exercise with a bicycle or the ability to attain a maximum heart rate of at least 99 beats per minute with exercise.[79]

Renal physiology is also progressively altered as one ages. A 30% decrease in renal mass is observed by age 90, primarily reflected in a loss of cortical mass with relative preservation of the medulla.[80,81] A progressive decrease in renal blood flow, out of proportion to any decline in cardiac output, may also be seen. These changes result in a gradual loss of renal function owing to progressive glomerular sclerosis and loss of plasma ultrafiltration. The glomerular filtration rate is thought to decrease by about 1 cc/minute per 1 year once a person reaches the age of 40.[82] These declines may not be reflected in the serum creatinine, which is also influenced by the loss of muscle mass seen in the elderly. Therefore, although the serum creatinine may remain unchanged with age, the creatinine clearance is generally inversely related to an individual's age and may be estimated by the following formula: creatinine clearance (cc/minute) = (140 – age) × body weight (kg) divided by 72 × serum creatinine (mg/dL) (Figure 15–7).[83] In women, this is adjusted by multiplying the result by 0.85 owing to the lower muscle mass in women. These physiologic changes result in a decreased ability to excrete a salt and water load and a decrease in renal drug clearance. Conversely, at the level of the distal convoluted tubule, there is a decreased ability to maximally

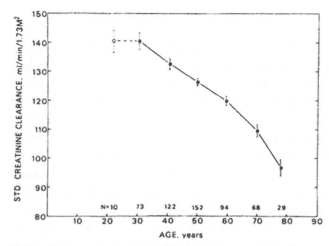

Figure 15–7. Cross-sectional differences in standard creatinine clearance with age. The number of subjects in each age group is indicated above the abscissa. Values plotted indicate mean ± SEM. Reproduced with permission from Rowe JW, Andres R, Tobin JD, et al. The effect of age on creatinine clearance in men: a cross-sectional and longitudinal study. J Gerontol 1976;31:155–63.

retain sodium and water, attributable at least in part to changes in the renin-angiotensin-aldosterone system.[4,84] The net effect, as in most other organ systems, is a decrease in the patient's reserve, such that perturbations in salt and water balance in either direction are tolerated less in the elderly than in younger patients.

Changes in the gastrointestinal system are not as dramatic as in other organ systems as one ages. There is a generalized decrease in motility, secretion, and absorptive capacity of the intestines as patients age.[5] However, the functional reserve of the bowel is large enough that this generally has little, if any, functional consequences. Nevertheless, there are motility changes in the esophagus and a slowing of gastric emptying, which put the elderly at slightly increased risk of aspiration. In addition, an increase in the circular and longitudinal muscles of the large bowel, coupled with an increase in elastin and connective tissue, collectively may result in the increased incidence of fecal impaction and diverticulosis in the elderly.[70] Pancreatic exocrine function is generally not significantly affected by age; however, serum levels of insulin tend to increase with age, whereas end-organ sensitivity to insulin decreases.[5] In the liver, there are a number of changes that all tend to decrease the "hepatic reserve" as patients age; however, this reserve is large enough that there is little loss of hepatic function clinically.[5]

Hematologically, there is a general involution of the bone marrow with age accompanied by a decrease in stem cell function.[85] This results in a decline in the hemoglobin level in patients over the age of 70 and a reduction in the bone marrow's reserve capacity and ability to respond to significant blood loss.[86] In addition, there is a reduction in the level of circulating lymphocytes, although usually not at the level of neutrophils.[87] There is also an overall reduction in cell-mediated immunity as patients age, accompanied by a paradoxical increase in response to self-antigens.[88] This suggests a progressive dysregulation of the immune system as patients age.

Collectively, these many physiologic changes result in an overall decline in the elderly's physiologic reserve. The ability to maintain homeostasis is lowered, such that patients do well under normal conditions but have greater difficulty maintaining homeostasis in the face of major stresses, such as surgery. This is particularly true in regard to pulmonary, cardiac, and renal function, all of which show a gradual decline with age. Cognitively, the elderly are more sensitive to centrally acting medications, and there is evidence for dysregulation of the immune system. An intimate knowledge of these many changes and close cooperation between the surgeon and the rest of the medical team are critical to successfully treating the elderly.

ANESTHETIC/SURGICAL CONSIDERATIONS

Anesthetic Risk

A number of studies have shown that elderly patients are at higher perianesthetic risk. Marx and colleagues demonstrated an 8.2% 1-week perioperative mortality among patients 81 years of age or older compared with an overall rate of 1.9% among younger surgical patients. Other data suggest that it is not chronologic age per se that confers this risk but the patient's comorbidities. A series by Farrow and colleagues demonstrated that when elderly patients over the age of 65 with no comorbid conditions were compared with those patients less than

65 years old, there was no significant difference in perioperative mortality.[89] A study by Cogbill and colleagues also compared elderly patients with no significant concurrent diseases to younger patients and found no difference in perioperative mortality.[90]

In general, there are three factors that consistently influence anesthetic risk.[70] These include whether the procedure is being performed on an emergent or elective basis (emergent cases increase the operative risk from approximately 1 to 45%), the type and scale of the surgery to be undertaken, and a patient's comorbid conditions.[91,92] Patient comorbidity is quantitated by the American Society of Anesthesiologists' Physical Status Classification or ASA class.[93] This classification groups patients into one of five classes as follows:

I: Healthy patient; operation planned involves a localized disease process without systemic disturbances
II: Mild to moderate systemic disease either from the condition to be operated on or another pathologic process
III: Severe disease that limits activity but is not incapacitating
IV: Severe and incapacitating systemic disease that is a constant threat to life.
V: Moribund patient not expected to survive more than 24 hours with or without surgery

An increasing ASA class has consistently been associated with increased perioperative mortality regardless of the patient's age. For example, a study by Djokovic and Hedley-White examined 500 patients over the age of 80 and found that in the 187 patients with an ASA class of II, there was only one perioperative death, whereas the rate was 25% in those with ASA class IV and 100% in ASA class V patients.[94] It appears that if there is an increase in perioperative mortality with age, it is secondary to the fact that older patients tend to have more comorbidities rather than to chronologic age per se. It is logical that when considering a patient for radical cystectomy, chronologic age alone should not be the sole factor determining patient eligibility. Rather, the overall risk, including consideration of the patient's comorbid conditions, should determine eligibility.

Anesthetic Considerations

Any decision to proceed with radical cystectomy must be preceded by a thorough and meticulous history and physical examination as well as pertinent laboratory and radiographic evaluations. A list of the patient's current medications is critical. This is important as a number of medications may need to be modified or stopped prior to the day of surgery. This should always be tailored to the patient's individual needs; however, in general, medications such as monoamine oxidase inhibitors should be stopped 2 weeks prior to surgery; aspirin, ticlopidine, and long half-life nonsteroidal anti-inflammatory drugs should be stopped 1 week prior to surgery; and warfarin should be stopped 3 to 5 days prior to surgery with or without conversion to intravenous anticoagulation with heparin, depending on the indication for anticoagulation.[77] Antidepressants are stopped 3 to 7 seven days prior to surgery, and drugs such as antipsychotics, benzodiazepines, and lithium are generally tapered and stopped the day prior to surgery. Drugs stopped the day prior to or on the day of surgery include oral hypoglycemics, diuretics, potassium supplements, and angiotensin-converting enzyme inhibitors. In all cases, communication between the surgeon and the anesthesiologist involved in the case helps ensure the optimal regimen for the individual patient.

In addition to optimizing the patient's medications, elderly patients in particular would benefit from admission to the hospital on the day prior to surgery for intravenous fluid administration during their bowel preparation. This avoids the problem of dehydration that the elderly are particularly sensitive to, as discussed previously. Although this is standard practice for all patients at USC, at many institutions, this is, unfortunately, no longer practical and not routinely undertaken.

An in-depth discussion of anesthesia in the elderly is beyond the scope of this chapter, and the interested reader is referred to several recent reviews on the subject in the literature.[68,70,77] Nevertheless, some general considerations are worth emphasizing. Achieving a satisfactory airway can be more difficult in the elderly owing to a number of factors, including loose teeth, temporomandibular joint dysfunction, cervical arthritis, and decreased neck mobility, as well as more difficult mask fit secondary to changes in facial contour, alveolar bone resorption, and loss of teeth as a person ages. Elderly patients with vertebrobasilar arterial insufficiency need to have neck extension kept to a minimum. The elderly have decreased protective airway reflex, which, coupled with changes in esophageal and gastric motility, can put them at increased risk of aspiration. The elderly have decreased tear production, putting them at increased risk of desiccation injury to the eyes, and have generalized skin atrophy, making them more prone to bruising, pressure injuries, and skin breakdown. The elderly are also more sensitive to hypothermia owing to a decreased metabolic rate and to changes in their cardiovascular reserve. Finally, although some have advocated the routine use of pulmonary artery monitoring in the elderly, no study has demonstrated that the use of such invasive monitoring improves outcomes, and it is generally felt that age alone is not an indication for more invasive monitoring beyond the standard protocol for a given operation.[95–97]

Surgical Technique

The technique for radical cystectomy with en bloc bilateral pelvic lymphadenectomy is well described in the literature (see Figures 15–8, 15–9, 15–10, 15–11, 15–12, and 15–13).[98,99] This technique is applicable in the elderly, with perhaps the only modification being a less aggressive lymph node dissection in those patients with significant arteriosclerosis.[58] With respect to the choice of urinary diversion, the trend in most series is toward performing an ileal conduit more often in elderly patients while performing continent diversions (cutaneous or orthotopic) in younger patients. Thus, most series of radical cystectomy in the elderly involve an incontinent form of urinary diversion, such as a conduit.[58,100–115] A recent review of the experience at USC demonstrated that 24% of patients less than 80 years old were diverted with an ileal conduit, whereas for patients older than 80, the rate was 46% ($p = .005$; Clark and colleagues, unpublished observation). Relatively fewer series have examined the use of various forms of continent diversion in the elderly; however, these have generally met with favorable results (see below).[113,116]

POSTOPERATIVE CONSIDERATIONS

Owing to the decline in renal physiology with age, some commonly used medications in the postoperative setting need to be adjusted to compensate for a decreased renal drug clearance.[117] Dosage of opiates such as morphine and fentanyl should be lowered in the elderly owing to the combination of decreased volume of distribution, decreased hepatic blood flow, and central nervous system changes increasing the sensitivity to the effects of narcotics, all of which result in a higher initial plasma level of opiates and reduced dose requirement to produce a given effect.[60] Similarly, there is a prolonged drug effect and reduced dose requirement for benzodiazepines such as diazepam and alprazolam owing to decreased liver mass and blood flow, as well as similar changes in the central nervous system that again increase the sensitivity to the effect of these sedatives.

As outlined previously, the physiologic reserve of the elderly is reduced compared with younger patients. The elderly rely more on end-diastolic volume to maintain and elevate cardiac output. They have a reduced capacity for oxygen delivery and tend toward a relative hypoxemia. Their response to inotropic drugs and ability to elevate their heart rate are reduced. These and other changes make it especially critical to minimize stress for the elderly in the

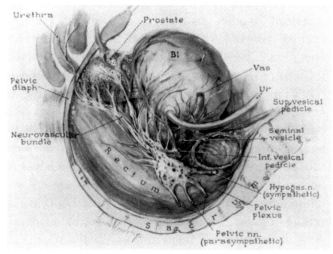

Figure 15–8. Schema of bladder and surrounding pelvic plexuses of importance in performance of anatomic radical cystectomy. With permission from Schlegel PN, Walsh, PC. Neuroanatomical approach to radical cystoprostatectomy with preservation of sexual function. J Urol 1987;138:1402.

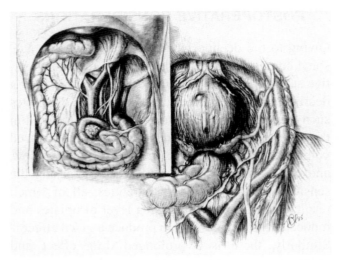

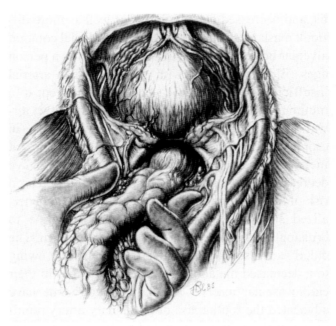

Figure 15–9. Proper patient positioning for cystectomy with the iliac crest located at the break of the table. Wide excision of the urachal remnant en bloc with the cystectomy specimen should be performed. Note, view of the pelvis from overhead; after the ascending colon and peritoneal attachments of the small bowel mesentery have been mobilized up to the level of the duodenum. This mobilization allows the bowel to be properly packed in the epigastrium and exposes the area of the aortic bifurcation, which is the starting point of the lymph node dissection.[98]

Figure 15–10. View of the pelvis from overhead; after the ascending colon and small bowel have been packed in the epigastrium. Note that the sigmoid mesentery is mobilized off the sacral promontory and distal aorta up to the origin of the inferior mesenteric artery.[98]

postoperative period. This includes minimizing hypovolemia, hypothermia, and acidosis.[67] Also important is adequate pain management, as well as avoiding inappropriate or overly hasty weaning from mechanical ventilation.

The exact postoperative medication regimen varies between institutions and from surgeon to surgeon. Although controversial and not universally practiced at other institutions, at USC, all patients over 65 years old are given prophylactic digoxin postoperatively.[58,113,118] All patients should have some form of prophylaxis against deep venous thrombosis (DVT) and other thromboembolic complications. At USC, patients routinely undergo prophylaxis with oral warfarin postoperatively, whereas at many institutions, sequential pneumatic compression devices, subcutaneous heparin, low-molecular-weight heparin, or some combination of the above are used.[58,113,119] Ultimately, the optimal prophylaxis for DVT in the setting of radical cystectomy for invasive bladder cancer remains to be defined and awaits the results of randomized, controlled, comparative trials.

Another source of controversy is in the use of nasogastric tubes after radical cystectomy versus the placement of a gastrostomy tube (G tube) at the time of cys-

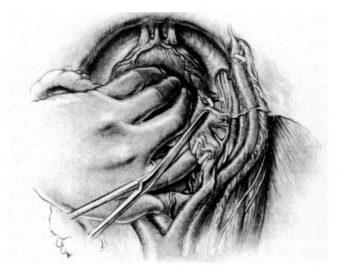

Figure 15–11. The pelvic iliac lymphadenectomy is then performed. The lymph node dissection is initiated 2 cm above the aortic bifurcations (superior limits of dissection), and extends laterally over the inferior vena cava to the genitofemoral nerve, representing the lateral limits of dissection. Distally, the lymph node dissection extends to the lymph node of Cloquet medially (on Cooper's ligament) and the circumflex iliac vein laterally. After the lymphadenectomy is completed, attention is directed to the lateral vascular pedicles. Note that the left hand is used to define the right lateral pedicle, extending from the bladder to the hypogastric artery. This plane is developed by the index finger (medial) and the middle finder (lateral), exposing the anterior branches of the hypogastric artery. This vascular pedicle is clipped and divided down to the endopelvic fascia. Traction with the left hand defines the pedicle, allows direct visualization, and protects the rectum from injury.[98]

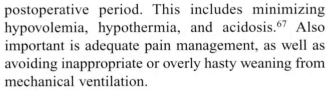

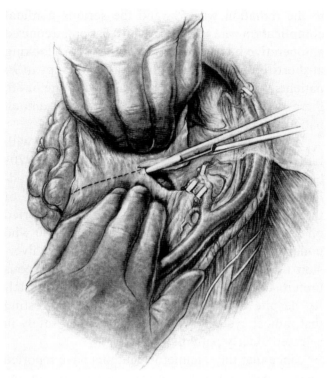

Figure 15–12. Following ligation of the lateral pedicles bilaterally, attention is then directed posterior in order to develop the posterior vascular pedicles. First, the peritoneum lateral to the rectum is incised down into the cul-de-sac, and carried anteriorly over the rectum to join the opposite side. Note that the incision should be made precisely so the proper plane behind Denonvilliers' fascia can be developed safely.[98]

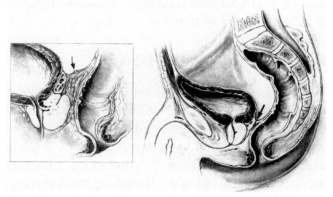

Figure 15–13. Illustration of the formation of Denonvilliers' fascia. Note that it is derived from a fusion of the anterior and posterior peritoneal reflections. Denonvilliers' space lies behind the fascia. To successfully enter this space and facilitate mobilization of the anterior rectal wall of Denonvilliers' fascia, the incision in the cul-de-sac is made close to the peritoneal fusion on the anterior rectal wall side, and not on the bladder side.[98]

tectomy. The practice at USC has been to place a G tube in all patients at the time of cystectomy, which remains in place until the complete return of bowel function, typically by postoperative days 5 to 7.[58,113] This has been demonstrated in a large series of 709 patients to be safe and effective, with a complication rate of 0.05%.[120] In the elderly, and for patients with a history of respiratory compromise, it may be important to consider the advantages in terms of patient comfort and improved pulmonary toilet offered by a G tube over a nasogastric tube. Nevertheless, G tubes are not routinely used at most institutions, and, to date, there are no randomized trials comparing the outcomes after radical cystectomy or other major urologic surgery between patients receiving a G tube versus nasogastric suction.

Another important consideration in all patients considering radical cystectomy is their nutritional status. In the elderly, this is particularly important because the incidence of malnutrition in Great Britain has been estimated to be as high as 5 to 6% in people aged 70 to 80 and 8 to 12% in people over 80 years old.[121] The comparable data in the United States for noninstitutionalized individuals are sparse, but the rate of malnutrition in elderly institutionalized individuals in the United States is estimated to be 52 to 85%.[122,123]

The reasons for this high rate in the elderly may include social factors (eg, living alone or social isolation); physical factors such as dysphagia, poor dentition, and a progressive decline in taste and olfactory function; financial constraints; and psychological disorders such as depression, dementia, and substance abuse (particularly alcohol) leading to anorexia.[124] In addition, disorders such as cerebrovascular accident, Parkinson's disease, congestive heart failure, and chronic pulmonary obstructive disease can all impact on the ability of patients to nutritionally support themselves.

Identifying and treating malnutrition in the elderly are critical prior to surgery because studies have shown that this improves outcome. A Veterans Administration study randomized 951 malnourished patients to receive either preoperative parenteral nutrition or a regular diet and demonstrated fewer postoperative infectious complications in the former group.[125] Postoperatively, elderly patients should be carefully monitored for their caloric intake, and the surgeon should have a lower threshold to initiate some form of parenteral nutrition while awaiting the return of bowel function

OUTCOMES

For years, there was great reluctance among urologic surgeons to perform radical cystectomy in the elderly. The potential morbidity and mortality of such a major operation were felt to be too large in the geriatric population.[126] Alternative therapies were frequently sought, including radiotherapy, chemotherapy, combinations of the two, or observation. It is now well established that the natural history of untreated invasive TCC of the bladder is rapid progression and death within 2 years.[112] Therefore, patients with invasive TCC and a life expectancy in excess of 2 years deserve consideration for definitive treatment. Although it is generally well accepted in the United States that radical cystectomy is the treatment of choice for invasive TCC, several authors have advocated the use of radiation therapy to decrease morbidity and mortality in the elderly. For example, a randomized study of 189 patients by Bloom and colleagues comparing radiation therapy (4,000 rads) plus cystectomy versus radiation therapy alone (4,000 rads plus 2,000 rad boost) found that there was an advantage to the combination therapy in patients less than 60 years old.[127] This advantage decreased but was still present in those between the ages of 60 and 64. Interestingly, no significant difference was observed between those treated with cystectomy and radiation versus radiation alone in patients 65 years of age or older. In addition, the operative mortality rate among those 65 years old or older was a disturbing 11%. Despite this, the overall results with radiation therapy for bladder cancer have been disappointing. For instance, in a series from the M.D. Anderson Cancer Center, the 3- and 5-year survival rates were only 22% and 14%, respectively, in 382 patients over the age of 60 with definitive radiation therapy for invasive bladder cancer.[128] The local recurrence rates reported after radiation therapy for bladder cancer have been as high as 50% or more.[108] Radiation therapy is also not without significant morbidity and mortality. In the M.D. Anderson series, the mortality rate owing

to the radiation was 5% and the serious nonfatal complication rate was 9%. Many patients required an operative intervention. In another study looking at short-term palliation with radiation therapy in 96 patients with invasive TCC and a median age of 80, there were 5 treatment related deaths, all among patients over the age of 80.[129]

As a result of the relatively poor results with radiation therapy, several centers in the 1970s began to explore the feasibility of performing radical cystectomy in the older population. In one of the earliest studies, Kursh and colleagues reported on 25 patients between the ages of 70 and 80 who underwent radical cystectomy and urinary diversion (23 with an ileal conduit, 2 with cutaneous ureterostomies).[100] There was no operative mortality despite a 40% complication rate, suggesting that radical cystectomy can be performed safely in selected elderly patients.

Since that time, numerous authors have reported their experience with radical cystectomy in the elderly (Table 15–2). The mortality rates among these series have varied between 0 and 18%. A total of 819 unique patients with mortality data are available among the series included in the table (the report by Figueroa and colleagues is an update of the series by Skinner and colleagues), and the mortality rate among these patients overall is 4%. One of the earliest reports to compare the operative mortality rates between younger and older patients was by Thomas and Riddle in 1982.[103] They found a 12% operative mortality rate among 41 patients over the age of 65 versus 3.4% among 59 patients less than 65 years old. With refinements in operative technique and perioperative care, all six reports since that time have found no significant difference in comparing the operative mortality between younger and older patients.[105,107,110,111,113,114]

The complication rates reported in the series from Table 15–2 vary considerably (between 7.7% and 54%). These differences may be related to the way in which complications were defined, how long the patients were followed, and whether the complications were divided into early versus late events. In the largest series by Figueroa and colleagues, the early and late complication rates among 404 patients 70 years old or older were 32% and 12.4%, respec-

Table 15–2. REPORTS ON RADICAL CYSTECTOMY IN ELDERLY PATIENTS						
Report	**# Patients**	**Definition of Elderly (yr)**	**Mortality Rate (%)**	**Difference vs Younger Patients**	**Complication Rate: Early/Late (%)**	**Difference vs Younger Patients**
Kursh et al, 1977[100]	25	70–80	0	—	40	—
Zingg et al, 1980[101]	24	≥ 70	18	—	54/—	—
Zincke et al, 1982[102]	19	≥ 80	5.3	—	47	—
Thomas and Riddle, 1982[103]	41	≥ 65	12	Yes	—	No*
Drago et al, 1983[104]	28	≥ 70	0	—	—	—
Tachibana et al, 1983[105]	9	≥ 80	0	No	67 (dementia)	Yes
Skinner et al, 1984[58]	77	≥ 65	3.9	—	34/—	—
Ogawa et al, 1985[106]	9	≥ 80	0	—	33	—
Wood et al, 1987[107]	38	≥ 70	5.3	No	34	No
Orihuela and Cubelli, 1987[108]	7	≥ 80	14	—	—	—
Jacqmin et al, 1989[109]	39	> 70	2.5	—	7.7 (reoperation)	—
Leibovitch et al, 1993[110]	42	≥ 70	9.5	No	—	No*
Navon et al, 1995[116]	21	≥ 75	9.5	—	28/48	—
Koch and Smith, 1996[111]	47	≥ 70	—	No*	—	No*
Stroumbakis et al, 1997[112]	44	≥ 80	4.5	—	51	—
Figueroa et al, 1998[113]	404	≥ 70	2.8	No	32/12.4	No
Rosario et al, 2000[114]	33	≥ 70	0	No	—	—
Lance et al, 2001[115]	36	> 80	0	—	62	—

*Rate not discernible from report, but statistical analysis indicates no. difference

tively.[113] There was no difference in the complication rates when compared with patients younger than 70 in the same series, and the mean length of stay in the hospital was comparable (10 days for patients less than 70 versus 11 days for those at least 70 years old).

Other series have also found no difference in the complication rates between younger and older patients.[103,107,110,111] The one exception was a small study by Tachibana and colleagues that reported on nine patients over the age of 80 and found a higher complication rate in this group (67%) than in younger patients, although the difference appeared to be mainly accounted for by psychiatric complications such as delirium.[105] In a different type of analysis, Malavaud and colleagues performed a multivariate analysis of predictors of complications after radical cystectomy and bilateral pelvic lymphadenectomy.[130] None of the patients in the study had preoperative chemotherapy or radiation. The only significant independent predictor of complications postoperatively was the patient's ASA class. Age was not an independent prognostic variable.

The choice of urinary diversion in the elderly patient remains controversial. Although many academic institutions perform continent urinary diversion, in particular continent orthotopic neobladders, most urologists will lean toward ileal conduits in the

elderly. Thus, the overwhelming majority in the reported series reviewed used incontinent urinary diversions (predominantly ileal conduits or cutaneous ureterostomies) or ureterosigmoidostomies.

Only two of the studies looked at continent cutaneous diversions using either a modified Indiana pouch or a Kock pouch.[113,116] In the series by Navon and colleagues, all 21 patients had undergone diversion via a modified Indiana pouch. In the large series from USC, 20% of the patients had undergone a continent cutaneous diversion (versus 41% conduits and 39% orthotopic diversion). This study is the largest reported series of elderly patients undergoing cystectomy and urinary diversion and the only series that includes patients undergoing orthotopic reconstruction. As noted previously, this study found no discernible difference in mortality or morbidity (either early or late) when stratified by the age of the patient. A recent update of the data from USC looking at early diversion-related complications stratified by four different age groups also found no difference between younger and older patients (Clark and colleagues, unpublished observation).

Additional support for continent diversion in the elderly comes from the multivariate analysis by Malavaud and colleagues, which found that the form of diversion was not an independent predictor of morbidity after radical cystectomy.[130] Although these results are encouraging, it has been shown in a separate report from USC that elderly patients do have an increased rate of incontinence after ileal neobladder urinary diversion than younger patients.[131] With increasing experience and refinements in both operative technique and perioperative care, it is likely that more and more elderly patients will be offered the option of a continent urinary diversion after radical cystectomy.

Overall, cystectomy in carefully selected elderly patients can be done safely. Similarly, continent urinary diversion can be performed in the elderly with no apparent increase in diversion-related complications. The importance of patient selection cannot be overemphasized. All of the reported series are retrospective reviews and, as such, include patients that were selected to undergo cystectomy with or without continent diversion. The selection of the appropriate elderly patient is, therefore, critical to long-term success. Physiologic age, not chronologic age per se, should guide the surgeon regarding both eligibility for cystectomy and the type of urinary diversion used.

CONCLUSIONS

As the population ages both in the United States and elsewhere, the importance of major surgery in the elderly, including radical cystectomy and urinary diversion, will continue to grow. Advances in molecular biology and genetics will continue to broaden our understanding of the aging process and the biologic basis of the physiologic changes observed clinically. Chronologic age should not be a contraindication for radical cystectomy. Rather, a thorough consideration of the patient's physiologic age in conjunction with the patient and the perioperative team should determine eligibility. An intimate knowledge of the unique challenges faced by the elderly patient combined with meticulous surgical technique and a team effort in the perioperative period and beyond will allow the urologic surgeon to perform radical cystectomy in the elderly safely and effectively. Further refinements in technique and perioperative care may allow more elderly patients in the future to undergo a continent form of urinary diversion.

REFERENCES

1. Ahmed A, Tollefsbol T. Telomeres and telomerase: basic science implications for aging. J Am Geriatr Soc 2001; 49:1105–9.
2. National Center for Health Statistics. US decennial life tables for 1989–1991. Vol. 1, No. 3. Some trends and comparison of United States life table data. Hyattsville (MD): US Department of Health and Human Services; 1999.
3. A health care debacle: lessons to learn from the retreat on the catastrophic health law. US News and World Report 1989; 107:16.
4. Koruda MJ, Sheldon GF. Surgery in the aged. Adv Surg 1991;24:293–331.
5. Evers BM, Townsend CM, Thompson JC. Organ physiology of aging. Surg Clin North Am 1994;74:23–39.
6. Dreicer R, Cooper CS, Williams RD. Management of prostate and bladder cancer in the elderly. Urol Clin North Am 1996;23:87–97.
7. Raghavan D. Management of advanced bladder cancer in the elderly. Urol Clin North Am 1992;19:797–806.
8. Greenlee RT, Murray T, Bolden S, Wingo PA. Cancer statistics, 2000. CA Cancer J Clin 2000;50:7–33.
9. Messing EM, Catalona W. Urothelial tumors of the urinary tract. In: Walsh PC, Retik AB, Vaughan EDJ, editors. Campbell's urology. Vol. 3. Philadelphia: WB Saunders Company; 1998. p. 2327–410.
10. Gompertz B. On the nature of the function expressive of the law of human mortality and on a new mode of determining life contingencies. Philos Trans R Soc Lond 1825; 115:513.
11. Cristofalo VJ, Gerhard GS, Pignolo RJ. Molecular biology of aging. Surg Clin North Am 1994;74:1–21.
12. Florini JR. Composition and function of cells and tissues. In: Florini JR, editor. Handbook of biochemistry in aging. Boca Raton (FL): CRC Press; 1981.
13. Bjorksten J. Cross linkage and the aging process. In: Rothstein M, editor. Theoretical aspects of aging. New York: Academic Press; 1974. p. 43.
14. Kohn RR. Aging of animals: possible mechanisms. Principles of mammalian aging. Englewood Cliffs (NJ): Prentice-Hall; 1978.
15. Strehler BL. Time, cells, and aging. New York: Academic Press; 1977.
16. Cristofalo VJ. An overview of the theories of biological aging. In: Birren JE, Bengston VL, editors. Emergent theories of aging. New York: Springer; 1988.
17. Hayflick L. How and why we age. New York: Ballantine; 1994.
18. Cummings DJ. Mitochondrial DNA in *Podospora anserina*: a molecular approach to cellular senescence. Monogr Dev Biol 1984;17:254–66.
19. Failla G. The aging process and carcinogenesis. Ann N Y Acad Sci 1958;71:1124–40.
20. Fairweather DS, Fox M, Margison GP. The in vitro lifespan of MRC-5 cells is shortened by 5-azacytidine-induced demethylation. Exp Cell Res 1987;168:153–9.
21. Morley AA. Is ageing the result of dominant or co-dominant mutations? J Theor Biol 1982;98:469–74.
22. Szilard L. On the nature of the aging process. Proc Natl Acad Sci U S A 1959;45:30–45.

23. Finkel T, Holbrook NJ. Oxidants, oxidative stress, and the biology of ageing. Nature 2000;408:239–47.

24. Armbrecht HJ. The biology of aging. J Lab Clin Med 2001; 138:220–5.

25. Sohal RS, Weindruch R. Oxidative stress, caloric restriction, and aging. Science 1996;273:59–63.

26. Yu BP, Masoro EJ, McMahon CA. Nutritional influences in aging of Fischer 344 rats: I. Physical, metabolic, and longevity characteristics. J Gerontol 1985;40:657–70.

27. Agarwal RS, Sohal RS. Relationship between susceptibility to protein oxidation, aging, and maximum life span potential of different species. Exp Gerontol 1996;31:365–72.

28. Pearl R. The rate of living. London: University of London Press; 1928.

29. Orr WC, Sohal RS. Extension of life-span by overexpression of superoxide dismutase and catalase in *Drosophila melanogaster*. Science 1994;263:1128–30.

30. Miller RA. Kleemeier award lecture: are there genes for aging? J Gerontol 1999;54A:B297–307.

31. Lithgow GJ, White TM, Melov S, Johnson TE. Thermotolerance and extended life-span conferred by single-gene mutations and induced by thermal stress. Proc Natl Acad Sci U S A 1995;92:7540–4.

32. Hayflick L, Moorehead PS. The serial cultivation of human dipoid cell strains. Exp Cell Res 1961;25:585–621.

33. Hayflick L. The limited in vitro lifetime of human diploid cell strains. Exp Cell Res 1965;37:614–36.

34. Cristofalo VJ, Palazzo R, Charpentier RL. Limited lifespan of human fibroblasts in vitro: metabolic time or replications? In: Adelman RC, Roberts J, Baker GT, et al, editors. Neural regulatory mechanisms during aging. New York: Alan R. Liss; 1980. p. 203.

35. Martin GM, Sprague CA, Epstein CJ. Replicative life span of cultivated human cells. Effects of donor's age, tissue, and genotype. Lab Invest 1970;23:86–92.

36. Rohme D. Evidence for a relationship between longevity of mammalian species and life spans of normal fibroblasts in vitro and erythrocytes in vivo. Proc Natl Acad Sci U S A 1981;78:5009–13.

37. Greider CW. Telomerase activity, cell proliferation, and cancer. Proc Natl Acad Sci U S A 1998;95:90–2.

38. Campisi J. Cancer, aging and cellular senescence. In Vivo 2000;14:183–8.

39. Bodnar AG, Ouellette M, Frolkis M, et al. Extension of life span by introduction of telomerase into normal human cells. Science 1998;279:349–52.

40. DePinho RA. The age of cancer. Nature 2000;408:248–54.

41. Hahn WC, Meyerson M. Telomerase activation, cellular immortalization and cancer. Ann Med 2001;33:123–9.

42. Brooks KM, Phillips PD, Carlin CR, et al. EGF-dependent phosphorylation of the EGF receptor in plasma membranes isolated from young and senescent WI-38 cells. J Cell Physiol 1987;133:523–31.

43. Carlin CR, Phillips PD, Knowles BB, Cristofalo VJ. Diminished in vitro tyrosine kinase activity of the EGF receptor of senescent human fibroblasts. Nature 1983;306:617–20.

44. Cristofalo VJ, Phillips PD, Sorger T, Gerhard G. Alterations in the responsiveness of senescent cells to growth factors. J Gerontol 1989;44:55–62.

45. Praeger FC, Gilchrest BA. Influence of increased extracellu-lar calcium concentration and donor age on density-dependent growth inhibition of human fibroblasts. Proc Soc Exp Biol Med 1986;182:315–21.

46. Brooks-Frederich KM, Ciancianulo FL, Rittling SR, Cristafola VJ. Cell cycle dependent regulation of Ca++ in young and senescent WI-38 cells. Exp Cell Res 1993;205:412–5.

47. De Tata V, Ptasznik A, Cristofalo VJ. Effects of the tumor promoter phorbol 12-myristate 13-acetate (PMA) on proliferation of young and senescent WI-38 human diploid fibroblasts. Exp Cell Res 1993;205:261–9.

48. Mann DMA. Molecular biology's impact on our understanding of aging. BMJ 1997;315:1078–81.

49. Goodwin JS, Samet JM, Key CR, et al. Stage at diagnosis of cancer varies with the age of the patient. J Am Geriatr Soc 1986;34:20–6.

50. Holmes FF. Clinical evidence for a change in tumor aggressiveness with age. Semin Oncol 1989;16:34–40.

51. Ershler WB, Socinski MA, Greene CJ. Bronchogenic cancer, metastases and aging. J Am Geriatr Soc 1983;31:673–6.

52. O'Rourke MA, Feussner JR, Feigl P, Laszlo J. Age trends of lung cancer stage at diagnosis: implications for lung cancer screening in the elderly. JAMA 1987;258:921–6.

53. Saitoh H, Shiramizu T, Hida M. Age changes in metastatic patterns in renal adenocarcinoma. Cancer 1982;50:1646–8.

54. Suen KC, Lau LL, Yermakov V. Cancer and old age: an autopsy study of 3,535 patients over 65 years old. Cancer 1974;33:1164–8.

55. Thrasher JB, Frazier HA, Robertson JE, et al. Clinical variables which serve as predictors of cancer-specific survival among patients treated with radical cystectomy for transitional cell carcinoma of the bladder and prostate. Cancer 1994;73:1708–15.

56. Takashi M, Murase T, Mizuno S, et al. Multivariate evaluation of prognostic determinants in bladder cancer patients. Urol Int 1987;42:368–74.

57. Narayana AS, Loening SA, Slymen DJ, Culp DA. Bladder cancer: factors affecting survival. J Urol 1983;130:56–60.

58. Skinner EC, Lieskovsky G, Skinner DG. Radical cystectomy in the elderly patient. J Urol 1984;131:1065–8.

59. Lipponen PK, Eskelinen MJ, Kiviranta J, Pesonen E. Prognosis of transitional cell bladder cancer: a multivariate prognostic score for improved prediction. J Urol 1991;146:1535–40.

60. Wallace DM, Raghavan D, Kelly KA, et al. Neo-adjuvant (pre-emptive) cisplatin therapy in invasive transitional cell carcinoma of the bladder. Br J Urol 1991;67:608–15.

61. Skinner DG, Daniels JR, Russell CA, et al. The role of adjuvant chemotherapy following cystectomy for invasive bladder cancer: a prospective comparative trial. J Urol 1991;145:459–67.

62. Geller NL, Sternberg CN, Penenberg D, et al. Prognostic factors for survival of patients with advanced urothelial tumors treated with methotrexate, vinblastine, doxorubicin, and cisplatin chemotherapy. Cancer 1991;67: 1525–31.

63. Loehrer PJS, Einhorn LH, Elson PJ, et al. A randomized comparison of cisplatin alone or in combination with methotrexate, vinblastine, and doxorubicin in patients with metastatic urothelial carcinoma: a cooperative group study. J Clin Oncol 1992;10:1066–73.

64. Watters JM, McClaran JC. The elderly surgical patient. In:

Wilmore DW, editor. Care of the surgical patient. New York: Scientific American; 1990.

65. Muravchick S. Anesthesia for the elderly. In: Miller RD, editor. Anesthesia. New York: Churchill Livingstone; 1990. p. 1969–83.

66. Stoelting RK, Dieredorf SF, McCammon RL. Geriatric patients. In: Stoelting RK, editor. Anesthesia and co-existing disease. New York: Churchill Livingstone; 1988. p. 885–906.

67. Watters JM, Bessey PQ. Critical care for the elderly patient. Surg Clin North Am 1994;74:187–97.

68. Burney TL, Badlani GH. Anesthetic considerations in the geriatric patient. Urol Clin North Am 1996;23:19–26.

69. Muravchick S. Current concepts. Anesthetic pharmacology in geriatric patients. Prog Anesthesiol 1987;1:2.

70. Buxbaum JL, Schwartz AJ. Perianesthetic considerations for the elderly patient. Surg Clin North Am 1994;74:41–58.

71. Clarke M, Lowry R, Clarke S. Cognitive impairment in the elderly—a community survey. Age Ageing 1986;15:278–84.

72. Turner JM, Mead J, Wohl ME. Elasticity of human lungs in relation to age. J Appl Physiol 1968;25:664–71.

73. Gerstenblith G, Frederiksen J, Yin FC, et al. Echocardiographic assessment of a normal adult aging population. Circulation 1977;56:273–8.

74. McMillan JB, Len M. The aging heart: I. Endocardium. J Gerontol 1959;14:268–83.

75. Skinner JS. The cardiovascular system with aging and exercise. In: Frunner D, Jake E, editors. Medicine and science in sport. Vol. 4. Baltimore: University Park Press; 1970. p. 100.

76. Evans TI. The physiologic basis of geriatric general anesthesia. Anaesth Intensive Care 1973;1:319–22.

77. Smith R, Osterweil D, Ouslander JG. Perioperative care in the elderly urologic patient. Urol Clin North Am 1996;23:27–41.

78. Goldman L, Caldera DL, Southwick FS, et al. Cardiac risk factors and complications in non-cardiac surgery. Medicine 1978;57:357–70.

79. Gerson MC, Hurst JM, Hertzberg VS, et al. Cardiac prognosis in noncardiac geriatric surgery. Ann Intern Med 1985;103:832–7.

80. Adkins BA, Davies J, Adkins RBJ. The anatomic and physiologic aspects of aging. In: Adkins RBJ, Scott HWJ, editors. Surgical care for the elderly. Baltimore: Williams & Wilkins; 1988. p. 10–28.

81. Dunnill M, Halley W. Some observations on the quantitative anatomy of the kidney. J Pathol 1973;110:113–21.

82. Adler S, Lindeman RD, Yiengst MJ, et al. Effect of acute acid loading on urinary acid excretion by the aging human kidney. J Lab Clin Med 1968;72:278–89.

83. Cockroft DW, Gault MN. Prediction of creatinine clearance from serum creatinine. Nephron 1976;16:31–41.

84. Epstein M. Effects of aging on the kidney. J Pathol 1979;38:168–72.

85. Hartstock RJ, Smith EB, Petty ES. Normal variations with aging on the amount of hematopoietic tissue in bone marrow from the anterior iliac crest. Am J Clin Pathol 1965;43:326–31.

86. Lipschitz DA, Udupa KB. Age and the hematopoietic system. J Am Geriatr Soc 1986;34:448–54.

87. Bender BS, Nagel JE, Adler WH, Andres R. Absolute peripheral blood lymphocyte count and subsequent mortality of elderly men. The Baltimore Longitudinal Study of Aging. J Am Geriatr Soc 1986;34:649–54.

88. Schwab R, Walter CA, Weksler ME. Host defense mechanisms and aging. Semin Oncol 1989;16:20–7.

89. Farrow SC, Fowkes FG, Lunn JN, et al. Epidemiology in anaesthesia II: factors affecting mortality in hospital. Br J Anaesth 1982;54:811–7.

90. Cogbill CL. Operation in the aged: mortality related to concurrent disease, duration of anesthesia, and elective or emergency operation. Arch Surg 1967;94:202–5.

91. Adkins R, Scott H. Surgical procedures in patients aged 90 years and older. South Med J 1984;77:1357–64.

92. Greenburg AG, Saik RP, Farris JM, Peskin GW. Operative mortality in general surgery. Am J Surg 1982;144:22–8.

93. American Society of Anesthesiologists. New classification of physical status. Anesthesiology 1963;24:111.

94. Djokovic JL, Hedley-White J. Prediction of outcome of surgery and anesthesia in patients over 80. JAMA 1979;242:2301–6.

95. Gore JM, Goldberg RJ, Spodick DH, et al. A community-wide assessment of the use of pulmonary artery catheters in patients with acute myocardial infarction. Chest 1987;92:721–7.

96. Robin ED. The cult of the Swan-Ganz catheter. Overuse and abuse of pulmonary flow catheters. Ann Intern Med 1985;103:445–9.

97. Schlegal PN, Walsh PC. Neuroanatomical approach to radical cystoprostatectomy with preservation of sexual function. J Urol 1987;138:1402–11.

98. Skinner DG. Technique of radical cystectomy. Urol Clin North Am 1981;8:353–66.

99. Stein JP, Quek ML, Skinner DG. Contemporary surgical techniques for continent urinary diversion: continence and potency preservation. Atlas Urol Clin North Am 2001;9:147–73.

100. Kursh ED, Rabin R, Persky L. Is cystectomy a safe procedure in elderly patients with carcinoma of the bladder? J Urol 1977;118:40–2.

101. Zingg EJ, Bornet B, Bishop MC. Urinary diversion in the elderly patient. Eur Urol 1980;6:347–51.

102. Zincke H. Cystectomy and urinary diversion in patients eighty years old or older. Urology 1982;19:139–42.

103. Thomas DM, Riddle PR. Morbidity and mortality in 100 consecutive radical cystectomies. Br J Urol 1982;54:716–9.

104. Drago JR, Rohner TJJ. Cystectomy and urinary diversion: a safe procedure for elderly patients. Urology 1983;21:17–9.

105. Tachibana M, Murai M, Deguchi N, et al. One-stage total cystectomy and ileal loop diversion in patients over eighty years' old with bladder carcinoma. Urology 1983;22:512–6.

106. Ogawa A, Yanagisawa Y, Nakamoto T, et al. Treatment of bladder carcinoma in patients more than 80 years old. J Urol 1985;134:889–91.

107. Wood DPJ, Montie JE, Maatman TJ, Beck GJ. Radical cystectomy for carcinoma of the bladder in the elderly patient. J Urol 1987;138:46–8.

108. Orihuela E, Cubelli V. Management and results in elderly patients with urologic cancer. Semin Urol 1987;5:134–40.

109. Jacqmin D, Cuvelier G, Bollack C. Radical cystectomy for

infiltrating bladder tumor in the elderly. J Urol 1989;141: 379A.

110. Leibovitch I, Avigad I, Ben-Chaim J, et al. Is it justified to avoid radical cystoprostatectomy in elderly patients with invasive transitional cell carcinoma of the bladder? Cancer 1993;71:3098–101.

111. Koch MO, Smith JAJ. Influence of patient age and comorbidity on outcome of a collaborative care pathway after radical prostatectomy and cystoprostatectomy. J Urol 1996;155:1681–4.

112. Stroumbakis N, Herr HW, Cookson MS, Fair WR. Radical cystectomy in the octogenarian. J Urol 1997;158:2113–7.

113. Figueroa AJ, Stein JP, Dickinson M, et al. Radical cystectomy for elderly patients with bladder carcinoma: an updated experience with 404 patients. Cancer 1998;83:141–7.

114. Rosario DJ, Becker M, Anderson JB. The changing pattern of mortality and morbidity from radical cystectomy. BJU Int 2000;85:427–30.

115. Lance RS, Grossman HB. Cystectomy in the elderly. Semin Urol Oncol 2001;19:51–5.

116. Navon JD, Weinberg AC, Ahlering TE. Continent urinary diversion using a modified Indiana pouch in elderly patients. Am Surgeon 1994;60:786–8.

117. Seely JF. Renal function in the elderly. In: Meakins JL, McClaran JC, editors. Surgical care of the elderly. Chicago: Year Book Medical Publishers; 1988. p. 143.

118. Deutsch S, Dalen JE. Indications for prophylactic digitalization. Anesthesiology 1969;30:648–56.

119. Chandhoke PS, Gooding GAW, Narayan P. Prospective randomized trial of warfarin and intermittent pneumatic leg compression as prophylaxis for postoperative deep venous thrombosis in major urological surgery. J Urol1992;147:1056–9.

120. Buscarini M, Stein JP, Lawrence MA, et al. Tube gastrostomy after radical cystectomy and urinary diversion: surgical technique and experience in 709 patients. Urology 2000; 56:150–2.

121. Department of Health and Social Security. A nutrition survey of the elderly. Rep Health Soc Subj (London) 1979;16:1–209.

122. Pinchcofsky-Devin GD, Kaminski MV. Incidence of protein calorie malnutrition in the nursing home population. J Am Coll Nutr 1987;6:109–12.

123. Shaver HJ, Loper JA, Lutes RA. Nutritional status of nursing home patients. JPEN J Parenter Enteral Nutr 1980; 4:367–70.

124. Rolandelli RH, Ullrich JR. Nutritional support in the frail elderly surgical patient. Surg Clin North Am 1994;74: 79–92.

125. The Veterans Affairs Total Parenteral Nutrition Study Group. Perioperative total parenteral nutrition in surgical patients. N Engl J Med 1991;325:525–32.

126. Dickinson AJ, Howe K, Bedford C, et al. A retrospective study of the investigation and management of muscle-invasive bladder cancer in the South-West region. Br J Urol 1996;77:70–5.

127. Bloom HJG, Hendry WF, Wallace DM, Skeet RG. Treatment of T3 bladder cancer: controlled trial of pre-operative radiotherapy and radical cystectomy versus radical radiotherapy. Second report and review (for the clinical trials group, Institute of Urology). Br J Urol 1982;54: 136–51.

128. Miller LS, Johnson DE. Megavoltage irradiation for bladder cancer: alone, postoperative, or preoperative? Proc Natl Cancer Conf 1972;7:771–82.

129. Holmang S, Borghede G. Early complications and survival following short-term palliative radiotherapy in invasive bladder carcinoma. J Urol 1996;155:100–2.

130. Malavaud B, Vaessen C, Mouzin M, et al. Complications for radical cystectomy: impact of the American Society of Anesthiologists Score. Eur Urol 2001;39:79–84.

131. Elmajian DA, Stein JP, Esrig D, et al. The Kock ileal neobladder: updated experience in 295 male patients. J Urol 1996;156:920–5.

132. Seshadri T, Campisi J. Repression of c-fos transcription and an altered genetic program in senescent human fibroblasts. Science 1990;247:205–9.

133. Riabowol K, Schiff J, Gilman MZ. Transcription factor AP-1 activity is required for initiation of DNA synthesis and is lost during cellular aging. Proc Natl Acad Sci U S A 1992;89:157–61.

134. Stein GH, Beeson M, Gordon L. Failure to phosphorylate retinoblastoma gene product in senescent human fibroblasts. Science 1990;249:666–9.

135. Chang CD, Phillips P, Lipson KE, Cristofalo VJ. Senescent human fibroblasts have a post-transcriptional block in the expression of the proliferating cell nuclear antigen gene. J Biol Chem 1991;266:8663–6.

136. Liu AY, Choi HS, Lee YK, Chen KY. Molecular events involved in transcriptional activation of heat shock genes become progressively refractory to heat stimulation during aging of human diploid fibroblasts. J Cell Physiol 1991;149:560–6.

137. Luce MC, Cristofalo VJ. Reduction in heat shock gene expression correlates with increased thermosensitivity in senescent human fibroblasts. Exp Cell Res 1992;202: 9–16.

16

Bladder-Sparing Approaches in Treatment of Muscle-Invasive Bladder Cancer

ARTHUR I. SAGALOWSKY, MD

KENNETH S. KOENEMANN, MD

Radical cystectomy and urinary diversion is the standard treatment for muscle-invasive bladder cancer. Earlier diagnosis, improved understanding of disease natural history and risk stratification, decreased surgical morbidity, and continent urinary diversion all enhance both patient acceptance and the efficacy of cystectomy. Effective systemic therapy of microscopic or gross metastatic disease, and strategies that prevent metastatic disease in the first place, are the most urgent needs for improving patient survival of muscle invasive bladder cancer. Nevertheless, bladder-sparing approaches to cystectomy that may also effectively treat local disease and prevent systemic progression represent idealized therapy, improvements in continent diversion notwithstanding. In recent years several comprehensive reviews on bladder-sparing approaches in the management of invasive bladder cancer have been published.[1–4] In the broadest context, bladder-sparing therapy for invasive bladder cancer may include transurethral resection of bladder tumor (TURBT) alone, TURBT plus intravesical immunotherapy or chemotherapy, TURBT plus neoadjuvant or adjuvant systemic chemotherapy, partial cystectomy, external beam radiotherapy, brachytherapy, or trimodal therapy of TURBT plus radiation plus systemic chemotherapy. Tables 16–1 to 16–4 adapted from the review by Feneley and Schoenberg present published results of series for each of these approaches.[4] The current authors wish to summarize emerging themes from the results of these various treatment approaches. In particular urologists must keep current with the tri-modality protocols for bladder sparing and the implications of chemotherapy plus cystectomy in the overall spectrum of results for management of invasive bladder cancer.

CYSTECTOMY

Authors in other chapters in this work (Chapters 13 and 15) discuss cystectomy in detail. However, a few brief observations on contemporary results are a necessary background for assessing bladder-sparing approaches in the following sections of this chapter. Stein and colleagues from the University of Southern California (USC) presented the results of cystectomy for bladder cancer in 1,054 patients treated from 1971 to 1997 with a median follow-up of 10.2 years.[5] Some patients with higher stage disease received adjuvant chemotherapy. Overall 5-year survival was 60%; detailed disease-specific 5- and 10-year survivals by P stage are shown in Table 16–5. Ten-year disease-specific survival was significantly lower among 246 node-positive patients than among 808 node-negative patients ($p < .001$). Postoperative mortality rate was 3%. Pelvic or distant relapse occurred in 7% (77 cases) and 22% (234 cases), respectively, for an overall recurrence rate of 30% (311 cases) at a median follow-up of 12 months (.04 to 11.1 years). Pelvic relapse following modern cystectomy alone is low overall, especially among node-negative patients. Historically, preoperative radiotherapy did not produce lower pelvic relapse than these results (data not shown).

Table 16–1. SURVIVAL AND BLADDER PRESERVATION RATES IN SELECTED SERIES OF TURBT ALONE FOR THE TREATMENT OF INVASIVE BLADDER CANCER

Investigator	n	Study Results
Herr HW[13]	45	Survival (5-yr median follow-up) Overall 82% With functioning bladder 67%
Solsona E, et al[14]	133	Cause-specific survival 5 yr: 80% 10 yr: 74% Bladder preservation 5 yr: 82% 10 yr: 79%
Henry K, et al[15]	43	Overall 5-yr survival by stage B1: 63% B2: 38%
O'Flynn JD, et al[16]	465	Overall 5-yr survival by stage T1: 65% T2 : 59% T3: 20% T4 : 0%
Marberger H, et al[17]	204	Overall 5-yr survival by stage < T2: 42% > T2: 10%
Barnes RW, et al[18]	151	5, 10, and 15-yr survival by stage B: 40%, 18%, 7% C: 5%, 0%, 0%

Adapted from Feneley MR and Schoenberg M.[4]

TURBT = transurethral resection of bladder tumor.

Nearly all patients with pelvic relapse die owing to systemic disease progression.

Skinner and colleagues reported on survival rates following cystectomy in a subset of 104 women and 422 men from the same USC series.[6] Muscle invasion or diffuse refractory superficial tumor was the indication for surgery in 66% and 33% of cases respectively. Whereas 54% of patients had $\leq$ pT2 disease, 25% were node positive. The percent 5-year overall and disease-free survival rate by sex is shown in Table 16–6. The findings reaffirm the significant risk of systemic disease among these patients.

Gschwend and colleagues reported cystectomy results in 493 bladder cancer patients treated at three centers.[7] Ten-year survival results shown in Table 16–7 again point out the limitations of cystectomy once disease becomes non–organ confined.

Analyses of outcome versus the timing of cystectomy are important in assessing the risk or penalty of bladder-sparing approaches that fail and require delayed cystectomy. Lin and colleagues recently reported the 8-year disease-specific survival follow-ing cystectomy in bladder cancer patients according to clinical and pathologic stage.[8] As shown in Table 16–8, there is a marked decline in survival when disease becomes deeply muscle invasive. Relapse occurred in 31% of patients and was associated with disease-related mortality in 81% of cases. Sanchez-Ortiz and colleagues recently reported that patients undergoing cystectomy later than 12 weeks after diagnosis versus earlier than 12 weeks have a higher rate of advanced disease ($\geq$ pT3 or N+; 48%, $p < .01$) and lower survival.[9] However, this was a nonrandomized retrospective review, and other factors that caused the delay before surgery might have influenced the outcome. Wei and colleagues from the University of Michigan recently reported that the timing of cystectomy per se did not correlate with tumor pathologic stage.[10] However, the senior author of that group has previously reported that cystectomy performed > 12 weeks after diagnosis is associated with lower survival.

Some of the most important observations on the importance of early versus late cystectomy when cystectomy becomes necessary are provided by Herr and colleagues from Memorial Sloan-Kettering Cancer Center (MSKCC). Herr and colleagues have reported extensively (see below) on a variety of bladder-sparing approaches in selected patients with high-risk bladder cancer (grade 3, stage T1; carcinoma in situ (CIS); stage T2). Recently Herr reported that early cystectomy (< 2 years after diagnosis) yielded improved 15-year survival rates compared to late cystectomy (> 2 years after diagnosis) in a subset of 90 out of 307 patients initially treated conservatively for noninvasive bladder cancer (Table 16–9).[11] In multivariate analysis, the timing of cystectomy was an independent variable in survival. Herr previously reported 15-year progression rates of 39% and 56%, respectively, following conservative therapy for patients with grades 2 or 3 Ta or grades 2 or 3T1 bladder tumors.[12] Disease-free survival rates among the same two patient groups at 15 years was 74% and 62%, respectively.

TURBT ALONE

No one should recommend TURBT alone as optimal current therapy with curative intent for patients with

Table 16–2. OUTCOME, SURVIVAL, AND RECURRENCE RATES FOLLOWING PARTIAL CYSTECTOMY FOR BLADDER CANCER TAKEN FROM SELECTED PUBLISHED SERIES

Investigator	Patients (n)	Survival Rates	Recurrence Rates and Outcome
Dandekar et al, 1995[26]	32 (All) 20 TCC 12 Adenocarcinoma	5-yr actuarial Overall 80% (n = 23) T2　100% (n = 5) T3a　88% (n = 18) T3b　45% (n = 9)	Overall 43% (n = 14) Bladder-superficial (n = 5) Bladder-invasive (n = 7) 　4 had cystectomy 　3 inoperable, later died Lung, bladder tumor free (n = 2) 　both died
Merrell RW, et al[28]	54	5- and 10-yr survival Overall 48% (n = 54), 30% (n = 37) B1　67% (n = 21), 33% (n = 18) B2　37% (n = 16), 25% (n = 12) C　25% (n = 8), 0% (n = 2) D　0% (n = 5), 0% (n = 3)	Overall 29% (n = 16) 　10 had radiotherapy 　4/10 alive at 5 yr 2 had cystectomy 1/2 developed metastases and died
Schoborg TW, et al[29]	45 (All) 36 TCC 7 SCC 2 Adenocarcinoma	5- and 10-yr survival Overall 39% (n = 44), 12% (n = 34) B1　29% (n = 21), 0% (n = 5) B2　50% (n = 6), 20% (n = 5) C　12% (n = 17), 0% (n = 15) D　100% (n = 1), 0% (n = 1)	Overall 70% (n = 31) B1/2 62% C/D　83%
Cummings KB, et al[30]	101	5-yr survival B1　80% (n = 21) B2　45% (n = 22) C　6% (n = 17) Diverticulum 33% (n = 3)	Overall 49% (n = 49) B1　48% B2　45% C　24% Diverticulum 66% 5 had diversion for reduced capacity 12 had adjuvant RT 9 had cystectomy
Novick AC, et al[31]	50	5- and 10-yr survival B　53% (n = 15), 44% (n = 9) C/D 20% (n = 10), 0% (n = 7)	Overall 50% (n = 25) 15 had pelvic recurrence or metastases 11 had radiotherapy 2 had cystectomy
Resnick MI, et al[32]	102	5-yr survival Overall 41% (n = 86) B1　76% (n = 13) B2　18% (n = 16) C　12% (n = 26) D　20% (n = 5)	5-yr recurrence Overall 75% B1　76% B2　87% C　79% D　80%
Utz DC, et al[33]	159 TCC	5- and 10-yr survival Overall 39% (n = 153) B1　47% (n = 38) B2　40% (n = 35) C　29% (n = 38) D　0% (n = 17)	

Adapted from Feneley MR and Schoenberg M.[4]
TCC = transitional cell carcinoma; SCC = squamous cell carcinoma; RT = radiotherapy.

muscle-invasive bladder cancer. Nevertheless, numerous series, as shown in Table 16–1, have demonstrated results in selected patients that are not greatly different from historical outcome with cystectomy. Barnes and colleagues were among the first to report 5-year survival of 20 to 40% in patients after TURBT alone for muscle-invasive bladder tumor.[18,19] Reported 5-year survivals range from 10 to 82%. However, the majority of series report

5-year survivals (after TURBT as definitive therapy) of 40 to 50% and 20% for path stage Ta to 2 and T3 to 4 tumors, respectively.

Herr[13] and Solsona and colleagues[14] noted particularly favorable results in patients who were either pT0 or pTa on repeat extensive TURBT. Herr reported 76% survival at a median follow-up of 61 months in 45 such patients.[13] Solsona and colleagues reported high 5- and 10-year disease-specific

Table 16–3. SELECTED SERIES OF SYSTEMIC CHEMOTHERAPY AND TURBT FOR TREATMENT OF INVASIVE BLADDER CANCER*

Investigator	Protocol	Re-evaluation	Surveillance	Survival	Bladder Preservation
Thomas DJ, et al[43]	Complete TURBT, CM, CM (n = 50) Radical TURBT + M (n = 61)	Complete TURBT, CM, 38/50 tumor free Radical TURBT + M 44/61 tumor free	22/38 recurrence 10/38 invasive recurrence (median 16 mo) 30/44 recurrence 15/44 recurrent invasive cancer (median 18 mo)	5-yr survival 25% persistent invasive cancer 75% no invasive cancer after chemotherapy	29/61 bladder preservation without local recurrence
Herr HW, et al[44]	MVAC (n = 111) ± TURBT or partial cystectomy (n = 43)	60/111 (54%) complete response TURBT/partial cystectomy (n = 43)	13/43 invasive recurrence 13 had salvage cystectomy 6/13 dead (median FU 10 yr)	32/43 (74%) survival (median FU 10 yr)	25/43 (28%) alive with intact functioning bladder
Uygur MC, et al[45]	Deep TURBT (n = 19) MVEC (n = 17)	13 tumor free 1 cystectomy 3 subsequently died	7 tumor free 5 superficial recurrence 1 invasive recurrence, later died with metastases		11 (mean, 36 mo FU) None with persistent or recurrent invasive disease
Angulo JC, et al[46]	TURBT (n = 71) CMV (n = 61)	20 tumor free 32 cystectomy 9 inoperable	4 had cystectomy	5-yr disease-specific survival T2-3a 75% T3b-T4 26%	11 without persistent or recurrent invasive disease (mean, 49 mo FU) 3 died of cancer 2 alive with active disease
Sternberg CN, et al[47]	TURBT, MVAC, partial cystectomy (n = 65)	28/65 (43%) complete response 21 cystectomy		73% 3-yr survival	Alive with functional bladder 64%
Dalal AV, et al[48]	TURBT, MVAC X 2 (n = 29)	7 tumor free 12 radical cystectomy 2 radiotherapy + salvage cystectomy 8 radiotherapy alone		86% survival 6 without persistent or recurrent invasive disease 1 died with metastases and normal bladder	With radiation, overall 34% bladder preservation
Lekili M, et al[49]	TURBT + MVAC (n = 32)	2 persistent tumor 1 cystectomy		Overall survival 84% and 97% for patients with functioning bladder. FU median, 2.8 yr	
Hall R, et al[50]	Radical TURBT/partial cystectomy + M (n = 57)	33 tumor free 13 invasive tumor 5 superficial tumor 3 progression at 6 mo	23/39 survival 79% tumor free 3 dead from treatment complications at 2 yr	83% actuarial survival at 3 yr	78% alive with native bladder at 3 yr

Adapted from Feneley MR and Schoenberg M.[4]

M = methotrexate; V = vinblastine; E = epirubicin; C = cisplatin; n = number of patients; TURBT = transurethral resection of bladder tumor; FU = follow-up

*Summarizing Protocol, Status after First Re-evaluation, Recurrence during Surveillance, Cystectomy, Survival, and Bladder Preservation Rates

Table 16–4. SELECTED SERIES OF RADIATION AND SYSTEMIC CHEMOTHERAPY FOR TREATMENT OF INVASIVE BLADDER CANCER*

Investigator	Protocol	Re-evaluation	Surveillance	Survival	Bladder Preservation
Zietman AL, et al[69]	TURBT, C + 5FU, RT (n = 18)	14/18 CR, 2 had cystectomy	0 Recurrence (at median 32 mo)	83% 3-yr actuarial survival	87% alive with native bladder
Serretta V, et al[70]	TURBT, CM + V, RT (n = 40)	27/40 (67%) CR, 13/40 (42%) persistent invasive bladder tumor	8/27 CR developed recurrence; 4/8 were invasive; 3 had cystectomy	53% 5-yr cancer-specific mortality; 43% 5-yr disease-free survival; 8 with CR dead from metastases; 13 with persistent tumor dead from metastases	14/19 (73%) with CR to chemotherapy were disease free with intact bladder at 5 yr
Danesi DT, et al[71]	TURBT, C + 5FU, RT (n = 24/25 completed)	21/24 (87.5%) CR 3/24 persistent tumor 1/3 had cystectomy	At median 31 mo 2/21 CR invasive local recurrence 3 CR had cystectomy 3 with persistent disease died had metastases	66% 4-yr actuarial disease-free survival 75% 4-yr actuarial disease-free survival for CR 18/21 (86%) having CR alive 2/3 with persistent tumor dead from metastases	81% 4-yr actuarial cystectomy-free survival 15/21 CR (71.4%) alive with tumor-free bladder 1/3 with persistent tumor alive after cystectomy
Fellin G, et al[72]	TURBT, CMV, RT (n = 56)	28/56 had CR 28/56 had persistent tumor 22/28 had cystectomy	22 metastases 16/28 CR developed bladder recurrence 9 were invasive 4/9 had cystectomy 2/4 developed metastases After cystectomy for persistent tumor, 10 had metastases	59% 5-yr actuarial disease-specific survival 54% 5-yr disease-free survival	41% bladder preservation
Kachnic LA, et al[73]	TURBT, MCV, RT (n = 106)	70% had CR	79% (n = 76) 5-yr freedom from invasive relapse in consolidated patients 336 had cystectomy	52% 5-yr actuarial overall survival 60% 5-yr disease-specific survival	43% 5-yr with preservation
Tester W, et al[74]	TURBT, MCV, RT (n = 91)	68/85 (80%) had CR; of those with persistent tumor, 14 had cystectomy	Recurrence in 36/70 consolidated (23 invasive); 23 had cystectomy	62% 4-yr survival	44% 4-yr survival with bladder preservation

continued

Table 16–4. CONTINUED

Investigator	Protocol	Re-evaluation	Surveillance	Survival	Bladder Preservation
Einstein AB Jr, et al[75]	TURBT, MCV, RT (n = 27/34 completed)	19/34 had CR; 15/34 had persistent tumor and 4/15 had cystectomy	11/19 developed bladder recurrence (at median 21 mo), 3/19 had metastases, 5/19 no recurrence; 3/19 CR developed metastases; 11/19 CR developed bladder recurrence; 6/19 CR had cystectomy	18% 36-mo overall survival	
Given RW, et al[76]	TURBT + C based chemotherapy + RT + partial cystectomy (n = 94)	40% had CR to chemotherapy; Chemotherapy, no radiotherapy; 4 had cystectomy for T0; 18 had cystectomy for persistent tumor; 6 partial cystectomy for T0; 2 partial cystectomy for persistent tumor; 4 died without further treatment; Chemotherapy with radiotherapy; 31/49 had CR; 18/49 had persistent tumor, and of these 4 died and 7 had cystectomy	53 bladder preserved; 30/53 developed bladder recurrence; 8/30 were invasive, and of these 7 had cystectomy; 22/30 were superficial, and of these 5 had cystectomy (for CIS); 3 had cystectomy for symptoms but no disease	49% relapse-free survival at median > 5 yr; 5-yr survival; 65% cystectomy group; 40% bladder preservation group	18% alive with preserved bladder at median > 5 yr
Orsatti M, et al[77]	TURBT, C + 5FU, RT (n = 70/76 completed)	57/70 had CR; 13/70 had persistent tumor, and of these 3 had cystectomy	15/70 (21%) had bladder recurrence only; 9/70 (13%) had metastases only; 7/70 (10%) had bladder recurrence + metastases; 7/14 cystectomy for invasive recurrence	33/76 (47%) alive and tumor free (at 45-mo median); 6-yr overall survival 42% (actuarial); 6-yr progression-free survival 40% (actuarial)	47% retained bladder continuously disease free at 48 mo
Vikram B, et al[78]	TURBT, MVC deoxyrubicin RT (n = 21)	16/18 had CR; 2 had CIS; 0 had cystectomy	1 developed pelvic recurrence; 2 developed metastases; 3 developed CIS; 0 cystectomy	60% 3-yr survival, 2 patients with metastases	At median 2 yr: bladder function preserved in 15 (84%)

continued

Table 16–4. CONTINUED

Investigator	Protocol	Re-evaluation	Surveillance	Survival	Bladder Preservation
Kaufman DS, et al[79]	TUR C + 5FU RT (n = 42/53 completed)	28/42 had CR 12/42 had persistent tumor, and of these 8 had cystectomy 4/11 who did not complete had cystectomy	3 had salvage cystectomy 22 metastases	Actuarial 5-yr overall survival 48% Survival at 4-yr median 28/53 alive 24/28 disease free 20/24 bladder preserved 11/53 died with bladder tumor free	At 4-yr median 31/53 bladder tumor free and functioning well 25/28 initial CR with functioning tumor-free bladder
Housset M, et al[67]	TURBT C + 5FU RT (n = 51/54 completed)	40/54 had CR 18/40 CR had cystectomy (pT0) 14/54 had persistent tumor, and of these 12 had cystectomy	4/40 CR developed pelvic recurrence (all salvaged) 6/40 CR developed metastases 12/14 with persistent tumor developed metastases	Survival at 3 yr 59% overall 62% disease free 77% disease free in responders 23% disease free in nonresponders	
Dunst J, et al[80]	TURBT, RT + C/carboplatin (n = 245)		53 salvage cystectomy	47% at 5 yr (total 60%, T2 64%, T3 43%, T4 16%) 26% at 10 yr	192 (79%) functioning bladder
Shipley W, et al[81]	TURBT, RT (n = 62/70 completed), cisplatin (n = 49/70) (70%)		In 36/49 CR (73%) bladder was maintained tumor free	At follow-up with median survival of 70 mo 36 alive, 33/36 tumor free 4-yr survival T2 64% T3/4 24% CR 57% non-CR 11%	

CIS = carcinoma in situ; CR = complete response; C = cisplatin; E = epirubicin; M = methotrexate; RT = radiotherapy; TURBT = transurethral resection of bladder tumor; V = vinblastin; 5FU = fluorouracil
Adapted from Feneley MR and Schoenberg M.[4]
*Summarizing Protocol, Status after First Re-evaluation, Recurrence during Surveillance, Cystectomy, Survival, and Bladder Preservation Rates for (a) All Patients, (b) Patients Achieving Complete Response, and (c) Patients with Persistent Tumor

Table 16–5. CONTEMPORARY SURVIVAL RATES OF CYSTECTOMY FOR BLADDER CANCER		
	% Disease-free Survival	
P Stage	**5-Year**	**10-Year**
T0N0	92	86
TisN0	91	89
TaN0	79	74
T1N0	83	78
T2N0	89	78
T3aN0	87	76
T3bN0	62	61
T4N0	50	45
TanyN+	31	23

Adapted from Stein et al.[5]

survival and high bladder preservation rates (see Table 16–1) after "radical" repeat TURBT.[14] Theoretic concerns that aggressive repeat TURBT may lead to pelvic or distant tumor dissemination are not supported in the literature. They noted that presence of CIS was a negative prognostic factor. Recently this concept of a favorable outcome if repeat TURBT is pT0 has been reaffirmed by Bravers and colleagues[20] in 42 high-risk patients with large tumors that were grades 2 to 3 pT1 or pTcis on initial resection. With a median follow-up of 60 months, tumor recurrence by P stage at the second TURBT was 33% for pT0, 57% for pTa, 75% for pTcis, and 88% for pT1. Bladder preservation was achieved in all of the one-third of patients who were pT0 at the second TURBT.

INTRAVESICAL THERAPY

Extensive TURBT to exclude muscle-invasive disease, followed by intravesical bacille Calmette-Guérin (BCG) immunotherapy for high-grade superficial tumor also may be considered a form of bladder sparing in the spectrum of bladder cancer that is headed toward invasion. Despite initial favorable responses to BCG in a majority of patients with CIS or papillary tumors, long-term results are sobering and sound a cautionary note for other bladder-sparing regimens. Herr and colleagues reported an 82% 5-year survival and 67% bladder preservation rate in a subset of stage T2 to 3a patients who were pT0 on radical repeat TURBT and who were then treated with BCG.[13] Only 21% of patients were pT0 on the second TURBT. The remaining 79% of

patients with residual tumor were recommended for immediate cystectomy. One wonders if radical repeat TURBT of pT0 tissue prevents some recurrences at the site of the original tumor or if it merely identifies patients who are going to respond well to BCG.

Cookson et al described the 15-year follow-up results in 86 patients with high-risk superficial disease treated at MSKCC by radical repeat TURBT with or without BCG.[21] Stage progression occurred in 53% of patients, and 36% underwent cystectomy. Disease-specific survival was 70% and 63% at 10 and 15 years, respectively. The 15-year disease-specific mortality rate was 37%. The 15-year survival rate with an intact bladder was 37%. The authors concluded that disease recurrence and progression are frequent and are associated with significant mortality risk despite subsequent cystectomy.

Recently Herr updated the 15-year results in 307 high-risk bladder tumor patients treated with a bladder-sparing approach at MSKCC between 1979 and 1984.[22] The tumor stage and grade was Ta grade 3 in 211 cases and T1 in 96 cases. Eighty-one percent of cases had CIS. All patients underwent a second extensive TURBT followed by 6 weeks of intravesical BCG. Overall 50% of patients experienced disease progression, and one-third died of bladder cancer. Forty-six of 90 patients who developed muscle invasion died owing to transitional cancer. Early cystectomy (< 1 year) for BCG failures resulted in better survival than late cystectomy (> 1 year) whether or not muscle invasion was present at the time of cystectomy. This suggests that persistence and/or recurrence of stage T1 disease and CIS are associated with ongoing risks of microscopic metastasis and death. Herr concluded that early cystectomy improves survival in BCG failures and is indicated if the bladder cannot be maintained tumor free for 2 years. Further, progression to muscle invasion dur-

Table 16–6. SURVIVAL RATE BY SEX FOLLOWING CYSTECTOMY FOR BLADDER CANCER		
	% 5-Year Survival	
Sex	**Overall**	**Disease-free**
Male	58.9	71.7
Female	63.5	69.1

Adapted from Skinner et al.[6]

Table 16–7. TEN-YEAR SURVIVAL RATE FOLLOWING CYSTECTOMY FOR ORGAN CONFINED AND NON–ORGAN CONFINED BLADDER CANCER

P Stage	Number	% 10-Year Survival		
		Disease Specific	Overall	
< T3a	274	75	50	p = .001
≥ T3a	219	43	28	p = .022
N+		28	21	NS

Adapted from Gshwend et al.[7]

ing bladder-sparing efforts is associated with a 50% death rate attributable to bladder cancer.

Tiguert and colleagues recently reported long-term follow-up in 77 patients who received BCG after resection of grade 3 T1 bladder tumors.[23] Only 18% of patients remained disease free at a mean follow-up of 44 months. Progression to muscle-invasive disease occurred in 30% (23/77) of patients; 52% of these patients had muscle invasion at the first disease recurrence. Among patients who were re-treated with BCG after superficial tumor recurrence, 39% and 9% developed invasive tumor after a second or third course of BCG, respectively. The authors concluded that there is a diminishing likelihood for invasion over time. However, a cautionary note is that there was a diminishing sample size over time. The findings are in agreement with the general observation that most bladder cancer patients who develop invasive disease have it at first presentation or soon thereafter.

Solsona and colleagues point out that persistence of disease at the 3-month restaging after intravesical therapy for superficial disease identifies a subset of patients who are at high risk for disease progression.[24] At a median follow-up of 73 months, recurrent invasive or superficial tumor occurred in 23% and 25% of cases, respectively. In a multivariate analysis, persistent disease at 3 months was the strongest predictor of progression to invasion. Progression to invasion was associated with a 46% disease-specific mortality rate despite cystectomy. The potential jeopardy of awaiting disease progression to invasion in any bladder-sparing protocol is clear even with vigilant surveillance.

The search for an effective and safe intravesical bladder-sparing alternative therapy in BCG refrac-

tory CIS of the bladder is ongoing. Steinberg and colleagues, reporting for the Valrubicin study group, noted a modest 21% complete response (19/90) at 30-month follow-up; however, there also was a 4.4% (4/90) death rate attributable to metastatic bladder cancer over the same interval.[25] Limited experience by Nseyo and colleagues with photodynamic therapy in patients with BCG refractory bladder CIS has shown responses in 58% of patients (21/36) at 3 months, but only 30% maintained the response for 1 year.[27] There was a 30% occurrence of overt bladder tumor and 10% incidence of bladder contracture in these patients.

PARTIAL CYSTECTOMY

The obvious theoretic advantage of partial cystectomy is potential tumor control with a lesser surgical procedure than radical cystectomy and retained native bladder function and sexual function. Partial cystectomy for invasive bladder cancer should be restricted to the subset of patients with a small, focal tumor away from the ureteral orifices and bladder floor and without any CIS or dysplasia on random bladder biopsies. The multifocal nature of most transitional cancer severely limits this treatment approach. Thorough TURBT may be as effective as partial cystectomy for truly focal lesions. Transurethral resection offers less surgical morbidity and lessens the risk of intraoperative tumor spillage. In various reports[4,26–34] the 5-year survival rates following partial cystectomy for invasive bladder tumor (T2–3) range from 18 to 100% as shown in Table 16–2. Recurrence rates vary from 20 to 75%

Table 16–8. EIGHT-YEAR DISEASE SPECIFIC SURVIVAL FOLLOWING CYSTECTOMY BY STAGE OF BLADDER CANCER

Stage	% 8-Year Disease-Specific Survival
cTis	93
cT1	70
cT2	55
cT3 pTa-1	100
pT2a	70
pT2b	58
pT3	30
pT4	20

Adapted from Lin et al.[8]

Table 16–9. IMPACT OF TIME OF CYSTECTOMY IN HIGH-RISK INITIALLY NONINVASIVE BLADDER CANCER

Time of Cystectomy after Diagnosis	N	% 15-Year Survival
Overall	90	
< 2 yr	48	69
> 2 yr	42	26
< pT2 at relapse	35	
< 2 yr		92
> 2 yr		56
≥ pT2 at relapse	55	
< 2 yr		41
> 2 yr		18

Adapted from Herr.[11]

and are invasive in approximately 20%. Thus vigilant bladder surveillance is required in follow-up.

Herr and Scher reported on a highly select group of 26 patients with T2 to 4 disease who underwent TURBT followed by systemic neoadjuvant chemotherapy (mostly with methotrexate, vinblastine, Adriamycin, and cisplatin [MVAC]) followed by partial cystectomy.[35] The 4-year survival was 65%, with bladder preservation in 50%. Overall, 33% of patients received additional salvage therapy.

EXTERNAL BEAM RADIATION THERAPY AND BRACHYTHERAPY

External beam radiation therapy after complete TURBT of superficial bladder cancer has obtained 5-year disease control rates of 40 to 64% in multiple series.[1,34,36–38] However, as definitive treatment following complete TURBT for muscle-invasive bladder cancer, it has been relatively ineffective. In review articles, noted 5-year survival rates range from 15 to 52% but are closer to 15% in most series. Doses of 60 to 70 Gy are used most often. Local control following radiation therapy has been reported in 40 to 50% of cases for stage T2 disease but has been poor for stage T3 disease. Radiation is ineffective when CIS is present. External beam radiation therapy prior to cystectomy did not produce lower rates of pelvic relapse than are seen in contemporary surgical series alone.[5,36,37]

Pollack and colleagues[39] studied the tumor molecular markers of spontaneous apoptosis rate, p53 and pRB, in patients who received definitive radiation therapy for stage T2 and T3b bladder cancer. The results regarding these individual markers and either radiosensitivity or outcome were inconsistent.

Data on interstitial radiotherapy in the treatment of invasive bladder cancer are quite limited and mainly consist of reports from a single center in Rotterdam.[1,36–42] Interstitial brachytherapy with and without afterloading has been reported to provide 5-year overall and disease-free survival rates of 47 to 66% and 62 to 81%, respectively.[41] The 5-year results in stage T2 are 70 to 88% local control and 55 to 73% survival. The 5-year results in stage T3 disease are 67 to 86% local control and 31 to 54% survival. Adjunctive brachytherapy following TURBT and partial cystectomy has been reported to offer 5-year overall and relapse-free survival rates of 50% and 70%, respectively.[41] The bladder preservation rate among survivors was 80%.

CHEMOTHERAPY AND BLADDER-SPARING SURGERY

Various neoadjuvant or adjuvant systemic chemotherapy regimens have been used as bimodality therapy with radical TURBT or partial cystectomy for treatment of invasive bladder cancer. Selected series are summarized in Table 16–3.[4,43–50] In an early series with cisplatin and methotrexate after TURBT for stage T3 and T4 disease, complete or partial responses of 11% and 34%, respectively, were obtained.[51] Over the past two decades the greatest experience has accrued with the MVAC or cisplatin, methotrexate, and vinblastine (CMV) regimens as shown in Table 16–3. Cystectomy alone for invasive disease often fails owing to the presence of microscopic metastases. The addition of systemic chemotherapy is a logical step to overcome this problem. Multiple single-center trials with either neoadjuvant or adjuvant chemotherapy plus cystectomy have been reported.[43–66]

Approximately 40% of patients receiving neoadjuvant combination chemotherapy after extensive TURBT for invasive tumor are stage pT0 at the time of cystectomy. Five-year survival among chemotherapy recipients who are stage pT0 at the time of cystectomy is 87%. This finding made consideration of chemotherapy as definitive treatment in some patients a logical step. However, a note of caution is required. In the early experience with neoadjuvant MVAC before cystectomy, 33% of patients who were tumor free on follow-up biopsy after completion of chemotherapy still had residual deeper tumor in the cystectomy specimen.[62]

Chemotherapy offers the prospect of eradication of distant microscopic disease as well as local control. The long-awaited results of Intergroup trial 0080 comparing cystectomy alone with neoadjuvant MVAC have been presented.[55] The chemotherapy group had a 50% or 2-year prolongation of survival and a hazard ratio of 0.74 compared to the surgery-alone group. However, this result does not negate the possible role played by cystectomy and lymphadenectomy in the overall outcome. Conclusions on the safety of leaving the bladder in place following MVAC cannot be drawn from this study.

Uygur and colleagues reported on 19 patients who received MVEC chemotherapy (methotrexate, vinblastine, epirubicin, cisplatin) after complete TURBT and who refused cystectomy.[45] Therapy was completed in 17 of 19 patients. One patient died of sepsis during the third treatment cycle, and one patient required dose reductions in the fourth cycle. Sixty-eight percent (13/19) of patients obtained an initial complete response, which was lasting in 7 of 13 cases at a mean follow-up of 41 months.

The results of Angulo and colleagues with CMV chemotherapy point out the limitations even among complete responders.[46] Thirty-three percent (20/61) of patients obtained initial complete response. However, 5-year disease-free survival was only 47%, overall bladder preservation rate was 26% (16/61), and survival with an intact bladder was 18%. In multivariate analysis, initial complete response to chemotherapy and tumor size were independent, statistically significant predictors of outcome, whereas tumor stage and grade were not. The investigators closed the trial early owing to unfavorable results compared to early cystectomy.

Many investigators have analyzed the neoadjuvant chemotherapy experience in bladder cancer patients to determine which patients are the best candidates for bladder sparing. Uncertainty of initial stage of tumor with regard to bladder penetration and pelvic lymph node status is inherent to bladder-sparing regimens. Millikan and colleagues reported on 23 patients who received neoadjuvant MVAC chemotherapy for clinical stage T2 bladder cancer with lymphovascular invasion on TURBT.[56] Pathologic upstaging at cystectomy to stage pT3 or N+ occurred in 36% (8/23) and 27% (6/23) of cases, respectively. Patients with lymphovascular invasion by tumor in the bladder wall may be less suitable candidates for bladder sparing.

Sternberg and colleagues reported on 88 patients who received three courses of MVAC and after TURBT were found to have invasive bladder tumor.[59] Patients were offered restaging TURBT after completion of chemotherapy. Bladder sparing was recommended for further surveillance only if the patients were tumor free. Partial or total cystectomy was recommended if there was persistent or recurrent tumor. Initial tumor stage was T2, T3, or T4 in 27%, 64%, and 9% of cases, respectively. One patient did not complete therapy, and eight others refused restaging. The stage after chemotherapy in 79 evaluable patients was T0, Ta to 1, Tis, and T2 to 3 in 58%, 28%, 11%, and 18% of cases, respectively. Five-year survival was 71% and 29% for stage pT0 or superficial versus invasive after chemotherapy, respectively (Table 16–10). The authors suggested that bladder preservation should be restricted to patients who are either tumor free or have only superficial tumor following chemotherapy.

Experience with neoadjuvant chemotherapy followed by partial cystectomy in highly selected patients also has been reported. Herr and colleagues administered four cycles of neoadjuvant MVAC combination chemotherapy to 111 patients with

Table 16–10. FIVE-YEAR SURVIVAL FOR INVASIVE BLADDER CANCER PATIENTS ACCORDING TO MVAC RESPONSE AND TYPE OF SURGERY

Parameter	% 5-Year Survival
MVAC Response	
pT0 or superficial	71
pT invasive	29
Further surgery	
TURBT alone	69
Partial cystectomy	69
Radical cystectomy	53

Adapted from Sternberg et al.[59]
MVAC = methotrexate, vinblastine, Adriamyein, and cisplatin;
TURBT = transurethral resection of bladder tumor.

stage T2 and T3 bladder cancer.[35] Restaging after chemotherapy included cystoscopy, urine cytology, and bladder biopsy. Fifty-four percent (60/111) of patients were pT0 on these studies. The published rate of false-negative staging in this setting varies from 0 to 30%.[67,68] Cystectomy was recommended in all patients with residual tumor. Among the 60 patients who were pT0 after chemotherapy, 28 refused cystectomy, whereas 15 and 17 patients underwent partial or total cystectomy, respectively. Ten-year survival was 65% (11/17) and 74% (32/43), respectively, among those who did or did not undergo cystectomy. Fifty-eight percent (25/43) of the latter group retained a functional bladder over 10 years. Bladder tumor recurred in 56% (24/43) at a median time of 41 months. Superficial tumor recurred in 26% (11/43) and responded to intravesical BCG in all cases. Invasive tumor developed in 30% (13/43) of cases. Seven of these patients were saved by delayed cystectomy, but the remaining six patients with invasive recurrence died of progressive bladder cancer. The authors felt that four of the six deaths, or 9% (4/43) of the retained bladder group, were a consequence of the recurrent invasive tumor. The need for careful patient follow-up, and the risk of possible decreased overall survival rate with delayed cystectomy, are evident.

The tumor suppressor gene *P53* has been among the most studied molecular markers for stratifying bladder cancer risk and outcome. Esrig and colleagues reported that abnormal p53 expression is associated with lower patient survival following cystectomy independent of stage.[65] Based on these findings, Herr and associates performed a blinded retrospective analysis of *P53* status in a selected group of 111 stage T2 and T3 bladder cancer patients who received MVAC chemotherapy after TURBT as part of a bladder-sparing program.[63] Ten-year survival was superior in the *p53*-negative patients as shown in Table 16–11. The authors concluded that bladder preservation for 10 years is safe in *p53*-negative, stage T2 patients who obtain a complete response after MVAC. In contrast, they recommend early cystectomy for *p53*-positive stage T2 and all stage T3 patients. One cannot extrapolate these results in a highly selected group of patients to all bladder cancer patients.[64] A prospective randomized multi-institutional trial of MVAC chemotherapy versus observation following cystectomy in *p53*-positive patients is in progress.

In a recent editorial, Sternberg provided a few final caveats regarding MVAC chemotherapy and bladder sparing.[58] Extensive TURBT renders some patients disease free, and additional chemotherapy represents overtreatment. Identification of patients who are pT0 after chemotherapy may be preselecting patients with an inherently better outcome. The long-term results show that approximately one-third of the MVAC-treated patients retained their bladder. The question is posed whether this result justifies exposing the remaining two-thirds of patients to MVAC with its 5 to 7% incidence of grade 3 or 4 granulocytopenia and sepsis.

TRIMODALITY THERAPY WITH SURGERY, CHEMOTHERAPY, AND RADIATION

The most comprehensive form of bladder-sparing therapy for invasive bladder cancer involves extensive TURBT followed by combination radiotherapy and chemotherapy. There is an extensive and growing literature on this approach as summarized for selected series in Table 16–4. Urologists need to be familiar with these results in counseling patients on treatment options. There is precedent for similar organ-sparing approaches in the management of esophageal, breast, oropharyngeal, limb sarcoma, and anorectal cancer. Agents such as 5-fluorouracil (5-FU), cisplatin, and gemcitabine are well-known radiosensitizers. The most common toxicity of 5-FU is mucositis. Myelotoxicity and nephrotoxicity are the major limitations of mitomycin. Nephrotoxicity is the most common toxicity of cisplatin. Even the most enthusiastic supporters of continent diversion, including the current authors, would admit to the

Table 16–11. TEN-YEAR SURVIVAL BY *P53* STATUS IN A BLADDER-SPARING COHORT

Stage	10-Year Survival	
	P53 Negative	*P53* Positive
T2	100 (19/19)	47 (9/19)
T3	67 (8/12)	60 (6/10)
Overall	87 (27/31)	52 (15/29)

Adapted from Herr et al.[63]

advantages of a natural bladder if its functional capacity and a tumor-free status could be maintained by "conservative" bladder-sparing therapy.

A variety of single-agent chemotherapies have been combined with radiation. Given and colleagues reported retrospective, nonrandomized results in patients who underwent TURBT followed by two to three cycles of cisplatin plus 64.8 Gy of radiotherapy.[76] Fifty-seven percent of patients had local relapse. Tumor recurrences were invasive in 15 cases and directly contributed to patient death in two cases. Survival among patients who eventually underwent cystectomy as compared with those who did not was 65% and 40%, $p = .009$. Overall 5-year disease-free survival for patients with stage T3 and T4 disease was 53% and 11%, respectively. Five-year disease-free survival by stage among patients with an intact bladder was 17% and 0% for stage T3 and T4, respectively. Tumors with mixed histology, including squamous and adenocarcinoma components, uniformly responded poorly to chemoradiation. The authors concluded that the overall results were not equivalent to those obtained by early cystectomy. The limitations in drawing conclusions are obvious owing to potential selection bias.

Coppin and colleagues compared cisplatin and radiotherapy versus radiotherapy alone in a prospective, randomized bladder cancer trial.[82] The group that received cisplatin had better local control at 5-year follow-up (59% versus 40%) but 3-year survival rates were not significantly different (47% versus 33%, $p = .34$). Systemic relapse occurred in 31% of patients overall.

Sauer and colleagues reported on radiotherapy plus either cisplatin or carboplatin in patients with invasive bladder cancer.[83] The group that received cisplatin had higher complete response rates (85% versus 70%, $p = .02$). Overall 5-year survival rates by stage were T1, 77%; T2, 55%; T3a, 50%; T3b, 41%; and T4, 22%.

Dunst and colleagues reported 10-year results in a retrospective series of 178 patients who received cisplatin plus 56 Gy of radiotherapy versus 67 patients who received radiotherapy alone.[80] Bladder preservation was achieved in 83% of patients at a median follow-up of 6 years. The overall and disease-free survival among the cisplatin and no-chemotherapy groups was not significantly different (52% versus 50% and 41% versus 35%, respectively).

Chauvet and colleagues treated 106 patients with stage T2 to 4 bladder cancer with cisplatin plus radiotherapy. Initial complete responses occurred in 71% of patients.[84] The overall 4-year disease-free survival was 41% (45/106), and the bladder preservation rate was 73% (77/106).

Kuehn and colleagues and Schrott and colleagues from Germany reported on the effectiveness of platinum-based chemotherapy and radiation in 272 patients and subsequent salvage cystectomy in 77 incomplete responders.[85,86] Patients received either cisplatin or carboplatin. The overall age-corrected 5-year survival rate was 64%; by stage and patient number (in parentheses) it was pT1, 82% (54); pT2, 71% (56); pT3, 59% (138); and pT4, 34% (24).

Five-year survival among the 73% (198/272) of patients who achieved an initial complete response was 83%. Conversely, 5-year survival was only 26% among patients with persistent disease that was stage pT3 or 4. A total of 77 salvage cystectomies were performed for 31 initial nonresponders and 46 patients with recurrent invasive disease. Thus, recurrent invasive disease developed in 23% (46/198) of initial complete responders. The 5-year survival rate in the salvage cystectomy group was overall, 44%; pT1 to 2, 88%; pT3, 42%; pT4, 16%; and pT(any) N+, 16 %. All forms of urinary division were employed including orthotopic neobladder. Surgical complication rates were not higher than those in most primary cystectomy series.

Hussain and colleagues in the Southwest Oncology Group performed a phase II trial of cisplatin plus 5-FU and radiation in a group of 56 patients with bladder cancer.[87] This was not an elective organ-sparing series. Patients either refused or were medically unfit for cystectomy, or had unresectable disease in 45%, 21%, and 34% of cases, respectively. Clinical stage was T3 to 4 or N+ in 68% and 22% of cases, respectively. Only 57% of patients completed the full treatment regimen. Results were reported by an intent-to-treat analysis, but only 35 patients were fully evaluated. The overall response rate was 51% (complete response [CR]: 49%; partial response [PR]: 2%). The overall 5-year survival rate was 32%, and estimated median survival was 27 months. Thus, eventual systemic relapse and death owing to disease were common with this regimen.

In a series of publications, Housset and colleagues[67,88] reported on combination cisplatin and 5-FU chemotherapy and twice daily radiation therapy with 3 Gy per day for 6 weeks. Bifractionation of low-dose radiation increases both cell kill and normal tissue tolerance. After 6 weeks, complete responders received further consolidation radiation to a total of 44 Gy. At 27 months follow-up, 86% (19/22) of patients had a retained bladder. Interpretation of this experience must be limited, as treatment was not randomized and initial complete responders underwent early cystectomy for unclear reasons.

Seretta and colleagues[70] from Palermo reported results with 10-year follow-up in 30 patients who received two-drug (platinum + methotrexate) and 10 patients who received three-drug (platinum + methotrexate + vinblastine) chemotherapy after complete TURBT for grade 3 T3 tumors. Forty-eight percent (19/40) of patients were tumor free after chemotherapy. The remaining patients with residual tumor received pelvic radiation to 60 to 65 Gy and eight of these became complete responders. Cystectomy was recommended for all patients with persistent disease. Ten-year overall and disease-free survival and bladder retention rate was 35%, 33%, and 55%, respectively. Disease-related mortality rate was 53%.

Vikram and colleagues treated 21 elderly patients with stage T2 and T3 tumors who were "medically unfit" for cystectomy with MVAC and twice daily radiation to 54 to 60 Gy.[78,89] The treatment-related mortality rate from sepsis was 5%. Tumor relapse occurred in 38% (8/21) of patients. The 5-year actual and disease-specific survival rates were 37% and 63%, respectively. Among survivors at 5 years, an intact bladder was achieved in 84% of patients.

Fellin and colleagues treated 56 patients with stage T2 to 4 tumors with two cycles of MCV and 40 Gy of radiation.[72] No patients had hydronephrosis or adenopathy on imaging studies. Sixty-one percent of the patients completed the treatment regimen and had a complete response rate of 50%. There were no treatment-related deaths. The 5-year overall, disease-free, and intact bladder survival rates were 55%, 59%, and 41%, respectively.

Over the past decade Shipley and colleagues at the Massachusetts General Hospital (MGH) and the multi-institutional Radiation Therapy Oncology Group (RTOG) have reported extensively on a series of studies using extensive TURBT, combination chemotherapy, and radiation trimodality therapy for bladder sparing.[79,74–76,82–85] Detailed review of these results is warranted as they represent the largest volume and most sustained experience with this approach.

In an early report Kaufman and colleagues described 5-year patient survival of 48% for the entire group and 29% for those with stage T3 and T4 disease.[79] Thirty-two percent of survivors developed recurrent disease and 38% retained their bladder at 5 years. Approximately 20% of patients were unable to complete the full regimen owing to toxicity. The consistency of subsequent results by these investigators with this early experience is noteworthy.

Shipley and colleagues reported phase 3 trial results on a select group of patients who were randomized to receive platinum plus radiation versus 2 cycles of neoadjuvant MCV chemotherapy followed by platinum plus radiation.[90] Nineteen and 33% of patients in the two respective groups failed to complete the regimen owing to toxicity, primarily neutropenia and sepsis. The trial was closed early because of this high complication rate. Five-year survival was 49% in both groups. Shipley and colleagues reported single-center phase 2 trial results for the same regimens in 106 patients.[91] Five-year overall and disease-specific survival was 52% and 60% respectively, with a median follow-up of 4.4 years. Forty-three percent of patients had an intact bladder at 5 years. No patient required cystectomy because of treatment-related symptoms rather than tumor. Two cycles of neoadjuvant MCV chemotherapy raised toxicity but did not produce higher survival or bladder retention rates than did platinum and radiation alone. Patients who underwent salvage cystectomy had a similar rate of subsequent metastases as patients in earlier primary cystectomy series. Shipley and colleagues cited that finding as evidence against any detrimental impact of delayed versus early cystectomy.[92] However, to the current authors this result suggests that the described bladder-sparing regimens had minimal impact on systemic micrometastases that were likely present at the time of initial diagnosis of invasive disease.

In two recent publications, Zietman and colleagues[92] and Zehr and colleagues[93] summarized in detail the MGH and RTOG results in 190 patients with stage T2 to 4 bladder cancer who were treated with one of five consecutive trimodality bladder-sparing regimens between 1986 and 1998. Patients underwent as complete a TURBT as possible followed by radiation therapy with 40 Gy using 10 to 23 MV photons in 1.2 to 1.8 Gy fractions. Concurrently patients received cisplatin at 20 mg/m^2 intravenously 2 days per week, every 3 weeks, to a total dose of 70 to 100 mg/m^2. Ninety-six patients also received two cycles of neoadjuvant MCV chemotherapy, and 29 patients received 5-FU and cisplatin. The initial tumor characteristics are shown in Table 16–12. Initial hydronephrosis, a known negative prognostic factor, was present in 14% of patients (27/190). Fifty-three percent of patients had locally advanced stage T3 to 4 disease, which carries a 30 to 64% risk of nodal metastases. In these regards the authors are justified in pointing out that the results should not be compared to those for immediate cystectomy in T2N0 patients. A visibly complete TURBT was possible in only 57% (106/190) of cases. The median follow-up was 6.7 years (range 1.3 to 12.1 years). Sixty-six percent (125/190) of patients had a complete response to the induction regimen. Cystectomy was recommended in patients with persistent tumor. Patients who refused cystectomy received further cisplatin and an additional 25 Gy of radiation as treatment consolidation.

Tumor relapse occurred in 39% (48/125) of the initial complete responders. Two-thirds of relapses were at the site of the original tumor. Tumor stage at the time of relapse in these 125 initial complete responders was < pT2 or ≥ pT2 in 32 (26%) and 16 (13%) of cases, respectively. The median time to relapse was 2.1 years. The presence of CIS in the original tumor did not lower the CR rate to trimodality therapy but it did increase the relapse rate (38% versus 25%). A similar effect of CIS was reported by Sauer.[83] A total of 57 superficial relapses occurred in 32 patients. Tumor grade was grade 2 to 3 in 29.9% (17/57), and CIS was present at relapse in 59.6% (34/57). Cystectomy was performed for eventual progression to invasive cancer or multiple tumor recurrences in 9% (3/32) and 22% (7/32) of relapsing patients. The cystectomy rate at 8 years for the entire group of 190 patients was twice as high in patients with superficial relapse compared with those who did not relapse (66% versus 31%). Cystectomy was recommended or performed in 47.9% (91/190) of the total trimodality therapy group for the reasons shown in Table 16–13. Pelvic relapse occurred in 9% of patients. These findings, that the presence of CIS did not decrease the CR rate after combined chemotherapy and radiation, are difficult to explain in view of the fact that each modality alone is ineffective against CIS. The fact that the relapse rate after chemoradiation was higher in patients with CIS suggests that the initial estimation of CR in patients with CIS was falsely high or that transient CR is less enduring in patients with CIS.

The 5- and 10-year overall and disease-specific survival rates for the total group of 190 patients in the MGH and RTOG series receiving trimodality therapy, and separated by T stage, are shown in Table 16–14. On the one hand, the majority of survivors had an intact bladder. However, the 5- and 10-year disease-specific survival rates with an intact bladder for all T stages, T2, or T3 to 4 were 46% and 45%, 57% and 53%, and 35% and 34%, respectively.

PITFALLS AND LIMITATIONS OF BLADDER SPARING

The initial clinical staging of invasive bladder cancer has a significant risk for either understaging or overstaging with currently available techniques such as computed tomography and magnetic resonance imaging of the abdomen and pelvis. These limitations are inherent in bladder-sparing regimens.

Table 16–12. INITIAL TUMOR CHARACTERISTICS IN 190 BLADDER-SPARING PATIENTS

Tumor	Number	Percent
G2	38	20
G3	152	80
T2	90	47
T3–4	100	53
Associated CIS	43	23

Adapted from Zietman et al.[92]

Table 16–13. INDICATIONS FOR CYSTECTOMY IN 190 PATIENTS WHO RECEIVED TRIMODALITY THERAPY FOR INVASIVE BLADDER CANCER		
Indication	**Number**	**Percent**
PR	65	71
Relapse after CR		
Early diffuse Ta	3	3
Late diffuse Ta	4	5
Early T2	16	18
Late T2	3	3
Total	91	100

PR = partial response, CR = complete response.
Adapted from Zietman et al.[92]

Laparoscopic pelvic lymphadenectomy could address the issue of identifying pelvic lymph node metastases but adds an additional surgical procedure, time, and associated costs. The problem of incomplete or inaccurate assessment of the local extent of the primary bladder tumor would still remain.

Following trimodality therapy for bladder sparing in patients with invasive bladder cancer, the risk of underdetection of persistent or recurrent disease also is problematic. Negative mucosal bladder biopsies may belie deeper residual invasive disease. Among apparent complete responders, the need for frequent comprehensive restaging is de rigueur and implies high patient compliance and high cost.

Favorable patient selection bias and tumor length bias must be acknowledged for a portion of treatment success in bladder-sparing regimens. Patients who become stage pT0 after TURBT, radiation, and chemotherapy may represent a subset of patients who were destined to do well with cystectomy or extensive TURBT alone.

Patients with CIS in the original bladder tumor are of special concern regarding attempts at bladder sparing. Neither radiation nor chemotherapy individually are effective against CIS. In general, oncologic treatment synergy is seen only among agents that are somewhat effective alone.

The risk or outcome penalty for delayed cystectomy if bladder-sparing trimodality therapy fails to eradicate tumor remains controversial. However, the surgical series cited above, with extensive repeat TURBT and intravesical therapy, document a worse outcome when delayed cystectomy becomes necessary compared with cystectomy performed earlier in comparable patient groups. The idea that a similar risk does not apply over time if chemoradiation fails to control the primary tumor is difficult to accept.

Comprehensive trimodality bladder-sparing regimens are complex, require a lengthy treatment interval, and are associated with treatment-limiting morbidity and toxicity in many patients. Trimodal therapy may represent overtreatment for many bladder cancer patients with the more favorable tumors. On the other hand, it may represent undertreatment leading to at least delayed cystectomy in the patients who are at greatest risk from the tumor and who need early cystectomy most of all.

If the original invasive bladder tumor was organ confined at the time of diagnosis, early cystectomy should offer the highest chance for disease control. Bladder-sparing regimens should offer an alternative for approximating the cystectomy outcome but should not exceed it unless the mortality rate associated with complications from surgery were high enough to offset any treatment advantage. The disease-specific patient survival rates in the most successful bladder-sparing reports do not equal those of contemporary cystectomy series.

SUMMARY AND CONCLUSIONS

From the multitude of series already referenced in this review, and a number of recent editorials,[58,96–98] several observations emerge on the current status of organ-sparing strategies for the treatment of invasive bladder cancer. The chemotherapy and radiotherapy regimens continue to evolve. The following elements are shared by most successful protocols. A complete, or as nearly complete as possible, TURBT

Table 16–14. FIVE- AND 10-YEAR SURVIVAL IN 190 PATIENTS RECEIVING TRIMODALITY THERAPY FOR INVASIVE BLADDER CANCER				
	Percent Survival			
	Overall		**Disease Specific**	
T Stage	**5 Year**	**10 Year**	**5 Year**	**10 Year**
All	57	36	63	59
T2	62	41	74	66
T3–4	53	31	53	52

Adapted from Zehr et al.[93]

is essential. Histopathologic features of tumor stage and grade are paramount. Presence of CIS greatly decreases CR rate and durability of response. Patients with small, focal stage T2 tumors have greater local systemic disease control than do those with large, multifocal or stage T3 to 4 tumors. Trimodality therapy bladder sparing is unlikely to succeed in patients with hydronephrosis or adenopathy on initial staging. Patients who do not obtain a CR should be recommended for early cystectomy if medically fit. Trimodality therapy requires a coordinated multidisciplinary approach involving urology, medical oncology, and radiation therapy. The full induction regimen requires approximately 6 months. Patients who obtain a CR must be carefully followed long term for detection of tumor relapse. Benefit from neoadjuvant chemotherapy prior to chemoradiation is unproven at this time. The role of adjuvant consolidation chemoradiation in maintaining a CR also is unproven. Cystectomy should be recommended in relapsing patients with CIS, high grade, multifocal, or greater than stage T1 disease at the time of relapse. The above idealized tumor features favoring bladder sparing are present in less than 20% of all patients with invasive bladder cancer. Further, contemporary 5-year survival rates for cystectomy alone in this "best" patient group are 70 to 80%.

The published 5-year initial CR rate for trimodality bladder-sparing therapy is 50 to 80%. The 5-year overall survival and bladder preservation rates are 30 to 83% and 36 to 78%, respectively. During the induction regimen 40 to 70% of patients experience nausea or neutropenia. Dose reductions in chemotherapy are required in 20 to 30% of patients. Treatment-related sepsis or death occur in 5 to 7% and 1% of patients, respectively. Among patients who achieve initial CR, tumor recurs in 20 to 50% of cases and is invasive in approximately one-third. Cystectomy eventually is performed for recurrent tumor or bladder dysfunction in 30% and 1% of patients. The net result is that 20 to 30% of the initial patient group achieve both long-term disease-free status and an intact bladder.

Whether delayed cystectomy following chemotherapy and radiation is more difficult or accompanied by higher complication rates is unsettled. There appears to be consensus that it does not preclude orthotopic neobladder urinary diversion.[5,94,96,98] Whether delayed cystectomy after bladder-sparing efforts is associated with lower survival[11,12,22,94,95] or equivalent survival[54,55,61,79,90–93] remains controversial.

A degree of uncertainty in initial staging is inherent to bladder-sparing protocols. Clinical staging errors occur in 30 to 50% of patients with current routine clinical imaging. Laparoscopic lymphadenectomy would add extra cost, morbidity, and delay prior to onset of induction therapy.

Evaluation of treatment outcomes for bladder-sparing regimens, or cystectomy alone for that matter, requires recognition that good results and poor results each may be attributable to inherent behavior of the tumor as well as effectiveness of the particular therapy. Further, initial risk stratification of the tumor based on molecular markers such as p53, Rb, Ki-67, apoptotic index, and others will make therapy more rational and effective in the future.

Quality of life as well as treatment efficacy also is important in management of patients with bladder cancer. Current chemotherapy is only moderately effective in patients with metastatic bladder cancer. Complete or major responses are few, and durability of response is limited to 18 to 24 months in most patients. The results of the multicenter randomized trial on cystectomy with or without neoadjuvant MVAC showed a survival advantage in the chemotherapy group and are quite provocative.[55] Yet the treatment-related toxicities in that trial and in the multitude of bladder-sparing trials reviewed in this chapter are considerable. Routine chemotherapy for all patients with invasive bladder cancer represents overtreatment for many patients. Cystectomy and orthotopic neobladder urinary diversion compare favorably to the bladder-sparing regimens from the standpoint of morbidity and quality of life. Following neobladder diversion, spontaneous voiding with daytime continence and nighttime continence is achieved in 90% and 85% of patients, respectively. For patients with locally advanced T3 to 4 disease and higher risk of pelvic relapse, contemporary cystectomy with or without neoadjuvant or adjuvant chemotherapy may well offer better disease control in the pelvis than does trimodality therapy bladder sparing.

Evaluation of cost associated with treatment is complex. Initial costs (trimodality versus cystectomy alone) are only one aspect. The costs of follow-up re-evaluation and additional treatment for local and/or systemic relapse all impact on the net financial "value" of a given regimen.

Cystectomy and continent urinary diversion for patients with invasive bladder cancer still offers highest patient survival and a high quality of life. Bladder-sparing regimens also are effective in selected patient groups and have a role in the armamentarium. However, the results are not equivalent to those of contemporary cystectomy. Bladder-sparing approaches should be offered in the context of organized clinical trials rather than as standard therapy.

Finally, and most importantly, the greatest need in management of patients with invasive bladder cancer is for improved treatment of microscopic and macroscopic systemic disease. Clinical trial and translational research efforts would be most productive if focused on this objective.

REFERENCES

1. Stackl W, Baierlein M, Albrecht W. Bladder preservation in muscle invasive bladder cancer. Br J Urol 1998;82:357–60.
2. Thurman SA, DeWeese TL. Multimodality therapy for the treatment of muscle invasive bladder cancer. Sem Urol Oncol 2000;18:313–22.
3. Kim HL, Steinberg GD. The current status of bladder preservation in the treatment of muscle invasive bladder cancer. J Urol 2000;164:627–32.
4. Feneley MR, Schoenberg M. Bladder-sparing strategies for transitional cell carcinoma. Urology 2000;56:549–60.
5. Stein JP, Lieskovsky G, Cote R, et al. Radical cystectomy in the treatment of invasive bladder: long-term results in 1,054 patients. J Clin Oncol 2001;19:666–75.
6. Skinner E, Grosben S, Skinner DG. Survival of women and men following radical cystectomy for bladder cancer. J Urol 2001;165:258,1064.
7. Gschwend JE, Dahm P, Fair WR. Disease specific survival as endpoint of outcome for bladder cancer patients following radical cystectomy. J Urol 2001;165:259,1065.
8. Lin JC, Bianco FJ, Reddy AY, et al. 8 year disease free survival of patients with transitional cell carcinoma of the bladder treated with radical cystectomy. J Urol 2001;165:303,1245.
9. Sanchez-Ortiz F, Van Arsdalen KN, Wein AJ, et al. A prolonged interval between the diagnosis of muscle invasion and cystectomy is associated with worse outcome in bladder carcinoma. J Urol 2001;105:259,1066.
10. Wei JT, Olapade-Olaopa O, Montie JE. Does delay in performing a radical cystectomy affect final pathologic stage? J Urol 2001;165:303,1246.
11. Herr HW. Does early cystectomy improve survival of patients with high risk non-muscle invasive bladder tumors? J Urol 2001;165:258,1061.
12. Herr H. Tumor progression and survival of patients with high grade, non-invasive papillary bladder tumors: 15 year outcome. J Urol 2000;163:60–2.
13. Herr HW. Conservative management of muscle-infiltrating bladder tumors: prospective experience. J Urol 1987;138:1162–3.
14. Solsona E, Iborra I, Ricos JV, et al. Feasibility of transurethral resection for muscle infiltrating carcinoma of the bladder: long term follow-up of a prospective study. J Urol 1998;159:95–8.
15. Henry K, Miller S, Mori M, et al. Comparison of transurethral resection to radical therapies for stage B bladder tumors. J Urol 1988;140:964–7.
16. O'Flynn JD, Smith JM, Hanson JS. Transurethral resection for the assessment and treatment of vesical neoplasms. Eur Urol 1975;1:38–40.
17. Marberger H, Marberger M Jr, Decristoforo A. The current status of transurethral resection in the diagnosis and therapy of carcinoma of the urinary bladder. Int Urol Neph 1972;4:35–44.
18. Barnes RW, Bergman RT, Hadley HT, Love D. Control of bladder tumors by endoscopic surgery. J Urol 1967;97:864–8.
19. Barnes RW, Dick AL, Hadley HL, Johnston OL. Survival following transurethral resection of bladder carcinoma. Cancer Res 1977;37:2985–97.
20. Bravers A, Buettner R, Jakse G. Second resection and prognosis of primary high risk superficial bladder cancer: is cystectomy often too early? J Urol 2001;165:808–10.
21. Cookson MS, Herr HW, Zhang ZF, et al. The treated natural history of high risk superficial bladder cancer: 15 year outcome. J Urol 1997;158:62–7.
22. Herr HW, Sogani PC. Does early cystectomy improve the survival of patients with high risk superficial bladder tumors? J Urol 2001;166:1296–9.
23. Tiguert R, Gheiler EL, Duncan R, Soloway MS. Tumor recurrence and progression following conservative management for T1G3 transitional cell carcinoma of the bladder. J Urol 2000;163:151,671.
24. Solsona E, Iborra I, Dumont R, et al. The 3 month clinical response to intravesical therapy as a predictive factor for progression in patients with high risk superficial bladder cancer. J Urol 2000;164:685–9.
25. Steinberg G, Bahnson R, Brosman S, et al. Efficacy and safety of valrubicin for the treatment of bacillus Calmette-Guérin refractory carcinoma in situ of the bladder. J Urol 2000:163:761–7.
26. Dandekar NP, Tongaonkar FIB, Dalal AV, Kulkarni SN. Partial cystectomy for invasive bladder cancer. J Surg Oncol 1995;60:24–9.
27. Nseyo VO, Shumaker B, Klein EA, Sutherland K. Photodynamic therapy using porfimer sodium as an alternative to cystectomy in patients with refractory transitional cell carcinoma in situ of the bladder. J Urol 1998;160:39–44.
28. Merrell RW, Brown HE, Rose JF. Bladder carcinoma treated by partial cystectomy: a review of 54 cases. J Urol 1979;122:471–2.
29. Schoborg TW, Sapolsky JL, Lewis CW Jr. Carcinoma of the bladder treated by segmental resection. J Urol 1979;122:473–5.
30. Cummings KB, Mason JT, Correa RJ Jr, Gibbons RP. Seg-

mental resection in the management of bladder cancer. J Urol 1978;119:56–8.

31. Novick AC, Stewart BH. Partial cystectomy in the treatment of primary and secondary carcinoma of the bladder. J Urol 1976;116:570–4.

32. Resnick MI, O'Connor VJ Jr. Segmental resection for carcinoma of the bladder: review of 102 patients. J Urol 1973;109:1007–10.

33. Utz DC, Schmitz SE, Fugelso PD, Farrow GM. A clinicopathologic evlution of partial cystectomy for carcinoma of the urinary bladder. Cancer 1973;32:1075–7.

34. Cespedes RD, McGuire EJ, Donat SM, Babaian RJ. Bladder preservation and continent urinary diversion in T3b transitional cell carcinoma of the bladder. Sem Urol Oncol 1996;14:103–11.

35. Herr HW, Scher HI. Neoadjuvant chemotherapy and partial cystectomy for invasive bladder cancer. J Clin Oncol 1994;12:975–80.

36. Gospodarowicz MK, Warde PR. A critical review of the role of definitive radiation therapy in bladder cancer. Semin Urol 1993;11:214–26.

37. Duncan W, Quilty PM. The results of a series of 963 patients with transitional cell carcinoma of the urinary bladder primarily treated by radical megavoltage x-ray therapy. Radiother Oncol 1986;7:299–310.

38. Gospodarowicz MK, Hawkins NV, Rawlings GA, et al. Radical radiotherapy for muscle invasive transitional cell carcinoma of the bladder: failure analysis. J Urol 1989; 142:1448–53.

39. Pollack A, Zagars GK, Swanson DA. Muscle invasive bladder cancer treated with external beam radiotherapy: prognostic factors. Int J Radiot Oncol Biol Phys 1994;30:267–77.

40. Pollack A, Zagars GK. Radiotherapy for stage T3b transitional cell carcinoma of the bladder. Semin Urol Oncol 1996;14:86–95.

41. Wijnmaalen A, Kruger CCGB. Organ preservation by external beam and after loading interstitial radiation in patients with muscle infiltrating bladder cancer. Semin Urol Oncol 2000;18:308–12.

42. van der Werf-Messing BHP, Van Putten WLJ. Carcinoma of the urinary bladder category $T_{2-3}N_xM_0$ treated by $40G_y$ external irradiation followed by cesium-137 implant at reduced dose (50%). Int J Radiat Oncol Biol Phys 1989;16:369–71.

43. Thomas DJ, Roberts JT, Hall RR, Reading J. Radical transurethral resection and chemotherapy in the treatment of muscle-invasive bladder cancer: a long term follow-up. BJU Int 1999;83:432–7.

44. Herr HW, Bajorin DF, Scher HI. Neoadjuvant chemotherapy and bladder-sparing surgery for invasive bladder cancer: 10 year outcome. J Clin Oncol 1998;16:1298–1301.

45. Uygur MC, Yaman I, Altug U, Erol D. Conservative management of stage T_2 or T_{3a} bladder cancer with deep transurethral resection followed by four cycles of chemotherapy. Br J Urol 1996;78:201–4.

46. Angulo JC, Sanchez-Chapado M, Lopez JI, Flores N. Primary cisplatin, methotrexate and vinblastine aiming at bladder preservation in invasive bladder cancer: multivariate analysis on prognostic factor. J Urol 1996;155: 1897–1902.

47. Sternberg CN, Pansadoro V, Calabro F, et al. Neo-adjuvant chemotherapy and bladder preservation in locally advanced transitional cell carcinoma of the bladder. Annals Oncol 1999;10:1301–5.

48. Dalal AV, Tongaonkar HB, Dandekar N, et al. Is bladder conservation feasible? An Indian experience. Eur J Surg Oncol 1995;21:301–6.

49. Lekili M, Ayder AR, Minareci S, et al. Conservative management of advanced bladder cancer. Int Urol Nephrol 1995;27:747–52.

50. Hall RR, Newling DW, Ramsden PD, et al. Treatment of invasive bladder cancer by local resection and high dose methotrexate. Br J Urol 1984;56:668–72.

51. Roberts JT, Fossa SD, Richards B, et al. Results of Medical Research Council phase II study of low dose cisplatin and methotrexate in the primary treatment of locally advance (T_3 and T_4) transitional cell carcinoma of the bladder. Br J Urol 1991;68:162–8.

52. Logothetis C, Swanson D, Amato R, et al. Optimal delivery of perioperative chemotherapy: preliminary results of a randomized prospective trial of preoperative and postoperative chemotherapy for invasive bladder carcinoma. J Urol 1996;155:1241–5.

53. Vogelzang NJ, Moormein JA, Awan AM, et al. Methotrexate, vinblastine, doxorubicin, and cisplatin followed by radiotherapy and surgery for muscle-invading bladder cancer: The University of Chicago Experience. J Urol 1993; 149:753–7.

54. Vogelzang N. Neoadjuvant MVAC: The long and winding road is getting shorter and straighter. J Clin Oncol 2001; 19:4003–4.

55. Natale RB, Grossman HB, Blumenstein B. SWOG 8710 (INT-0080) Randomized phase III trial of neoadjuvant MVAC + cystectomy versus cystectomy alone in patients with locally advanced bladder cancer. Proc Am Soc Clin Oncol 2001;20:2–3.

56. Millikan R, Dinney C, Swanson D, et al. Integrated therapy for locally advanced bladder cancer: final report of a randomized trial of cystectomy plus adjuvant MVAC versus cystectomy with both preoperative and postoperative MVAC. J Clin Oncol 2001;79:4005–13.

57. Bajorin D. Plenary debate of randomized phase III trial of neoadjuvant MVAC plus cystectomy versus cystectomy alone in patients with locally advanced bladder cancer. J Clin Oncol 2001;19:17s–20s.

58. Sternberg CN, Parmar MKB. Neoadjuvant chemotherapy is not (yet) standard treatment for muscle-invasive bladder cancer. J Clin Oncol 2001;19:21s–6s.

59. Sternberg CN, Pansadoro V, Calabro F, et al. Can we select patients for bladder preservations based on response to chemotherapy? J Urol 2000;163:216.

60. Sternberg CN, Pansadoro V, Calabro F, et al. Neoadjuvant chemotherapy and bladder preservation in locally advanced transitional cell carcinoma of the bladder. Ann Oncol 1999;10:1301–5.

61. Schultz PK, Herr HW, Zhang ZF, et al. Neoadjuvant chemotherapy for invasive bladder cancer: prognostic factors for survival of patients treated with MVAC with 5 year follow-up. J Clin Oncol 1994;12:1394–1401.

62. Scher HI, Yagoda A, Herr HW, et al. Neoadjuvant MVAC

(methotrexate, vinblastine, doxorubicin, and cisplatin) effect on the primary bladder lesion. J Urol 1988;139: 470–1.

63. Herr HW, Bajorin DF, Scher HI, et al. Can p53 help select patients with invasive bladder cancer for bladder preservation? J Urol 1999;161:20–3.

64. O'Donnell M. Editorial comment. J Urol 1999;161:22–3.

65. Esrig D, Elmajian D, Groshen S, et al. Accumulation of nuclear p53 and tumor progression in bladder cancer. New Engl J Med 1994;331:1259–64.

66. Martinez-Pineiro JA, Martinez-Pineiro L. The role of neoadjuvant chemotherapy for invasive bladder cancer. Br J Urol 1998;82:33–42.

67. Housset M, Maulard C, Chretein Y, et al. Combined radiation and chemotherapy for invasive transitional cell carcinoma of the bladder: a prospective study. J Clin Oncol 1993;11: 2150–7.

68. Splinter TA, Scher HI, Denis L, et al. The prognostic value of the response to combination chemotherapy before cystectomy in patients with invasive bladder cancer. J Urol 1992;147:606–8.

69. Zietman AL, Shipley WU, Kaufman DS, et al. A phase I/II trial of transurethral surgery combined with concurrent cisplatin, 5-fluorouracil and twice daily radiation followed by selective bladder preservation in operable patients with muscle invasive bladder cancer. J Urol 1998;160:1673–7.

70. Serretta V, Greco GL, Pavone C, Pavone-Macaluso M. The fate of patients with locally advanced bladder cancer treated conservatively with neoadjuvant chemotherapy, extensive transurethral resection and radiotherapy: 10 year experience. J Urol 1998;159:1187–91.

71. Danesi DT, Arcangeli G, Cruciani E, et al. Combination treatment of invasive bladder carcinoma with transurethral resection, induction chemotherapy, and radical radiotherapy plus concomitant protracted infusion of cisplatin and 5-fluorouracil: a phase I study. Cancer 1997;80:1464–71.

72. Fellin G, Groffer U, Bolner A, et al. Combined chemotherapy and radiation with selective organ preservation for muscle invasive bladder carcinoma. A single institution phase II study. Br J Urol 1997;80:44–9.

73. Kachnic LA, Kaufman DS, Heney NM, et al. Bladder preservation by combined modality therapy for invasive bladder cancer. J Clin Oncol 1997;15:1022–9.

74. Tester W, Caplan R, Heaney J, et al. Neoadjuvant combined modality program with selective organ preservation for invasive bladder cancer: results of Radiation Therapy Oncology Group phase II trial 8802. J Clin Oncol 1996;14:119–26.

75. Einstein AB Jr, Wolf H, Halliday KR, et al. Combination transurethral resection, systemic chemotherapy, and pelvic radiotherapy for invasive (T2–T4) bladder cancer unsuitable for cystectomy: a phase I/II Southwestern Oncology Group study. Urology 1996;47:652–7.

76. Given RW, Parson JT, McCarley D, Wajsman Z. Bladder-sparing multimodality treatment of muscle-invasive bladder cancer: a five year follow-up. Urol 1995;46:499–505.

77. Orsatti M, Curotto A, Canobbio L, et al. Alternating chemoradiotherapy in bladder cancer: a conservative approach. Int Radiot Oncol Biol Phys 1995;33:173–8.

78. Vikram B, Malamud S, Silverman P, et al. A pilot study of chemotherapy alternating with twice a day accelerated radiation therapy as an alternative to cystectomy in muscle infiltrating (stages T_2 and $_3$) cancer of the bladder: preliminary results. J Urol 1994;151:602–4.

79. Kaufman DS, Shipley WV, Griffin PP, et al. Selective bladder preservation by combination treatment of invasive bladder cancer. N Engl J Med 1993;329:1377–82.

80. Dunst J, Sauer R, Schrott KM, et al. Organ-sparing treatment of advanced bladder cancer: a 10 year experience. Int J Radiat Oncol Biol Phys 1994;30:261–6.

81. Shipley WU, Prout GR Jr, Einstein AB, et al. Treatment of invasive bladder cancer by cisplatin and radiation in patients unsuited for surgery. JAMA 1987;258:931–65.

82. Coppin CM, Gospodarawicz MK, James K, et al. Improved local control of invasive bladder cancer by concurrent cisplatin and preoperative or definitive radiation: The National Cancer Institute of Canada Clinical Trial Group. J Clin Oncol 1996;14:2901–7.

83. Sauer R, Birkenhake S, Kuhn R, et al. Efficacy of radiochemotherapy with platin derivatives compared to radiotherapy alone in organ-sparing treatment of bladder cancer. Int J Radiot Qual Biol Phys 1998;40:121–7.

84. Chauvet B, Brewert Y, Felix-Faure C, et al. Concurrent cisplatin and radiotherapy for patients with muscle invasive bladder cancer who are not candidates for radical cystectomy. J Urol 1996;156:1258–62.

85. Kuehn R, Brod JL, Schrott KM, et al. Organ sparing treatment of invasive bladder cancer by TUR and radiochemotherapy. J Urol 1999;161:265,1025.

86. Schrott KM, Schafhauser W, Brod JL, et al. Results of salvage cystectomy after radiochemotherapy in locally invasive transitional cell carcinoma of the bladder. J Urol 1999;161:265,1024.

87. Hussain MHA, Glass TR, Forman J, et al. Combination cisplatin, 5-fluorouracil and radiation therapy for locally advanced unresectable or medically unfit bladder cancer cases: A Southwest Oncology Group Study. J Urol 2001;165:56–61.

88. Houssett M, Dufour B, Maulard-Durtux C. Concomitant 5-fluorouracil cisplatin and bifractionated split course radiation therapy for invasive bladder cancer. Proc Am Soc Clin Oncol 1997;16:319,1139.

89. Vikram B, Chadha M, Malamud SC, et al. Rapidly alternating chemotherapy and radiotherapy instead of cystectomy for the treatment of muscle-invasive carcinoma of the urinary bladder; long term result of a pilot study. Cancer 1998;82:918–22.

90. Shipley WU, Winter KA, Kaufman DS, et al. Phase III trial of neoadjuvant chemotherapy in patients with invasive bladder cancer treated with selective bladder preservation by combined radiation therapy and chemotherapy: initial results of Radiation Therapy Oncology Group 89-03. J Clin Oncol 1998;16:3576–83.

91. Shipley WU, Kaufman DS, Heney NM, et al. An update of combined modality therapy for patients with muscle invading bladder cancer using selective bladder preservation or cystectomy. J Urol 1999;162:445–51.

92. Zietman AL, Grocela J, Zehr E, et al. Selective bladder conservation using transurethral resection, chemotherapy,

and radiation: management and consequences of T_a, T_1, and T_{is} recurrence within the retained bladder. Urol 2001;58:380–5.

93. Zehr E, Shipley WU, Heney NM, et al. Combined modality therapy for selective bladder preservation in patients with T_2-T_{4a} invasive bladder cancer: The MGH experience. J Urol 2001;165:260,1071.

94. Hautmann RE. Complications and results after cystectomy in male and female patients with locally invasive bladder cancer. Eur Urol Suppl 1998;33:23–4.

95. Abrott RP, Wilson JA, Pontin AR, Barnes RD. Salvage cystectomy after radical irradiation for bladder cancer: prognostic factors and complications. Br J Urol 1993;72: 756–60.

96. Lerner S. [Editorial comment]. J Urol 1998;160:1673–7.

97. Raghavan D. Editorial: Bladder preservation in patients with bladder cancer–quality versus quantity of life? J Urol 1998;160:1678–9.

98. Montie JE. Against bladder sparing surgery. J Urol 1999; 162:452–7.

17

Laparoscopic Aproaches in Cystectomy for Urethelial Cancer

JIHAD H. KAOUK, MD
INDERBIR SINGH GILL, MD, MCH

Radical cystectomy remains the most effective modality of treatment for localized muscle invasive bladder cancer. However, radical cystectomy and urinary diversion is a major abdominal surgery with significant postoperative morbidity and protracted recovery period. Laparoscopy is now a viable option for most urologic ablative surgeries while intracorporeal reconstructive techniques are still evolving. With increased surgical experience especially in intracorporeal suturing and improvements in laparoscopic instruments, major advances in laparoscopic reconstructive urology including urinary diversion have been made.

Although laparoscopic radical cystectomy has been reported in patients with bladder cancer, the accompanying technically challenging urinary diversion has uniformly been performed by open-assisted techniques.[1–4] Completely intracorporeal performance of the entire radical cystectomy and urinary diversion procedure is a recent development after several animal studies.[5,6] To date, laparoscopically-constructed urinary diversions include ileal conduit, rectal sigmoid (Mainz II) pouch, and orthotopic ileal (Studer) neobladder. Also, an Indiana pouch with continent catheterizable umbilical stoma has been performed, wherein the Indiana pouch was constructed extracorporeally.[7–11]

INDICATIONS FOR SURGERY

Criteria for cystectomy and type of urinary diversion are similar to indications followed during the stan-dard open surgical technique. In general, acute intraperitoneal infectious process and uncorrected coagulopathy represent a contraindication for the laparoscopic approach. Previous abdominal surgery is not an absolute contraindication, but extra care should be taken during initial trocar insertion. Obesity is not, in itself, a contraindication to the laparoscopic approach; however, difficulty may be encountered while gaining intraperitoneal access or due to a smaller working space especially when operating in the pelvis.

PATIENT PREPARATION AND POSITIONING

On the day prior to surgery, a liquid diet is initiated. A mechanical bowel preparation is undertaken using 4 liters of polyethylene glycol (GoLytley). Intravenous broad-spectrum antibiotics and subcutaneous heparin are administered prior to anesthesia induction. The patient is placed in the supine, modified low lithotomy position with thighs abducted and arms adducted to the sides of the patient. All bone prominences are carefully padded and bilateral sequential compression devices are applied to both calfs. During surgery, the operative table is placed in a Trendelenburg position. A Foley catheter is placed in the bladder after the patient is prepped and draped.

The surgeon is situated on the left side of the patient. The first assistant is on the right side of the patient and the second assistant is positioned next to the surgeon. Monitors are placed on either side of the patient's pelvis for the cystoprostatectomy part of the operation and on either side of the patient's shoulders when laparoscopic bowel work is being performed.

TECHNIQUE

Port Placement

A six-port transperitoneal approach is used (Figure 17–1). A primary 10 mm port is placed at the umbilicus for the 0° laparoscope. Four secondary ports are placed under visualization: a 12 mm port to the left of the umbilicus, lateral to the rectus muscle, and two ports in the left (10 mm) and right (5 mm) lower quadrants, approximately 2 finger-breadths medial to the ipsilateral anterior superior iliac spines. At the pre-selected stoma site, a 12 mm port is placed in the right rectus muscle. Finally, a 5 mm port is placed in the midline infra-umbilical location approximately 2 finger-breadths cephalad to the symphysis pubis.

Laparoscopic Radical Cystectomy

The posterior peritoneal fold is incised posterior to the bladder in the rectovesical pouch and the prerec-

tal plane is dissected (Figure 17–2). The vasa deferentia are divided and dissection is continued along the posterior aspect of the seminal vesicles toward the bladder base. Denonvilliers' fascia is incised and dissection along the anterior rectal surface is followed distally towards the apex of the prostate. Upon completion of the posterior dissection, the initial peritoneal incision is carried laterally on either side, up to the common iliac artery at the point of crossing of the ureter. Generous mobilization of the ureters is done bilaterally. Both ureters are mobilized down close to the bladder wall. Adequate mobilization of the left ureter is assured to allow subsequent tension-free retroperitoneal transfer to the right side for the ureteroileal anastomosis.

The bladder is distended with 200 mL of saline and the parietal peritoneum lateral to the medial

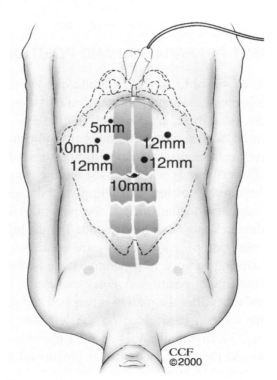

Figure 17–1. Transperitoneal 6-port approach. Adapted with permission, CCF 2001.

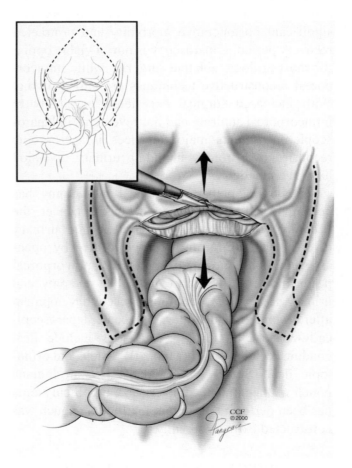

Figure 17–2. Initial peritoneal incision is made in the rectovesical pouch. A plane is identified between the bladder and the rectum. Dashed line represents subsequent incision, laterally up to the common iliacs. Inset represents extension of peritoneotomy onto the undersurface of the abdominal wall. Adapted with permission, CCF 2001.

umbilical ligaments is incised and extended anteriorly onto the undersurface of the abdominal wall to include the entire urachus close to the umbilicus (Figure 17–3). The Retzius space is entered and the bladder is mobilized keeping all the extraperitoneal perivesical fat attached to the bladder.

The lateral and posterior pedicles of the bladder are dissected with serial Endo-GIA firing (vascular 2.5 mm stapler, US Surgical, Norwalk, CT). Both ureters are clipped close to the bladder and divided. The distal ureteral margin is sent for frozen pathological examination. The clip-occluded ureters are allowed to hydro distend for easier subsequent ureteroileal anastomosis. The endopelvic fascia is incised bilaterally and the dorsal venous complex is then controlled with either the Endo-GIA (for non orthotopic urinary diversion) or by applying a suture (for orthotopic urinary diversion). The Foley catheter is removed and the urethra is transected using the Endoshears. In women, a sponge stick inserted into the vagina helps to identify the anterior vaginal wall and subsequent plane of dissection. The anterior vaginal wall along with the uterus is excised. A frozen section evaluation of the urethral margin is performed. The specimen is entrapped in an Endocatch-II bag (US Surgical, Norwalk, CT) for later extraction at the end of the procedure. In women, the specimens could be extracted intact through the already open vaginal vault then the vaginal wall defect is reconstructed.

Pelvic Lymphnode Dissection

Bilateral extended pelvic lymphadenectomy is performed including lymphatic tissue from the pubic bone distally to the bifurcation of the common iliac artery proximally and from the genitofemoral nerve laterally and the obturator nerve inferiorly.

Laparoscopic Ileal Conduit

During ileal conduit urinary diversion, a 15–20 cm segment of ileum is identified 15 cm from the ileocecal junction. Division of the isolated segment of bowel and the mesentery is performed using the Endo-GIA (3.5 mm stapler) for the bowel and (2.5 mm stapler) for the mesentery (Figure 17–4). Ileotomies are made in both ileal stumps and intestinal continuity is re-established by creating a generous side-to-side ileoileal anastomosis with

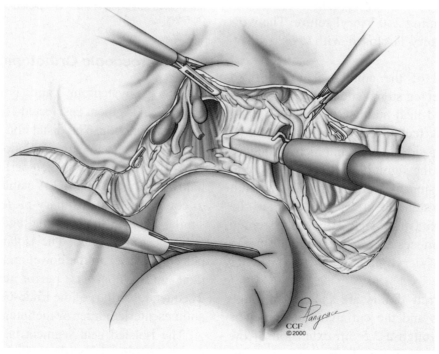

Figure 17–3.   Generous mobilization of the ureters is done. The lateral and posterior pedicles are secured with an Endo-GIA stapler. Adapted with permission, CCF 2001.

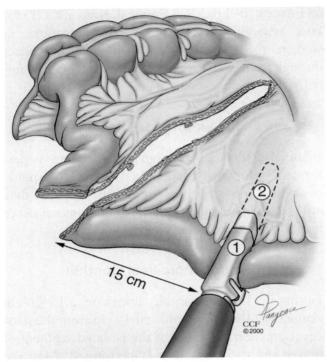

Figure 17–4. Division of the isolated bowel segment and mesentery is performed with serial firings of the Endo-GIA stapler. Adapted with permission, CCF 2001.

two sequential firings of the Endo-GIA stapler. The open ends of the bowel are closed with transverse firings of the Endo-GIA stapler. This edge is then oversewn with running 2–0 Vicryl suture. The window in the mesentery is closed with 2 or 3 interrupted stitches.

The distal end of the conduit is exteriorized through the preselected stoma site at the right rectus muscle and an end-ileal stoma is fashioned using conventional open techniques. The left ureter is passed to the right side of the abdomen through a window created in the sigmoid mesentery. A 90 cm, 7 French single-J stent is inserted into the conduit lumen then used to stent the ureter at the desired site of ureteroileal anastomosis. Bilateral stented ureteroileal anastomoses are completed in a running fashion using 4–0 Vicryl sutures on RB-1 needles (Figure 17–5).

Two Jackson-Pratt drains are inserted through different port sites and the entrapped specimen is extracted intact through a 3.5 cm extension of the umbilical port-site incision. Hemostasis is confirmed and port sites are closed in standard fashion.

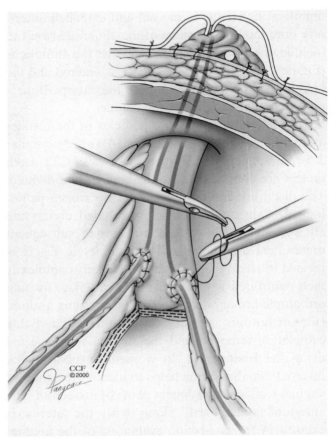

Figure 17–5. Ileal conduit urinary diversion. The distal end of the ileal loop is exteriorized through the preselected stoma site and is secured to the skin using standard technique. Stented bilateral ureteroileal anastomoses are completed. Adapted with permission, CCF 2001.

Laparoscopic Orthotopic Neobladder

Following cystectomy and lymphadenectomy, a 65 cm ileal segment is selected 15 cm proximal to the ileocecal junction. The distal end of the selected segment is transected with an Endo-GIA stapler. Division of the mesentery is then performed by 2 sequential firings of the Endo-GIA stapler. Care is taken not to compromise the primary mesenteric vessels. In a similar manner, the proximal end of the 65 cm ileal segment is transected. The isolated ileal segment is placed posterior to the bowel and a side-to-side ileoileal anastomosis is performed anteriorly with 2 sequential firings of the Endo-GIA stapler along the antimesenteric border of the intestinal segments.

The isolated ileal segment is detubularized along the antimesenteric border using the endoshears and harmonic scalpel. The proximal 10 to 15 cm of the ileal segment is reserved for the isoperistaltic Studer limb of the neobladder. The posterior wall of the neobladder is created by continuous intracorporeal suturing of adjacent detubularized ileal wall using 2–0 Vicryl suture on a CT-1 needle. The segment is then brought into the pelvis, and the most dependent portion is selected for the urethroileal neobladder anastomosis using 2–0 Vicryl on a UR-6 needle. Prior to completing the anastomosis, a 22 French silicone Foley catheter is inserted per urethra. In female patients, two 90 cm single-J ileoureteral stents are inserted via the external urethral meatus alongside the Foley catheter and delivered into the neobladder. In the male, the two ileoureteral stents are inserted through the right lateral port, which is then removed and re-inserted alongside the stents. The anterior wall of the neobladder is folded forward and the free edges are sutured to achieve a spherical configuration (Figure 17–6). Prior to completion of the neobladder suturing, the ileoureteral stents are delivered into the Studer limb and passed through ileotomies created at the site of the future ureteroileal anastomosis. Bilateral ureteroileal anastomoses are performed in a continuous manner using two separate 3–0 Vicryl sutures (RB-1 needle) for each ureter. A suprapubic catheter is inserted into the neobladder through the midline port-site incision. Two Jackson-Pratt drains are inserted, one through each lateral port site.

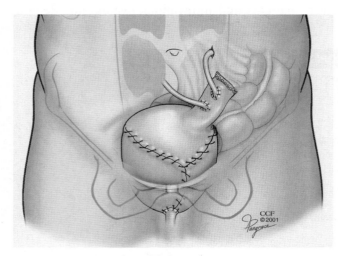

Figure 17–6. Orthotopic neobladder urinary diversion. After isolation of the ileal segment and detubularization of the distal portion, the posterior plate is created and urethroileal anastomosis is completed using a running suture. The anterior wall of the neobladder is folded to achieve a spherical configuration of the neobladder. Adapted with permission, CCF 2001.

POSTOPERATIVE CARE

The neobladder is irrigated through the Foley and suprapubic catheters every 4 to 6 hours during the first 2 to 3 days and every 8 hours thereafter. The Jackson-Pratt drains are removed as their drainage decreases appropriately. The ureteral stents are removed at approximately 1 to 2 weeks. A cystogram is obtained at 4 to 6 weeks postoperatively to confirm complete healing prior to removal of the Foley catheter. An intravenous pyelography is obtained at 3 months after surgery.

RESULTS

Several authors have described laparoscopic cystectomy after Parra and colleagues[9] reported the initial case in 1992.[9] However, completely intracorporeal radical cystectomy and urinary diversion was not performed till a decade later. At the Cleveland Clinic, we reviewed our first 11 cases (9 males and 2 females) of laparoscopic radical cystectomy with ileal conduit.[12] The entire procedure was completed intracorporeally as previously described (see technique section) for all cases. Mean surgical time was 8.3 hours. The estimated blood loss was only 330 mL with no blood transfusions required. Five patients (4 males and 1 female) have been followed for 2 years.[13] Of these five, three patients are alive with no evidence of recurrent disease. The remaining two patients died of unrelated causes (septicemia following unrelated pulmonary infection and multiorgan failure at 9 months in one patient and myocardial infarction 12 months after surgery in the other). Both of these patients had normal renal function and no evidence of recurrent disease up to the time of death.

Postoperative complications consisted of bowel obstruction (n = 1) developed on the fifth postoperative day. Exploratory laparotomy revealed concerns regarding viability of bowel proximal to the ileoileal anastomosis. A temporary diverting ileostomy was done. After intensive postoperative care, the patient recovered, and bowel continuity was restored at 12 weeks. At 3 weeks postoperatively, one patient had abdominal distension and low-grade fever (that responded to antibiotics) for a period of 10 days. One patient developed transient left adductor spasm postoperatively and recovered within a week. The average hospital stay was 7 days (range 6–22 days). Histopathology revealed transitional cell carcinoma in four patients (stage pT3bN0 in 2 patients, pT3aN1 in 2) and squamous cell carcinoma (stage pT3bN0) in one patient. Surgical margins of the bladder specimen were negative for cancer in all five cases. All surviving patients are doing well with normal upper tracts on intravenous urography and no evidence of local recurrence or metastatic disease.

Although the total surgical time was longer than is usually expected with open surgery, blood loss was less and none of the patients required any blood transfusion. The videoendoscopic vision provided excellent identification of tissue planes allowing superb hemostasis. The Endo-GIA stapler significantly facilitated control of vascular pedicles of the bladder. We believe that the combination of decreased bowel manipulation, minimal postoperative pain, and the resultant reduction in narcotic analgesics, are potential benefits of laparoscopic surgery that may reduce postoperative ileus. However, it is a technically demanding procedure that requires extensive experience in laparoscopic surgery.

More recently, we have performed laparoscopic cystectomy with orthotopic ileal neobladder in two patients (1 male and 1 female). All suturing was performed exclusively using free-hand laparoscopic techniques and the entire procedure was completed intracorporeally. One additional patient underwent an Indiana pouch continent diversion, wherein the pouch was constructed extracorporeally.[10]

Total operative time for laparoscopic radical cystectomy and orthotopic neobladder was 8.5 and 10.5 hours, with a blood loss ranging from 200 to 400 mL, respectively. Neither patient required any blood transfusion. Hospital stay was between 5 and 12 days, and surgical margins of the bladder specimen were negative in each case. Postoperative renal function was normal and intravenous pyelograms revealed unobstructed upper tracts. The solitary postoperative complication was upper gastrointestinal bleeding in one patient from a known, pre-existing duodenal ulcer, that responded to conservative measures resulting in a 12-day hospital stay. Both patients resumed ambulation on the first postoperative day, and oral liquids were resumed between day 2 and day 4. The ileoureteral stents were removed at 1 to 2 weeks, and the urethral Foley catheter was removed at 4 to 6 weeks, after a cystogram confirmed watertight healing. In the patient with Indiana pouch, operative time was 7 hours, blood loss was 300 mL, hospital stay was 6 days and surgical margins of the bladder specimen and lymph nodes were negative for cancer. Histopathology revealed pT1G1 transitional cell carcinoma with carcinoma-in-situ in two patients, and infiltrating Gleason 7 prostate adenocarcinoma in one. Postoperatively, renal function was normal in all three patients and intravenous pyelograms demon-

No.	Instrument	Size
	Table 17–1. LAPAROSCOPIC INSTRUMENTS	
1	0° Laparoscope	10 mm
3	Trocars	10–12 mm
3	Trocars	5 mm
1	Electrosurgical monopolar scissors	5 mm
1	Electrosurgical hook	5 mm
2	Atraumatic grasping forceps	5 mm
1	Right-angle dissector	5 mm
1	Right-angle dissector	10 mm
1	Fan retractor	10 mm
1	Weck clip applicator with disposable clip cartridges	10 mm
2	Needle holders	5 mm
1	Endoshears	5 mm
1	Maryland grasper	5 mm
1	Endoclip applier	11 mm
1	Articulated Endo-GIA vascular stapler (US Surgical, Norwalk, CT) with multiple reloads	12 mm
1	Irrigator/aspirator device	5 mm
1	Endocatch II bag (US Surgical, Norwalk, CT)	15 mm

strated unobstructed upper tracts. Both patients with the orthotopic neobladder had complete daytime continence. Nocturnal continence was achieved with timed voiding. The patient undergoing Indiana pouch diversion remains completely continent with no complications from his catheterizable ileal stoma at the umbilicus. Over a follow-up ranging from 5 to 13 months, one patient expired from metastatic disease. The other two patients are doing well with normal upper tracts and without local or systemic progression.

Laparoscopic continent diversion using the Mainz pouch II technique was reported by Turk and colleagues.[7] In five patients, creation of a rectal sigmoid pouch and bilateral ureteral implantation was performed completely intracorporeally. Median operative time was 7.4 hours, blood loss was 190 to 300 mL and hospital stay was 10 days. In all five patients, lymph nodes and surgical margins were tumor free. No complications were reported and patients were continent for urine and/or feces.[9]

CONCLUSON

Laparoscopic radical cystectomy and urinary diversion is an evolving technique in laparoscopic reconstructive surgery. The procedure can be achieved by completely intracorporeal techniques in a manner duplicating open surgical principles and following the established oncologic principles. With more experience, critical evaluation of surgical outcomes and comparison to standard open surgical techniques are important to determine the advantages of laparoscopic techniques in the management of patients with bladder cancer.

REFERENCES

1. Kozminski M, Partamian K. Case report of laparoscopic ileal loop conduit. J Endourol 1992;6:147.
2. Puppo P, Perachino M, Ricciotti G, et al. Laparoscopically assisted transvaginal radical cystectomy. Eur Urol 1995; 27:80–4.
3. Sanchez de Badajoz E, Gallego Perales JL, Reche Rosado A, et al. Laparoscopic cystectomy and ileal conduit: case report. J Endourol 1995;9:59–62.
4. Denewer A, Kotb S, Hussein O, El-Maadawy M. Laparoscopic assisted cystectomy and lymphadenectomy for bladder cancer: initial experience. World J Surg 1999;23:608–11.
5. Gill IS, Fergany A, Klein EA, et al. Laparoscopic radical cystoprostatectomy with ileal conduit performed completely intracorporeally: the initial 2 cases. Urology 2000;56:26–9; discussion 29–30.
6. Potter SR, Charambura TC, Adams JB 2nd, Kavoussi LR. Laparoscopic ileal conduit: five-year follow-up. Urology 2000;56:22–5.
7. Turk I, Deger S, Winkelmann B, et al. Laparoscopic radical cystectomy with continent urinary diversion (rectal sigmoid pouch) performed completely intracorporeally: the initial 5 cases. J Urol 2001;165:1863–6.
8. Gill IS, Kaouk JH, Meraney AM, et al. Laparoscopic radical cystectomy and continent ileal neobladder performed completely intracorporeally–the initial experience. J Urol 2002;168(1):13–8.
9. Parra RO, Andrus CH, Jones JP, Boullier JA. Laparoscopic cystectomy: initial report on a new treatment for the retained bladder. J Urol 1992;148:1140–4.
10. Fergany AF, Gill IS, Kaouk JH, et al. Laparoscopic intracorporeally constructed ileal conduit after porcine cystoprostatectomy. J Urol 2001;166:285–8.
11. Kaouk JH, Gill IS, Desai MM, et al. Laparoscopic orthotopic ileal neobladder. J Endourol 2001;15:131–42.
12. Gill IS, Meraney AM, Fergany A, et al. Laparoscopic radical cystectomy with ileal conduit performed completely intracorporeally–the initial experience in 11 patients [abstract]. J Urol 2001;165:284.
13. Gupta NP, Gill IS, Fergany A, Nabi G. Laparoscopic radical cystectomy with intracorporeal ileal conduit diversion: 5 cases with 1.5 year follow up. [2001; submitted to Br J Urol]

Demographics and Epidemiology of Urothelial Cancer of the Renal Pelvis and Ureter

NEIL FLESHNER, MD, MPH, FRCSC

Urothelial tumors of the upper tracts refer to transitional cell carcinoma, adenocarcinoma, and squamous cell cancers of the renal pelvis and ureters. Unlike urothelial carcinoma of the bladder, much less is known about the risk factors for these neoplasms. The reason for this relative paucity of knowledge relates to the fact that these tumors are rare; thus, the statistical power required to determine associations is prohibitive. Nonetheless, some observations about upper tract urothelial cancers raise some important etiologic hypotheses about cancer ontogeny and biology.

INCIDENCE AND DEMOGRAPHICS

Cancer registry figures regarding the incidence and mortality of upper tract tumors have been notoriously unreliable. In most cancer registries, renal pelvic tumors are grouped together with renal cortical neoplasms, which possess a vastly different etiology, histology, and biology.[1] Tumors of the renal pelvis and ureter represent approximately 5% and 1 to 2% of urothelial tumors, respectively.[2] Similar to urothelial tumors of the bladder, upper tract cancers are most common among whites and men.[3] Incidence also appears to be increasing over the past 20 years, although this may reflect better registry data input.[4] If the incidence of upper tract urothelial tumors is increasing, it likely reflects a true increase and is not related to more sophisticated medical imaging and case ascertainment. Asymptomatic "autopsy" tumors of the upper tracts are exquisitely

rare.[5,6] Similar to bladder cancer, sex-specific mortality figures indicate that women have a 25% increased chance of death from this disease in comparison with men.[3] This gender difference may relate to later onset of diagnosis or to hormonally mediated differences in disease biology. Certain countries seem to have a higher incidence of upper tract cancers. This is especially true in the Balkans but is also prevalent in areas such as Taiwan.[7,8]

Patients at highest risk of upper tract tumors are those with bladder cancer. The estimated risk of upper tract tumors is 2 to 4% at 5 years.[9] Bilateral involvement, either synchronous or metachronous, is, fortunately, rare at 5%.[6] Patients with high-grade superficial bladder cancer are particularly at increased risk of upper tract cancers. Cookson and colleagues reported that 21% of patients with diffuse carcinoma in situ (CIS) and T1 disease developed upper tract cancers at 15 years.[10] Shinka and colleagues reported that 13% of patients with CIS of the bladder developed tumors of the upper tracts.[11]

Patients with upper tract tumors are also at high risk for subsequent distal disease in the bladder. Reported rates of bladder cancer after upper tract cancer are 25 to 75%.[12–14] There are no reliable data assessing this risk in relation to the location of the upper tract cancer, but tumors of the distal ureter likely have a higher incidence of bladder recurrence as a result of local extension. This high incidence has led to the routine use of cystoscopy in the surveillance of patients with urothelial upper tract tumors.

UPPER TRACT UROTHELIAL CANCER BIOLOGY: TUMOR SEEDING

The discordant rates of upper tract recurrence among bladder cancer patients compared with bladder recurrence among patients with upper tract cancers raise some interesting biologic issues about the possibility of tumor cell shedding and implantation as a mechanism of cancer recurrence. Molecular analyses provide a hypothetical means of distinguishing the ontogeny of tumor recurrence among patients with upper tract disease. The most interesting work in this field was reported by Takahashi and colleagues, who performed microsatellite marker analysis among 19 incident cases of patients with low-grade upper tract cancers who had subsequent bladder "recurrence."[15] Using this technique, approximately half of the recurrent bladder lesions seemed to emanate from the upper tract primary tumor. Consistent with the natural history of upper tract disease, this rate appears to be higher than bladder recurrences from bladder cancer. These data have been further reinforced by the study from Hafner and colleagues, who showed that both monoclonal and oligoclonal cancerization occurs.[16] Although molecular analyses cannot definitely conclude that the origin of bladder tumors is from the upper tract primary tumor, these data would indicate that both tumor implantation and generalized urothelial field change play an important role in urothelial carcinogenesis.

UPPER TRACT UROTHELIAL CANCER BIOLOGY: MECHANISM OF CARCINOGENESIS

The upper tracts of the urinary system are lined with transitional epithelium.[17] The hypothesized mechanism of upper tract carcinogenesis is that of contact between urine-containing carcinogens and the epithelial mucosae. Because of relatively diminished contact time between the urine and the mucosae in the upper tracts compared with the bladder, the incidence of these cancers is less. Consistent with this paradigm is the observation that renal pelvic contact time exceeds that of the ureter. This may explain why renal pelvic tumors are four times more common than ureteral tumors.

Given the aforementioned hypotheses, it would stand to reason that virtually any well-accepted risk factor for urothelial cancer of the bladder (except schistosomiasis, which is limited to the bladder) is also probably a risk factor for upper tract cancers. This observation is pragmatic as there are no metabolic or physical changes in the composition of urine between the collecting ducts and the bladder. Unlike bladder cancers, a second mechanism of urothelial cancers exists that seems to be somewhat specific for the upper tracts. In these cases, inflammation of the collecting system usually as a result of nephrotoxin exposure (and tubulointerstitial nephritis) leads to upper tract cancers.[18] These cancers are more common in the renal pelvis and are often associated with end-stage renal disease. In this chapter, we review the evidence for associations between putative upper tract carcinogens and upper tract cancers. Similar to Chapter 1, we classify the evidence as sufficient, limited, or inadequate for a causal association.

ENVIRONMENTAL RISK FACTORS

Geography (Balkan Nephropathy)

The incidence and mortality figures for upper tract cancers are vastly higher in certain areas of southern Europe and parallel the incidence of an endemic form of tubulointerstitial nephropathy known as Balkan endemic nephropathy (BEN).[7] In one study by Petronic and colleagues, incidence rates of upper tract cancers were 100 to 200 times higher in areas afflicted with BEN.[19] BEN is confined to a relatively well-circumscribed rural areas in the Balkans incorporating parts of Serbia, Croatia, Bosnia, Bulgaria, and Romania.[20] For unknown reasons, incidence has dramatically fallen in certain areas over the past 10 years.[20] BEN-associated tumors trend toward lower histologic grade and bilaterality compared with non–BEN-associated tumors. Considerable debate exists as to whether BEN is also a risk factor for urothelial bladder cancer (see Chapter 1).

Although there is sufficient evidence to indicate that residents of BEN-endemic areas are at higher risk for upper tract tumors, the etiologic agent responsible for BEN remains elusive. Hypothetical factors include aristolochic acid, mycotoxins (ochratoxin A), viral vectors, and defective embryogenesis.[21–24]

Ochratoxin A

Ochratoxin A is the most well-studied candidate agent for BEN. This nephrotoxic fungal metabolite (mycotoxin) is known to be present in high concentrations in the Balkans and is a common contaminant among foods, drink, and animal feed.[21,25] This compound is both a known genotoxin and nephrotoxin. Exposure of pigs to ochratoxin A causes porcine nephropathy, which is histologically similar to human BEN.[26,27] In one international study, tumor tissues from patients from France and Bulgaria were compared for levels of ochratoxin-DNA adducts. No adducts were detected in the tissue of French patients, and high levels were found among the tumors of Bulgarian patients.[28] There is sufficient evidence that ochratoxin A is the etiologic agent for BEN and urothelial upper tract cancers.

Viral Etiology

The cyclical and sporadic nature of the BEN incidence has led some investigators to pursue the possibility of a viral origin.[23] Most attention has been directed toward a coronavirus termed endemic Balkan nephropathy virus. This virus has been isolated from kidney tissue among patients with BEN.[29] One recent study demonstrated that 87% of patients with end-stage renal disease in endemic areas had evidence of viral exposure, compared with 74% of people in the endemic area who did not have the disease.[29] Only 14% of individuals outside the nephropathic endemic areas demonstrated serologic evidence of exposure. Although these data suggest that people within the endemic areas are infected with this agent, the lack of significant differences between cases and controls within the endemic area raises many questions about whether this is the responsible agent.

Aristolochic Acid

Aristolochic acid is a known urothelial carcinogen and is primarily discussed in the context of Chi-

nese herb nephropathy (CHN).[22] Because of epidemiologic similarities between CHN and BEN, investigators have attempted to determine if aristolochic acid could be the agent that causes BEN. No firm scientific investigation has confirmed this hypothesis.

Renal Embryologic Anomalies

Nenov and Nenov have hypothesized that BEN may be a form of renal dysplasia.[24] The evidence for this hypothesis is based on the observation of a high incidence of renal dysplasia and hypoplasia among patients with BEN. There is also a reported higher incidence of renal vascular anomalies and Fanconi-type syndrome in renal tubular dysfunction.[24] They rationalize that because BEN is a relatively new condition (has never affected more than two generations) and has recently declined in incidence, it may represent the effects of an environmental agent.[20] Although this hypothesis is attractive, there is little evidence aside from circumstantial. It is also plausible that the agent responsible for BEN could also induce renal dysgenesis.

Cigarette Smoking

As mentioned earlier in this chapter, it is pragmatic to assume that almost all well-recognized carcinogens for bladder cancer are also risk factors for upper tract tumors. It is thus not surprising that smokers have a threefold increased risk. Some studies suggest that the risk is higher within the ureter versus the renal pelvis, although confirmatory studies do not exist.[30,31]

Laxatives

Laxatives have been implicated as uroepithelial carcinogens. Although there is no convincing evidence for laxative use as a risk factor for urothelial cancer, some studies suggest that an association may exist. In the Berlin Urothelial Cancer Study, habitual users of laxatives had a ninefold increased risk of upper tract cancer compared with only a twofold increased risk for bladder cancer.[32] These interesting observations require further study.

Analgesic Nephropathy

Phenacetin, a commonly consumed over-the-counter analgesic in the 1960s and 1970s, is a well-accepted uroepithelial carcinogen.[32-34] Although it may be a weak bladder carcinogen, the preferential urothelial target associated with phenacetin is the upper tracts. Phenacetin is primarily a tubulointerstitial nephrotoxin.[34] An epidemic of end-stage renal disease secondary to analgesic abuse occurred in the Western world in the 1970s and 1980s secondary to this phenomenon. Phenacetin users are at particular risk of renal pelvic tumors. One recent German study suggested that the elevated risk was approximately fivefold, with an appropriate dose-response relationship.[32]

The removal of phenacetin from the analgesic market in Scandinavia, Australia, and New Zealand has had dramatic effects on the incidence of analgesic nephropathy.[34] The metabolic relatives of phenacetin, acetaminophen, and paracetomol; are currently the analgesics of choice in the Western world. There is currently insufficient evidence linking these two agents with urothelial cancer; however, latency issues mandate that this association be continuously monitored.[35]

Aristolochia Fangchi

CHN is a progressive form of renal insufficiency secondary to tubulointerstitial nephropathy.[36-38] This form of nephropathy is associated with the consumption of a variety of weight reducing over-the-counter herbal products. *Aristolochia fangchi* is the herb that has been identified as being the likely candidate for CHN, likely as a result from exposure to aristolochic acid. Aristolochic acid is also a uroepithelial carcinogen.[36] Laboratory and molecular epidemiologic studies have shown that this agent is a potent genotoxin and nephrotoxin.[36,37]

It has recently been recognized that *Aristolochia fangchi* exposure significantly raises the risk of urothelial cancers, particularly of the upper tracts. In one study by Nortier and colleagues, among 39 patients with CHN, 46% had evidence of urothelial cancer, 94% of which were either in the ureter or renal pelvis.[39] The association of CHN and upper tract cancers illustrates a rare example of which the causal association is so strong that standard epidemiologic studies are of minimal value. The strong causal association coupled with similarities between CHN and BEN has led investigators to examine whether this agent may be playing a role in BEN; studies to date have been negative.[40]

Cyclophosphamide

Although primarily associated with urothelial bladder cancers, cyclophosphamide is probably also a significant upper tract carcinogen. Fifteen reported cases of upper tract tumors have been reported.[41] Because the denominator is unknown, it is difficult to know whether the association is causal or not.

Chronic Infection/Stones

Although never formally studied using traditional epidemiologic methods, most investigators believe that patients with chronic upper tract inflammation from recurrent or persistent stone disease or ureteritis cystica are at elevated risk for upper tract tumors.[42,43] These tumors tend to be squamous cell carcinoma or adenocarcinoma secondary to metaplastic change. Although the denominator is not known, few doubt the validity of this observation. The relative increase in risk associated with these conditions is largely unknown.

Hypertension

It has long been hypothesized that patients with hypertension are at higher risk of renal tumors.[44] Recent studies have suggested that hypertensive patients may also be at higher risk for upper tract urothelial tumors.[45] Hypothetical causes for this association include renal inflammation, drugs used to treat hypertension, and chronic dehydration (secondary to diuretics).[46] This association is also often confounded by cigarette smoking. Although ascertainment bias owing to microhematuria is plausible, the lack of asymptomatic upper tract tumors makes this unlikely. There is currently insufficient evidence for this association; however, further investigation is warranted.

HEREDITARY FACTORS

There are no-well accepted familial cancer syndromes associated with bladder cancer. Upper tract cancers have, however, been linked with the Lynch syndrome type II.[47] This syndrome is characterized by colonic tumors at early onset, which tend toward a right-sided distribution. Although it appears that these tumors are associated with Lynch syndrome, the rarity of cases makes a causal association difficult to implicate.

SUMMARY

Upper tract urethelial carcinomas are relatively uncommon. Tumors of the renal pelvis and ureter represent approximately 5% and 1 to 2% of urothelial tumors, respectively. The rare incidence has made the determination of epidemiologic associations difficult. Nonetheless, some observations about upper tract urothelial cancers raise some important etiologic hypotheses about cancer ontogeny and biology. This chapter has presented a comprehensive review of the epidemiology of upper tract urothelial carcinoma. We have reviewed the mechanisms of upper tract carcinogenesis and evidence for epidemiologic associations between a host of environmental and genetic risk factors.

It stands to reason that virtually and well-accepted risk factor for urothelial cancer of the bladder (except schistosomiasis, which is limited to the bladder) is also probably a risk factor for upper tract cancers. This observation is pragmatic as aside from contact time with exposed urothelium; there are no metabolic or physical changes in the composition of urine between the collecting ducts and the bladder. Unlike bladder cancers, however, a second mechanism of carcinogenesis exists that seems to be somewhat specific of the upper tracts. In this case, inflammation of the collecting systems, usually as a result of nephrotoxin exposure (and tubulo-interstitial nephritis), leads to upper tract cancers.[18] These cancers are more common in the renal pelvis, and are often associated with end-stage renal disease.

Epidemiologic-associated environmental risk factors reviewed in this chapter included, smoking, laxatives, analgesics, cyclophosphamide, chronic inflammation, and hypertension. An extensive review of Balkan Endemic Nephropathy, and its hypothesized causes, have also been included.

REFERENCES

1. Maranchie JK, Linehan WM. Genetic disorders and renal cell carcinoma. Urol Clin North Am 2003;30:133–41.
2. Huben RP. Tumor markers in bladder cancer. Urology 1984; 23:10–7.
3. Jemal A, Tiwari RC, Murray T, et al. Cancer statistics, 2004. CA Cancer J Clin 2004;54:8–29.
4. Munoz JJ, Ellison LM. Upper tract urothelial neoplasms: incidence and survival during the last 2 decades. J Urol 2000;164:1523–5.
5. Resseguie LJ, Nobrega FT, Farrow GM, et al. Epidemiology of renal and ureteral cancer in Rochester, Minnesota, 1950–1974, with special reference to clinical and pathologic features. Mayo Clin Proc 1978;53:503–10.
6. Messing EM. Urothelial tumors of the urinary tract. In: Walsh P, Retik A, Vaughan D, Wein A, editors. Campbell's urology. 8th ed. Philadelphia: WB Saunders; 2002. p. 2732.
7. Djukanovic L, Bukvic D, Maric I, et al. Open questions on Balkan nephropathy. Nephrol Dial Transplant 2001;16 Suppl 6:27–9.
8. Yang MH, Chen KK, Yen CC, et al. Unusually high incidence of upper urinary tract urothelial carcinoma in Taiwan. Urology 2002;59:681–7.
9. Solsona E, Iborra I, Ricos JV, et al. Extravesical involvement in patients with bladder carcinoma in situ: biological and therapy implications. J Urol 1996;155:895–9; discussion 899–900.
10. Cookson MS, Herr HW, Zhang ZF, et al. The treated natural history of high risk superficial bladder cancer: 15-year outcome. J Urol 1997;158:62–7.
11. Shinka T, Uekado Y, Aoshi H, et al. Occurrence of uroepithelial tumors of the upper urinary tract after the initial diagnosis of bladder cancer. J Urol 1988;140:745–8.
12. Abercrombie GF, Eardley I, Payne SR, et al. Modified nephro-ureterectomy. Long-term follow-up with particular reference to subsequent bladder tumours. Br J Urol 1988;61:198–200.
13. Huben RP, Gaeta J. Pathology and its importance in evaluating outcome in patients with superficial bladder cancer. Semin Urol Oncol 1996;1 Suppl 1:23–9.
14. Holmang S, Hedelin H, Anderstrom C, et al. Long-term followup of a bladder carcinoma cohort: routine followup urography is not necessary. J Urol 1998;160:45–8.
15. Takahashi T, Kakehi Y, Mitsumori K, et al. Distinct microsatellite alterations in upper urinary tract tumors and subsequent bladder tumors. J Urol 2001;165:672–7.
16. Hafner C, Knuechel R, Zanardo L, et al. Evidence for oligoclonality and tumor spread by intraluminal seeding in multifocal urothelial carcinomas of the upper and lower urinary tract. Oncogene 2001;20:4910–5.
17. Uchida T, Wang C, Wada C, et al. Microsatellite instability in transitional cell carcinoma of the urinary tract and its relationship to clinicopathological variables and smoking. Int J Cancer 1996;69:142–5.

18. Thon WF, Kliem V, Truss MC, et al. Denovo urothelial carcinoma of the upper and lower urinary tract in kidney—transplant patients with end-stage analgesic nephropathy. World J Urol 1995;13:254–61.

19. Petronic VJ, Bukurov NS, Djokic MR, et al. Balkan endemic nephropathy and papillary transitional cell tumors of the renal pelvis and ureters. Kidney Int Suppl 1991;34:S77–9.

20. Cukuranovic R, Petrovic B, Cukuranovic Z, Stefanovic V. Balkan endemic nephropathy: a decreasing incidence of the disease. Pathol Biol (Paris) 2000;48:558–61.

21. Abouzied MM, Horvath AD, Podlesny PM, et al. Ochratoxin A concentrations in food and feed from a region with Balkan endemic nephropathy. Food Addit Contam 2002;19:755–64.

22. Arlt VM, Ferluga D, Stiborova M, et al. Is aristolochic acid a risk factor for Balkan endemic nephropathy-associated urothelial cancer? Int J Cancer 2002;101:500–2.

23. Riquelme C, Escors D, Ortego J, et al. Nature of the virus associated with endemic Balkan nephropathy. Emerg Infect Dis 2002;8:869–70.

24. Nenov VD, Nenov DS. Balkan nephropathy: a disorder of renal embryogenesis? Am J Nephrol 2002;22:260–5.

25. Iavicoli I, Brera C, Carelli G, et al. External and internal dose in subjects occupationally exposed to ochratoxin A. Int Arch Occup Environ Health 2002;75:381–6.

26. Stoev SD, Vitanov S, Anguelov G, et al. Experimental mycotoxic nephropathy in pigs provoked by a diet containing ochratoxin A and penicillic acid. Vet Res Commun 2001; 25:205–23.

27. Stoev SD. The role of ochratoxin A as a possible cause of Balkan endemic nephropathy and its risk evaluation. Vet Hum Toxicol 1998;40:352–60.

28. Pfohl-Leszkowicz A, Grosse Y, Castegnaro M, et al. Ochratoxin A-related DNA adducts in urinary tract tumours of Bulgarian subjects. IARC Sci Publ 1993;124:141–8.

29. Uzelac-Keserovic B, Spasic P, Bojanic N, et al. Isolation of a coronavirus from kidney biopsies of endemic Balkan nephropathy patients. Nephron 1999;81:141–5.

30. McLaughlin JK, Silverman DT, Hsing AW, et al. Cigarette smoking and cancers of the renal pelvis and ureter. Cancer Res 1992;52:254–7.

31. Jensen OM, Knudsen JB, McLaughlin JK, Sorensen BL. The Copenhagen case-control study of renal pelvis and ureter cancer: role of smoking and occupational exposures. Int J Cancer 1988;41:557–61.

32. Pommer W, Bronder E, Klimpel A, et al. Urothelial cancer at different tumour sites: role of smoking and habitual intake of analgesics and laxatives. Results of the Berlin Urothelial Cancer Study. Nephrol Dial Transplant 1999;14:2892–7.

33. Stewart JH, Hobbs JB, McCredie MR. Morphologic evidence that analgesic-induced kidney pathology contributes to the progression of tumors of the renal pelvis. Cancer 1999;86:1576–82.

34. McCredie M, Stewart J, Smith D, et al. Observations on the effect of abolishing analgesic abuse and reducing smoking on cancers of the kidney and bladder in New South Wales, Australia, 1972–1995. Cancer Causes Control 1999;10:303–11.

35. Linet MS, Chow WH, McLaughlin JK, et al. Analgesics and cancers of the renal pelvis and ureter. Int J Cancer 1995; 62:15–8.

36. Arlt VM, Stiborova M, Schmeiser HH. Aristolochic acid as a probable human cancer hazard in herbal remedies: a review. Mutagenesis 2002;17:265–77.

37. Stiborova M, Hajek M, Frei E, Schmeiser HH. Carcinogenic and nephrotoxic alkaloids aristolochic acids upon activation by NADPH: cytochrome P450 reductase form adducts found in DNA of patients with Chinese herbs nephropathy. Gen Physiol Biophys 2001;20:375–92.

38. Lord GM, Cook T, Arlt VM, et al. Urothelial malignant disease and Chinese herbal nephropathy. Lancet 2001;358: 1515–6.

39. Nortier JL, Martinez MC, Schmeiser HH, et al. Urothelial carcinoma associated with the use of a Chinese herb (*Aristolochia fangchi*). N Engl J Med 2000;342:1686–92.

40. Arlt VM, Pfohl-Leszkowicz A, Cosyns J, Schmeiser HH. Analyses of DNA adducts formed by ochratoxin A and aristolochic acid in patients with Chinese herb nephropathy. Mutat Res 2001;494:143–50.

41. Shiga Y, Suzuki K, Tsutsumi M, Ishikawa S. Transitional cell carcinoma of the renal pelvis in a patient with cyclophosphamide therapy for malignant lymphoma: a case report and literature review. Hinyokika Kiyo 2002;48:301–5.

42. Beyer-Boon ME, Cuypers LH, de Voogt HJ, Brussee JA. Cytological changes due to urinary calculi: a consideration of the relationship between calculi and the development of urothelial carcinoma. Br J Urol 1978;50:81–9.

43. Richmond HG, Robb WA. Adenocarcinoma of the ureter secondary to ureteritis cystica. Br J Urol 1967;39:359–63.

44. McCredie M, Stewart JH. Risk factors for kidney cancers in New South Wales, Australia II. Urologic disease, hypertension, obesity and hormonal factors. Cancer Causes Control 1992;3:323–31.

45. Liaw KL, Linet MS, McLaughlin JK, et al. Possible relation between hypertension and cancers of the renal pelvis and ureter. Int J Cancer 1997;70:265–8.

46. Grossman E, Messerli FH, Goldbourt U. Carcinogenicity of antihypertensive therapy. Curr Hypertens Rep 2002;4: 195–201.

47. Rohde D, Jaske G. Involvement of the urogenital tract in patients with five or more separate malignant neoplasms. Eur Urol 1998;34:512–7.

Diagnosis and Staging of Upper Tract Urothelial Cancer

MURALI K. ANKEM, MD
KENNETH B. CUMMINGS, MD

Carcinomas of the renal pelvis and ureter are rare malignant tumors that account for only 2 to 5% of all urothelial tumors.[1,2] As per the American Cancer Society statistics, renal pelvic transitional cell carcinoma (TCC) accounted for 15% of renal tumors.[3] Ureteral tumors are even more uncommon, occurring with one quarter the incidence of renal pelvic tumors, and account for less than 1% of all genitourinary malignant tumors.[4] There has been a 30-fold increase in the incidence of upper tract TCC secondary to improvement in the diagnostic techniques and higher survival rates of bladder cancer patients, who are at a greater risk than the general population.[5] The incidence in white males is 10 cases per 100,000 per year. Ureteral tumors are twice as common in men as in women and twice as common in whites as blacks.[6] The peak incidence is in the fifth and sixth decades with a mean age of occurrence at 67 years.[3] The distal ureter is reported as the primary site in 73%, the mid ureter in 24%, and the proximal ureter in only 3% of the patients.[7] Bilateral involvement (synchronous or metachronous) occurs in 2 to 5% of upper tract TCC cases.[8] Upper tract tumors occur in 2 to 4% of patients with bladder cancer.[9] Although intravenous urograms are not routinely recommended after diagnosis of bladder cancer, certain high-risk groups such as patients with high grade, multiple, recurrent tumors and tumors involving the ureteral orifice should be evaluated with an intravenous urogram to rule out upper tract lesions. About 30 to 75% of patients with upper tract TCC will have concurrent or subsequent bladder tumors.[10]

Tumors of the urothelium represent a diffuse instability of the entire urothelium and careful monitoring with intravenous urography, endoscopy, and cytology on a periodic basis is highly recommended. Environmental exposure to substances like aromatic amines, tobacco, phenacetin, association with chronic inflammation, and Balkan nephropathy have been linked to the genesis of upper tract urothelial tumors.

CLINICAL PRESENTATION

The most common presenting symptom of upper urinary tract tumor is gross or microscopic painless hematuria, which is seen in 80% of patients (Table 19–1)[1,8,11] Total hematuria suggests upper tract or bladder bleeding. The duration of symptoms prior to diagnosis may be relatively short, because hematuria is usually a sudden, dramatic, and anxiety producing event that compels the patient to seek urgent medical care. Flank pain is seen in one third of the patients and is usually dull continuous pain secondary to gradual development of hydronephrosis. Uremia sec-

Table 19–1 CLINICAL MANIFESTATIONS OF UPPER TRACT UROTHELIAL CANCER	
Symptom	Incidence (%)
Hematuria	80
Flank pain	30
Incidental finding	10–15
Irritative voiding symptoms	5–10
Constitutional symptoms	5
History of urothelial tumor	16
Uremia	4

ondary to obstructed solitary or poorly functioning kidneys may be the initial presentation. Acute flank pain with passage of vermiform blood clots is not an uncommon presenting symptom. Upper tract tumors are detected in 10 to 15% of patients as an incidental finding on imaging studies done for other reasons.[12] Irritative voiding symptoms are seen in 5 to 10% of patients and constitutional symptoms in approximately 5% of patients.[13] Usually physical findings are absent, but occasionally a flank mass secondary to hydronephrosis may be present. Occasionally TCC of kidney may present as a large renal mass similar to renal cell cancer (Figure 19–1); urine cytology would be useful in these circumstances.

EVALUATION

Renal pelvic and ureteral tumors are not uncommon and at times are difficult diagnostic challenges for the urologist. The differentiation between benign and malignant causes of upper tract filling defects is critical to avoid unnecessary nephroureterectomy.

The diagnostic evaluation of the patient presenting with hematuria and recurrent irritative voiding symptoms is straightforward. Excretory urography (IVP) has been the standard method for diagnosing ureteral and renal pelvic tumors and is routinely performed early in the evaluation of patients with suspected neoplasia. A radiolucent filling defect on excretory urography is the most common radiologic finding in upper tract urothelial cancer (Figure

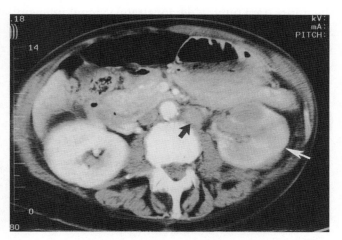

Figure 19–1. Transitional cell carcinoma (TCC) of kidney presenting as a large left renal mass (*arrow on the right*) with lymph node involvement (*arrow in the middle*).

19–2). These defects tend to be irregular and in continuity with the wall of the collecting system.[8] The differential diagnosis of a radiolucent filling defect in the collecting system (Table 19–2) includes malignancy, blood clot, radiolucent calculi, fungus ball, air bubble, artifact, overlying bowel gas, sloughed papilla, malakoplakia, external compression of collecting system by a crossing vessel, or a benign lesion such as ureteritis cystica.[12] A tumor may produce incomplete filling or nonfilling of an infundibulum or a calyx. It is noteworthy that ureteral obstruction on an IVP is a sign of advanced disease[11] and nonvisualization of collecting system is seen in 10 to 30% of cases.[7]

Abnormal findings on excretory urography falls into one of five categories (Table 19–3): (1) a filling defect within the renal collecting system (35%); (2) filling defects in the distended calyces (26%); (3) calyceal obliteration and amputation (19%); (4) hydronephrosis with soap bubble nephrogram; or (5) reduced or nonfunction without enlargement of kidney (13%). Contrast caught in the papillary fronds gives a stippled appearance on the urograms (Stipple sign).[5] An obstructing lesion with a dilated ureter distal to the lesion is known as Goblet sign or Champagne-glass sign.[5] Bergman's sign, coiling of the ureteral catheter immediately distal to the tumor, has been reported as pathognomonic for this neoplasm.[5]

In the clinical scenario of poor renal function, contrast allergy, or partial or complete nonvisualization of the collecting system, a retrograde pyelogram (RPG) is indicated. Overall, retrograde pyelogram is accurate in establishing the diagnosis of upper tract TCC in 75% of cases (Figures 19–3 and 19–4).[8] It is prudent to study the contralateral side and look for multiple tumors on either side, which might alter the treatment options.[13]

Percutaneous antegrade pyelography is not recommended because of the theoretical risk of seeding the needle tract. It may be considered as a last resort when the excretory urogram is inconclusive and retrograde pyelography could not be done. Even then computed tomography (CT) is a better alternative in those situations.[12]

Ultrasonography is occasionally used to differentiate a calculus from a neoplasm, but its role in the diagnosis and staging of upper tract neoplasia is minimal.[12]

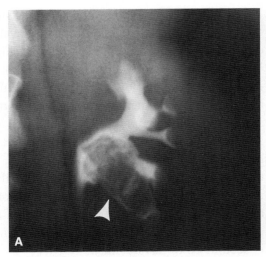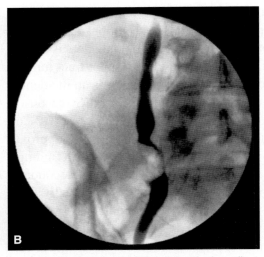

Figure 19–2. *A*, Radiolucent filling defect on excretory urography. *B*, Radiolucent filling defect in the collecting system.

Computed tomography scan is useful for both diagnostic and staging purposes. It is helpful in determining the local extent of the primary tumor as well as in evaluating the metastases by showing extension into the renal parenchyma, periureteral soft tissues, venous involvement,[14] lymph node involvement (see Figure 19–1) and liver metastasis. CT offers good sensitivity (87.5%) and specificity (98%) in the detection of lymph node involvement, and 64% sensitivity and 97% specificity for the detection of renal parenchymal invasion.[15] CT scanning usually shows soft tissue masses of an average density of 46 Hounsfield units (range, 10–70) as shown in Figures 19–5 and 19–6.[16] Three classic patterns can be noted on a CT scan: (1) a focal intraluminal mass, (2) ureteral/pelvic wall thickening, and (3) an infiltrating mass. It is very important to perform thin CT slices (3–5mm) at adjacent levels through the abnormality before and after administration of intravenous contrast material. As the urothelial tumors are usually hypovascular, compared to renal cell carcinomas, they usually do not enhance after intravenous contrast administration. Takebayashi and colleagues reported their experience with an innovative technique called CT ureteroscopy. CT or virtual endoscopy using surface rendering techniques enables imaging of the interior of a target organ by extracting CT data from only the boundary regions between the organ walls and contrast material. CT ureteroscopy is a practical and acceptable technique that is promising for the detection of ureteral tumors and distinction from ureteral stricture.[17]

On magnetic resonance imaging (MRI) scans, the upper tract tumors demonstrate a signal intensity similar to muscle on T_1-weighted images and slightly higher relative signal intensity on T_2-weighted images. This is similar to signal character-

Table 19–2. DIFFERENTIAL DIAGNOSIS OF A FILLING DEFECT ON IVP/RGP
Malignant lesion
Blood clot
Radiolucent calculi
Fungus ball
Air bubble
Artifact
Overlying bowel gas
Sloughed papillae
Malakoplakia
Ureteritis cystica
Vascular impression
Inflammatory process

Table 19–3. FINDINGS ON EXCRETORY UROGRAM	
Defect	Number Shown (%)
Discrete filling defect	35
Filling defects in the distended calyces	26
Calyceal obliteration and amputation	19
Hydronephrosis with soap bubble nephrogram	
Reduced or nonfunction	13
Stipple sign	
Goblet or Champagne-glass sign	
Bergman's sign	

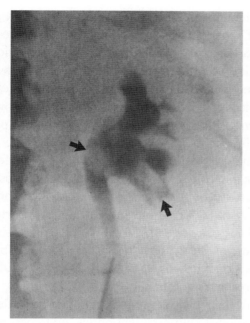

Figure 19–3. Arrows depict filling defect on retrograde pyelogram.

istics of transitional cell carcinomas (TCCs) of bladder. Ureteral carcinomas may also present as diffuse, usually symmetric wall thickening, which is readily demonstrated by MRI. However, MRI has not proved to be superior to CT scanning either in diagnosis or staging of upper tract urothelial cancer.[18]

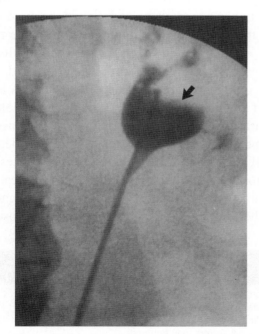

Figure 19–4. Arrow shows calyceal amputation on retrograde pyelogram.

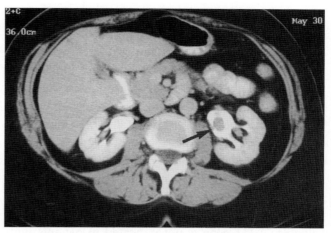

Figure 19–5. CT scan showing an intraluminal lesion in continuity with the wall of the renal pelvis (*arrow*).

The role of cross-sectional imaging (CT and MRI) in the diagnosis and staging of upper tract TCC is controversial. Proponents claim that these modalities not only can demonstrate the tumor, but also can accurately stage the disease unlike IVP and RPG. CT and MRI depict streaking in the periureteral fat adjacent to tumor, which in the absence of prior surgery, inflammation, or radiation, is indicative of periureteral spread. CT and MRI are accurate in identifying spread to lymph nodes or other distant sites. These modalities are also important in the evaluation of an obstructed ureter secondary to tumor in the bladder, and scarring and/or distortion of the ureter secondary to resection of the ureteral orifice in the bladder. CT and MRI are also important in the evaluation of a response to neoadjuvant chemotherapy for advanced upper tract

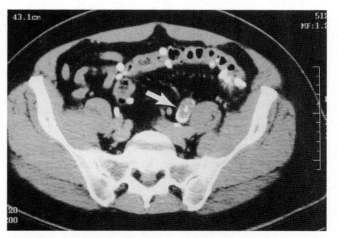

Figure 19–6. CT scan showing an intraluminal lesion with thickening of the ureter (*arrow*).

TCC.[16] The inaccuracy of CT in the preoperative staging of upper tract urothelial cancer has been previously reported.[19–22] Scolieri and colleagues[23] reported that the accuracy of a preoperative CT scan in patients with upper tract urothelial tumors is poor, and that routine performance of CT scanning is not recommended. They felt that the CT scan of the abdomen and pelvis did not accurately predict the tumor node metastasis (TNM) stage, and the ability to base treatment decisions is limited. They also suggested that if the clinical suspicion for advanced disease is high, for example with elevated liver function tests, a CT scan might be valuable. A CT scan is not indicated in patients with very low suspicion for advanced disease and in whom open surgery is being considered, because it is rarely used to guide the management decisions. The authors of this chapter have found the use of CT and MRI are immensely helpful in the diagnosis and staging of upper tract TCC and we routinely use these imaging studies for follow-up as well.

Renal arteriography is an invasive test and it is not commonly employed in the evaluation of upper tract urothelial cancer. Cummings and colleagues[24] described three classic findings on selective arteriogram for renal pelvic tumors, that included (1) encasement of intrarenal arteries, (2) hypertrophy of renal pelvic artery, and (3) tumor blush for tumors larger than 3 cm in diameter.

Cystoscopy is a mandatory component of complete evaluation of upper tract TCC because of the significant association with bladder tumors. Ideally, cystoscopy should be performed during an episode of hematuria so that the source of bleeding can be lateralized.

Routine voided or catheterized urinary cytology studies are of limited value because of the high incidence of false positive and negative results. Low-grade TCC is believed to have greater cell-to-cell adherence than high-grade disease. This may, in part, account for the lower sensitivity of urinary cytology in low-grade TCC.[25] On the other hand, urine cytology often is useful in detecting high-grade, more aggressive malignancies because such cell types will be present in voided or catheterized urine collections owing to their lack of cell-to-cell cohesiveness. Urine cytology sensitivity increases as tumor anaplasia increases, varying from 11% for grade 1 to 83% for grade 4 lesions.[26]

Even though the urine cytology is positive in a given case of upper tract filling defect, one cannot be certain of the origin of those cells. Ureteral catheterization for collection of urine from the renal collecting system provides more accurate results.[26] Gill and colleagues introduced a concept of brush biopsy to improve the sampling. A brush mounted on a guide wire is passed through a ureteric catheter under fluoroscopic guidance and used to brush the suspected filling defects.[27] Sheline and colleagues reported that brush biopsy has a sensitivity of 91%, a specificity of 88%, and an accuracy of 89%.[28] Blute and colleagues reported an overall accuracy rate of 78%.[29] With the increased use of endoscopic techniques for visualization and biopsy of upper tract lesions, the use of retrograde catheters with brushes is questionable.

With the recent development of rigid and flexible ureteroscopes with excellent optics, ureteroscopy has become a valuable tool in the diagnosis of upper tract tumors. Ureteroscopy can be used to access upper tract filling defects for inspection and sampling (Figure 19–7). It has been a highly successful diagnostic technique with few (7%) serious complications.[33] Using endourologic techniques, Blute and colleagues demonstrated improved diagnostic accuracy with renal pelvic tumors (86%) and ureteral tumors (90%) over the standard evaluation with IVP, RPG, and cytology.[2,30–33] Nevertheless, diagnostic ureteroscopy is an invasive procedure and should be used only when the diagnosis is in doubt, and when the treatment would be influenced by the results of ureteroscopy. A potential problem associated with endoscopic management of upper tract tumors is the lack of reliability in staging.[2,34] Addition of endoluminal ultrasonography to the endourology armamentarium increased the accuracy of staging and demonstrated invasion of tumor in a few cases.[35,36] Nephroscopy via pyelotomy or percutaneous nephrostomy tract has been reported as a valuable diagnostic and therapeutic tool.[28,37,38] However, nephrostomy

Table 19–4. APPEARANCE OF TRANSITIONAL CELL CARCINOMA ON CT

Intraluminal mass
   Ureteral/pelvic wall thickening
Infiltrating renal mass
   Regional spread to lymph nodes
   Metastatic spread to liver or other sites

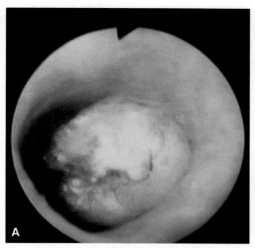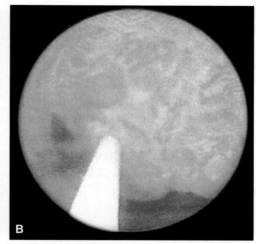

Figure 19–7.   Ureteroscopy showing a solid intraluminal lesion in a patient.

tube tract and retroperitoneum tumor cell implantation have been noted in some patients.[39] We have been reluctant to recommend percutaneous nephroscopy for diagnosis and treatment of upper tract tumor for any but the most exceptional cases (Figure 19–8).

Regarding biomarkers, data are not available to demonstrate their clinical utility as diagnostic or prognostic tools that can assist in the management of upper tract urothelial cancer.

TUMOR GRADING AND STAGING

Tumor stage and grade are clinically the most useful prognostic variables in patients with upper tract urothelial tumors.[24] A strong correlation exists between the grade and the stage, and the tumor stage

is more important than the grade.[24,40] Huben and associates[40] observed that the median survival for low-grade tumors was 67 months; for high-grade tumors, median survival was only 14 months. The median survival for low-stage tumors was 91 months and for high-stage tumors only 13 months. In the Mostofi system (devised for and adopted by the World Health Organization [WHO]) there are three grades depending on the cellular anaplasia, highly differentiated to poorly differentiated.[41] In grade 1 tumors, the cells resemble normal transitional cells. Papillary configuration and increase in the number of cell layers, (ie, more than seven layers) helps the pathologist to diagnose grade 1 TCC. Moderately differentiated (grade 2) has a wider fibrovascular core, disturbance of cellular maturation, loss of polarity, occasional mitotic figures, and more nuclear pleomorphism with prominent nucleoli. Grade 3 tumors have cells with poor differentiation, marked pleomorphism, and more frequent mitotic figures.[41]

The difficulty in establishing the diagnosis as well as the limited accuracy of staging procedures

Figure 19–8.   Percutaneous nephroscopy showing a papillary lesion in the renal pelvis.

Table 19–5. EVALUATION OF SUSPECTED UPPER TRACT UROTHELIAL NEOPLASM
Excretory urogram
Retrograde pyelogram
Voided urine cytology
Cytoscopy with selective upper tract cytology
Ureteropyeloscopy and biopsy
CT scan/MRI

has precluded the development of a useful clinical staging system. Staging is thus usually based on the pathologic findings. Batata and Grabstald proposed a classification, which is similar to the Jewett and Marshall system for bladder cancer (Table 19–6).[1] This was later modified by Cummings and colleagues (Figure 19–9).[24,42] TNM staging sponsored by the American Joint Committee on Cancer (AJCC) and the International Union against Cancer (UICC) is more widely used by clinicians and pathologists.[43,44]

AJCC–UICC TNM CLASSIFICATION

Two different but related staging systems are now generally accepted for renal pelvic, and ureteral tumors: the TNM system of the UICC and the somewhat more convenient system of the AJCC. These systems apply only to carcinomas. Papillomas are excluded, as are nonepithelial and metastatic tumors. Histologic or cytologic confirmation is essential. The TNM classification derives its name from the three components of the staging system: T—tumor size and extent; N—regional lymph nodes involved, if any; and M—metastases to distant sites, if any.[45] By convention, the prefix "p" is used when staging is based on pathologic rather than exclusively clinical findings (ie, pT or pN) physical examination, imaging, and endoscopy are used for assessing the TNM categories. The current TNM staging by AJCC/UICC is summarized in Table 19–7.

Table 19–6. MODIFIED JEWETT SYSTEM

Stage	Description	5-Year Survival (%)
0	Confined to mucosa	100
A	Involvement through lamina propria	80-–95
B	Into muscular wall	40-–80
C	Periureteral spread	15-–33
D	Metastatic disease	0

Reprinted with permission from Crawford ED, Das S. Current genitourinary cancer surgery.[45]

PROGNOSIS

The 5-year survival rate for patients with Grade 1 TCC of the renal pelvis approaches 100%, for grade 2 it is 60 to 70%; and for grade 3, it is under 5%.[46] Corresponding 5-year survival rates for carcinoma of the ureter are 95% for stage A, 82% for stage B, 29% for stage C, and 0% for stage D.[47] Das and colleagues observed that there is no significant difference in survival by stage between patients with TCC of the renal pelvis or the ureter.[48] However, the data from TNM staging suggested that T3 renal pelvic TCC had a better prognosis than stage T3 ureteral TCC because of the renal parenchymal barrier.[3]

Nephroureterectomy has been the "gold standard" treatment for upper tract TCC; however, endoscopic treatment has been generally accepted in patients with a solitary kidney, bilateral disease, poor renal function or comorbidities precluding an open surgical procedure. Elliott and colleagues reported a local recurrence rate of 33%, with a mean time to recur-

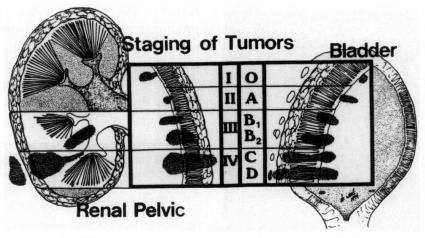

Figure 19–9. Proposed classification of renal and ureteral tumors modified from Grabstald and Jewett and Strong.[1]

Table 19–7. TNM STAGING SYSTEMS FOR CANCER OF RENAL PELVIS AND URETER

Primary Tumor [T]

TX	Primary tumor cannot be assessed
T0	No evidence of primary tumor
Ta	Papillary noninvasive carcinoma
Tis	Carcinoma in situ
T1	Tumor invades subepithelial connective tissue
T2	Tumor invades the muscularis
T3	(For renal pelvis only) Tumor invades beyond the muscularis into peripelvic fat or renal parenchyma
T3	(For ureter only) Tumor invades beyond muscularis into periureteric fat
T4	Tumor invades adjacent organs, or through the kidney into the perinephric fat

Regional Lymph nodes [N]*

NX	Regional lymph nodes cannot be assessed
N0	No regional lymph node metastasis
N1	Metastasis in a single lymph node, 2 cm or less in the greatest dimension
N2	Metastasis in a single lymph node, more than 2 cm but not more than 5 cm in the greatest dimension; or multiple lymph nodes none more than 5 cm in greatest dimension
N3	Metastasis in a lymph node more than 5 cm in greatest dimension

Distant Metastasis [M]†

MX	Distant metastasis cannot be assessed
M0	No distant metastasis
M1	Distant metastasis

Stage Grouping

Stage 0a	Ta	N0	M0
Stage 0is	Tis	N0	M0
Stage 1	T1	N0	M0
Stage 2	T2	N0	M0
Stage 3	T3	N0	M0
Stage 4	T4	N0	M0
	Any T	N1	M0
	Any T	N2	M0
	Any T	N3	M0
	Any T	Any N	M1

Histopathologic Grade

GX	Grade cannot be assessed
G1	Well differentiated
G2	Moderately differentiated
G3	Poorly differentiated or undifferentiated

*Note: The following nodes are considered regional for renal pelvis: hilar, abdominal-paraaortic and paracaval nodes, and for ureter intrapelvic nodes as well. Laterality does not affect the N classification
†Note: The most common sites of distant metastases, in decreasing order of frequency, are lung, bone, and liver.
Source: From Renal pelvis and Ureter. American Joint Committee on Cancer-Manual for Staging of Cancer. Fifth ed. Philadelphia: Lippincott-Raven, 1997.[43]

rence of 7.3 months. Tumor progression occurred in 6% of cases and ultimately 19% of cases required a nephroureterectomy for the recurrence. Overall, 81% of target renal units were preserved.[49] High recurrence rates were noted after endoscopic surgery by several investigators. Chen and colleagues observed a 65% recurrence rate and 17% eventually required open radical surgery, with a renal salvage rate of 65%.[50] Stoller and colleagues reported that 44% of patients with renal pelvic tumors and 80% of ureteric tumors experienced recurrence.[51]

The use of endoscopic surgery for the management of upper tract TCC in patients with normally functioning kidneys remains extremely controversial. Existing data are from retrospective studies with only small numbers of patients and long-term results are not very clear. At this stage, endourologic treatment of upper-tract TCC should be limited to patients with a solitary kidney and low grade (Grade 1), low stage, small (less than 2 cm) completely visible and resectable lesions or to those who are poor surgical candidates. Despite the encouraging results from many studies, it remains our strong opinion that unless the aforementioned criteria are met and a skilled endourologist is available, nephroureterectomy remains the treatment of choice for the patient with upper-tract TCC and a normal contralateral kidney.

REFERENCES

1. Batata M, Grabstald H. Upper urinary tract urothelial tumors. Urol Clin North Am 1976;3:79–86.
2. Tawfiek ER, Bagley DH. Upper-tract transitional cell carcinoma. Urology 1997;50(3):321–29.
3. Guinan P, Vogelzang NJ, Randazzo R, et al. Renal pelvic cancer: a review of 611 patients treated in Illinois 1975–1985: Cancer Incidence and End Results Committee. Urology 1992;40:393–9.
4. Huben RP, Mounzer AM, Murphy GP. Tumor grade and stage as prognostic variables in upper tract urothelial tumors. Cancer 1988;62:2016–20.
5. Babaian RJ. Primary carcinoma of the upper urothelium: an overview. In: Crawford ED, editor. Current genitourinary cancer surgery. Philadelphia: Lea & Febiger; 1990. p. 93.
6. Annual cancer statistics review: including cancer trends: 1950–1985. Bethesda, MD; National Cancer Institute, US Department of Health and Human Services, NIH Publication no. 88–2789, 1987.
7. Babaian RJ, Johnson DE. Primary carcinoma of the ureter. J Urol 1980;123:357–9.
8. Murphy DM, Zincke H, Furlow WL. Management of high-grade transitional cell cancer of the upper urinary tract. J Urol 1981;125:25–9.
9. Shinka T, Uekado Y, Aoshi H, et al. Occurrence of uroepithelial tumors of the upper urinary tract after the initial diagnosis of bladder cancer. J Urol 1988;140:745–8.
10. Anderstrom C, Johansson SL, Pettersson S, Wahlquist L. Carcinoma of the ureter: a clinico-pathological study of 49 cases. J Urol 1989;142:2 pt 1:280–3.

11. Bloom NA, Vidone RA, Lytton B. Primary carcinoma of the ureter. A report of 102 cases. J Urol 1970;103:590–8.

12. Messing EM, Catalona WJ. Urothelial tumors of the urinary tract. In: Walsh PC, Retik AB, Vaughn ED Jr, Wein AJ, editors. Campbell's urology. Vol 3. 7th ed. Philadelphia: WB Saunders; 1998. p. 2327.

13. Haskell CM, Berek S, editors. Cancer treatment. 5th ed. Philadelphia: WB Saunders; 2001. p. 828–53

14. Williams JH, Frazier HA 2nd, Gawaith KE, et al. Transitional cell carcinoma of the kidney with tumor thrombus into the vena cava. Urology 1996;48(6): 932–5.

15. Millan-Rodruigez F, Palou J, de la Torre-Holguera P, et al. Conventional CT signs in staging transitional cell tumors of the upper urinary tract. Eur Urol 1999;35:318–22.

16. Lantz EJ, Hattery RR. Diagnostic imaging of urothelial cancer. Urol Clin North Am 1984;11:567–83.

17. Takebayashi S, Hosaka M, Kubota Y, et al. CT ureteroscopy for diagnosing ureteral tumors. J Urol 2000;163:42–6.

18. Milestone B, Friedman AC, Seidmon EJ, et al. Staging of ureteral transitional cell carcinoma by CT and MRI. Urology 1990;36(4):346–50.

19. McCoy JG, Honda H, Reznicek M, Williams RD. Computerized tomography for detection and staging of localized and pathologically defined upper tract urothelial tumors. J Urol 1991;146:1500–3.

20. Planz B, George R, Adam G, et al. Computerized tomography for detection and staging of transitional cell carcinoma of the upper urinary tract. Eur Urol 1995;27:146–50.

21. Baron RL, McClennan BL, Lee JK, et al. Computerized tomography of transitional carcinoma of the renal pelvis and the ureter. Radiology 1982;144:125–30.

22. Badalment RA, Bennett WF, Bova JG, et al. Computed tomography of primary transitional cell carcinoma of upper urinary tracts. Urology 1992;40:71–5.

23. Scolieri MJ, Paik ML, Brown SL, Resnick MI. Limitations of computed tomography in the preoperative staging of upper tract urothelial carcinoma. Urology 2000;56:930–4.

24. Cummings KB, Correa RJ Jr, Gibbons RP, et al. Renal pelvic tumors. J Urol 1975;113:158–62.

25. Rife CC, Farrow GM, Utz DC. Urine cytology of transitional cell neoplasms. Urol Clin North Am 1979;6(3):599–612.

26. Zincke H, Aguillo JJ, Farrow GM, et al. Significance of urinary cytology in the early detection of transitional cell cancer of the upper urinary tract. J Urol 1976;116:781–3.

27. Gill WB, Lu CT, Thomsen S. Retrograde brushing: a new technique for obtaining histologic and cytologic material from ureteral, renal pelvic and calyceal lesions. J Urol 1973;109:573–8.

28. Sheline M, Amendola MA, Pollack HM, et al. Flouroscopically guided retrograde brush biopsy in the diagnosis of transitional cell carcinoma of the upper urinary tract: results in 45 patients. AJR Am J Roentgenol 1989;153:313–6.

29. Blute RD Jr, Gittes RR, Gittes RF. Renal brush biopsy: survey of indications, techniques, and results. J Urol 1981; 126:146–9.

30. Streem SB, Pontes JE, Novick AC, Montie JE. Ureteropyeloscopy in the evaluation of upper tract filling defects. J Urol 1986;136:383–5.

31. Bagley DH, Rivas D. Upper urinary tract filling defects: flex-ible ureteroscopic diagnosis. J Urol 1990;143:1196–2000.

32. Kavoussi L, Clayman RV, Basler J. Flexible, actively deflectable fiberoptic ureterorenoscopy. J Urol 1989;142:949–54.

33. Blute ML, Segura JW, Patterson DE, et al. Impact of endourology on diagnosis and management of upper urinary tract urothelial cancer. J Urol 1989;141:1298–301.

34. Huffman JL, Bagley DH, Lyon ES, et al. Endoscopic diagnosis and treatment of upper tract urothelial tumors. A preliminary report. Cancer 1985;55:1422–8.

35. Bagley DH, Liu JB, Godberg BB. The use of endoluminal ultrasound of the ureter. Semin Urol 1992;10:194–8.

36. Liu JB, Bagley DH, Conlin MJ, et al. Endoluminal sonographic evaluation of ureteral and renal pelvic neoplasms. J Ultrasound Med 1997;16:515–21.

37. Gittes RF. Retrograde brushing and nephroscopy in the diagnosis of upper tract urothelial cancer. Urol Clin North Am 1984;11:617–22.

38. Smith AD, Orihuela E, Crowley AR. Percutaneous management of renal pelvic tumors. A treatment option in selected cases. J Urol 1987;137:852–6.

39. Huang A, Low RK, deVere White R. Nephrostomy tract tumor seeding following percutaneous manipulation of ureteral carcinoma. J Urol 1995;153:1041–2.

40. Huben RP, Mounzer AM, Murphy GP. Tumor grade and stage as prognostic variables in upper tract urothelial tumors. Cancer 1988;62:2016–20.

41. Mostofi FK, Sabin LH, Torloni J. Histological typing of urinary bladder tumors. In: WHO international histological classification of tumors, No.10. Geneva: WHO; 1973:1–274.

42. Cummings KB. Nephroureterectomy: rationale in the management of transitional cell carcinoma of the upper urinary tract. Urol Clin North Am 1980;7(3):569–78.

43. Renal pelvis and Ureter. American Joint Committee on Cancer. In: Manual for staging of cancer. 5th ed. Philadelphia: Lippincott-Raven; 1997. p. 235–7.

44. Sobin LH, Wittekind CH. Renal pelvis and ureter. TNM classification. In: TNM classification of malignant tumors/UICC, International Union Against Cancer. 5th ed. New York: Wiley-Liss; 1997. p. 183–6.

45. Crawford ED, Das S. Current genitourinary cancer surgery. Malvern, PA: Lea & Febiger; 1990. p. 106.

46. Grabstald H, Whitmore WF, Melamed MR. Renal pelvic tumors. JAMA 1971;218:845–54.

47. Heney NM, Nocks BN, Daly JJ, et al. Prognostic factors in carcinoma of ureter. J Urol 1981;125:623–6.

48. Das AK, Carson CC, Bolick D, Paulson DF. Primary carcinoma of the upper urinary tract: effect of primary and secondary treatment on survival. Cancer 1990;66:1919–23.

49. Elliott DS, Segura JW, Lightner D, Patterson DE, Blute ML. Is nephroureterectomy necessary in all cases of upper-tract transitional cell carcinoma? Long-term results of conservative endourologic management of upper-tract transitional cell carcinoma in individuals with a normal contralateral kidney. Urology 2001;58:174–8.

50. Chen GL, Bagley DH. Ureteroscopic management of upper tract transitional cell carcinoma in patients with normal contralateral kidneys. J Urol 2000;164(4):1173–6.

51. Stoller ML, Gentle DL, McDonald MW. Endoscopic management of upper tract urothelial tumors. Tech Urol 1997; 3:152–7.

Endoscopic and Radiologic Imaging of Urothelial Cancer of the Upper Urinary Tract and Bladder

DAVID I. LEE, MD

JAIME LANDMAN, MD

Recent advances in radiologic imaging and improvements in endoscopic technology offer the urologist of today a wide spectrum of powerful diagnostic tools for the detection of urothelial malignancies. The most common clinical presentation of patients with urothelial cancer is microscopic or gross painless hematuria.[1] Standard evaluation begins with: history and physical examination, urinalysis, microscopic urine evaluation, urine cytopathology, and urine culture. In the majority of cases, the presence of gross hematuria and sterile microscopic hematuria prompt further evaluation with radiologic imaging and cystoscopy to rule out a possible malignancy.

This chapter will discuss in detail the efficacy and utility of the various endoscopic and radiographic modalities that are currently clinically available to the practicing urologist. Although the standard evaluation of hematuria seeks to detect pathology throughout the entire urinary tract, evaluation for bladder and upper tract malignancy will be addressed specifically.

UPPER TRACTS

Upper Tract Endoscopy

The mainstay of diagnosis and surveillance for upper urinary tract transitional cell carcinoma (TCC) has been reliant on radiographic evaluation. The evolution of ureteroscopy with the widespread availability of small highly maneuverable flexible ureteroscopes has altered the urologist's complete dependence on radiologic findings, and has allowed the management of upper tract disease to become more similar to that of bladder cancer. The endoscopic appearance of TCC in the upper tract is similar to that in the lower urinary tract (Figure 20–1). The differential diagnoses of upper tract neoplasms include TCC, squamous cell carcinoma, adenocarcinoma, and fibroepithelial polyps. The first retrograde diagnostic

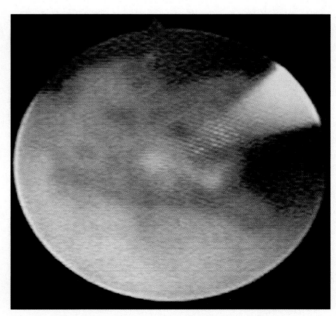

Figure 20–1. Ureteroscopic view of low-grade transitional cell carcinoma of the renal pelvis with laser fiber poised to resect the tumor.

333

endoscopy of the upper tracts was performed by Hugh Hampton Young in 1912.[2] Early work has demonstrated that the diagnostic sensitivity of an evaluation with ureteroscopy is increased from 58 to 83% over a work-up without ureteroscopy.[3]

The ability of flexible ureteroscopes to not only visualize, but also biopsy and ablate lesions of the upper urinary tracts has allowed selected patients to avoid highly morbid ablative procedures (open or laparoscopic nephroureterectomy) (Figure 20–2). Additionally, selected patients with solitary or functionally solitary kidneys may be spared dialysis or renal transplantation with ureteroscopic management of upper urinary tract disease. These indications have been extended to patients with normal contralateral kidneys in certain well-selected cases.

Chen and Bagley have described a technique to manage upper tract TCC ureteroscopically. The procedure begins with cystoscopy where cytology is taken. The retrograde pyelogram is performed with a cone-tip ureteral catheter. This serves as a "road map" for the rest of the case. A 6.9F semi-rigid ureteroscope is then carefully passed to visualize the distal ureter. An aspirated urine specimen is taken through the ureteroscope for cytologic evaluation. A floppy-tip guide wire is then placed carefully through the scope into the collecting system under fluoroscopic guidance. The flexible ureteroscope is then passed over the guidewire and the rest of the collecting system is endoscopically inspected. The delayed passage of the guidewire prevents confusion of areas of wire trauma and true urothelial lesions. If tumor is identified, it is biopsied with a 2.4F flat wire basket or 3F cup biopsy forceps. As the working channel of the currently available flexible ureteroscopes is very small, specimens are extracted by removal of the entire ureteroscope as a unit to maximize specimen recovery. After adequate biopsies have been achieved, combination laser therapy with the holmium and noedymium/yttrium-aluminum-garnet (Nd:YAG) are used to ablate all remaining visible tumor.[4]

The authors of this chapter use a similar technique, but find that a combination of the holmium laser and electrovaporization of lesions results in a more expeditious treatment with improved hemostasis. Additionally, we apply a ureteroscope that is currently available with a 4.3F working channel (Wolf model number 7330.072) (Figure 20–3). This ureteroscope allows passage of a 4.0F biopsy device which allows for a much more robust sample of tissue to be extracted than is possible with standard small caliber flexible ureteroscopes. The relatively large working channel of this ureteroscope permits application of larger caliber laser fibers and electrosurgical probes while still permitting good irrigant flow. We have found this ureteroscope very valuable for the diagnosis and treatment of TCC. For renal lesions, after inspection of the ureter, a ureteral access sheath (Applied Medical Resources, Rancho Santa Margarita, CA) is commonly placed if renal lesions are identified. The access sheath allows the

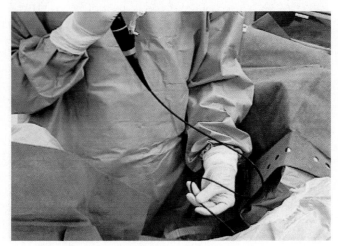

Figure 20–2. Demonstration of flexibility of small diameter, actively deflectable flexible ureteroscope.

Figure 20–3. Shown here is the tip of the Wolf flexible ureteroscope. Note the very large working channel.

operator repeated access to the renal collecting system throughout the case without additional trauma to the urethra, bladder, and ureter. The ureteral access sheath also maximizes irrigant flow while maintaining decreased intra-renal pressures. At the termination of the procedure, we unroof the ipsilateral ureteral tunnel. This maneuver facilitates future diagnostic and therapeutic procedures, and, in selected patients, will permit office ureteroscopic surveillance of the upper urinary tracts.

Chen and colleagues also compared the efficacy of urinary cytopathology, radiographic surveillance, and ureteroscopy.[5] In their series, 23 patients with previously resected upper tract TCC underwent a total of 88 surveillance procedures. Patients provided urine for microscopic examination and underwent cystoscopy, retrograde pyelography, and ureteroscopy every 3 months until they were tumor-free. Patients subsequently underwent ureteroscopy every 6 months with office cystoscopy every 3 months. In this series, ureteroscopy was the standard; if a tumor was visualized this was considered a recurrence. Of the modalities evaluated, bladder cytology manifested a sensitivity of 50% and specificity of 100%. Retrograde pyelography had a sensitivity and specificity of 72% and 85%, respectively, when read by the urologist in the operating room. Of interest, a radiologist reading the film at a later date yielded a sensitivity and specificity of 27% and 89% respectively. The authors of that study concluded that ureteroscopy is essential for follow-up of endoscopically managed upper tract TCC.

Percutaneous nephroscopy has also been applied for both the visualization and the treatment of upper tract TCC. Liatsikos and colleagues reported the largest series published.[6] Over the last 14 years, 69 patients have been treated percutaneously for upper tract TCC. Complications included a 37% transfusion rate. With a mean follow-up of 49 months there have been no cases of tract seeding with tumor cells. Survival depended on grade with 100% survival of grade I tumors. Disease specific survival was 96% and 64% for grade II and III tumors, respectively.

The authors' technique involves initial retrograde placement of a ureteral catheter into the renal pelvis. The patient is placed into the prone position, and percutaneous access is obtained with an 18-gauge needle under fluoroscopic guidance. A guide wire is placed and the tract is balloon dilated to admit a 30F working sheath. The ureteral catheter is then grasped via the nephroscope and used to pass another working wire for through and through access. A 24F resectoscope is used to resect all visible tumor. When flexible endoscopy is required the holmium:yttrium laser is employed. A nephrostomy tube is left in place and a nephrostogram is performed via this tube within 48 hours. A second look is then performed within the first week. Follow-up involves cytology, CT scan, retrograde pyelography and ureteroscopy every 3 months for 1 year and biannually thereafter. Liatsikos recommend nephroureterectomy for patients with high-grade disease upon subsequent evaluations.[8]

Upper Tract Imaging

The imaging of the upper urinary tracts has traditionally started with IVP. This involves the administration of intravenous contrast that is quickly filtered by the kidneys. The resultant opacity on plain films of the excreted contrast in the collecting system can provide clues to diagnosis of upper tract pathology. Upper tract tumors are usually diagnosed by the presence of a radiolucent filling defect.[7] Obstruction or nonvisualization of the collecting system can occur in 10 to 30% of patients, and this portends a higher risk of invasive disease.[8–10]

For patients with allergies to iodinated contrast, an equivocal intravenous pyelogram is suggested, or in cases of renal insufficiency where intravenous contrast is to be avoided, retrograde ureteropyelography is recommended. Contrast material is diluted to one-half strength or one-third strength to prevent over-opacification of the upper tract that may obscure subtle filling defects.[11] Retrograde pyelography has been shown to have a sensitivity of 85%.[12] Elliot and colleagues demonstrated that in patients with known renal pelvic tumors, an IVP or retrograde pyelogram revealed the lesion in 95% of cases. In patients with ureteral tumors, the lesions were visualized 65% of the time.[13] Gaboardi and co-workers found a 36% false-positive rate for radiographic diagnosis of upper tract tumors. Of the 28 patients that were studied with positive filling defects, only 18 were ultimately diagnosed with upper tract TCC.[14] Igawa and colleagues performed ureteroscopy to assess 37 filling defects identified radiographically and found only 15 to be tumors.[15] False-positive filling defect results may result from hyperplasia, inflammation, cysts, fibroepithelial polyps, and hemangiomas. Thus, nephroureterectomy should not be performed for radiographically identified filling defects alone, and further evaluation is warranted before initiating definitive therapy to better guide treatment.

Antegrade pyelography is not recommended for routine imaging of a nonvisualized kidney on an IVP. It may be used when a percutaneous approach is planned from the outset or when access through the bladder is not possible. However, due to concern of tumor seeding along the access tract this approach is not recommend.[11]

The CT scan has greater utility in cases of upper tract TCC than it does with bladder cancer. CT can be used for both diagnostic and staging purposes.[16] Pure uric acid calculi may be radiolucent on conventional x-rays and may manifest as a filling defect on IVP. The CT density of uric acid stones is typically greater than 100 Hounsfield units (HU) whereas soft tissue masses, such as tumors, have an average density of 46HU.[17] Also, TCC tends to be hypovascular, in contrast to renal cell carcinomas that are typically hypervascular, and therefore will usually not enhance on CT to the same extent. TCCs present as filling defects that do not distort the renal outline, masses with ureteral or pelvic wall thickening, or infiltrative masses.[18] Cases of TCC indistinguishable from renal cell carcinoma have however been reported.[19] Although the sensitivity of CT for diagnostic purposes has been reported to be as high as 90%, CT has not been able to show differentiation between superficial and muscle invasive disease; missing muscle

invasion in 59% of cases.[20] Additionally, the detection of tumor invasion into perinephric fat is often only seen with very large tumors.[21,22] Planz and colleagues examined a series of patients who underwent nephroureterectomy with preoperative CT scans. This cohort of 26 patients had a total of 28 tumors. Twenty-six (93%) of the tumors were correctly identified using IVP. Using CT, 86% of the tumors were diagnosed. Correct staging however revealed an accuracy of only 43%. CT resulted in overstaging of 36% of cases and understaging in 7% of cases.[21] Criteria used by this group for staging is found in Table 20–1.

Takebayashi and colleagues evaluated 23 patients with suspected upper tract TCC with a new interactive 3-dimensional image acquisition technique modified CT scan.[23] The procedure was called CT endoscopy, and the technology uses helical CT scans with and without contrast to provide data for computer software to extract information only about the interior surface of target hollow organs. This type of scan has been used previously on the colon, tracheobronchial tree, and ventricles of the brain.[24,25] In this study, final histopathologic examination was compared retrospectively to preoperative virtual endoscopic findings. CT endoscopy correctly detected 92% of the carcinomas whereas standard helical CT detected 83%. This method could act as an adjunct, or even replacement, for IVP as the technology becomes more readily available. However, further investigation and direct comparison to IVP will be required (Figure 20–4).

The same group has published a series of CT ureteroscopy for diagnosis of ureteral tumors.[26] They retrospectively compared final surgical histopathologic results with preoperative scans in a blinded fashion. The vast majority of lesions ranging from ureteral tumors, stricture, and lymph node metastasis were correctly identified using CT ureteroscopy. The

Table 20–1. CT RESULTS CORRELATED WITH THE PATHOLOGICAL CLASSIFICATION (pTNM)		
CT Results	T Stage	pTNM Classification
Tumor with thickening of the collecting system wall and tissue density filling defects	pTis, pTa, pT1, pT2	Carcinoma in situ, no invasion, lamina propria invasion, invasion of the muscularis propria
Tumor with invasion of periureteral, peripelvic or renal sinus fat, or renal parenchyma	pT3	Invading periureteral, peripelvic or renal sinus fat or renal parenchyma
Tumor with invasion of perirenal fat or adjacent organs	pT4	Invading perirenal fat or adjacent organs

Data from Planz B, George R, Adam G, et al. Computed tomography for detection and staging of transitional cell carcinoma of the upper urinary tract. Eur Urol 1995;27:146.

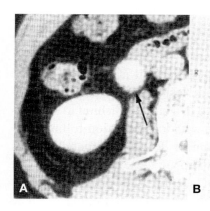
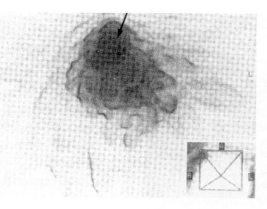

Figure 20–4. *A*, Axial CT of right kidney of patient with positive urinary cytology reveals dilitation of extrarenal pelvis and thickening of pelvic wall (*arrows*). Involvement of renal pelvic wall interior is unclear. *B*, CT nephroscopic image demonstrates diffuse, irregular pelvic interior indicating infiltrative carcinoma. *Arrow* indicates ureteropelvic junction. (Reprinted from Takebayashi S et al.[26])

overall sensitivity and specificity of CT ureteroscopy were 81% and 100% respectively (Figure 20–5).

Endoluminal ultrasonography has been performed in the setting of ureteroscopic procedures.[27] The currently available probes are 6.2 French catheters that are passed intraluminally to provide imaging of the ureter and periureteral structures. Liu and colleagues studied 38 patients that had suspected upper tract pathology (Figure 20–6). Due to the small number of final pathology specimens (ie, nephroureterectomy specimens) the effectiveness of staging could not be determined, but there was a correlation between the sonogram results and available pathology. The technique requires specialized and costly equipment and expertise, therefore endoluminal ultrasonography in this setting has not yet become widely available.

Though transabdominal ultrasound has historically been of limited value for ureteral pathology, a recently published small series of 16 patients reported by Hadas-Halpern and colleagues demonstrated that transabdominal ultrasound can be of clinical utility.[28–30] A single experienced examiner under conditions of good patient hydration was able to identify all 16 tumors in all areas of the ureter without false-positive or false-negative results. Rare reports of Doppler sonography for differentiation of vascular versus nonvascular masses of the ureter exist.[31] However, it is well known that ultrasonography is highly dependent on the experience of the sonographer. As such, it is unlikely that such excellent results can be achieved on a widespread basis.

Standard MRI still does not provide any significant advantages over CT in the evaluation of patients with upper tract carcinoma.[16] Unfortunately standard MRI and CT as of yet do not seem to provide enough accurate data to select patients who would benefit from nephron sparing techniques. They do provide a useful alternative, however, when the ureteral orifice is obstructed and direct visualization and biopsy is impossible.[16] New techniques that involve a fast, heavily T_2-weighted sequence are being examined for cases of urinary obstruction.[32,33] In a series comparing 14 patients with urinary obstruction and 20 patients without obstructions, MR urography was applied and detected neoplasms in 4 patients: a TCC of the bladder, a TCC of the ureter, a lymphoma of the bladder,

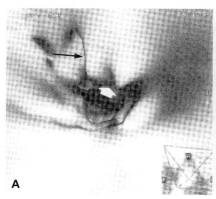
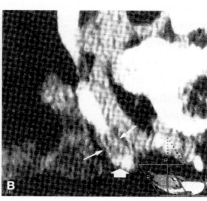

Figure 20–5. *A*, CT ureteroscopy in a 53-year-old man reveals sessile tumor (*black arrow*) with ulceration (*white arrow*). *B*, reformatted oblique CT ureterogram shows filling defect (*thin arrows*) with preserved periureteral fat and stage T2 or less disease. *Short arrow* indicates viewpoint of CT ureteroscopy in *A*. (Reprinted with permission from Takebayashi S et al.[26])

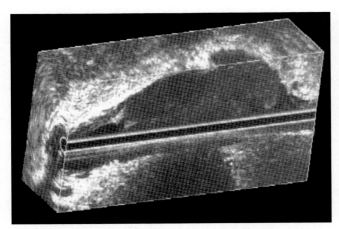

Figure 20–6. Ureteral mass diagnosed as transitional cell carcinoma is well demonstrated in this 3D reconstruction of endoluminal ultrasound data. (Reprinted with permission from Lee DI, Bagley DH, Liu JB. Experience with endoluminal ultrasonography in the urinary tract. J Endourol 2001;15:67–74.)

and a nephrogenic adenoma of the bladder.[34] Obstruction seems to be reliably detected with MR urography but the technique is not of utility in cases of high urinary flow.[35] Larger trials evaluating patients with upper tract tumors will be required prior to defining the clinical utility of this technology.

Upper Tract Follow-up

There is no clearly defined standard for follow-up after treatment of upper tract TCC. Bladder tumor recurrence rates as high as 75% have been reported after the diagnosis of upper tract TCC.[36] Therefore, a schedule of cystoscopy similar to that of bladder cancer is justified.

If nephroureterectomy is chosen as treatment for a particular upper tract TCC, the contralateral recurrence rate is less than 2%.[12] As such, continued imaging of the contralateral kidney in combination with cystoscopy is prudent in this patient population.

Patients managed by minimally invasive techniques that are used to spare renal units require a much more rigorous follow-up regimen. Huffman and colleagues reported on an initial series of 8 patients where low-grade tumors were managed ureteroscopically.[37] Since that time many series have been published demonstrating the success rate in the carefully selected patient.[13,38,39] These authors agree that repeated ureteroscopic examination along with retrograde pyelography and urine cytology are

mandatory. Advances in flexible ureteroscope technology and surgical expertise have made flexible endoscopic visualization of the upper urinary tract increasingly routine. As such, it is likely that in the future many low-grade lesions of the ureters or kidneys may be managed in a similar fashion to superficial bladder cancers, with local ablation followed by endoscopic surveillance. Regarding percutaneous treatment and follow-up of these tumors, there are anecdotal reports of seeding; however, the largest series of treatment reported no tract seeding.[40–43] The only reported case of seeding after planned resection were reported by Fulgsig and Krarup.[44] That patient had a grade III, T4 lesion. The remainder of reported cases of tract seeding have been after pyeloscopy only or in cases of long-term nephrostomy drainage for obstructed systems.[45] Jarrett and associates did however observe a correlation between increasing tumor grade and the number and severity of complications as a result of treatment.[42] These complication were likely due to the more extensive resections required for the higher grade tumors.

CONCLUSION

Detection and subsequent surveillance of upper tract TCC continue to be dependent on time-honored evaluations such as cystoscopy, IVP, and CT scan. Technologic advances in endoscopes have allowed the use of ureteroscopy to not only diagnose, but in many instances, to ablate and perform surveillance of TCC, thus sparing many patients of dialysis or eventual renal transplantation.

REFERENCES

1. Messing E, Valencourt A. Hematuria screening for bladder cancer. Journal of Occup Environ Med 1990;23:838–45.
2. Young H, McKay R. Congenital valvular obstruction of prostatic urethra. Surg Gynecol Obstet 1929:509–35.
3. Streem S, Pontes J, Novick A, Montie J. Ureteropyeloscopy in the evaluation of upper tract filling defects. J Urol 1986;136:383–5.
4. Chen G, Bagley D. Ureteroscopic surgery for upper tract transitional cell carcinoma: complications and management. J Endourol 2001;15:399–404.
5. Chen G, El-Gabry E, Bagley D. Surveillance of upper urinary tract transitional cell carcinoma: the role of ureteroscopy, retrograde pyelography, cytology and urinalysis. J Urol 2000;164:1901–4.

6. Liatsikos E, Dinzenc C, Kapoor R, Smith A. Transitional-cell carcinoma of the renal pelvis: ureteroscopic and percutaneous approach. J Endourol 2001;15:377–83.

7. Fein A, McClennan B. Solitary filling defects of the ureter. Semin Roentgenol 1986; 21:201–13.

8. Haleblian G, Skinner E, Dickenson M, et al. Hydronephrosis as a prognostic indicator in bladder cancer patients. J Urol 1998; 160:2011–14.

9. Babaian R, Johnson D. Primary carcinoma of the ureter. J Urol 1980;123:357–9.

10. Bloom N, Vidone R, Lytton B. Primary carcinoma of the ureter: a report of 102 new cases. J Urol 1970;103:590–8.

11. Messing E, Catalona W. Urothelial tumors of the urinary tract. In: Walsh P, editor. Campbell's urology. Philadelphia: WB Saunders 1998:p. 2327–410.

12. Murphy D, Zincke H, Furlow W. Management of high-grade transitional cell cancer of the upper urinary tract. J Urol 1981;135:25–9.

13. Elliott D, Blute M, Patterson D, et al. Long-term follow-up of endoscopically treated upper urinary tract transitional cell carcinoma. Urology 1996; 47:819–25.

14. Gaboardi F, Bozzola A, Dotti E, Galli L. Conservative treatment of upper urinary tract tumors with Nd:YAG laser. J Endourol 1994;8:37–41.

15. Igawa M, Urakami S, Shiina H, et al. Limitations of ureteroscopy in diagnosis of invasive upper tract urothelial cancer. Urol Int 1996;56:13–15.

16. Milestone B, Friedman A, Seidmon E. Staging of ureteral transitional cell carcinoma by CT and MRI. Urology 1990;36:346–9.

17. Lantz E, Hattery R. Diagnostic imaging of urothelial cancer. Urol Clin North Am 1984; 11:567–83.

18. Leder R, Dunnick N. Transitional cell carcinoma of the pelvicalices and ureter. AJR Am J Roentgenol 1990;155:713–22.

19. Roberts C, Collins J, Lidner T, Larson T. Transitional cell carcinoma obstructing a calyceal diverticulum: unusual presentation as a peripheral cystic mass. J Ultrasound Med 1999;18:19–21.

20. Badalament R, Bennett W, Bova J, et al. Computed tomography of primary transitional cell carcinoma of upper urinary tracts. Urology 1992;40:71–5.

21. Planz B, George R, Adam G, et al. Computed tomography for detection and staging of transitional cell carcinoma of the upper urinary tract. Eur Urol 1995;27:146–50.

22. McCoy J, Honda H, Reznicek M, Williams R. Computerized tomography for detection and staging of localized and pathologically defined upper tract urothelial tumors. J Urol 1991;146:1500–3.

23. Takebayashi S, Hosaka M, Takase K, et al. Computerized tomography nephroscopic images of renal pelvic carcinoma. J Urol 1999;162:315–8.

24. Kimura F, Shen Y, Date S, et al. Thoracic aortic aneurysm and aortic dissection: new endoscopic mode for three-dimensional CT display of aorta. Radiology 1996;198:573–8.

25. Jolesz F, Lorensen W, Shinmoto H, et al. Interactive virtual endoscopy. AJR Am J Roentgenol 1997;169:1229–35.

26. Takebayashi S, Hosaka M, Kubota N, et al. Computed tomographic ureteroscopy for diagnosing ureteral tumors. J Urol 2000;163:42–6.

27. Liu J, Bagley D, Conlin M, et al. Endoluminal sonographic evaluation of ureteral and renal pelvic neoplasms. J Ultrasound Med 1997;16:515–21.

28. Holm H, Torp-Pederson S, et al. Transabdominal and endoluminal ultrasonic scanning of the lower ureter. Scand J Urol Nephrol 1994;157:19–25.

29. Wong-You-Cheong J, Wagner B, Davis C. Transitional cell carcinoma of the urinary tract: radiologic-pathologic correlation. RadioGraphics 1998;18:123–42.

30. Hadas-Halpern I, Farkas A, Patlas M, et al. Sonographic diagnosis of ureteral tumors. J Ultrasound Med 1999; 18:639–45.

31. Killi R, Cal C, Pourbagher A, Yurtseven O. Doppler sonographic diagnosis of primary transitional cell carcinoma of the ureter. J Clin Ultrasound 2000;28:361–4.

32. Friedburg H, Henning J, Frankenschnidt A. RARE-MR urography: imaging of the urinary tract with a new fast non-tomographic MR technique. Radiologe 1987;27:45–57.

33. Sigmund G, Steover B, Zimmerhackl L, et al. RARE-MR-urography in the diagnosis of upper urinary tract abnormalities in children. Pediat Radiol 1991;21:416–20.

34. Rothpearl A, Frager D, Subramanian A, et al. MR urography: technique and application. Radiology 1995;194:125–30.

35. Regan F, Bohlman M, Khazan R, et al. MR urography using HASTE imaging in the assessment of ureteric obstuction. AJR Am J Roentgenol 1996;167:1115–20.

36. Abercrombie G, Eardley I, Payne S, et al. Modified nephroureterectomy : Long-term follow-up with particular reference to subsequent bladder tumours. Br J Urol 1988;61:198–200.

37. Huffman J, Bagley D, Lyon E, et al. Endoscopic diagnosis and treatment of upper tract urothelial tumors. Cancer 1985;55:1422–28.

38. Martinez-Pineiro J, Matres M, Martinez-Pineiro L. Endourological treatment of upper tract urothelial carcinomas: Analysis of a series of 59 tumors. J Urol 1996;156:377–85.

39. Keeley FX, Bibbo M, Bagley D. Ureteroscopic treatment and surveillance of upper urinary tract transitional cell carcinoma. J Urol 1997;157:1560–5.

40. Clark P, Streem SB, Geisinger MA. 13-year experience with percutaneous management of upper tract transitional cell carcinoma. J Urol 1999;161:772–6.

41. Patel A, Soonwalla P, Shepherd SF, et al. Long-term outcome after percutaneous treatment of transitional cell carcinoma of the renal pelvis. J Urol 1996;155:868–74.

42. Jarrett TW, Sweetsea PM, Weiss GH. Percutaneous management of transitional cell carcinoma of the renal collecting system: 9-year experience. J Urol 1995;154:1629–35.

43. Lee B, Jabbour M, Marshall F, et al. 13-year survival comparison of percutaneous and open nephroureterctomy approaches for management of transitional cell carcinoma of renal collecting system: equivalent outcomes. J Endourol 1999;13:289–94.

44. Fulgsig S, Krarup T. Percutaneous nephroscopic resection of renal pelvic tumors. Scand J Urol Nephrol 1995;172 Suppl:15–7.

45. Jabbour M, Smith A. Primary percutaneous approach to upper urinary tract transitional cell carcinoma. Urol Clin North Am 2000;27:739–50.

21

Percutaneous Upper Tract–Preserving Approaches in Urothelial Cancer

ROBERT MARCOVICH, MD
AVRUM JACOBSON, MD
ARTHUR SMITH, MD

HISTORICAL PERSPECTIVE

The traditional treatment for upper tract urothelial carcinoma has been total nephroureterectomy with excision of a cuff of bladder tissue surrounding the ureteral orifice.[1] In 1941, faced with a patient with a renal pelvic tumor in a solitary kidney, Ferris and Daut performed the first conservative procedure to treat such a tumor, preserving the kidney.[2] Soon after, Vest performed the first conservative excision of a tumor in the ureter.[3] Subsequently, numerous series on conservative surgery for renal pelvic and ureteral tumors reported acceptable outcomes in highly selected cases. In 1985, Huffman and colleagues reported the first truly endoscopic treatment of renal pelvic cancer using a transurethral ureteroscopic approach.[4]

In 1955, Goodwin and colleagues published the first report on percutaneous trocar access to the kidney.[5] However, percutaneous resection of upper tract tumors was not reported until the mid-1980s, by Streem and Pontes and by Smith and colleagues.[6,7] The latter group also was the first to systematically instill antineoplastic agents into the renal pelvis percutaneously, based on prior anecdotal reports of topical thiotepa and bacille Calmette-Guérin (BCG) administered in the ureter and kidney.[8,9]

Percutaneous surgery for upper tract urothelial carcinoma has been controversial owing to a number of factors, including the theoretical risk of tumor seeding of the nephrostomy tract. Nevertheless, several centers have undertaken this approach, and focus has shifted to defining the role of percutaneous resection in the treatment of upper tract cancer based on prognostic variables and outcomes analysis.

THEORETICAL CONSIDERATIONS

There are several factors to consider prior to committing a patient to a treatment course involving percutaneous or ureteroscopic resection. The concept of treating urothelial cancers of the upper urinary tract by an endoscopic approach arose out of the need for renal preservation in some patients, as well as a desire to provide a less invasive and less morbid form of therapy wherever possible.

Renal preservation, although an admirable goal, is not necessary in all situations. The presence of bilateral synchronous tumors certainly mandates a renal-sparing approach, but the risk of a tumor occurring subsequently in a contralateral kidney is rare. The incidence of metachronous tumors is only 1 to 2%, considerably lower than the incidence of ipsilateral recurrence after percutaneous resection of even low-grade tumors.[10,11] Therefore, the risk of developing a metachronous tumor is insufficient as the sole reason to undertake a renal-sparing approach in a patient with two normal kidneys. Furthermore, it is clear from long-term follow-up of patients who have undergone nephrectomy for renal cell carcinoma or for organ donation that there is essentially no risk of developing renal insufficiency or hypertension years after removal of the kidney.[12] Thus, the risk of leaving a patient with a solitary kidney may also be insufficient reason to perform renal-sparing therapy for upper tract urothelial carcinoma.

There are, however, cases that certainly warrant a conservative approach. The 5-year survival rate for patients 65 years and older on hemodialysis ranges from only 10 to 20%.[13] Although upper tract urothelial carcinoma can occur in younger patients, it is most commonly diagnosed during the seventh or eighth decades of life. An elderly patient with renal insufficiency or a solitary kidney who is treated for upper tract cancer with nephroureterectomy and subsequent hemodialysis is likely to fare no better than if he were treated with conservative resection, even for high-grade disease, and retained enough renal function to avoid dialysis. It is also arguable that from a quality of life standpoint alone, renal preservation in such patients, regardless of the grade of disease, is a better treatment than nephroureterectomy and dialysis.

Another argument for conservative therapy stems from the report of Zincke and Neves, who showed that patients with tumors of high grade and stage do equally poorly whether they undergo conservative or radical surgery.[14] They postulated that an improvement in outcome might be influenced by the use of adjuvant chemotherapy, and, certainly, patients whose renal function is preserved by conservative resection would be able to tolerate a more aggressive chemotherapeutic regimen.

Another consideration is the accuracy of staging and grading of upper tract urothelial tumors using an endourologic approach. The theoretical basis of local resection of upper tract cancers is similar to that of superficial bladder cancer. The efficacy of conservative local therapy is predicated on accurate staging because recognition of invasive disease would necessitate nephroureterectomy. A percutaneous approach would likely provide better staging than a retrograde ureteroscopic approach because of the improved visibility and ability to use larger instruments. Nevertheless, an accurate survey of the entire pelvicalyceal system is much more difficult to perform than an accurate survey of the bladder.

One must also consider the issue of tumor recurrence after conservative therapy. Excluding metastatic disease, a urothelial tumor can recur only if there is urothelium still present. Indeed, the basis for removal of the distal ureter as part of standard extirpative surgery for renal pelvic cancer is the high reported rates of recurrence in the retained ureter.[15] Endourologic therapy leaves behind the majority of urothelium, and as such, recurrence rates, especially for higher-grade disease, are significant, as is addressed in a later section of this chapter. On the other hand, low-grade disease tends to recur at low grade. The risk of progression for low-grade disease is small; therefore, nephroureterectomy in such cases is an overly aggressive approach.

It is also important to consider the issue of post-treatment surveillance. After nephroureterectomy, surveillance is no more complicated than after resection of a superficial bladder tumor, but because urine cytology, intravenous urography, and even retrograde pyelography are inadequate to detect upper tract recurrences after conservative therapy, the patient undergoing percutaneous or endoscopic treatment must undergo lifelong periodic ureteroscopic examinations. This not only has implications for the accumulated morbidity of this regimen over time but, most importantly, requires that conservative therapy be reserved for highly reliable and compliant patients.

Lastly, the advent of laparoscopic nephroureterectomy in the past several years has dealt a blow to the concept that only conservative therapy can be minimally invasive. Currently, specialists at most tertiary referral centers have the ability to perform a purely laparoscopic or a hand-assisted nephroureterectomy. Studies comparing laparoscopic and open nephroureterectomy confirm the equivalence of the two modalities in terms of cancer control and the superiority of the former in terms of decreased morbidity and convalescence.[16–18] Laparoscopic nephroureterectomy has been shown to be well tolerated even by patients in their eighties and nineties and by those with significant comorbidity, as assessed by American Society of Anesthesiology score.[19] Therefore, the number of patients who are offered an endourologic approach solely because they are a poor risk for open surgery may decrease. Nevertheless, laparoscopy is certainly not without morbidity, and, in certain cases, an endourologic approach, especially a ureteroscopic one, will undoubtedly be more appropriate.

INDICATIONS FOR THE PERCUTANEOUS APPROACH

The development of endoscopic surgical techniques has not changed the basic tenet of solid tumor therapy, that of complete extirpation of neoplastic tissue. Endourologic techniques have merely given urologists a less invasive tool for removing cancer. Percutaneous and ureteroscopic resection of urothelial carcinoma as performed today are merely less invasive methods to accomplish what practitioners of old were attempting to do with open surgical excision of tumor: preserve renal parenchyma. As such, there is agreement that the main indication for any endoscopic approach to the treatment of upper tract urothelial carcinoma is preservation of functional renal tissue.

Situations in which conservative surgery for upper tract urothelial carcinoma has been advocated, and is generally accepted, include bilateral synchronous disease, tumor in a solitary kidney, and in patients with impaired renal function in whom nephrectomy would result in an unacceptable risk of necessitating subsequent hemodialysis. An endoscopic approach should also be considered in patients whose comorbidities would preclude radical surgery, although, as mentioned previously, the advent of laparoscopic nephroureterectomy has now made this less of an issue.

Additionally, there is now general agreement that endoscopic surgery for upper tract carcinoma is indicated in situations when tumor characteristics alone are likely to result in a favorable outcome with local excision. As will be discussed in more detail later in this chapter, patients with small grade 1, and to some extent grade 2, lesions may be safely treated by endoscopic resection as long as such patients are willing to undergo rigorous post-treatment surveillance.

CONTRAINDICATIONS TO THE PERCUTANEOUS APPROACH

Contraindications to percutaneous surgery can be categorized as tumor related or patient related.

Tumor-related contraindications include high-grade (grade 3 or 4) lesions and tumors that appear to be invasive on radiographic imaging or direct endoscopic inspection. If a tumor is found to be unre-sectable on either anatomic or technical grounds, nephroureterectomy should follow. Recurrence at a higher grade of a previously resected tumor or a tumor that recurs rapidly after resection and BCG instillation portends aggressive disease, and further attempts at conservative therapy are ill advised.

Patient-related contraindications to percutaneous resection of upper tract urothelial carcinoma include the presence of active infection, bleeding diathesis or coagulopathy, and uncontrolled hypertension, which may increase the risk of perioperative hemorrhage. Although morbid obesity is not a contraindication, standard instrumentation may be of inadequate length to effectively access the tumor, and extra-long instruments may be required in such cases.

Finally, the inability or unwillingness of a patient to undergo a rigorous follow-up regimen after treatment should definitively exclude that patient from any form of endoscopic therapy.

PERCUTANEOUS VERSUS URETEROSCOPIC APPROACH

Both the antegrade percutaneous approach and the retrograde ureteroscopic approach can effectively accomplish the goal of tumor excision, but each has particular advantages and disadvantages. Percutaneous access with dilation of the tract to 30 French allows for the use of larger endoscopes with more rapid flow of irrigant, resulting in improved visualization. Both rigid and flexible endoscopes may be inserted through the percutaneous sheath, allowing for complete inspection of all calyces for tumor-bearing tissue. Should one percutaneous tract be inadequate for access to all calyces, one or more additional tracts can be created. Percutaneous tracts facilitate resection of larger tumors and ease repetitive passage of the endoscope in and out of the system. Therefore, tissue removal or multiple biopsies from the upper urinary tract are essentially hassle free. In patients with a prior urinary diversion, the percutaneous approach may be the only way to access the collecting system. Furthermore, a wider array of instruments can be used percutaneously, especially large-bore resectoscopes, graspers, and biopsy forceps, in addition to those instruments that can be used ureteroscopically, such as lasers and wire baskets. The percutaneous approach allows for sampling of all layers of tissue, including epithelium, stroma, muscle, fat, and renal parenchyma, potentially improving local tumor staging. It also facilitates so-called "second-look" and "third-look" nephroscopy. Second-look nephroscopy is performed within 2 or 3 days of the initial resection, through the existing percutaneous tract, and allows the surgeon to assess the completeness of the initial resection and obtain biopsies to document absence of residual disease and, if necessary, provides an opportunity to remove any gross remaining tumor. Similarly, third-look nephroscopy is performed through the existing nephrostomy tract 2 weeks after adjuvant percutaneous instillation of antineoplastic agents. Again, the efficacy of treatments to date can be assessed and biopsies taken.

The main advantages of retrograde ureteroscopy are its lesser degree of invasiveness, decreased theoretical potential for tumor spillage into the retroperitoneum, and the fact that the majority of contemporary urologists are technically facile in gaining access to the upper urinary tract with both rigid and flexible ureteroscopes. Ureteroscopy is the best initial method of obtaining tissue for diagnosis and grading, thus differentiating those patients who might benefit from further renal-sparing approaches and those who will require total nephroureterectomy. Flexible ureteroscopy is the most thorough method of surveying the entire ipsilateral collecting system for recurrence during post-treatment follow-up. A ureteroscopic approach is well suited to treating low-volume lesions of the ureter or renal pelvis.[20]

Although ureteroscopy lacks the versatility of percutaneous resection in the treatment of upper tract urothelial cancer, it is associated with fewer potential complications. Ureteroscopy poses no risk of injury to solid organs, bowel, or pleura, whereas colonic puncture, hydrothorax, and hemothorax, although rare, are known pitfalls with the percutaneous approach. The incidence of stricture after ureteroscopic tumor resection is low and should continue to decrease as smaller-caliber instruments become more widely available. The possibility of ureteral or collecting system perforation exists with both approaches, and, owing to the risk of tumor spillage into the retroperitoneum, care should be taken to avoid this occurrence with either modality.

It has been the practice at the authors' institution to initially approach all upper tract urothelial tumors that appear to be noninvasive using ureteroscopy. If the tumor is not completely resectable ureteroscopically, a percutaneous resection is undertaken.

PATIENT COUNSELING

Experience with percutaneous management of urothelial carcinoma of the upper urinary tract is expanding and gaining acceptance in the urologic community. It offers great advantages to patients with solitary kidneys, chronic renal failure, or significant comorbidity and to those with low-grade, low-stage disease. Despite this, at present, nephroureterectomy remains the "gold standard" treatment. Patients electing percutaneous therapy should be made aware that this deviates from the gold standard and must understand that, at some point, a nephroureterectomy may yet be required. He or she must also be prepared to undergo an intense follow-up regimen, including frequent ureteroscopy.

The patient should also be made aware of the risks inherent in percutaneous renal surgery. Of these, the most commonly encountered are bleeding and fever. Others, rarely encountered, include failed access and adjacent organ injury. The theoretical risk of tract seeding should also be discussed.

PREOPERATIVE PREPARATION

Preparation for surgery can be divided into that which is required for any percutaneous procedure and that which is specific to the treatment of urothelial carcinoma.

As in any patient presenting for percutaneous surgery, it is important to minimize the risk of hemorrhage and sepsis. Anticoagulants should be stopped prior to surgery and any bleeding diathesis should be corrected. As well, hypertension may contribute to bleeding and should be medically controlled. Active infection is also a contraindication. Positive urine cultures should be treated prior to surgery, and, even in the absence of positive cultures, a broad-spectrum antibiotic should be administered preoperatively.

Unlike in endoscopic management of bladder carcinoma, it is important to obtain a thorough metastatic evaluation prior to resection. At minimum, this should include a computed tomographic (CT) scan of the abdomen and pelvis, chest radiograph, liver function tests, and serum alkaline phosphatase and calcium levels. Endoscopic management should be reserved for localized superficial disease.

TECHNIQUE

After general anesthesia is induced and an endotracheal tube is placed, the patient is positioned in dorsal lithotomy. Cystoscopy is performed and a ureteral catheter is passed up into the affected collecting system. The ureteral catheter is secured to a Foley catheter, and the patient is repositioned prone. All pressure points must be appropriately padded. A retrograde pyelogram is then performed delineating the collecting system, and an appropriate calyx is selected for percutaneous access. When the tumor is located within a peripheral calyx, access should be obtained directly onto that calyx. When the renal pelvis is involved, we recommend access through a middle or upper calyx so that the ureteropelvic junction (UPJ) can be inspected and manipulation down the ureter can be accomplished. Others, however, have recommended that renal pelvic tumors be approached though lower or middle calyceal accesses.[21] Once a calyx is selected, using biplanar fluoroscopy, a needle is advanced into the collecting system and a guidewire is coiled in the pelvis or, preferably, passed down the UPJ (Figure 21–1). The tract is enlarged using either balloon dilators or progressive Amplatz dilators, and a nephroscopy sheath is placed. Whenever possible, access should be accomplished with one puncture. As well, care should be taken to ensure that the nephroscopy sheath never slips out of the collecting system. These precautions may decrease the risk of tumor seeding.

Once the tract is established, the collecting system is thoroughly inspected to identify any area of involvement that was not previously suspected (Figure 21–2). The ureteral catheter is grasped and brought out through the access tract. A Teflon-coated guide wire is passed down the ureteral catheter so that "through-and-through" access is ensured. The tumor is then biopsied extensively using cold-cup forceps (Figure 21–3). The base is carefully resected (Figure 21–4)

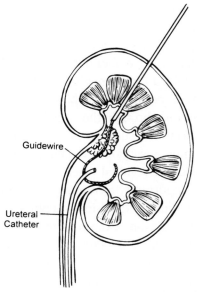

Figure 21–1. Retrograde ureteral catheter has been placed and nephrostomy needle introduced into collecting system through the upper calyx. A guidewire is passed into the renal pelvis through the nephrostomy needle.

and cauterized using an electrocautery loop or laser (Figure 21–5). Deep resection should be avoided as bleeding can be extremely difficult to control. A flexible cystoscope or nephroscope can be used to survey the entire collecting system for tumors (Figure 21–6). At the end of the procedure, a Re-entry catheter

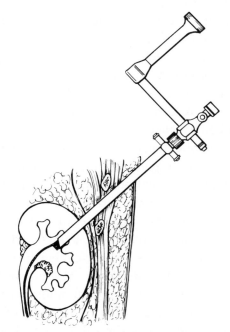

Figure 21–2. After placement of a nephrostomy sheath, the nephroscope is used to inspect the collecting system.

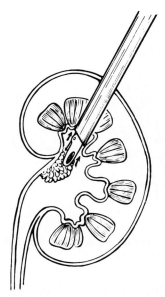

Figure 21–3. Biopsy forceps are used to remove the bulk of the tumor.

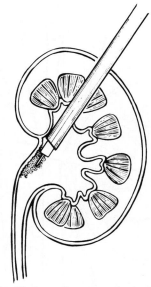

Figure 21–5. The tumor base may also be fulgurated with the neodymium:yttrium-aluminum-garnet (Nd:YAG) laser.

(Boston Scientific/Microvasive, Natick, MA) is placed to facilitate a future second-look procedure (Figure 21–7). It is important to verify correct positioning of the Re-entry tube with fluoroscopy.

If pathology reveals invasive or high-grade disease or if the tumor is deemed unresectable, a nephroureterectomy is performed. Otherwise, the patient is brought back to the operating room within 3 to 7 days for a second-look nephroscopy. If any gross residual tumor is identified, it is resected. The base of the prior resection site is biopsied as well.

Again, if high-grade or invasive disease is present, the patient is offered a nephroureterectomy.

If adjuvant BCG therapy is planned, a nephrostomy tube is left in place, and, 2 weeks later, a course of six weekly installments is initiated. The patient is admitted to the hospital for each BCG treatment. It is important to administer prophylactic intravenous antibiotics prior to beginning BCG infusion. Beta-lactam antibiotics (penicillins and cephalosporins) are acceptable because BCG is not susceptible to them, but fluoroquinolones, gentamicin, and doxycycline

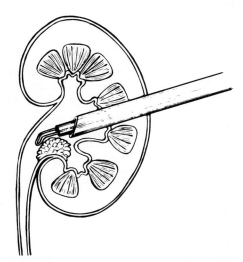

Figure 21–4. Tumor can also be removed by electrosurgical resection. The base of the tumor may be fulgurated with the cautery loop.

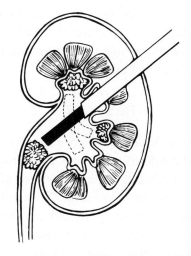

Figure 21–6. Calyces adjacent to the nephrostomy tract may be inspected with a flexible nephroscope or cystoscope placed through the nephrostomy sheath.

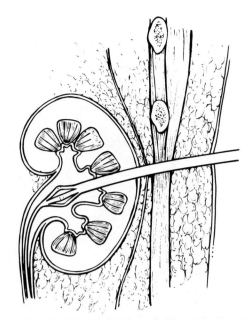

Figure 21–7. After resection and fulguration, a nephrostomy tube with a ureteral extension is placed through the percutaneous tract to drain the collecting system.

should be avoided as they will inactivate BCG.[22] An infusion of normal saline into the nephrostomy tube is begun at 10 cc per hour and increased by 10 cc/hr every hour until the infusion rate reaches 50 cc per hour. The intrarenal pressure is closely monitored to ensure that it remains below 25 cm H_2O (Figure 21–8). If the patient tolerates the saline infusion without difficulty, 50 cc of 1×10^8 colony-forming units of BCG is administered over 1 hour. The patient voids after instillation and is discharged home the next day. Two weeks after completion, the patient undergoes a third-look nephroscopy. Figure 21–9 summarizes the algorithm used to manage upper tract urothelial cancer at the authors' institution.

RESULTS

To date, there have been no prospective studies examining the role of percutaneous management of upper tract urothelial cancer. Almost all patients treated had solitary kidneys, bilateral disease, chronic renal failure, or significant comorbid disease contraindicating major open surgery. At present, however, this is representative of patients considered for a percutaneous approach. Very few institutions have expanded the indications to include motivated,

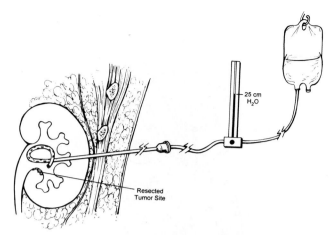

Figure 21–8. Schematic diagram of percutaneous infusion of bacille Calmette-Guérin.

otherwise healthy patients with superficial low-grade disease who elect a nephron-sparing, minimally invasive approach.[23] Despite the limitations of the available data, it is clear that patients with grade 1 disease have an excellent prognosis, whereas the prognosis of those with grade 3 is guarded.

The effect of grade on recurrence after percutaneous resection can be seen in Table 21–1. Grade 1 disease has a reported recurrence rate of 5 to

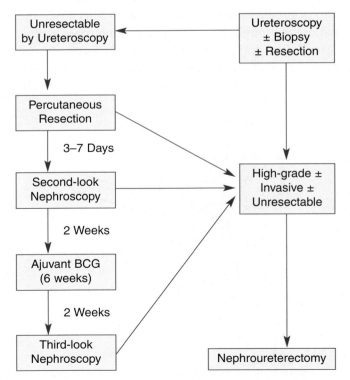

Figure 21–9. Treatment algorithm for upper tract urothelial carcinoma. BCG = bacille Calmette Guérin.

33%.[11,21,23–26] However, despite recurrences, death from low-grade urothelial carcinoma is rare. In four reported series with a total of 50 grade 1 patients, only one patient died of cancer-related causes, and this patient was found on second-look nephroscopy to actually have grade 2 histology.[11,23,25,26] Furthermore, renal retention rates have been excellent. Liatsikos and colleagues reported on 15 patients with grade 1 disease. Two of three recurrences were treated successfully endoscopically, and only one patient underwent nephroureterectomy.[23]

The prognosis of grade 2 disease is also good. The recurrence rate in 94 patients from seven different series is 22%.[11,21,23–27] In four of the five studies in which disease-specific survival is reported or can be calculated, patients with grade 2 pathology die of cancer-related causes in less than 5% of cases. Renal retention, however, is a serious consideration. Jarrett and colleagues reported that of 12 patients with grade 2 histology, 6 (50%) required nephroureterectomy, 3 within days of their percutaneous resection and 3 for recurrence.[11] Jabbour and colleagues published a study that specifically addressed grade 2 disease managed with percutaneous resection. They found that 7 of 24 patients (29%) underwent nephroureterectomy, 4 immediately and 3 for recurrence.[27]

No matter how grade 3 urothelial carcinoma of the upper urinary tract is managed, the prognosis is poor. Nephroureterectomy data have shown that patients with high-grade disease have a 5-year survival of 24.2 to 28.3%.[28,29] Lee and associates found no statistically significant survival difference between grade 3 patients treated with nephroureterectomy or initial percutaneous resection.[26] However, patients treated with percutaneous resection were offered a nephroureterectomy when high-grade disease was

diagnosed. In the largest published series of grade 3 patients, Liatsikos and colleagues reported disease-specific survival of 64% and a recurrence rate of 56%.[23] Jarrett and colleagues included 13 grade 3 patients in their series. Eight of them died during follow-up, six of disease-related causes (46%). As well, of those who had no evidence of disease at the time of publication, only one patient still retained the affected kidney.[11] In the authors' opinion, percutaneous resection should not be offered for high-grade renal urothelial carcinoma, except as a last resort in elderly patients with a solitary kidney, who would fare quite poorly on hemodialysis.

Tumor stage is another important prognostic variable. There are, appropriately, very few cases of invasive (T2/T3) disease treated percutaneously. Often in such cases, patients have been treated with immediate nephroureterectomy. The following discussion is therefore limited to stage Ta and T1. Ta has a strong correlation with grade 1 disease. Jarrett and colleagues reported that all nine grade 1 patients in their study had Ta disease.[11] Plancke and colleagues and Martinez-Pineiro and colleagues also found a strong correlation; Ta was associated with grade 1 in 76% and 86% of cases, respectively.[25,30] T1 disease, however, is not as consistently associated with a specific grade. Jarrett and colleagues found grade 2 and 3 disease in 14% and 86% of cases, whereas Martinez-Pineiro and colleagues found that T1 was associated with grade 1, 2, and 3 histology in 32%, 55%, and 14% of cases, respectively.[11,30]

Jabbour and colleagues recently published their results in 54 patients with a mean follow-up of 50 months who underwent percutaneous management of upper tract urothelial cancer. Patients with stage Ta had a recurrence rate of 30% and a disease-free

Series	No. of Patients	Follow-Up (mo)	Grade 1 (%)	Grade 2 (%)	Grade 3 (%)	Total (%)
Plancke et al, 1995[25]	10	28	1/6 (17)	0/3	—	1/9 (11)
Jarrett et al, 1995[11]	34	56.4	2/11 (18)	3/9 (33)	5/10 (50)	10/30 (33)
Patel et al, 1996[24]	26	44.7	2/11 (18)	3/11 (27)	—	6/25* (24)
Clark et al, 1999[21]	18	20.5	2/6 (13)	2/8 (25)	2/4 (50)	6/18 (33)
Lee et al, 1999[26]	50	—	1/20 (5)	1/16 (6)	4/13 (31)	6/49 (12)
Jabbour et al, 2000[27]	20	48	—	5/20 (25)	—	5/20 (25)
Liatsikos et al, 2001[23]	69	49	3/15 (20)	7/27 (26)	14/25 (56)	24/67 (36)

Table 21–1. RECURRENCE RATES AFTER PERCUTANEOUS RESECTION OF UPPER TRACT UROTHELIAL CARCINOMA, STRATIFIED ACCORDING TO TUMOR GRADE

*1 of 3 patients with tumors of an unknown grade had a recurrence.

survival of 93%. Stage T1 was associated with a recurrence rate of 57% and a disease specific survival of 64%. Grade for grade, stage retained its prognostic significance.[31] Other authors have also reported worse prognosis with higher stage. Patel and colleagues found that T1 had a higher recurrence rate than Ta (30% versus 12.5%), and Jarrett and colleagues found worse disease-specific survival (92% versus 57%).[11,24]

Finally, an issue that must be addressed in any discussion of the outcome of percutaneous resection of urothelial carcinoma is recurrence in the percutaneous tract. Initially, percutaneous management was regarded with great skepticism, and many believed that tract seeding would limit the usefulness of this approach. Woodhouse and colleagues described the use of tract irradiation to limit seeding in patients treated percutaneously.[32] Patel and colleagues reported the use of tract irradiation in 24 of 26 patients, and no patient had any evidence of tract recurrence.[24] Other authors have treated patients without tract irradiation. In multiple series of 10 to 69 patients, no tract seeding has been noted.[11,21,23–27,30,31] Two cases of tract seeding, however, have been reported. Both cases had a past history of high-grade urothelial cancer of the bladder. Percutaneous resection in one revealed moderate grade but indeterminate stage. Nephroureterectomy, performed for recurrence 3 months later, revealed high-grade carcinoma with penetration into the parenchyma and infiltration of the perirenal fat at the site of the prior nephroscopy tract.[33] The other patient had a nephrostomy tube inserted for renal obstruction caused by a ureteral mass. Antegrade ureteroscopy demonstrated a high-grade unresectable lesion. One month after placement of the nephrostomy tube, nephroureterectomy was performed and revealed grade 3 stage T3b ureteral tumor.[34] Three weeks after this, a tract recurrence was noted. Despite wide resection, this recurred again, and the patient eventually succumbed to his disease. Although these cases highlight the potential for seeding, they are, in fact, not typical of the current protocols being followed. In one case, the tract was exposed to unresected high-grade disease for a month. In the other, there is no mention of a second-look procedure to ensure that all disease was actually treated. Therefore, growing experience with specific protocols has shown that this risk is minimal.

COMPLICATIONS OF PERCUTANEOUS RESECTION

The most common complication of percutaneous tumor resection is hemorrhage requiring blood transfusion. Bleeding can occur from resection of tumor or from vessel injury during percutaneous puncture. If bleeding from creation of the nephrostomy tract is so brisk as to hamper adequate visualization, the procedure should be aborted and postponed until a later date. This type of hemorrhage can usually be managed by tamponade of the tract with a large-bore nephrostomy catheter or a Kaye balloon catheter (Cook Urological, Spencer, IN). If ongoing bleeding remains a problem despite these measures, the patient should undergo angiography and selective embolization of the responsible vessel.

The transfusion rate for percutaneous resection of upper tract urothelial carcinoma ranges from 11 to 37%.[21,24,31] The extent and grade of tumor, as well as depth of resection, are significant factors in determining the severity of the hemorrhage.[31] Bleeding as a consequence of tumor excision, in contrast to bleeding from the nephrostomy tract, can be managed only by adequate tumor excision or fulguration. Care should be taken not to resect too deeply into the renal parenchyma as invasive disease will require nephroureterectomy anyway. Fulguration of the tumor base with a neodymium:yttrium-aluminum-garnet (Nd:YAG) laser or vaporization electrode may help to reduce the incidence of significant bleeding.[31]

Other complications related to percutaneous resection of upper tract urothelial carcinoma are fever with or without urinary tract infection, failure to obtain access, perforation of the renal pelvis, and injury to adjacent structures. Perforation of the renal pelvis may theoretically predispose to spillage of tumor into the retroperitoneum, but sequelae from this have not been reported in the literature.

SURVEILLANCE

Because of the potential for tumor recurrence, patients treated endourologically for upper tract urothelial cancer must undergo a rigorous, lifelong follow-up regimen. This regimen should be tailored to the recurrence pattern of upper tract tumors. Although long-term (> 5 year) recurrences have been reported, most recurrences occur in the first 3 years following initial therapy.[35] Therefore, the follow-up regimen may be tailored to this pattern.

Patients with upper tract disease are at significant risk of developing urothelial carcinoma of the urinary bladder, so cystoscopy should be performed every 3 months during the first year, every 6 months during the second year, and then yearly thereafter, providing that no tumors recur during the surveillance period. Excretory urography and retrograde pyelography have been advocated to follow the upper tracts, but they lack sensitivity. Based on a study of 23 patients undergoing 88 surveillance procedures over a 30-month period, Chen and colleagues determined that the sensitivity of ureteroscopy and biopsy was 93.4%, compared with 71.7% for retrograde pyelography.[36] Keeley and colleagues diagnosed only 4 of 16 recurrences (25%) using retrograde pyelography.[37] Thus, ureteroscopy is the best modality to survey the upper tract. The authors recommend that ureteroscopy be performed every 6 months, that the contralateral kidney (if present) be imaged at least annually with either retrograde or excretory pyelography, and that an abdominal CT scan be done yearly.

INSTILLATION THERAPY IN UPPER TRACT UROTHELIAL CARCINOMA

In 1985, Herr reported a case of a patient with a solitary kidney who had been treated for muscle-invasive urothelial carcinoma with wide excision of the renal pelvis and entire ureter followed by creation of a pyelovesical anastomosis. The margins of the resected pelvis and infundibula were positive for carcinoma in situ, so the patient underwent a 6-week course of BCG instillation via the bladder. The patient's urinary cytology normalized and remained negative for over 13 months.[8] In 1986, Streem and Pontes reported on a patient with urothelial carcinoma of a solitary kidney treated with percutaneous resection followed by adjuvant mitomycin C.[6] The following year, Smith and colleagues published results on a series of nine patients treated with percutaneous resection; five of these patients received adjuvant BCG.[7] Since that time, a number of institutions have reported the use of instillation therapy with BCG, mitomycin, or thiotepa, either as primary treatment for carcinoma in situ or as adjuvant therapy after resection or ablation of papillary tumors. Currently, BCG is the most commonly used agent.

The rationale for instillation therapy in upper tract urothelial carcinoma mirrors that for instillation therapy in superficial cancer of the urinary bladder. BCG therapy after transurethral resection (TUR) of bladder carcinoma has been shown to decrease tumor recurrence and prolong the time to recurrence when compared with TUR alone.[38] It has also been demonstrated to decrease tumor progression and prolong survival.[39] Adjuvant therapy in bladder cancer is indicated in patients with multiple tumors, high-grade disease, carcinoma in situ, or recurrent tumors. Although high-grade disease in the upper tract is most effectively treated with nephroureterectomy, it still remains an indication for adjuvant therapy in situations when conservative treatment is absolutely necessary for preservation of renal function (such as in the case of a solitary kidney). The indications for adjuvant therapy in upper tract urothelial cancer have evolved over the years. Currently, grade 2 tumors, multifocal disease, T1 tumors, carcinoma in situ, and bilateral disease constitute the main indications for adjuvant therapy at the authors' institution.

The authors' technique for percutaneous administration of BCG has been outlined previously in this chapter. Other techniques have been advocated, including retrograde instillation through a ureteral catheter or by creation of vesicoureteral reflux with an indwelling stent. Use of a retrograde catheter requires the patient to undergo cystoscopy at the time of each instillation. Patel and Fuchs described a technique in which the distal end of a single-J ureteral stent was passed through a percutaneous cystotomy and secured to the skin of the abdomen, allowing weekly instillations without the need for endoscopic intervention each time.[40] The retrograde techniques are useful when a percutaneous nephrostomy is not used, such as when the initial resection is performed ureteroscopically or for primary therapy of carcinoma in situ. However, Studer and colleagues use a small-bore nephrostomy tube for all instillations, even those in which a percutaneous resection is not required, feeling that contact of the agent with the urothelial surface is maximized by antegrade administration.[41] Other purported disadvantages of the retrograde instillation techniques include interference of contact between agent and urothelium by the retrograde catheter itself and the uncertainty of how much agent actually refluxes up to the kidney when the vesicoureteral reflux method is used. The former allegation has never been proven. Regarding the latter issue, Irie and colleagues performed cystograms to determine the amount of fluid required to induce reflux in each of their patients after placement of a double-J stent. This volume, which averaged 120 cc (range 80–250 cc), was used to guide the subsequent instillation volume of BCG.[42] With regard to percutaneous administration of agents, the main critique has been the potential for seeding of the nephrostomy tract during the 6 or more weeks that the tube is in place; however, no such cases have been reported in the literature. It is unclear from a survey of the literature that any one administration technique holds an advantage over the others in terms of outcome. However, there is a theoretical possibility that retrograde instillation, which is done into a closed system, may predispose to gram-negative septicemia.

When BCG instillation is used as primary therapy for upper tract carcinoma in situ, positive initial response rates, based on normalization of selective urinary cytology, range from 60 to 100%, with an overall response rate of 84% for all studies reported (Table 21–2). Of the patients in these studies who responded, 25.8% eventually experienced an upper tract recurrence. Almost 10% of patients in these studies developed metastatic disease. Fifteen percent died of urothelial carcinoma and 13.5% died of other causes within an overall mean follow-up period of 35 months.

The benefit of BCG as adjuvant therapy after resection of the primary upper tract tumor has not been fully determined. There have been no randomized trials assessing the efficacy of adjuvant therapy, and it is unclear whether such a trial would even be feasible, given the relative rarity of the condition. At a minimum, a multi-institutional effort would be required to conduct such a study. A total of six series in the literature assess the efficacy of BCG as adjuvant therapy for upper tract disease (Table 21–3). The recurrence rate in these studies is quite variable, ranging from 11 to 85%, although recurrence rates in the two largest series are closer to 30%. Stratified by grade of the resected tumor, recurrence rates are 17% for grade 1, 20% for grade 2, and 44% for grade 3 from 76 total patients. These numbers do not include the study by Thalmann and colleagues, in which recurrence was not stratified by grade but which had the highest overall recurrence rate (85%).[43] In fact, the high rate of recurrence in this series may be explained by the presence of mostly high-grade cases (U.E. Studer, personal communication, 2002).

Thus far, there has been only one report comparing outcomes of patients who received postresection BCG versus those who did not receive it, and this study failed to show any benefit for grade 2 or grade 3 disease. However, there was a lower recurrence rate in grade 1 patients who received BCG than in those who did not (14% versus 50%, $p < .05$).[31] This analysis lacked sufficient power to definitively exclude an advantage for the higher grades.

Despite the lack of strong evidence to support the practice in grade 2 or 3 disease, the mere potential existence of a benefit is enough for most practitioners to use BCG instillation as an additional tool to prevent recurrence because the stakes are so high for

Table 21–2. POSITIVE RESPONSE AND LOCAL RECURRENCE RATES AFTER PRIMARY THERAPY OF UPPER TRACT CARCINOMA IN SITU WITH BACILLE CALMETTE-GUÉRIN			
Series	No. of Patients	Positive Response (%)	Upper Tract Recurrence (%)
Sharpe et al, 1993[44]	11	8 (73)	0/8
Yokogi et al, 1996[47]	5	3 (60)	0/3
Nishino et al, 2000[45]	6	6 (100)	0/6
Nonomura et al, 2000[48]	11	9 (82)	2/9 (22)
Okubo et al, 2001[49]	11	8 (73)	3/8 (37)
Irie et al, 2002[42]	9	9 (100)	0/9
Thalmann et al, 2002[43]	21	19 (90)	11/19 (58)
Total	74	62 (84)	16/62 (26)

Table 21–3. LOCAL RECURRENCE RATES FOR UPPER TRACT UROTHELIAL CARCINOMA TREATED BY PRIMARY PERCUTANEOUS OR ENDOSCOPIC RESECTION FOLLOWED BY ADJUVANT BACILLE CALMETTE-GUÉRIN

Study	No. of Patients	Upper Tract Recurrence (%)
Schoenberg et al, 1991[50]	9	1 (11)
Martinez-Pineiro et al, 1996[30]	8	1 (12.5)
Patel and Fuchs, 1998[40]	12	2 (16.7)
Clark et al, 1999[21]	18	6 (33)
Jabbour and Smith, 2000[31]	30	9 (30)
Thalmann et al, 2002[43]	14	12 (85.7)
Total	91	31 (34)

patients undergoing conservative therapy. The relative safety of adjuvant therapy, when appropriate techniques of administration are employed, also does not detract from its application. The major complications of BCG therapy in the upper tract are BCG dissemination and gram-negative sepsis, although these are relatively rare. Sharpe and colleagues experienced one case of BCG dissemination from a total of 11 cases treated.[44] Thalmann and colleagues reported two cases of sepsis and one case of BCG dissemination of 37 patients perfused, and the authors have experienced one case of sepsis and one BCG dissemination of 30 patients.[43] Much more common are fever unrelated to infection and irritative voiding symptoms. Urinary frequency and dysuria occur transiently for 2 to 3 days postinstillation in the majority of patients, and fever has been reported in up to 67% of patients in one series.[45] Renal granulomas have been found on biopsy during third-look procedures, but these have not been clinically significant.[46]

CONCLUSION

Local therapy for upper tract urothelial carcinoma continues to evolve. The majority of patients with this condition can now be offered a minimally invasive approach to their disease with ureteroscopy, percutaneous resection, laparoscopic nephroureterectomy, or a combination of these modalities. Endourologic techniques are ideal for managing noninvasive, resectable tumors that are well- or moderately differentiated in patients who are willing and able to undergo a careful, long-term follow-up regimen. These modalities are particularly well suited to patients with renal compromise, as well as to patients with two normally functioning kidneys and favorable tumor characteristics.

REFERENCES

1. Kimball FN, Ferris HW. Papillomatous tumor of the renal pelvis associated with similar tumors of the ureter and bladder: review of the literature and report of two cases. J Urol 1934;31:257–9.
2. Ferris DO, Daut RV. Epithelioma of the pelvis of a solitary kidney treated by electrocoagulation. J Urol 1948;59:577–9.
3. Vest SA. Conservative surgery in certain benign tumors of the ureter. J Urol 1945;53:97–9.
4. Huffman JL, Bagley DH, Lyon ES, et al. Endoscopic diagnosis and treatment of upper tract urothelial tumors. A preliminary report. Cancer 1985;55:1422–8.
5. Goodwin WE, Casey WC, Woolf W. Percutaneous trocar (needle) nephrostomy in hydronephrosis. JAMA 1955; 157:891–4.
6. Streem SB, Pontes EJ. Percutaneous management of upper tract transitional cell carcinoma. J Urol 1986;135:773–5.
7. Smith AD, Orihuela E, Crowley AR. Percutaneous management of renal pelvic tumors: treatment option in selected cases. J Urol 1987;137:852–6.
8. Herr HW. Durable response of a carcinoma in situ of the renal pelvis to topical bacillus Calmette-Guérin. J Urol 1985;134:531–2.
9. Powder JR, Mosberg WH, Pierpoint RZ. Bilateral primary carcinoma of the ureter: topical and ureteral thiotepa. J Urol 1984;132:349–52.
10. Clayman RV, McDougall EM, Nakada SY. Endourology of the upper urinary tract: percutaneous renal and ureteral procedures. In: Walsh PC, Retik AB, Vaughan ED, Wein AJ, editors. Campbell's urology. Vol. 3. Philadelphia: WB Saunders; 1998. p. 2831–6.
11. Jarrett TW, Sweetser PM, Weiss GH, Smith AD. Percutaneous management of transitional cell carcinoma of the renal collecting system: 9-year experience. J Urol 1995; 154:1629–35.
12. Wishnow KI, Johnson DE, Preston D, Tenney D. Long-term serum creatinine values after radical nephrectomy. Urology 1990;35:114–6.
13. Fenton S, Desmeules M, Copleston P, et al. Renal replacement therapy in Canada: a report from the Canadian Organ Replacement Register. Am J Kidney Dis 1995;25:134–50.
14. Zincke H, Neves RJ. Feasibility of conservative surgery for transitional cell cancer of the upper urinary tract. Urol Clin North Am 1984;11:717–24.
15. Mazeman E. Tumors of the upper urinary tract calyces, renal pelvis, and ureter. Eur Urol 1976;2:120–8.
16. Shalhav AL, Dunn MD, Portis AJ, et al. Laparoscopic nephroureterectomy for upper tract transitional cell cancer: the Washington University experience. J Urol 2000; 163:1100–4.
17. Seifman BD, Montie JE, Wolf JS. Prospective comparison between hand-assisted laparoscopic and open surgical nephroureterectomy for urothelial cell carcinoma. Urology 2001;57:133–7.

18. Gill IS, Sung GT, Hobart MG, et al. Laparoscopic radical nephroureterectomy for upper tract transitional cell carcinoma: the Cleveland Clinic experience. J Urol 2000;164: 1513–22.

19. Hsu TH, Gill IS, Fazeli-Matin S, et al. Radical nephrectomy and nephroureterectomy in the octogenarian and nonagenarian: comparison of laparoscopic and open approaches. Urology 1999;53:1121–5.

20. Elliot DS, Segura JW. Lightner D, et al. Is nephroureterectomy necessary in all cases of upper tract transitional carcinoma? Long-term results of conservative endourologic management of upper tract transitional cell carcinoma in individuals with a normal contralateral kidney. Urology 2001;58:174–8.

21. Clark PE, Streem SB, Geisinger MA. 13-year experience with percutaneous management of upper tract transitional cell carcinoma. J Urol 1999;161:772–6.

22. Durek C, Rusch-Gerdes S, Jocham D, Bohle A. Sensitivity of BCG to modern antibiotics. Eur Urol 2000;37:21–5.

23. Liatsikos EN, Dinlenc CZ, Kapoor RK, Smith AD. Transitional cell carcinoma of the renal pelvis: ureteroscopic and percutaneous approach. J Endourol 2001;15:377–83.

24. Patel A, Soonawalla P, Shepherd SF, et al. Long-term outcome after percutaneous treatment of transitional cell carcinoma of the renal pelvis. J Urol 1996;155:868–74.

25. Plancke HR, Strijbos WE, Delaere KP. Percutaneous endoscopic treatment of urothelial tumours of the renal pelvis. Br J Urol 1995;75:736–9.

26. Lee BR, Jabbour ME, Marshall FF, et al. 13-year survival comparison of percutaneous and open nephroureterectomy approaches for management of transitional cell carcinoma of renal collecting system: equivalent outcomes. J Endourol 1999;13:289–94.

27. Jabbour ME, Desgrandchamps F, Cazin S, et al. Percutaneous management of grade II upper urinary tract transitional cell carcinoma: the long-term outcome. J Urol 2000; 163:1105–7.

28. Lee SH, Lin JS, Tzai TS, et al. Prognostic factors of primary transitional cell carcinoma of the upper urinary tract. Eur Urol 1996;29:266–70.

29. Huben RP, Mounzer AM, Murphy GP. Tumor grade and stage as prognostic variables in upper tract urothelial tumors. Cancer 1988;62:2016–20.

30. Martinez-Pineiro JA, Matres MJG, Martinez-Pineiro L. Endourological treatment of upper tract urothelial carcinomas: analysis of a series of 59 tumors. J Urol 1996;156: 377–85.

31. Jabbour ME, Smith AD. Primary percutaneous approach to upper urinary tract transitional cell carcinoma. Urol Clin North Am 2000;27:739–50.

32. Woodhouse CRJ, Kellett MJ, Bloom JG. Percutaneous renal surgery and local radiotherapy in the management of renal pelvic transitional cell carcinoma. Br J Urol 1986;58:245–9.

33. Sharma NK, Nicol A, Powell CS. Tract infiltration following percutaneous resection of renal pelvic transitional cell carcinoma. Br J Urol 1994;73:597–8.

34. Huang A, Low RK, White R. Case reports: nephrostomy tract tumor seeding following percutaneous manipulation of a ureteral carcinoma. J Urol 1995;153:1041–2.

35. Mills IW, Laniado ME, Patel A. The role of endoscopy in the management of patients with upper urinary tract transitional cell carcinoma. BJU Int 2001;87:150–62.

36. Chen GL, El-Gabry EA, Bagley DH. Surveillance of upper urinary tract transitional cell carcinoma: the role of ureteroscopy, retrograde pyelography, cytology, and urinalysis. J Urol 2000;164:1173–6.

37. Keeley FX, Bibbo M, Bagley DH. Ureteroscopic treatment and surveillance of upper urinary tract transitional cell carcinoma. J Urol 1997;157:1560–5.

38. Shelley MD, Kynaston H, Court J, et al. A systematic review of intravesical bacillus Calmette-Guérin plus transurethral resection vs. transurethral resection alone in Ta and T1 bladder cancer. BJU Int 2001;88:209–16.

39. Herr HW, Schwalb DM, Zhang ZF, et al. Intravesical bacillus Calmette-Guérin prevents tumor progression and death from superficial bladder cancer: ten year follow-up of a prospective randomized trial. J Clin Oncol 1995;13: 1404–8.

40. Patel A, Fuchs GJ. New techniques for the administration of topical adjuvant therapy after endoscopic ablation of upper urinary tract transitional cell carcinoma. J Urol 1998;159:71–5.

41. Studer UE, Casanova G, Kraft R, Zingg EJ. Percutaneous bacillus Calmette-Guérin perfusion of the upper urinary tract for carcinoma in situ. J Urol 1989;142:975–7.

42. Irie A, Iwamura M, Kadowaki K, et al. Intravesical instillation of bacillus Calmette-Guérin for carcinoma in situ of the urothelium involving the upper urinary tract utilizing vesicoureteral reflux created by a double-pigtail catheter. Urology 2002;59:53–7.

43. Thalmann GN, Markwalder R, Walter B, Studer UE. Long term experience with bacillus Calmette-Guérin therapy of upper urinary tract transitional cell carcinoma in patients not eligible for surgery. J Urol 2002;168:1381–5.

44. Sharpe JR, Duffy G, Chin JL. Intrarenal bacillus Calmette-Guérin therapy for upper urinary tract carcinoma in situ. J Urol 1993;149:457–60.

45. Nishino Y, Yamammoto N, Komeda H, et al. Bacillus Calmette-Guérin instillation treatment for carcinoma in situ of the upper urinary tract. BJU Int 2000;85:799–801.

46. Bellman GC, Sweetser P, Smith D. Complications of intracavitary bacillus Calmette-Guérin after percutaneous resection of upper tract transitional cell carcinoma. J Urol 1994;151:13–5.

47. Yokogi H, Wada Y, Mizutani M, et al. Bacillus Calmette Guérin perfusion therapy for carcinoma in situ of the upper urinary tract. Br J Urol 1996;77:676–9.

48. Nonomura N, Ono Y, Nozawa M, et al. Bacillus Calmette-Guérin perfusion therapy for the treatment of transitional cell carcinoma in situ of the upper urinary tract. Eur Urol 2000;38:701–5.

49. Okubo K, Ichioka K, Terada N, et al. Intrarenal bacillus Calmette-Guérin therapy for carcinoma in situ of the upper urinary tract: long-term follow-up and natural course in cases of failure. BJU Int 2001;88:343–7.

50. Schoenberg MP, Van Arsdalen KN, Wein AJ. The management of transitional cell carcinoma in solitary renal units. J Urol 1991;146:700–3.

22

Ureteroscopic Upper Tract–Preserving Approaches in Urothelial Cancer

DEMETRIUS H. BAGLEY, MD

Ureteroscopy has gained a valuable role in the diagnosis and treatment of upper urinary tract neoplasms. There are many radiologic techniques and urinary markers that can help define upper tract lesions. Cytology can be helpful, especially with high-grade lesions, but direct endoscopic inspection and biopsy is the only definitive technique. The same endoscopic access can deliver ablative techniques to the upper tract to treat neoplasms. The value and the limitations of ureteroscopic treatment, as well as the appropriate postoperative surveillance, are being defined. Similarly, the appropriate selection of patients for endoscopic therapy is growing with the development of instruments and techniques for therapy.

DIAGNOSIS OF UPPER TRACT NEOPLASMS

During the evaluation of patients with suspected upper tract neoplasms, a filling defect is the most common lesion found. Many radiographic features have been considered characteristic of neoplasms, such as the Goblet sign.[1] Renal sonography can distinguish lucent calculi from soft tissue lesions.[2,3] Computed tomography can detect renal calculi and masses as the cause of a filling defect even more effectively.[4,5] Yet there is no single pathognomonic configuration that can define a neoplasm. Direct endoscopy, however, allows visual identification and can give access for biopsy.

URETEROSCOPIC ACCESS

The endoscopic approach for the diagnosis of an upper tract filling defect includes cystoscopy to give access through the bladder, which is inspected. Any suspicious area is biopsied as necessary. Attention is then turned to the upper tract in question. A retrograde pyelogram may, in some cases, give additional information regarding the extent and presence of a lesion. A cone tip retrograde ureteropyelogram is preferred because it can outline the entire collecting system. Initial ureteral catheterization with a pull-out contrast study runs the risk of traumatizing any small lesions present. It may be necessary to use multiple injections of contrast and different volumes and different concentrations of the contrast to prevent overfilling or overly dense radiopacity, which may obscure some filling defects. Generally, 30% iodinated contrast in saline give an adequate density.

The ureter is then inspected endoscopically. A small diameter (approximately 7 French) rigid endoscope is passed under direct vision transurethrally and into the affected ureter. It is best to proceed without initial dilation to avoid trauma to the ureter or any neoplasm within the dilated segment. A small-diameter rigid endoscope can usually be passed directly into the ureter without dilation.[6,7] It may be necessary to introduce a wire through the ureteroscope to help open the orifice. This instrument is then passed along the ureter, inspecting the lumen as far as possible. If it becomes difficult to pass the instrument, as it often is when the ureter leaves the pelvis, then a guidewire is left in place and the rigid endoscope is removed. A flexible ureteroscope is then passed over the wire to inspect the more proximal portions of the ureter and the intrarenal collecting system.[8] There the lumen is inspected in a sequential atraumatic pattern. As the ureteropelvic junction is passed, the pelvis is first inspected. Then the upper infundibula followed by the mid- and finally the lower calyces are inspected. With this careful systematic inspection, small, otherwise undetected lesions may be found, and the primary lesion causing the filling defect is approached without trauma, which might obscure the lesion.[9]

Ureteroscopy was applied to the diagnosis of upper tract filling defects early in its development. Aso and Bagley and their colleagues reported the benefits of the ureteroscopic visualization of upper urinary tract in providing a diagnosis.[10,11] Huffman and colleagues reported experience with both diagnosis and treatment of upper tract lesions.[12] Streem and colleagues demonstrated that ureteroscopy could be used to provide the correct diagnosis in evaluation of upper tract filling defects in 83% of patients with upper tract filling defects.[13] In comparison, the standard diagnostic regimen, which included cystoscopy, retrograde pyelography with upper tract cytology in all patients, and computed tomographic scans or ultrasonography in those patients when indicated, gave the correct diagnosis in only 58% of patients in the smaller group of 12. Bagley and Rivas reviewed 62 patients evaluated for upper urinary tract filling defects.[14] All patients were studied with flexible ureteropyeloscopes to reach a lesion for direct visualization. A diagnosis was made in each patient who had been studied by standard radiographic and cytologic techniques previously, thus indicating the value of endoscopy in providing the endoscopic diagnosis in 62 upper urinary tract filling defects. (Table 22–1).

With ureteroscopic visualization, typical papillary tumors can be recognized and distinguished from calculi or some forms of edema (Figure 22–1). However, other lesions may not be so easily recognized. For example, high-grade transitional cell carcinoma (TCC) may have a smooth, less papillary surface appearance and be indistinguishable by appearance alone from benign lesions such as fibroepithelial polyps or inverted papillomas. Others can be nearly identical to inflammatory lesions.

URETEROSCOPIC BIOPSY

Ureteroscopy with direct inspection of an upper tract neoplasm also provides a mechanism for biopsy of

Table 22–1. ENDOSCOPIC DIAGNOSIS OF UPPER URINARY TRACT FILLING DEFECTS

Etiology	No. of Patients
Calculi	11
Tumor	
Transitional cell carcinoma	25
Renal adenocarcinoma	1
Inverted papilloma	1
Fibroepithelial polyp	1
Vascular impression	7
Edema or submucosal hemorrhage	5
Emphysematous blebs	2
Ureteral stenosis	1
Unremarkable urothelium	8

Adapted from Bagley and Rivas.[14]

the tumor. Earlier studies by Gill and colleagues and Gittes had demonstrated that sampling of upper tract neoplasms with a brush placed cystoscopically and followed radiographically could provide a diagnosis more often than voided or catheterized cytology alone. This technique gave small tissue samples, which could be prepared to be read as histologic specimens with an architecture of the neoplasm and not just the individual cells. These studies gave an accuracy in diagnosing upper tract tumors of approximately 60%.[15,16]

Under the direct vision of ureteroscopy, several techniques are used to sample the neoplasm.[17] The brush appears to be relatively inefficient because it often just moves the tumor without really sampling it. Other devices such as a cup forceps, a grasper, or, most effectively, a basket, can sample tumors to give a larger specimen. The choice of instrument is guided by the architecture of the neoplasm. For example, a papillary tumor in the ureter, or even intrarenal collecting system, can usually be sampled easily with a flat wire basket (Table 22–2 and Figure 22–2). A relatively large sample of a few millimeters can often be obtained.

A cup forceps also can give an adequate sample. Although the tissue enclosed within the cup is 1 mm or less, often there is tissue extending beyond the cup itself, providing a larger sample. The cup forceps is also particularly useful to sample a sessile lesion, which is not amenable to sampling with a basket (Figure 22–3). The wire-pronged grasper is reserved for papillary tumors, which are not accessible for a basket such as those at the base of a calyx. A brush

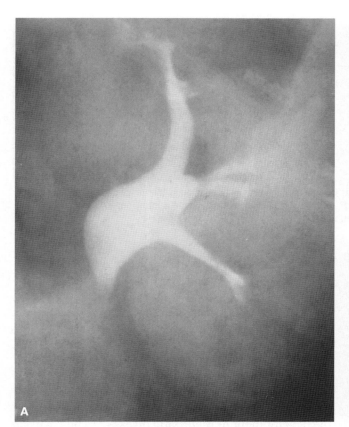

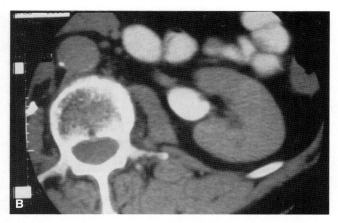

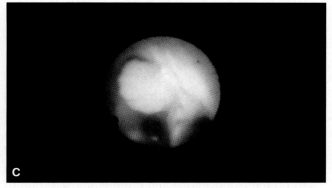

Figure 22–1. *A*, A 56-year-old female was found to have microscopic hematuria. Contrast study demonstrated a filling defect in the renal pelvis. The patient had previously undergone a right nephroureterectomy for transitional cell carcinoma of the kidney. *B*, A computed tomographic scan also demonstrates a filling defect based on the anterior wall of the renal pelvis. *C*, Visualization by ureteroscopy shows a small papillary neoplasm consistent with a low-grade transitional cell carcinoma.

may be useful to sample a flat, erythematous, or sessile lesion. After any biopsy, the irrigant within the collecting system near the tumor should be aspirated as a sample (Table 22–3). All samples are studied with cytopathologic techniques, including preparation of a slide with Cytospin and preparation of a cell block with any macroscopic tissue sample.[18–20]

These biopsy and cytopathologic techniques have provided considerable information in the diagnosis of upper tract tumors. Keeley and colleagues reviewed 42 patients who had ureteroscopic visualization and biopsy and subsequent surgical resection of the upper tract neoplasm.[21] Among 30 ureteroscopic specimens read as showing low- or moderate-grade neoplasms, 27 (90%) were also read as low- or moderate-grade TCC on the final surgical specimens. At the other end of the scale, 11 of the 12 tumors read as high grade on the ureteroscopic biopsy were also high grade in the final specimen (Table 22–4). It was of note that two of

the patients had T0 tumors in the final surgical specimens after the diagnosis had been made and the tumor treated endoscopically. The patients, both with normal contralateral kidneys, had chosen a nephroureterectomy as definitive therapy. These findings support the endoscopic approach to the treatment of upper tract neoplasms with the demonstrative ability to evaluate tumors. Guarnizo and colleagues had stressed the need for multiple ureteroscopic biopsies.[22] The preferred technique has included multiple biopsies and the careful cytopathologic handling of the specimens to give both cytologic and histologic samples.

Table 22–2. URETEROSCOPIC BIOPSY OF UPPER TRACT NEOPLASMS
Place basket onto neoplasm
Close snugly but not fully
Withdraw to avulse fragment of tumor
Remove entire unit, tumor, basket, and ureteroscope

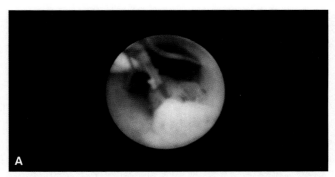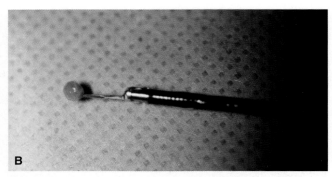

Figure 22–2.   *A,* A midureteral papillary tumor is biopsied using a flat wire basket, which is placed around the neoplasm and closed snugly but not fully. A portion of the tumor can then be avulsed from the wall. *B,* In this way, a larger piece of tissue approximately 3 to 4 mm in diameter is retrieved with removal of the entire unit of ureteroscope, basket, and tumor.

Hara and colleagues have compared the value of ureteropyeloscopy in the diagnosis of upper urinary tract tumors to the results with radiography and urinary cytology (Table 22–5).[23] The safety of ureteroscopy combined with accurate diagnosis with high positive predictive value and negative predictive value rendered a very valuable technique.

The risks of ureteroscopy and biopsy of upper tract TCC have been controversial. One report speculated on the pyelovenous and lymphatic migration of TCC during flexible ureteroscopy because in the one patient reported, tumor was found in an unusual pattern outside the renal pelvis at surgery.[24] However, in

a review of patients treated surgically after ureteroscopic biopsy, Kulp and Bagley could not detect any unusual spread of tumor.[25] In a more definitive comparative study, Hendin and colleagues found no difference in long-term or disease-specific survival of patients with upper tract TCC who had surgical treatment preceded either by ureteroscopic biopsy or none (Table 22–6).[26] Hara and colleagues added 50 patients to those who have had ureteroscopic biopsy without the development of metastatic disease.[23] Thus, we can conclude at this time that ureteroscopic biopsy can be a safe and very valuable procedure without any documented evidence of tumor dissemination.

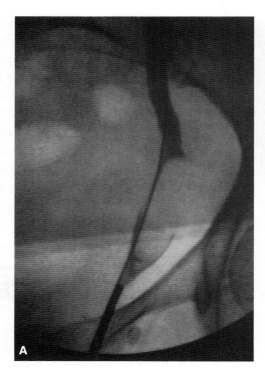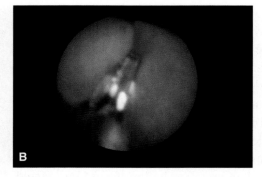

Figure 22–3.   A 64-year-old female experienced an episode of gross painless hematuria. *A,* Intravenous contrast study demonstrated a filling defect in the left distal ureter, which is better defined with injection of contrast during ureteroscopy. *B,* Multiple biopsies of the lesion with a cup forceps on two episodes showed only fibrous and stromal tissue consistent with fibroepithelial polyp. The entire tumor was treated ureteroscopically with laser coagulation and ablation.

Table 22–3. SAMPLING FOR CYTOPATHOLOGY IN PATIENTS WITH UPPER TRACT NEOPLASMS
Bladder urine
Aspirate at tumor
Biopsy with selected device
Aspirate
Treat (if appropriate)
Aspirate

Table 22–5. DIAGNOSTIC STUDIES FOR UPPER TRACT TUMORS		
Study	Sensitivity	Specificity (%)
Radiography	96	12
Cytology	60	84
Ureteroscopy	92	88

Adapted from Hara I et al.[23]

PATIENTS FOR URETEROSCOPIC BIOPSY

There is some question as to which patients suspected of having an upper tract tumor to biopsy. Our policy has been to do a ureteroscopy and biopsy in any patient in whom the diagnosis of an upper tract filling defect is in question. This includes any patient with a filling defect and voided urinary cytology with or without any abnormality less than definitive (positive) for malignant cells. The presence of individually malignant-appearing cells (positive cytology) indicates the presence of a high-grade tumor or carcinoma in situ (CIS). It is probably not necessary to biopsy those patients who have cytology definitely positive for malignant cells and a large irregular filling defect, which, in itself, may be nearly definitive for TCC.

URETEROSCOPIC TREATMENT

Ureteroscopic access to the upper urinary tract also offers access for treatment with ablative techniques. Many devices are now available that can be placed through ureteroscopes, such as small-diameter graspers, electrodes, and appropriate laser fibers, which can be used to treat neoplasms. Selection of the appropriate patient and acceptance of these techniques are being developed.

Selection of the appropriate patient for ureteroscopic treatment of an upper tract neoplasm depends on several factors (Table 22–7). The earliest experience was driven by interest and need for a nephron-sparing procedure. These patients remain the strongest candidates for this treatment. They are patients with a solitary kidney or compromised contralateral kidney. Those with a small tumor are technically easier and generally less likely to have recurrences. The urinary cytology should be negative for high-grade cells, which, by their presence, would indicate either a high-grade tumor or associated CIS.

In contrast, there are findings that argue strongly against a ureteroscopic resection. These include a large tumor, a sessile high-grade lesion, or a neoplasm that extends more than half of the circumference of a ureter or infundibulum. Treatment of the latter in a single stage is likely to result in stricturing. Some neoplasms cannot be treated ureteroscopically because they are inaccessible, too extensive, or obviously too large and advanced (Figure 22–4 to 22–8).

The patient must participate in any decision on the form of therapy. There is a risk to the patient's life with any upper tract neoplasm, and that must be balanced with the risks and demands of treatment. If the patient is rendered anephric by treatment, the risks and changes in lifestyle from future management with dialysis or transplantation must be taken into account. However, the risk of recurrence and the

Table 22–4. GRADING OF UPPER URINARY TRACT TRANSITIONAL CELL CARCINOMA ON URETEROSCOPIC BIOPSY			
Grade on Ureteroscopic Biopsy	Grade on Histopathology From Surgical Specimen (No. of Patients)		
	1	2	3
Low	5	—	—
1–2	1	6	1
Biopsy 2	2	6	2
High		1	11

Adapted from Keeley FX et al.[21]

Table 22–6. LONG-TERM SURVIVAL WITH UPPER TRACT TRANSITIONAL CELL CARCINOMA: EFFECT OF URETEROSCOPIC BIOPSY		
	Biopsy	None
No. of patients	48	48
Metastases	12.6%	18.8% (NS)
Died with recurrence	10.4%	10.4% (NS)

Adapted from Hendin BN et al.[26]
NS = not significant.

Table 22–7. CANDIDATES FOR URETEROSCOPIC TREATMENT OF UPPER TRACT TRANSITIONAL CELL CARCINOMA		
Tumor factor	Good	Poor
Size	Small	Large
Configuration	Papillary	Sessile
Number	Solitary	Multiple
Distribution	Single	Circumferential or extensive
Grade	Low	High
Cytology	Negative	Positive (for high-grade cells)

need for surveillance must be considered and accepted by the patient before any endoscopic treatment can be undertaken.

Several instruments and techniques are available for resection or ablation of upper tract tumors ureteroscopically. The first technique employed was electroresection. Ureteroscopic resectoscopes are available that are similar to a pediatric resectoscope but in a longer design. These are rigid and relatively large, with an outer dimension of 12 to 13 French. However, these can be used effectively to resect ureteral neoplasms and are the first instruments employed for successful resection of TCC of the upper tract.[11,22]

Experience with biopsy techniques has demonstrated that a significant volume of papillary neoplasm can be removed mechanically. Multiple samples are removed to remove tumor volume. The base of the tumor can then be fulgurated lightly to eradicate the base yet maintain the integrity of the ureter with minimal scarring.

LASER RESECTION

Laser techniques have proven to be most efficient for treating upper tract neoplasms ureteroscopically. The small fibers (200 or 365 micron) can be passed through the working channel of a small-diameter rigid ureteroscope or flexible ureteroscope with suf-

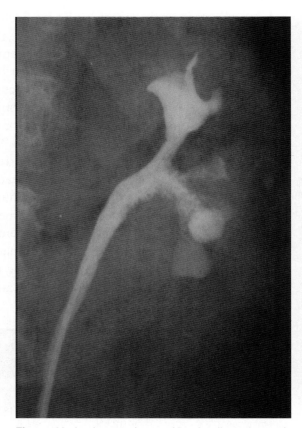

Figure 22–4. Low-grade transitional cell carcinoma is scattered extensively throughout the renal pelvis and the mid- and lower infundibula. It is impossible to reach and treat the entire neoplasm ureteroscopically.

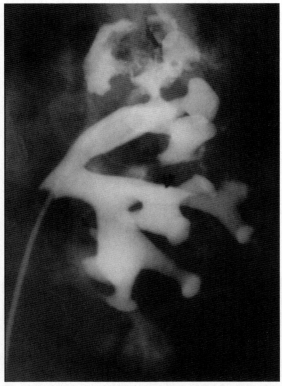

Figure 22–5. An episode of gross hematuria prompted evaluation in this 70-year-old male. His urinary cytology showed only atypical cells. Ureteroscopic visualization and biopsy demonstrated a papillary grade 1 to 2 transitional cell carcinoma, which is clearly too large to resect. The patient was treated with nephroureterectomy.

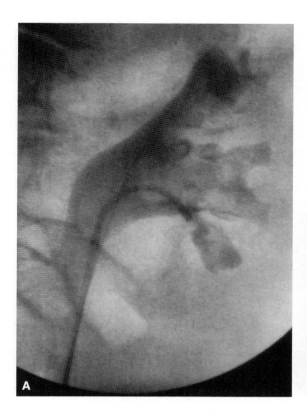

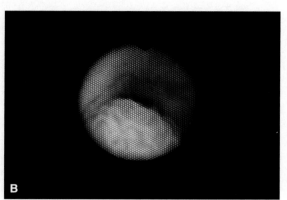

Figure 22–6. Ureteroscopy was performed in a patient with gross hematuria after an excretory urogram suggested a filling defect in the lower infundibulum, *A*. Inspection of this area demonstrated a papillary neoplasm, *B*. Because of the difficulty in reaching the medial wall of the lower infundibulum with surveillance and treatment, the patient was treated with a nephroureterectomy. Ureteroscopes that deflect with active secondary deflection may improve access to the entire lower pole and permit treatment of neoplasms at that location.

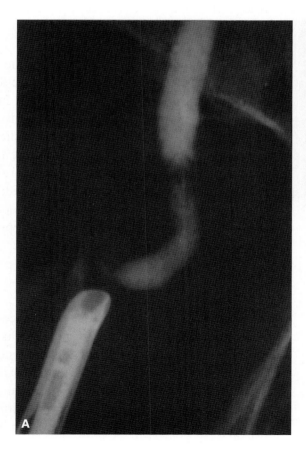

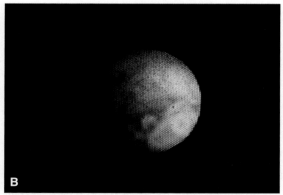

Figure 22–7. A filling defect in the left distal ureter was found to be a papillary neoplasm encompassing nearly the entire circumference of the ureter. After ureteroscopic treatment using the neodymium:YAG and holmium:YAG lasers, the patient developed a short stricture, which was not obstructive.

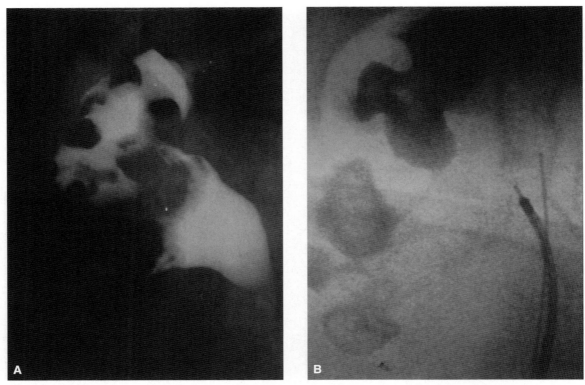

Figure 22–8.   This patient presented with gross hematuria and was found on a abdominal radiogram (KUB) to have renal calculi. His gross hematuria persisted. Further evaluation with a computed tomographic scan had demonstrated clot or mass within the renal pelvis in addition to several calyceal calculi. *A,* Because the hematuria was excessive for calculi alone, he underwent diagnostic retrograde ureteropyelography, which demonstrated a filling defect in the upper pelvis and upper infundibulum. *B,* Ureteroscopic inspection and biopsy demonstrated a grade 2 transitional cell carcinoma, which was treated by nephroureterectomy.

ficient space left for irrigating fluid. The lasers available for urologic application can effectively coagulate and ablate tissue throughout the urinary tract.

The neodymium: yttrium-aluminum-garnet (Nd: YAG) laser can coagulate tissue. Although it can penetrate several millimeters into tissue, this effect depends on a time factor with several seconds of exposure necessary for greater penetration. The beam must also be aimed directly toward the tissue to penetrate more deeply. It is quite possible to control the exposure both by positioning the fiber onto the tumor without directly aiming toward the wall of the ureter and by moving the fiber across the surface of the tumor to avoid prolonged exposure.[27,28] Ureteral damage is also limited because the laser fiber and beam are usually aimed at the tumor parallel to the surface of the ureter.[29–40] Within the kidney, where there is less risk of scarring and stricturing, the neoplasm can be coagulated safely with the Nd:YAG laser.[41]

The holmium laser offers additional advantages. It can coagulate tissue more superficially than the Nd:YAG laser. Additionally, it can ablate tissue. This dual-modality effect is controlled by the selection of energy and the positioning of the fiber.[42–44] A higher energy applied more closely to the tissue gives an ablative effect, whereas a lower energy applied by removing the fiber short a distance from the tissue enhances the coagulative effect.[28] Lasers are also available with the capability to produce the Nd:YAG and holmium:YAG wavelengths. Thus, the optimal effect can be achieved by selection of the appropriate laser with activation of a dual foot pedal.

RECURRENCES

Upper tract neoplasms are prone to recurrences just as locally treated bladder tumors are. This is presumably because of the field change seen generally in TCC. Endoscopic treatment then should aim to treat the neoplasm thoroughly with minimal damage to the normal tissue, particularly within the ureter. The success of treatment is based on eradication of the primary tumor and on the local recurrence of neoplasm as well as the potential for metastatic spread.

In considering the risks of local recurrence, we must compare earlier series of local surgical removal of single upper tract TCC. With surgical removal, we would expect the best chance for local control. In those series, there is a high recurrence rate after the treatment of ureteral or renal pelvic neoplasms.[45–47] In the ureter, the recurrence was reported at 12 to 18%. It was higher when more proximal lesions were removed. After treatment of lesions within the renal pelvis, the recurrence rate was very high at 48 to 64%.

The size of a primary tumor, the grade of a primary TCC, and the grade of the lesion are known to affect the risk of recurrence in the bladder. A similar pattern is seen for upper tract tumors. The risk of recurrent disease was considerably higher with tumors over 1.5 cm in diameter than those that were smaller. Similarly, there was a lower risk of recurrence for low-grade tumors than for grade 2 or 3 TCC treated ureteroscopically (Figure 22–9).[39]

Large tumors have been treated successfully ureteroscopically by staging treatment at intervals of 6 to 8 weeks (Figures 22–10 and 22–11). This period is necessary to permit acute inflammatory changes to resolve and is also long enough to detect additional tumor growth. Lesions too large to be treated successfully by staging may be treated by percutaneous nephroscopy, as discussed in Chapter 19, or may require nephroureterectomy.

Reported series of ureteroscopic treatment of upper tract TCC are summarized in Table 22–8. It is notable that among the time periods studied, the recurrences of the treatment of renal pelvic lesions remain at approximately 40%. However, after treatment of ureteral lesions, recurrences increased from 25 to 43%. This may be the result of treating more proximal and larger lesions in the more recent series. New bladder tumors developed in approximately 40% of patients in each time period, although this

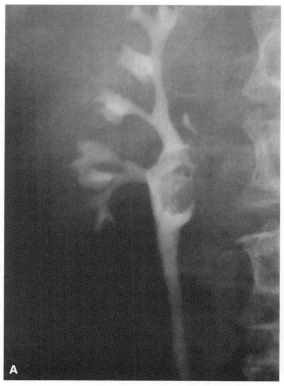 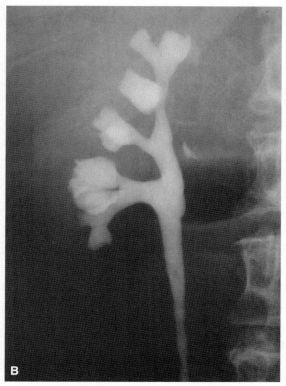

Figure 22–9. A 73-year-old patient with a solitary functioning right kidney was found to have a large filling defect in the right renal pelvis after evaluation for an episode of gross hematuria (*A*). The neoplasm was biopsied ureteroscopically and resected with a combination of the holmium:YAG and neodymium:YAG lasers (*B*). After a single treatment on this grade 1 transitional cell carcinoma, the patient remained free of recurrent disease for 3 years.

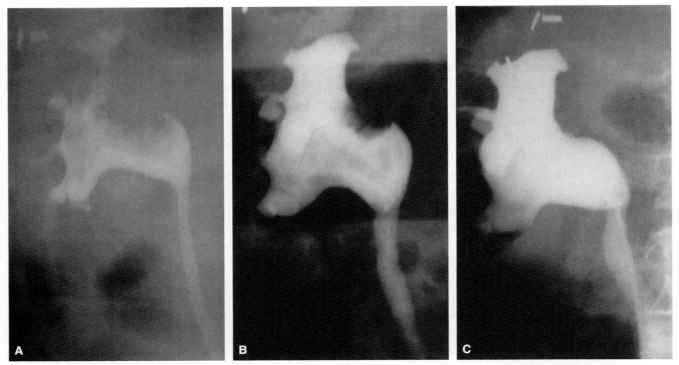

Figure 22–10.   Six years after a left nephroureterectomy for transitional cell carcinoma of the kidney, an octogenarian presented with an episode of gross hematuria. *A,* Retrograde ureteropyelography demonstrates a large filling defect in the renal pelvis that was grade 1 to 2 transitional cell carcinoma. The filling defect extended into the upper infundibulum represents clot. The neoplasm was treated ureteroscopically with a combination of the neodymium:YAG and holmium:YAG lasers. *B,* Eight weeks later, there was residual tumor on the upper margin of the renal pelvis. *C,* This was similarly treated, and 8 weeks later, the irregularity along the pelvis represented only edematous mucosa. The patient remained free of recurrent neoplasm for another 6 years before he died of unrelated causes.

rate is very similar to that reported after surgical treatment with nephroureterectomy, nephrectomy, or segmental ureteral resection of upper tract tumors. Among reported series, the risks of the bladder tumors ranged from 9 to 36%, depending in some series on the grade of the tumor.[48–52] Their relationship was not studied in other series. In one series, the rate of bladder neoplasms could be related to a previous history of bladder cancer, where a 53% recurrence rate was noted. Thus, the observed 40% in patients treated ureteroscopically can be expected because it represents a blend of these many factors. Ureteroscopic treatment does not appear to provoke new bladder tumors.

NORMAL CONTRALATERAL KIDNEY

This relatively positive experience in patients with some compromise of renal function has been the basis for the interest in treating patients with a normal contralateral kidney. Elliott and colleagues reviewed 21 patients with two renal units and found that 37% of the patients developed a local recurrence on an average of 7 months after treatment.[53] Among 13 ureteral tumors, 46% recurred, whereas only 1 of 8 (12%) renal pelvic tumors recurred. They demonstrated a high mortality rate of 11 of 20 patients dying of unrelated causes, whereas 1 died from invasive bladder cancer. No one died because of the endoscopic tumor treatment regimen. Kidneys were preserved in 17 patients (81%), whereas 4 (19%) required nephroureterectomy.

In another series by Chen and Bagley, 23 patients with 2 functional kidneys had an upper tract TCC treated ureteroscopically.[54] Although these patients had numerous local recurrences, there was no significant grade increase and no patient developed metastatic disease. At the time of follow-up, 61% of patients were free of disease, whereas 17% had an ipsilateral recurrence and 5% (one patient) a new contralateral neoplasm (Figure 22–12). Four, or 17%, of patients had been treated with nephroureterectomy. Thus, from both series, it is possible to conclude that ureteroscopic treatment of upper urinary tract TCC can be safe and effective in very carefully selected patients.

ADJUVANT THERAPY

There has been interest and certainly a need for adjuvant therapy after the endoscopic treatment of upper tract neoplasms. There is hope that the high rate of recurrences of new tumors developing in patients after local endoscopic therapy can be minimized. A similar approach has been used in patients with positive upper tract cytology, although these really represent a separate subset of patients.[55] Intraluminal immunotherapy has been initiated with

bacille Calmette-Guérin (BCG) by placing an indwelling ureteral stent and then instilling the BCG into the bladder. Because reflux with this technique can be quite variable, there is no certainty that it ever reaches the upper tract. Patel and Fuchs have placed a diversionary catheter into the affected segment, bringing the distal end out through the bladder and abdominal wall to the skin to allow introduction of BCG directly into the intrarenal collecting system at the desired scheduled.[56]

Mitomycin has also been used as an adjuvant. Eastham and Huffman reported on percutaneous instillation of mitomycin and also a technique for retrograde instillation with 5 mg delivered to patients in the first and second postoperative days.[57] Keeley and

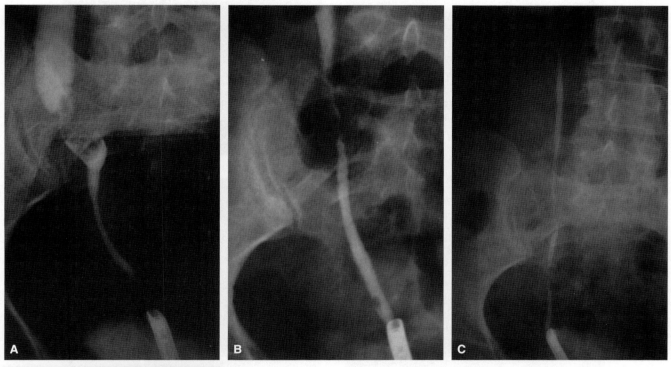

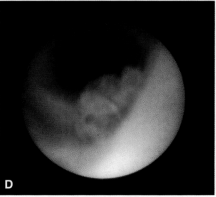

Figure 22–11. *A,* A large right midureteral filling defect was evident on evaluation for an episode of hematuria in a patient who had previously had a distal left ureterectomy and resection of multiple bladder tumors. The tumor was treated ureteroscopically. *B,* Because the entire lesion was not resected, a repeat retrograde ureterogram demonstrated some irregularity of the midureter. Additional grade 1 to 2 transitional cell carcinoma was biopsied and removed at that time. *C* and *D,* Under inspection at 3 months, once again there was a small papillary tumor in the midureter. This was also treated, and the patient remained free of disease for 4 years. She has remained free of disease in that ureter.

Table 22–8. TUMOR RECURRENCE AFTER URETEROSCOPIC TREATMENT OF UPPER TRACT TRANSITIONAL CELL CARCINOMA		
	To 1995 (%)	To 2000 (%)
RP	6/15 (40)	22/60 (37)
Ureter	22/87 (25)	33/77 (43)
New BT	11/28 (39)	41/101 (41)
NU	4/102 (4)	19/137 (14)

Adapted from references 28 to 40, 43, and 48 to 54. BT = bladder tumor; NU = nephroureterectomy; RP = renal pelvis.

colleagues have used a higher dose of mitomycin C (40 mg) instilled through a ureteral catheter on the first or second postoperative day.[58] In that retrospec- tive series, there was suggestive evidence of fewer recurrences in the high-risk patients treated.

There are no prospective randomized trials sup- porting the use of adjuvant therapy after the endo- scopic treatment of upper tract neoplasms. Its use has been based on the evidence found in patients with TCC of the bladder.

SURVEILLANCE

Because there is a high recurrence rate after uretero- scopic treatment of upper tract neoplasms, a close surveillance protocol is necessary. The need for cys-

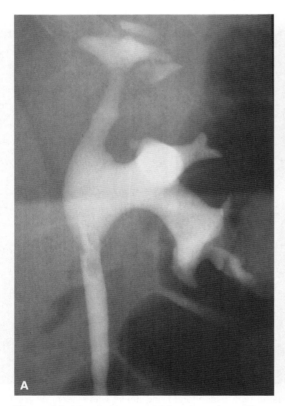
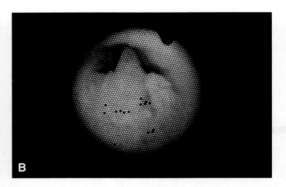
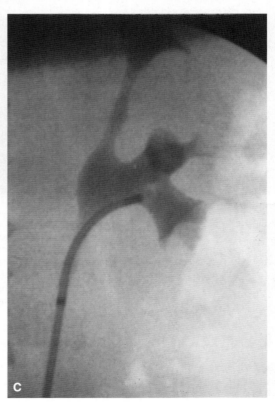

Figure 22–12. A 45-year-old female patient with an episode of gross hematuria had been evaluated 1 year earlier without findings. At the more recent episode, a filling defect was found at the ureteropelvic junction (*A*). Ureteroscopic inspection reveals the papillary neo- plasm at that level (*B*). It was treated with laser resec- tion and followed ureteroscopically (*C*). The patient has been free of recurrent disease for 6 years

toscopy to detect new bladder neoplasms after excisional surgical treatment of upper tract tumors has been well defined. After endoscopic treatment, a similar program of surveillance with cystoscopy must be maintained in addition to surveillance of the upper tract.

Ureteroscopy has been the most sensitive technique to detect and then to treat upper tract neoplasms (Figure 22–13). In an initial retrospective study, Keeley and colleagues noted that the sensitivity of retrograde pyelography for detecting recurrent upper tract tumors was only 25%.[39] In another later series, surveillance was evaluated with urinalysis, voided cytology, retrograde ureteropyelography, and ureteroscopic biopsy in patients with ureteroscopically visualized and treated neoplasms.[59] None of these tests detected all of the tumors (Table 22–9). However, the high specificity of the noninvasive urinalysis and voided urinary cytology support their value as screening studies. There may also be value in their use at an interval when ureteroscopy is not otherwise planned.

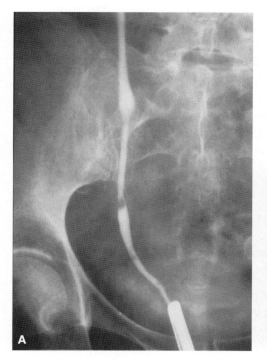

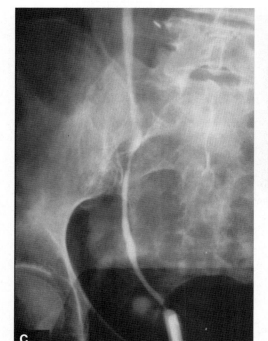

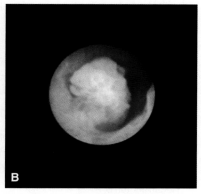

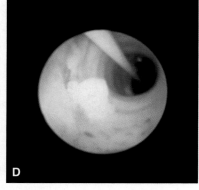

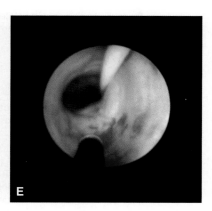

Figure 22–13. A 65-year-old female who previously had a segmental ureterectomy for a grade 1 to 2 transitional cell carcinoma was found to have a filling defect in the distal ureter (*A*). Ureteroscopic inspection demonstrated a papillary tumor, which was removed with a ureteral resectoscope (*B*). On follow-up, a retrograde pyelogram demonstrates a possible irregularity in that area, but ureteroscopic inspection confirmed the presence of a small papillary tumor (*C* and *D*). This was removed with a cup forceps and the base was fulgurated (*E*). The patient remained free of disease in that area for an additional 5 years.

Table 22–9. SURVEILLANCE OF UPPER TRACT TRANSITIONAL CELL CARCINOMA

	Sensitivity	Specificity
Urinalysis	38	85
Bladder cytology	50	100
Retrograde pyelogram		
Urologist	72	85
Radiologist	27	89
Ureteroscopic biopsy	93	65

Adapted from Chen GL et al.[59]

Ureteroscopic evaluation is an essential part of the follow-up surveillance after endoscopic treatment of upper tract neoplasms. The optimal surveillance protocol has not been determined. A protocol for surveillance using cystoscopy, ureteroscopy, and imaging of a contralateral kidney, if present, has been suggested (Figure 22–14 and 22–15).

COMPLICATIONS

Complications of ureteroscopic treatment consist predominantly of ureteral stricture and, to a lesser extent, perforation.[60] With an overall complication rate of 19%, stricture occurred in 13.6% of patients treated and perforation in 4.2%. The significance of perforation is not known, although the presence of tumor cells within any extravasated fluid must be considered, and a risk of extraluminal recurrence exists. This has not been reported or observed in those series that have commented on it. However, it still must be considered a risk. Ureteral stricture, on the other hand, has been reported in every series. The rate of 13% is considerably higher than the 0.5% seen after ureteroscopic treatment of stones. This can be expected because the ureter itself is being affected by the treatment of

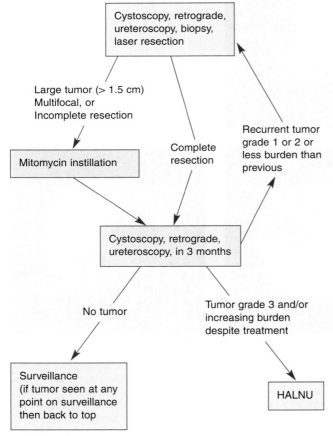

Figure 22–14. Algorithm for patients presenting with bilateral tumors, renal failure, solitary kidney or compromised contralateral kidney. HALNU = hand-assisted laparoscopic nephroureterectomy. Adapted from Lee et al.[61]

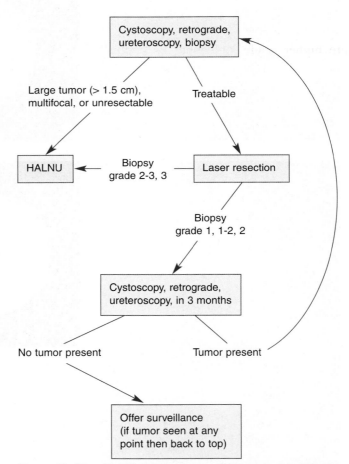

Figure 22–15. Algorithm for patients with normal contralateral kidneys. HALNU = hand-assisted laparoscopic nephroureterectomy. Adapted from Lee et al.[61]

Table 22–10. TOTALLY ENDOSCOPIC TREATMENT OF UPPER URINARY TRACT TRANSITIONAL CELL CARCINOMA

Biopsy: ureteroscopy
Treatment: ureteroscopy or percutaneous nephroscopy
Surveillance: ureteroscopy
Nephroureterectomy: laparoscopy

the neoplasm, whereas the ureter is carefully avoided when treating stones. The risk is probably considerably higher when there is a circumferential tumor being treated.

TOTALLY ENDOSCOPIC MANAGEMENT OF UPPER TRACT TCC

TCC of the upper urinary tract is increasingly diagnosed and treated endoscopically (Table 22–10).[61–63] Suspected lesions are visualized and biopsied ureteroscopically. Tumors can also be treated endoscopically, smaller lesions ureteroscopically, and larger tumors by staging or percutaneously. Tumors that are larger, are higher grade, or cannot be controlled are then treated with nephroureterectomy, usually with hand-assisted laparoscopic nephroureterectomy. After endoscopic treatment, surveillance is with cystoscopy and ureteroscopy. This represents the first urologic disease, which can be managed entirely endoscopically in many patients.

REFERENCES

1. Malek RS, Aguilo J, Hattery RR. Radiolucent filling defects of the renal pelvis: classification and report of unusual cases. J Urol 1975;114:508–13.
2. Pollack HM, Arger PH, Goldberg BB, Mulholland SG. Ultrasonic detection of nonopaque renal calculi. Radiology 1978;127:233–7.
3. Mulholland SG, Arger PH, Goldberg BB, Pollack HM. Ultrasonic differentiation of renal pelvic filling defects. J Urol 1979;122:14–16.
4. Pollack HM, Arger PH, Baumer MP, et al. Computed tomography of renal pelvic filling defects. Radiology 1981;138:645–51.
5. Segal AJ, Spataro RJ, Linke CA, et al. Diagnosis of nonopaque calculi by computed tomography. Radiology 1978;129:447–50.
6. Abdel-Razzak OM, Bagley DH. The 6.9F semi-rigid ureteroscope in clinical use. Urology 1993;41:45–8.
7. Bagley DH. Flexible ureteroscopy. Semin Urol 1989;7:7–15.
8. Bagley DH, Huffman JL, Lyon ES. Combined rigid and flexible ureteropyeloscopy. J Urol 1983;130:243–4.
9. Bagley DH, Allen J. Flexible ureteropyeloscopy in the diagnosis of benign essential hematuria. J Urol 1990;143:549–53.
10. Aso Y, Ohtawara Y, Suzuki K, et al. Usefulness of fiberoptic pyeloureteroscope in the diagnosis of the upper urinary tract lesions. Urol Int 1984;39:355–7.
11. Bagley DH, Lyon ES, Morse MJ, et al. Endoscopic diagnosis and treatment of upper tract urothelial tumors—a preliminary report. Cancer 1985;55:1422–8.
12. Huffman JL, Morse MJ, Herr HW, et al. Ureteropyeloscopy: the diagnostic and therapeutic approach to upper tract urothelial tumors. World J Urol 1985;3:58–63.
13. Streem SB, Pontes JE, Novick AC, Montie JE. Ureteropyeloscopy in the evaluation of upper tract filling defects. J Urol 1986;136:383–5.
14. Bagley DH, Rivas DA. Upper urinary tract filling defects: flexible ureteroscopic diagnosis. J Urol 1990;143:1196–2000.
15. Gill WB, Bibbo M, Thomsen S, Lu CT. Evaluation of renal masses including retrograde renal brushing. Surg Clin North Am 1976;56:149–74.
16. Gittes RF. Retrograde brushing and nephroscopy in the diagnosis of upper tract urothelial cancer. Urol Clin North Am 1984;11:617–22.
17. Abdel-Razzak OM, Ehya H, Cubler-Goodman A, Bagley DH. Ureteroscopic biopsy in the upper urinary tract. Urology 1994;44:451–7.
18. Bian Y, Ehya H, Bagley DH. Cytologic diagnosis of upper urinary tract neoplasms by ureteroscopic sampling. Acta Cytol 1995;39:733–40.
19. Low RK, Moran ME, Anderson KR. Ureteroscopic cytologic diagnosis of upper tract lesions. J Endourol 1993;7:311–14.
20. Tawfiek ER, Bibbo M, Bagley DH. Ureteroscopic biopsy: technique and specimen preparation. Urology 1997;50:117–9.
21. Keeley FX, Kulp DA, Bibbo M, et al. Diagnostic accuracy of ureteroscopic biopsy in upper tract transitional cell carcinoma. J Urol 1997;157:33–7.
22. Guarnizo E, Pavlovich CP, Seiba M, et al. Ureteroscopic biopsy of upper tract urothelial carcinoma: improved diagnostic accuracy and histopathological considerations using a multi-biopsy approach. J Urol 2000;163:52–5.
23. Hara I, Hara S, Miyake H, et al. Usefulness of ureteropyeloscopy for diagnosis of upper urinary tract tumors. J Endourol 2001;15:601–5.
24. Lim DJ, Shattuck MC, Cook WA. Pyelovenous lymphatic migration of transitional cell carcinoma following flexible ureteroscopy. J Urol 1993;149:109–11.
25. Kulp DA, Bagley DH. Does flexible ureteropyeloscopy promote local recurrence of transitional cell carcinoma? J Endourol 1994;8:111–13.
26. Hendin BN, Streem SB, Levin HS, et al. Impact of diagnostic ureteroscopy on long term survival in patients with upper tract transitional cell carcinoma. J Urol 1999;161:783–5.
27. Bagley DH. Ureteroscopic laser treatment of upper urinary tract tumors. J Clin Laser Med Surg 1998;16:55–9.
28. Bagley DH. Laser treatment of urothelial tumors. In: Bagley DH, Das AK, editors. Endourologic use of the holmium laser. Jackson (WY): Teton NewMedia; 2001. p. 29–36.
29. Blute ML, Segura JW, Patterson DE, et al. Impact of endourology on diagnosis and management of upper tract urothelial cancer. J Urol 1989;141:1298–301.

30. Schmeller NT, Hofstetter AG. Laser treatment of urethral tumors. J Urol 1989;141:840–3.

31. Papadopoulos I, Wirth B, Bertermann H, Wand H. Diagnosis and treatment of urothelial tumors by ureteropyeloscopy. J Endourol 1990;4:55–60.

32. Grossman HB, Schwartz SL, Konnak JW. Ureteroscopic treatment of urothelial carcinoma of the ureter and renal pelvis. J Urol 1992;148:275–7.

33. Kauffman RP, Carson CC. Ureteroscopic management of transitional cell carcinoma of the ureter using the neodymium:YAG laser. Lasers Surg Med 1993;13: 625–8.

34. Gaboardi F, Bozzola A, Dotti E, Galli L. Conservative treatment of upper urinary tract tumors with Nd:YAG laser. J Endourol 1994;8:37–41.

35. Bales GT, Lyon ES, Gerber GS. Conservative management of transitional cell carcinoma of the kidney and ureter. Diagn Ther Endo 1995;1:121–3.

36. Engelmyer EL, Belis JA. Long-term ureteroscopic management of low grade transitional cell carcinoma of the upper urinary tract. Tech Urol 1996;2:113–6.

37. Elliott DS, Blute ML, Patterson DE, et al. Long-term follow up of endoscopically treated upper urinary tract transitional cell carcinoma. Urology 1996;47:819–25.

38. Martinez-Pineiro JA, Matres Garcia MJ, Martinez-Pineiro L. Endourological treatment of upper tract urothelial carcinomas: analysis of a series of 59 tumors. J Urol 1986; 156:377–85.

39. Keeley FX, Bibbo M, Bagley DH. Ureteroscopic treatment and surveillance of upper tract transitional cell carcinoma. J Urol 1997;157:1560–5.

40. Tasca A, Zattoni F, Garbeglio A, et al. Endourologic treatment of transitional cell carcinoma of the upper urinary tract. J Endourol 1992;6:253–6.

41. Malloy TR, Schultz RE, Wein AJ, Carpiniello VL. Renal preservation utilizing neodymium:YAG laser. Urology 1986;27:99–103.

42. Johnson DE. Use of the holmium:YAG laser for treatment of superficial bladder carcinoma. Lasers Surg Med 1994;14: 213–8.

43. Razvi HA, Chun SS, Denstedt JD, Sales JL. Soft-tissue applications of the holmium:YAG laser in urology. J Endourol 1995;9:387–90.

44. Bagley DH, Erhard M. Use of the holmium laser in the upper urinary tract. Tech Urol 1995;1:25–30.

45. Johnson DE, Babayan RJ. Conservative surgical management for noninvasive distal ureteral carcinoma. Urology 1979; 13:365–7.

46. Zincke H, Neves RJ. Feasibility of conservative surgery for transitional cell cancer of the upper urinary tract. Urol Clin North Am 1984;11:717–24.

47. Mazeman E. Tumours of the upper urinary tract calyces, renal pelvis and ureter. Eur Urol 1976;2:120–8.

48. Williams CG, Mitchell JP. Carcinoma of the ureter: a review of 54 cases. Br J Urol 1973;45:377–80.

49. Charbit L, Gendreau M-C, Mee S, et al. Tumors of the upper urinary tract: 10 years of experience. J Urol 1991;146: 1243–6.

50. Nielsen K, Ostri P. Primary tumors of the renal pelvis: evaluation of clinical and pathological features in a consecutive series of 10 years. J Urol 1988;140:9–21.

51. Murphy DM, Zincke H, Furlow WL. Primary grade I transitional cell carcinoma of the renal pelvis and ureter. J Urol 1980;123:629–31.

52. Murphy DM, Zincke H, Furlow WL. Management of high grade transitional cell cancer of the upper urinary tract. J Urol 1981;125:25–9.

53. Elliott DS, Segura JW, Lightner D, et al. Is nephroureterectomy necessary in all cases of upper tract transitional cell carcinoma? Long-term results of conservative endourologic management of upper tract transitional cell carcinoma in individuals with a normal contralateral kidney. Urology 2001;58:174–8.

54. Chen GL, Bagley DH. Ureteroscopic management of upper tract transitional cell carcinoma in patients with normal contralateral kidneys. J Urol 2000;164:1173–6.

55. Okubo K, Ichioka K, Terada N, et al. Intrarenal bacillus Calmette-Guérin therapy for carcinoma in situ of the upper urinary tract: long-term follow-up and natural course in cases of failure. BJU Int 2001;88:343–7.

56. Patel A, Fuchs GJ. New techniques for the administration of topical adjuvant therapy after endoscopic ablation of upper urinary tract transitional cell carcinoma. J Urol 1998;159:71–5

57. Eastham JA, Huffman JL. Technique of mitomycin C instillation in the treatment of upper urinary tract urothelial tumors. J Urol 1993;150:324–5.

58. Keeley FX, Bibbo M, Bagley DH. Adjuvant mitomycin C following endoscopic treatment of upper tract transitional cell carcinoma. J Urol 1997;158:2074–7.

59. Chen GL, El-Gabry EA, Bagley DH. Surveillance of upper urinary tract transitional cell carcinoma: the role of ureteroscopy, retrograde pyelography, cytology and urinalysis. J Urol 2000;165:1901–4.

60. Chen GL, Bagley DH. Ureteroscopic surgery for upper tract transitional cell carcinoma: complications and management. J Endourol 2001;15:399–404.

61. Lee D, Trabulsi E, McGinnis D, et al. Totally endoscopic management of upper tract transitional cell carcinoma. J Endourol 2002;16:37–41.

62. Keeley FX, Tolley DA. Laparoscopic nephroureterectomy: making management of upper tract transitional cell carcinoma entirely minimally invasive. J Endourol 1998;12:139–41.

63. Liatsikos EN, Dinlenc CZ, Kapoor R, Smith AD. Transitional cell carcinoma of the renal pelvis: ureteroscopic and percutaneous approach. J Endourol 2001;15:377–83.

23

Laparoscopic versus Open Nephroureterectomy for the Treatment of Upper Tract Transitional Cell Carcinoma

MICHAEL C. OST, MD

STEPHEN J. SAVAGE, MD

Radical nephroureterectomy, including en bloc excision of the ipsilateral ureter with a surrounding bladder cuff, is the standard treatment for upper tract transitional cell carcinoma (TCC).[1,2] The oncologic basis for such treatment emerged from the observation of Kimball and Ferris in 1934 that ureteral stump TCC recurrences following incomplete nephroureterectomy for upper tract TCC could be avoided if the entire ureter was excised.[3] Numerous studies in the last quarter of the century validated complete ureterectomy as an essential part of the procedure, citing the 30 to 60% risk of recurrent tumors in any remaining portion of the ipsilateral ureter.[1,4–7]

Le Dentu and Albarran are credited with performing the first nephroureterectomy for upper tract urothelial cancer in 1898.[8] Almost a century later, open radical nephroureterectomy (ONU) by either two separate incisions or a lengthy single incision continued to be the standard of care for this disease, despite the significant associated postoperative morbidity and prolonged convalescence.[9] Within the latter half of the last decade, however, urologic laparoscopic surgery has emerged as a viable alternative to many open procedures.[10] Technological advancements and increasing experience with minimally invasive surgery have provided an impetus to performing urologic procedures with reduced perioperative morbidity, shorter hospital stays, and efficacious oncologic results. In light of this, at multiple centers of excellence, laparoscopic nephroureterectomy (LNU) has evolved into a new standard for the surgical management of upper tract TCC.

BACKGROUND FOR COMPARISON

A clinical evaluation of a new oncologic surgical technique is based primarily on efficacy and secondarily on morbidity. For upper tract TCC, treatment efficacy is determined by disease-free survival rates (local and distant) and, ultimately, survival. In the absence of long-term data, surrogate end points include the adequacy of the surgical specimen, recurrence rates, and, in the case of laparoscopic surgery, the incidence of port-site seeding.[11] The limited number of patients with upper tract TCC makes the organization of randomized, prospective trials comparing surgical technique unlikely; consequently, useful information must be obtained from retrospective or prospective case series reviews and case reports.

The once justifiable criticism of using laparoscopy in treating patients with urologic malignancies pointed at the paucity of data demonstrating equivalent efficacy when compared with traditional open surgery. Although 5-year follow-up data are not available for reported series on radical LNU, there is certainly no longer a scarcity of evidence regarding technique and outcomes. Concern has largely centered on the capability of laparoscopy coupled with minimally invasive techniques to effectively remove the entire distal ureter along with the adjacent bladder cuff, while maintaining the established onco-logic principles of open surgery.[10] In this regard, the most challenging and controversial aspect of mini-mally invasive treatment of upper tract TCC is the correct oncologic management of the distal ureter.[12]

Many laparoscopic management options exist for treatment of upper tract TCC. Whether transperi-toneal, retroperitoneal, or hand assisted, all have been thoroughly described, reporting their strengths and shortcomings. The purpose of this chapter is not only to report on differing technique but to compare reported outcomes as a result of such procedures with regard to oncologic efficacy, complications, and patient recovery. To appreciate such data, an understanding of the natural history of upper tract TCC and historical outcomes from ONU is critical.

NATURAL HISTORY OF UPPER TRACT TCC

Upper tract TCC accounts for less than 5% of urothe-lial tumors.[13] Ureteral TCC is even less common than tumors of the renal pelvis by a ratio between 1:3 and 1:4.[5,13] During the last two decades, the incidence of renal pelvic tumors has remained stable, although there has been a slight increase in the incidence of ureteral cancer.[14] Although rare, upper tract transi-tional cell tumors can be aggressive, with a tendency toward high-grade disease, multifocality, local recur-rences, and distant metastasis.[15] It is reported that as many as 30% of patients may present with advanced disease. A history of bladder TCC is present in 20 to 30% of patients, and contralateral tumor can present synchronously in up to 2.5%.[16]

Survival and recurrences following radical nephroureterectomy depend on pathologic tumor stage, which is strongly correlated with tumor grade. Hall and colleagues reviewed a large single-center experience involving 252 patients over a 30-year period treated for upper tract TCC by surgical means, 77% of whom underwent ONU with removal of a bladder cuff.[9] Patients had extensive follow-up, with a median of 64 months. Disease relapses occurred in 27% of patients at a median time of 12 months. Recurrences occurred in the retroperi-toneum (9%), bladder (51%), and remaining upper tract (18%) or metastatic to the lung, bone, or liver

in 22% of patients. Notably, all patients with local retroperitoneal relapses had either pT3 or pT4 tumors and died of metastatic TCC at a median of 37 months from the time of diagnosis.

Hall and colleagues determined that significant prognostic indicators for recurrence by univariate analysis were both tumor grade and stage.[9] On mul-tivariate analysis, however, only tumor stage and treatment modality were predictors of recurrence. Actuarial 5-year disease-specific survival rates by primary tumor stage were 100% for Ta/cis, 92% for T1, 73% for T2, and 41% for T3. Survival of patients with primary T4 was dismal, with a median of 6 months. Earlier studies by Batata and colleagues similarly reported that local extension outside the renal pelvis or ureter into renal parenchyma, peripelvic fat, perihilar tissue (T3 or T4), or lymph nodes (N1 or N2) portended a poor 5-year survival rate of 10 to 23% irrespective of treatment modal-ity.[17] As a result, extended surgical resection is per-formed typically for prognostic assessment only.

Whether complete ureterectomy does, however, have any influence on the incidence of subsequent TCC of the bladder is far from clear.[18] Are bladder recurrences manifestations of the multifocal nature of urothelial TCC or the result of tumor spillage and implantation from an operative procedure?[19,20] Despite the availability of advanced technology, treatments are all too often ineffective. To a large extent, this is probably attributed to our inability to predict the intrinsic biologic potential of many of these conditions and the limitations in therapeutic options that might otherwise make the application of some of these new technologies more effective.[21]

Prior to the development of laparoscopic tech-niques, ONU, whether modified or complete, resulted in subsequent bladder tumor recurrences of approximately 30%.[5,7,18,22,23,24] This percentage may vary depending on the location of the primary lesion. The rate of invasive bladder recurrences after ONU without employment of endoscopic techniques is infrequently documented, but some series report the rate as between 2 and 3%.[7,25,26]

Minimally invasive techniques of using retro-grade uretereroscopic or percutaneous antegrade approaches to treat TCC of the upper urinary tract are well established and are certainly indicated in special clinical circumstances. Such techniques are best reserved for patients with high anesthetic risks, a solitary kidney, bilateral upper tract disease, or decreased renal reserve who have tumors of low volume, grade, and stage.[27] This is expertly reviewed elsewhere in this atlas.

An alternate nephron-sparing approach to upper tract TCC is distal ureterectomy with ureteral reimplantation for tumors limited to the distal third of the ureter. This approach has proven to be effective in regard to avoiding upper tract tumor recurrence because the majority of recurrences occur distal to the primary lesion.[4] Radical nephroureterectomy with ipsilateral en bloc excision of a bladder cuff, however, is the gold standard of treatment when an upper urinary tract tumor is not suitable to endoscopic technique or conservative open surgery. It is the benchmark against which other treatment approaches to upper tract tumors must be compared.

The standard open surgical approach to nephroureterectomy involves either two separate incisions (flank and lower abdominal) or one lengthy incision. Although highly efficacious, open surgery results in a significant amount of postoperative pain, pulmonary complications, and a lengthy convalescence.[9,28,29] With the intention to minimize the morbidity related to ONU while maintaining oncologic principles, radical LNU for treatment of upper tract tumors has been adopted. LNU is no longer an investigational or experimental procedure but has become a standard practice at many major medical centers throughout the world.[30]

HISTORY OF RADICAL LNU

Since Clayman and colleagues performed the first laparoscopic nephrectomy for a renal tumor in 1991, urologists have performed more advanced laparoscopic oncologic procedures such as radical nephroureterectomy, radical prostatectomy, and radical cystectomy.[10,27,29,31–47] LNU for upper tract TCC was first reported in the same year as laparoscopic nephrectomy, both of which were performed by a transperitoneal approach.[31,48]

Radical nephroureterectomy differs from radical nephrectomy because the dissection must be extended caudally to include the entire distal ureter.

In this regard, technical approaches to LNU are extensions of those developed for laparoscopic nephrectomy. The technique itself has been successful as a pure transperitoneal procedure with no incision > 12 mm, a hand-assisted procedure via a 7 to 10 cm incision, and a retroperitoneal procedure with intact specimen removal via a specimen-appropriate incision.[49] The recapitulation of laparoscopic surgical themes is obvious. Tierny and colleagues and Nakada and colleagues reported on the first clinical hand-assisted laparoscopic (HAL) nephrectomies.[50,51] Keeley and colleagues subsequently described the feasibility of HAL nephroureterectomy.[52] Similarly, Kerbl and colleagues and Gaur and colleagues reported on the first retroperitoneal laparoscopic nephrectomies in 1993, leading the way for successful nephroureterectomies by the same approach.[10,32,38,53,54]

Attempts to make total nephroureterectomy minimally invasive can be traced back to 1952. McDonald and colleagues described a technique for nephroureterectomy based on the endoscopic resection of the ureteral orifice through the bladder into the perivesical fat.[55] Gentle traction on the ureter allowed for completion of the operation through a single ordinary kidney incision. Operative time was shortened, and two incisions were not required. Concern over tumor seeding was addressed by use of a punctate electrode through a McCarthy panendoscope to seal off the open end of the ureter by fulguration.

A modification of this "pluck" approach by Abercrombie included resection of the intramural ureteral roof after placement of a ureteral catheter.[22] Ureteral intubation allowed for better endoscopic control during endoscopic dissection while theoretically minimizing tumor spillage. Larger series in the last decade employing "modified pluck" nephroureterectomy have demonstrated the ease in performing this combined endourologic and open approach.[56,57] Of concern, however, are the few reports of invasive bladder recurrences and tumor implantation at the site of endoscopic resection using this technique.[18,58–60]

Other novel endoscopic means of ureteral dissection facilitating ONU have been described over the last two decades. Clayman and colleagues reported their results on a series of 18 patients who underwent one incision nephroureterectomy with transvesical ureteral intussusception.[61] During a 5-year follow-up, 3 of 14 patients (21%) developed bladder tumor recurrences; however, no extravesical recurrences were reported. Angulo and colleagues described a ureteral intussusception technique in which a wire stone basket was used to secure the ureter cystoscopically at the beginning of the procedure.[62] On completion of the nephrectomy, the distal ureter and surrounding bladder cuff are excised by pulling the already clipped and divided ureter through the urethra and circumferentially detaching it with a Collins knife mounted on a resectoscope. Tumors treated by this method were limited to the renal pelvis. At a mean follow-up of 44.6 months, 3 patients (20%) had bladder tumor recurrences.

The most modern of endoscopic methods to distal ureteral management in LNU are based on older and contemporary techniques that aim at decreasing the morbidity associated with the open approach.[55–57] During the evolution toward more minimally invasive methods, concern over maintaining oncologic principles and avoiding tumor seeding has always been stressed. Presently, the question is not whether a nephroureterectomy can be accomplished laparoscopically but which management options for the distal ureter are most efficacious.

DISTAL URETERAL MANAGEMENT AND COMPARISON OF RESULTS FROM SERIES ON LNU FOR TREATMENT OF UPPER TRACT TCC

As previously discussed, mobilization of the kidney and proximal ureter during nephroureterectomy may be accomplished transperitoneally, retroperitoneally, or hand assisted. To date, these techniques have been compared with regard to convalescence as it relates to incision size. Techniques for optimal methods of mobilization and excision of the distal ureter with a surrounding bladder cuff, however, are still evolving, with much controversy with regard to tumor seeding. Although the series reporting on LNU continue to mature, to date, approximately 10 series of LNU for treatment of upper tract TCC have been reported with a maximum follow-up of close to 4 years. Table 23–1 summarizes these studies with

respect to patient characteristics, oncologic outcomes, and convalescence data. Herein, techniques regarding handling of the distal ureter and laparoscopic surgical outcomes are discussed.

Open Technique

After performing the laparoscopic radical nephrectomy portion of the operation, the ureter is mobilized at least to the level of the pelvic brim. The distal ureter and bladder cuff are then dissected through a Gibson or lower abdominal incision through which an intact specimen is delivered.

The bladder cuff may be secured by placement of a right-angled clamp extravesically or through an anterior cystotomy. Opening the bladder has the potential to locally seed tumor because a closed system is breeched. An additional shortcoming of the procedure is the potential compromise of the contralateral ureteral orifice if using a right-angled clamp extravesically.[38] Furthermore, it is possible to leave a small portion of intravesical ureter if the entire dissection is performed extravesically.

Chung and colleagues were the first to describe the feasibility of a retroperitoneoscopic approach to radical nephroureterectomy.[32] They combined this technique with an open infraumbilical excision of the distal ureter and bladder cuff. The six patients in this series underwent cystotomy for bladder cuff excision with a mean operative time for the laparoscopic portion of the procedure of 4.6 hours with one open conversion. Average hospital stay was 9 days because patients remain in the hospital until the time of catheter removal. During a mean follow-up of 12.6 months, one patient developed a bladder tumor recurrence at 5 months. Follow-up data in this study are short, and pathologic tumor stage and grade were not recorded.

Similarly, Salomon and colleagues used a laparoscopic retroperitoneal approach, without balloon dilation of the retroperitoneal space, on four patients with upper tract TCC limited to the renal pelvis.[38] There were no complications and no open conversions. A Gibson incision was used to mobilize the distal ureter and excise the bladder cuff. A right-angled clamp was used extravesically to secure the bladder cuff with the thought of minimizing tumor

Table 23–1.   WORLDWIDE EXPERIENCE OF LAPAROSCOPIC NEPHROURETERECTOMY FOR UPPER TRACT TRANSITIONAL CELL CARCINOMA

	Keeley et al (1998)[29] McNeil et al (2000)[64]		Gill et al (2000)[10] Hsu et al (1999)[34]		Jarrett et al (2000)[35]	Chung et al (1996)[32]
	LNU	ONU	LNU	ONU	LANU/LNU	LNU
Period	1993–2000		9/97–1/00	2/91–12/99	1993–99	12/93–5/95
Number of Patients	25	42	42	35	25	7
Average Age (yrs)	NR	NR	71.6	64.3	63	64.3
Technique	Trans	NA	Retro	NA	Trans	Retro
Number of Ports	4	NA	3	NA	3/4	4
Management of Distal Ureter	Pluck Open		Transvesical (27) Open (15)	NA	Open (n=20) EndoGIA (n=4)	Open
Specimen Extraction	NR	NR	Intact	NA	Intact (n=20) Morcellation (n=4)	Intact
Mean Surgical Time (hrs)	2.8	2.8	3.7	4.7	5.5	4.6
Mean Blood Loss (cc)	NR	NR	242	696	440	Minimal
Mean Specimen Weight (gms)	NR	NR	559	388	NR	NR
Pathologic Stage	T1–T3	T1–T3	Ta–T4	Ta–T4	Ta–T3	NR
Pathologic Grade	G1–G3	G1–G3	G1–G3	G1–G3	G1–G3	NR
Mean Narcotic Dose						
Morphine Sulphate (mg)	NR	NR	26	228	NR	11.6
Ketorolac (mg)	NA	NR	NA	NA		NA
Paracetamol (mg)	NA	NR	NA	NA		NA
Mean Hours to Resume Oral Intake	NR	NR	38.4	76.8	NR	NR
Mean Hospital Stay (days)	9.1	10.7	2.3	6.6	4 (median)	9
Mean Time to Convalesence (wks)	NR	NR	4.7	8.2	NR	NR
Mean Time to Full Recovery (mo)	NR	NR	2	3.5	NR	NR
Complications (%) Overall	16	17	12	29		
Major	NR	NR	4.8	0	13	NR
Minor	NR	NR	7.2	29	25	NR
Open Conversions (%)	12	NA	4.8	NA	4	1 (14)
Tumor Recurrences (%)	NR	NR				1 (14)
Bladder			23	37	50	1
Grade			NR	NR	NR	NR
Stage			NR	NR	NR	NR
Local			0	0	4	0
Distant metastases	NR	NR	8.6	13	17	0
Patients Available for Follow-up	NR	NR	NR	NR	24	NR
Mean Follow-up (mos)	32.9	43.2	11.1	34.4	24.2	12.6
% Positive Margins	NR	NR	7	15	NR	NR
% Survival	84	79	97	87	88	NR

(continued)

Table 23–1. CONTINUED

	Salomon et al (1999)[38]	Seifman et al (2001)[39]		Chen et al (2001)[33]		McDougall et al (1995)[37]	
	LNU	LNU	ONU	HALNU	ONU	LNU	ONU
Period	7/95–6/97	3/97–9/99	3/97–9/99	1/00–?	1/00–?	5/91–8/94	1/93–9/94
Number of Patients	4	16	11	7	15	10	13
Average Age (yrs)	68	71	71	66.5	58.1	68	65
Technique	Retro	Hand Assisted	Extraperitioneal Flank	Tran	NA	Trans	NR
Number of Ports	5	NR	NA	2 or 3	NA	6	NA
Management of Distal Ureter	Open	Endo staple (1) TUR (12) Open (3)	TUR (4) Open (7)	Open(Gibson)	NA	Ureteral Unroofing	NR
Specimen Extraction	Intact	Intact	NA	Intact	NA	Intact	NA
Mean Surgical Time (hrs)	3.7	5.3	3.32	3.7	NR	8.3	3.9
Mean Blood Loss (cc)	220	557	345	140	455	233	590
Mean Specimen Weight (gms)	NR	581	364	NR	NR	408	NR
Pathologic Stage	T2b–T3	T0–T3	Ta–T3	NR	NR	Ta–T3	NR
Pathologic Grade	G2–G3	G1–G3	G1–G3	NR	NR	NR	NR
Mean Narcotic Dose							
Morphine Sulphate (mg)	10	48	81	38	70	16	117
Ketorolac (mg)	NA	NA	NA	NA	NA	0	58
Paracetamol (mg)	3.5	NA	NA	NA	NA	NA	NA
Mean Hours to Resume Oral Intake	NR	33	38	33	61	18	103.2
Mean Hospital Stay (days)	5.7	3.9	5.1	7.33	9.1	5	11
Mean Time to Convalesence (wks)	NR	2.6	5.4	3.7	5.6	2.8	6
Mean Time to Full Recovery (mo)	NR	1.5	NR	NR	NR	1.5	7.4
Complications (%) Overall				NR	NR		NR
Major	0	19	45			10	NR
Minor	0	19	27			0	NR
Open Conversions(%)	0(0)	1(6)	NA	0	NA	0	NA
Tumor Recurrences (%)	1(25)	3(19)	7(64)	1(14.3)	3(20)	5(62.5)	2(33.3)
Bladder	0	3	3	14.3	20	4	2
Grade	NA	G2–G3	G2–G3	NR	NR	atypia, G1-2	atypia, G1
Stage	NA	NR	NR	NR	NR	Ta	Ta
Local	1	0	3	NR	NR	1	NR
Distant metastases	0	0	1	NR	NR	1	NR
Patients Available for Follow-up	4	15	11	NR	NR	8	6
Mean Follow-up (mos)	18	19.3	15.8	NR	NR	25	16
% Positive Margins	NR	NR	NR	NR	NR	0	NR
% Survival	NR	NR	NR	NR	NR	87.5	NR

(continued)

Table 23–1. CONTINUED

	Shalhav et al (2000)[40]		Stifelman et al (2000)[41] Stifelman et al (2001)[27]	
	LNU	ONU	HALNU	ONU
Period	5/91–6/98	3/90–1/97	5/98–?	5/98–6/99
Number of Patients	25	17	22	11
Average Age (yrs)	69.7	62	65	NR
Technique	Trans	NR	Tran	NA
Number of Ports	5–6	NA	4	NA
Management of Distal Ureter	Ureteral Unroofing (24) Pluck (1)		Transvesical Endoscopic Dissection (19) Extravesical Laparoscopic Dissection (3)	
Specimen Extraction	Intact	NA		NA
Mean Surgical Time (hrs)	7.7	3.9	4.5	3.9
Mean Blood Loss (cc)	199	441	180	311
Mean Specimen Weight (gms)	445	380	457	392
Pathologic Stage	Ta–T4	T1–T3	Ta–T3	Ta–T4
Pathologic Grade	G1–G4	G2–G4	G1–G3	G1–G3
Mean Narcotic Dose	37	144	55	44
Morphine Sulphate (mg)	NA	NA	NA	NA
Ketorolac (mg)	NA	NA	NA	NA
Paracetamol (mg)	NA	NA	NA	NA
Mean Hours to Resume Oral Intake	23	116	2.1	2.3
Mean Hospital Stay (days)	3.6	9.6	4.1	6.1
Mean Time to Convalesence (wks)	2.8	10	2.7	NR
Mean Time to Full Recovery (mo)	NR	NR	NR	NR
Complications (%) Overall				
Major	8	29	0	0
Minor	40	29	0	0
Open Conversions(%)	0	NA	0	NA
Tumor Recurrences (%)	7(29)	10(77)	6(32)	4(36)
Bladder	3	6	4	4
Grade	G1–?	NR	NR	NR
Stage	Ta–T1	NR	NR	NR
Local	3	0	0	0
Distant metastases	2	3	2	0
Patients Available for Follow-up	24	13	22	11
Mean Follow-up (mos)	24	43	13	17
% Positive Margins	4	NR	0	0
% Survival	77	77	NR	9

HALN = hand-assisted laparoscopic nephrourectomy; LANU = laparoscopic-assisted nephrourectomy; LNU = laparoscopic nephroureterectomy; ONU = open nephroureterectomy; NA = not available; NR = not reported; TUR = transurethral resection.

seeding. The authors report an average total operative time of 3.7 hours, a mean blood loss of 220 cc, and a mean hospital stay of 5.7 days. One patient with a pT3G3 tumor had a local recurrence 1 year postoperatively. He subsequently underwent reoperative excision with adjuvant chemotherapy. At an average follow-up of 1.6 years, no bladder recurrences were recorded.

Most recently, Chen reported on a small series in which an innovative combination of an open approach and HAL was used in the surgical management of upper tract TCC.[33] The distal ureter and bladder cuff are first excised through a 7 cm Gibson incision without placement of a ureteral stent. The patient is kept in a 60-degree oblique position to implement HAL following ureteral dissection. At a mean follow-up of 7.8 months for the HAL group and 6.5 months for a contemporary ONU group, bladder tumor recurrences were 14.3% and 20%, respectively. Although this study favored this modified HAL technique over ONU in regard to convalescence data, specimen pathologic data were not available and follow-up time was short.

Ureteral Unroofing Technique: The Washington University Approach

The intramural ureter and bladder cuff are first mobilized cystoscopically. Under fluoroscopic guidance, a 7 French (F) ureteral dilating balloon catheter is inserted over a guidewire. Within the intramural ureter, the balloon is inflated with dilute contrast material to < 1 atmosphere of pressure. A 24 F resectoscope equipped with an Orandi electrosurgical knife is used to unroof the ureteral tunnel at 12 o'clock from the intramural level of the ureterovesical junction down through the ureteral tunnel (Figure 23–1). After removal of the balloon, a roller ball electrode is used to cauterize the edges and the floor of the intramural ureter (Figure 23–2). With the intention to prevent tumor seeding prior to the nephrectomy portion of the operation, a 7 F 11.5 mm occlusion balloon catheter is passed into the renal pelvis and placed to gravity drainage.

On average, ureteral unroofing lasts 50 minutes. The procedure is intended to facilitate ureteral identification and dissection in preparation for stapling of the bladder cuff following the transperitoneal laparoscopic nephrectomy portion of the operation. Use of the endoscopic gastrointestinal anastomosis (GIA) tissue stapler at the conclusion of en bloc tissue resection secures the bladder cuff with a watertight seal.[63] It has the advantage of potentially avoiding spillage of cancer cells into the extraperitoneal and peritoneal spaces. However, the contralateral ureteral orifice is not visualized when firing the stapler over the trigone. This technique, therefore, carries risk of injury to the unaffected collecting system. Although the staple line in the bladder has the theoretical potential for stone formation, this complication is yet to be reported in the literature. Other disadvantages

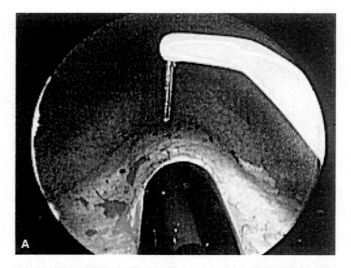

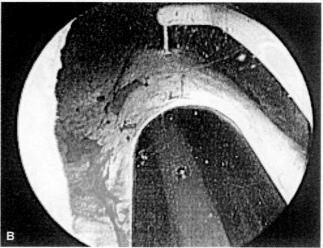

Figure 23–1. *A,* Cystoscopic view of electrosurgical knife above intramural ureter that has been dilated with ureteral balloon catheter. *B,* First incision of intramural ureter over balloon catheter. (Courtesy of J. Landman, MD)

include the need for fluoroscopy and the requirement of a transperitoneal approach, with resultant risks to intraperitoneal organs, especially bowel injury during colon reflection.

In 1995, McDougall and colleagues reported on their experience with 10 patients who underwent LNU with ureteral unroofing for upper tract TCC.[37] They retrospectively compared outcomes over a 2-year period to a contemporary group of 8 patients undergoing ONU for the same disease. This was the first series in the urologic literature on LNU for upper tract TCC. In light of this, lengthy operative times were reported with a mean of 8.3 hours compared with a mean of 3.9 hours

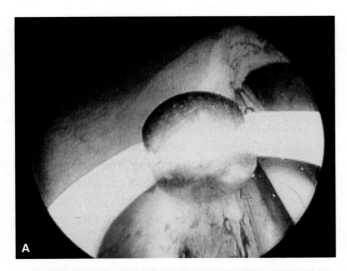

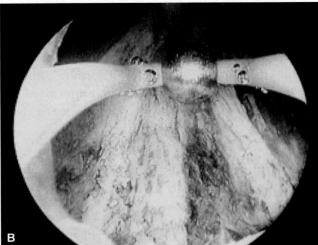

Figure 23–2. *A,* Cystoscopic view of roller ball electrode cauterizing anterior portion of ureteral tunnel over balloon catheter. *B,* Image demonstrating subsequent cauterization of the floor of the ureteral tunnel after removal of the balloon catheter. (Courtesy of J. Landman, MD.)

for the open group. Impressively, blood loss, postoperative analgesia requirements, time to resume oral intake, and length of hospital stay were all significantly lower in the laparoscopic group. There were no intraoperative complications in the laparoscopic group; however, one patient required re-exploration for bleeding attributed to adrenal gland hemorrhage.

Average postoperative surveillance was 25 months in the laparoscopic group. One patient developed a local retroperitoneal recurrence 9 months postoperatively. This patient was noted to have pT3 disease on final pathology and died 3 months later despite adjuvant chemotherapy. Final pathology of the remaining patients was pTa in six and pT2 in one. Thirty-eight percent of these patients developed subsequent superficial bladder tumors (pTa grade 1). Six patients were available in the open group for an average follow-up of 16 months, 2 (33%) of whom developed recurrent superficial bladder cancer (pTa grades 1 and 3).

Time to tumor recurrence was not recorded in the McDougall and colleagues study.[37] Regardless, bladder recurrence rates were similar in the laparoscopic (38%) and open (33%) groups, reflecting overall recurrence rates in the literature. The authors of this study subsequently updated this cohort of patients with the addition of more subjects.[40] At a mean cystoscopic follow-up of 24 months for the laparoscopic group and 43 months for the ONU group, the rate of lower tract recurrence was 23% and 54%, respectively. However, the authors pointed out that at 24 months, there was only a 24% lower tract recurrence rate for the open group, reported to be comparable to the laparoscopic group.

In Washington University's follow-up study, the average operative times for laparoscopy were still almost twice as long as those for ONU.[40] Not surprisingly, convalescence data continued to favor the laparoscopic group. More importantly, the overall recurrence rates were similar for the laparoscopic (31% at 1.5 years) and open (23% at 1.8 years) groups. Specifically, there were three cases of retroperitoneal metastasis in the laparoscopic group and none in the open. All retroperitoneal recurrences had either high grade (grade 3–4) or advanced pathologic stage (pT3b–T4). In an effort to relate the pathologic grade and stage of the disease to the subsequent development of metastatic disease, patients were stratified to risk categories: low, medium, or high. Interestingly, regardless of the type of nephroureterectomy performed, in each category at least one patient had metastatic disease, and the risk of bladder recurrence was equivalent.

Although disease-specific survival was equivalent (77%) for both groups, the higher incidence of retroperitoneal recurrences in those treated laparoscopically in this series is concerning. Whether such local recurrence is attributable to laparoscopic technique or to the natural history of high-grade, high-stage disease cannot be determined owing to the relatively small sample size.

Pluck Technique

Keeley and Tolley first reported on a series of 22 patients who underwent transperitoneal LNU using a pluck technique and compared outcomes with those of a contemporary ONU series ($n = 26$).[29] Patients with mid- or distal ureteral tumors were excluded from the study. For these patients, distal ureteral dissection was performed through a lower abdominal incision.

A standard 26 F resectoscope was used to resect the affected ureteral orifice until it was completely detached from the trigone. During the laparoscopic portion of the procedure, the ureter was identified and clipped but not divided to minimize the risk of tumor spillage. Following completion of the nephrectomy portion of the operation, the ureter was dissected down into the pelvis using gentle traction to assist in mobilization. When the ureter was completely freed, an incision was made at the inferior port site to remove the specimen.

McNeil and colleagues addressed oncologic data of this series by retrospectively reviewing the case records and pathology reports of all patients who underwent either LNU or ONU during an 8-year period.[64] This included a total of 25 patients who underwent ONU versus 42 who underwent LNU with a pluck technique. At a mean follow-up of 32.9 months for LNU and 42.3 months for ONU, 9 (21%) of the ONU group and 4 (16%) of the LNU group died, with a mean disease-specific survival of 15.1 months and 17 months, respectively. Comparative disease-specific survival times were not significantly different, and, interestingly, all deaths were associated with grade 3 pT1 to 3 disease. Further analysis of this cohort demonstrated that tumor grade was closely correlated with pathologic stage ($r = .74$, $p < .001$), imparting prognostic significance. Such findings reproduce those of Hall and colleagues for ONU and hence support LNU using the pluck as a reasonable treatment option for upper tract TCC limited to the renal pelvis based solely on the natural history of the disease.[9] Data on bladder and local recurrences, a specific concern when using the pluck technique, were not available in these series.

Operative time in LNU using the pluck technique in this series is shorter or equivalent to that of ONU. However, at all times following cystoscopic ureteral mobilization, the distal ureter remains unoccluded. It is speculated that this may contribute to tumor spilling and seeding.

Concern over tumor spillage resulting in perivesical recurrence and seeding in the retroperitoneum was raised by four reports of local recurrences following ONU using the pluck technique.[18,58–60] However, Palou and colleagues reported on a series of 31 patients who underwent endoscopic excision of the distal ureter before ONU, the majority of whom ($n = 17$) had high-grade (grade 3) disease.[56] Although bladder recurrence rates were consistent with other studies at 27%, no patients had either local or retroperitoneal tumor relapses. It is also speculated that because there is no identifiable marking of the distal ureter with a suture, it may be difficult to determine whether cephalad traction has resulted in removal of the entire ureter or if some portion of the ureter has been unknowingly torn and left behind.[12]

Transvesical Ureteral Dissection: The Cleveland Clinic Approach

Step 1: Securing the Bladder Cuff

Following cystoscopy to rule out concomitant bladder tumor(s), two 5 mm suprapubic ports are inserted into the bladder under direct vision. These ports are arranged transversely one fingerbreadth above the pubic symphisis and attached to wall suction. A 5 mm endoloop is inserted through an introducer sheath into the ipsilateral suprapubic port and positioned around the ureteral orifice. A 6 F open-ended ureteral catheter is passed over a 0.038-inch guidewire, through the endoloop, and into the renal pelvis

Step 2: Detachment of the Bladder Cuff

Using a resectoscope and a Collins knife, an oval bladder cuff is marked by scoring the urothelium circumferentially around the ureteral orifice. Care is always taken not to damage the contralateral ureteral orifice. A 5 mm Allis clamp inserted through the contralateral suprapubic port providing anterior traction is necessary to incise the full thickness of the bladder wall along the scored margin. Using this technique, the intramural ureter and bladder cuff are mobilized en bloc from the bladder. The ureteral catheter serves as a guide to prevent inadvertent entry into the intramural ureter while also providing scaffolding for traction by the Allis clamp. To minimize the potential for tumor seeding as well as fluid absorption syndrome, it is critical to ensure that the bladder stays relatively decompressed throughout the procedure

Step 3: Mobilization of the Juxtavesical Ureter

Transurethral dissection is continued transvesically into the extravesical fatty tissue. Established firm anteromedial traction delivers the intact intramural and juxtavesical ureter into the bladder and permits additional mobilization of the extravesical ureter. Using this technique, approximately 3 to 4 cm of the intact extravesical ureter are circumferentially mobilized into the bladder (Figure 23–3). It is important to judiciously use coagulating current when needed to achieve hemostasis of the vessels commonly found at the incised bladder edge and in the pelvic extraperitoneal fat.

Step 4: Preparation of the Ureter for Removal

The previously positioned endoloop is cinched tightly around the ureter as the ureteral catheter is removed, thereby occluding its lumen. Alternatively, the catheter may be left within the ureter to facilitate subsequent identification and cephalad traction on the pelvic ureter. The now detached ureteral orifice, bladder cuff, and 1 cm margin of the adjacent bladder urothelium are cauterized to prevent pelvic seeding. After the suprapubic ports are removed, a 24 F Foley catheter is inserted and left indwelling.

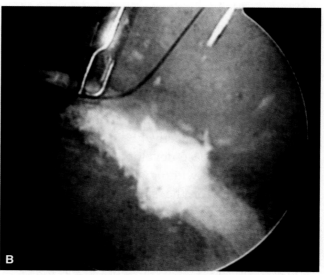

A

B

Figure 23–3. *A,* Schematic drawing demonstrating cystoscopic detachment of juxtavesical ureter traction through suprapubic port. *B,* Cystoscopic image showing dissection depicted in A. (Courtesy of I. Gill, MD.)

Results

In the largest single-institution series comparing LNU with ONU, Gill and colleagues determined that laparoscopy was superior in regard to surgical time (3.7 versus 4.7 hours, $p = .003$).[10] This follows the typical trend of longer operative times in initial laparoscopy series, followed by a rapid decrease, approaching or even surpassing open operative times. Laparoscopy using transvesical ureteral dissection in 42 patients was also found to have a significant advantage in regard to blood loss, resumption of oral intake, narcotic analgesic requirement, hospital stay, return to normal activities, and overall convalescence. Of the 12% of complications in the laparoscopic group, their initial patient undergoing cystoscopic detachment of the bladder cuff had significant extravasation of irrigant, which was drained through the extraction incision. The extravasation was attributed to a 2 mm suprapubic port that had slipped out of the bladder. In addressing this complication, 5 mm balloon ports were subsequently used to avoid extravasation and potential tumor seeding.

At a mean follow-up of 11.1 months for the laparoscopic group and 34.4 months for the open group, there was no difference in rates of bladder tumor recurrences (23% versus 37%). Of note, follow-up was significantly longer for the open group, and time to bladder recurrence was not reported. In addition, the pathologic grade of the recurrences was not stratified by initial pathology. Unlike previous series, however, there was no reported incidence of local retroperitoneal recurrences in either group. This may have been attributed to occlusion of the distal ureter, although it is impossible to determine this retrospectively.

Metastatic disease developed in 8.6% of LNU and 13% of ONU, without statistical significance. After adjusting for the shorter follow-up in the LNU group, cancer-specific survival was found to be comparable (97% versus 87%). The Gill and colleagues study demonstrated the technical efficiency of the procedure without compromise of short-term oncologic efficacy.[10] Longer oncologic follow-up is needed is needed, however, to truly measure efficacy.

HAL with Transvesical Laparoscopic Ureteral Dissection

The advent of HAL has provided an additional laparoscopic alternative for patients with upper tract urothelial tumors (Figure 23–4). Multiple devices for hand assistance, each with recognizable strengths and weaknesses, are currently used, and modifications are continually being made. Proponents of HAL contend that having the ability to place a hand in the operative field avoids some of the problems associated with pure laparoscopy, including loss of proprioception, tactile sensation, and three-dimensional orientation.[27] Furthermore, for the urologist not experienced in laparoscopy, a hand in the operative site may allow for additional comfort in the development of laparoscopic skills.

Stifelman and colleagues reported on their initial series of 11 patients who underwent HAL for upper tract TCC using transvesical laparoscopic ureteral dissection.[27] Outcomes were compared with those of a contemporary group of 11 patients undergoing ONU for the same disease. As with previous series using pure laparoscopy, postoperative recovery favored HAL with regard to analgesia requirements and length of hospital stay.

At a mean follow-up of 13 months for HAL and 17 months for ONU, bladder recurrences were equivalent, at 27% and 36%, respectively. There were no positive margins on final pathologic evaluation of the HAL specimens, although a patient with a pT3 grade 3 lesion subsequently developed metastatic disease and was lost to follow-up. Consistent with the finding of the Cleveland Clinic series, no patients developed retroperitoneal recurrences. In a later study, Stifelman and colleagues expanded their series to include 11 additional patients from a second institution.[41] In 19 patients, the distal ureter and bladder cuff were managed by transvesical ureteral dissection. Earlier findings were confirmed with 18% of patients developing superficial bladder recurrences at an average of 13 months follow-up. Once again, there were no recurrences in the retroperitoneum; however, an additional patient with a pT3 grade 3 tumor developed metastatic disease. All patients

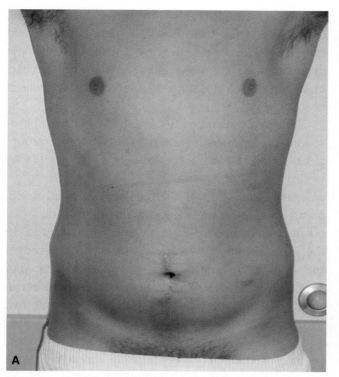
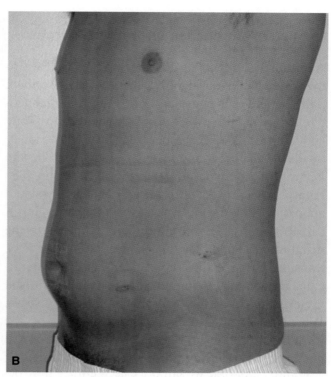

Figure 23–4. *A,* Postoperative abdominal appearance 2 weeks after hand-assisted left laparoscopic nephroureterectomy. *B,* Same patient with an oblique view demonstrating lateral port-sites. (Courtesy of M. Stifelman, MD.)

were reported to be alive at 18 months, although one patient who developed metastatic disease was lost to follow-up.

Most recently, Landman and colleagues conducted a nonrandomized retrospective review comparing HAL and standard laparoscopy in the treatment of upper tract TCC.[36] In the HAL group, 13 of 16 (81%) of the distal ureters were managed by laparoscopic dissection to the bladder and transection with an endoscopic GIA stapler. The ipsilateral ureteral orifice was subsequently unroofed using an Orandi or Collins resectoscope. In the standard laparoscopic group, the ureter was managed by ureteral unroofing and electrocoagulation of the opened ureteral tunnel in 9 of 11 (82%) of the cases. Convalescence data, including mean time to oral intake, analgesic requirements, and overall hospital stay, were similar between both groups, although mean time (weeks) to partial and complete convalescence in the standard and HAL groups was 2.4 and 5.2 and 3.5 and 8.0, respectively. Total operative time was reported to be more than 1 hour shorter for HAL than for standard laparoscopy (4.9 hours versus 6.1 hours, $p = .055$). This difference in operative time, however, may have been attributed to all of the participating surgeons' experience with standard laparoscopic nephroureterectomy before application of the HAL technique. Furthermore, operative times in other pure laparoscopic groups compare favorably with their HAL group.

Definitive conclusion from Landman and colleagues' oncologic data cannot be made as follow-up in the standard and hand-assisted groups was 27.4 and 9.6 months ($p = .038$), respectively.[36] At the time of follow-up, 60% of the HAL patients were disease free and 27% developed Ta grade 2 to 3 bladder recurrences, and three patients subsequently developed metastasis. In the one instance of an ipsilateral retroperitoneal recurrence, a pT1 grade 3 to 4 tumor was managed by stapling and cystoscopic fulguration. In the standard laparoscopic group, 80% of patients were disease free at follow-up, whereas 30% of patients developed Ta grade 1 to 3 bladder recurrences and distant metastasis developed in two patients.

Studies Reporting on Mixed Approaches to the Distal Ureter

Additional series using a variety of approaches to the distal ureter during LNU have been described. Seifman and colleagues described the first prospective comparison between hand-assisted laparoscopy and surgical ONU for upper tract TCC.[39] The study involved 27 nonrandomized patients, 16 in the laparoscopic group and 11 in the open group. The laparoscopic procedure used a hand-assisted approach using the Pneumo Sleeve (Dexterity Surgical, Roswell, GA) with multiple approaches to the distal ureter, including endoscopic stapling ($n = 1$), transurethral resection ($n = 12$), and an open surgical approach ($n = 3$) in the instance of mid- or distal ureteral tumors and or extensive high-grade disease. When performing transurethral resection of the intramural ureter and bladder cuff, intravesical chemotherapy with mitomycin (5–10 mL of 1 mg/mL solution in saline) was instilled into the upper tract using an occlusion catheter. This is the first report of mitomycin used during an LNU for upper tract disease. The open surgical procedures used a standard extraperitoneal flank incision. A second incision was used to resect the ureter in seven patients, whereas the remaining four patients underwent transurethral incision without mitomycin.

Operative times were significantly greater for the HAL group (mean = 5.3 hours) versus the open group (mean = 3.3 hours) and one laparoscopic patient required open conversion for a splenectomy after sustaining a capsular injury. The specimen weight tended to be greater in the laparoscopic group (mean 581 g versus 364 g), although the difference was not statistically significant. Excluding the splenic injury (estimated blood loss [EBL] 4,600 cc), estimated blood loss was similar between the two groups.

Major complications occurred in 19% of the laparoscopic group and in 27% of the open group. In the laparoscopic patients, such complications included respiratory failure in two patients requiring intubation and one death owing to a cardiac arrhythmia. Adrenal insufficiency with subsequent respiratory failure requiring reintubation in one patient and a cerebrovascular accident in a second patient were the major complications in those patients who underwent ONU. Convalescence data demonstrated much more favorable outcomes for the laparoscopic group as there was less postoperative morphine use, quicker time to resume oral intake, and decreased hospital stay.

Follow-up averaged 19.3 months in the laparoscopic group and 15.8 months in the open group. Urothelial carcinoma recurred in 3 of 16 (19%) laparoscopic patients and 7 of 11 (64%) open surgical patients ($p = .04$). In the laparoscopic group, recurrences were limited to the bladder (grade 2–3); no port-site or retroperitoneal seeding occurred. In the open group, however, recurrences occurred in the bladder (graded 2–3), retroperitoneum, and pelvis and as metastatic disease to bone. The mean time to recurrence was similar between the two groups: 55.3 and 43.3 weeks for the laparoscopic and open groups, respectively ($p > .3$). All patients with recurrences in the open group had initial surgical specimens with high pathologic stages (T2–3), yet those with equivalent pathologic stages (T2–3) in the laparoscopic group had no recurrences. Overall, cancer control rates appeared equivalent at a mean follow-up of 69 weeks; however, recurrence data were not stratified within each treatment group with regard to management of the distal ureter, and the short-term follow-up precludes meaningful analysis of cancer control rates.

LYMPHADENECTOMY, SPECIMEN RETRIEVAL, MORCELLATION, AND PORT-SITE SEEDING

The role for lymphadenectomy in the surgical treatment of upper tract TCC remains somewhat controversial. Lymph nodes are the most common site for upper tract TCC metastasis, and the prognosis for those with such advanced disease is grim. Komatsu and colleagues retrospectively evaluated the efficacy of lymphadenectomy in conjunction with ONU in patients with upper tract TCC.[66] When stratified by grade, it was determined that regional lymphadenectomy offered no survival benefit beyond identifying candidates for possible adjuvant chemotherapy.

Similarly, in evaluating patients who had nephroureterectomy with ONU, Miyake and colleagues identified lymph vessel invasion on surgical specimens to be correlated with tumor grade, stage, and incidence of distant metastasis.[67] It was determined that lymphadenectomy might provide a therapeutic advantage only to those patients without lymph vessel invasion through the prophylactic eradication of minimal metastatic disease. Given these observations, Shalhav recommended that the laparoscopic surgeon should not feel compelled to perform lymphadenectomy and should continue to perform intact specimen retrieval to allow for full pathologic analysis.[30]

Some controversy exists regarding specimen retrieval at the conclusion of LNU. Many urologists are concerned that tissue specimen morcellation may risk tumor seeding and compromise pathologic staging. Shalhav and colleagues have modified their specimen retrieval techniques, limiting intact removal to suspected high-grade or higher-stage renal pelvic tumors.[40] They propose that in these cases, accurate staging and grading are needed as they may lead to effective adjuvant chemotherapy. In the instance of ureteral tumors or biopsy-proven grade 1 renal pelvic tumors, they use an intracorporeal high-speed electrical morcellation via a 12 mm port site within an organ entrapment device. Similarly, Jarrett and colleagues have used a total laparoscopic approach with tissue morcellation for patients in whom the tumor was located proximally and/or was low grade.[35]

The laparoscopy sack is constructed with a double layer of plastic and nondistensible nylon and is reported to remain impermeable even after tissue morcellation.[68] Despite the development of such specialized bags, sack perforations have been reported.[69,70] Although intracorporeal seeding has not been described with morcellation, the potential to compromise cure by tumor spillage certainly exists. Furthermore, the impermeable sack requires multiple ports for effective manipulation and is often difficult to employ when using a retroperitoneoscopic approach.

At present, the adequacy of a surgical specimen and the margin status cannot be determined after morcellation. Jarrett and colleagues, for example, could only estimate the pathologic stage of four patients who had tumor morcellation following LNU by rigor-

ous examination of the morcellated specimens of the collecting system.[35] In an attempt to address this criticism of inaccurate pathologic staging after morcellation, Meng and colleagues described a novel method of inking laparoscopic specimens before morcellation with subsequent "piecemeal" extraction from organ retrieval bags.[71] In an animal model, their technique allowed for pathologic determination of the surgical margin status. Perhaps further advancements in molecular analysis will ultimately obviate the need for intact organ removal.

Proponents of morcellation also contend that the importance of pathologic staging has decreased in the era of improved preoperative imaging. This may apply to renal cell carcinoma. However, with respect to upper tract TCC, the most modern imaging modalities cannot accurately assess tumor grade or stage. Computed tomography (CT), for example, may be sensitive in diagnosing upper tract TCC but is of limited value with respect to accurate staging. Planz and colleagues assessed the value of CT in the preoperative staging of upper tract TCC.[72] They found that although CT accurately detected upper tract urothelial tumors 86% of the time, staging was correct in only 43% of the cases. An early study by Badalament and colleagues also reported on the low sensitivity of CT in staging with the exception of obvious tumor extension through the real pelvic or ureteral wall; in this instance, it is a sensitive marker of a high-stage tumor.[73] The inability of CT to assess grade or microscopic infiltration and the low sensitivity of endoscopic biopsy in advanced disease preclude any accurate assumptions on preoperative staging that would support morcellation at the present time.

Other techniques regarding specimen retrieval following LNU have been described. Dauleh and Townell reported on the utility of a vaginal incision at the conclusion of either LNU or nephrectomy in females.[74] Although dependent on an adequately sized vagina, this technique bypasses the shortcomings and criticisms of morcellation while minimizing fascial incisions.

Location of specimen extraction following retroperitoneal LNU is based on tumor location. As a rule of thumb, an appropriate muscle-splitting flank incision is used for tumors primarily located in the renal pelvis, upper ureter, or midureter. For distal tumors, however, specimen extraction is usually accomplished through a small, muscle-splitting, extraperitoneal Gibson incision in the ipsilateral iliac fossa. From an oncologic standpoint, this technique is performed because the retroperitoneal laparoscopic approach may not allow adequate, wide periureteral dissection when the primary tumor is in the distal ureter.[10]

The best method of organ removal has yet to be established. Intact specimen retrieval with an entrapment device is preferred because it minimizes the risk of tumor seeding and allows for adequate pathologic staging. Morcellation may hold promise in the future if improvements in technology allow for accurate pathologic staging without tumor spillage.

Port-site seeding of TCC following LNU is a rarity but has been reported.[75,76] In one report using transurethral resection of the ureteral orifice and intact specimen removal for a high-grade tumor, the patient presented 8 months postoperatively with a painful incisional hernia in the periumbilical laparoscopic port. Exploration revealed a metastatic deposit of TCC. In a second report, a port-site urothelial recurrence was found months after a laparoscopic nephrectomy for an atrophic tuberculous kidney in which an unsuspected upper tract TCC was found on final pathology. Such reports are concerning but only re-emphasize the importance of precautions that must be undertaken in specimen retrieval at the conclusion of laparoscopic cases.

COST

A criticism of laparoscopy is the increased operative times and cost associated with the operation. Seifman and colleagues reported that the mean operative cost was 56% greater for the laparoscopic procedure than the open procedure ($p < .001$).[39] These expenses were attributed to the laparoscopic equipment and longer operative times. However, when factoring in the shorter hospital stay and the reported fewer complications requiring treatment, total hospital costs were only 8% greater in the laparoscopic group. In an early financial analysis from the Cleveland Clinic, Meraney and colleagues reported on an overall 24% cost increase for LNU when compared with ONU.[77] Most recently, however, Meraney and Gill re-evaluated

LNU from a financial standpoint by performing a detailed cost analysis of ONU versus LNU.[78] Compared with radical ONU, mean total costs associated with initial laparoscopic cases were 28% greater. This was a reflection of mean intraoperative costs that were 65% greater and mean postoperative costs that were 27% less. Interestingly, when analyzing the more recent laparoscopic nephrectomies and nephro-ureterectomies, there was an overall 6% cost benefit over open surgery.

It is evident, that cost-effectiveness correlates with learning curves for laparoscopic procedures. Because increased operative time is directly related to increased costs, the experienced laparoscopic surgeon can dramatically decrease costs over time. The general surgery literature, for example, reports a learning curve of up to 50 cases for laparoscopic cholecystectomy to stabilize operative times.[79]

Cost data may also be misleading if not viewed with a global perspective. Costs such as operative time and disposable laparoscopic instruments are not easily compared to the financial benefits to an individual, employer, or society at large if one may return to work earlier or require less assistance owing to the benefits of a minimally invasive procedure.

OVERVIEW

To date, it is already indisputable that patients undergoing LNU for upper tract TCC fare better than their counterparts having open surgery in regard to a number of factors: hospital stay, analgesic requirements, intraoperative blood loss, and convalescence.[80] Interestingly, immunologic benefits of laparoscopy in urologic surgery have also been reported, giving further support for the use of minimally invasive techniques.[28] Studies comparing laparoscopic to open techniques for treatment of upper tract TCC show equivalent oncologic outcomes with respect to bladder recurrences, retroperitoneal recurrences, and subsequent metastatic disease. The natural history of upper tract TCC, especially in the instances of higher grade and stage, is perhaps the more powerful predictor of oncologic failures rather than if a laparoscopic or an open approach is used. When considering this observation and the obvious intraoperative and postoperative advantages of laparoscopy, it is clear that LNU is emerging as a first-line treatment for upper tract TCC.

The question as to which management options for the distal ureter are most efficacious is not yet answered. There may be a trend toward retroperitoneal and local recurrence in high-grade and -stage disease in which the distal ureter is not occluded when performing a transurethral resection. Although the natural history of the disease is not controllable, it would be wise to take definitive steps to minimize the potential for tumor seeding. Occlusion of the distal ureter, regardless of the method chosen, at the onset of cystoscopic ureteral mobilization should become the standard of care when choosing to manage the distal ureter and bladder cuff transurethrally. Alternatively, one may elect an open approach to the distal ureter, especially in the setting of distal ureteral tumors.

The general urology community may feel that LNU is too technically challenging. Along with the low incidence of upper tract TCC, this may cause urologic surgeons to view the learning curves associated with this procedure as a Herculean task. However, many urologists espouse hand-assisted laparoscopic surgery (HALS) as a tool to help bring LNU into the mainstream of urologic surgery. Pure proponents of laparoscopy view HALS as an educational bridge that helps the novice laparoscopist get comfortable with minimal access surgery.[81]

Whether the approach is hand-assisted, transperitoneal, or retroperitoneal, short-term results indicate that LNU is an effective method with pathologic specimens and complication rates comparable with those of the open approach. Easier postoperative courses are evidenced by less blood loss, earlier oral intake, less analgesia consumption, and shorter hospital stays and convalescence. Although longer oncologic follow-up is required before LNU can truly be considered as the new standard of care for the definitive management of upper tract TCC, the complication rates are acceptable, and the risk of tumor recurrence appears to parallel that reported in open surgical series

CONCLUSION

LNU for the treatment of upper tract TCC respects oncologic principles and is efficacious with regard to risk of tumor recurrences. Concern regarding port-site seeding is unsubstantiated in a properly controlled setting, and the ideal surgical approach for management of the distal ureter continues to evolve. Perioperatively, patients undergoing LNU fare better than those who undergo open treatments. Although continued follow-up and prospective multi-institutional studies are needed to verify long-term efficacy, LNU is emerging as the new standard of care for the treatment of upper tract TCC.

REFERENCES

1. Cummings KB. Nephroureterectomy: rationale in the management of transitional cell carcinoma of the upper urinary tract. Urol Clin North Am 1980;7:569–78.
2. Anderstrom C, Johansson SL, Petterson S, Wahlquist L. Carcinoma of the ureter: a clinicopathological study of 49 cases. J Urol 1989;142(2 Pt 1):280–3.
3. Kimball FN, Ferris HW. Papillomatous tumors of the renal pelvis associated with similar tumors of the ureter and bladder: review of the literature and report of two cases. J Urol 1934;31:257–304.
4. Mazeman E. Tumors of the upper urinary tract calyces, renal pelvis and ureter. Eur Urol 1976;2:120–8.
5. Murphy DM, Zincke H, Furlow WL. Primary grade I transitional cell carcinoma of the renal pelvis and ureter. J Urol 1980;123:629–31.
6. Murphy DM, Zincke H, Furlow WL. Management of high grade transitional cell carcinoma of the renal pelvis and ureter. J Urol 1981;125:25–9.
7. Strong DW, Pearse HD. Recurrent urothelial tumors following surgery for transitional cell carcinoma of the upper urinary tract. Cancer 1976;38:2173.
8. Haupt G. Editorial comment—transitional cell carcinoma of the ureter. J Endourol 2001;15:409.
9. Hall MC, Womack S, Sagalowsky AI, et al. Prognostic factors, recurrence, and survival in transitional cell carcinoma of the upper urinary tract: a 30-year experience in 252 patients. Urology 1998;52:594–601.
10. Gill IS, Sung GT, Hobart MG, et al. Laparoscopic radical nephroureterectomy for upper tract transitional cell carcinoma: the Cleveland Clinic experience. J Urol 2000; 164:1513–22.
11. Schulam PG, DeKernion JB. Laparoscopic nephrectomy for renal cell carcinoma: the current situation. J Endourol 2001;15:375–6.
12. Kaouk JH, Savage SJ, Gill IS. Retroperitoneal laparoscopic nephroureterectomy and management options for the distal ureter. J Endourol 2001;15:385–90.
13. Huben RP, Mounzer AM, Murphy GP. Tumor grade and stage as prognostic variables in upper tract urothelial tumors. Cancer 1988;62:2016–20.
14. Munoz JJ, Ellison LM. Upper tract urothelal neoplasms: incidence and survival during the last 2 decades. J Urol 2000;164:1523–5.

15. Wagle DG, Moore RH, Murphy GP. Primary carcinoma of the renal pelvis. Cancer 1974;33:1642–6.

16. Laguna MP, Rosette JJ. The endoscopic approach to the distal ureter in nephroureterectomy for upper urinary tract tumor. J Urol 2001;166:2017–22.

17. Batata MA, Whitmore WF, Hilaris BS, et al. Primary carcinoma of the renal pelvis: a prognostic study. Cancer 1975;35:1626.

18. Abercrombie GF, Eardley SR, Payne SR, et al. Modified nephro-ureterectomy. Long-term follow-up with particular reference to subsequent bladder tumours. Br J Urol 1988;61:198–200.

19. Kakizoe T, Fujita J, Muraseb T, et al. Transitional cell carcinoma of the bladder in patients with renal pelvic and ureteral cancer. J Urol 1980;124:17–9.

20. Auld GM, Grigor KM, Fowler JW, et al. Histopathological review of transitional cell carcinoma of the upper urinary tract. J Urol 1984;56:486–9.

21. Droller MJ. Editorial comment: extending the domain of minimally invasive surgery: bladder cancer. J Endourol 2001;15:425.

22. Abercrombie GF. Nephroureterectomy. Proc R Soc Med 1972;65:1221–2.

23. Carr T, Powell PH, Ramsden PD, et al. Letter to the editor. Br J Urol 1987;59:99–100.

24. Williams CB, Mitchell JP. Carcinoma of the renal pelvis: a review of 48 cases. Br J Urol 1973;45:370–6.

25. Charbit L, Gendreau MC, Mee S, et al. Tumors of the upper urinary tract: 10 years of experience. J Urol 1991;146:124.

26. Krough J, Kvist E, Rye B. Transitional cell carcinoma of the upper urinary tract: prognostic variables and postoperative recurrences. Br J Urol 1991;67:32.

27. Stifelman MD, Hyman MJ, Shichman S, et al. Hand-assisted laparoscopic nephroureterectomy versus open nephroureterectomy for the treatment of transitional-cell carcinoma of the upper urinary tract. J Endourol 2001;15:377–83.

28. Dunn MD, Shalhav AL, McDougall EM, et al. Laparoscopic nephrectomy and nephroureterectomy for renal and upper tract transitional cell cancer. Semin Laparosc Surg 2000;7:200–10.

29. Keeley FX, Tolley DA. Laparascopic nephroureterectomy: making management of upper-tract transitional-cell carcinoma entirely minimally invasive. J Endourol 1998;12:139–41.

30. Shalhav AL, Portis AJ, McDougall EM, et al. Laparoscopic nephroureterectomy—a new standard for the surgical management of upper tract transitional cell cancer. Urol Clin North Am 2000;27:761–73.

31. Clayman RV, Kavoussi LR, Soper NJ, et al. Laparoscopic nephrectomy: initial case report. J Urol 1991;146:278–82.

32. Chung HJ, Chiu AW, Chen KK, et al. Retroperitoneoscopy-assisted nephroureterectomy for the management of upper urinary urothelial cancer. Min Invas Ther Allied Technol 1996;5:266–71.

33. Chen J, Chueh S, Hsu WT, et al. Modified approach of hand-assisted laparoscopic nephroureterectomy for transitional cell carcinoma of the upper urinary tract. Urology 2001;58:930–4.

34. Hsu TH, Gill IS, Fazeli-Matin S, et al. Radical nephrectomy and nephroureterectomy in the octogenarian and nonagenarian: comparison of laparoscopic and open approaches. Urology 1999;53:1121–5.

35. Jarrett TW, Chan DY, Cadeddu JA, Kavoussi LR. Laparoscopic nephroureterectomy for the treatment of transitional cell carcinoma of the upper urinary tract. Urology 2001;57:448–53.

36. Landman J, Lev RY, Bhayani S, et al. Comparison of hand assisted and standard laparoscopic radical nephroureterectomy for the management of localized transitional cell carcinoma. J Urol 2002;167:2387–91.

37. McDougall EM, Clayman RV, Elashry O. Laparoscopic nephroureterectomy for upper tract transitional cell cancer: the Washington University experience. J Urol 1995;154:975–80.

38. Salomon L, Honek A, Cicco A, et al. Retroperitoneoscopic nephroureterectomy for renal pelvic tumors with a single iliac incision. J Urol 1999;161:541–4.

39. Seifman BD, Montie JE, Wolf JS. Prospective comparison between hand assisted laparoscopic and open surgical nephroureterectomy for urothelial cell carcinoma. Urology 2001;57:133–7.

40. Shalhav AL, Dunn MD, Portis AJ, et al. Laparoscopic nephroureterectomy for upper tract transitional cell cancer: the Washington University experience. J Urol 2000;163:1100–4.

41. Stifelman MD, Sosa RE, Andrade A, et al. Hand assisted laparoscopic nephroureterectomy for the treatment of transitional cell carcinoma of the upper urinary tract. Urology 2000;56:741–7.

42. Guillonneau B, Rozet F, Cathelineau X, et al. Perioperative complications of laparoscopic radical prostatectomy: the Mountsouris 3-year experience. J Urol 2002;167:51–6.

43. Turk I, Deger S, Winkelman B, et al. Complete laparoscopic approach for radical cystectomy and continent urinary diversion (sigma rectum pouch). Tech Urol 2001;7(1):2–6.

44. Kaouk JH, Gill IS, Desai MM, et al. Laparoscopic orthotopic ileal neobladder. J Endourol 2001;15:131–42.

45. Turk I, Deger S, Winkelman B, et al. Laparoscopic radical cystectomy with continent urinary diversion (rectal sigmoid pouch) performed completely intracorporeally: the initial 5 cases. J Urol 2001;165(6 Pt 1):1863–6.

46. Gill IS, Kaouk JH, Meraney AM, et al. Laparoscopic radical cystectomy and continent orthotopic ileal neobladder performed completely intracorporeally: the initial experince. J Urol 2002;168:13–8.

47. Gupta NP, Gill IS, Fergany A, Nabi G. Laparoscopic radical cystectomy with intracorporeal ileal conduit diversion: five cases with a 2-year follow up. BJU Int 2002;90:391–6.

48. Clayman RV, Kavoussi LR, Figenshau RS, et al. Laparoscopic nephroureterectomy: initial clinical case report. J Laparoendosc Surg 1991;1:343–9.

49. Portis AJ, Elnady M, Clayman RV. Laparoscopic radical/total nephrectomy: a decade of progress. J Endourol 2001;15:345–54.

50. Tierney JP, Oliver SR, Kusminsky RE, et al. Laparoscopic radical nephrectomy with intra-abdominal manipulation. Min Invas Ther 1994;3:303–5.

51. Nakada SY, Moon TD, Gist M, Mahvi D. Use of Pneumosleeve

as an adjunct in laparoscopic nephrectomy. Urology 1997;49:612–3.

52. Keeley FX, Sharma NK, Tolley DA. Hand-assisted laparoscopic nephroureterectomy. BJU Int 1999;83:504–5.

53. Kerbl K, Figenshau RS, Clayman RV, et al. Retroperitoneal laparoscopic nephrectomy: laboratory and clinical experience. J Endourol 1993;7:23.

54. Gaur DD, Agarwal DK, Purohit KC. Retroperitoneal laparoscopic nephrectomy: initial case report. J Urol 1993; 149:103–5.

55. McDonald HP, Upchurch WE, Sturdevant CE. Nephroureterectomy: a new technique. J Urol 1952;67:804–9.

56. Palou J, Caparros J, Orsola BX, Vicente J. Transurethral resection of the intramural ureter as the first step of nephroureterectomy. J Urol 1995;154:43–4.

57. Kural AR, Demirkesen OD, Arar O, et al. Modified "pluck" nephroureterectomy for upper urinary tract disorders: combined endourologic and open approach. J Endourol 1997;11:131–9.

58. Hetherington JW, Ewing R, Philp H. Modified nephroureterectomy: a risk of tumor implantation. Br J Urol 1986;58:368–70.

59. Jones DR, Moisey CU. A cautionary tale of the modified "pluck" nephroureterectomy. Br J Urol 1993;71:486.

60. Arango O, Bielsa O, Carles J, Gelabert-Mas A. Massive tumor implantation in the endoscopic resected area in modified nephroureterectomy. J Urol 1997;157:1839.

61. Clayman RV, Garske GL, Lange PH. Total nephroureterectomy with ureteral intussusception and transurethral ureteral detachment and pull-through. Urology 1983;21:482.

62. Angulo JC, Hontoria J, Sanchez-Chapado M. One incision nephroureterectomy endoscopically assisted by transurethral stripping. Urology 1998;52:203S.

63. Figenshau RS, Albala DM, Clayman RV, et al. Laparoscopic nephroureterectomy: initial labarotory experience. Min Invas Ther 1991;1:93.

64. McNeil SA, Chrisofos M, Tolley DA. The long-term outcome after laparascopic nephroureterectomy: a comparison with open nephroureterectomy. Br J Urol Int 2000; 86:619–23.

65. Gill IS, Soble JJ, Miller SD, Sung GT. A novel technique for management of the en bloc bladder cuff and distal ureter during laparoscopic nephroureterectomy. J Urol 1999; 161:430–4.

66. Komatsu H, Tanabe N, Kubodera S, et al. The role of lymphadenectomy in the treatment of transitional cell carcinoma of the upper urinary tract. J Urol 1997;157: 1622–4.

67. Miyake H, Hara K, Gohji S, et al. The significance of lymphadenectomy in transitional cell carcinoma of the upper urinary tract. Br J Urol 1998;82:494–8.

68. Urban DA, Kerbl K, Mc Dougall EM, et al. Organ entrapment and renal morcellation: permeability studies. J Urol 1993;150:1792.

69. Parekh AR, Moran ME, Newkirk RE, et al. Tissue removal utilizing Steiner morcellator within a LapSac: effects of a fluid filled environment. J Endourol 2000;14:185–9.

70. Ordorica RC, Moran ME. Vital–dye sham intrarenal lesions: assessment of risk of intraabdominal tumor spread during laparoscopic nephrectomy and morcellation. MIT 1994;3: 105–9.

71. Meng MV, Kopie TM, Duh QY, Stoller ML. Novel method of assessing surgical margin status in laparoscopic specimens. Urology 2001;58:677–81.

72. Planz B, George R, Adam G, et al. Computed tomography for detection and staging of transitional cell carcinoma of the upper urinary tract. Eur Urol 1995;27:146–50.

73. Badalament RA, Bennett WF, Bova JG, et al. Computed tomography of primary transitional cell carcinoma of upper urinary tracts. Urology 1992;40:71–5.

74. Dauleh MI, Townell NH. Laparoscopic nephroureterectomy for malignancy: vaginal route for retrieval of intact specimen. Br J Urol 1993;72(5 Pt I):667–8.

75. Ahmed I, Shaikh NA, Kapadia CR. Track recurrence of renal pelvic transitional cell carcinoma after laparoscopic nephrectomy. Br J Urol 1998;81:319.

76. Otani M, Irie S, Tsuji I. Port site metastasis after laparoscopic nephrectomy: unsuspected transitional cell carcinoma within a tuberculous atrophic kidney. J Urol 1999;162:486.

77. Meraney AM, Gill IS. Financial analysis of open versus laparoscopic radical nephrectomy and nephroureterectomy. J Urol 2002;167:1757–62.

78. Merany AM, Gill IS. Financial analysis of laparoscopic vs open radical nephroureterectomy for upper tract TCC [abstract]. J Endourol 1999;13 Suppl 1:A64.

79. Cagir B, Rangraj M, Maffuci L, et al. The learning curve for laparoscopic cholecystectomy. J Laparoendosc Surg 1994; 4:419.

80. Savage SJ, Gill IS. Laparoscopic radical nephroureterectomy. J Endourol 2000;14:859–64.

81. Gill IS. Hand-assisted laparoscopy: con. Urology 2001;58: 31–7.

24

Systemic Chemotherapy for Metastatic Urothelial Cancer

GURKAMAL S. CHATTA, MD
DONALD L. TRUMP, MD

Metastatic bladder cancer is sensitive to chemotherapy, and high response rates are obtained following combination chemotherapy: response rates of 70% are reported in metastatic disease and pathologic complete response (CR) rates of over 30% in the neoadjuvant setting.[1–3] Despite this, chemotherapy has yet to impact overall survival in patients with metastatic disease; the total number of deaths attributable to bladder cancer continues to be over 12,000 patients/year in the United States.[4] Multiple cytotoxic agents have single-agent response rates in the 15 to 30% range in bladder cancer. Combination regimens comprised of these single agents have response rates in the 30 to 70% range. The best known of these regimens is MVAC (methotrexate, vinblastine, Adriamycin [doxorubicin], and cisplatin), which was first developed by Yagoda and colleagues at Memorial Sloan-Kettering Cancer Center (MSKCC), in the early 1980s.[5–7] In the setting of metastatic transitional cell carcinoma (TCC), MVAC is the only combination reported to be associated with occasional survivorship (3.7%) beyond 5 years. Furthermore, MVAC-associated tumor response rates are unsurpassed by other regimens. Hence, despite its toxicity, this multiagent regimen continues to remain the "gold standard," against which all new combinations are evaluated.

During the 1990s, a plethora of new agents and new combinations were described.[1,2] An important advance is the development of the gemcitabine + cisplatin (GC) regimen, which is significantly less toxic and apparently of equivalent efficacy when compared with MVAC.[8] The challenge for the next decade is to integrate these cytotoxic regimens with the emerging "target-specific" agents to improve survival rates in bladder cancer.[9,10] We review agents with activity in TCC of the bladder and subsequently discuss the combinations currently in use. More than 90% of bladder tumors are transitional cell in histology and typically have a better response to chemotherapy. The other histologies include squamous cell carcinoma (SCC), adenocarcinomas, and small cell cancer, all of which are associated with lower response rates and have a uniformly poor prognosis.[11–13] There are few reports evaluating cytotoxic combinations specifically in non-TCC histologies; these are briefly discussed.

SINGLE AGENTS IN BLADDER CANCER

Several cytotoxic agents have activity in bladder cancer.[14] Cisplatin was one of the first agents to be evaluated in bladder cancer and continues to be a key component of most combination regimens. Taxanes and gemcitabine are the newer agents with impressive single-agent activity in TCC. Combinations based on these two agents are currently under intense investigation.

Cisplatin and Platinum Analogues

Cisplatin is a planar inorganic compound; it binds to deoxyribonucleic acid (DNA) and produces intrastrand crosslinks and DNA adducts, which interfere with DNA replication. Cisplatin is administered intravenously and has a biphasic disappearance curve. Over 90% of the drug is bound to plasma proteins, and less than 10% of the drug is cleared by renal mechanisms. Free drug is rapidly cleared with a half-life of 50 to 60 minutes. Protein-bound drug is neither bioactive nor toxic and is gradually cleared by a renal mechanism with a half-life well over 24 hours. Less than 10% of the drug is excreted in the bile. The principal dose-limiting toxicity of cisplatin is nephrotoxicity, which peaks 2 weeks after administration and is usually reversible. Cisplatin-associated nausea and vomiting, which were formerly dose limiting, can now be well controlled by premedicating with steroids in conjunction with 5-hydroxytryptamine$_3$ antagonists. Single-agent cisplatin has been evaluated in both phase II and phase III trials of metastatic bladder cancer.[15–18] In more than 10 phase II trials, with an aggregate of over 250 patients, the median response rate is 25% (range 15–33%). There were few (< 10%) CRs, and median time to disease progression is 3 to 4 months. Predictably, the response rate (RR) in five phase III trials (*n* > 300) was even lower (< 20%), once again with few CRs. In the largest of these trials, cisplatin had an overall response rate of only 12%, with 3% CRs. Cisplatin was administered at a dose of 50 to 120 mg/m^2 intravenously either on a weekly schedule or every 3 to 4 weeks in the above trials. The schedule of cisplatin administration does not appear to impact its efficacy. Although higher doses of cisplatin produce higher response rates, these have not been shown to correlate with increased survival.

Carboplatin is a cisplatin analogue that also binds to DNA, forming DNA adducts and intrastrand crosslinks, thereby hampering DNA replication.[19,20] Unlike cisplatin, little carboplatin is protein bound, and after intravenous administration, free drug is eliminated from the plasma, with a half-life of 90 minutes. The major route of elimination is renal, and unlike cisplatin, the clearance of carboplatin is directly related to the glomerular filtration rate (GFR). Hence, carboplatin can be accurately dose modified for decrements in renal function. In ovarian cancer, optimal tumor responses occur at carboplatin areas under the curve (AUC) of 5 to 7.[21]

Higher AUC increase toxicity without enhancing response rates. Similar studies have not been carried out in TCC. The principal dose-limiting toxicity is marrow suppression, particularly thrombocytopenia. The use of carboplatin in TCC is driven by (1) its lack of nephrotoxicity, (2) the ability to dependably achieve a therapeutic AUC by individualized dosing based on GFR, and (3) the convenience of administering it in the ambulatory setting: unlike cisplatin, prolonged hydration and extensive antiemetic premedications are not required to administer carboplatin. In phase II trials, carboplatin was administered as a 30-minute infusion at doses of 200 to 400 mg/m^2 or dosed to achieve AUC of 5 and 6. In pooled data from 274 patients, the median response rate was 14% (8 to 23%), with a CR rate of 3%. As with cisplatin, the time to progression (TTP) with carboplatin was in the 3- to 5-month range. Given the dose variability and the lack of direct comparative data, it is unclear whether the two platinum analogues are of equivalent efficacy in the treatment of urothelial cancers.[22,23] In testicular cancer, two randomized studies have clearly shown the superiority of cisplatin over carboplatin in nonseminomatous germ cell tumors.[24,25] Equivalence of cisplatin and carboplatin in TCC has not been demonstrated, and caution must be used in considering replacement of cisplatin by carboplatin.

Taxanes

Paclitaxel is a diterpene plant product that is poorly water soluble.[26,27] Paclitaxel antitumor activity depends on its binding to the β subunit of tubulin, promoting the assembly of microtubules and stabilizing them against depolymerization. This blocks the cell cycle in mitosis. Paclitaxel is typically administered as a 3-hour infusion at doses ranging from 175 mg/m^2 to 225 mg/m^2 every 3 weeks. It is > 90% protein bound and is rapidly cleared from the plasma by the hepatobiliary route. Paclitaxel's plasma half-life is 4 to 5 hours. Limiting toxicities are hypersensitivity, peripheral neuropathy, and myelosuppression. Single-agent paclitaxel has one of the highest reported response rates in urothelial malignancies. In the initial Eastern Cooperative Oncology Group (ECOG) phase II trial, 26 chemotherapy-naive patients were treated with a 24-hour infusion of paclitaxel (250 mg/m^2). The total RR was 42% (95% CI = 23–63%), with 27% patients achieving a CR (95% CI = 12–48%) and 15% experiencing a partial response (PR). The median duration of response was 7 months. The RRs were higher in patients with nodal disease; no response was seen in patients with liver metastasis. Follow-up studies with single-agent paclitaxel have primarily been in either previously pretreated patients or patients with renal insufficiency. The response rates in an aggregate of more than 50 patients ranged between 7 and 30%.

Docetaxel is a semisynthetic taxane that also blocks mitosis by preventing microtubule depolymerization.[28] It mediates its actions by binding to a different set of microtubule-associated proteins. It is administered every 3 weeks as a 30-minute infusion at doses between 60 and 75 mg/m^2. Its toxicity includes hypersensitivity reactions, marrow suppression, and asthenia. Studies of single-agent docetaxel in metastatic TCC are scant. It is currently being investigated in several multiagent regimens in urothelial malignancies.

Gemcitabine

The pyrimidine antimetabolite gemcitabine (2',2'-difluorodeoxycytidine) is a cytidine analog. Gemcitabine is converted to 5'-guanosine triphosphate in tumor cells and thereby inhibits DNA synthesis. It can also block the conversion of ribonucleotides to deoxyribonucleotides. Gemcitabine is infused weekly as a 30-minute infusion at doses ranging between 800 and 1,200 mg/m^2. The plasma half-life is less than 30 minutes, and most of the gemcitabine is deaminated to difluorodeoxyuridine, which is rapidly eliminated from the plasma. Myelosuppression is the dose-limiting toxicity. Recent evidence suggests that gemcitabine-related toxicity can be minimized by maintaining the rate of infusion of the drug at less than 10 mg/m^2/minute. Gemcitabine has broad antitumor activity and has been extensively studied in metastatic bladder cancer. The RR to single-agent gemcitabine in phase II studies is in the 22 to 28% range.[29–31] In 31 patients previously treated with cisplatin, the median RR was 22% (95% CI = 8–37%). In two trials of chemotherapy-naive patients, the response rates were 28% (95% CI = 15–45%) and 24% (95% CI = 15–45%), respectively. In both of these trials, gemcitabine was administered at 1,200 mg/m^2 weekly for 3 of every 4 weeks, and a total of 76 patients were treated. In both of these studies, a third of the responses were CRs and included patients with metastatic disease to the liver. The dose-limiting toxicity was myelosuppression; nonhematologic toxicity consisted primarily of fever, nausea, and liver function abnormalities. Gemcitabine is an active agent in previously treated patients.

Anthracyclines

Doxorubicin is the most thoroughly studied compound in this class.[32,33] It is an anthracycline antibiotic that mediates its antitumor activity by inhibiting nucleic acid synthesis by multiple mechanisms: intercalation of DNA, intercalation of induction of DNA strand breaks by inhibiting DNA topoisomerase II, formation of heavy metal complexes, and generation of free radicals. It is cytotoxic in all phases of the cell cycle. Typically, in TCC, it has been used at dosages of 30 to 60 mg/m^2 intravenously every 3 weeks. It has a plasma half-life of 30 to 40 hours, and myelosuppression and cardiotoxicity are its principal side effects. In pooled analyses from over 250 patients, single-agent doxorubicin was associated with a median RR of 17% (95% CI = 11–25%). Thus, doxorubicin has modest single-agent activity in TCC, but it is a component of the multiagent regimen MVAC, although its necessity in this regimen is uncertain.

Epirubicin, the 4'-epimer of doxorubicin, has been extensively studied in Europe, primarily as a substitute for doxorubicin in combination regimens, owing to its favorable cardiac toxicity profile.[34] Epirubicin also intercalates DNA and induces DNA strand breaks. It is administered intravenously in doses of 75 to 90 mg/m^2 every 3 weeks, with myelosuppression being its principal toxicity. Like doxorubicin, it is excreted by the hepatobiliary tract, necessitating dosage adjustments in the presence of biliary obstruction. It has a plasma half-life of 30 hours, and single-agent activity is ~10 to 15% in a variety of solid tumors.

Table 24–3. GEMCITABINE + CISPLATIN VERSUS MVAC		
	n = 203	*n* = 202
Patient characteristics		
Median age (yr)	63	63
PS < 80 (%)	20	18
> 80 (%)	80	82
Prior surgery/radiation therapy (%)	51	50
Disease characteristics (%)		
Extravesical primary	16	18
Visceral metastases	49	46
Four or more sites	21	17
Bone metastases	28.6	26
Responses		
Overall response (%)	49	46
Complete response (%)	12	12
Partial response (%)	37	34
Time to progression (mo)	9.6	11
Overall survival (mo)	13.8	14.8
At 3 yr	12.3–15.8	13.2–16.8

Adapted from von der Maase H et al.[11] PS = Performance status.

and greater use of supportive measures and hospitalizations. Furthermore, the GC arm was better tolerated, with less fatigue, less constitutional sequelae, and better preservation of performance status (Table 24–4). Hence, the study suggests that the GC combination has a favorable toxicity profile and is an acceptable alternative to MVAC in the setting of metastatic TCC. Longer follow-up is needed to determine whether, like MVAC, long-term survivorship is also associated with GC. Building on the results of this study, EORTC and SWOG are plan-

Table 24–4. GEMCITABINE + CISPLATIN VERSUS MVAC		
	Gemcitabine + Cisplatin	MVAC
Tolerability		
Median cycles of chemotherapy	6	4
Patients receiving 6 cycles (%)	53	36
No dose adjustment (%)	63	37
Drug toxicity, death rate (%)	1	3
Safety (%)		
Hematologic grade 3/4 neutropenia	71	82
Neutropenic fever ± sepsis	2.5	25
Growth factor	6.4	21
Grade 3/4 thrombocytopenia	57	21
Hemorrhage	1.5	1.5
Nonhematologic toxicity (%)		
Mucositis	1	22
Alopecia	11	55
Nausea/vomiting	22	21

Adapted from von der Maase H et al.[11]
MVAC = methotrexate, vinblastine, Adriamycin (doxorubicin), cisplatin.

ning an international phase III study that will randomize patients with metastatic TCC to either GC or GC and paclitaxel.

Gemcitabine + Taxanes

Individually, paclitaxel and gemcitabine have high single-agent activity in TCC. Hence, both "doublets" and "triplets" incorporating these agents are being investigated in advanced TCC.[1,2,49,58,59] In small phase I/II trials, an aggregate of approximately 70 patients has been treated with the paclitaxel + gemcitabine regimen, with response rates in the 40 to 60% range and a median survival of 15 months. Confirmatory trials with both paclitaxel + gemcitabine and docetaxel + gemcitabine are currently under way. Triplets incorporating these two agents have generated even more enthusiasm (see below).

Other Combination Regimens

These combinations have been primarily used in the salvage setting. Although initially promising, they were ultimately abandoned owing to unacceptable toxicity or unproven efficacy.[1,2,14] Thus, the combination of vinblastine, ifosfamide, and gallium nitrate (VIG) was associated with RRs of 67% (95% CI = 46–84%).[60] However, toxicity was severe and included febrile neutropenia and anemia in a third of the patients, nephrotoxicity in 15%, and encephalopathy and blindness in 2 of 27 patients. Given the activity of 5-FU and interferon-α in refractory bladder cancer patients, a combination of 5-FU, interferon-α, and cisplatin (Platinol) (FAP) was developed by investigators at MDACC. In an initial phase II trial, a response rate of 61% (95% CI = 41–78%) was noted. However, in a follow-up EORTC study of patients with refractory disease, overall response rates were just under 15% with this regimen. In a recently reported phase III trial, 172 previously untreated patients with metastatic TCC were randomized to either FAP or MVAC. In the FAP arm, the RR was 42%, with a CR of 10%; in the MVAC arm, the RR was 59%, with a CR of 24%. The two regimens were equally toxic, and median survival was 12.5 months in both arms.[61]

New Regimens

TCC is known to be highly responsive to a number of single agents: cisplatin, taxanes, gemcitabine, ifosfamide, and doxorubicin. Combinations of these agents are known to produce high response rates in metastatic TCC, but impact on survival has been minimal. To extend the durability of these responses, the focus is now shifting from "doublets" to "triplets" and sequential "doublets." The following are some of the regimens currently being investigated (Table 24–5).[1,2,49,62]

Gemcitabine + Carboplatin + Paclitaxel or GC + Paclitaxel

The regimens above seek to build on the favorable results of the pivotal GC trial. In essence, they add a third active agent, a taxane, to two active agents. In the recently published gemcitabine + carboplatin + paclitaxel trial, 46 patients with a median age of 63 years received paclitaxel 200 mg/m^2 over 3 hours on day 1, carboplatin dosed to an AUC of 5 on day 1, and gemcitabine 800 mg/m^2 on days 1 and 8 of a 21-day cycle. In 43 evaluable patients, the overall RR was 63% (including a 31% CR), and the toxicity profile was acceptable.[58,59]

Results of the phase I/II trial of GC + paclitaxel in advanced TCC were also recently reported by Bellmunt and colleagues.[58] The phase II regimen consisted of cisplatin 70 mg/m^2 on day 1, paclitaxel 80 mg/m^2 over 1 hour on days 1 and 8, and gemcitabine 1,000 mg/m^2 on days 1 and 8 of a 21-day cycle. In the 58 evaluable patients, the overall RR was 78% (95% CI = 60–98%), with a CR rate of 28%. Median survival for the phase I component was over 20 months. Based on the activity and tolerability of this triplet, an international phase III study randomizing patients with metastatic TCC to either GC or GC + paclitaxel is being launched jointly by EORTC and SWOG.

Ifosfamide + Paclitaxel + Cisplatin

Bajorin and his colleagues at MSKCC developed ifosfamide + Taxol (paclitaxel) + Platinol (cisplatin) (ITP) for the treatment of patients with advanced TCC.[63] The regimen is composed of cisplatin 70 mg/m^2 on day 1, paclitaxel 200 mg/m^2 over 3 hours on day 1, and ifosfamide 1.5 g/m^2/day for 3 days (days 1–3) on an every 21- to 28-day schedule. Results from the first 44 patients reported an overall RR of 68% (95% CI = 52–81%). At 28 months of follow-up, the median survival was 20 months. All of the patients required growth factor support, and the major toxicities were hematologic, renal, and neuropathic.

Sequential Doxorubicin + Gemcitabine, followed by ITP

This is the companion trial to ITP, also developed by investigators at MSKCC.[64] In the phase I setting, doxorubicin 50 mg/m^2 and gemcitabine 2,000 mg/m^2 were administered on day 1 every 2 weeks for a total of six cycles. Granulocyte colony-stimulating factor support was necessary to maintain the delivery of chemotherapy on schedule. This was followed by the 21-day ITP regimen for a total of four cycles. In the 15 patients treated, the overall RR was 64%. The phase II component of this trial is ongoing.

Table 24–5. NEWER REGIMENS IN TRANSITIONAL CELL CARCINOMA	
Ifosfamide/paclitaxel/cisplatin (ITP) Bajorin et al[63] (n = 44; RR = 68%)	Cisplatin 70 mg/m^2 day 1 Paclitaxel 200 mg/m^2 day 2 Ifosfamide 1.5 g/m^2/d days 1–3 Every 21 to 28 d
Gemcitabine/carboplatin/paclitaxel Hussain et al[59] (n = 46; RR = 63%)	Gemcitabine 800 mg/m^2 days 1 & 8 Paclitaxel 200 mg/m^2 day 1 Carboplatin AUC 5 day 1 Every 21 d
Sequential doxorubicin + gemcitabine Dodd et al[64] (n = 15; RR 64%)	Doxorubicin 50 mg/m^2 day 1 followed by ITP Gemcitabine 2,000 mg/m^2 day 1 Every 2 wk × 6 cycles followed by ITP every 21 d × 4 cycles

Targeted Therapies

A better understanding of the molecular and genetic alterations underlying bladder cancer has increased the repertoire of targets and potential therapies available for the treatment of bladder cancer. Loss of heterozygosity of chromosome 9 and mutations in *P53* are crucial events in the transition of normal urothelium to TCC and subsequent disease progression.[65] Mutations in *H-RAS* and overexpression or amplification of erbB-2 and the epidermal growth factor receptor (EGFR) also occur in up to 40% of patients with bladder cancer and are thought to be associated with a poor prognosis. Hence, both farnesyl transferase inhibitors and blockade of the EGFR and erbB-2 are currently being investigated either alone or in combination with cytotoxics in metastatic TCC. Other potential candidates for targeted therapy in TCC include antiangiogenic agents, differentiation agents, and cyclooxygenase-2 (COX-2) inhibitors.[70]

SPECIAL ISSUES IN METASTATIC UROTHELIAL CANCER

Risk Stratification

Both response rates and survival data vary widely between different trials of metastatic TCC, even when they employ the same treatment regimen. Investigators at MSKCC have analyzed their database of MVAC-treated patients ($n = 203$) with metastatic TCC, using a prognostic factor–based model of survival.[42] On multivariate regression analysis, two factors had independent prognostic value for survival: Karnofsky performance status less than 80% and the presence of visceral metastasis ($p = .0001$). Patients were stratified into low-, intermediate-, or high-risk categories based on the presence of zero, one, or both risk factors. Median survival for patients in the low-, intermediate-, and high-risk subsets was 33, 13.4, and 9.3 months, respectively. Thus, risk stratification may be imperative in patient selection for maximizing the benefit of aggressive therapy and in providing balance between treatment arms in randomized clinical trials.

Another important prognostic factor is the status of the *P53* tumor suppressor gene in the primary tumor.[65,66,68] Fifty percent of muscle-invasive tumors have a mutated *P53* gene, and preliminary evidence also suggests that stratification based on *P53* status may help in selecting patients with muscle-invasive TCC who are appropriate candidates for either neoadjuvant or adjuvant chemotherapy. Investigators at the University of Southern California reported on a *P53* analysis of 243 patients who underwent radical cystectomy (pT1 to pT4): 12% of pT2 tumors and 13% of pT3a tumors recurred in patients with wild-type *P53*; in contrast, 56% of pT2 and 80% of pT3a tumors recurred in patients with mutant *P53* expression ($p = .001$). Overall survival was inferior in patients with mutant *P53* expression ($p < .001$), and adjuvant chemotherapy in the setting of muscle-invasive tumors conferred a survival advantage in patients with mutant *P53*. In a smaller study from MSKCC, the *P53* status of the tumors of 90 patients treated with neoadjuvant chemotherapy was evaluated. Patients with tumors that were positive for wild-type *P53* had a threefold higher survival than patients with a mutant *P53*. A SWOG trial evaluating adjuvant therapy with MVAC in muscle-invasive, *P53* positive TCC is currently accruing.

Role of Local Treatment in Advanced Disease

The role of surgery following complete responses of locally advanced TCC to combination chemotherapy is unclear. In the absence of definitive surgery or radiation, local failure is common, and patients eventually succumb to metastatic disease. Investigators from MSKCC recently reported a 15-year experience with postchemotherapy surgery in patients with locally advanced TCC.[71] Between 1984 and 1999, a total of 207 patients were treated with cisplatin-based intensive chemotherapy. Eighty of the 207 patients (39%) elected to undergo a cystectomy. At surgery, 24 of the 80 cases (30%) had a pathologic CR with no evidence of residual disease; 49 patients (61%) had residual disease, which was resected; and 7 patients (9%) had unresectable disease. A subset of 60 from the original group of 80 chemotherapy-treated patients received MVAC. A third of these patients were disease free at 5 years. Long-term survival in a similar setting has also been reported in isolated cases in smaller studies. Thus cystectomy following combination chemotherapy may be a reasonable approach in highly selected patients with locally advanced and/or node-positive TCC, for example, in *P53*-positive patients.

Systemic Treatment of Micrometastatic Disease

Half of all patients with muscle-invasive TCC relapse within 2 years of cystectomy and subsequently die of metastatic disease. The pathologic stage of the tumor at the time of diagnosis is perhaps the single best predictor of future outcome. Thus, 5-year survival, which is 63% for pT2 tumors, falls to 18% for pT4 tumors. Node-positive disease is also associated with dismal 5-year survival rates, that is, 15 to 30%. Hence, there has been a high level of enthusiasm for integrating active cytotoxic regimens with definitive local therapy for attempting cure in muscle-invasive TCC and improving survival rates in locally advanced disease. The availability of highly active chemotherapy regimens has seen a number of neoadjuvant and adjuvant trials in TCC during the last decade. Until very recently, the fundamental question of whether adjunctive chemotherapy improves survival was unclear. A number of combination regimens have been tested in both the adjuvant and neoadjuvant settings.[3,72,78] The adjuvant studies are difficult to interpret, either because of insufficient numbers or because of premature termination.[75] On the other hand, the neoadjuvant experience has been much larger, and, to date, a little over 2,500 patients have been treated in a randomized manner. Although the data are somewhat conflicting, two recent studies suggest that MVAC in either the adjuvant or the neoadjuvant setting has a survival benefit. In the first study conducted by the SWOG, 307 patients were randomized to either MVAC × 3 cycles versus no MVAC, followed by cystectomy, over an 11-year time span. Median survival, as well as 5-year survival, was superior in the MVAC arm: 6.2 years versus 3.5 years and 51% versus 42% ($p = .04$, one-tailed t-test; $p = .08$, two-tailed t-test).[3] Furthermore, 37% of the MVAC-treated patients were reported to have a pathologic CR at surgery. In the second study, investigators at MDACC randomized 140 patients to

either two cycles of neoadjuvant and three cycles of postcystectomy adjuvant MVAC or five cycles of adjuvant MVAC after radical cystectomy. Follow-up at 7 years revealed that there was no difference between the two arms, with 58% of all of the patients showing no evidence of disease. Additionally 40% of the patients treated with two cycles of neoadjuvant MVAC achieved a pathologic complete remission (pCR).[74]

Finally, the results of the largest neoadjuvant trial to date were also recently updated. In the joint Medical Research Council and EORTC trial, 976 patients were randomized to CMV × 3 cycles versus no CMV prior to definitive local therapy.[73] At 4 years, survival in the CMV arm was superior but not statistically significant (5%; $p = .07$). However, at 6 years, survival in the CMV arm was both superior and statistically significant: 56% versus 50% ($p < .048$). Collectively, these studies point to the benefit of chemotherapy in the setting of muscle-invasive and locally advanced TCC. The next challenge is to confirm this result with less toxic, more generalizable, and equally, if not more, effective regimens than MVAC.

Nontransitional Cell Histologies

Over 90% of bladder tumors are transitional cell in histology. The non-TCC histologies include SCC, adenocarcinomas, and small cell cancer; these histologies are less chemoresponsive than TCC and have a uniformly poor prognosis. In most large series, median survival in the setting of metastatic non-TCC of the urogenital tract is a few months, with no survivors beyond 2 years.

SCC of the bladder is the most prevalent cancer in Africa and constitutes 25 to 30% of all cancers.[8,79] The median age at diagnosis is 46 years, with a 5:1 male preponderance. These tumors usually arise in the context of bladder schistosomiasis or bilharziasis. The optimal cytotoxic regimen(s) for SCC of the bladder remain to be defined. Typically, cisplatin-based regimens are used to treat SCC of the bladder. Given the high expression of COX-2 in SCC, regimens incorporating COX-2 inhibitors are currently being investigated in SCC of the bladder.[70]

Adenocarcinomas are notoriously refractory to chemotherapy (including MVAC), and optimal treatment remains to be developed.[9] Small cell cancers are treated with small cell regimens.[10,80] Typically, these tumors are widespread at the time of diagnosis, and median survival despite treatment is less than a year.

SUMMARY

TCC of the bladder is a highly chemosensitive neoplasm, with the potential for cure in some patients. Multiple cytotoxic agents and multiple combinations have activity in this disease. The challenge for the next decade remains the development of regimens and schedules that confer a survival advantage in the setting of both micrometastatic and metastatic disease. Given the proliferation of newer target-specific agents, the potential exists for developing combination regimens, which induce high response rates that are durable and which also translate to improved survival.

REFERENCES

1. Vaughn DJ, Malkowicz SB. Recent developments in chemotherapy for bladder cancer. Oncology (Huntingt) 2001;15: 763–71; discussion 775–6, 779–80.
2. Maluf FC, Bajorin DF. Chemotherapy agents in transitional cell carcinoma: the old and the new. Semin Urol Oncol 2001;19:2–8.
3. Vogelzang NJ. Neoadjuvant MVAC: the long and winding road is getting shorter and straighter. J Clin Oncol 2001; 19:4003–4.
4. Jemal A, Tiwari RC, Murray T, et al. Cancer Statistics, 2004. CA Cancer J Clin 2004;54:8–29.
5. Sternberg CN, Yagoda A, Scher HI, et al. Preliminary results of M-VAC (methotrexate, vinblastine, doxorubicin and cisplatin) for transitional cell carcinoma of the urothelium. J Urol 1985;133:403–7.
6. Sternberg CN, Yagoda A, Scher HI, et al. M-VAC (methotrexate, vinblastine, doxorubicin and cisplatin) for advanced transitional cell carcinoma of the urothelium. J Urol 1988; 139:461–9.
7. Yagoda A. Chemotherapy of urothelial tract cancer: Memorial Sloan-Kettering Cancer Center experience. Important Adv Oncol 1988;143–59.
8. el-Mawla NG, el-Bolkainy N, Khaled HM. Bladder cancer in Africa: update. Semin Oncol 2001;28:174–8.
9. McMahon RF, Hunt CR. In situ adenocarcinoma of the bladder: the role of the urachus. Am J Surg Pathol 2002;26:271–2.
10. Lohrisch C, Murray N, Pickles T, Sullivan L. Small cell carcinoma of the bladder: long term outcome with integrated chemoradiation. Cancer 1999;86:2346–52.
11. von der Maase H, Hansen SW, Roberts J, et al. Gemcitabine and cisplatin versus methotrexate, vinblastine, doxorubicin, and cisplatin in advanced or metastatic bladder cancer: results of a large, randomized, multinational, multicenter, phase III study. J Clin Oncol 2000;18:3068–77.
12. Lunec J, Challen C, Wright C, et al. C-erbB-2 amplification and identical p53 mutations in concomitant transitional carcinomas of renal pelvis and urinary bladder. Lancet 1992;339:439–40.
13. Nicholson RI, Gee JM, Harper ME. EGFR and cancer prognosis. Eur J Cancer 2001;37 Suppl 4:S9–15.
14. Stadler WM, Roth BJ. Chemotherapy for metastatic disease. In: Vogelzang, NJ, Scardino PT, Shipley WV, et al, editors. Comprehensive textbook of genitourinary oncology. Philadelphia: Lippincott Williams & Wilkins; 2000. p. 513–24.
15. Oliver RT, Newlands ES, Wiltshaw E, Malpas JS. A phase 2 study of cis-platinum in patients with recurrent bladder carcinoma. The London and Oxford Co-operative Urological Cancer Group. Br J Urol 1981;53:444–7.
16. Herr HW. Cis-diamminedichloride platinum II in the treatment of advanced bladder cancer. J Urol 1980;123:853–5.
17. Fagg SL, Dawson-Edwards P, Hughes MA, et al. Cis-diamminedichloroplatinum (DDP) as initial treatment of invasive bladder cancer. Br J Urol 1984;56:296–300.
18. Peters PC, O'Neill MR. Cis-diamminedichloroplatinum as a therapeutic agent in metastatic transitional cell carcinoma. J Urol 1980;123:375–7.
19. Mottet-Auselo N, Bons-Rosset F, Costa P, et al. Carboplatin and urothelial tumors. Oncology 1993;50 Suppl 2:28–36.
20. Calvert AH, Newell DR, Gumbrell LA, et al. Carboplatin dosage: prospective evaluation of a simple formula based on renal function. J Clin Oncol 1989;7:1748–56.
21. Jodrell DI, Egorin MJ, Canetta RM, et al. Relationships between carboplatin exposure and tumor response and toxicity in patients with ovarian cancer. J Clin Oncol 1992;10:520–8.
22. Bellmunt J, Ribas A, Eres N, et al. Carboplatin-based versus cisplatin-based chemotherapy in the treatment of surgically incurable advanced bladder carcinoma. Cancer 1997;80:1966–72.
23. Petrioli R, Frediani B, Manganelli A, et al. Comparison between a cisplatin-containing regimen and a carboplatin-containing regimen for recurrent or metastatic bladder cancer patients. A randomized phase II study. Cancer 1996;77:344–51.
24. Bajorin DF, Sarosdy MF, Pfister DG, et al. Randomized trial of etoposide and cisplatin versus etoposide and carboplatin in patients with good-risk germ cell tumors: a multiinstitutional study. J Clin Oncol 1993;11:598–606.
25. Horwich A, Sleijfer DT, Fossa SD, et al. Randomized trial of bleomycin, etoposide, and cisplatin compared with bleomycin, etoposide, and carboplatin in good-prognosis metastatic nonseminomatous germ cell cancer: a Multiinstitutional Medical Research Council/European Organization for Research and Treatment of Cancer Trial. J Clin Oncol 1997;15:1844–52.
26. Roth BJ, Dreicer R, Einhorn LH, et al. Significant activity of paclitaxel in advanced transitional-cell carcinoma of the urothelium: a phase II trial of the Eastern Cooperative Oncology Group. J Clin Oncol 1994;12:2264–70.
27. Dreicer R, Gustin DM, See WA, Williams RD. Paclitaxel in advanced urothelial carcinoma: its role in patients with

renal insufficiency and as salvage therapy. J Urol 1996; 156:1606–8.

28. de Wit R, Kruit WH, Stoter G, et al. Docetaxel (Taxotere): an active agent in metastatic urothelial cancer; results of a phase II study in non-chemotherapy-pretreated patients. Br J Cancer 1998;78:1342–5.

29. Moore MJ, Tannock IF, Ernst DS, et al. Gemcitabine: a promising new agent in the treatment of advanced urothelial cancer. J Clin Oncol 1997;15:3441–5.

30. Stadler WM, Kuzel T, Roth B, et al. A phase II study of single-agent gemcitabine in previously untreated patients with metastatic urothelial cancer. J Clin Oncol 1997;15:3394–8.

31. Lorusso V, Pollera CF, Antimi M, et al. A phase II study of gemcitabine in patients with transitional cell carcinoma of the urinary tract previously treated with platinum. Italian Co-operative Group on Bladder Cancer. Eur J Cancer 1998;34:1208–12.

32. Yagoda A, Watson RC, Whitmore WF, et al. Adriamycin in advanced urinary tract cancer: experience in 42 patients and review of the literature. Cancer 1997;39:279–85.

33. Knight EW, Pagand M, Hahn RG, Horton J. Comparison of 5-FU and doxorubicin in the treatment of carcinoma of the bladder. Cancer Treat Rep 1983;67:514–5.

34. Jones WG, Sokal MP, Ostrowski MJ, Newling DW. A phase II study of epirubicin in advanced transitional cell bladder cancer. The Yorkshire Urological Cancer Research Group. Clin Oncol (R Coll Radiol) 1993;5:25–9.

35. Witte RS, Elson P, Bono B, et al. Eastern Cooperative Oncology Group phase II trial of ifosfamide in the treatment of previously treated advanced urothelial carcinoma. J Clin Oncol 1997;15:589–93.

36. Hall RR. Methotrexate treatment for advanced bladder cancer. A review after 6 years. Br J Urol 1980;52:403.

37. Feun LG, Savaraj N, Benedetto P, et al. Oral piritrexim in advanced bladder cancer: an effective drug after progression on MVAC chemotherapy? Am J Clin Oncol 1994; 17:448–51.

38. Misset JL. Brief communication: use of the multitargeted antifolate pemetrexed (Alimta) in genitourinary cancer. Semin Oncol 2002;29:36–9.

39. Blumenreich MS, Yagoda A, Natale RB, Watson RC. Phase II trial of vinblastine sulfate for metastatic urothelial tract tumors. Cancer 1982;50:435–8.

40. Richards B, Newling D, Fossa S, et al. Vincristine in advanced bladder cancer: a European Organization for Research on Treatment of Cancer (EORTC) phase II study. Cancer Treat Rep 1983;67:575–7.

41. Saxman SB, Propert KJ, Einhorn LH, et al. Long-term follow-up of a phase III intergroup study of cisplatin alone or in combination with methotrexate, vinblastine, and doxorubicin in patients with metastatic urothelial carcinoma: a cooperative group study. J Clin Oncol 1997;15: 2564–9.

42. Bajorin DF, Dodd PM, Mazumdar M, et al. Long-term survival in metastatic transitional-cell carcinoma and prognostic factors predicting outcome of therapy. J Clin Oncol 1999;17:3173–81.

43. Loehrer PJ Sr, Einhorn LH, Elson PJ, et al. A randomized comparison of cisplatin alone or in combination with methotrexate, vinblastine, and doxorubicin in patients with metastatic urothelial carcinoma: a cooperative group study. J Clin Oncol 1992;10:1066–73.

44. Logothetis CJ, Dexeus FH, Finn L, et al. A prospective randomized trial comparing MVAC and CISCA chemotherapy for patients with metastatic urothelial tumors. J Clin Oncol 1990;8:1050–5.

45. Harker WG, Meyers FJ, Freiha FS, et al. Cisplatin, methotrexate, and vinblastine (CMV): an effective chemotherapy regimen for metastatic transitional cell carcinoma of the urinary tract. A Northern California Oncology Group study. J Clin Oncol 1985;3:1463–70.

46. Logothetis CJ, Finn LD, Smith T, et al. Escalated MVAC with or without recombinant human granulocyte-macrophage colony-stimulating factor for the initial treatment of advanced malignant urothelial tumors: results of a randomized trial. J Clin Oncol 1995;13:2272–7.

47. Loehrer PJ Sr, Elson P, Dreicer R, et al. Escalated dosages of methotrexate, vinblastine, doxorubicin, and cisplatin plus recombinant human granulocyte colony-stimulating factor in advanced urothelial carcinoma: an Eastern Cooperative Oncology Group trial. J Clin Oncol 1994;12:483–8.

48. Seidman AD, Scher HI, Gabrilove JL, et al. Dose-intensification of MVAC with recombinant granulocyte colony-stimulating factor as initial therapy in advanced urothelial cancer. J Clin Oncol 1993;11:408–14.

49. Hussain, M, Vaishampayan U, Smith DC. Novel gemcitabine-containing triplets in the management of urothelial cancer. Semin Oncol 2002;29:20–4.

50. Dreicer R, Manola J, Roth BJ, et al. Phase II study of cisplatin and paclitaxel in advanced carcinoma of the urothelium: an Eastern Cooperative Oncology Group Study. J Clin Oncol 2000;18:1058–61.

51. Sternberg CN. Second-line treatment of advanced transitional cell carcinoma of the urothelial tract. Curr Opin Urol 2001;11:523–9.

52. Pycha A, Grbovic M, Posch B, et al. Paclitaxel and carboplatin in patients with metastatic transitional cell cancer of the urinary tract. Urology 1999;53:510–5.

53. Redman BG, Smith DC, Flaherty L, et al. Phase II trial of paclitaxel and carboplatin in the treatment of advanced urothelial carcinoma. J Clin Oncol 1998;16:1844–8.

54. Small EJ, Lew D, Redman BG, et al. Southwest Oncology Group Study of paclitaxel and carboplatin for advanced transitional-cell carcinoma: the importance of survival as a clinical trial end point. J Clin Oncol 2000;18:2537–44.

55. Vaughn DJ, Malkowicz SB, Zoltick B, et al. Paclitaxel plus carboplatin in advanced carcinoma of the urothelium: an active and tolerable outpatient regimen. J Clin Oncol 1998;16:255–60.

56. Kaufman D, Raghavan D, Carducci M, et al. Phase II trial of gemcitabine plus cisplatin in patients with metastatic urothelial cancer. J Clin Oncol 2000;18:1921–7.

57. Moore MJ, Winquist EW, Murray N, et al. Gemcitabine plus cisplatin, an active regimen in advanced urothelial cancer: a phase II trial of the National Cancer Institute of Canada Clinical Trials Group. J Clin Oncol 1999;17:2876–81.

58. Bellmunt J, Guillem V, Paz-Ares L, et al. Phase I-II study of paclitaxel, cisplatin, and gemcitabine in advanced transitional-cell carcinoma of the urothelium. Spanish Oncology Genitourinary Group. J Clin Oncol 2000;18:3247–55.

59. Hussain M, Vaishampayan U, Du W, et al. Combination paclitaxel, carboplatin, and gemcitabine is an active treatment for advanced urothelial cancer. J Clin Oncol 2001;19:2527–33.

60. Einhorn LH, Roth BJ, Ansari R, et al. Phase II trial of vinblastine, ifosfamide, and gallium combination chemotherapy in metastatic urothelial carcinoma. J Clin Oncol 1994;12:2271–6.

61. Siefker-Radtke AO, Millikan RE, Tu SM, et al. Phase III trial of fluorouracil, interferon alpha-2b, and cisplatin versus methotrexate, vinblastine, doxorubicin, and cisplatin in metastatic or unresectable urothelial cancer. J Clin Oncol 2002;20:1361–7.

62, Von der Maase H. Current and future perspectives in advanced bladder cancer: is there a new standard? Semin Oncol 2002;1:3–14.

63. Bajorin DF, McCaffrey JA, Dodd PM, et al. Ifosfamide, paclitaxel, and cisplatin for patients with advanced transitional cell carcinoma of the urothelial tract: final report of a phase II trial evaluating two dosing schedules. Cancer 2000;88:1671–8.

64. Dodd PM, McCaffrey JA, Hilton S, et al. Phase I evaluation of sequential doxorubicin gemcitabine then ifosfamide paclitaxel cisplatin for patients with unresectable or metastatic transitional-cell carcinoma of the urothelial tract. J Clin Oncol 2000;18:840–6.

65. Cote RJ, Esrig D, Groshen S, et al. P53 and treatment of bladder cancer. Nature 1997;385:123–5.

66. Esrig D, Elmajian D, Groshen S, et al. Accumulation of nuclear p53 and tumor progression in bladder cancer. N Engl J Med 1994;331:1259–64.

67. Jimenez RE, Hussain M, Bianco FJ Jr, et al. Her-2/neu overexpression in muscle-invasive urothelial carcinoma of the bladder: prognostic significance and comparative analysis in primary and metastatic tumors. Clin Cancer Res 2001;7:2440–7.

68. Knowles MA. The genetics of transitional cell carcinoma: progress and potential clinical application. BJU Int 1999;84:412–27.

69. Wolf HK, Stober C, Hohenfellner R, Leissner J. Prognostic value of p53, p21/WAF1, Bcl-2, Bax, Bak and Ki-67 immunoreactivity in pT1 G3 urothelial bladder carcinomas. Tumour Biol 2001;22:328–36.

70. Xu XC. COX-2 inhibitors in cancer treatment and prevention, a recent development. Anticancer Drugs 2002;13:127–37.

71. Herr HW, Donat SM, Bajorin DF. Post-chemotherapy surgery in patients with unresectable or regionally metastatic bladder cancer. J Urol 2001;165:811–4.

72, McCaffrey JA, Bajorin DF. Adjuvant and neoadjuvant chemotherapy for invasive bladder cancer. In: Vogelzang NJ, Scardino PT, Shipley WU, et al, editors. Comprehensive textbook of genitourinary oncology. Philadelphia: Lippincott Williams & Wilkins; 2000. p. 473–82.

73. International Collaboration of Trialists. Neoadjuvant cisplatin, methotrexate, and vinblastine chemotherapy for muscle-invasive bladder cancer: a randomised controlled trial. Lancet 1999;354:533–40.

74. Millikan R, Dinney C, Swanson D, et al. Integrated therapy for locally advanced bladder cancer: final report of a randomized trial of cystectomy plus adjuvant M-VAC versus cystectomy with both preoperative and postoperative M-VAC. J Clin Oncol 2001;19:4005–13.

75. Skinner DG, Daniels JR, Russell CA, et al. The role of adjuvant chemotherapy following cystectomy for invasive bladder cancer: a prospective comparative trial. J Urol 1991;145:459–64; discussion 464–7.

76. Bajorin DF. Plenary debate of randomized phase III trial of neoadjuvant MVAC plus cystectomy versus cystectomy alone in patients with locally advanced bladder cancer. J Clin Oncol 2001;19:17S–20S.

77. Natale RB. Adjuvant and neoadjuvant chemotherapy for invasive bladder cancer. Curr Oncol Rep 2000;2:386–93.

78. Domopoulos MA, Galani E. Randomized trials of adjuvant and neoadjuvant chemotherapy in bladder cancer. Semin Urol Oncol 2001;19:59–65.

79. Corral DA, Sella A, Pettaway CA, et al. Combination chemotherapy for metastatic or locally advanced genitourinary squamous cell carcinoma: a phase II study of methotrexate, cisplatin and bleomycin. J Urol 1998;160:1770–4.

80. Trias I, Algaba F, Condom E, et al. Small cell carcinoma of the urinary bladder. Presentation of 23 cases and review of 134 published cases. Eur Urol 2001;39:85–90.

Index

Page numbers followed by f indicate figure. Pages numbers followed by t indicate table.

Accu-Dx, 164, 180, 189
Acetaminophen, 9
Acetylation, 10
Acetyltransferase genes, 10, 30
Adenocarcinoma, 85f, 398–399
  bladder
    cystoscopy, 74
  cytologic grading of, 122
  mesonephric, 86f
    histopathology, 84–85
  moderately differentiated, 123f
  urachal *vs.* nonurachal, 108t
Adriamycin, 211–213, 213t, 265. *See also*
  Doxorubicin (Adriamycin); Methotrexate
  vinblastine adriamycin cisplatin (MVAC)
  vs. MVAC
    for metastatic urothelial cancer, 393
AE1/AE3, 104
Africa, 1
African bladder cancer, 8
Aging, 279. *See also* Elderly
  chemotherapy, 276–277
  cognition, 279
  free radical theory of, 272
  genetic theory of, 274
  molecular biology of, 272–273
  oxidative stress theory of, 272
  physiology of, 277–278
  radical cystectomy, 276
  tumor biology, 275–276
AgNOR, 144
Airway
  elderly, 280
AJCC
  TNM classification
    upper tract urothelial cancer staging,
      330
ALA, 77, 77f
  clinical studies of, 79t
  induced PPIX fluorescence, 78
Alcohol
  bladder urothelial cancer, 6
Alimta, 391
Alprazolam
  elderly, 281
American Joint Committee on Cancer (AJCC)
  TNM classification
    upper tract urothelial cancer staging,
      330
American Society of Anesthesiologists'
  Physical Status Classification, 280
American Urological Association (AUA)
  Best Practice Policy Panel on
  Asymptomatic Microscopic Hematuria,
  170
Aminolevulinic acid (ALA), 77, 77f
  clinical studies of, 79t
  induced PPIX fluorescence, 78
Amphiregulin, 194
Amyloid, 89f
Analogy, 4

Ancona (Italy) refinement
  WHO classification, 92, 93t
Aneuploidy, 133, 135
  DNA histogram, 134f
Angiogenesis, 52
Angiotensin-converting enzyme inhibitors
  with anesthesia, 280
Aniline dye industry, 28
Anthracyclines, 390
AntiBCG, 229, 231
Antidepressants
  with anesthesia, 280
Antifolates, 391
Antigen-presenting cell (APC)
  BCG, 222–223
Antikeratin immunostaining (AE1/AE3), 104
Antioxidants, 273
Antipsychotics
  with anesthesia, 280
APC
  BCG, 222–223
Apoptosis, 151
Apoptosis index, 164
Apoptosis silver-staining nucleolar organizer
  regions, 144
Aristolochia fangchi, 8
  causing BEN, 321
Aristolochic acid
  causing BEN, 320
Aromatic amine manufacturing, 11
Arsenic
  bladder cancer, 8
Asia, 1
Aspiration
  elderly, 281
Asymptomatic individuals
  screening of, 126–127
Atypia of unknown clinical significance,
  93–94, 126f
AUA
  Best Practice Policy Panel on
  Asymptomatic Microscopic Hematuria,
  170
Automobile industry, 11

Bacille Calmette-Guerin (BCG), 118, 118f,
  163, 210–238
  cell-mediated Th1 immune response,
    221–224
  cellular immunity, 220–221
  vs. chemotherapy
    clinical trials, 226
  CIS, 225–226
  clinical science of, 224–229
  combination therapy, 234–235
  danger signal generated, 222
  disease-risk analysis, 219
  dose-reduction strategies, 231–234,
    232t–233t
  effector cell killing malignant cells,
    223–224

  failure of, 235–238, 236t
  high-risk superficial bladder cancer,
    228–229
  history of, 220
  IFN-alpha, 237f
  instillation therapy
    upper tract urothelial cancer,
      350–351, 350t, 351t
  intravasation into bloodstream, 230
  intravesical chemotherapy trials, 224–229
  intravesical TURB, 225
  invasion, 222
  invasive bladder carcinoma, 297–298
  leukocyte recruitment, 222–223
  local cancer phenotype alteration, 223
  maintenance therapy, 227–228, 228f
  mechanism of action, 223f
  megadose vitamins following, 235
  new prospectives, 231–235
  percutaneous infusion of, 346f
  rechallenge, 224
  regimen modifications, 234
  residual disease, 225
  restoration or repression, 224
  survival, 226–227
  toxicity, 229–230
    treatment of, 229–230, 230t
  tumor progression, 226–227
  tumor recurrence, 226–227
  for upper tract cancer, 363
Bacteria, 116
Balkan endemic nephropathy (BEN), 8,
  319–320
  renal embryologic anomalies, 320
  viral etiology, 320
Barbotage. *See* Bladder washings (Barbotage)
Basic fibroblast growth factor (bFGF), 48–49
BCG. *See* Bacille Calmette-Guerin (BCG)
BCGitis, 231
BCGosis, 230–231
bcl2, 154, 155f, 192–195
BEN. *See* Balkan endemic nephropathy (BEN)
Benign prostatic hyperplasia, 137
Benign urothelial cells, 114f, 115f
  abnormal cytology, 116–118
Benzodiazepines
  with anesthesia, 280
  elderly, 281
Beta-catenin, 194–195
Beta-human chorionic gonadotrophin, 104
bFGF, 48–49
Bimanual examination, 65–66
Bio-dot-test, 177
Biologic plausibility, 4
Biomarkers, 107
  quantitative
    bladder cancer, 144
    TCC, 143–156
Biopsy
  bladder, 65
  cold cup, 74

forceps, 345f
multiple, 127–128
ureteroscopic, 354–356
patients for, 357
Birth control pills
oral, 256
Bisulfan, 117
Bladder
adenocarcinoma
cystoscopy, 74
biopsy, 65
contrast filled
filling defects, 81–82
rhabdomyosarcoma, 80
TUR, 74–76
Bladder cancer. *See also* Bladder urothelial
cancer; Invasive urothelial bladder
cancer; Urothelial cancer
African, 8
biologic significance of various forms of,
69–70
cell-based morphologic findings, 107–108
cytologic findings in, 119–122
detection and surveillance
standard care for, 160–161
high-grade
detection of, 168
high-risk superficial
BCG, 228–229
locally advanced
cisplatin, 264f
low-grade
detection of, 168
muscle-invasive
bladder-sparing approaches, 290–307
cystectomy, 290–291
prognostic markers, 191–196
quantitative biomarkers, 144
recurrence
bladder tumor markers, 162–163
staging, 59–60
objectives of, 58
superficial, 206, 206f
Bladder cuff
detachment of, 379
securing, 378–379
Bladder Tumor Antigen (BTA) tests, 173
Bladder tumor markers, 160–198, 171t–172t
accuracy, 166
bladder cancer recurrence, 162–163
cancer screening, 161–162
chi-squared analysis, 167
combination
cost, 163
comparative analysis, 184–191
cost, 163
with cystoscopy, 163
disease-specific survival, 192–195
early detection, 167
efficiency, 164–165
false-negatives, 164–166
false-positives, 163, 165
hematuria, 170–173
ideal, 164–168
incidence rate, 166
individualized treatment selection,
163–164
odds ratio, 167–168
progression prediction, 192–195
rationale, 161–162
recurrence, 192–195

risk ratio, 167–168
sensitivity, 165
specificity, 165–166
technical simplicity of detection, 164
tests
comparative analysis, 187t
treatment response prediction, 195–196
true-positives, 164–165
urine cytology, 168–170
variability, 164
Bladder tumors
recurrence, 160
resection
cytology, 129–130
Bladder urothelial cancer
case control studies, 3
casual criteria, 3
causation, 2–4
clinical appearance of, 71
clinical pathogenesis and staging of, 58–70
correlational studies, 2–3
demographics of, 1–2
diagnosis of, 71–90
ecological studies, 2–3
environmental factors, 4–5
etiology of, 4–5
gender differences, 1
iatrogenic causes of, 9–10
incidence of, 1
lifestyle, 5–8
risk factors for, 5t
staging schema for, 60–62, 61f
strength, 3
Bladder wall thickening, 82
CT, 83f
MRI, 82f
virtual cystoscopy, 83f
Bladder washings (Barbotage), 114, 114f,
115f, 168
with cystoscopy, 127, 127t
fields of applications for, 113t
BLCA-4, 164, 177
Blue-light cystoscopy, 78t
Body composition
aging, 277
Body image
satisfaction with, 256
sexual function, 256t
Body weight
aging, 277
Bone marrow
aging, 279
Bone scans, 64
Botryoid sarcoma, 80
Brachytherapy
interstitial
invasive bladder carcinoma, 299
BTA-Stat, 84, 162–164, 185, 188–191
cost, 173
prognosis, 174
sensitivity, 173–174
specificity, 174
BTA-TARK, 84, 173–175
sensitivity, 174–175
specificity, 175
with urine cytology, 162–163
BTA tests, 173
Bulgaria, 1
Bunch of grapes appearance, 80
Buschke-Löwenstein tumor
cystoscopy, 74

Calyceal amputation, 327f
Cancer
cytologic features, 120t
cytologic findings in, 119–124
Cancer screening
bladder tumor markers, 161–162
Carbon black, 11
Carboplatin, 262, 389, 396
with paclitaxel
for metastatic urothelial cancer, 394
Carcinogenesis, 29–32
hypothetical model of, 30f
Carcinoma in situ (CIS), 32, 61, 68f, 93–96,
95f
BCG, 225–226
cystoscopy, 75
cytology, 129
diagnostic criteria, 93–96
follow-up, 130
progression of, 96
symptoms of, 73
Carcinosarcoma 1, 87f
Carcinosarcoma 2, 87f
Cardiovascular system
aging, 278
Catenin, 194–195
CDK4, 22
CDK6, 22
CDN2A gene, 20
CD44v6, 102
Cell cycle, 17–20
aberrations, 17–25
clinical implications, 25
pathways, 20f, 22f
growth signals, 20–23
Cell-mediated Th1 immune response
BCG, 221–224
Cellular senescence theory, 274
Centrifuge, 168
Chemical dye manufacturing, 11
Chemoprevention
surrogate end-point markers, 155
Chemotherapy. *See also* Intravesical
chemotherapy
age, 276–277
vs. BCG
clinical trials, 226
systemic, 117–118
with TURBT
invasive bladder carcinoma,
293t–296t
Chills
BCG, 229, 230t
Chinese herb nephropathy (CHN), 320
Chinese herbs *(Aristolochia fangchi)*, 8
CHN, 320
Chromatin patterns
electron microscopy, 148f
nuclear signatures representing, 148f
Chromatin texture analysis, 147–148, 154f
chemoprevention clinical trials, 154
Chromosomal alterations, 164
Chromosome 9
FISH, 149f
Cigarette smoking, 161, 166
causing BEN, 320
CIS. *See* Carcinoma in situ (CIS)
CISCA
vs. MVAC
for metastatic urothelial cancer, 393

Cisplatin, 24, 261, 262, 265, 388–389, 396.
    See also Methotrexate vinblastine
    adriamycin cisplatin (MVAC);
    Methotrexate vinblastine epirubicin
    cisplatin (MVEC)
    with docetaxel
        for metastatic urothelial cancer, 394
    with 5-FU and radiation, 302
    with gemcitabine
        for metastatic urothelial cancer,
            394–395
        vs. MVAC, 395t
    for locally advanced bladder cancer,
        264f
    for metastatic urothelial cancer, 392
    vs. MVAC
        for metastatic urothelial cancer,
            392–393
    with paclitaxel
        for metastatic urothelial cancer, 394
    with radiotherapy
        vs. radiotherapy alone, 302
    toxicity of, 301
    with TURBT, 302
Cisplatin cyclophosphamide adriamycin
    (CISCA)
    vs. MVAC
        for metastatic urothelial cancer, 393
Cisplatin methotrexate vinblastine (CMV),
    262, 263, 299–301
    for metastatic urothelial cancer, 393
    for micrometastatic disease, 398
Cleveland Clinic
    laparoscopic cystectomy
        urethelial cancer, 315–317
    transvesical ureteral dissection, 378–380
CMV. *See* Cisplatin methotrexate vinblastine
    (CMV)
Coal gasification, 11
Coffee
    bladder urothelial cancer, 6–7
Cognition
    aging, 279
Coherence, 4
Cohort studies, 3
Cold cup biopsy, 74
Collins knife, 372
Collins resectoscope, 381
Columnar cells, 115
Combination therapy, 248
Complement factor H-related protein,
    173–175
Complications
    NMP22, 176–177
Computed tomography (CT), 62, 63, 63t,
    81–84
    virtual cystoscopy, 82–83
Computer-assisted fluorescent image
    analysis, 135
Condyloma acuminatum
    cystoscopy, 74
Consistency, 4
Continent cutaneous urinary diversion, 250
Continent diversion
    elderly, 285
Contrast filled bladder
    filling defects, 81–82, 81f
Cost
    bladder tumor markers, 163
    BTA-Stat, 173
    cystoscopy, 160–161
    NMP22, 175

upper tract transitional cell carcinoma
    laparoscopic *vs.* open
        nephroureterectomy, 384
CT. *See* Computed tomography (CT)
Cup forceps, 354
Cyclin D1, 194
Cyclin-dependent kinase 4 (CDK4), 22
Cyclin-dependent kinase 6 (CDK6), 22
Cyclophosphamide, 9–10, 117, 261, 262, 265
    causing BEN, 321
    vs. MVAC
        for metastatic urothelial cancer, 393
CYFRA 19, 164, 179–180, 186
Cystectomy. *See also* Laparoscopic
    cystectomy; Radical cystectomy
    cytologic analysis after, 131
    elderly, 272–286
        anesthesia, 280–281
        anesthetic risk, 279–280
        outcomes, 284–285, 285t
        postoperative considerations, 281–282
        radical cystectomy, 258t
        surgical technique, 281
        urinary diversion in, 258t
    invasive bladder carcinoma
        survival, 297t
    muscle-invasive bladder cancer, 290–291
    partial, 248
        invasive bladder carcinoma, 292t,
            298–299
    patient position for, 282f
Cystitis, 93–94, 229, 230t, 231
    denuding, 95
    malignant, 73
    recurrent, 8–9
Cystitis glandularis
    signet-ring cell carcinoma, 85
Cystoscopy, 65, 74–76, 75f, 160–161
    with bladder wash cytology, 127, 127t
    blue-light, 78t
    condyloma acuminatum, 74
    cost, 160–161
    CT-virtual, 82–83
    flexible, 160–161, 345f
    fluorescence
        technical setup for, 78f
    photodynamic, 76–79
    with urinary wash cytology, 127, 127t
    white-light
        lesions missed during, 78t
Cytochrome P-450, 11, 30
Cytokeratin 7, 194–195
Cytokeratin 8, 178
Cytokeratin 18, 178
Cytokeratin 19 (CYFRA 19), 164, 179–180,
    186
Cytokeratin 20, 178–179, 194–195
    RT-PCR, 190
Cytokeratins, 177–178
Cytologic analysis
    accuracy of, 131–132
    after cystectomy, 131
    clinical usefulness of, 126–131
    vs. histologic analysis, 127
    objective grading in, 150–151
    subjectivity of, 143
    of symptomatic patients, 127–128
Cytologic consultation
    clinical information accompanying, 113t
Cytologic interpretation, 114–124
    abnormal cytology in benign urothelial
        cells, 116–118

chemotherapy, 117–118
    dysplasia, 118–119
    immunotherapy, 117–118
    irradiation, 117
    laser therapy, 117
    urinary sediment, 115–116
Cytologic specimens
    collection and processing of, 112–114
    noncancerous conditions interfering with,
        116t
Cytology, 66
Cytology report, 124–126
    terminology, 124–125, 125t
Cytomegaloviruses, 116

Deep vein thrombosis (DVT)
    elderly, 282
Dehydration
    elderly, 280
Denonvilliers' fascia, 283f
    urethelial cancer
        laparoscopic cystectomy, 312f
Denuding cystitis, 95
Diazepam
    elderly, 281
Digital image analysis
    nuclei, 145
Digital images, 146f
Digital texture analysis
    features measured during, 148t
    recurrence, 152
Digitized image analysis, 135–136
Digoxin
    elderly, 282
Dihydropyrimidine dehydrogenase,
    194–195
Disease-specific survival
    bladder tumor markers, 192–195
Diuretics
    with anesthesia, 280
Diversion. *See also* Urinary diversion
    comparison of, 254t
    continent
        elderly, 285
    educational literature about, 256
    in elderly patients, 257–258
    in female patients, 256–257
    ileal conduit, 314f
DNA
    microsatellite, 164, 182–183, 182*f*
DNA analysis, 132–135
DNA flow cytometry, 149–150, 149f
    prognosis, 152
DNA histogram
    aneuploidy, 134f
    classification of, 147t
DNA image cytometry, 146–147
    with cytology, 153
DNA ploidy
    recurrence, 151
DNA replication, 274f
Docetaxel, 261, 390
    with cisplatin
        for metastatic urothelial cancer, 394
Dose response, 4
Doxorubicin (Adriamycin), 24, 155,
    261–262, 268, 390
    and gemcitabine
        followed by ITP, 396
Dry cleaning industry, 11
DVT
    elderly, 282

Dysplasia, 93, 118f
    cytologic findings, 118–119

Eastern Cooperative Oncology Group
    (ECOG), 265, 389–390
E-cadherin, 32, 36, 45–47, 194, 195f
Educational literature
    about diversions, 256
EGF. *See* Epidermal growth factor (EGF)
EGFR. *See* Epidermal growth factor receptor
    (EGFR)
18F-2-fluoro-2-deoxy-D-glucose, 64
Elderly. *See also* Aging
    cystectomy, 272–286
        anesthesia, 280–281
        anesthetic risk, 279–280
        outcomes, 284–285, 285t
        postoperative considerations, 281–282
        radical cystectomy, 258t
        surgical technique, 281
        urinary diversion in, 258t
    diversions in, 257–258
Electrosurgical knife, 376f
Electrosurgical resection, 345f
ELISA, 52
    ideal monoclonal UBC, 178
Endocatch-II bag, 313
Endo-GIA firing, 313
Endo-GIA stapler, 313, 314f, 316
Endometriosis, 90f
Endoscopy
    upper tract, 333–335
Endoshears, 313
Enzyme-linked immunosorbent assay
    (ELISA), 52
    ideal monoclonal UBC, 178
EORTC, 253, 263, 268
Epidermal growth factor (EGF), 20, 20f,
    49–52, 50f
    senescent cells, 275–276
Epidermal growth factor receptor (EGFR),
    20, 32, 36–37
    signaling and angiogenesis, 51
Epiregulin, 194
Epirubicin, 213–214, 390. *See also*
    Methotrexate vinblastine epirubicin
    cisplatin (MVEC)
Epithelial tissues
    homeostasis of, 18–19
ERBB2 gene, 38
Erectile dysfunction, 256
Ethambutol, 231
Etoposide (VP-16), 392
EUA, 65
Eukaryotic cell cycle, 18f
Europe, 1
European Organization for Research and
    Treatment of Cancer (EORTC), 253, 263,
    268
Examination under anesthesia (EUA), 65
Excretory urography, 62
Exophytic tumors, 81
Experimental evidence, 4
External beam radiation therapy
    after BCG failure, 238
    invasive bladder carcinoma, 299

FACT-G, 253
FDG, 64
FDP, 84, 164, 180
Females
    diversions in, 256–257

orthotopic bladder reconstruction in, 257t
Fentanyl
    elderly, 281
Feulgen reaction, 147, 147f
    recurrence, 152
Fever and chills
    BCG, 229, 230t
18F-2-fluoro-2-deoxy-D-glucose (FDG), 64
FGF-2. *See* Basic fibroblast growth factor
    (bFGF)
Fibrin, 180
Fibrinogen degradation products (FDP), 84,
    164, 180
Filling defects, 325, 326f, 327f
    contrast filled bladder, 81–82, 81f
    of contrast medium, 79–80, 80f
    differential diagnosis, 326t
Filtration, 168
FISH. *See* Fluorescence in situ hybridization
    (FISH)
Flank pain
    in upper tract urothelial cancer, 324
Flat lesions
    CIS, 93–96
    dysplasia, 93
    grading, 92–96
    reactive changes, 92–93, 94f
Flat wire basket, 354, 356f
Flexible cystoscopy, 160–161, 345f
Flexible nephroscope, 345f
Flexible ureteroscopes, 334, 334f
    Wolf, 334f
Flow cytometry, 132–135
Flu-like symptoms
    BCG, 229, 230t
Fluorescence cystoscopy
    technical setup for, 78f
Fluorescence in situ hybridization (FISH),
    36, 135–137, 148–149, 164, 190
    schematic representation of, 136f
    vs. washing cytology, 136
Fluorescent image analysis
    computer-assisted, 135
5-fluorouracil (5-FU), 261, 262, 392
    with cisplatin and radiation, 302
    toxicity of, 301
Free radical theory of aging, 272
5-FU, 261, 262, 392
    with cisplatin and radiation, 302
    toxicity of, 301
Functional Assessment of Cancer Therapy
    general score (FACT-G), 253
Fungi, 117

G-actin, 162
Gallium nitrate, 261, 392
    for metastatic urothelial cancer, 395
Gastrointestinal anastomosis (GIA) tissue
    stapler
    endoscopic, 376
Gastrointestinal system
    aging, 279
Gastrostomy tube (G tube)
    elderly, 282–283
GC paclitaxel, 396
Gemcitabine, 261, 268, 390
    with cisplatin
        for metastatic urothelial cancer,
        394–395
        vs. MVAC, 395t
    with taxanes
        for metastatic urothelial cancer, 395

Gemcitabine carboplatin paclitaxel, 396
Genetic localizations, 70t
Genetics
    upper tract urothelial cancer, 322
Genetic theory of aging, 274
GIA tissue stapler
    endoscopic, 376
Gibson incision, 372
Glomerular filtration rate
    aging, 278
Glutathione-S-transferase M1, 10, 31
Grading, 92–102
    grade 1 urothelial carcinoma, 98–100
    grade 2 urothelial carcinoma, 100–102
    grade 3 urothelial carcinoma, 102
    papillary lesions, 96–98
GTPase, 20, 31
G tube
    elderly, 282–283
Guanosine triphosphatase (GTPase), 20, 31
GUONE, 263

HA. *See* Hyaluronic acid (HA)
HAase. *See* Hyaluronidase (HAase)
Hair dyes, 11
HAL. *See* Hand-assisted laparoscopy (HAL)
Hand-assisted laparoscopy (HAL), 376
    nephrectomy, 371
    nephroureterectomy
        postoperative abdominal appearance,
        381
        with transvesical laparoscopic ureteral
        dissection, 380–381
Hautmann neobladder with chimney
    modification, 251f
hCG, 104
Hematoporphyrin, 76
Hematuria, 71, 160, 229, 230t
    bladder tumor markers, 170–173
    filling defect, 355f, 356f
    in upper tract urothelial cancer, 324
    ureteroscopy, 358f, 359f
Hemoglobin dipstick, 170
Hemorrhage
    after percutaneous resection, 348
Heredity
    upper tract urothelial cancer, 322
High-grade bladder cancer
    detection of, 168
High-grade neuroendocrine carcinoma,
    102–103
High-grade tumors, 121f
    follow-up, 130
High-risk superficial bladder cancer
    BCG, 228–229
Hill criteria, 3t, 4
Histologic analysis
    vs. cytologic analysis, 127
    objective grading in, 150–151
    subjectivity of, 143
Histologic field, 145f
Histology
    nontransitional cell, 398–399
Histopathology, 84–86
Hob-nail appearance, 86f
Holmium laser, 334, 360
Homeostasis
    aging, 279
Host factors, 10
HPV, 9, 116, 116f
H-RAS, 31
hTERT, 181, 189

Human chorionic gonadotrophin (hCG), 104
Human papillomavirus (HPV), 9, 116, 116f
Human polyomavirus, 117f
Human telomerase reverse transcriptase (hTERT), 181, 189
HYAL1 type hyaluronidase
    immunohistochemical localization, 186f
Hyaluronic acid (HA), 183
    hyaluronidase (HAase) test, 162, 164, 183–184, 190–191
    immunohistochemical localization of, 185f
    test, 183f
Hyaluronidase (HAase), 183
    hyaluronic acid (HA) test, 162, 164, 183–184, 190–191
    immunohistochemical localization, 186f
    test, 183f
Hypertension
    causing BEN, 321
Hypothermia
    elderly, 281
Hypoxia
    aging, 277

ICAM
    BCG, 223
Ideal monoclonal UBC ELISA, 178
IFN-alpha
    after BCG failure, 236
    BCG, 234–235, 237f
IFN-gamma
    BCG, 221, 223
Ifosfamide, 9–10, 261, 262, 391
    for metastatic urothelial cancer, 395
Ifosfamide paclitaxel cisplatin, 396
IL-2
    BCG, 221
IL-8, 53–54
    BCG, 222
Ileal conduit, 249, 249f
    diversion, 314f
    elderly, 281
    in elderly patients, 257–258
    urethelial cancer laparoscopic cystectomy, 313–314
Ileal neobladder
    urinary tract symptoms after, 255t
Image analysis, 144–145
Image processing algorithms, 146f
IMMUNO-4 analysis, 156
ImmunoCyt, 137–138, 137f, 153, 164
Immunohistochemistry, 184f
Immunotherapy
    intravesical, 117–118
Indiana pouch, 250–251, 250f
Inflammatory reactive urothelial cells, 119f, 125f
INH, 229, 231
Instillation therapy
    upper tract urothelial cancer, 349–351
Interferon-alpha (IFN-alpha)
    after BCG failure, 236
    BCG, 234–235, 237f
Interferon-gamma (IFN-gamma)
    BCG, 221, 223
Interleukin-2 (IL-2)
    BCG, 221
Interleukin-8 (IL-8), 53–54
    BCG, 222
International Union against Cancer (UICC)
    TNM classification
        upper tract urothelial cancer staging, 330

Interstitial brachytherapy
    invasive bladder carcinoma, 299
Intracellular adhesion molecules (ICAM)
    BCG, 223
Intravenous pyelogram (IVP), 62
Intravenous urography, 79–80
Intravesical bacille Calmette-Guerin
    TURB, 225
Intravesical chemotherapy, 117–118, 206–215
    adriamycin, 211–213
    BCG, 210–238
    epirubicin, 213–214
    idealized goals of, 219–220
    mitomycin C, 209–211
    thiotepa, 207–209
    trials
        BCG, 224–229
    valrubicin, 214
Intravesical immunotherapy, 117–118
Intravesical therapy
    invasive bladder carcinoma, 297–298
Invasive bladder carcinoma, 299–301
    bladder sparing
        limitations of, 304–305
    chemotherapy with bladder-sparing
        surgery, 299–301
    CT, 82
    cystectomy
        surgery, 298t
        survival, 297t, 299t
    external beam radiation therapy, 299
    interstitial brachytherapy, 299
    intravesical therapy, 297–298
    MRI, 82
    MVAC
        survival, 300t
    partial cystectomy, 298–299
        outcome, 292t
    surgery with chemotherapy with
        radiation, 301–304
    trimodality therapy
        cystectomy indications, 305t
        survival, 305t
    TURBT, 291–297
        with chemotherapy, 293t–296t
        survival, 291t
Invasive carcinoma
    gross features, 104–105
Invasive urothelial bladder cancer
    adjuvant chemotherapy, 265–267
    adjuvant chemotherapy and radical
        cystectomy
        randomized trials, 266t, 268t
    chemotherapy of, 261–262
    neoadjuvant chemotherapy, 262–263
    neoadjuvant chemotherapy and radical
        cystectomy
        randomized trials, 263t
    perioperative chemotherapy, 264–265
Invasive urothelial cancer
    cystoscopy, 76f
    molecular carcinogenesis and
        pathogenesis of, 28–39
    molecular pathogenesis of, 44–54, 46f
    prognosis, 106–107
IP-10
    BCG, 222, 223
Irradiation
    cytology, 117
Isoniazid, 229, 231
IVP, 62

Juxtavesical ureter
    mobilization of, 379
    traction
        cystoscopic detachment of, 379f

Kaye balloon catheter, 348
Keyhole limpet hemocyanin (KLH)
    after BCG failure, 238
Ki67, 192–195
    labeling index, 38, 164
    prognosis, 195–196
Kidneys
    aging, 278
    compromised contralateral
        treatment algorithm, 366f
    CT, 337f
    failure
        treatment algorithm, 366f
    normal contralateral, 362–363
        treatment algorithm, 366f
Kidney stones, 360f
Kidney ureter and bladder (KUB), 62
KLH
    after BCG failure, 238
Koch pouch
    elderly, 285
K-RAS, 31
KUB, 62

Lamina propria
    inflammation, 92
    invasion of, 105–106
Laparoscopic cystectomy
    urethelial cancer, 311–322
        patient preparation, 311–312
        postoperative care, 315
        results, 315–317
        technique, 312–315
Laparoscopic instruments, 316t
Laparoscopic nephroureterectomy (LNU)
    radical
        history of, 371–372
        TCC, 369–385
Laparoscopy sack, 383
Laser therapy
    cytology, 117
Latin America, 1
Laxatives, 10
    causing BEN, 320
LCM, 64
Leiomyosarcoma 1, 87f
Leiomyosarcoma 2, 88f
Lithium
    with anesthesia, 280
L-(methyl)-11C-methionine (LCM), 64
LNU
    radical
        history of, 371–372
        TCC, 369–385
Locally advanced bladder cancer
    cisplatin, 264f
Loss of heterozygosity (LOH), 22, 36
Low-grade bladder cancer
    detection of, 168
Low-grade papillary transitional cell
    carcinoma, 69–70
Low-grade tumor, 121f
    follow-up, 130
LY231514, 391
Lymphadenectomy, 66
    upper tract transitional cell carcinoma, 382–383

Lymphoma, 88f

MAC, 152
Macrophage inhibitory protein -1 (MIP-1)
    BCG, 222
Magnetic resonance imaging (MRI), 63–64,
    81–84
Mainz pouch II technique, 317
Malakoplakia 1, 89f
Malakoplakia 2, 89f
Malignancy. *See* Cancer
Malignancy-associated changes (MAC), 152
Malignant cystitis, 73
Malignant melanoma, 124f
Malnutrition
    elderly, 283
Markers. *See also* Bladder tumor markers
    urine, 84
Massachusetts General Hospital (MGH), 303
Matrix metalloproteinase (MMP), 47–48,
    194–195
MCP-1
    BCG, 222
M.D. Anderson Cancer Institute
    cystectomy
        elderly, 284
        MVAC, 261–262
MDM2, 39
Mechanical ventilation
    elderly, 282
Melanoma, 89f
Memorial Sloan-Kettering Cancer Center, 268
    early *vs.* late cystectomy, 291
    MVAC, 276–277
Metastatic urothelial cancer
    combination chemotherapy, 392–397
    local treatment, 397–398
    risk stratification, 397
    systemic chemotherapy for, 388–399
Methionine, 64
Methotrexate, 24, 261, 262, 391. *See also*
    Cisplatin methotrexate vinblastine
    (CMV)
    with platinum, 303
Methotrexate vinblastine adriamycin
    cisplatin (MVAC), 261, 263, 266,
    276–277, 299–301
    vs. CISCA
        for metastatic urothelial cancer, 393
    vs. cisplatin
        for metastatic urothelial cancer,
        392–393
    invasive bladder carcinoma
        survival, 300t
    for metastatic urothelial cancer, 392, 393
    for micrometastatic disease, 398
    neoadjuvant, 300
    phase III clinical trials of, 392t
    with radiation, 303
Methotrexate vinblastine epirubicin cisplatin
    (MVEC), 266, 300
Methyl-11C-methionine, 64
MGH, 303
Microinvasive carcinoma, 105
Micrometastatic disease
    systemic treatment, 398
Microsatellite DNA, 164, 182–183, 182*f*
Microsatellite instability, 33
Microvessel density, 145
Micturition, 257
MIP-1
    BCG, 222
Mitomycin C, 154, 154f, 209–211, 210t, 261

after BCG failure, 236
    toxicity of, 301
    for upper tract cancer, 363–364
MMP, 47–48, 194–195
Modified Grabstald system, 330f
Modified Indiana pouch
    elderly, 285
Modified Jewett system, 330f, 330t
Monocyte chemotactic protein-1 (MCP-1)
    BCG, 222
Morcellation, 383
Morphine
    elderly, 281
Morphometry, 144–145
Mortality, 2
Mostofi system
    upper tract urothelial cancer staging, 329
MRI, 63–64, 81–84
Mucositis, 301
Multiple biopsies, 127–128
Muscle-invasive bladder cancer
    bladder-sparing approaches, 290–307
    cystectomy, 290–291
Muscle-invasive cancer, 61, 160
    follow-up, 130
Muscularis mucosa, 105
Muscularis propria, 68
    invasion
        staging, 106
MVAC. *See* Methotrexate vinblastine
    adriamycin cisplatin (MVAC)
MVEC, 266, 300
Mycobacterium bovis, 220
Myelosuppression, 208

N-acetyl-transferse genes (Nat1), 10, 30
Nasogastric tubes
    elderly, 282
Neoadjuvant MVAC, 300
Neobladder
    Hautmann
        with chimney modification, 251f
    ileal
        urinary tract symptoms after, 255t
    orthotopic, 251, 257
        urinary diversion, 313–314, 314f
    Studer ileal, 252f
Neodymium yttrium-aluminum-garnet
    (Nd:YAG) laser, 334, 345f, 348, 360
Neovagina, 256
Nephroscope, 344f
    flexible, 345f
Nephrostomy catheter, 348
Nephrostomy tube, 346f
Nephroureterectomy
    radical
        retroperitoneoscopic approach, 372
Nervous system
    aging, 277
Neuroendocrine carcinoma
    high-grade, 102–103
NMP22, 84, 164, 185–189
    complications, 176–177
    cost, 175
    sensitivity, 176
    specificity, 176
Noninvasive tumors
    follow-up, 130
Non-muscle invasive urothelial carcinoma,
    206
Nonsteroidal anti-inflammatory drugs
    (NSAID), 229
Nontransitional cell histology, 398–399

Nordic Cooperative Bladder Cancer Study
    Group, 262
North Eastern Uro Oncological Group
    (GUONE), 263
NSAID, 229
Nuclei
    digital image analysis, 145
    interactive tracing of, 145, 145f
Nutrition
    elderly, 283

Object counting, 144
Object identification algorithms, 146f
Occupational risk factors, 11–12, 161, 166
Ochratoxin A
    for BEN, 320
Oil industry, 11
Oncogenes
    tissue specificity of, 19–20
Oral birth control pills, 256
Oral hypoglycemics
    with anesthesia, 280
Orandi resectoscope, 381
Orthotopic bladder reconstruction
    in females, 257t
Orthotopic neobladder, 251, 257
    urinary diversion
        urethelial cancer laparoscopic
        cystectomy, 313–314, 314f
Oxidative stress theory of aging, 272

P27
    prognosis, 195–196
P53, 22, 31–33, 37–38, 163–164, 195–196
    pathway, 23–24, 23f
    prognosis, 195–196
    survival status, 301t
P-300, 162
Paclitaxel, 261, 262, 389–390, 396
    with carboplatin
        for metastatic urothelial cancer, 394
    with cisplatin
        for metastatic urothelial cancer, 394
PAH, 10, 30
Pain
    elderly, 282
Papillary lesions, 96–98, 359f
    clinical significance, 97–98
    diagnostic criteria, 96–97
    flat wire basket, 356f
    ureteroscopy, 354
Papillary neoplasm of low malignant
    potential (PUNLMP), 120f
Papilloma, 98f
    inverted urothelial, 97
    urothelial
        diagnostic features, 97t
Paracetamol, 9
Parasites, 117f
Partial cystectomy, 248
    invasive bladder carcinoma, 298–299
        outcome, 292t
Pathology, 92–108
    grading, 92–102
    staging, 104–106, 105t
    urachal cancer, 107
PCNA, 151, 192–195
PDT, 76
    after BCG failure, 238
PE1001, 155
Pedicles
    posterior vascular, 283f
Pelvic iliac lymphadenectomy, 282f

Pelvic lipomatosis
    intravenous urography, 80f
Pelvic lymph node dissection
    urethelial cancer laparoscopic cystectomy,
        313
Pelvic radiotherapy, 10
Peritoneal incision
    urethelial cancer
        laparoscopic cystectomy, 312f
PET, 64–65
Phenacetin, 9
    causing BEN, 321
Pheochromocytoma 1, 88f
Pheochromocytoma 2, 88f
Photodiagnosis, 76
Photodynamic cystoscopy, 76–79
Photodynamic therapy (PDT), 76
    after BCG failure, 238
Photofrin, 76
Piritrexim, 391
Pixels, 146f
Plastic manufacturing, 11
Platinum
    with MCV and radiation, 303
    with methotrexate, 303
    with radiation, 302
Pluck technique, 371, 378
Pneumonia
    aging, 278
Pneumo Sleeve, 382
Polycyclic aromatic hydrocarbons (PAH), 10,
    30
Ports
    urethelial cancer
        laparoscopic cystectomy, 312, 312f
Port-site seeding
    TCC, 383–384
Positron emission tomography (PET), 64–65
Potassium supplements
    with anesthesia, 280
PPIX, 77
Procedure, 151–152
Prognosis
    DNA flow cytometry, 152
    S-phase cells, 152
    staging, 106–107
Prognostic markers
    bladder cancer, 191–196
Progression prediction, 151–152
    BCG, 226–227
    bladder tumor markers, 192–195
Proliferating cell nuclear antigen (PCNA),
    151, 192–195
Propidium iodide, 147, 150f
Prostate adenocarcinoma, 124f
    locally advanced, 122
Prostatic hyperplasia
    benign, 137
Prostatic involvement
    staging, 106
Protoporphyrin IX (PPIX), 77
Pseudosarcoma, 89f
Pulmonary system
    aging, 277
PUNLMP, 120f
Pyridoxine (vitamin B6)
    BCG, 235

QLQ-C30, 253
Quality of life
    sexual function, 255–256
    urinary continence, 254–255

urinary diversion, 252–254
Quality of Life survey
    SF-36, 253
Quanticyt, 138–139, 138f, 164
Quantitative biomarkers
    bladder cancer, 144
    TCC, 143–156

Radiation therapy
    vs. cisplatin and radiotherapy, 302
    external beam
        after BCG failure, 238
        invasive bladder carcinoma, 299
    with 5-FU and cisplatin, 302
    with MVAC, 303
    with platinum, 302
    with platinum and MCV, 303
    with TURBT, 304
Radiation Therapy Oncology Group (RTOG),
    263, 303
Radical cystectomy, 263, 263t, 266t
    age, 276
    anatomic, 281f
    in elderly, 257–258, 258t
    outcomes and quality of life following,
        248–259
Radical laparoscopic nephroureterectomy
    history of, 371–372
Radical nephroureterectomy
    retroperitoneoscopic approach, 372
Radiographic staging, 62–65
Radiologic imaging, 79–84
    intravenous urography, 79–80
    ultrasonography, 80–81
RANTES
    BCG, 222
Rat-bitten cells, 119, 126f
Rb, 20, 22, 37
    pathway, 21–22
RDC, 173
Reactive oxygen species (ROS), 273f
Recurrence
    BCG, 226–227
    bladder tumor markers, 192–195
    digital texture analysis, 152
    DNA ploidy, 151
    Feulgen reaction, 152
    prediction, 151–152
        urothelial carcinoma, 107t
    screening, 152–153
Recurrent cystitis, 8–9
Red cell volume distribution curves (RDC),
    173
Regulated on activation normal T expressed
        and secreted (RANTES)
    BCG, 222
Renal calculi, 360f
Renal failure
    treatment algorithm, 366f
Renal pelvis
    cancer, 327f
        cytologic grading of, 122–123
        papillary lesion, 329f
        TNM classification, 331t
    monitoring, 131
    urothelial cancer
        demographics and epidemiology,
            318–322
Retinoblastoma (Rb), 20, 22, 37
    pathway, 21–22
Retrograde pyelography, 74
Rhabdomyosarcoma, 88f

bladder, 80
Rhabdomyosarcoma 2, 88f
Rifampin, 231
Risk factors, 29–32
Roller ball electrode cauterizing, 377f
ROS, 273f
RTOG, 263, 303
Rubber manufacturing, 11

SAKK, 267
Sarcoma
    botryoid, 80
Schistosoma haematobium, 8, 117
Screening
    recurrence, 152–153
Self-perception, 256
Senescent cells, 275–276
    molecular changes in, 276t
Sexual function, 255–256
    body image, 256t
SF-36 Quality of Life survey, 253
Sickness Impact Profile (SIP), 253
Sigmoid mesentery
    mobilization of, 282f
Sigmoid pouch, 252f
Signet-ring cell carcinoma, 85, 86f
Silver-staining nucleolar organizer regions
    (AgNOR), 144
SIP, 253
Skin
    elderly, 281
Small cell carcinoma, 87f, 102–103,
    398–399
    immunohistochemistry of, 104t
Smoking, 161, 166
    causing BEN, 320
SOGUG, 268
Solitary kidney
    treatment algorithm, 366f
Southwestern Oncology Group (SWOG),
    264, 302
    8507 trial, 227–228, 228f
Spanish Oncology Genitourinary Group
    (SOGUG), 268
Specificity, 4
S-phase cells, 134
    prognosis, 152
Squamous cell carcinoma, 86f, 123f
    cystoscopy, 74
    cytologic grading of, 122
    histopathology, 85–86
Staging, 104–106, 105t
    invasive carcinoma gross features,
        104–105
    lamina propria invasion, 105–106
    muscularis propria invasion, 106
    prognosis, 106–107
    prostatic involvement, 106
    urachal adenocarcinoma, 108t
    urachal cancer, 107
    vascular/lymphatic lamina propria
        invasion, 106
Staging algorithm, 66–69, 67f
Staging modifiers, 60t
Staging tools, 62–65
Stanford trial, 267
Stoma
    care of, 249–250
Stones, 117
Stress
    elderly, 281–282
Studer ileal neobladder, 252f

Sudan, 1
Superficial bladder cancer, 206, 206f
Superficially invasive tumors
 follow-up, 130
Superficial tumor recurrence
 molecular basis of, 34–35
Surgical staging, 65–66
Survival
 BCG, 226–227
Survivin, 164, 177
Swiss Group for Clinical Research (SAKK), 267
SWOG, 264, 302
 8507 trial, 227–228, 228f
Systemic chemotherapy, 117–118
Systemic immunotherapy, 117–118

Tar distillation, 11
Targeted therapies, 397
Taxanes, 389–390
 with gemcitabine
  for metastatic urothelial cancer, 395
 for metastatic urothelial cancer, 393–394
TCC. See Transitional cell carcinoma (TCC)
Tears
 elderly, 281
Telomerase, 164, 180–182
Telomeres
 de novo synthesis of, 275f
Terminology
 cytology report, 124–125, 125t
Textile industry, 11
TGF-alpha, 51, 194
Th1 immune response
 cell-mediated
  BCG, 221–224
Thiotepa, 207–209, 208t
Thymidylate synthase, 194–195
Time order, 4
TNF-alpha
 BCG, 221, 223
TNM classification. See Tumor, nodes, and
 metastases (TNM) classification
Tobacco, 5
Transforming growth factor alpha
 (TGF-alpha), 51, 194
Transfusion rate
 after percutaneous resection, 348
Transitional cell carcinoma (TCC), 2, 69–70,
 85, 169f, 193f, 206, 261, 272, 324,
 325f. See also Upper tract transitional
 cell carcinoma
 biologic continuum of, 68f
 bladder washings, 114
 CT, 84f, 328t, 336–337, 336t
 cytologic findings in, 119–120
 cytologic grading of, 120–122
 endoluminal ultrasound, 338f
 endoscopy, 331, 333–335
 grading systems, 122t
 histologic grading of, 119t
 industrial development, 28
 low-grade papillary, 69–70
 newer regimens, 396, 396t
 percutaneous nephroscopy, 335
 progression
  cytogenetic changes associated with,
   35–36
  molecular and immunohistochemical
   changes, 36
 quantitative cell biomarkers, 143–156
 tissue-confirmed, 132t

ureteroscopic view of, 333f
urinary cytology, 328
virtual cystoscopy, 84f
Transurethral resection (TUR), 59, 65
 bladder, 74–76
Transurethral resection of bladder (TURB),
 82, 105, 248
 BCG, 234
 intravesical BCG, 225
Transurethral resection of bladder tumor
 (TURBT), 67
 with chemotherapy
  invasive bladder carcinoma, 293t–296t
 with cisplatin, 302
 invasive bladder carcinoma, 291–297
  survival, 291t
 with neoadjuvant combination
  chemotherapy, 299–300
 with radiation, 304
Transvesical laparoscopic ureteral dissection
 HAL with, 380–381
Transvesical ureteral dissection
 Cleveland Clinic approach, 378–380
TRAP assay, 189
TRAP-ELISA, 190
Treatment response
 prediction
  bladder tumor markers, 195–196
 prediction of, 153–155
Tumor, nodes, and metastases (TNM)
 classification, 59t, 60
 upper tract urothelial cancer staging, 331t
  upper tract urothelial cancer, 330
Tumor development
 genetics of, 32–34
 molecular basis of, 28–34
 pathway for, 29f, 33f
Tumor markers. See Bladder tumor markers
Tumor necrosis factor-alpha (TNF-alpha)
 BCG, 221, 223
Tumor progression
 molecular basis of, 35–39
Tumor suppressor genes, 19–20
TUR, 59, 65
 bladder, 74–76
TURB. See Transurethral resection of
 bladder (TURB)
TURBT. See Transurethral resection of
 bladder tumor (TURBT)
Tyrosine kinase
 senescent cells, 275–276

UBC, 164, 185, 188–189
UICC
 TNM classification
  upper tract urothelial cancer staging,
   330
Ultrasonography, 64, 80–81
 heterogeneous echogenic area, 81f
Umbrella cells, 115, 115f, 123f
Unicellular organisms
 evolutionary transition to metazoons,
  17–18
University of Southern California (USC)
 adjuvant chemotherapy trial, 265–267
 age
  cystectomy, 276
 ileal conduit, 281
UPJ, 344
Upper tract
 antegrade pyelography, 336
 CT, 337f

endoluminal ultrasonography, 337
endoscopy, 333–335
follow-up, 338
IVP, 335
MRI, 337
transabdominal ultrasound, 337
ureteroscopic treatment, 357–358
Upper tract cancer
 adjuvant therapy, 363–364
 cytopathology sampling, 357t
 diagnosis of, 353, 357t
 laser resection, 358–360
 recurrence, 360–362
 treatment algorithm, 346f
 ureteroscopic biopsy, 355t
 ureteroscopic surgery
  complications of, 366–367
  surveillance, 364–366
Upper tract filling defect
 cone tip ureteropyelogram, 353
 cystoscopy, 353
 endoscopic diagnosis, 354t
 retrograde pyelogram, 353
 ureteroscopy, 354
Upper tract imaging, 335–338
Upper tract transitional cell carcinoma
 grade 1, 361f
 laparoscopic vs. open
  nephroureterectomy, 369–385
   cost, 384
   distal ureter, 382
   lymphadenectomy, 382–384
   morcellation, 383
   pluck technique, 378
   port-site seeding, 383–384
   postoperative surveillance, 377
   results, 380
   specimen retrieval, 382–384
   time to tumor recurrence, 377
   transvesical ureteral dissection,
    378–380
 LNU
  distal ureteral management, 372–382
  open technique, 372–376
  worldwide experience, 373t–375t
 low-grade, 358f
 natural history of, 370–371
 recurrence, 361, 362f
 surveillance, 366t
 totally endoscopic management of, 367,
  367t
 ureteral unroofing, 376–378
 ureteroscopic biopsy of, 356
  grading, 357t
 ureteroscopic surgery
  candidates for, 358t
  recurrence, 364t, 365f
  survival, 357t
Upper tract urothelial cancer
 carcinogenesis mechanism, 319
 clinical presentation of, 324–325, 324t
 CT, 326–328
 cystoscopy, 328
 diagnosis and staging of, 324–331
 environmental risk factors, 319–321
 evaluation, 325–329, 329t
 excretory urogram, 325t
 hereditary factors, 322
 instillation therapy, 349–351
 IVP, 325
 MRI, 326–328
 nephroureterectomy, 330–331

prognosis, 330–331
renal arteriography, 328
retrograde pyelogram, 325
tumor grading and staging, 329–330
tumor seeding, 319
ultrasonography, 325–326
ureteroscopy, 328, 329f
urinary cytology, 328
Urachal adenocarcinoma
diagnostic criteria, 107t
staging, 108t
Urachal cancer
pathology, 107
staging, 107
Ureter
endoscopy, 353–354
filling defect, 363f
preparation for removal, 379
thickening, 327f
upper tract transitional cell carcinoma
laparoscopic *vs.* open
nephroureterectomy, 382
urothelial cancer
demographics and epidemiology,
318–322
Ureteral access sheath, 334–335
Ureteral cancer
cytologic grading of, 122–123
recurrence, 364f
TNM classification, 331t
Ureteral catheterization
cytology of, 113
Ureteral unroofing
upper tract transitional cell carcinoma,
376–378
Ureteral washing, 114f
Ureteritis cystica
causing BEN, 321
Ureterocele
IV urography, 74f
Ureteropelvic junction (UPJ), 344
Ureteroscopes
flexible, 334, 334f
Wolf flexible, 334f
Ureteroscopic biopsy, 354–356
patients for, 357
Ureters
mobilization of, 313f
monitoring, 131
Urethelial cancer
laparoscopic cystectomy, 311–322
patient preparation, 311–312
postoperative care, 315
results, 315–317
technique, 312–315
surgery indications, 311
Urethral cancer
cytology, 124f
Urethral catheter
retrograde, 344f
Urinary continence
quality of life, 254–255
Urinary cytokeratin 19, 164, 179–180, 186
Urinary cytology
fields of applications for, 113t
Urinary diversion, 118
bladder preservation, 248–249
continent cutaneous, 250
elderly, 285
in elderly, 258t

orthotopic neobladder
urethelial cancer laparoscopic
cystectomy, 313–314, 314f
outcomes and quality of life following,
248–259
types of, 248–249
Urinary leaks, 254–255
Urinary sediment
normal
cytologic findings of, 115–116
Urinary wash cytology
with cystoscopy, 127, 127t
Urine cytology
bladder tumor markers, 168–170
Urine markers, 84
Urine specimens, 112–113
Urine stabilizer kit, 175
Urography
excretory, 62
intravenous, 79–80
Urolithiasis, 117
Uroplakin II, 194
Urothelial barrier
maintenance of, 18–19
Urothelial cancer. *See also* Bladder urothelial
cancer; Metastatic urothelial cancer
percutaneous upper-tract preserving
approaches, 340–351
complications of, 348
contra indications for, 342
historical perspective, 340
indications for, 342
patient counseling, 343
preoperative preparation, 343–344
recurrence, 347t
results, 346–348
surveillance, 348–349
technique, 344–346
theoretical considerations, 340–341
percutaneous *vs.* ureteroscopic approach,
342–343
ureteroscopic upper tract-preserving
approaches, 353–366
Urothelial carcinoma
histologic differential diagnosis, 86t
non-muscle invasive, 206
recurrence prediction, 107t
renal pelvis and ureter
demographics and epidemiology,
318–322
with syncytiotrophoblastic giant cells, 104
variants of, 102–104, 104t
Urothelial carcinoma grade 1, 99f, 120f, 123f
clinical significance, 99–100
diagnostic criteria, 98–100
diagnostic features, 97t
grading, 98–100
Urothelial carcinoma grade 2, 101f, 120f,
123f, 126f
clinical significance, 101–102
diagnostic criteria, 100–101
DNA histogram, 133f
grading, 100–102
Urothelial carcinoma grade 3, 102, 103f,
121f, 123f, 126f
Urothelial cells
benign, 114f
abnormal cytology, 116–118
inflammatory reactive, 119f, 125f
Urothelial neoplasia

cellular features of
WHO classification, 122t
Urothelial tumors
quantitative and analytical assessment,
132–139
USC
adjuvant chemotherapy trial, 265–267
age
cystectomy, 276
ileal conduit, 281

Valrubicin, 214
after BCG failure, 236
Vascular endothelial growth factor (VEGF),
52–53, 52f
Vascular/lymphatic lamina propria invasion
staging, 106
VEGF, 52–53, 52f
VIG
for metastatic urothelial cancer, 395
Vinblastine, 24, 391–392. *See also* Cisplatin
methotrexate vinblastine (CMV)
Vinblastine ifosfamide gallium nitrate (VIG)
for metastatic urothelial cancer, 395
Vinca alkaloids, 261, 391–392
Vincristine, 391–392. *See also* Methotrexate
vinblastine adriamycin cisplatin (MVAC);
Methotrexate vinblastine epirubicin
cisplatin (MVEC)
Viruses, 116
Vitamin A
BCG, 235
Vitamin B6
BCG, 235
Vitamin C
BCG, 235
Vitamin E
BCG, 235
Voided urine
cytology of, 113, 127–128, 161
variability, 168
Voiding reeducation, 257
Von Brunn's nests, 96
VP-16, 392

Warfarin
elderly, 282
Washington University
ureteral unroofing
upper tract transitional cell carcinoma,
376–378
Well-differentiated grade 1 tumors, 133
White-light cystoscopy
lesions missed during, 78t
WHO classification, 92
Ancona refinement, 93t
urothelial neoplasia, 122t
Wilcoxon test, 266
Wire basket, 354, 356f
Wire-pronged grasper, 354–355
Wolf flexible ureteroscope, 334f
Women
continence mechanism in, 257
World Health Organization (WHO)
classification, 92
Ancona refinement, 93t
urothelial neoplasia, 122t

Yugoslavia, 1